Stopping to window jambs
and moniads.

(over.)

The Law Courts

The Architectural
History Foundation
New York, New York

The MIT Press
Cambridge, Massachusetts
and London, England

The Law Courts

The Architecture of George Edmund Street

David B. Brownlee

The Architectural History Foundation/MIT Press Series

American Monograph Series

Special thanks go to the National Endowment for the
Humanities, whose generous grant helped make possible
the publication of this book.

Library of Congress Cataloging in Publication Data

Brownlee, David Bruce.
The Law Courts.
(The Architectural History Foundation/MIT Press
series; v. 8)
Bibliography: p. 423
Includes index.
1. Street, George Edmund, 1824–1881. 2. Court-houses
—Great Britain. I. Title. II. Series.
NA4475.G7B78 1984   725'.15   83-25625
ISBN 0-262-02199-4 (MIT Press)

Designed by James Wageman

David B. Brownlee is Assistant Professor of the History of
Art at the University of Pennsylvania.

Pages 2–3: Royal Courts of Justice. Air view.
(Aerofilms Ltd.) Pages 4–5: The Strand façade, from
the great portal to the clock tower.

Contents

Preface

THE DOMINATING monument of an important quarter of London and the largest commission won by one of the most noteworthy British architects of the nineteenth century, the Royal Courts of Justice have naturally been the subject of earlier inquiry. However, previous studies have not tapped the vast archives of the Public Record Office nor explored the parallel stories that the law courts can tell about law reform, political patronage of the arts, and the theory and practice of architecture in the High Victorian era.

Although important, the law courts have never been a popular building. Erected in a time of changing taste, they were quickly surrounded by controversy, and, like Victorian architecture as a whole, their reputation has not yet been fully rehabilitated. Sir John Summerson's analysis is little short of savage: "The . . . exterior design . . . is as totally incoherent as the great hall is eloquent. It represents the pathetic collapse of an overstrained imagination."[1] Sir Nikolaus Pevsner was only slightly kinder: "The Law Courts is not a popular building now and perhaps never will be. Yet it is serious and competent. . . . Moreover, in its composition it is not without sensitivity. . . . Street's façade to the Strand is an object lesson in free composition, with none of the symmetry of the classics, yet not undisciplined where symmetry is abandoned."[2]

It is not my purpose to enter into this debate, for the importance of the law courts is intrinsic, not relative, and their study should not be made subject to the shifting tastes of architectural historians. However, insofar as the controversy itself began in the nineteenth century, it will receive discussion and analysis.

1983

Acknowledgments

I HAVE incurred debts to the kindness and services of many people while completing this study. My greatest indebtedness is to Neil A. Levine, who has constantly challenged me to think more searchingly about nineteenth-century architecture. Every aspect of the project has also benefited from John Coolidge's generosity and wisdom. Paul Joyce has freely shared his great knowledge of G. E. Street and of Victorian architecture generally, and Lynn Hollen Lees reviewed the portions of the text devoted to political and legal matters. However, I remain responsible for my own errors.

I am grateful to Harvard University for the Frank Knox Memorial Traveling Fellowship which enabled me to work in Britain in 1977–78 and to the University of Pennsylvania for a faculty Summer Fellowship in 1982. The following institutions and individuals have also provided essential assistance: Aerofilms Limited; the Architectural Association (Elisabeth Dixon); the Boston Public Library, Fine Arts Division; the British Architectural Library, Royal Institute of British Architects; the British Architectural Library Drawings Collection, Royal Institute of British Architects (Nicholas M. E. Antram, James Bettley, and Jill Lever); the British Library, Manuscript, Newspaper, Official Publications, and Printed Book divisions; the British Library of Political and Economic Science; the Fine Arts Library, Harvard University; the Fine Arts Library, University of Pennsylvania; the House of Lords Record Office (D. Johnson); the University of Kentucky Libraries; the Lambeth Palace Library; the Law Society Library (F. P. Richardson); the National Monuments Record; the Northamptonshire Record Office (P. I. King); the Property Services Agency Library, Department of the Environment (B. D. Charlton); the Public Record Office; the Royal Academy Library (Constance-Ann Parker); the Royal Commission on Historical Manuscripts; the Royal Courts of Justice (M. R. Cockrem, M.B.E., and J. F. Warwick); the Southampton Civic Record Office (S. D. Thomson); the Victoria and Albert Museum, Department of Prints, Drawings and Photographs, and Paintings, and Department of Furniture (Clive Wainwright); the Watkinson Library, Trinity College, Hartford (Margaret F. Sax); and the Westminster City Libraries. I extend my thanks to them all.

Much of the wearisome work of preparing the manuscript was borne by Susan Nally, Mary Buttrick, and Michal Truelsen. William Clough printed many of the photographs, and Daniel McCoubrey drew two plans. Victoria Newhouse, Julianne Griffin, Karen Banks, and Lauren T. Klein of the Architectural History Foundation have overseen the production of the book with intelligence, ingenuity, and tact; they have made my task much easier. In this and in all else I have been sustained by Ann Blair Brownlee.

Abbreviations

AES	Arthur Edmund Street
AES, *Memoir*	Arthur Edmund Street. *Memoir of George Edmund Street, R.A., 1824–1881.* London: John Murray, 1888. Reprinted by Benjamin Blom, New York, 1972
BAL	British Architectural Library, Royal Institute of British Architects, London
BL	Manuscript Department of the British Library, London
BPP	British Parliamentary Papers. The pagination cited is the printed pagination of each blue book, not the cumulative pagination in manuscript which has been added in some sets of this series.
GES	George Edmund Street
NMR	National Monuments Record, London
PRO	Public Record Office, Kew, Surrey

The Law Courts

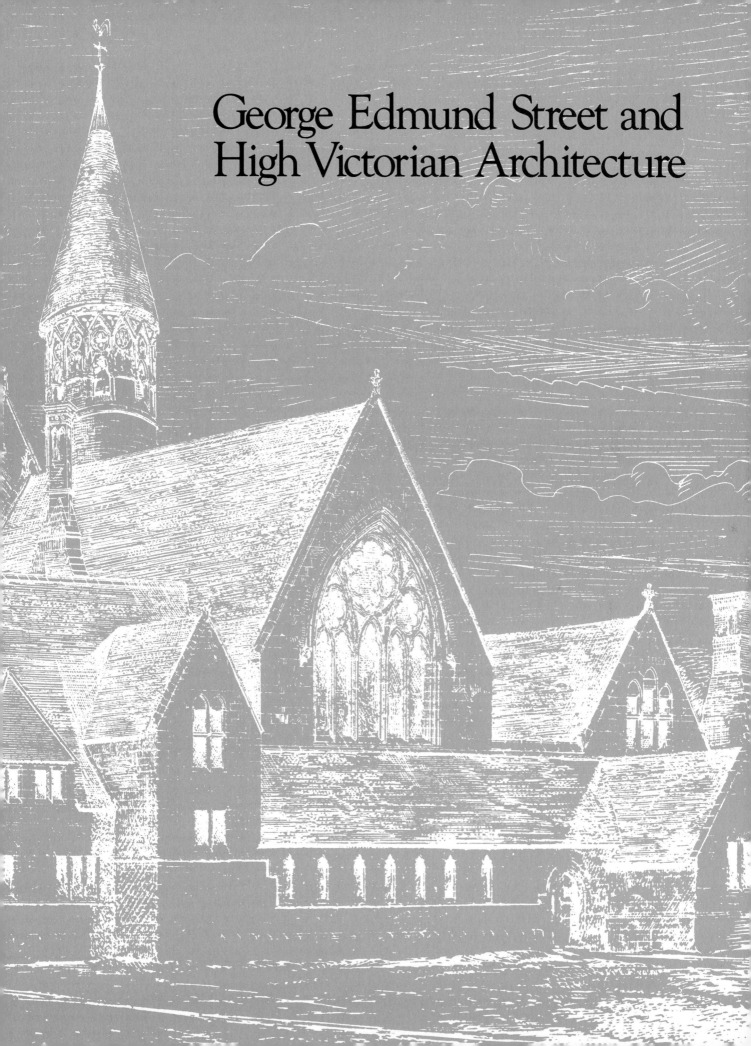

George Edmund Street and
High Victorian Architecture

"The Central Building of the World."
—John Ruskin, 1851

GEORGE EDMUND STREET (1824–81) won the commission to design the Royal Courts of Justice in a competition conducted in 1866–67. For his generation, the law courts possessed a symbolic and real importance nearly equal to that which the Houses of Parliament held for early Victorians, and his building still mirrors the complex vitality of British civilization in the middle years of Queen Victoria's long reign.

Tied to the political and institutional history of the Victorian era, the courts are a monument to the Age of Reform—particularly to legal reform. They are a memorial to the national leaders who promoted their construction and most especially to William Ewart Gladstone, who befriended Street. And they reflect the nature of the bureaucracy that oversaw official patronage of the arts.

The law courts are also an artistic milestone. A correspondent to the *Times* correctly predicted in 1867 that they would prove to be "a perpetual monument of English art as understood and practised in the latter half of the 19th century," and the building can now be identified as the climax of High Victorian architecture.[1] In the 1850s and 1860s that movement strove to broaden the Gothic Revival to encompass all forms of secular and monumental design. The Gothic law courts, the greatest public building of the time, symbolized the achievement of that objective.

The creative and intellectual leader of High Victorianism was G. E. Street, whose enormous artistic and literary productivity overshadowed the work of his colleagues (Fig. 1). The most important of those contemporaries were the more prolific but artistically and intellectually duller George Gilbert Scott, the brilliant but intensely private William Butterfield, the flamboyant but seemingly unbusinesslike William Burges, and the enormously efficient but visually straitened Alfred Waterhouse. It was clear from the outset that Street accepted the commission for the law courts, the greatest prize of his generation, as a test of his leadership and a challenge to his ability.

However, the Royal Courts of Justice were built late in the High Victorian period and late in Street's career. The building was partially influenced by the new tastes that supplanted High Victorianism, and thus, while it was the climax of the movement, it was also its finale. It was fitting that the last phase of Street's career should produce such a transitional monument, for his office had been the training ground for the leaders of the new Queen Anne style that emerged in the 1870s. Richard Norman Shaw, Philip Webb, and William Morris had all worked for him as assistants or pupils during the fifties and early sixties, and he continued to be a friend and admirer of his erstwhile protégés.[2]

The climactic and transitional character of the law courts was recognized soon after they were completed in 1882, a year after Street's death. In a speech that Robert Kerr delivered to a conference of architects in 1884, he identified the building as the swan song of the entire Gothic revival:

1 George Edmund Street in 1877. (AES. Memoir.)

Street [was appointed] to build the Courts of Justice in an Academic [i.e., historicist] style, probably the most severely uncompromising that had ever been attempted in the world of archaeological art. The edifice has but recently been finished. It is a monument of artistic resolution, and, of course, of artistic skill. But it is much more than this. Such is the fearless muscularity of its artistic attitude, such the vehemence of its characteristic Gothic force—let me at once say ruthless violence—that without it the whole process of the Revival had been quite incomplete. But, for that very reason, the consummation at length accomplished, it was fit that the great movement should confess itself exhausted. Street died at the very goal, and his cause died with him. Except in ecclesiastical work, our modern Gothic of any high pretension is now no more; it has done its service, and done it well.[3]

George Edmund Street, the architect of the Royal Courts of Justice, was born in Woodford, Essex, in 1824.[4] His father, Thomas Street, was a City solicitor who had just moved to that suburban London town with his wife and Street's two older brothers. A sister was born a year later, and in 1830 the Streets relocated in Camberwell in South London. Street was enrolled in school at Mitcham, six miles away, but after a collegiate school opened in Camberwell he was registered there as a day student. When his father retired in 1839 and moved the family to Crediton in Devon, Street's schooling came to an end.

Street's career had several false starts. In Crediton that first autumn the family was joined by Thomas Henry, the eldest son, who had just succeeded his father as a partner in the London law firm. Thomas Street was an enthusiastic amateur ecclesiologist, and in Devon he took his youngest brother on the first of what were to be many walking tours of medieval monuments. Street's interest in architecture may have been kindled, but law was the more obvious career, and early in 1840 he was sent to London with Thomas Street to begin work in the family office.

In May the death of Street's father upset these plans, and he returned to live with his mother in Crediton, moving with her to nearby Exeter a few months later. There, the dominating form of the great cathedral seems to have captured his imagination, and, after a second tour with his brother, he moved to Taunton to take lessons in perspective and painting from Thomas Haseler, a local painter who was related to the Streets by marriage. However, this training did not immediately suggest a course for his future. In fact, Street now hoped for a life of service to the Church, but there was no money to send him to a university, and he returned to the law office in London.

Street's mother recognized her son's predicament, and, after he had resumed his place in the City, she consulted Haseler and arranged for Street to be articled to Owen Carter (1806–59), an architect in Winchester who was Haseler's cousin. Street eagerly accepted this more congenial proposal, joining Carter in the spring of 1841. In Winchester, another cathedral town, he spent three years, two years as a pupil and one as a somewhat unwilling assistant. Carter was a competent but unremarkable designer with a substantial provincial practice. His best-known work was the Winchester Corn Exchange (1836–38), modeled on Inigo Jones's St. Paul's, Covent Garden, but he was also an antiquarian and the architect of a number of unsophisticated Gothic churches. From Carter, Street learned the fundamentals of construction and professional practice. He also continued to study medieval architecture on his own. Thomas Street came to Winchester on every possible occasion, and the two brothers tramped across most of England together in the course of the next few years, giving up this pleasant holiday routine only after Thomas Street married in 1849.

In 1844 Thomas Street took a house at Lee, south of Greenwich, and the family reassembled near London. Mrs. Street came up from Exeter, and Street moved from Winchester. Having obtained an introduction, he presented himself at the office of G. G. Scott and W. B. Moffatt, who were pressed with work on the competition for the Nicholaikirche in Hamburg. They took on the nineteen-year-old as a temporary assistant, and he earned the right to stay permanently. Together with his fellow assistants, William White and George F. Bodley, Street was now introduced to the caliber of architecture that he wished to practice. He spent five years in the office in Spring Gardens at the time when Scott was closest to the artistic and intellectual leadership of the architectural profession. A committed Gothicist of the Ecclesiological stamp, Scott attracted men of the quality of Street, Bodley, and White to work for him, and the respect which they developed for their master during those years never faded, even when Scott could no longer be considered an artistic innovator. At the same time Street became an active member of the Ecclesiological Society, making his first contribution to the *Ecclesiologist* in 1848.[5]

In 1846 the Streets moved across South London to Peckham, and although the young architect moved with them, he now began to cut professional and family ties and to proceed toward greater independence. In 1847, at the age of twenty-three, he obtained his first commission in his own name for a church at Biscovey (Par), Cornwall, through a chance acquaintance which his sister had made while visiting Bath. Other work in that part of England followed, and in 1848 he exhibited for the first time at the Royal Academy, showing a view of his new church at Treverbyn, Cornwall. Street listed his address as Hampstead, and in 1849, encouraged by his success, he decided to leave Scott and establish his own office. He thus began his independent career in the pivotal year in which William Butterfield started the church of All Saints, Margaret Street, and John Ruskin published the *Seven Lamps of Architecture.* High Victorian architecture was being born.

From Cornwall the architect found that the focus of his practice soon began to shift toward Oxfordshire and Berkshire, where he had made the acquaintance of the influential vicar of Wantage, William Butler. Butler commissioned him to build a vicarage, and, more importantly, he introduced him to Samuel Wilberforce, the bishop of Oxford. In 1850 Wilberforce appointed Street his diocesan architect, and in November of that year Street moved to Wantage to be near his new work. His position insured him a continuous supply of substantial commissions.

During the years that he spent in the Oxford diocese, Street established the habit of taking his holidays abroad. He was motivated by a typical High Victorian curiosity about foreign architecture and by the need to find a substitute for the hikes across England which he had shared with his brother. In 1850 he made his first tour, to France, and he visited Germany and Belgium in 1851. In almost every succeeding year, except when war interfered, he spent at least a few weeks on the Continent.

Hoping to expand his private practice, Street moved from Wantage into Oxford in May 1852. There he obtained his first regular assistants, Edmund Sedding and Philip Webb, both of whom were friendly with the band of Pre-Raphaelite undergraduates then in residence. Up until that time his friend George Bodley had lent an occasional hand when the work was heavy. A month after settling in Oxford, Street married Mariquita Proctor, and their only child, Arthur Edmund, was born three years later. The architect prospered, and in 1856, when he won the second prize in the international competition for Lille Cathedral, he began to think about moving to London. Late that summer the young family took up residence at 33 Montague Place, Bloomsbury, not far from Thomas Street's new house in Gordon Square. Street's national reputation now began to grow, as he established himself as both a major artist and an important theorist.

The fundamental theoretical problem confronting the High Victorian architect was how to make medievalism the universal architectural vocabulary of the nineteenth century. A large measure of acceptance for Gothic had been won by the preceding generation, but while churches and rural houses were now medieval by general preference, many of the most important commissions for urban and monumental buildings were still reserved for classical architects. The challenge was a romantic one—to make the Middle Ages relevant to all aspects of an assertively modern culture—and High Victorian art was born of the ensuing struggle. High Victorian culture was similarly shaped by the confrontation of moral, material, and social polarities: imperial expansion and laissez-faire industrialism coexisted with political and social reform, and science flourished beside the arts. G. E. Street was especially well adapted to this prickly environment, for he possessed what one posthumous review called "that thoroughly robust English spirit which . . . confronts difficulties and dangers as incentives only to greater effort, greater self-confidence, and greater endurance."[6]

As the theoretician of High Victorian architecture, Street was practically unchallenged. Ruskin and Scott were the only other authors to discuss seriously the complex issues with which the movement was concerned, and he thought and wrote more about the problems than either of them. Street reserved a full measure of energy for architectural theory and did not allow this to be redirected to the demands of his practice, as did Scott, or to other artistic and social issues, as did Ruskin.

Street's theoretical writings are an excellent monitor of the architectural times. His first major publications, three seminal essays in the *Ecclesiologist* and a pamphlet, all written between 1850 and 1853, coincided with the beginnings of High Victorianism.[7] These were followed by a long series of articles and two books in the later fifties and sixties that explored the medieval architecture of Italy, Germany, France, and Spain, reflecting the widened stylistic horizons of his generation.[8] Finally, Street was given the opportunity to summarize his views as the architectural lecturer at the Royal Academy, first as a replacement for the ailing G. G. Scott in 1871, and in the last year of his life as the appointed lecturer.[9] To these must be added a host of other essays and lectures on ancillary issues, letters to magazines and newspapers, and his often quoted remarks at public meetings.[10]

This great outpouring was remarkably consistent. As in his architecture, changes of nuance revealed Street's later sympathy with some ideas of the younger architects, but there was a strong basic continuity between the first essay of 1850, written when High Victorianism was being defined, and the last lectures of 1881, delivered when the Queen Anne had been in fashion for a decade. As his son noted in his biography of Street, "With the literature of architecture, art, and religion he was widely conversant. He had read and studied these subjects diligently as a young man, and had thought them over so seriously that the views he then formed underwent comparatively little change."[11] In an era marked by complexity and change, Street was constitutionally equipped to provide stability and continuity.

At the heart of Street's High Victorian reconciliation of medievalism and modernity lay the fundamental, romantic belief that, as Ruskin wrote, "truths may be and often are *opposite,* though they cannot be contradictory."[12] For Street the most important opposed truths of architecture had been formulated by Early Victorian theorists in the forties, when his own architectural ideas were first shaped. That decade experienced a reaction against the gentle pluralism of the early nineteenth century, and two opposite points of view had emerged: that of Augustus Welby Northmore Pugin and the Ecclesiological Society on the one hand, and that of critics like Robert Kerr and James Fergusson on the other. Pugin, after defining the necessary underpinnings of good architecture, had specified, "It is in *pointed* architecture alone that these great principles have been carried out."[13] But Fergusson had countered that the objective of architects must be "to give up all imitation of past styles, and to start at once with the determination to surpass all that has hitherto been done."[14] High Victorian architecture was founded on the daring premise that somehow both Pugin's absolute medievalism and Fergusson's unconditional demand for a new style could be accommodated.

Street's intellectually taxing response to this dilemma refuted some of what Pugin and Fergusson had said while respecting their central arguments. He agreed with Fergusson that "copyism," the derogatory term of the day for Pugin's type of strict historicism, was indefensible. However, he also believed that the creation of a new style *ex nihilo* was impossible and that medieval architecture provided the best demonstration of correct architectural principles. Street maintained that medievalism could be made modern by extracting these principles from the study of Gothic, by admitting a wider historical and geographical range of precedents than the purists of the forties had allowed, and by permitting a process called "development" to transform Gothic architecture to meet the needs of the nineteenth century.

Street's strong stand against vesting absolute authority in a narrow body of precedent set him apart from Pugin and the Ecclesiological admirers of English "Middle Pointed." In 1852 Street attacked their kind of copyism: "The study to revive what is defunct, simply on antiquarian grounds, will never take deep root, or prosper. Unless it use fairly, and grapple with, all that is put before it to do, it cannot and will not succeed."[15] Nearly thirty years later he told the students at the Royal Academy, "I would never have you draw or sketch existing examples with a view to copying or reproducing them. That is wholly contrary to right principles."[16]

However, Street could also boast, "We *are* mediaevalists and rejoice in the name."[17] Like Pugin, Street believed fervently in the general superiority of Gothic architecture, which he thought was more technically sophisticated than classicism.

In 1852 he wrote: "Surely no man can pretend to say, that when once the arch had been discovered, men could truthfully persist in such clumsy expedients as those of the old Greeks soon came to be. The Romans of course felt this, but their style was not much more than that of the Greeks compatible with common sense after the invention of the pointed arch."[18] His argument was that the arch, with its ability to cover wide openings with small building stones, was the most ingenious type of construction, and that the pointed arch, which allowed architects to vault irregularly shaped spaces, was its most highly developed form. With this in mind, in his lectures at the Royal Academy he admitted only, "If you have such magnificent material that you can obtain it in masses of sufficient bulk, I can conceive no reason for objecting to the employment of trabeated systems of architecture."[19] And he strongly implied that economy and common sense would favor arcuated construction in the vast majority of cases.

Street's position was thus full of potential contradictions, but, by emphasizing architectural principles rather than precedents, he carefully balanced his medievalism between the copyism of Pugin and the antihistoricism of Fergusson. It was because of the demonstrable excellence of Gothic architecture, not because revivalism was an objective in itself, that Street proclaimed so proudly that he was a Goth. He stressed structural values, declaring in 1852, "In all architecture, the first principles are most eminently constructional."[20] These principles were best expressed in medieval architecture, for, as he later explained, the Gothic builder had accepted that construction must be "(1) permanent; (2) exhibited rather than concealed; (3) natural; (4) suitable to its purpose and material; and (5) it must avail itself of the latest discoveries and inventions where it is clear that they are usable under or consistently with the first four conditions."[21] The caveat attached to the final principle ruled out the extensive use of iron, at least as a concealed strengthener.

High Victorian medievalism, thus defined as a system of structural principles, had little need for the "associational" arguments which had been advanced by Pugin and the Ecclesiological Society. Such arguments justified the Gothic Revival on the basis of the connections between medieval architecture and the ancient and presumably better state of the Church and of society as a whole. Early in his career, as an ardent Ecclesiologist, Street believed in this himself. He wrote in 1852 that "Art must be considered generally in her religious aspect more than any other."[22] But already he tempered this sentiment with the observation: "While there is great danger that one class of men may think that they may prosper in a religious branch of art without religion, there is perhaps an almost equal danger lest others should mistake religion for art and deem that so an architect be religious, his success must be certain, and his work always good."[23] Street grew increasingly secure in this opinion as he learned more about the realities of medieval practice. In 1865, in his book on the Gothic architecture of Spain, he concluded,

> The common belief in a race of clerical architects and in ubiquitous bodies of freemasons, seems to me to be altogether erroneous. The more careful the inquiry that we make into the customs of the architects of the middle ages, the more clear does it appear that neither of these classes had any general existence; and in Spain, so far as I have examined, I have met with not a single trace of either. I am glad that it is so; for in these days of doubt and

perplexity as to what is true in art, it is at least a comfort to find that one may go on heartily with one's work, with the honest conviction that the position one occupies may be, if one chooses to make it so, as nearly as possible the same as that occupied by the artists of the middle ages.[24]

A few years later, during his work at Christ Church Cathedral, Dublin, Street reached an understanding of the motivation and character of medieval masons that contributed further to his skepticism: "The workmen absolved themselves of all responsibility, worked the stones they were ordered to work, and ate their meals between times with the same absolute *sang froid* that marks their successors at the present day. They had no more pleasure in their work, no more originality in their way of doing it, than our workmen have at the present time, all pretty fables to the contrary notwithstanding."[25] Thus did he dismiss the connections that the romantics had seen between religion, society, and art in the Middle Ages. For Street, the architecture had to stand on its own.

Imbued with principles and shorn of artistically irrelevant associations, Street's medievalism was also of great historical and geographic breadth. He could admire almost any architecture in which the pointed arch was employed, and while he favored certain periods and national schools, he was contemptuous of the narrow preference for English Middle Pointed that Pugin and the Ecclesiological Society had promoted.

In his first theoretical paper, a discussion of urban churches in 1850, Street lamented the unthinking adoption of the English rural church as a model.[26] He recommended the study of examples from the Continent, where many more large, urban churches had been built during the Middle Ages, a pursuit furthered by Street's own detailed reports on the architecture of Germany, Italy, France, and Spain. The national chauvinism that pervaded much of the early revival—reflected in the style adopted for the Houses of Parliament—must have seemed very parochial to him. He wrote feelingly and without bigotry about the architecture of the Île de France in 1858: "It is that which I have studied the most carefully, and love the most of any architecture that I know; it is one which presents no features unsuitable for our country or inconsistent with the demands of our climate."[27]

Having swept away the significance of national boundaries, Street was scarcely more respectful of chronological limits. Even in his apprenticeship days, when the Middle Pointed or Decorated style of about 1300 was the canonical model for most medievalizing architects, Street remembered that he and his drafting room colleagues had used to "swear by first-pointed; and we called Scott's work 'ogee' because we thought it too late in character."[28] He also appreciated late medieval architecture, noting in his early papers in the *Ecclesiologist* that fifteenth- and even sixteenth-century examples could teach useful lessons.[29] The large fifteenth-century churches that he found in the towns of Catalonia received special praise in his later book on Spain.[30]

Street insisted, however, that architects should not employ these historically and geographically diverse examples as the basis for a "hybrid and mixed style."[31] By adhering faithfully to structural principles and by thinking out all new problems afresh, he believed that a single, unified, and coherent style could be evolved that did not specifically quote bits of detail from unrelated sources. As he explained in

1858, the medieval traditions must be revived, but from them would develop a new art: "My aim has been to study old examples everywhere, and to throw myself, as much as possible, into the frame of mind and feeling about art which so nobly distinguished our old architects; and as they never copied, so I refuse to copy."[32] Street's wide-ranging curiosity about architecture even extended into some areas that lay well beyond the Gothic, and it was in this realm that he broke new ground. He was convinced, almost from the first, that the challenge of the High Victorian period—to produce a monumental, urban, secular architecture in the Gothic style—could be met only by adopting a large number of formal characteristics that were usually thought of as classical. He argued that such programs required "breadth," "uniformity," "symmetry," "regularity," "repose," and "horizontal lines."[33] To be sure, in keeping with his warning against hybridization, Street refused to accept the use of actual classical details in the architecture that he wished to see founded upon medieval principles. Yet he openly admitted that he was flirting with classicism. In 1852 he even proposed that "that architecture is best which best combines the verticality of Pointed with the repose of Classic architecture."[34] What he had in mind was a tempering of the picturesque and vertical qualities that were usually associated with Gothic in order to adapt it to the monumental, secular, and urban needs of the time. But Street perceived this in characteristically High Victorian terms as the reconciliation of opposite stylistic forces. To him the infamous "Battle of the Styles" seemed old-fashioned, and so he proposed a truce—admittedly on terms which were rather pro-Gothic—to be followed by an alliance of the once warring parties.

Where this alliance might lead would be determined, Street believed, by what we call "development."[35] This Darwinian process guaranteed that while "no style has ever been invented," new architecture nevertheless could be evolved "gradually and systematically" out of the architecture of the past.[36] Thus Street argued that medievalism could be made modern, noting that Gothic architects had historically "adapted themselves to the requirements of convenience with a novelty of resource and invention which is astonishing."[37] In the nineteenth century these processes of adaptation and development required consideration of "modern appliances and facilities," and Street denied that his medievalism implied "any desire to refuse to this age what its history really entitles it to demand."[38]

The concept of development, proposed as a solution to the contemporary historicist dilemma, also shaped Street's theory of architectural history. Rather than a sequence of "classical" moments, he interpreted the past as a dynamic system activated by the same process. In history Street found endless examples of the interaction of divergent stylistic forces and of architects caught between tradition and contemporary necessities. History offered a continuous record of the old giving birth to the new. This interpretation made the past an analogy for the present, and it supported his contention that architecture could evolve smoothly to meet new challenges. In 1881 Street described poetically this enlivened view of architectural history:

> The course of art is like a stream with endless back currents and eddies, which
> interrupt us on our way. It takes us from Egypt to Greece, from Greece to
> Rome, thence to Grecian art again at Byzantium, to Syria and the Holy Land.

Then it crosses again to Europe, taking possession of the south and west of France, and, joining two streams, one of mixed Byzantine and Roman from Ravenna and Venice, and the other of pure Romanesque from Rome, flows northward to the German Ocean. There these streams of art, rich in their combined developments, find another art establishing itself, founded upon an independent use of Roman work. At the same time, Moor and Christian are fighting for dear life in Spain, and wherever either plants his foot he builds in his own style, either in the most complete Moorish or in the severest Romanesque borrowed from his neighbours on the other side of the Pyrenees, but each showing occasional evidence in some part of his work of the influence of his enemy.[39]

Accordingly, wherever Street directed his study of medieval architecture, he focused on the dynamic forces of influence and change. In the Île de France he was fascinated by the patterns of influence exerted by the Rhenish Romanesque and by the Byzantine architecture of the south. In his published notes on his French travels in the late fifties, he described this region as "the meeting point as it were of these two developments, which made it the centre from which the best Gothic architecture of the world naturally sprung."[40] Similarly, Street justified the study of Le Puy in 1861 on the basis of its "special value as illustrating, among other things, the way in which French Gothic was developed from Romanesque and Byzantine buildings."[41]

In German architecture Street attributed stylistic changes to successive waves of foreign influence.[42] And he confessed that when he began his researches in Spain, "I fully expected . . . that I should find evidence . . . that if the Moors were . . . influenced by the sight of Christian art, the Christians would not be less so by the sight of theirs."[43] In fact, he found that Christian and Islamic art rarely interacted, but he did establish the existence of a decisive French influence on the great Spanish churches of Toledo, Burgos, and León.[44]

As a High Victorian, Street was particularly intrigued by those patterns of historical development in which seemingly opposite forces had been reconciled. This led him naturally to medieval Italy, where strong recollections of Roman classicism had survived the nominal triumph of Gothic taste. Italian medieval architecture possessed many of the same characteristics that Street believed should mark a classically tempered Gothic for the nineteenth century. He first visited Italy in 1853, and in 1855 his first book discussed the special eclecticism of Italian medieval architects, who, "conversant alike with the beauties of the best pointed architecture of the North and the best classic examples of Italy, worked in an eclectic fashion, taking what they deemed best from each, and endeavouring to unite the perfections of both."[45] This was very nearly Street's formula for the architecture of his own time. However, in following the Italian example, the contemporary architect must take pains to preserve the underlying medieval constructional principles and to adopt only those formal classical qualities appropriate for modern monumental architecture. While the architect was to explore both Gothic and classical examples, he was only to

gather from each that which is best in principle, and . . . combine them—not in the production of a hybrid and mixed style of architecture, but only in the development of our application of those true principles of construction, of which the architects of the pointed style were the first to acknowledge the necessity, and the first to introduce . . . . Nothing on earth would ever convince me that we ought ever to give up the use of the pointed arch—unless, indeed, some better principle of construction could be invented, which I believe to be impossible.[46]

Italy thus proved that apparently irreconcilable objectives could be accommodated, an achievement that John Ruskin had first identified in these High Victorian terms in his *Stones of Venice.* The second volume, published in July 1853, provided the first thorough discussion of Venetian medieval architecture, and helped to inspire Street's initial trip to Italy a few months later. In the first volume Ruskin had already described the convergence of European and Asian architectural taste at Venice in an unforgettable passage:

> Opposite in their character and mission, alike in their magnificence of energy, they came from the North and from the South, the glacier torrent and the lava stream; they met and contended over the wreck of the Roman empire; and the very centre of the struggle, the point of pause of both, and the dead water of the opposite eddies, charged with the embayed fragments of the Roman wreck, is VENICE. The Ducal palace of Venice contains the three elements in exactly equal proportions—the Roman, Lombard, and Arab. It is the central building of the world.[47]

The central building of the world—for Ruskin the Palazzo Ducale, a secular and urban building—was the ideal of High Victorian architecture expressed in its most romantic terms. Street, too, dreamed of such architecture, a disciplined eclecticism, in which all the elements of a diverse past and a demanding present might be equally alive.

John Ruskin was eloquent, and the spark of his eloquence burned within all of High Victorian architecture. However, his views did not comprise a coherent body of theory, and Street's own High Victorian theoretical position was an original synthesis of ideas culled from Ruskin and a variety of other sources. From Pugin and the Ecclesiological Society he had learned to believe that much of the importance of Gothic architecture derived from its superior principles. Indeed, for an early essay Street borrowed his title phrase, "true principles," from one of Pugin's most celebrated books.[48] However, Street could not accept the concomitant emphasis placed by those earlier authorities on the religious and cultural associations of medievalism, nor could he condone their copyism.

It was from Gilbert Scott, in whose office Street worked from 1844 until 1849, that he probably learned to treat historical precedents with High Victorian self-assurance. In a seminal essay, apparently written in 1849, Scott had enunciated many of the more important parts of the High Victorian argument before Street had published any theoretical papers of his own. After asserting his belief in the "perfect adaptation of pointed architecture to the altered requirements of our day," Scott went on to plead for "the amalgamation of all which is really beautiful and intrinsically valuable in the hitherto attained developments of pointed architecture; and, while we may take one period as our nucleus or groundwork, the engrafting upon it of all the essential beauties of earlier or later periods."[49] He accepted the study of Continental architecture as well, and he proscribed "mere copying of ancient examples."[50] As in Street's formulation only a few years later, Scott believed in Gothic as a universally valid system, and he broadened Gothic to include a wide historical and geographical range of examples. He also proposed the notion that medievalism could be made thoroughly up-to-date through a process specifically called "development." Indeed, Scott was to make the theme of development almost his own, devoting much of his *Remarks on Secular and Domestic Architecture* (1857) to that subject.[51]

Scott was thus a father of High Victorian architecture, and his office in the forties, with Street, Bodley, and White in attendance, was one of its nurseries. Nevertheless, Street did not adopt Scott's arguments without embellishing them. The older architect had little to say about the question of principles, which Street emphasized strongly. Scott's greater pragmatism was also reflected in his relative lack of interest in seeking out examples of transition and cross-fertilization in history, where Street sought analogies for the present situation. Thirteen years Street's senior, he did not feel as sharply the High Victorian urgency for reconciling opposites; Scott was a genial man who would rather yield a point than induce a tedious argument. Thus, while loyal to Gothic, he readily accepted the use of iron, and, to disarm his modernist critics, he was even willing to vow, "I am no mediaevalist."[52] As we have seen, Street held the opposite view.

Much of this new, more uncompromising spirit was Ruskin's contribution to High Victorian architecture.[53] From him, too, it is likely that Street learned to see history as a dynamic process, and his more spirited phrases owe a great deal to the writing style of the famous critic. Street thus took Pugin's medieval fervor, tempered it with Scott's broadmindedness, and then rekindled its flame from Ruskin's fire.

In practice and in theory Street faced the same High Victorian challenge—that of producing designs for the wide range of urban and monumental programs created in the nineteenth century. But until the mid-1860s, when he simultaneously entered competitions for the National Gallery and the law courts, his architecture did not correspond very closely to his espoused philosophy. In particular, he rarely attempted to imbue medieval architecture with classical clarity, as he proposed so forcefully in his writings, perhaps because of the relative scarcity of appropriate commissions. But Street also had an abiding taste for the picturesque and the ability to design brilliantly in that mode. He could not easily give up what he did so well. As a result, it was left to G. G. Scott to design the first and paradigmatic High Victorian public building, his symmetrical and strongly corniced entry in the Hamburg Rathaus competition of 1854. The Oxford Museum (Thomas N. Deane and Benjamin Woodward, 1854–61) adopted a similar solution.

Street's picturesque taste was clearly expressed in his early religious work, much of it strongly influenced by the popularity that the English Middle Pointed style enjoyed during the 1840s. His pretty little church of St. Peter, Treverbyn, of 1848–50, undertaken before he set up his own office, was an ideal Decorated country

2 *St. Peter, Treverbyn, Cornwall.*
1848–50. (Courtesy of Paul Joyce.)

3 *Sketch for the Oxford*
Museum. 1853. (GES. An
Urgent Plea for the Revival
of True Principles of
Architecture in the Public
Buildings of the University of
Oxford. *Oxford and London:*
John Henry Parker, 1853.
Sterling Memorial Library, Yale
University.)

church of Puginian character (Fig. 2). The clear and picturesque articulation of parts and the simple and obvious construction reflected the best that could be learned from the preceding generation, and these same elements were given enlarged treatment in his own sketch design of a few years later for the Oxford Museum (Fig. 3). Here the program for a major public building on a town site seemed to demand just the kind of quasi-classical discipline that Street had described in his first theoretical papers. The long stretches of horizontal molding and the large expanses of roof did provide a measure of repose. But, perhaps mirroring the somewhat informal architecture typical of college towns, the overall effect was determined by the juxtaposition of two dissimilar towers, by the dramatically varied fenestration patterns of the two lateral wings, and by the placement of the main entrance in a corner of a collegiate courtyard. The model for this design appears to have been Pugin's palace for the Roman Catholic bishop of Birmingham of 1839–41.

The same picturesque qualities prevailed even when Street, the nascent High Victorian, began to replace the English prototypes of his first few years of practice with foreign sources. Although he revered Italian Gothic for its echoes of classicism, that reverence is hard to detect in the buildings designed after his first trip to northern Italy in 1853. His church of All Saints, Boyne Hill (Maidenhead), Berkshire (1854–56), is an English Decorated prototype injected with a large dose of Italian structural polychromy of the kind that Butterfield had made famous only a few years earlier at All Saints, Margaret Street. This Italian color superficially

identifies the building as High Victorian, but All Saints reveals little of Street's more complex, theoretical High Victorianism. Most notably, it is impossible to find in this picturesque suburban design and its straggle of related houses and school buildings any of the underlying classicism that he so praised in his book of 1855 on Italian Gothic. In his urban church of St. James-the-Less, Westminster (1859–61), in which an admiration of Italian forms mixes with a sympathetic understanding of the great brick churches of northern Germany, broken rooflines and pronounced asymmetries also dominate the composition (Fig. 4). Most surprising of all, when given the opportunity to design a vast public building for London in the government offices

4 St. James-the-Less, Westminster. 1859–61. (Ecclesiologist 20 [1859].)

5 *Foreign Office competition, London. 1856–57. West façade. (Illustrated London News, 24 October 1857.)*

competition of 1856–57, Street still resisted his theoretician's conscience and produced a picturesque ensemble (Fig. 5). To be sure, he maintained that the north elevation (now lost) of his Foreign Office design possessed a "general effect of uniformity," but he proposed a resolutely irregular façade where the building faced St. James's Park.[54] Although Street provided insistent horizontal bands of constructional polychromy and an explicitly Italian campanile and upper story arcade, the roofline was repeatedly broken and interrupted by towers and spires, and the masses of the building were arranged around a series of railed courtyards like that of his project for the Oxford Museum.

Indeed, despite his strong theoretical position, Street's Italian Gothic was largely a matter of color and motifs, and his taste for it was of short duration. By the mid-fifties, in the company of architects like William Burges and his close friend George F. Bodley, Street was drawn increasingly toward the early Gothic of France. This style, which grew into the High Victorian submovement called "Early French," afforded an alternative solution for the urban and monumental programs of the era. Unlike the Italian quasi-classicism that Street had embraced in theory, the Early French achieved monumentality through strong massing and picturesque vigor. That is what Street admired about Laon cathedral in 1859: "The stern, solemn majesty of its art is just what we modern men ought to endeavour to impress ourselves with."[55]

6 *Theological College, Cuddesdon, Oxfordshire. 1852–54. Entrance façade of original wing.*

Street's Early French had its roots in his general interest in early Gothic, with which he began to experiment in the later 1840s, when he was an assistant in Scott's progressive office. This appreciation of a sterner, almost primitive architecture, though not yet French in source, was reflected in another Cornish commission that Street accepted before going out on his own, the church of St. Mary, Biscovey (Par), of 1847–48. The lancets, plate tracery, and broad expanses of rustic masonry at Par contrasted sharply with the details of his nearly contemporary work at Treverbyn. Some of this almost blunt simplicity was retained in the initial wing of the diocesan Theological College of Oxfordshire, in the village of Cuddesdon, which Street built in 1852–54 (Fig. 6). This was his first major building and the cornerstone of his national reputation, but although its forms were simple and the composition was powerful, it remained picturesque. It scarcely fulfilled his theoretical guidelines for secular architecture.

This taste for early Gothic assumed a strong Gallic flavor in the wake of the competition for Lille cathedral in 1855–56, in which Burges and Street won the first and second prizes, respectively.[56] The instructions specified that the designs should be in the French style of the early thirteenth century, and Burges's and Street's successes catapulted that idiom to popularity in Britain. A year later Street won another second prize in the Crimean War Memorial Church competition with a massive, heavily buttressed design of a decidedly "early" character; and in 1859 he began two churches, one in Howsham, Yorkshire, and the other in a growing suburb of Oxford, that were among the first realizations of the new style.

The most splendid example of Street's work in this mode was the actual Crimean Memorial Church which he built in Istanbul in 1863–68, after the authorities had changed the site and discovered that they could not get along with Burges, who had originally won the commission (Fig. 7). The invigorated picturesque qualities of the Early French also permeated Street's design of the Convent of St. Margaret, East

7 *Crimean Memorial Church, Istanbul. Revised design, 1863–68. (Building News, 21 August 1868.)*

Ground Plan.

Scale.

VESTRY CLOISTER

CHANCEL NAVE

PULPIT

FONT

10 5 0 10 20 30 40 FEET

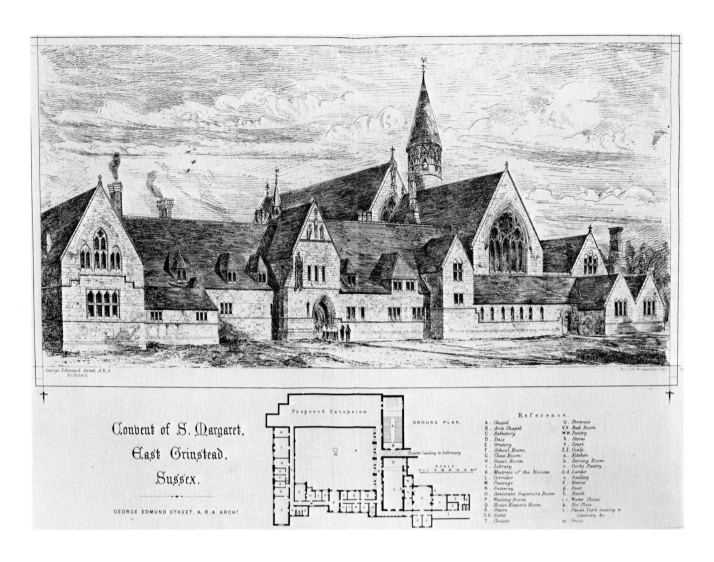

Convent of S. Margaret.
East Grinstead.
Sussex.

GEORGE EDMUND STREET, A.R.A. ARCH.ᵗ

8 Convent of St. Margaret,
East Grinstead, Sussex. 1864–
90. Chapel built to revised de-
sign, 1878–83. (Building
News, 18 December 1868.)

Grinstead, Sussex (1864–90), his largest work before he entered the great law courts and National Gallery competitions in 1866 (Fig. 8). There again Street produced an informal composition, justified by the rural setting of the building.

The Early French achieved monumentality without resorting to the proposed synthesis of classical and Gothic, and this "muscular" and "masculine" style thus drove a wedge between Street's High Victorian theory and practice.[57] It nevertheless became the preferred architectural idiom for Street and many other architects in the early sixties, for it possessed both extraordinary visual power and a timely congruence with High Victorian cultural values. At that time, the intellectualization of the Early Victorian period was gradually yielding to a more vigorous, outgoing attitude. A symptom of these new values was the emphasis on physical exercise and sport at public schools, a movement led by Rugby School under Thomas Arnold and celebrated by Thomas Hughes in *Tom Brown's School Days* (1857). Another sign of the times was the challenge offered to theological ritual and symbolism made by what was significantly called "muscular Christianity." This term was aptly defined by Charles Kingsley in 1865 as "a healthful and manful Christianity; one which does not exalt the feminine virtues to the exclusion of the masculine."[58]

To these currents of thought Street remained alert, and his work for Edward Thring, the famous headmaster of Uppingham School, brought him into direct contact with one of the leaders of the movement. Thring had taken over the then tiny school in Rutland in 1853, and on his first day he played a symbolically important cricket match with the boys.[59] He revised the curriculum in order to attract students, increasing the contact between the masters and their pupils, and he also launched an important building program. In 1859 Uppingham erected the first gymnasium of any public school in Britain, followed a few years later by a carpentry shop. In 1861 Thring obtained the appointment of Street, over the objections of the board of supervisors, to design a new school room and a chapel.[60] It is easy to imagine why Thring, who wrote that education must strike a "balance of manliness and intellect," was impressed by Street's work of that period, and why Street produced a muscular design for Uppingham.[61]

Reinforcement of this kind helped to sustain the Early French and delayed Street in putting his theories completely into practice until 1866 and the competition for the law courts. Only then did he face squarely what he had identified as the High Victorian challenge and impose classical order on the architecture of the Middle Ages; this gave his contest entry peculiar poignancy and significance. Thereafter, Street was beset by the great political and bureaucratic forces that shape most of the following story. But in the midst of that storm, Street continued to reconsider his artistic position, as reflected in the slow evolution of the revised and final designs. The law courts as built returned to the muscular and picturesque, and that final transformation signaled Street's abandonment of his quest for the "central building of the world."

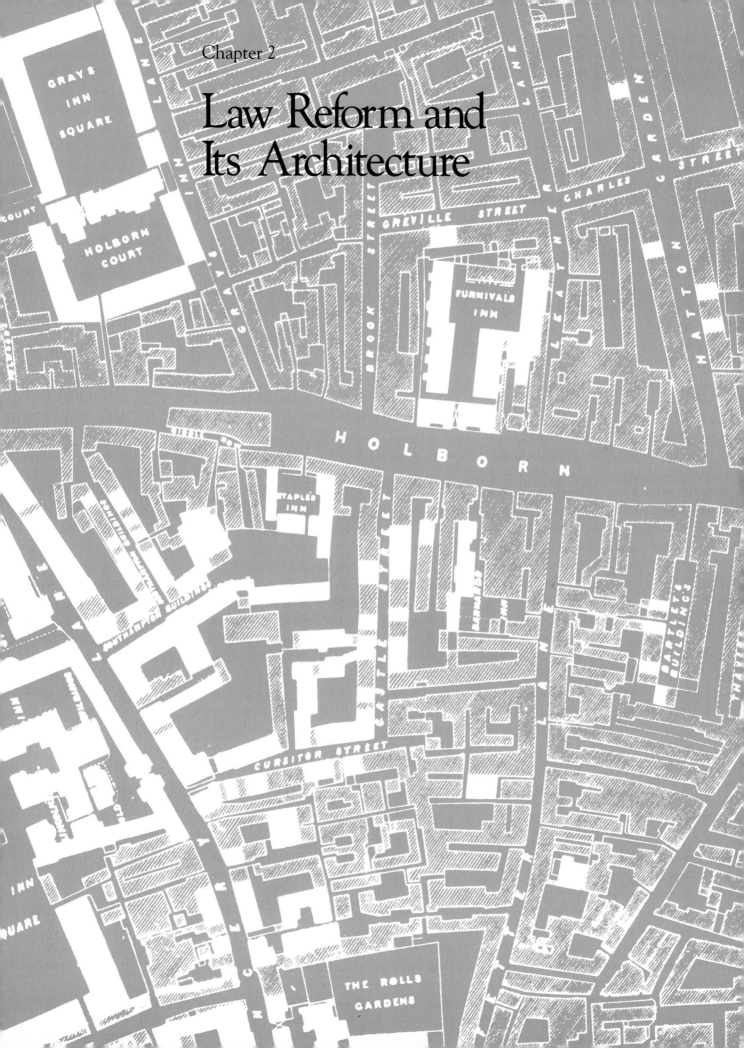

Chapter 2

Law Reform and
Its Architecture

"The Staff of Honesty and the Shield of Innocence."
—Henry Peter Brougham, 1828

I saw crimes of the most pernicious nature pass unheeded by the law: acts of
no importance put in point of punishment upon a level with the most baneful
crimes: punishments inflicted without measure and without choice: satisfaction denied for the most crying injuries: the doors of justice barred against a
great majority of the people by the weight of wanton and unnecessary expense: false conclusions ensured in most questions of fact by hasty and inconsistent rules of evidence: light shut out from every question of fact by fantastic
and ill considered rules of evidence: the business of hours spun out into years:
impunity extended to acknowledged guilt and compensation snatched out of
the hands of injured innocence by . . . impertinent and inscrutable exemp-
tion: the measure of decision in many cases unformed: in others locked up and
made the object of a monopoly: the various rights and duties of the various
classes of mankind jumbled together into one immense and unsorted heap:
men ruined for not knowing what they are neither enabled nor permitted even
to learn: and the whole fabric of jurisprudence a labyrinth without a clew.[1]

THUS WROTE Jeremy Bentham of English law in the 1770s, when he was a
young barrister. Six decades later, when Queen Victoria ascended to the throne,
the legal system was still a labyrinth, but enormous improvements had been made
by the time she celebrated her Golden Jubilee. By that time two generations of
reformers, aroused by Bentham's critique and guided by his utilitarian philosophy,
had almost entirely reshaped the law and its administration.[2] A new building to
house the reformed superior courts had become the symbol of their efforts, just as
the reform of suffrage, enacted in 1832, took the Houses of Parliament as its symbol.

The history of nineteenth-century law reform is bound up inextricably with
Street's commission for the law courts. The nature of the legal reforms determined
the program of the building, and the reform agenda included its construction. The
politics of the broader movement called "Reform," which transformed almost every
public institution in Britain, shaped the system of government controls under which
Street labored. More abstractly, the law reformers' progressive habits of thought and
modes of analysis are so typical of the age that they also found expression in Street's
architecture.

The connections between Street and the legal profession were personal. His
father, Thomas Street, was a solicitor in the City of London who established his
office in Philpot Lane in 1784. His eldest brother, Thomas Henry (eight years his
senior), became a partner in the firm in 1839 and eventually inherited the business.
Although his own legal career was brief—Street himself spent several months in the

office in 1840—family ties kept him in touch with the world of the law. Through Thomas, Street would have learned of the great campaign mounted during the first decades of the reign of Victoria to correct the manifold inequities of the law and to mend the defects of the system through which it was administered. He would also have learned of the reformers' plans for a new, centrally located building for the courts, plans in which he became uniquely prepared to play a leading role.

The Legal Labyrinth ENGLISH law as Street first learned of it was a great, creaking apparatus encumbered by redundancies in some areas but entirely powerless in many others. On the local level two distinct systems of courts survived. First, justices of the peace, amateur officials appointed both to maintain order and to render justice, sat in quarterly "quarter sessions" hearing minor criminal cases. Second, traveling judges of the King's central courts presided over the assizes, a separate set of courts where major criminal suits and civil cases were heard. The assizes brought the King's justice to the major county towns, and their work grew as the demands of an increasingly complex society began to overtax the competence of the nonprofessional quarter sessions. In London a permanent assize court, devoted solely to criminal cases, was established in 1834 to serve the large needs of the capital city. This was popularly called the "Old Bailey."

The most serious and complicated civil cases from the country were referred to the national superior courts which sat in London, although in certain instances this responsibility could be delegated to the assizes by a process called *nisi prius*. The London courts were divided into two major divisions, common law and equity, which administered two separate bodies of law. The common law division was further subdivided into the courts of common pleas, King's bench, and Exchequer, and there was a third, less important branch of the superior courts that considered matters of ecclesiastical law. By the early years of the nineteenth century, the lines that divided these various jurisdictions had grown indistinct and confusing.

While the court system was organized according to a hierarchy of authority, presided over by the lord chancellor, the chief judge of the equity court, no clear process of appeal existed. Indeed, except in cases of judicial error, appeals were very rare in Britain before the last hundred years, although the House of Lords had established appellate jurisdiction over most of the courts and the Privy Council reserved final authority over the ecclesiastical and colonial courts. Only in 1830 was the Court of Exchequer Chamber established as an appeals court for matters of common law, and in 1851 a Court of Appeals was created for questions of equity. Criminal cases had no explicit avenue of appeal until 1907, although important trials were often transferred from the assizes to the King's bench, and the home secretary might be petitioned to grant clemency.

The legal profession which served this judicial system was also divided into two branches: the bar, composed of barristers who argued cases in court but did not usually consult directly with the parties, and the solicitors (or attorneys) who were retained by clients to handle nonlitigious business and to engage the assistance of a barrister if a case was to be heard before a judge. Both branches of the profession were concentrated in London, the home of the superior courts and the headquarters for those judges assigned to the assize circuits. Barristers for the most part had their offices in the Inns of Court, the dozen or so collegiate institutions that had been erected just west of the City of London on the land previously occupied by the great medieval monasteries. The largest of the inns were Lincoln's Inn, Gray's Inn, the Inner Temple, and the Middle Temple. They served a variety of functions—educational, fraternal, and professional—and membership was a prerequisite for admission to the bar. Their concentration in a small geographical area induced the majority of London solicitors to establish their offices in the same quarter. However, in the beginning of the nineteenth century, the superior courts themselves were clustered in the vicinity of the royal Palace of Westminster, more than a mile to the southwest of the inns, where their location reflected their origin as an extension of the King's personal judgment. After the Napoleonic Wars, Sir John Soane designed a new building for them adjacent to Westminster Hall, but this was quickly overcrowded as the courts struggled to accommodate the soaring legal demands of the nineteenth century. A piecemeal exodus of courts and offices from Westminster began almost immediately after the new building was completed, and, by the time Street took his place in the family office, these facilities were scattered across the length and breadth of London.

The condition of the law and legal practice in these courts during the time of Street's youth was trenchantly captured in the novels of Charles Dickens, particularly *Bleak House* (1852) and *Pickwick Papers* (1836–37).[3] Dickens fanned the eighteenth-century indignation of Bentham into an inferno of cruder nineteenth-century rage: an intensification of feeling that was to produce reform. In *Bleak House*, the complacent hypocrisy of the Court of Chancery was laid bare:

> To see everything going on so smoothly, and to think of the roughness of the suitors' lives and deaths; to see all that full dress and ceremony, and to think of the waste, and want, and beggared misery it represented; to consider that, while the sickness of hope deferred was raging in so many hearts, this polite show went calmly on from day to day, and year to year, in such good order and composure; to behold the Lord Chancellor, and the whole array of practitioners under him, looking at one another and at the spectators, as if no one had ever heard that all over England the name in which they were assembled was a bitter jest; was held in universal horror, contempt, and indignation: was known for something so flagrant and bad, that little short of a miracle could bring any good out of it to any one.[4]

The common law courts were portrayed no more favorably in *Pickwick Papers*.

Complex, Slow, and Costly

THIS WAS the legal world in which Street's father and brother worked, captured on the eve of its demise. Its faults, as observed by Dickens or by any informed critic, can be discussed under three headings: technicality, delay, and expense.

The technicalities of the law in the early nineteenth century were chiefly the products of historical survival. They were often the enlightened reforms of earlier times, rendered obsolete and even counterproductive by changed conditions. The division of the superior courts into two separate branches, equity (or chancery) and common law, was the most striking and awkward of these survivals, the petrification of a sixteenth-century innovation. At that time, the medieval custom of providing a more flexible alternative to the precedent-bound justice of the common law courts was institutionalized in the form of an equity court, presided over by the lord chancellor (hence the alternative name, "chancery"), the traditional keeper of the King's conscience. At first the chancellor was not bound by any precedent, and he could thus decide cases where there was none or where the peculiarities of circumstance demanded greater latitude for judgment. But over the years the equity court created its own body of precedent, and by the time of Lord Eldon, lord chancellor in 1801–06 and 1807–27, it had become at least as inflexible as the courts of common law. But worse than the rigidity of equity law was its frequent conflict with common law. The problem was not merely the slight possibility that a single case might be decided differently under the two systems. The greater, everyday problem was that different procedures and separate but sometimes poorly defined jurisdictions led to endless confusion, creating a private realm in which only the initiates of the legal profession could hope to find their way. In this realm abuse flourished, isolated from effective public scrutiny.

Under common law, much of the public bewilderment and dismay—and, ultimately, anger—was directed at the unnecessary complications involved in committing a case to the courts. A report written in 1829 concluded that there were five usual maneuvers with which proceedings might be begun in the King's bench or common pleas divisions, and six in the Exchequer division. These did not include the most straightforward method, the issuance of an "original writ," for that procedure left the plaintiff without recourse if the defense counsel could find a minute defect in the papers. It was necessary to be more devious.[5]

Other qualms beset the suitor contemplating an action in chancery, although committing a case there was less complex. In chancery law the principle of "complete justice" was the stumbling block. The court had to decide every aspect of cases referred to it, even those not in dispute between the parties.[6] This led to long proceedings, to unexpected results, and to the resolution of many cases by private arbitration.

In the conduct of the trial itself, the method of collecting evidence was the greatest obstacle. Although similarly obtuse, common law and equity procedures in this area were vastly different. Common law was very much dependent upon the jury's consideration of oral testimony. This simple and fair-minded principle was crippled, however, by the rule that parties and interested witnesses could not give evidence at all, a paradox illustrated in a case cited by Lord Bowen: "If a farmer in his gig ran over a foot-passenger in the road, the two persons whom the law singled out to prohibit from becoming witnesses were the farmer and the foot-passenger."[7] In theory, this rule protected otherwise honest persons from the temptation of perjury, but in practice some justice was inevitably sacrificed.

Chancery observed no such nicety of distinction between eligible and ineligible witnesses; it simply prohibited oral (or *viva voce*) testimony altogether. Rather, it employed a cumbersome, time-consuming, costly, and unjust system of taking written depositions. Special commissions were sent to examine witnesses at a place near their homes. When dispatched outside of London, the members of the commissions were paid a two guinea per diem by the parties, with an additional fifteen shillings for each clerk. Parties and their counsel were not allowed to accompany the commissions, and testimony was returned to the court written in the third person, in words chosen by the commissioners. Cross-examination in any useful sense was impossible, and it was often necessary to transfer questions of disputed fact to a common law court for decision.[8]

These technicalities were only overcome by the use of elaborate fictions. For example, because there was no satisfactory equity machinery for deciding questions between amicable parties, fictitious injuries had to be invented in order to obtain judgment. Real property law was full of such inventions, such as the procedure for recovering possession of a piece of land, again as detailed by Lord Bowen:

> The claimant began his action by delivering to the defendant a written statement narrating the fictitious adventures of two wholly imaginary characters called John Doe and Richard Roe, personages who had in reality no more existence than Gog and Magog. The true owner of the land, it was averred, had given John Doe a lease of the property in question, but John Doe had been forcibly and wrongly ejected by Richard Roe, and had in consequence begun an action of trespass and ejectment against him. Richard Roe, meanwhile, being a "casual ejector" only, advised the real defendant to appear in court and procure himself to be made defendant in place of the indifferent and unconcerned Richard Roe, otherwise the defendant would infallibly find himself turned out of possession.[9]

Ultimately, even if the technicalities of procedure could be overcome with the aid of such elaborate fictions, a court might decline to make a decision and refer the case to the other branch of the legal system. More commonly, a decision would be forthcoming, but the court would lack the power to enforce its own judgment. Equity courts were not empowered to award damages, and common law courts could not issue injunctions.[10]

While these complications made the achievement of justice uncertain, they also conspired with other factors to make it agonizingly slow. The antiquated court system was unable to keep up with the enormously enlarged demands placed upon it by a growing and increasingly complex society. The necessary personnel and procedures were lacking even to maintain the eighteenth-century pace of business at a time when most institutions were accelerating the rate at which they worked.

Symbolic of this problem, as it was of the legal system, was the office of the lord chancellor. At the beginning of the nineteenth century the chancellor was the sole fully qualified equity judge, aided by a master of the rolls with only some of the same powers. In addition to his primary judicial responsibility, he was also the Speaker of the House of Lords and its chairman when it heard appeals from the lower courts. Lord Eldon, who held the office for most of the first quarter of the century, was a methodical jurist and fond of the intricate system over which he presided. But he was unable to keep up with an increasing burden of equity cases, even after the appointment of a vice chancellor in 1813. The common law courts were similarly understaffed.

In addition, the long survival of an impossibly short judicial year—four terms of three weeks each on the common law side—resulted in prodigious arrears. In the beginning of 1839, just a year before G.E. Street entered the family office, 859 cases were waiting to be heard in the equity courts. Those at the top of the list had been ready for hearing for anywhere between eighteen months and three years, depending on the specific court. Owing to the cumbersome system of taking written testimony, two hearings were usually required for each case, necessitating a minimum of three years to obtain judgment. But even greater delay was anticipated for the future, when it was predicted that the increase in litigation would lengthen the time required for a two-hearing case to thirteen years or more. The backlog in common law was not quite as large, but at the beginning of 1837 there were three hundred cases waiting to be heard before the Queen's bench, its most heavily used court, and delays of more than a year were usual.[11] In scale, the predicament resembles that which afflicts American courts in the 1980s, where civil cases face a median pretrial waiting period of 19 months in the federal judiciary and as much as 4 years and 135 days at the state level.[12]

Finally, justice was not only difficult and slow, it was also prohibitively expensive. Even without considering the costs of delay itself, the financial burden of extended litigation could bankrupt the ultimately victorious party. An estate of £60,000 could be liquidated in a trial testing the will, such as Dickens narrated in the case of *Jarndyce v. Jarndyce* in *Bleak House,* for, in addition to the double expense of retaining a solicitor and a barrister, the suitor was devastated by innumerable court fees. These fees supported a great number of legal sinecures, chiefly the common law clerks and chancery masters, who had to be paid to file papers and to make the many requisite but often useless copies of documents. The labor was, of course, performed by poorly paid subordinates. Moreover, in chancery, there were the expenses of the commissions appointed to record testimony. Because the intricacies of the law frequently required the repetition of certain steps in a proceeding, these payments to both lawyers and the courts often had to be made more than once.

The detriments of complication, delay, and expense combined effectively to deny justice to all but the well-educated, the unhurried, and the well-to-do. The fault was not that the courts of England failed to do justice, but that they bestowed it only on these fortunate few.

Reform

THE FIRST step to eradicate these evils was taken by Henry Peter Brougham, a Whig, who made an important motion in Parliament on February 7, 1828. In a speech lasting six hours and three minutes, during which he consumed a hatful of oranges, Brougham won support for the creation of two commissions to investigate the multiple shortcomings of English law. His peroration was memorable:

> It was the boast of Augustus—it formed part of the glare in which the perfidies of his earlier years were lost—that he found Rome of brick and left it of marble; a praise not unworthy a great prince, and to which the present reign also has it claims. But how much nobler will be the sovereign's boast when he shall have it to say that he found law dear and left it cheap; found it a sealed book, left it a living letter; found it the patrimony of the rich, left it the

> inheritance of the poor; found it the two-edged sword of craft and oppression, left it the staff of honesty and the shield of innocence.[13]

The work of the resulting royal commissions was less stirring, but when Brougham was named lord chancellor two years later (as Lord Brougham) reform began to gain momentum.

Brougham (1778–1868), attorney general for Queen Caroline in her "trial" before the House of Lords in 1820 and a strong supporter of the reform of suffrage in 1831 and 1832, accomplished more by personal exertion and example than by altering the legal system. He initiated a number of institutional and procedural reforms, some of which were enacted, but he was best remembered for the zest with which he attacked the great backlog of cases waiting to be heard in his own court. At the beginning of his tenure of office, Brougham sat without vacation from November 22, 1830, until September 27, 1831, hearing arguments even on Good Friday and Easter Monday.[14] He characteristically worked from 10 A.M. to 11 P.M. or midnight, and so successful was he in demolishing the court's arrears that twice he was reportedly able to adjourn due to lack of business.[15]

This earned Brougham high respect in some circles, where it was perceived that "a new spirit was introduced into the realms of Chaos and Old Night."[16] But others questioned whether much true reform was taking place and pointed out that in his enthusiasm for dispatch Brougham was apt to be careless. In fact, his conduct of the case of *Brookman v. Rothschild*, heard while he was preparing his great speech in support of the Whig (Suffrage) Reform Bill of 1831, demonstrated such negligence that Lord Kingsdown wrote that it merited impeachment.[17]

Brougham's flamboyance and independence were also a liability to his political colleagues. His unauthorized lobbying efforts for the renewal of the Coercion Bill in 1834 acutely embarrassed and forced the resignation of Lord Grey, the prime minister. Lord Holland, the great Whig leader, had reason to recall his prediction of 1830, made after it had been decided to offer the Great Seal of the chancellorship to Brougham: "I suppose it must be so, but this is the last time we shall meet in peace."[18] Brougham's concrete achievements were also questioned, and late in 1834 it was revealed in Parliament that there were still two hundred outstanding cases in the court of chancery and that even more appeals were waiting for hearing in the House of Lords, despite his fabled exertions to reduce the backlog.[19]

At least, Brougham's efforts had drawn much attention to the problem of law reform. Unfortunately, the same could not be said of the work of Brougham's immediate successors. After a brief Tory interlude he was succeeded by Charles Christopher Pepys (Lord Cottenham, chancellor 1836–41) and then by a Conservative, John Singleton Copley (Lord Lyndhurst, chancellor 1841–46). Cottenham made an unsuccessful effort to rationalize the lord chancellor's duties in 1836, and Lyndhurst made some modest administrative reforms, but their only substantial contribution to law reform was the appointment of two additional vice chancellors, a measure proposed by Cottenham and enacted by Lyndhurst. For fifteen years after Brougham the impetus for reform rarely originated with the lord chancellor.

However, the momentum was not entirely lost, for law reform in the late 1830s and 1840s was taken up by the lawyers, and specifically by the new professional organizations of the solicitors. The growing importance of these organizations paralleled early Victorian developments in other professions.[20] The Incorporated Law Society, founded in 1825 and granted a royal charter in 1831, and the Provincial Law Association (later the Metropolitan and Provincial Law Association), founded in 1847, were created to improve the standards and social prestige of solicitors, to whom the Inns of Court were closed. They almost immediately began to promote legal reform as a demonstration of their professional responsibility; in this they were consistently in advance of their more socially secure colleagues of the bar.[21]

Both the Law Society and the Law Association assigned committees to the task of studying reform issues, although the lead was taken by the older Law Society in London, with its clubhouse in Chancery Lane and a membership drawn from superior court practitioners. Their objectives were also furthered by another, specialist organization of solicitors, barristers, and judges—the Society for Promoting the Amendment of the Law—which was founded in 1844. Lord Brougham was its first president. The *Law Times*, which first appeared in 1843, provided a public forum for the reformers, and its first ten years of publication recorded a steadily growing clamor for change.

These law reforming lawyers were given an enormous incentive to action when, at long last, a plan originally drafted by Brougham in 1830 was passed as the County Courts Act of 1846. This, the first substantial piece of law reform legislation, replaced the creaking, understaffed system of quarter sessions with about five hundred new provincial courts, grouped in sixty circuits. Each court had a judge appointed by the lord chancellor. The London-centered legal profession had steadfastly opposed this reform, fearing that efficient rural courts would reduce their business. However, provincial politicians, with the support of Lord Lyndhurst, who was anxious to have the new judgeships within his patronage, defeated the London interests.[22] This reform challenged the Londoners to set their own house in order. Looking back on recent events in 1852, the *Law Times* observed: "The County Courts were established; they speedily became formidable rivals of the still unreformed Superior Courts; they stole away the best of the business; they have reduced them to the condition in which we now behold them—one Court without business in the second week of the Term, the others almost exhausted, the Bar already half destroyed, and the prospect darker even than the dark present."[23] As a result of this competition, those advocating reform of the superior courts called for the comprehensive restructuring of the legal system, including nothing less than the abolition of the troublesome distinction between common law and equity.

Such a unification of the legal system had been implicit in the Benthamite critique of English institutions, but it was only after the shock of the County Courts Act that the eradication of the nonsensical separation of common law and equity was seriously contemplated. Reformist attention now turned to what was called "fusion," a typically High Victorian designation. To this end, the Society for Promoting the Amendment of the Law, still headed by Brougham, created a Committee on Law and Equity Procedure in 1850. Following its first report, the society passed a series of resolutions on May 12, 1851, including the recommendation "that justice, whether it relate to matters of legal or equitable cognizance, may advantageously be administered by the same tribunal."[24]

By the summer of 1851 lobbying efforts had already rallied an impressive list of fusion proponents. Lord Brougham, of course, headed the roster, but Richard Bethell (a Peelite M.P. and the future Lord Chancellor Westbury) and both the solicitor general and the attorney general of the Whig administration were also counted among the prominent supporters of the planned reform. The original skepticism of the *Law Times* had been quickly overcome, and it had declared that the separation of common law and equity was "purely arbitrary and artificial."[25]

The Government responded swiftly to the pressure for change by entrusting the reform of the legal system to the same species of institution that was responsible for most of the great reform legislation in nineteenth-century Britain, the royal commission. These commissions were "blue ribbon" panels, not Parliamentary committees, appointed to investigate areas of critical interest and propose remedies. In turn, factories, schools, coal mines, hospitals, prisons, the civil service, the army, and the electoral process were subjected to such scrutiny. Brougham had prompted the formation of two commissions on matters of law reform with his rousing speech in 1828, and Lords Cottenham and Lyndhurst had appointed informal commissions to advise them. In May 1850, amid growing talk of fusion, Lord Cottenham (in his second, more active term as chancellor) established a formal commission with the mandate to consider the complete reorganization of the administration of common law.

Cottenham retired before this commission reported, but his successor, fellow Whig Thomas Wilde (Lord Truro, 1850–51), immediately took up the torch of fusion. In December 1850 he appointed a second commission to study the equity courts as well. The blue books filled by these two panels (two on common law and five on chancery) provided the basis for the Common Law Procedure and Chancery Amendment Acts of 1852. These measures removed many of the inconveniences of the divided judiciary without abolishing the division altogether.

The result was not a comprehensively reformed legal system, but justice was made cheaper, quicker, and more easily understood. The *Law Times* was at first convinced that the inadequacy of the new measures, especially with respect to common law, would drive even more business into the county courts.[26] However, these fears proved to be unjustified, and the new laws inaugurated a period of gradually increasing prosperity for the legal profession in London.[27] A second Chancery Act followed in 1858 and two additional Common Law Acts in 1854 and 1860.

At this point in the process of reform, the new law courts were designed, following a program defined by the needs of a legal system in a state of semifusion. Once the architectural effort was underway, however, attention returned to the postponed ideal of uniting common law and equity. In 1867 the Tories were prompted by a Parliamentary question from Roundell Palmer, the attorney general for the preceding administration, to appoint a powerful Judicature Commission to review the state of law reform. The commission was chaired by Hugh McCalmont Cairns and sparked by the active participation of Palmer. Their ideas were embodied first in the Appellate Judicature Bill of 1870, introduced by Gladstone's first Government, which proposed a unified high court and the abolition of diverse procedures and jurisdictions. The bill foundered in an intense debate over the system of appeals, but in 1873 Roundell Palmer himself (now Lord Chancellor Selborne) secured the passage of the Judicature Act, creating a fused high court. The names of equity and common law were retained for its divisions united beneath a single Court of Appeal.

Implementation of this law was delayed until 1875 by the Tories, however, who succeeded to power before it was put into force. Their efforts at amendment were generally unsuccessful, although in 1876 Disraeli's Government was able to insure the continued role of the House of Lords as the ultimate court of appeal, contrary to Selborne's intention. But complete fusion was at last a reality, and very little of the cruel absurdity that Dickens had portrayed was transferred into Street's new building when it opened in 1882. Since the Royal Courts of Justice were designed before the reforms were completed, however, the building was already slightly obsolete when it began service.

A Palace for Justice;
Sir John Soane

THE CONSTRUCTION of a new building for the courts was an essential component of the law reform agenda from the beginning. A commodious Royal Courts of Justice was a practical necessity for the Benthamite reformers, but the great building also became the popular symbol of their efforts and of the majesty of the law. The *Law Times* concluded, after reviewing the construction of the new government offices in Whitehall, the Houses of Parliament, and the National Gallery, "Surely Justice is entitled to be lodged in a palace, if Government and Legislation and Art are to be so domiciled."[28]

Like the legal system itself, the courtrooms that Dickens had portrayed were inadequate for the increased demands of the nineteenth century. They were inconveniently located, unsatisfactory in design, and simply too small. The solicitors once more took the initiative in investigating these deficiencies, and the government responded by appointing a series of royal commissions and Parliamentary committees. For several decades the question of a new building was subjected to almost continuous scrutiny, and these long deliberations largely settled the issues of location and funding, as well as many aspects of architectural planning. Moreover, during this period five experimental designs for the law courts were created and evaluated, and these plans established the context in which Street and the other eventual competitors worked when legislation for the new building finally passed in 1865.

The starting point for all thinking about architecture for the courts of law during the campaign for reform was the building for the superior courts of common law and equity that Sir John Soane had woven between the buttresses on the west side of Westminster Hall (Figs. 9, 10).[29] His plan had incorporated John Vardy's "Stone Building" of 1755–99, and he had preserved its western façade. (In Fig. 10 the Stone Building is the unshaded portion of the plan.) Soane had fitted new courtrooms and offices between Vardy's block and the great medieval hall (1394–1401), and he had designed his only new façade for the north end of this complex. An "attached architect" of the Office of Works, he had begun work on these first new law courts of the nineteenth century in 1820, when the temporary wooden partitions that closed off parts of Westminster Hall for the courts of King's bench and chancery had to be removed for the coronation ceremonies of George IV. This necessity spurred the government to clear the hall permanently and to provide a more appropriate home for the courts. Further impetus for a new building came from the need to prepare a courtroom for the new vice chancellor, whose position was created in 1817.

Elevation of the Front of the New Courts next New Palace Yard altered agreeably to the directions of the Select Committee.
5ᵗʰ May 1824.

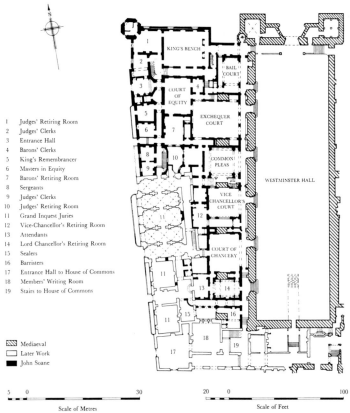

1 Judges' Retiring Room
2 Judges' Clerks
3 Entrance Hall
4 Barons' Clerks
5 King's Remembrancer
6 Masters in Equity
7 Barons' Retiring Room
8 Sergeants
9 Judges' Clerks
10 Judges' Retiring Room
11 Grand Inquest Juries
12 Vice-Chancellor's Retiring Room
13 Attendants
14 Lord Chancellor's Retiring Room
15 Sealers
16 Barristers
17 Entrance Hall to House of Commons
18 Members' Writing Room
19 Stairs to House of Commons

Mediaeval
Later Work
John Soane

Scale of Metres
Scale of Feet

9 John Soane. The law courts at Westminster, as built. 1823–26. North elevation, 6 May 1824. (The Trustees of Sir John Soane's Museum.)

10 Soane. The law courts at Westminster, as built. 1823–26. Redrawn plan. (Crown copyright. With the permission of the Controller of Her Britannic Majesty's Stationery Office.)

The executed design did not, however, reflect Soane's original intention, in which the building was to extend further north and receive a façade that would complement the Palladian Stone Building. This scheme had been hammered out in consultation with the Treasury, and construction was allowed to begin in 1823. But in that same year the fifteen-year campaign to restore the roof and exterior of Westminster Hall was completed. In addition to structural repairs and the replacement of ornament, the huddled coffee houses and taverns that had encumbered the north façade of the Hall were swept away. The awakening respect for medieval architecture reflected in these efforts soon came into conflict with Soane and his classical design. The criticism of his plans culminated in the House of Commons on March 1, 1824, when Henry Bankes rose to object to "the abominable taste in which new buildings of a different order of architecture had been grafted onto the old Gothic."[30] After an unsuccessful defense by the Treasury, a select committee was created to revise Soane's design. That committee, which included Bankes, promptly ordered the elimination of much of the northern part of the new building, lest it obstruct views of the hall, and the Gothicization of the north façade. Soane's protests enabled him to preserve more of his northern rooms than the committee initially intended, but everything north of the King's bench courtroom was lost, and he was compelled to follow their precise instructions as to the fenestration and detailing of the exterior. Such as they were, the new law courts opened in 1826. The executed design established a precedent which was followed in 1835, after the destruction of the Houses of Parliament, when the Government again decreed that only Gothic might be built in the shadow of Westminster Hall.

The altered plan lacked the law library, the consultation rooms, and some of the retiring rooms of the original project. A separate entrance for judges and lawyers was sacrificed. In short, many of the deficiencies that would be the subject of Parliamentary inquiry for decades to come were the result of Parliamentary action in the first place. However, given the restraints imposed by the select committee and the even greater problems imposed by the small, irregular site, the plan devised by Sir John Soane was ingeniously successful, and it established, if primitively, some of the principles that would guide future planning for the law.

Soane utilized Westminster Hall, now freed of the clutter of temporary screens, as the entrance concourse and *salle des pas perdus* of his design. He aligned five of the seven new courtrooms along its west flank, sandwiched between the great exterior buttresses and reached through doorways cut in the western wall. The two additional courts were added in a second tier at the northern end of the building, where the site was wider. A narrow but continuous corridor ran between the hall and the inner line of courts, allowing the passage of barristers and attorneys who might be engaged in more than one case. A second, tortuously-routed hallway ran behind the courts, permitting judges and court officers to penetrate the warren of offices that lay further to the west, including those in the Stone Building. Although muddled by circumstance, a rational order, based on an increasing degree of privacy, is apparent behind this plan: there is first the great hall, then a quasi-public corridor with the courts beyond, and, beyond them, the private office corridor and the offices themselves.

At least the romantic interior spaces of the courts were unhampered by the difficulties of planning and untrammeled by official taste.[31] Soane used many of his characteristic shallow domes, with surfaces taut and tentlike, pilasters shorn of their orders, and austere moldings that framed undecorated sections of the wall. The effect was dry, thin, and nonarchitectonic. The lack of room for interior courtyards and lightwells called Soane's genius for skylights and indirect lighting into play, and his method for lighting courtrooms was frequently adopted by later architects. But the fine interiors themselves were lost when the courts were razed in 1883.

Imperfect from the start, the building was quickly subjected to new demands for which it was inadequate. In the 1830s the creation of a separate Court of Bankruptcy and the new custom by which the master of the rolls sat as an equity judge demanded two additional courtrooms. In 1841 two more vice chancellors were named, and the miserble courtrooms improvised for them out of record storage areas came to be called the "dog hole" and the "cock loft." The number of common law judges was also increased, requiring further makeshift arrangements. Some courts simply gave up sitting in Soane's building, but the new Probate and Divorce Court and the High Court of the Admiralty moved in to fill their places. Dignity and convenience were regularly sacrificed under these circumstances, as suggested by a disastrous story reported by the *Law Times* in 1864:

> Those who were unfortunate enough to have business in the Court of Queen's Bench on June 14, must have been deeply scandalised at the manner in which the court was hustled from one place to another until it found rest for its weary foot in a little room in some out-of-the-way part of the building.
>
> It had been announced that the Q. B. would hold its sittings in the Bail Court, a wretched enough place, but this court happened to be occupied by Mr. Justice Mellor as a second court of Nisi Prius; consequently the Q. B. had to find some other place of sitting, and the only available room was a mere shed occasionally used by one of the Vice-Chancellors, where, though the learned Judges were in the shade, the Bar and those in the body of the room were scorched by the heat of the sun.[32]

While annoyance and comic opportunism colored such reports, the seriousness of the problem was scarcely exaggerated. Even the health of those attending the law courts was placed in jeopardy. A few years later Dr. Angus Smith determined that there was less oxygen in a sample of air taken from the Queen's bench court than in any sample he had ever taken from an inhabited space above ground. The only comparable conditions were in coal mines.[33]

Not only were decent courtrooms in short supply, the building also lacked lobbies and waiting rooms, consultation rooms, an adequate law library (except in chancery), refreshment rooms, or even a convenient jury room.[34] The usher of the Exchequer court testified in 1841 that he was accustomed to charging five shillings for the use of the Exchequer master's room for client consultations.[35]

The exodus of courts and legal offices from Soane's overcrowded building began almost immediately, and it accelerated as the years passed. By the 1840s the legal system had established outposts all over London. Few of the new offices and court-rooms were conveniently located for lawyers, whose chambers were concentrated in and around the Inns of Court, although in 1849 the equity courts did take up permanent quarters in Lincoln's Inn itself, the traditional home of equity barristers. In 1860 a royal commission described this chaotic dispersion of the legal establishment:

> Practically, the Courts of Equity have ceased to sit at Westminster, and now sit in convenient neighbourhood to each other in Lincoln's Inn, with the exception of the Rolls, the Court for which is in Chancery Lane, at a short distance only. Their offices and chambers, 14 in number, are scattered about in Chancery Lane, Quality Court, the Rolls Yard, Lincoln's Inn and Staple Inn. To these must be added the offices of the Master in Lunacy in Lincoln's Inn Fields; of the Registrar in Lunacy, and that of the Bankrupt Appeals in Quality Court; and the Patent Office in Southampton Buildings. The Courts of Common Law sit in Westminster Hall, conveniently near to each other; but the Judges' Chambers are in the Rolls Garden; the Masters' Offices of the Queen's Bench are in King's Bench Walk and Mitre Court Buildings in the Temple; those of the Common Pleas, in Serjeant's Inn and Chancery Lane; those of the Exchequer, in Stone Buildings, Lincoln's Inn; that of the Queen's Remembrancer, in Chancery Lane; that of the Registrar of Acknowledgments of Married Women, in Lancaster Place; that of the Registry of Judgments, in Serjeant's Inn; that of the Associates and Marshals, in Chancery Lane.
>
> The Judge of the Probate and Divorce Courts has no Court of his own, but sits for the present, by permission of the Lord Chancellor, in the Lord Chancellor's Court in Westminster Hall; his Registrar's office, however, and the Depository of wills are still remaining in Doctors' Commons. The Judge of the High Court of Admiralty is also without any Court of his own; he has been used to sit by permission of the College of Advocates in their Hall, and now sits by permission in the Court of the Master of Rolls, at Westminster; but the office of his Registrar, and that of the Admiralty Marshals, are still in Doctors' Commons.[36]

In addition, some common law cases were heard at the Guildhall, the Insolvent Debtors' Court was located in Portugal Street, south of Lincoln's Inn Fields, and, until the year of the report just quoted, the Admiralty court and the ecclesiastical courts had been quartered in Doctors' Commons.

The result of this fantastic diffusion of the courts and offices was further delay and expense for the suitors. Lawyers had to ply back and forth among the scattered courts of common law and equity (for some practiced in both) and the court offices. The long journey prevented them from waiting in their chambers, preparing pleadings, until cases in which they were involved were called. Instead they were forced to spend most of the day in crowded waiting rooms and taxicabs. This wasted time was charged to the suitors at a high rate, in fees levied for useless meetings at which the other conferees were absent due to business at a distant office or court, and in the cost of delay generally. Edwin Wilkins Field, a solicitor and longtime crusader for reform, calculated that a single day of delay for all suitors cost them an aggregate of £25,000.[37]

It could not even be said that by moving out of Westminster the various courts and offices had much improved their physical circumstances. Perhaps the best accommodated refugees were the equity courts, but for them the Society of Lincoln's Inn built only temporary courtrooms in their hall and nearby. These makeshift arrangements prompted one critic to rage, "The Lord Chancellor of England now sits, by sufferance, in a dining hall!!"[38] Moreover, the courtroom at Lincoln's Inn used by Vice Chancellor Wood was too small for the many exhibits required in complex and technical trials, was insufficiently ventilated for use in the summer, and possessed no accommodation for witnesses or for the juries that equity procedure now permitted.[39]

The inhabitants of the other scattered legal offices were no better off. In 1841 the five masters of the Exchequer court had only three rooms among them, and only one of these was equipped with a fireplace.[40] The two chancery registrars shared a single office.[41] And in 1860 Vice Chancellor John Stuart complained that his own office was poorly ventilated and only large enough for three persons, making it impossible to conduct his "in chambers" business in his chamber. Moreover, because Stuart's room was located underground, he charged that his books had decayed on account of the constant damp and that his own face had been "disfigured."[42]

These dreadful conditions received as much attention from ardent law reformers as did the technical deficiencies of the legal system itself. They recognized that it was necessary to satisfy the rudimentary needs of judges, lawyers, and clients, and they also realized that the scattering of courts and offices that had resulted from the poor conditions at Westminster was an obstacle to the achievement of fusion, their ultimate objective. As a barrister argued in a letter to the *Law Times* in 1852, the fusion of common law and equity could be promoted most effectively if they were housed in a single, adequate building, in which "Each would learn of the other, and each would be competing with the other, and the Profession no less than the public would be the gainers."[43] So, although Soane's law courts survived the fire that destroyed the adjoining Houses of Parliament in 1834, they failed the test of fire imposed on them by the growing requirements of the legal system. Within five years of their completion, at a cost of £100,000, their replacement was already being discussed.

The Wilde and Buller Committees; The Barry Plans

THE DISCUSSION of the architectural component of law reform began in earnest in the 1830s, and this first decade of work culminated in the appointment of two select committees by the House of Commons in the early 1840s. These committees considered proposals drafted by the Law Society and plans for a building prepared by Charles Barry.

As early as July 7, 1830, Henry Brougham, on the eve of his epochal term as lord chancellor, had presented to the House of Commons a petition from more than 250 solicitors who complained against the Westminster courts.[44] There was as yet no great enthusiasm to replace an almost new building, and no action was taken. A similar petition in 1832 was similarly ignored, and the economist Joseph Hume stirred no interest in the Commons when he proposed that the law courts be relocated in Lincoln's Inn Fields during the debate on the reconstruction of the Houses of Parliament in 1836.[45] However, as with the reform of the law itself, this official lethargy was an inspiration to private exertion.

The suggestion made by Hume had aroused a very positive response among solicitors, who again took the lead in agitating for reform. The Incorporated Law Society had already established a committee to study the courts in 1835, and in May 1840 a general meeting of the society voted to petition Parliament for the construction of new courts for both common law and equity in Lincoln's Inn Fields, close to the Inns of Court and to many of the existing court offices. They also voted to ask Charles Barry, the recently chosen architect of the Houses of Parliament, to prepare a plan, elevation, and estimate for such a building.[46] Further, they strongly lobbied for their idea with Thomas Wilde, the Whig attorney general who would later serve as Lord Chancellor Truro.[47] The solicitors convinced Wilde to support their petition and to move for the creation of a select committee in the Commons on April 27, 1841.[48] The motion carried, and Wilde was named chairman of the committee, the first legislative victory in what would be a twenty-four-year campaign to erect a new building and concentrate all the courts in the traditional legal quarter of London.

The Wilde Select Committee heard testimony during May and June 1841, and for two additional days in June and July 1842. The defects of the existing courts were first given exhaustive publicity in this forum, and architectural considerations were established as an integral part of law reform.

The Incorporated Law Society dominated the proceedings of the committee, exploiting them to publicize the plan they had formulated for their petition of May 1840 and explained in pamphlets in 1840 and 1841.[49] Solicitors, including several past and present officers of the society, were numerous among the witnesses, and they strongly and nearly unanimously endorsed the Law Society's three-part program: execution of the design prepared by Charles Barry, placement of the building in Lincoln's Inn Fields, and payment for the project out of the interest accumulated on fees paid to the Court of Chancery. The discussion of these proposals before the Wilde Committee established the general parameters of design, site, and finance for the new courts of law.

The best received component of the Law Society proposal was their plan to employ Charles Barry, whose widely admired design offered the first visual impression of what the new courts might be like. If the new law courts had been erected promptly, this second great commission would almost certainly have gone to the architect of the Houses of Parliament. Such was his status that a surveyor retained by the Law Society blandly asserted in his testimony to the Wilde Committee, "Of course . . . Mr. Barry is likely to have the erection of the building."[50]

The design, ordered by the Incorporated Law Society sometime after their May 1840 general meeting, was evidently completed by April 27, 1841, when Thomas Wilde referred to it. Barry testified before the Wilde Committee on June 8, and the printed transcript of the hearings includes illustrations of the design (Figs. 11, 12).[51] Barry estimated that construction would cost £200,000.

The building—a low, symmetrical, and solidly massed Doric structure, with entrance porticoes on four sides—was to be placed in the very center of Lincoln's Inn Fields. The long axis of the building ran east–west, as did that of the central hall, whose dimensions (200 by 80 feet) approximated those of Westminster Hall (230 by 62 feet). Indeed, the overall plan demonstrated that Barry had understood the underlying logic of Soane's design, which incorporated that great medieval hall

C. Barry, Arch.t   . J. Basire, Lith.

ELEVATION of THE NEW LAW COURTS, PROPOSED TO BE ERECTED in LINCOLN'S INN FIELDS.

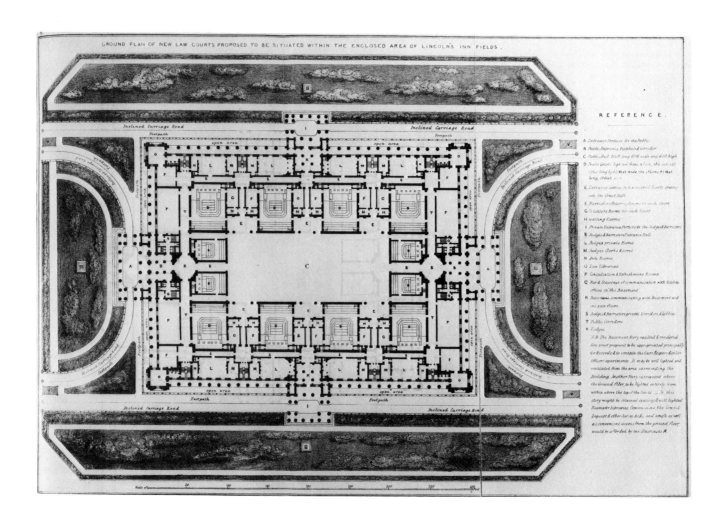

in its functional system. Around his own central hall, Barry arrayed twelve court-rooms in a manner analogous to that adopted by Soane at Westminster. Behind the courts ran a private corridor for judges and the bar, and behind that lay the judges' chambers; this was again a clarification of Soane's plan. But, with a building of more than three times the overall floor area, Barry was able to provide more completely for those ancillary services with which the Parliamentary committee had interfered twenty years earlier. He designed judges' chambers of enormous proportions, placed retiring rooms for both barristers and solicitors between the larger courtrooms, provided bar libraries in each corner pavilion, and planned consultation rooms and refreshment facilities at the east and west ends of the building. In addition, small waiting rooms for witnesses were included adjacent to the lawyers' retiring rooms, jury rooms were placed on an upper floor, and record depositories were located in the basements. Barry contrived his plan so that the great hall and all courtrooms were lit from above.

11 Charles Barry. Proposed law courts, Lincoln's Inn Fields. 1840–41. South elevation. (BPP, volume 10 in 1842.)

Barry's design was not merely a more generously scaled and more intelligently organized version of that prepared by Soane. It was infused with one vital concept that had been only adumbrated in the plan for the Westminster courts: the provision of wholly separate circulation patterns for the different types of people who might have business in the building. Soane had intended to provide a separate entrance for the legal professionals at the north end of his building, but that feature was lost in the ordered revision. Barry revived that notion, admitting judges and barristers through the north and south entrances and the public through the east and west, but he also extended the principle of separation throughout the entire building. The entrances for the law profession connected directly with private corridors that led to the judges' chambers and to the outer ends of the courtrooms. Judges might ascend to the bench directly from these corridors, while barristers could enter their retiring rooms and pass through them to the side entrances of the courts. The doorways for the public at large, through which witnesses, jurymen, and solicitors were also admitted, gave access to circular vestibules at each end of the building. Straight ahead, wide corridors led to the short sides of the central hall, while public hallways to the right and left led to the consultation rooms and refreshment facilities. Solicitors could enter their retiring rooms from the central hall and then pass into the courtrooms via a side door. Witnesses might also enter their waiting rooms from the hall, from which they would be taken by counsel into the courtrooms for examination. The curious public was to enter the spectator galleries at the rear of the courts from lobbies adjoining the central hall. The system was deficient in several important matters, however, for the large courtrooms at the ends of the building had no adjacent bar retiring rooms, and the four smaller courts were entirely without these complex provisions, save for a private entrance to the bench for judges.

12 Barry. Proposed law courts, Lincoln's Inn Fields. 1840–41. Plan. (BPP, volume 10 in 1842.)

Barry's somewhat Byzantine circulation pattern was designed to meet the needs of legal protocol, which were badly served in the existing building. Barristers frequently complained that their passage was blocked by the press of spectators, and within the courtrooms reporters and even witnesses and jurors were often left to find seats for themselves. On one later occasion, a judge recommended that jurymen who complained that they had had difficulty finding places in his court should come early to secure good seats. They replied that they had done just that but that the

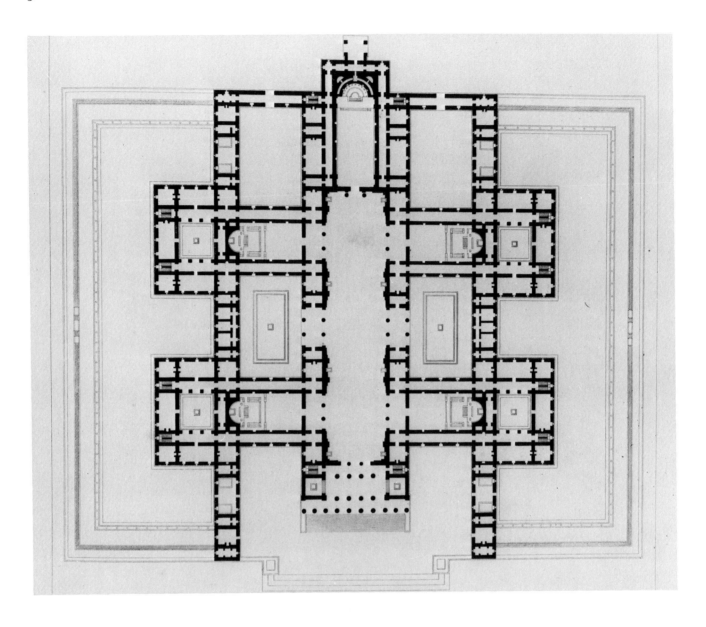

13 *Abel Blouet. Palais de Justice. Premier Grand Prix, Ecole des Beaux-Arts. 1821. Plan. (Grands prix d'architecture: Projets couronnés par l'Académie Royale des Beaux-Arts de France. Liège: D. Avanzo, 1842.)*

witnesses had usurped their chairs during lunch.[52] Barry clearly took all of this into account, just as he carefully corrected most of the other evident faults of the courts at Westminster. Remarkably, his ingenious plan was devised before the hearings of the Wilde Committee publicly aired these problems. He evidently worked very closely with the experienced solicitors of the Law Society who had commissioned the design, and studied parallel examples wherever he could find them.

Barry may seem to have had contemporary French planning in mind when he took the organizational principles that Soane had striven for at Westminster and rearranged them around an armature of separate circulation patterns. His apparently un-English discipline does bear some striking similarities to the ordering symmetry and repetition that shaped the three recent Premier Grand Prix designs of law courts (1782, Pierre Bernard; 1821, Abel Blouet; and 1824, Henri Labrouste).[53] These had been published, and Barry's own central hall is particularly like that of Blouet (Fig.

13). In both cases the hall elevation is an alternation of solid wall and distyle in antis, although in Blouet's characteristically more logical solution the paired columns frame the entrances to the courts, whereas Barry places them in front of vestibules that lead into the courtrooms obliquely.

However, while such formal similarities do exist, the underlying process by which Barry's plan was generated was not very Gallic. The French designs, despite an initial appearance of linear abstraction, are the taut expressions of their interior spaces. The concept of *marche,* the dynamic succession of spatial units that was emphasized in French architectural criticism in the second quarter of the nineteenth century, gives their interiors a wholeness despite their evident articulation.[54] The overall composition and the exterior aspect of these buildings are shaped by the almost physical pressure exerted by this conception of dynamic interior space. Especially in the two later designs, axes are pushed out through courtrooms and their ancillary chambers from great central, spatial reservoirs, and they are stopped only when a state of fluid equilibrium is reached. This defines the exterior of the building. In marked contrast, the Barry plan is spatially inert. Its two great, simple axes are broken and constricted by elaborate vestibules, while, significantly, it is not the courtrooms but their lobbies that are strung on the minor axes of the design. The major spaces are conceived as positive figures of a detached nature, and they are allowed to hang in a kind of limbo, unaffected by what would be the lines of spatial organization in a French plan. This is the case despite the fact that Barry very successfully ordered his internal spaces in terms of actual use. The practical needs of circulation and not the more abstract notion of spatial *marche* underlie his planning. Such pragmatism is perhaps an English trait, and it was certainly encouraged in the case of this design, fostered by the Incorporated Law Society and guided by their very precise vision of proper law courts.

Barry's design for the law courts fits most easily into an English artistic tradition. Its long Doric colonnade merits comparison with the Ionic British Museum of Robert Smirke, designed in 1823 but still under construction when Barry made his plans, and with Barry's own Manchester Royal Institution, also of 1823, with its Ionic portico and short Ionic colonnades on either side. But although generically related to these two buildings, the denser and more plastically varied law courts are closer to the tastes of mid-century. The courts reject the thin detailing of even Barry's own Houses of Parliament, and, to achieve a more sculptural appearance, they adopt the freestanding classical order that was usually shunned by Barry, the famed architect of Renaissance palazzi.

The design is best seen in conjunction with two more nearly contemporary projects by other architects, in which the new taste is also evident. The first is the design made by George Basevi for the Fitzwilliam Museum, Cambridge, a commission that he won in a competition in 1834 and for which he had produced what was almost the final scheme by 1837. Although Corinthian rather than Doric, the Fitzwilliam façade displays a nearly Baroque plasticity that must have intrigued Barry when he set to work on his building for Lincoln's Inn Fields. The organization of the orders, with a portico advanced in front of colonnaded wings and with pilastered pavilions at the corners, is much like that adopted for the law courts.

But an even closer parallel, in both plan and elevation, can be made with the

14 Henry Lonsdale Elmes.
Liverpool Assize Courts com-
petition. 1839. Perspective.
(BAL)

design that won the competition for the Liverpool Assize Courts in 1839 for Harvey
Lonsdale Elmes, an architectural prodigy nearly twenty years younger than Barry
(Figs. 14, 15). Here the Fitzwilliam *parti* is translated into the lowered proportions
of Doric, with a concomitant increase in apparent solidity. Save for the attic and
podium, this is virtually the façade designed a year later by Charles Barry. The plans
are related almost as closely, and it was from Elmes, working out of the pragmatic
English tradition, that the clarity of Barry's planning evidently derived. In this
respect the law courts project was no more French than the Houses of Parliament. It
was Elmes who first worked out the means by which different types of visitors could
be kept apart through the use of separate entrances and corridors. He accomplished

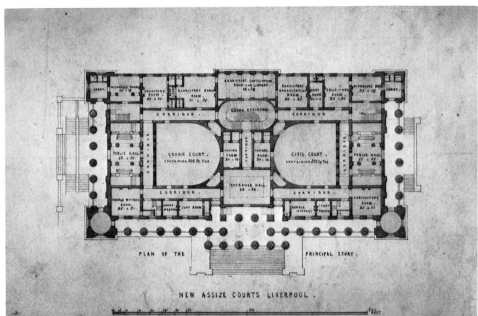

15 Elmes. Liverpool Assize Courts.
Revised design, c. 1840. Plan. (BAL)

this on a smaller scale than Barry, with only four courtrooms (two were on an upper floor), but the overall similarity in outline and arrangement is striking. Elmes perfected his plan through several revisions, culminating in the plan shown here of about 1840—just about the time that Barry began work.

The central portico on the long side provided a private entrance for the judges. Beyond the entrance hall were located their offices, and these connected directly, to the left and right, to the two main courtrooms. Lawyers might enter either at the corners of the main portico or through minor doorways at the rear of the end colonnades, and they could then walk to their retiring rooms, consultation rooms, the library, and the courts by means of a private internal circuit of corridors. The major entranceways within the colonnades at the ends of the building were for the use of the general public, who were also provided with stairs leading directly to the galleries of the courts.

Much of the elegance of Elmes's plan was sacrificed when the assize courts were ultimately combined with a concert room to form one great edifice called St. George's Hall, but Charles Barry must have been familiar with the earlier stages of this work, and his popular design for Lincoln's Inn Fields adopted its innovations. In architecture for the law as in law reform itself, the provinces exerted a catalytic and even formative influence over events in London. In more ways than one, the proposal Barry presented to the Wilde Committee was a young man's design.

While Barry's design was applauded, the other two elements of the Law Society scheme, pertaining to site and finance, were subjected to more critical scrutiny. Lincoln's Inn Fields, as first suggested by Joseph Hume in 1836, initially seemed to be the logical site, for it offered a large, unoccupied area in a convenient location.

The Inns of Court were nearby, and by 1841 most of the sixty-seven houses that surrounded the fields had been converted into offices by solicitors. Not surprisingly, a survey of leaseholders and freeholders showed that a large majority would favor the construction of the law courts in what amounted to their front yard. Harvey Gem, a solicitor with offices at No. 1 Lincoln's Inn Fields and the probable author of the Law Society's pamphlets of 1840–41, emerged as the leading proponent of this site.[55]

However, the trustees of Lincoln's Inn Fields, in whom the control of the park land was vested, were much less enthusiastic about the project at first, and the Wilde Committee heard a number of arguments against it.[56] The critics proposed several alternative locations, and the process of weeding out the most unlikely of these was begun. First, some preferred to remain close to the present courts, including Lord Denman, chief justice of the court of Queen's bench, who testified, "We all have a prejudice in favour of Westminster Hall, and feel besides, a general notion, that it is convenient [that the courts] should be near the Houses of Parliament."[57] In this spirit, hope was expressed that the new Houses of Parliament might be able to provide the necessary additional accommodation for the courts. But not all judges were infatuated with their historic surroundings. Vice Chancellor Sir Lancelot Shadwell responded, when asked about Westminster Hall, "I like to see the building, but that is all; but I had rather have a good and comfortable court elsewhere, than one not so there."[58]

Others preferred the Rolls Estate, the block of publicly owned land on the eastern side of the legal quarter, east of Chancery Lane. On this location, James Pennethorne's Public Record Office would later be erected. However, a surveyor told the Wilde panel that this site was too small.[59]

The most important alternative suggested by witnesses was the large tract of land south of Lincoln's Inn Fields that was ultimately chosen for the courts. This property was bounded on the south by the Strand and on the north by Carey Street. (Figure 16 shows the outline of the site.) The Strand provided the "Carey Street site" with good communication to Westminster in the west and to the City in the east, but the property itself was a labyrinth of courtyards and lanes, and the houses were some of the poorest in London. Matthew Davenport Hill, a radical M.P. who was anxious to eradicate such a notorious slum, first proposed the site on May 11, 1841.[60] William Cadogan, a surveyor apparently hired by the Law Society, inspected the tract and estimated that a sufficient portion could be obtained and cleared for £288,364. But he characterized it as the "second best site" after Lincoln's Inn Fields, the preferred site of the Law Society. Charles Barry, who assisted Cadogan with the survey, shared this opinion.[61] Nevertheless, the committee members, eager to find an alternative to building in the green oasis of Lincoln's Inn Fields (called one of the "lungs" of London), were quickly attracted by the Carey Street proposal.[62]

The Law Society's financial proposal—that the project should be paid for out of the Suitors' Fund of the Court of Chancery—was subjected to similar investigation. A vast accumulation of unclaimed money, which was itself a reflection of the failings of the legal system, the fund had resulted from the chancery practice of requiring the deposit of money that was the object of a suit with the court. Since the second quarter of the eighteenth century, suitors had been able to request that this money be invested by the court on their behalf. Some suitors, however, did not instruct that their money be invested, either out of fear of loss or out of negligence, and their funds were invested by the government at public risk and for public profit. More than £1 million had been accumulated in this way by the time the debate for the new law courts began, and, from time to time, some of this money had been siphoned off to improve legal offices or to pay the salaries of certain law officers.

However, the Wilde Committee heard an intense debate concerning the propriety of diverting nearly all of this fund to build new law courts. The Law Society argued that the money could be employed properly in constructing a building that would benefit future suitors, since it had been generated in the past by the investment of suitors' funds. This attractive theory was attacked by chancery judges, who defined three areas of dissatisfaction. First, some argued that the fund was simply inadequate for the intended purpose, a subject that was only lightly touched upon in the hearings of this first law courts committee.[63] A second, more strenuous objection, raised by Lord Chancellor Cottenham, was that present-day suitors would benefit more from applying the money to the reduction of the onerous chancery court fees.[64] And his colleague, Lord Langdale, the master of the rolls, presented a third argument—that it was unjust to devote the funds earned by the court of chancery to a building that would also house new common law courts.[65] Such doubts about the financing of the law courts were to continue.

Although the Wilde Committee did much to define the issues of design, site, and funding for the new courts of law, this preliminary work did not bear fruit immediately. Whatever its feelings may have been, the committee made no formal recommendations, and the House of Commons did not discuss the subject. The House of Lords briefly debated the issue of removing the courts from Westminster in 1843, when they received another petition from the Incorporated Law Society, but the conservatism of the Peers was evident in the tone of the discussion. Lord Campbell even argued that lawyers already worked too hard and that building new courts near the inns would encourage them to increase their workload dangerously. The long walk between their chambers and the courts provided necessary recreation, he suggested, quoting the old adage, "All work and no play, makes Jack a dull boy."[66]

The impetus for new courts was not much increased by the creation of a second Commons select committee in 1845, although the Law Society, which once again dominated the proceedings, revealed that it would transfer its support to the Carey Street site. Chaired by Charles Buller, the Whig M. P. for Liskeard, the committee heard from only five witnesses in its one day of hearings on July 31, 1845. Charles Barry and William Cadogan, both still employed by the Law Society, and the secretary of the society gave testimony, all vigorously supporting the new site.

The argument for Carey Street took many forms. It was pointed out that this location would not involve the sacrifice of the greenery and open space of the fields. Moreover, the new site was closer to the Temples and thus nearer the real geographical center of the legal district. (Gray's Inn, inconveniently far to the north, had already been abandoned by barristers and was not considered in this argument.) Barry warned that the new Houses of Parliament in Westminster had no room for additional courts, and Cadogan gave a colorful account of the Carey Street property, designed to convince the committee that it would be desirable to clear it.[67] He reported,

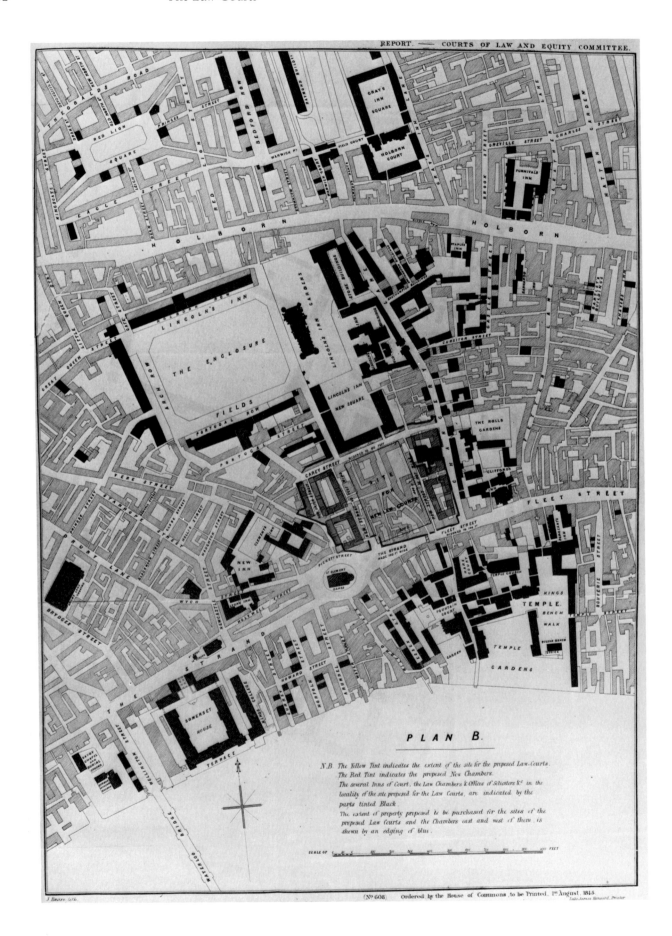

PLAN B.

N.B. The Yellow Tint indicates the extent of the site for the proposed Law Courts.
The Red Tint indicates the proposed New Chambers.
The several Inns of Court, the Law Chambers & Offices of Solicitors &c. in the
locality of the site proposed for the Law Courts, are indicated by the
parts tinted Black
The extent of property proposed to be purchased for the sites of the
proposed Law Courts and the Chambers east and west of them is
shown by an edging of blue.

SCALE OF   FEET

(Nº 608)   Ordered by the House of Commons, to be Printed, 1ˢᵗ August, 1845.

16 Barry. Proposed
law courts, Carey Street site.
1845. Map. (BPP, volume
12 in 1845.)

The dirt and filth are so abominable, that sometimes in hot weather you have
difficulty in walking through those places; they are dreadfully bad, and the
circumstances of having pulled down so much in St. Giles's [the adjacent
parish], has driven so many more of the poor into that neighbourhood. . . .
There is a great deal of it that has no drainage, no sewerage at all, and there
being a current down towards the Strand, a great deal of water and filth has to
find its way down.[68]

The Buller Committee was told that this 7¾-acre slum could be acquired for
£675,074. But Barry cleverly argued that the real expense of the site could be
calculated as only £172,224 if part of the purchased land were devoted to new
chambers for lawyers (at a ground rent of £316,474), and if account were taken of
both the savings to be made by vacating the present offices (£100,350) and the
value of the land on which the Westminster courts were built (£86,000).[69]

Barry also presented a brief indication of the type of architecture he envisioned
at this new location, and his block plan was included on the map published in the
report of the committee (Fig. 16). The center of the cleared land was occupied by
the law courts themselves, organized on the same principles as the project for Lincoln's Inn Fields, with twelve to fourteen courtrooms arranged around a central hall
that would presumably run north–south, following the longer axis of the building.
The more crowded site would require a taller, four-story structure, but the courts
and the central hall would still be lit from above. The exterior, Barry suggested
presciently, might be treated in "the Medieval style of architecture," and although
he did not explain this change of intention, it is likely that he was motivated by the
tightly enclosed, urban site, on which only oblique views of the building would be
possible. Presumably Gothic was better adapted to such picturesque siting. To the
east and west of the courts proper, Barry planned detached quadrangles of income-
producing offices for lawyers, one of which he showed absorbing the Law Society's
new clubhouse on Chancery Lane. The cost of the law courts themselves—only a
part of the entire project—was calculated by him at approximately £300,000.[70]

Further Site Debate; The Scott Plan

LIKE THE Wilde Committee, the Buller Committee published only a transcript
of testimony, which received no discussion in Parliament. For a while after
1845 the attention of most law reformers turned away from architecture and toward
the partial fusion of common law and equity, but when this was achieved, interest
returned to architectural matters. The debate focused again on the site. Although
this question had seemingly been settled by the almost unanimous evidence heard
by the Buller panel, the strong endorsement given to Carey Street by the Law
Society was now challenged by other powerful interest groups who wished to see the
courts built in Lincoln's Inn Fields or in Lincoln's Inn itself.[71]

In January 1854 a deputation of officers from the Law Society had exacted a
generally favorable response to the Carey Street plan in separate meetings with the
earl of Aberdeen, the prime minister, and Sir John Molesworth, the first commissioner of works.[72] However, Harvey Gem, the leading proponent of Lincoln's Inn
Fields, also conferred privately with Molesworth, advising him that impending events
would make the Lincoln's Inn Fields site irresistibly attractive.[73] Gem's prediction
came true at a meeting on February 1 of the trustees of the fields. Awakened to the

PROPOSED NEW LAW COURTS.
PERSPECTIVE SKETCH FROM THE NORTH WEST.

17 George Gilbert Scott. Proposed chancery courts, Lincoln's Inn. 1859. (BPP, 1s, volume 10 in 1859.)

lucrative possibilities that placement of the law courts on their land would create, they overcame their earlier misgivings and voted overwhelmingly to offer three acres of land, ready for immediate construction, in exchange for an expenditure of only £300,000 for road-widening.[74] This, Gem reasoned in a pamphlet, was a good deal cheaper than the estimated £675,074 for the Carey Street site, and he argued that Barry had exaggerated the offsetting credits.[75]

Despite these inducements, the Lincoln's Inn Fields proponents, most of whom had a speculative or professional interest in the matter, lost the site debate. The Law Society continued to lobby for Carey Street, and Molesworth did not place himself in the hands of Gem and his allies.[76] Asked in the House of Commons in 1855 whether the Government had any plan to provide new law courts, Molesworth replied that their long-term goal was still closely related to the Barry proposal for the Carey Street site.[77]

However, after Lincoln's Inn Fields was out of contention, the barristers of Lincoln's Inn erected a second obstacle to the Law Society plan for Carey Street by offering to build new premises in the inn itself for the chancery courts already housed there. The Tory administration which took office in February 1858 was sympathetic to this less expensive proposal, which made no provision for the other courts and offices. Lord John Manners, first commissioner for the Tories, explained to the Law Society that there were "insuperable objections," chiefly of a financial nature, to the Carey Street site.[78]

To enact the Lincoln's Inn plans, Lord Chelmsford, the chancellor, introduced a bill in the House of Lords in March 1859, where it received a second reading.[79] Lincoln's Inn was to expend £100,000 of its own money to build new courtrooms for the three vice chancellors, in return for which the courts would pay an annual rent. The plain brick building erected for the two newest vice chancellors by the inn in 1842, a structure that wags labeled the "Lord Chancellor's official stables," was to be replaced, along with the building constructed for the first vice chancellor by the inn in 1816.[80] The chancellor was to be provided with new offices, although his court would continue to sit in Lincoln's Inn Hall. For the members of Lincoln's Inn, a majority of whom were chancery barristers, this promised to be a most agreeable arrangement.

Lincoln's Inn went so far as to order a design from George Gilbert Scott, to whom the Tory administration had just awarded the much contested commission for the new government offices (Fig. 17). Scott prepared floor plans and a perspective sketch for a building in his usual mixture of French and Italian Gothic. Two of the required new courtrooms for the vice chancellors were provided in one wing, and the third court, together with offices for the lord chancellor, were placed in a second wing. The wings were separated by a courtyard, hindering effective internal communication, and the design adopted few of the sophisticated provisions for circulation made by Barry. However, Scott's project was the first full representation of what the new courts might look like in twenty years, and he was the first High Victorian architect to tackle the problem.

Although this scheme appeared attractive to the barristers of Lincoln's Inn and to the opponents of using chancery funds to build common law courts, the supporters of an entirely new building found it unacceptable. In the first place, locating new chancery courts by themselves in Lincoln's Inn would be a step away from the ideal of fusion. As the Law Society characterized the plan in a broadside of January 1859, it "would amount to a practical decision against that blending of Law and Equity, which most thoughtful people consider desirable."[81] Moreover, many believed strongly that the nation ought to provide its own courts rather than remain the tenant of a private society of lawyers. The *Law Times* editorialized, "The age of court-squatting in Lincoln's Inn is past."[82]

The Coleridge Commission

THE PROPOSALS to reconsider the use of Lincoln's Inn Fields and to build separate equity courts in Lincoln's Inn rallied the supporters of law reform to defeat the special interest groups. In February 1859 Lord Derby, the prime minister, received a deputation from the Society for Promoting the Amendment of the Law, and they convinced him to withhold his support from the Lincoln's Inn bill. Instead, the prime minister created a royal commission on April 21. Its work, largely completed under the Liberal Government with which Lord Palmerston returned to office in June, laid the groundwork for the passage of the law courts bills in 1865.

The commission, chaired by Sir John Coleridge, a judge of the Queen's bench, heard testimony in May and July 1859, and again in December 1859 and February 1860. Part of its report, issued on July 3, 1860, was a complete set of recommendations.[83] Like the select committees of the 1840s, it listed the complaints against the existing courts and called for their removal to the Inns of Court area. More importantly, it endorsed the essential provisions of the Law Society's newest plan. The commissioners recommended the Carey Street site with perfect conviction, and,

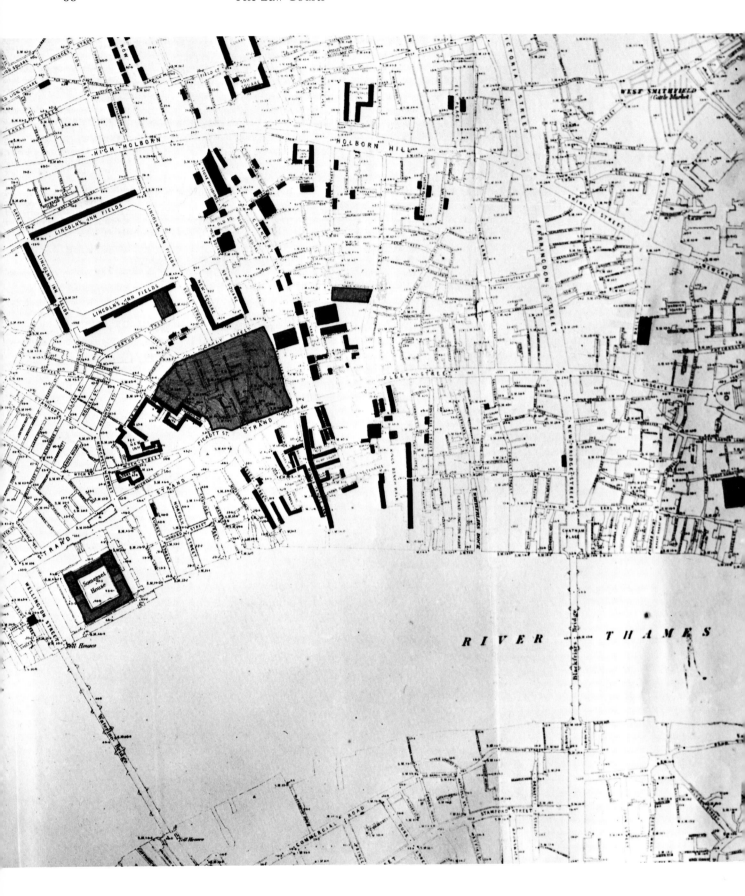

with somewhat less sureness, approved the use of the Chancery Suitors' Fund to pay for the new building.

The hearings of the Coleridge Commission were dominated by two men who would continue to play leading roles in the story of the law courts. Sir Richard Bethell (1800–73), Palmerston's first attorney general and lord chancellor (with the name of Westbury) after the death of Lord Campbell in 1861, was the sponsor of the eventual legislation. He had already attempted to win official approval for the Law Society plan in 1856.[84] A fellow of Wadham College, Oxford, Bethell's stately manner of speaking earned him the nickname "Miss Fanny," and while he was respected in the House of Commons, his abrasive temperament earned him few friends. By contrast, Edwin Wilkins Field (1804–71), was both admired and liked.[85] A prosperous solicitor and a leading member of the Law Society, he had worked for law reform since 1840 and testified briefly before the Wilde Committee in 1841. He later helped to draft the law courts legislation and then served as the secretary of the royal commission that supervised the design of the building.

The powerful testimony of Bethell and Field stressed the importance of concentrating common law and equity courts in the same building, an ideal that would be impossible with new equity courts in Lincoln's Inn.[86] Although well-briefed witnesses testified on behalf of the Lincoln's Inn plan, they could not overcome the impression that it was selfishly motivated. As Bethell pointed out, the presence of the equity courts already had "augmented the wealth of Lincoln's Inn twenty-fold above the wealth of the other societies."[87]

With similar fervor, Bethell and Field argued that the Lincoln's Inn Fields site was inconvenient for barristers who had chambers in the Inner and Middle Temples.[88] Field took this position despite a personal interest in the fields, where his own office was established. Their arguments were sufficient to overwhelm those of Harvey Gem, who once again testified.[89]

The royal commission thus endorsed the more centrally located Carey Street site, where common law and equity courts might both be accommodated. Instead of the somewhat larger site of 1845 on which Charles Barry had proposed to erect both new law courts and additional chambers for lawyers, the acquisition of 7½ acres was now contemplated, excluding the property to the east, lying between Bell Yard and Chancery Lane. The price was again estimated at £675,000, the same as that put on the larger site fifteen years earlier (Fig. 18).[90]

The general outlines of the building program were also briefly discussed, including the addition of numerous courts and offices that had not been accommodated in Barry's plan of 1840–41 or in his sketch proposal of 1845. Barry himself testified briefly before the commission in February 1860, less than a year before his death. But neither Barry nor any other architect gave architectural substance to the program. Only a rough estimate of £675,000 for the building was therefore possible.[91]

The royal commission had greater difficulty resolving the funding proposal for the new courts. The Incorporated Law Society continued to support the appropriation of the Chancery Suitors' Fund and certain other associated resources, and Edwin Field testified strongly in support of their use. He reasoned that the greater efficiency of the new building would save more money for the suitors than spending the same funds to reduce court fees.[92] In the end, the commission majority approved

18 The Carey Street site and the legal district. Detail. 1860. (BPP, volume 31 in 1860. Sterling Memorial Library, Yale University.)

the use of £1.5 million from these sources, more than enough to cover the estimated costs. However, one commissioner, Vice Chancellor Sir William Page Wood, disagreed so vigorously that he submitted a minority report on finances. Wood sided with the chancery judges who doubted the propriety of taking chancery funds for the construction of a new building for all the courts.[93] This vexatious question thus remained unsettled, but the other unequivocal recommendations of the Coleridge Commission sufficed to bring the law courts to legislative attention at last.

The First Legislative Season and the Abraham Plan

THE STRUGGLE for the law courts now shifted to Parliament, where the battle for approval took five years. Bills based on the royal commission's report were introduced in 1861 and 1862, and were promised but not introduced in 1863 and 1864. Only in 1865 was legislation debated and passed. Although a few final hours were lost in continuing the debate on the site issue, the delay derived chiefly from difficulty in winning approval for the financial part of the proposal, which was always embodied in a separate bill. This created a chaotic situation for landowners and tenants on the intended site, who were served each year with official notices to vacate. However, the architectural discussion of the proposed building was furthered, for the architects who surveyed the site for the government in 1861 and 1865, H. R. Abraham and James Pennethorne, each presented a sketch design for the new law courts. Although neither proposal was seriously considered, they joined with the plans of Soane, Barry, and Scott to comprise a substantial library of precedents from which the competitors would work in 1866.

The initiative for the first legislative testing of the finance and site bills in 1861 came from Attorney General Richard Bethell, for Lord Chancellor Campbell was not enthusiastic about the project. In the summer of 1860 Bethell prompted the Treasury to prepare financial legislation, and the Office of Works was asked to draft a site bill. The site bill required a surveyor, and Henry Robert Abraham (ca. 1804–77), Bethell's brother-in-law, was retained. The architect of the Middle Temple Library (1858–61), Abraham probably owed that appointment to Bethell as well, for the attorney general was a member of the Middle Temple. Apparently on his own initiative, Abraham prepared an outline plan for the law courts in addition to the surveying work, and when this was publicized, suspicions of nepotism flourished.[94] However, Bethell could never have steered the commission to his meagerly talented relative, especially after an architect of Barry's stature had been mooted for the job, and the small scandal that ensued precluded any such maneuvering.

Nevertheless, Abraham's design did have some lasting influence. It was recognized as an expression of up-to-date court planning, and the government purchased copies of his drawings (the originals having been lost by the luckless architect on an omnibus in the summer of 1862) for study by the eventual competitors. No copy of Abraham's project survives, but he showed four floor plans and a section to his brother-in-law on April 9, 1861, leaving the designs in the House of Lords library. On the 15th he discussed his plans with Gladstone, the chancellor of the Exchequer, whom Abraham later said was critical of his work. The architect also presented his drawings to the Council of the Law Society and explained them to the select committee that was studying the legislation.

Abraham's plan was large. To provide the 21 courtrooms and 710 other rooms and offices that he calculated would be necessary for the growing requirements of the law courts, he designed a building with 617,500 square feet of floor space, more than twice what Barry proposed in 1841.[95] Records were to be stored in a separate depository, and the general layout of the main body of the building was later described as "an outer shell of buildings containing the departments less connected with the courts, an internal street within this shell, and a central block containing the courts, with their appurtenances, and such departments, &c., as are more connected with them."[96] This was certainly based on Barry's concentric arrangement of central hall, courts, and offices, although it differed from the earlier projects in the use of an internal "street" to divide the growing bulk of the building and in the addition of a detached store for records. Abraham even produced an ideal version of the concentric plan, circular in form and derived from the Colosseum, but this proved too large for the site. No record or description survives of Abraham's elevations, and he may have limited his work to the questions of plan.

Abraham was an architect of modest talent, but he showed considerable ability as a surveyor of property and population and gave lively testimony on these subjects to the law courts select committee of 1861. He reported that the Carey Street site could be acquired for £678,044, and he vividly described the qualities that made metropolitan improvers so anxious to clear the tract:

> It is almost impossible to remain for any length of time on some parts, the stench is so dreadful. The condition of the people is, I can use no other word than, terrible; the vice and wretchedness in the young, the decrepitude in those of middle age, and the dreadful condition of those in premature old age is appalling. . . . There are very few work-people in the common acceptation of that term; they are people who gain a livelihood by hawking and letting lodging, and writing occasionally for law stationers; women who wash, and sweeps; in fact, a most extraordinary combination of the most unfortunate characters in the metropolis. . . . I was attacked during my survey, and had a very narrow escape of being robbed near Plough-court. In Shire-lane there are some of the worst houses in the metropolis. The other day there was a violent robbery at the south end of Shire-lane. There are houses there of the worst possible description, where the youngest girls are taken in numbers. . . .
> There are a great many [houses of ill-repute], but the condition of a large number of the houses is such, that it is a place of ill-fame altogether. There are some recognised houses of ill-fame, old established houses I may call them. But almost every house in the court is more or less badly occupied. . . . I believe there is no system of drainage at all; I cannot detect any system of drainage, and I believe there is no system of drainage in the courts.[97]

Such conditions argued strongly for passage of the site bill.

Despite this supporting evidence, the progress of the legislation for the law courts was halting. By January 2, 1861, the first notices to vacate had been served on the unhappy Carey Street residents, but Bethell had to needle his colleagues continuously to keep the bills on track.[98] Later in the month he wrote Prime Minister Palmerston: "I will remind you that there is another measure . . . which has engaged much of my time, and in which I am most anxious to have a meeting with your Lordship and the Chief Commissioner of Works—I mean the Law Courts Concentration Bill."[99] On April 19 the site bill was finally read for the first time in the House of Commons.

Once this hurdle had been cleared, the consideration of the site bill in Parliament proceeded smoothly. To be sure, Lincoln's Inn petitioned against Carey Street, reiterating their offer of 1859, two Tory M.P.'s attacked the bill when it was read for a third time in the House of Commons on June 27, and Harvey Gem doggedly repeated the case for Lincoln's Inn Fields before the Commons select committee.[100] But Palmerston threw his weight behind the measure, and the bill was passed by the lower house and received a second reading by the Peers on July 9.[101] The site defined by the legislation was basically that suggested by the Coleridge Commission, slightly enlarged to the west to accommodate Abraham's plan. Henry A. Hunt, the surveyor of the Office of Works, estimated the cost of this property at £700,000–£750,000, a bit more than Abraham had calculated.[102]

However, the finance bill faced tougher opposition. Even before any funding legislation had been introduced, Lord St. Leonards went on record with the usual argument that the expenditure of the Chancery Suitors' Fund could not be justified for courts that were not solely for the use of chancery suitors.[103] Charles Selwyn, a member of Lincoln's Inn, argued similarly in the House of Commons, labeling as "confiscation" the proposal to divert any part of the chancery fund to the construction of common law courts.[104] The master of the rolls, Sir John Romilly, repeated to the select committee his view that it was better to reduce court fees than to build.[105]

The Government was also uncertain about the financial plan for the law courts. Officials delayed introducing the money bill until June 17, two months after the introduction of the site bill, while they worked out some unforeseen problems. Their difficulties began with the determination that only £1,400,000 could be obtained from the various suitors' funds, rather than the £1,500,000 estimated by the Coleridge Commission, but the spending ceiling of the proposed bill was simply reduced to match this lower figure. A more intractable problem was that the interest from these funds was still being used to pay the salaries of a number of court officials. Many of these positions had been discontinued by the recent legal reforms, but the present jobholders had been promised an income for life, and they were apparently surviving longer than the commission had reckoned. Insuring these incomes would cost £410,000, a sum that the introduced legislation had to guarantee from tax revenue, supplemented by continuing court fees. This made it impossible to abolish those fees immediately, delaying a needed reform.

The situation was distressing for William Ewart Gladstone, the chancellor of the Exchequer. Throughout his long and celebrated chancellorship of 1859–66 he resisted the cries that echoed through Parliament and across the nation for increased expenditure—particularly for armament against the imagined threat of Napoleon III. The reduction of tariffs to promote free trade, the keystone of the Liberal economic policy, required this powerful control over government spending, but the law courts now threatened to upset his cautious budget. While allowing legislation for the new building to go forward, Gladstone prepared a paper for the Cabinet on

April 27 which predicted that the project might drain £1 million from tax revenues.[106] This fearful prospect was detailed in a Treasury minute of July 16, which warned that the site and the new building might cost £2 million.[107] To this had to be added the £410,000 in salaries that would have to be paid from other sources after the appropriation of the suitors' funds, making a total expenditure of £2,410,000. This exceeded the available funds by even more than Gladstone's £1 million.

The July Treasury minute gave necessary ammunition to the Parliamentary foes of the legislation, and on July 2 Lord John Manners, speaking for the Opposition, called attention to the Government's deep misgivings about its own bill and demanded an exhaustive debate on the subject.[108] The press of business in the final weeks of the session made this impossible, and so the matter had to be postponed until 1862.

Setbacks and Gladstone's Magic

IN 1862 the Liberal Government tried to rescue the financial portion of the legislation, but despite their stout defense the money bill was again rejected. This second defeat prompted Gladstone to draft a new funding plan in 1863 and 1864, paving the way for the eventual success of the Parliamentary campaign in 1865.

Both the site and money bills were introduced once more in 1862, but interest was concentrated on the latter. Lincoln's Inn did petition again in favor of their own site scheme, and a Westminster landowner named Rigby Wason conducted a long but futile campaign to retain the courts in their traditional locale.[109] But more typical of the growing consensus on the site issue was the decision by the trustees of Lincoln's Inn Fields to withdraw their offer of the gardens as a site for the courts.[110]

However, the more heated consideration of the money bill began as soon as it was introduced in the House of Commons on March 14. Gladstone, apparently fulfilling promises made to Palmerston and to Bethell, now Lord Chancellor Westbury, threw his full support behind the project that he had torpedoed the year before. He backed away from the bleak estimates contained in his Treasury minute, and he also argued that, in any case, "the concentration of our law courts was a scheme of practical improvement, which was worthy of being prosecuted, even at the hazard of considerable public charge." He had "no hesitation," he said, in recommending the bill to the House.[111]

Not surprisingly, legislators were not equally confident, and the second reading on April 10 was the occasion of a major debate. William Cowper, the first commissioner of works and sponsor of the bill, began with a long attempt to dispel the fears engendered by the Treasury minute.[112] However, the leader of the Opposition forces and a longtime foe of the concentration plan, Charles Selwyn, showed no sign of being persuaded by these arguments. Instead, he repeated the objections against the use of chancery funds to build common law courts and reiterated his belief that the reduction of court fees was a more important objective. He also doubted whether the stated program could be realized with the available money.[113] Selwyn was seconded by Sir Henry Willoughby, who called the intended system of finance "the most fishy and rotten ever submitted to a deliberative assembly."[114] Edward Pleydell Bouverie, his finger on the pulse of a Francophobic population, suggested that

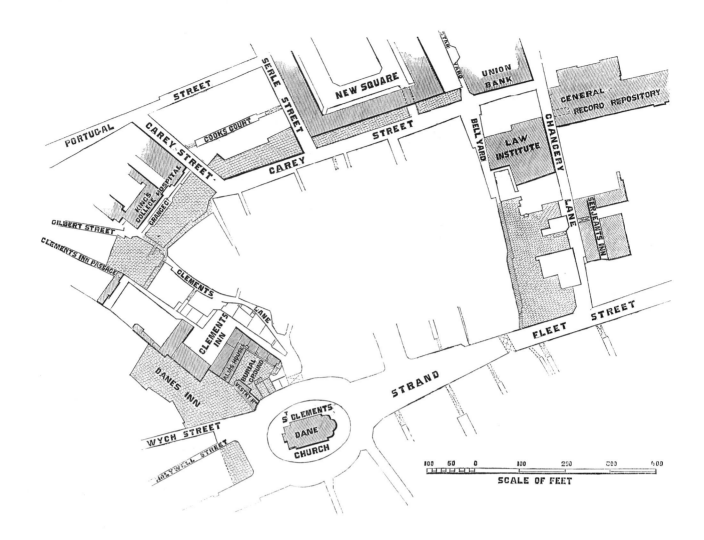

SCALE OF FEET

Parliament was then "building new ships, erecting batteries, re-organizing and re-arming the army, and this expenditure could well be deferred until they had an overflowing Exchequer."[115]

The Government supported the money bill strenuously against this onslaught. Gladstone assured the House that he assumed personal "responsibility . . . at its maximum" for the bill—a strong argument in the context of the ingenuity and popularity of his recent budgets.[116] The attorney general and solicitor general also spoke, but to no avail. The strong impression made by the Treasury report in the preceding session could not be eradicated, and the bill was defeated at its second reading by a narrow margin of eighty-three to eighty-one.

Lord Chancellor Westbury was dismayed at this turn of events, and he was particularly annoyed by the disastrous interference of the Treasury in what he presumed to be his own sphere of authority. Of course, British central administration in this period was largely exercised through authority over the purse strings, so that many ministers and department heads shared Westbury's predicament.[117] As in the case of the law courts, they found that Treasury control was usually negative in character, halting projects in progress rather than starting new programs on a firm footing. But Westbury felt that an essential piece of reform had been sacrificed, and he complained about the fate of the law courts in a letter to Palmerston on December 26, 1862: "This the greatest improvement, whether regarded in a legal, moral, sanitary, or architectural point of view, has been utterly defeated, and, as I have been compelled to give it up . . . , now lies utterly derelict. In lieu of it, I suppose Mr. Gladstone proposes to expend £700,000 in a building for the surplus rubbish of the British Museum [referring to plans for the Natural History Museum]."[118] Westbury's criticism was at least partially misdirected, for his own unpopularity and the suspicion that he intended to make his brother-in-law a gift of the architectural commission for the new building also contributed to the defeat of the bill.[119]

Having failed twice in as many years, the Government did not intend to introduce legislation again in 1863. Only after relentless questioning in Parliament did William Cowper make a halfhearted and unfulfilled promise to introduce a bill in June.[120]

Before proceeding with the law courts, the Government waited for Gladstone to prepare a new, more acceptable financial scheme. In the expectation that he would produce such a plan in time for the session of 1864, the surveyor Charles R. Cheffins was directed in the fall of 1863 to prepare the necessary plans and books of reference, as Abraham had done for the bills of 1861 and 1862. This time, however, the site was to be exactly that recommended by the Coleridge Commission, without enlargement (Fig. 19).[121] As the session of 1864 began, Cowper, anticipating the readiness of the new proposal, once more promised prompt legislative action.[122] However, the weeks of spring passed, and, anxious lest another year go by without progress, the Law Society maintained steady pressure on the Government.[123]

Although the work was slower than expected, preparation of the new money bill proceeded, aided by the report in February of a royal commission that had been studying the use of chancery funds since 1861.[124] By June 18 Gladstone had prepared a new Treasury minute, and the Office of Works was directed to draft the bills.[125] Although too little time remained in the session for a full debate, the Government unveiled Gladstone's brilliant solution to the finance muddle on June 27, 1864.[126] The forthcoming money bill, as explained to the Commons, would not ask taxpayers to pay the salaries heretofore drawn from the interest earned by the Suitors' Fund. Instead, enough of the fund would be left intact to meet that expense, and the reduction that this would effect in the money available for construction of the new courts would be made up from two other sources. First, the savings that would accrue after the courts and offices vacated their present accommodations were now to be officially counted as part of the building fund. These future savings would be advanced to the law courts from tax revenue and repaid later. Secondly, small additional fees were to be levied on the suitors in all courts except the courts of chancery, and, in consideration of these, a second loan from tax monies would be made. Thus the major objections to the bills of 1861 and 1862 were ingeniously struck down. No permanent expense was to fall on the taxpayers, and, while the new fees were anathema to some law reformers, they did distribute part of the cost of the new building to the nonchancery courts that would share it.

The proposal, the foundation for the legislation that was eventually approved, was further proof of the financial genius of Gladstone and of his ability to direct Governmental policy from the Treasury. With his pessimistic minute of 1861 he had been, as the *Law Times* said, "The dreadful man . . . Mr. Gladstone, who, when he frowns, darkens all financial Olympus."[127] But with the legerdemain of this new scheme, he had transformed the situation into one in which economy and legal reform might happily coexist. As Gladstone himself wrote of his solution, "Law and Finance are two beautiful damsels. How charming to see them hand in hand!"[128]

Successful Legislation;
The Pennethorne Plan

ARMED with its new financial proposal, the Government hoped for a well-earned success in the 1865 session, and officials prepared for the legislative campaign with unequaled thoroughness. The Privy Council solicited support from all quarters, and, at the behest of law reformers, petition campaigns or lobbying efforts were launched by the Incorporated Law Society, the Society for Promoting the Amendment of the Law, the Metropolitan and Provincial Law Association, the Law Students Debating Society, and the Manchester Law Association. Moreover, petitions were received from the Middle and Inner Temples and, most surprising of all, from Lincoln's Inn, which voted to support the Carey Street site on February 15, 1865.[129] The Government recruited the tireless Edwin Wilkins Field to draft the legislation, and he served as a nearly full-time lobbyist for the bills. As Field explained to a friend in April 1865, "Out of the ordinary work of my profession, or just fringing it, my principal occupation, last summer and this year, has been looking after the measure now before Parliament for concentrating all the offices and Courts of law in one building."[130] Of course, Palmer and Westbury also played major roles in the Parliamentary struggle.

In the summer of 1864, the Government ordered James Pennethorne (1801–71) to prepare a site plan and book of reference such as Abraham and Cheffins had compiled for previous legislation.[131] As a civil servant, the salaried architect and surveyor of the Office of Works, Pennethorne had designed the Public Record Office in Chancery Lane (1850–58). He was now also asked to prepare a more careful estimate for the purchase of the Carey Street site, and on February 3, 1865, he submitted a calculation of £702,938, which was in the lower part of the range predicted by Hunt.[132]

Moreover, on December 3, the Office of Works ordered Pennethorne to prepare an estimate for the building itself. To facilitate this, he immediately began to draw up a set of architectural plans.[133] He was able to enclose a block plan with his site estimate on February 3, and reported on February 18 that the necessary building would cost £892,895.[134] Before the end of the month Pennethorne submitted eight floor plans to the Office of Works, and although these have not been preserved, his written description and his testimony to the select committee that studied the legislation permit an analysis of his design.[135] His work provided the contestants in the impending competition with one further image of what the new building might be like.

While Abraham had enlarged the site to the west to accommodate his building, Pennethorne accepted the limits set by the Coleridge Commission, whose recommendations formed the basis of the new site bill (see Fig. 19). On the shallower, western portion of the property he planned a small, separate building, containing two courtrooms, 31 depository rooms, and 91 offices for the Matrimonial and Probate Court. On the eastern part of the site, divided from the smaller building by a new north–south roadway, would stand the major block of 18 courts and 616 offices, a trapezoid with a 450-foot frontage on the Strand, a 480-foot front on Carey Street, and a depth of 430 feet. The total area of his two buildings was 744,080 square feet, a substantial increase over Abraham's 617,500 and an indication of the relentless enlargement of the program.

Pennethorne's drawings were returned to him in late June 1865, but the competitors in the eventual design contest were evidently familiar with his work, described in his published testimony.[136] Some of the contestants even adopted his division of the building into smaller blocks, and almost all of them learned something from his cogent explanation of the now familiar concentric zone *parti*, utilized in his main structure. As usual, Pennethorne centered his plan on a great hall— 300 feet long, 50 feet wide, and 70 feet high—which he compared specifically to Westminster Hall. It was to run north-south, and to the east and west he proposed to place the equity and common law courts, respectively, with judges' chambers, jury rooms, retiring rooms for lawyers, and witness rooms immediately behind the courtrooms on two levels. The outer precincts of the upper three floors of the four-story building were to be devoted to court-related offices. Pennethorne added some new sophistication to this almost standard plan by taking full advantage of the topography of the site, which rose substantially between the Strand and Carey Street. The gradient permitted ground level entrances on two floors: to the courtrooms from Carey Street and to a lower floor of offices, refreshment rooms, and official residences from the Strand. Later competitors took careful note of this innovation.

Like Abraham, Pennethorne left no record of whether he intended the elevations of the new law courts to be Gothic in the manner of his Public Record Office or Italian after the fashion of his slightly earlier Museum of Economic Geography. He limited his studies to those plans that were needed in making an estimate, testing the sufficiency of the site, and, as he wrote to Cowper, "defin[ing] the principles which ought to dictate the arrangement of the Building."[137] Unlike Abraham, Pennethorne was probably not scheming for the commission, but, nonetheless, the Site Select Committee severely questioned him. Charles Selwyn, the nemesis of the law courts, apparently concluded that Pennethorne had been promised the job, and Roundell Palmer had to take some pains to explain to the House of Commons that this was not the case.[138] Although it was never made public, Pennethorne's estimate of £900,000 for his building gave the Government a special reason to distance itself from his work. Coupled with his site estimate of more than £700,000, this figure pushed the total expense well over the ceiling of £1.5 million. In apparent response to this concern, Pennethorne prepared a second estimate totaling £1,386,540 for what he termed a "plain brick building."[139]

With this preparatory material in hand, the Government introduced the site and money bills in the House of Commons on the first business night of the session, February 10, 1865. Roundell Palmer made a long opening statement, reviewing the findings of past committees in favor of concentration and fleshing out the details of the finance plan that he had outlined to the House the preceding June. With the aim of defusing the economic controversy that had blocked passage of all previous legislation, he now quoted exact figures for the three sources of funding on which the new scheme relied. The Chancery Suitors' Fund would provide £900,000 (leaving enough to pay the salaries of officers), the reuse or sale of the present offices and courts would account for £200,000, and the slight increase in nonchancery court fees would raise £400,000.[140] The £1.5 million ceiling proposed by the Coleridge Commission remained in force.

This solution to the financial tangle satisfied the majority in both houses. Some Tory opposition existed, and Lord St. Leonards contributed one memorable phrase to the debate, when he spoke against the "fusion, or as [I] . . . should call it, the confusion—of law and equity," but the Government had no real difficulty in winning approval for the money bill.[141]

Somewhat surprisingly, two questions related to the site bill did delay final approval of the legislative package until late June. The first matter was the proposal of an attractive alternative to the centrally placed Carey Street site, what Westbury, in his long opening speech in the Lords, had called "the *umbilicus* of the legal locality."[142] The alternative was a quayside tract on the new Thames Embankment, first suggested to Parliament a year earlier by Charles Selwyn.[143] In the 1865 debate Frederick Lygon in the Commons and Lord Stanhope in the Lords renewed the discussion of this spacious site, adjacent to the new Embankment roadway and the railway line beneath it, and close to the piers used by the Thames steamers.[144] The House defeated Lygon's motion for a select committee to examine the Embankment site because the members apparently interpreted his action as another effort to block the law courts legislation altogether. Although the Government was sufficiently discomfited to direct Pennethorne to survey a large, sharply inclined piece of property on the Embankment east of Somerset House, he reported an unpromising estimate of more than £1 million, and the Embankment site did not become the subject of serious consideration until 1869.[145]

The second delay stemmed from a discussion of the fate of those who would be displaced by the construction of the new building. This matter was raised automatically because the House of Lords had enacted a standing order in 1851 that required a census of the working-class population evicted by any Parliamentary action. The mandated survey of the 7½ acres of the Carey Street site further documented the frightening conditions vividly described by Abraham in 1861. Although the exact population of the maze of lanes and courtyards between Carey Street and the Strand was difficult to ascertain, the surveyor reported an approximate figure of 4175, accommodated in 343 houses. Of these people, roughly three-quarters (3082) were considered working class, and these inhabited only half (172) the houses, comprising 1163 rooms.[146] And this squalid average of 18 persons per house and of nearly 3 per room was better than conditions on the most overcrowded parts of the site. In Middle Serle's Place, 19 houses sheltered 385 souls, in Robin Hood Court 52 people lived in just 2 houses, and 189 people were packed into the 9 houses of Lower Serle's Place.[147] This crush of humanity was increased nightly by the transient residents of three lodging houses, accommodating as many as 140 people, where, the surveyor reported, "any person who can produce 4d. has a bed to himself."[148]

The plight of this multitude, should the tightly crowded houses of the Carey Street site be removed, excited enough concern within the Liberal party to slow the passage of the law courts bill. The discussion was initiated by Sir Francis Goldsmid, the M.P. for Reading who was the first Jewish barrister and also a leader of the campaign for Jewish enfranchisement, and by Arthur F. Kinnaird, the M.P. for Perth and a philanthropist interested in working-class affairs. On February 28 Kinnaird moved: "That it be an Instruction to the Select Committee on the Courts of Justice

Concentration (Site) Bill, that they have power to make provision for appropriating or obtaining sites, and for the erection of lodging-houses or other suitable dwellings for the working classes proposed to be displaced by the said Bill."[149] The leadership of the Liberal Government placed their prestige against Kinnaird's proposal, with Roundell Palmer urging the legislators to "take a practical and not merely a sentimental view of such subjects" and warning that the motion would effectively block construction of the law courts.[150] Prime Minister Palmerston seconded him, and the House adjourned at 1 A.M. without a substantive vote. The issue was not raised again. The poor, many said, would make their own way to better lodgings after Carey Street was cleared, and the Liberal party, straight-jacketed by Gladstonian economics, was unable to devise any more active policy to assist them. Government subsidies to housing were instituted only at the end of the century, and, meanwhile, the support of such projects as model lodgings remained the work of private philanthropy, led by progressive Conservatives like Lord Shaftesbury.

After the site issue had been quite easily set aside and the fate of the Carey Street residents had been coolly dismissed, the bills moved on toward approval. Only at the last moment, when they were read for a third time in the House of Lords on May 8, was the legislation even slightly threatened by the largely Tory opposition. At that time mischievous amendments were attached to both bills, but when these were rejected by the Commons, the upper house withdrew them rather meekly. Lords Redesdale and St. Leonards, the authors of the amendments, made a final gesture of complaint by attaching long dissenting briefs to the two bills, but little of this last skirmish was remembered after the measures received the royal assent on June 19. At last, the long-dreamed-of law courts were to be built.

Lord Chancellor Westbury was in office only a few days to enjoy this victory, for on July 3 he resigned the Great Seal, leaving in disrepute. Westbury was undone by two charges of abuse of power, leveled against him in the spring of 1865. In each case he was guilty of allowing malfeasant officers under his authority to resign without penalty and without sacrificing their pensions. In one of the instances, Westbury appointed one of his son's major creditors to the newly vacated position. Select committees reported unfavorably on his conduct, and, after a motion of censure, Westbury's continued participation in the Government became impossible.[151] His downfall was speeded by the suspicions of nepotism raised by his favors to H. R. Abraham in 1860–62.

The Royal Commission and the Competition Instructions

LORD WESTBURY was thus denied the privilege of presiding over the powerful Royal Commission formed on June 25 to oversee the first concrete preparations for the new law courts. The role of this commission was defined by an amendment that Roundell Palmer had added to the site bill in February: "The plan upon which the said buildings shall be erected, and the necessary arrangements for the proper and convenient accommodation of all the courts and offices to be provided for therein, shall be determined upon by the Treasury, with the advice and concurrence of such persons as Her Majesty shall think fit to authorize in that behalf."[152] "Such persons" were the Royal Commission, chaired by the new lord chancellor, Lord Cranworth (ex officio), and comprised of a cross-section of the leadership of the legal community. The commissioners included all the judges of the superior courts, the attorney general, the solicitor general, numerous officers of the courts, the chancellor of the Exchequer (Gladstone), the first commissioner of works, the president of the Law Society, and representatives of all the Inns of Court. To assist them, Edwin W. Field was appointed secretary, and he asked to serve without remuneration. It was assumed that the commission would offer their "advice" to the Treasury in the matter of the plan by conducting a competition, and their first major responsibility was thus to draft a program and a set of instructions for the competing architects.

However, the commission's first meeting, held on July 5, 1865, was devoted almost entirely to a hollow formality. In deference to Lord Redesdale's unsuccessful eleventh-hour amendment, which would have required approval of a plan and estimate by Parliament, the Government had agreed to ask the Royal Commission to certify the adequacy of both the site and the available funds. This was the business addressed on July 5, although the commissioners heard no new testimony and formed no opinion independent of that of the administration.[153] They certified the sufficiency of the appropriated land and cash, but then drafted instructions that could not be obeyed without exceeding both. This guaranteed that none of the competing designs would be executed.

To assist in drafting the instructions, the commission appointed the son of H. R. Abraham as their architectural clerk. But young Abraham soon fell ill, and Field recruited the services of Alfred Waterhouse, whose recently completed assize courts in Manchester were widely admired by lawyers. Waterhouse, however, accepted the appointment with the proviso that he should remain eligible to join the competition. At first this seemed to be accepted, but on November 29 William Cowper wrote to Field to warn that Waterhouse's "appointment would be considered by many to be hardly compatible with the position of one of the competing architects." Aware of the earlier charges of favoritism, he argued that it was essential to avoid "any suspicion of unfairness."[154] These concerns were communicated to Waterhouse, and on December 1 he tendered his resignation, to be replaced by the nonentitive William Burnet, formerly of the Office of Works.[155] On Burnet fell the enormous editorial burden of making intelligible instructions out of the recommendations of the commission and out of the mountains of information that it collected.

Information gathering was the backbone of the commission's work, but its omnium gatherum approach to the drafting of the instructions nearly crippled the competition. The members consulted a variety of outside experts, and thus their instructions became a voluminous anthology rather than a set of interrelated directions. For example, the commission based its vast tables of necessary accommodation on a raw compilation of questionnaires that were addressed to the existing legal departments. Naturally, the requests for space were exaggerated. Similarly, separate reports from the police and the fire brigade concerning the provisions they would desire in the new law courts were passed on to the competitors in toto. The Incorporated Law Society, which continued to be closely identified with the project, was also asked to submit recommendations, and these were largely adopted and included in the instructions. The resulting compilation emphasized such practical matters as the provision of adequate light, ventilation, and quiet, and the necessary separation of the different types of people who would visit the law courts. But these considerations had already been made obvious by the work of the preceding committees and the Coleridge Commission.

The commission did take a firm stand on the overall scope of the program for the new building, and this posed its own difficulties. While the legislation of 1865 had only authorized provisions for the courts and offices of common law and equity, together with the new Divorce and Probate Court and the Admiralty court, the commission greatly inflated this program in response to lobbying by the most utopian law reformers. It added the offices of the masters of lunacy, the Middlesex land registry, a depository of wills for the probate department, the bankruptcy court and its offices, the ecclesiastical courts and their offices, and several extra courts, one of which might be used by the Judicial Committee of the Privy Council when it met to hear appeals. It also considered including the copyhold, charity, enclosure, and tithe commissioners in the program, but decided that these were not a necessary part of law courts concentration. According to the tables published by the commission, this inflation of the program would result in a building of 683,000 square feet, falling between the areas of the designs prepared by Abraham and Pennethorne, who had similarly contrived to satisfy the wishes of the most ardent reformers.

The generosity of the commission and its acceptance of the large accommodation requests submitted by the legal departments strained both the authorized budget and the borders of the approved site, whose sufficiency the commission had begun by certifying. Accordingly, these Parliamentary guidelines were referred to only in passing in the instructions published for the competitors. With respect to the £750,000 ceiling for the building, the instructions merely advised: "The Architect is requested, if possible, to design such a Building as may be erected for that sum, and to state the cost at which he estimates his design could be carried out." Further on it was observed with optimism that "The number of Departments to be accommodated, and consequently the extent of accommodation required, has been increased since the above estimate of £750,000 was made, but it is hoped that the additions will not much increase the amount."[156] However, the Treasury never authorized any increase in expenditure, nor did it approve the commission's concomitant territorial ambitions with respect to the site. To contain the expanded program and permit the widening of roads in the vicinity of the new building, it recommended the purchase of additional land on each side of the approved site, at an estimated additional cost of £488,620.[157] That Gladstone refused to accept this increase by nearly two-thirds of the amount originally allowed for land is hardly surprising. But the commission portrayed the matter in a misleading light in the instructions: "The Treasury have not yet come to a decision on the subject, but it may be assumed that their assent will be given to such additional purchases as in the Architect's opinion may be found essential to the efficient carrying out of the scheme."[158]

The instructions, which thus encouraged the competitors to ignore both the wishes of Parliament and the scruples of the Exchequer, passed through three drafts during the first months of 1866. In a characteristic effort to solicit a full range of opinions, four hundred copies of one version were circulated for comment among lawyers. On April 17, Lord Cranworth signed the final draft. The Treasury, apparently satisfied that its desires had not been altogether ignored in the vaguely worded document, approved the instructions on April 21, and they were forwarded to the invited architects.

Having been shaped by the most extreme faction of law reformers, the published guidelines were remarkable chiefly for what they did not prohibit rather than for what they specified. The very substantial uniformity in planning later observed in the competition designs was not inspired by these vague instructions. Instead, that similarity reflected a common image of the law courts that had evolved over four decades in the designs of Soane, Barry, Abraham, and Pennethorne. By 1865 the formula was traditional, and any architect who designed a courtroom was likely to adopt it. But, conveniently, on November 27, 1865, on the eve of the competition, the formula was once more clearly set forth in a paper on the new courts read by Thomas Webster, Q.C., at a meeting of the Society for Promoting the Amendment of the Law. Sensing its significance, the Royal Commission printed copies of Webster's talk for the competitors, so that no architect was allowed to remain ignorant of the evolved principles of law court design.[159]

Webster, who praised the new courts in Manchester by Waterhouse as an embodiment of his views, stressed the now familiar objective of separating the various types of visitors to the building. To effect this, he recommended a plan based on the scheme of "four concentric circles." Centermost was to be a great hall, located two floors above the Strand, with adjacent courtrooms. The ordinary public would be restricted to this hall and to the spectator galleries of the courts. Behind the courtrooms, and together with them comprising the second "concentric circle," were located the judges' chambers, jury rooms, witness rooms, and retiring rooms for barristers and solicitors, all placed on two floors. Beyond them was a corridor, the third circle, restricted to law professionals and those with official business. Around the perimeter of the building, in the fourth circle, were the subsidiary offices of the courts. This was a crystallization of the plan intended by Soane, sketched by Barry, and expanded and refined by Abraham and Pennethorne. It was to be the plan adopted by most in the competition.

Lessons Architectural and Political

GEORGE EDMUND STREET surely followed the architectural and procedural ramifications of law reform with interest. As an architect he would have been intrigued by the prospect of a great public commission, and through his family's legal connections he would have been kept abreast of the technical reforms. What Street learned of the lawyers' requirements and of the preliminary plans to satisfy them was to be of practical value when he prepared his own design for the new law courts. What he saw of the politics of the broader Reform movement was also useful, for the Governments that built the courts were shaped by that confusing issue.

Street's political perspective on these events is not entirely clear. His son recorded that he was a High Churchman and a high Tory, but Street also admired William Ewart Gladstone, the greatest Liberal politician of his era. Gladstone and Street developed a close personal acquaintance, and their relationship was of substantial importance in the later history of the law courts. Street showed surprising sympathy for Liberal causes, and in 1879, after a visit from Gladstone, he wrote in his diary that he had vowed to his guest that he would not interfere with a passerby who broke the lock on a gate blocking a public thoroughfare across private land.[160] Thus Street was probably not opposed to certain aspects of the Reform movement. Like his brother Thomas, a prospering solicitor who moved the family firm in 1861 to Lincoln's Inn Fields, he likely supported law reform in particular. This individual example demonstrates that party distinctions in this period were not ironclad, and that legal reform, which would appear to be the clear ideological property of the Liberals, was not without support among Tories.

The blurring of ideology was also apparent on the national level. While most of the Benthamite law reformers were Whigs or Liberals—including Brougham, Cottenham, Truro, and Selborne—and while most reforms were at least initiated under their ministries, the Tories never entirely renounced law reform. For example, under Derby's brief ministry in 1852 they seized the then accelerating cause of fusion as their own. Similarly, Disraeli's Government attempted in 1874 to place their own stamp on the monumental Judicature Act of 1873, formulated under Gladstone.

Part of this was pure political competition with little ideological significance, the favorite Conservative game of "dishing the Whigs" by beating them to the enactment of certain kinds of reform legislation. Dramatic instances of this were the repeal of the Corn Laws in 1846 and the passage of the Second (Suffrage) Reform Bill in 1867, both under Tory Governments. But the Reform movement had also gained such great breadth by the second or third decade of Victoria's reign, that it overstepped the still uncertain boundaries of party philosophy. It is a truism that the liberal policy of one generation is the conservative policy of the next, and mid-century Conservatives, brought up in the progressive "Young England" movement, were ready to initiate many reforms, especially those of a paternalistic nature.[161] Their opportunities were increased since the Liberals had sacrificed tariff income in order to promote free trade, and were compelled to act as fiscal conservatives.

Street's personal feelings may have given him special insight into this unsettled political situation, and this was certainly of value when he began to work on the law courts, for the story of their construction was a classic case study of Reformist political rivalry. The building was first proposed and authorized by the Liberals in 1865, but a short-lived Tory Government unscrambled the competition and appointed an architect in 1868. The victim of subsequent Liberal economizing, the project fared much better when the Tories came to power again in 1874. But while they were rivals in promoting the needed reform, the two parties were also allies on several occasions in defeating nonpartisan objections to the plan in Parliament.

Street's interest in studying the efforts of law reformers was perhaps further strengthened by the realization that his work and theirs shared the same premise: that it was essential to cull material for a synthetic solution to contemporary problems from a broad range of precedent. In High Victorian architecture, too, this eclecticism was sometimes called "fusion," a philosophy that emerged in both fields about 1850.[162] At the same time that Street, in his first writings, was calling for the "harmonious combination of ideas derived from different sources" in architecture, the movement to unite common law and equity in one legal system was getting underway.[163] Moreover, the arguments for legal fusion and High Victorian architectural eclecticism also shared the same romantic assumption that even opposite and antagonistic historical elements could be conjoined. Street believed that medieval and quasi-classical properties were necessary complements in architecture, in the same way that Roundell Palmer thought that common law and equity were equally essential to a comprehensive legal system. Like John Ruskin, High Victorian architects and law reformers were inclined to believe that "truths may be and often are *opposite*, though they cannot be contradictory."[164]

Chapter 3

The Competition

"More Intricate and Incomprehensible
than the Labyrinth of Crete."
—*Times*, November 19, 1867

T HE COMPETITION for the Royal Courts of Justice introduced the political
campaigners for legal reform to the architects who would give substance to their
dreams. Their meeting was turbulent. The political background was filled by the
events of a great episode of the Reform movement, while the architectural world was
beset by the dilemmas that marked the end of the High Victorian era.[1]

*The Politics of
Electoral Reform*

T HE COMPETITION took place during a strenuous political contest over the
further extension of suffrage, the greatest Reform activity since the passage of
the First Reform Bill in 1832. In 1866, the year in which the instructions were
drafted and the architects were invited to compete, Gladstone's Representation of
the People Bill was defeated, precipitating the fall of the Liberal Government that
had worked so long for the law courts legislation. In 1867, the year in which the
designs were judged, the succeeding Tory administration successfully enacted its own
representation proposal, a measure called the Second Reform Bill. But the Conservatives were themselves defeated in 1868, after they had decided to award the
commission to George Edmund Street. Gladstone and Benjamin Disraeli confronted
each other as national leaders for the first time during these years.[2]

This stormy interchange began when the Liberals took up the cause of electoral
reform with fresh enthusiasm after their victory in the general election of July 1865.
Gladstone, the chancellor of the Exchequer, was the Parliamentary leader of this
effort, but his reform legislation of 1866 was sabotaged by a group of about a dozen
Liberal deserters who were named the "Cave of Adullam," after David's refuge from
Saul. Led by Lord Elcho and Robert Lowe, they united with the Tories to defeat the
Government on June 18. Reform League supporters rioted in Hyde Park, and Gladstone challenged the incoming Conservative administration, in which Disraeli served
as chancellor of the Exchequer and leader in the Commons, to push through a
suffrage bill of their own. To the horror of the Adullamites who had brought the
Tories to power, that is precisely what they did.

The resulting Conservative Reform Bill of 1867 created virtual household suffrage, boosting the voting rolls by more than even Gladstone had intended. Disraeli
and his party thus succeeded in "dishing" the Liberals by beating them at their own
game. But they also seem to have been motivated by the belief that such reform was
compatible with Tory paternalism and that it was the duty of the Conservatives to
keep up with public opinion in order to preserve their political legitimacy. "The
dream of my life," Disraeli explained, was "reestablishing Toryism on a national
foundation."[3] For less adventuresome Conservatives, however, the Second Reform
Bill remained a senseless leap into the dark of republicanism, a program that Thomas
Carlyle likened to "shooting Niagara."[4]

The Tory Reform Bill did not immediately improve the party's political position. The next April, Gladstone defeated them with a first resolution on the disestablishment of the Irish (Anglican) Church. Crippled, the Tories, now led by Disraeli, limped into the general elections of November 1868 which were conducted with the newly expanded voting registers. The predictable Liberal victory was recorded, and Gladstone formed his first Government in December. There followed five years of significant Reform legislation, reshaping education, the civil service, and university admissions. Among the achievements, the Judicature Act of 1873 finally fused common law and equity. Ironically, this Liberal Reform program had been robbed of its cornerstone when the Conservatives snatched the suffrage bill away in 1867.

The major events of this political struggle shaped the law courts competition. But its story is surprisingly full of instances of bipartisan cooperation, just as other reform issues often straddled the political fence. Moreover, by this date, architectural competitions had become such a notorious nuisance that they could arouse an unusual kind of solidarity among politicians. The law courts were thus able to rise a little above the storm of Parliamentary warfare.

Designing the Competition; Judges and Judging

THE HISTORY of competitions for public buildings had been a gloomy one, and the Royal Commission took pains to insure that the law courts broke with this unhappy tradition. The judges of the competition for the General Post Office in 1819 had been unable to recommend the acceptance of any design, and the commission ultimately went to an attached architect of the Office of Works, Robert Smirke.[5] The Royal Exchange competition of 1838 also produced no acceptable design, and that commission was eventually given to William Tite, who was first associated with the contest as the surveyor who checked cost estimates.[6] The decision of the judges in the scandalous War and Foreign Offices competition of 1856 was not sustained by a Parliamentary select committee, and the Government transferred the award to G. G. Scott. Even the contest for the Houses of Parliament had been spoiled by the later dispute over the relative responsibilities of Charles Barry and A. W. N. Pugin in the design.

In their effort to benefit from the lessons of the past, the Royal Commission voted on December 21, 1865, to limit the competition to six architects. The commissioners explained that the competitors should visit the existing courts and offices while preparing their designs, and that a larger number of visitors would have disrupted the transaction of legal business.[7] But they also hoped that inviting a smaller number of thoroughly qualified architects would free the competition from some of the confusion attendant upon the unsuccessful contests for the General Post Office, the Royal Exchange, and the government offices, each of which had been open to all comers.

The commission also drafted particularly thorough instructions, which were expected to reduce the risk of receiving unusable designs still further. But the resulting massive compilation of facts and figures, several times larger than the instructions in the War and Foreign Office competition, was full of exaggerated expectations and hazy priorities. Scott complained about their "unprecedented . . . voluminousness," and the *Building News* agreed.[8] As a correspondent to the *Times* observed after the competition was over, the program had been "elaborate . . . in detail, but vague and inconclusive in the most important particulars."[9] For practical guidance, the competitors turned instead to the earlier designs of Soane, Barry, Abraham, and Pennethorne.

Moreover, the Royal Commission sought to establish an unimpeachable system of judging for the competition, based on its Parliamentary mandate to provide the Treasury with "advice and concurrence" in selecting the design for the building. Lest this ambiguous description of its relationship with the Treasury be allowed to interfere with the acceptance of its work, a delegation from the commission met with the financial secretary of the Treasury on December 23, 1865, to define the formula for judging the competition.[10] They authorized a five-member jury to which the Treasury and the commission were each to appoint two judges, with the first commissioner of works, William Cowper, serving as chairman. The judges, in turn, were to select the competitors. In February, in accordance with this plan, the commission appointed two lawyers, Sir Roundell Palmer, the attorney general, and Sir Alexander Cockburn, the lord chief justice of the Queen's bench, to serve as judges, and Gladstone appointed himself and Sir William Stirling-Maxwell, M.P., to represent the Treasury.[11] But although this jury effectively represented both the interests of the Government and of the lawyers on the Royal Commission—nicely settling the problem of joint responsibility—its members brought with them prejudices that ultimately prevented them from reaching a conclusive decision. Moreover, Cowper, Palmer, Cockburn, Stirling-Maxwell, and Gladstone did not possess the necessary architectural credentials to win acceptance for the awkward solution which they did propose. Despite the good intentions of the commission, these deficiencies combined with the weaknesses of the instructions to insure that the law courts would join the list of disastrous competitions.

The chairman of the judges, William Cowper (1811–88), served his stepfather, Lord Palmerston, as first commissioner of works from 1860 until 1865, and after Palmerston's death he continued in that office until 1866. Although his earlier work as vice president of the Committee of Council on Education and as president of the Board of Trade is probably a better indication of his personal interest, he exhibited an active concern for architecture and played an important role in winning passage of the law courts bills. Cowper was a tool of his stepfather in the insensitive manipulation of G. G. Scott's Foreign Office design, but Scott maintained that Cowper's sympathies had lain with the original Gothic version.[12] This medieval sympathy was revealed again in February 1866, when he appointed Alfred Waterhouse to succeed the classicist Francis Fowke as the architect of the Natural History Museum. Cowper was known to be considerate and accessible, and he even seems to have established a good working relationship with the young and temperamental Edward M. Barry, who became the architect of the Houses of Parliament upon his father's death in 1860.[13] Because of his official position, Cowper must have known most of the eventual competitors for the law courts, but he would have known Scott, Waterhouse, and Barry best, for they were in charge of the large public architectural projects of the sixties.

Sir Roundell Palmer (1812–96) was attorney general from 1863 until 1866, and in that position he guided the successful law courts money bill through the

House of Commons in 1865. Later, as lord chancellor, he oversaw the passage of the Judicature Act of 1873, which effected judicial fusion. Despite these actions, he was a High Churchman with only moderately Liberal views, and he had differed sharply with Gladstone over the disestablishment of the Irish Church. Palmer's rise to the chancellorship was delayed by this dispute. His architectural preferences may be inferred from his employment of Alfred Waterhouse to design "Blackmoor," his home in Hampshire. Waterhouse submitted his first drawings in November 1866, in the midst of preparing for the law courts competition, and during the period of assessment by the competition judges he was in regular consultation with Palmer and his wife. He was the recipient of their hospitality, and his commission ultimately included other buildings on the estate, and the school and the church of St. Matthew in the adjacent village.[14]

No such evidence can be adduced for the artistic taste of Sir Alexander Cockburn (1802–80), who is not known to have taken any special interest in architecture. He sat as chief justice of the court of Queen's bench from 1859 until 1873, but although his early reputation as a Liberal M.P. was based on his advocacy of law reform, he never endorsed fusion, the final step of that process. Accordingly, Cockburn disliked the Judicature Act and did not promote its implementation. Nevertheless, he was a respected lawyer, and Gladstone had considered him as a possible lord chancellor.

Sir William Stirling-Maxwell (1818–78), Gladstone's appointee to the jury, was its only Conservative and its only *bona fide* art critic.[15] Educated at Cambridge where his tutor was William Whewell, the pioneering medieval antiquarian, he traveled extensively in the Middle East and in Spain. His *Annals of the Artists of Spain* (1848) presented to the English public for the first time that nation's achievements in painting. Seventeen years later, George Edmund Street's *Some Account of Gothic Architecture in Spain* did the same for its architecture. A hint of what Stirling-Maxwell felt about architecture may be seen in his service on the select committee headed by A. J. Beresford-Hope that studied the government offices competition and made a report favorable to G. G. Scott. Scott later counted him among the supporters in Parliament of his Gothic design.[16]

William Ewart Gladstone (1809–98), as chancellor of the Exchequer, was the ranking minister among the competition judges. His must have been the most influential voice. His first great biographer recorded that "he was a collector of ivories, of China, of Wedgwood, but in architecture in all its high historic bearings I never found him very deeply interested."[17] This opinion must now be modified. Gladstone's curiosity encompassed almost every aspect of Victorian intellectual life, and, like many High Church leaders, he kept himself informed about the course of the medieval revival in architecture that was providing appropriate settings for the revised Anglican liturgy. Gladstone was, in fact, almost certainly the best tutored in architectural matters of all the jurors, not excepting William Cowper. This heretofore little studied aspect of Gladstone's life and of Victorian official patronage explains his decision to appoint himself to the law courts jury, and his diaries reveal that not a few of the architects who were invited to compete, or who might have been considered for invitations, were already known to him.[18]

William Butterfield, long the favored architect of the Ecclesiological Society, was one of those High Church architects with whom such an acquaintance might have been expected. Indeed, Gladstone's papers show that in May 1858 Butterfield had breakfast with the future prime minister, being thus initiated into the ritual of morning hospitality that Gladstone reserved for those with whom he wished to speak but whom he had no official reason to entertain. Butterfield was again at breakfast in May 1860, and, in the meantime, Gladstone's diaries show that on April 1, 1859, they had together visited All Saints, Margaret Street, the architect's newly opened masterpiece and the model church of the Ecclesiological Society.[19] But Butterfield was not the only architect who was acquainted with Gladstone.

As early as May 1854, G. G. Scott had also received an invitation to breakfast, and he prepared a report on Westminster Abbey for Gladstone shortly thereafter.[20] When the church on Gladstone's estate in North Wales was destroyed by fire on October 29, 1857, Scott was given the job of reconstruction. The diaries show that Scott visited the estate at Hawarden, which included the ruins of a medieval castle on the grounds, on November 11; and when the work was completed, Gladstone wrote that the church had been "admirably rebuilt and restored."[21] While the restoration was under way, Gladstone read and praised Scott's *Remarks on Secular and Domestic Architecture* as well as an unspecified lecture by him on the Gothic revival.[22] Gladstone's High Church partiality to Gothic encouraged Scott to appeal for his assistance in 1859–60, when Palmerston insisted that the Foreign Office be given a classical façade. As chancellor of the Exchequer, Gladstone surveyed this altercation with divided loyalties, but he was guardedly supportive of Scott and evinced none of the presumed Liberal preference for classicism that Palmerston symbolized. In one letter he even implied that it would be more honorable for the architect to resign than to allow the Foreign Office design to be tampered with.[23]

Although Gladstone's preference for Gothic architecture seems to have been in part religiously motivated, he did not limit his acquaintance with architects to the narrow circle of High Church practitioners, among whom even Scott was not truly at home. His diaries show that on October 14, 1864, he visited the nearly completed Manchester Assize Courts with their young Quaker architect, Alfred Waterhouse. Gladstone described as "beautiful" this new architectural ornament of the city that he would later represent in Parliament, and his relationship with its architect, a local man, was said to be a close one.[24] From a study of the assize courts, Gladstone learned the latest thinking in court design, and this information was valuable when he assumed his responsibilities as a competition juror.

In light of the final outcome of the law courts contest, the most interesting of Gladstone's architectural connections was certainly his relationship with G. E. Street. Their friendship and mutual respect were by no means inconsiderable, even though their politics were different. Street was a Conservative, who, as his son explained, had "an intense personal admiration for one great man, Mr. Gladstone, with whose political career he could not feel any sympathy."[25] But, ideology did not prevent them from agreeing on an occasional controversial issue. Above all, the bond of common religious principles drew them together, as did a shared interest in religious architecture. Indeed, the first recorded letter from Gladstone to Street, on December 18, 1855, was probably an inquiry concerning the architect's new book on the Gothic of Italy.[26] Street was subsequently invited to breakfast on June 17,

1858, and he wrote of the occasion that "Gladstone was very friendly, and the whole party quite informal."[27]

Most likely, Samuel Wilberforce, the bishop of Oxford and Street's patron as diocesan architect, introduced Gladstone to Street's architectural work as well as to Street himself. The rising politician was entertained on several occasions at the bishop's palace in the little village of Cuddesdon, where Street completed his first large commission, the Theological College of 1852–54. During a visit in 1857 the Gladstone diaries record simply: "We went over the Diocesan College," and, more revealingly: "Certainly Cuddesdon with its Bishop and all that he is doing is a goodly sight."[28] Gladstone's strong Oxfordshire connections also included the Convent of St. Mary at Wantage, to which he often sent his "rescue cases," the prostitutes to whom he devoted a large, politically risky amount of effort. Wantage was another town in which Street had built much, beginning with the rectory in 1849–50 and including several buildings for the Convent, with which Gladstone must have been familiar. And, as chancellor of the Exchequer, Gladstone is known to have visited Street's early masterpiece of All Saints, Boyne Hill, Maidenhead (1854–65), where he worshiped while staying at Cliveden in 1863.[29]

Out of regard for Gladstone, Street dedicated his book on Spanish architecture to him in 1865, and in asking permission to make the dedication he praised him as "the statesman for whom I have the greatest respect."[30] A later letter eulogized "your work—public and private," making it clear that the two could minimize their political differences.[31] Gladstone was charmed by the offered dedication and even interested in the contents of the book. Although Street expressed a fear that "so dry and technical a subject" would prove boring, Gladstone spent three days reading the book in February and March 1865.[32] Less than a year later Street was invited to compete for the law courts.

Gladstone and Street were not close friends, but their acquaintance was peculiarly vibrant. Fired by a common faith and by a common interest in building for it, their relationship was also strengthened by similar intellectual dilemmas. Both faced a variant of the quintessentially High Victorian quandary—the need to reconcile contradictions. While Gladstone sought to combine economic conservatism with reformist liberalism, Street's challenge was to practice medieval and modern architecture at the same time. Perhaps the admiration each felt for the other's success in meeting this challenge helped to overcome their differences.

Thus was a jury assembled that had personal ties to many of the leading architects of the day and prejudices that would handicap them in reaching a consensus. At the time of their appointment, however, these prejudices were undetected, and the general criticism centered on their lack of architectural knowledge. Cavendish Bentinck, a Tory M.P. and a noted connoisseur of French and Italian paintings, made this argument in the Commons in March 1866. He demanded that the judges "should have such a knowledge of the subject that their decision should command the respect, not of artists only, but of the artistic world in general."[33] He made no complaint about the qualifications of Stirling-Maxwell, and he did not discuss Gladstone and Cockburn, but he suggested that Cowper and Palmer would both fail a "competitive architectural examination."[34] In defense of the judges, A. J. Beresford-Hope could only say that a panel composed of amateurs might be able to avoid the pitfalls encountered by the Foreign and War Offices jury, which had included an architect, William Burn, and an engineer, Isambard Kingdom Brunel. This reasoning blunted the attack, but the expertise of the judges continued to be questioned.

FOR THE purpose of inviting six architects to compete for the Royal Courts of Justice commission, the jury met for a first time on February 19, 1866.[35] Although the Liberal majority, and Gladstone in particular, must have been preoccupied with the new Reform Bill which was then being discussed in the Cabinet and which would be introduced in Parliament only three weeks later, the judges chose six architects, whose names were announced in the House of Commons the following day: Edward M. Barry, Philip Charles Hardwick, George Gilbert Scott, George Edmund Street, Alfred Waterhouse, and Thomas Henry Wyatt.[36] At the same time, they named first and second alternates, Raphael Brandon and Thomas N. Deane, respectively. The official letters of invitation were not dispatched until February 27, but most of the architects heard the news earlier. On February 21, for example, Street wrote to his sister:

> Today . . . I see by the *Times,* that it was announced in the House of Commons last night that I was one of the six architects selected to make plans for the New Courts of Law. . . . It is a great distinction, I consider, to be asked to make a design, and though the chances of competitions are always doubtful, still, of course, there is a fair chance of success. . . . It is all the more gratifying because I have never moved in the matter at all.[37]

Given the date of the competition and the known architectural preferences of the judges, the selection of these architects is not surprising. Among them were all of the architects with whom the judges had personal contact, save for Butterfield, who avoided competitions. Three of the eight named (six invitees and two alternates) had had previous success in official competitions, with Scott, Street, and Deane all having won prizes in the government offices contest. However, the pro-Gothic prejudice of the jury was such that the two first place winners in that earlier competition, the classicists Henry Edward Coe and Henry B. Garling, were notably excluded. Only three of the chosen architects, Barry, Hardwick, and Wyatt, had established their reputations with classical works. As a group the competitors were rather young. Wyatt, the eldest, was still a year short of sixty, and the two youngest, Barry and Waterhouse, were thirty-six. Their average age was forty-six and Street was forty-two. Despite their relative youth, the contestants all had established reputations, and among them were many of the best-known architects of the day.

Edward M. Barry (1830–80), the son of Sir Charles, was at that time closely identified with the monster hotels that he had built at the Cannon Street (1861) and Charing Cross (1864) railway stations, and for the Royal Opera House, Covent Garden, whose rapid rebuilding after a fire he had directed in 1857, at the precocious age of twenty-seven.[38] He had also taken the second prize in the Oxford Museum competition. Already an associate of the Royal Academy, he was characterized by the unsympathetic *Building News* as a "pushing young man."[39] Like his father and like T. H. Wyatt, in whose office he trained, Barry was a classicist at heart, despite his occasional medieval excursions. He had succeeded to the position held by his father at the Houses of Parliament and thus established his reliability in government work, to which Cowper could testify. He was probably selected by the judges as a safe representative of both youth and classical taste.

Philip C. Hardwick (1820–90) was the architect of another railway hotel, the Great Western at Paddington Station (1851–53), whose mansard roofs had provided the model for Barry at Cannon Street and Charing Cross.[40] But in the context of the law courts competition, his most important work was the Tudor hall and library at Lincoln's Inn (1839–45), where he supervised and augmented his father's design. His new campus for the Charterhouse School, which he began in 1865, was also Tudor and Gothic. The judges may have hoped that he would produce a medieval design for the courts, despite the Great Western and the numerous Italianate commercial buildings he erected in London. His invitation was perhaps a gesture toward the powerful Society of Lincoln's Inn, which had only recently given up its opposition to the concentration of both common law and equity on the Carey Street site. Roundell Palmer was a Lincoln's Inn bencher.

Gilbert Scott (1811–78) was not only the most prominent Gothic architect, but, owing to his dispute with Palmerston over the design of the Foreign Office, he had become the symbol of the struggle for the adoption of the Gothic style in secular buildings. Next to Wyatt, he was the oldest on the list of invitees. Scott had already designed a building for the equity courts for Lincoln's Inn, and, with his personal association with Gladstone and support from Cowper and Stirling-Maxwell, he was an inevitable choice.

G. E. Street (1824–81) was the second most prolific contemporary Gothic architect after Scott, and, although he had been responsible for few large secular buildings, he was a longtime proponent of secular medievalism. In the government offices contest he had only tied for the fifth award for the Foreign Office, but his numerous church commissions kept him constantly in the public eye. His recent book on Spanish Gothic architecture would have attracted the attention of Stirling-Maxwell, and it was dedicated to Gladstone, whom Street had known for several years. Conceivably, the architect foresaw Gladstone's role in the competition for the long-awaited law courts when he proposed the book's dedication in December 1864, but his sincere admiration for the statesman provides an adequate and more honorable explanation for the gesture. Street may have been included in the roster of contestants to represent the group of serious, High Church architects, such as Bodley and Butterfield, of whom he was the most prominent. It is barely possible that he was also selected as the representative of the avant-garde of Early French "art architects," which also included such men as William Burges and E. W. Godwin.

Alfred Waterhouse (1830–1905) was another young architect who had rapidly achieved national recognition, having triumphed in the competition of 1859 for the Manchester Assize Courts (Figs. 20, 21).[41] Opened less than two years before the law courts competitors were named, this was the first major building to benefit from the ongoing discussion of courthouse planning. Unlike other recent large public buildings that included courtrooms, such as H. L. Elmes's executed version of St. George's Hall, Liverpool (1841–56), and Cuthbert Brodrick's Leeds Town Hall (1853–58), the Manchester courts adopted the concentric circle scheme. While

20 *Alfred Waterhouse.*
Manchester Assize Courts.
1858–64. Perspective. (Papers
Read at the Royal Institute of
British Architects 1864–65.)

this was simplified and reduced for application in a provincial setting, the arrangement of the central hall with adjacent courtrooms served by a rear corridor was preserved, and its success was widely acclaimed by jurists. The building was explicitly praised in the instructions for the law courts competition, and the *Times* later called the Manchester Assizes "the best courts of law in the world."[42] As a result of these accolades, Edwin Field asked Waterhouse to serve as the architectural clerk of the Royal Commission, and it was at first intended that he would draft outline plans to guide the competitors.[43] Waterhouse was also a provincial architect, and, although he opened a London office in 1865 to serve his growing national practice, his appointment was probably seen as a gesture toward geographic equity. To be sure, his candidacy could not have been hurt by the fact that since 1865 Gladstone had been his M.P.[44]

Thomas H. Wyatt (1807–80), the older and less well-known brother of Matthew Digby Wyatt, is best remembered for the Lombard Romanesque church of SS. Mary and Nicholas, Wilton, which he designed with David Brandon in 1840. He may have been brought to the attention of the judges by his collaboration with Brandon on the assize courts of Devizes (1835) and Cambridge (1840–43), Greek and Italianate buildings, respectively, of no great merit. Possessed of few stylistic scruples, Wyatt's more recent works included the French Renaissance Liverpool

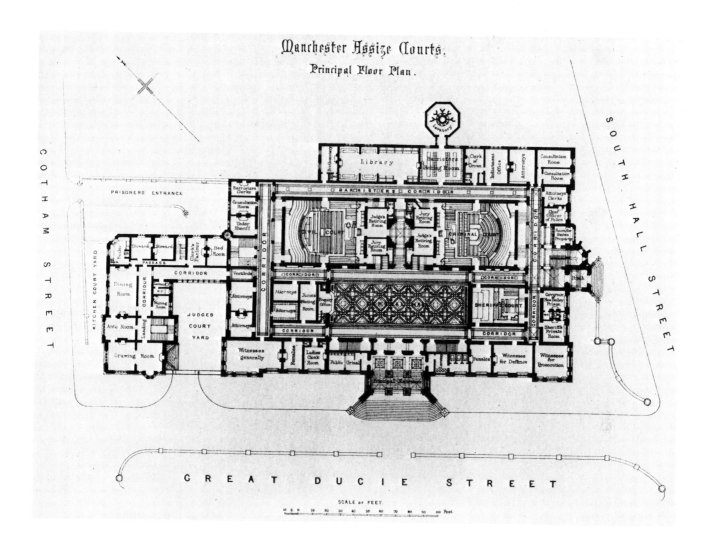

Manchester Assize Courts.
Principal Floor Plan.

COTHAM STREET · SOUTH HALL STREET · GREAT DUCIE STREET · SCALE of FEET · PRISONERS ENTRANCE · KITCHEN COURT YARD · JUDGES COURT YARD · Library · Laboratory · Civil Court · Criminal Court · Sheriff's Court · BARRISTERS CORRIDOR · CORRIDOR

21 Waterhouse. Manchester Assize Courts. 1858–64. Plan. (Papers Read at the Royal Institute of British Architects 1864–65.)

Exchange (1863–67) and a number of churches which demonstrated his appreciation of High Victorian Gothic. Wyatt served as president of the Royal Institute of British Architects for several years in the early seventies and was the winner of the institute's Royal Gold Medal in 1873. His listing among the competitors was probably an effort to include a member of the professional old guard, for he could scarcely have been considered a strong opponent for the younger Goths.

The two alternates, Raphael Brandon (1817–77) and Thomas N. Deane (1828–99) were both medievalists. Brandon, who was unrelated to David Brandon, had built one large and admired building, the Catholic Apostolic Church in Gordon Square, London (1851–55), and he was the architect and surveyor of little Clement's Inn, whose buildings on the west side of the site for the law courts were already threatened by the expansion-minded Royal Commission. Moreover, like Waterhouse, he had specifically asked to be invited, and his name may have been brought up at an opportune moment.[45] Brandon had trained in France—a very rare preparation for an English architect of his generation. Deane was a predictable choice, for he had gained wide recognition through his association with the Oxford Museum (1854–61), designed by his late partner, Benjamin Woodward. His name was also linked with that of Woodward in the design that won fourth place in the Foreign Office division of the government offices competition, and since his partner's death his own Meadows Building at Christ Church, Oxford (1862–65), had been favorably noticed. A Dubliner, consideration of Deane may also have been a gesture to architects on the other side of the Irish Sea.

At nearly the same time that the competitors for the law courts were selected, a roster of contestants was drawn up for the rebuilding of the National Gallery. Only Street, Barry, and Scott were invited to enter both competitions, and Scott promptly declined the gallery. When formal invitations for the law courts were at last issued, Street was already embarked on a two-week tour of Antwerp, Munich, Vienna, Prague, Dresden, Berlin, Hannover, and Hildesheim, studying the principles of modern museum design.

With the announcement of the law courts invitations, the work of designing the new building should have begun. But dissatisfaction with the competition and with the invitations themselves soon spread among the architects, in the press, and in Parliament, and these forces combined to upset both the original ground rules of the contest and to modify the list of participants. On March 3, while Street was still abroad, Scott, Barry, Waterhouse, and Wyatt resolved to protest against the clause in the draft instructions that permitted the Government to decide against using any of the submitted designs. It was just such a clause that had allowed the judgment in the government offices competition to be overturned, and those earlier competitors had complained in vain. On this occasion the Royal Commission read the architects' letter with understanding, and the redrafted instructions of March 7 omitted the offending provision.[46]

Despite this procedural victory, in early March both Hardwick and Wyatt decided to decline the invitation. No explanation was published, but they probably realized that the thinking of younger and more medieval architects would dominate the competition.[47] Shortly thereafter Scott and Barry also withdrew, protesting a second clause in the instructions that would prohibit the selected architect from accepting other new work for a period of three years. Their complaint against this probably unnecessary guarantee of devoted service was also favorably considered by the Treasury and the commission; a sign that the long campaign by architects for professional recognition was at last bearing fruit.[48] However, the four vacancies had been filled before the rules were revised, blocking out the protesters.

The resignations of Hardwick and Wyatt had automatically propelled Brandon and Deane into the contest, joining Street and Waterhouse, the only survivors of the original six. But this exhausted the alternate pool, so that when Scott and Barry resigned, the judges had to nominate new competitors. They accomplished this without another formal meeting, for the Reform Bill debate was then taxing their energies. Through informal consultation, the judges chose Henry B. Garling and George Somers Clarke to fill the places vacated by Scott and Barry, and selected John Gibson and John P. Seddon as alternates. These names were announced on March 21.[49] While the first invitees had included three competitors and two alternates who were committed Goths, the new roster included five Gothic competitors and one alternate. The judges had thus allowed themselves a further concession to medieval prejudices.

The newly chosen architects had neither the national prominence nor the personal associations with the judges of the first group. The process of selection had

22 *Henry Garling. War Office competition, London. 1856–57. (Builder, 1 August 1857.)*

clearly become more difficult. Henry B. Garling (1821 or 1822–1909) had won the War Office division of the government offices competition with a design which, like many in that contest, reflected a naive appreciation of the recently completed additions to the Louvre (Fig. 22). Aside from that moment of glory, he had no public reputation. George Somers Clarke (1825–82) was a somewhat better known architect who had built a prosperous practice in London designing commercial buildings in the Italian Gothic mode. However, Somers Clarke had already been invited to participate in the National Gallery competition, and he chose not to accept the law courts in addition. His place was then automatically filled by John Gibson (1814–92), the first of the new alternates and a pupil of Sir Charles Barry. He, too, had developed a lively commercial practice, but his preferred style was a rich Renaissance classicism. With the advance of Gibson to the competition, the classic-to-Gothic ratio was restored to its original balance of three-to-three. The remaining alternate, John P. Seddon (1827–1906), had placed fourth in the War Office contest, and he was just beginning to receive national recognition for the buildings that he had erected in Wales, of which the new hotel at Aberystwyth (1864) was the best known. It ranked among the largest and most powerful secular Gothic buildings of the time.

Even after this dizzy reshuffling, the competition had not attained its final form. While this game of rotation had been played, outside criticism had mounted against the limitation of the contest to only six architects. On March 10, the *Law Times*— in a campaign that quickly gained momentum—called on lawyers to demand an open competition.[50] Twelve days later, Cavendish Bentinck brought the matter to the attention of the House of Commons. His attack on the management of the contest included a resolution that "In the opinion of this House, it is not expedient that the competition for the building of the New Courts of Justice should be limited to six architects only."[51]

Bentinck argued that there should be a sufficient number of competitors to permit the judges "a full latitude of choice"—almost certainly a plea for more classicists—and he pointed out that contemporary architecture, unlike that in the days of Sir Christopher Wren, was not dominated by a very small number of artists. He was seconded in this argument by two spokesmen for the architectural profession. A. J. Beresford-Hope, president of the R.I.B.A. and an M.P., recommended, however, that the number of invitees be increased without declaring an unwieldy open competition. William Tite, a past president of the R.I.B.A. and also an M.P., argued similarly for increasing the number of architects to ten or twelve. This was necessary because "the number of six architects was so extremely limited that it certainly created in the minds of the architectural profession an impression that, to a great extent, a foregone conclusion had been arrived at." It is likely that Tite, the architect of the Royal Exchange, feared that the "foregone conclusion" was that the law courts were to be medieval. He hoped that more classicists might be invited in an expanded competition.

Two of the competition judges, Cowper and Palmer, attempted in debate to refute these implications of prejudice and jobbery. Cowper undiplomatically suggested that Parliament had relinquished its authority in the matter when it authorized a royal commission to oversee the competition. Palmer made the more persuasive argument that the two hundred or three hundred architects who might enter an unlimited competition would seriously interfere with the work of the courts and offices when they came to inspect the present arrangements. But the House clearly believed that at least a small increase in the number of entrants was practical, and passed the Bentinck motion by a vote of 101 to 70.

After consultation, the Treasury and the Royal Commission agreed to increase the number of competitors to twelve, and on April 21 the six architects who had already been invited were advised of the intended change.[52] Two complained, but no further resignations were precipitated.[53]

The judges were again called upon to nominate new competitors, but their principal attention surely remained riveted on the Reform Bill debates. Again, no record of a full jury meeting exists, but Gladstone's diary records a conference with Roundell Palmer in the wake of the passage of Bentinck's resolution.[54] On April 30 Cowper announced to the House of Commons that six additional architects had been chosen: Gilbert Scott and E. M. Barry, who no longer found the instructions objectionable, had rejoined the competition; John Seddon had advanced from his position as an alternate; and Henry Robert Abraham, Henry F. Lockwood, and William Burges were newly invited.[55] No further competitors would be selected for the law courts, although Bentinck made a bid to have the roster increased to twenty-four on May 18.[56] When John Gibson retired on July 31, owing to "pressure of urgent professional engagements and other claims upon my time," his place was allowed to remain vacant, and the competition field was thereby set at eleven.[57] Edward W. Godwin's last minute application to take Gibson's place was turned down.[58]

The final selections of the judges had been made easier by the willingness of Barry and Scott to re-enter the competition and by the presence of one remaining architect, Seddon, on their list of alternates. For the additional three, the choice was more difficult, and, after the publicity of the Parliamentary debate, the judges were inundated with requests for invitations. H. R. Abraham and H. F. Lockwood had already submitted such requests, and now letters were received from Thomas Goodchild, the architect of the Guildford Assize Courts, from John and Horace Francis, the designers of the National Discount Offices in London, from the firm of F. R. Beeston and F. S. Brereton, and from John Dales.[59] It is unlikely that the later requests received much attention, but the early letters of Abraham and Lockwood may have had something to do with their selection.

In inviting Henry Robert Abraham (c. 1804–77), the architect of the robust Middle Temple Library (1858–61), the judges continued the pattern of looking to the architects employed by the Inns of Court (Fig. 23). Of course, Abraham had also prepared a plan for the law courts in 1860–61, but this must have counted very little in his favor, given the charges of favoritism that surrounded his appointment and the subsequent resignation of his patron, Lord Westbury, in disgrace.

Henry F. Lockwood (1811–78) had designed a series of public buildings in Bradford like those that Waterhouse built in Manchester. His choice probably reflected the desire of the judges to increase the number of provincials in step with the increase in the overall size of the competition. Lockwood's St. George's Hall,

23 Henry R. Abraham. Middle Temple Library, London. 1858–61. (Builder, 15 December 1860.)

Bradford (1851–52), was classical, but he had kept pace with changing tastes and the design with which he won the Bradford Exchange competition in 1864 was of a florid Ruskinian Gothic.[60] He had expanded his practice to a national scale, and at the time of the law courts contest he was building the Inns of Court Hotel between Holborn and Lincoln's Inn Fields. It may have been this strategically placed edifice that attracted the attention of the jurors.

William Burges (1827–81) was the most important of the last three to be selected. In some respects it is puzzling that he did not receive earlier consideration, but he was still a young man and his work was associated with that of those who were younger still. Moreover, he had designed no large secular buildings, and his reputation rested on three great churches, only one of which he had been able to build. The winner of the competitions for both Lille cathedral (1855–56) and the Crimean Memorial Church (1856), he had seen those commissions diverted to other architects. But Burges's victory in the 1862 contest for the Anglican cathedral at Cork, Ireland, had been crowned with a commission to build, and that building was now rising as a tangible representative of the powerful, somewhat eccentric style that many younger architects admired. The law courts competition was to provide the opportunity for Burges's art to win an even wider following.

These last three to be selected were all medievalists, giving their group a nine-to-three majority in the final list. With the retirement of Gibson, that majority was increased to nine-to-two. The predominantly Liberal judges thus conclusively dispelled the impression, created by the Foreign Office controversy, that Gothic was the architectural language of the Tories alone. In terms of public acceptance, Gothic architecture was then at the peak of its popularity, and, when prompted by a little High Church feeling, even the descendants of Palmerston were inclined to favor the pointed arch.

Preparation and Interpretation

WITH THE NAMING of the last competitors on April 30, the competition began in earnest. While the architects turned to their drawing tables, the Royal Commission continued to play an active role in interpreting the instructions and in providing further information. The deadline was December 15, 7½ months away.

Two of the competitors, Street and Waterhouse, had had a nominal two-month head start on those who were named after the expansion of the contest, but the final instructions had not been published until April 21. Street had spent some of his extra time in Europe, inspecting art galleries, and although the reams of hearing testimony and commission reports provided some basis on which to begin planning, the few additional weeks of preparation time did not substantially lessen the task. Scott later recalled the vastness of the work:

> It took me, I think, from April to September to get up my information and throw it into anything like shape, and at length I succeeded in packing together, in what I had reason to think a good form, every room required, to the number, I should think of some thousands. Then . . . I took [the purely architectural work] vigorously in hand, working at it at odd times, while my own more practical study was going on, and then taking a month at the seaside for

this department exclusively, besides much subsequent work, upon my return home. No previous competition had involved me in such an amount of labour.[61]

In all, he estimated that his design for the law courts had required "almost continuous study for three-quarters of a year, involving absence for fully half my time from ordinary business, and the almost entire absorption of my thoughts from other subjects."[62] Waterhouse, who admitted that in late November he had not yet decided how to arrange the courts, spent December evenings with his staff, remaining in the office until midnight.[63]

While the architects worked, the commission attempted to provide them with a number of services. Its eagerness to accumulate vast quantities of information was now reflected in a large but in great part useless effort to study courts of law in foreign countries. On March 1, after the first architects had been invited, the Foreign Office was asked to make inquiries abroad, and replies were received almost until the submission date for the designs.[64] No comprehensive report could thus be prepared for the competitors, and, moreover, William Burnet, the architectural clerk of the commission, concluded that foreign courts could only provide negative examples.[65] Nothing of comparable size and complexity could be found elsewhere (the new Palais de Justice in Paris was inexplicably ignored), nor were the provisions made abroad suitable for the business of English justice. The similar inquiry made by the commission at this time into the planning of British assize courts also turned up little that was considered worthy of emulation. Manchester alone was warmly praised, and its virtues were already well known.[66]

The commission was only slightly more successful in interpreting the vague but voluminous instructions. The most important issue to be settled now was the extent of the site, a question that the instructions had left to the architects by providing them with a site map which showed the land approved by Parliament and the Treasury in yellow, but which also included the commission's large recommended parcels of adjacent property, tinted pink. The yellow land was the 7½ acres proposed by the Coleridge Commission, bounded on the north by Carey Street, on the east by Bell Yard, on the south by the Strand, and on the west by the irregular boundary of Clement's Inn (see Fig. 19). The supplemental pink land, which the Treasury had failed to approve because of an estimated purchase price of £488,620, was dangled before the architects with the request that they decide for themselves whether its acquisition was necessary.[67]

Sensing that they were being lured into the crossfire of an intragovernmental dispute, the architects prudently chose to confer on June 1 before responding.[68] The eleven competitors elected Scott as their chairman and then predictably voted to side with the commission and ask for the purchase of the pink land. This would provide a nearly rectangular parcel, about an acre larger than the yellow site, with dimensions of 700 and 510 feet. In addition, they proposed the acquisition of yet further property, colored blue on a map which they submitted to the commissioners. The commission responded on June 8, asking the Treasury to reconsider the purchase of the pink land and allowing the architects to decide individually how much of the blue land was needed for their designs. They were to submit plans, showing their use of the blue land, by October 20.

The Treasury was understandably unenthusiastic about the prospect of increased expenditure, but they did press a piece of general enabling legislation through Parliament in July. However, they were far less complaisant after the architects met again on September 13 and decided that the use of all of the blue and all of the pink property was "essential for the success of the scheme." The competitors now also proposed that several other adjacent parcels should be acquired, including a large tract north of Carey Street which was to be resold to a group of private developers who intended to erect several blocks of offices. These further lands were colored green on the map submitted with the architects' proposal.[69] To this polychromatic self-indulgence, totaling more than thirteen acres, the Treasury replied sternly on October 5. George Hamilton, a Treasury secretary, advised the Royal Commission that while some further land would be required, it was still desirable to adhere as closely as possible to the original site estimate of £750,000. He wrote, "However the acquisition of the land now proposed to be purchased might add to the effect of the designs of the competing Architects, it can scarcely be said, at least at present, that such an acquisition is necessary for proper accesses to the intended buildings."[70] The wishful thinking of the architects, fostered by the indulgence of the commission, had been identified for what it was. Although the Treasury was induced to prepare specific legislation for the acquisition of additional lands in the next Parliamentary session, the measure was never pursued.[71] By 1867 interest had shifted to the enormous controversy surrounding the selection of the architect.

It was easier to resolve smaller questions which involved less expenditure. Thus, the competitors had little difficulty in winning commission and Treasury approval for the widening of Carey Street in order to provide better light for the lower stories of the building.[72] The architects were also successful in obtaining an extension of the deadline, after protesting the December 15 date in a letter of October 23 which was signed by Abraham, Barry, Burges, Deane, Garling, Lockwood, Seddon, and Waterhouse. They cited the enormous number of requirements that had to be fulfilled and the delay in defining the site boundaries. Scott concurred with their petition in a separate letter, and Brandon and Street did not dissent. Responding favorably to their request, Henry A. Hunt, the surveyor of the Office of Works, pointed out, "It may be that those who desire further time are the very parties who could produce the best designs . . . and it is fair to assume that those who will not be ready are for the most part men in considerable private practice and probably of larger experience and knowledge than those who are less engaged."[73] Hunt recommended an extension until March 1, and the commission and Treasury approved a less generous postponement until January 15 at 1 P.M.[74]

In the closing months of the competition, the Royal Commission also prepared for the public exhibition of the drawings. Such displays had become a tradition in public competitions, at least since the hanging of the designs for the Houses of Parliament in Westminster Hall. The commission and the architects were anxious that the exhibition be located near the Carey Street site, and they proposed the erection of a temporary building for that purpose. The Treasury preferred the Royal Gallery in the Palace of Westminster, but they eventually approved the expense of erecting a temporary structure. The contract was signed for this building on November 20, and the design prepared by Burnet was quickly executed in the center of New Square, Lincoln's Inn, only a few steps away from the intended site (Fig. 24).[75]

24 *William Burnet. Exhibition building for the law courts competition, New Square, Lincoln's Inn. 1866–67. (Illustrated London News, 16 February 1867.)*

25 *Burnet. Exhibition building for the law courts competition, New Square, Lincoln's Inn. 1866–67. (Illustrated London News, 16 February 1867.)*

Although all of the competitors seem to have been able to submit their drawings on time—indeed Waterhouse overcame his slow start and submitted his early—and although Burnet's building was completed on schedule, the exhibition did not open until February 8, 1867.[76] In the intervening weeks the plans and elevations were photolithographed, a process that at that time required waiting for sunny weather, and the prints were made up into booklets for the use of the judges. The architects themselves supervised the hanging of their designs, each within a designated 12 by 30 foot alcove in the skylit exhibition building (Fig. 25). Scott submitted the largest number of drawings, approximately forty, followed closely by Street, Waterhouse, and Lockwood, in roughly that order. Seddon alone had models built of his design, as the instructions had permitted. After the exhibition closed that summer, the drawings were returned to the architects, and out of the 250 or more that were hung in New Square, only 13 are known to exist today. However, most of the other designs are well recorded by surviving photographs and publications.[77]

Special viewing hours were established for members of Parliament and other dignitaries, for the press, and for architects and lawyers. The general public was admitted on Thursdays, after having obtained tickets, like the other visitors, from the office of the commission. Fridays were reserved for the purposes of the Royal Commission and the jury.

Gothic Designs

THE EXHIBITION in New Square was a great popular success. The scores of beautiful drawings, the work of the best architectural talent of the nation, attracted large crowds and extensive press coverage. But the interest of most observers was focused on the question of style and on the artistry of the renderings, rather than on what the *Times* called "plans ten times more intricate and incomprehensible than the Labyrinth of Crete."[78] As the *Saturday Review* judged, the program requirements had made the planning of the law courts "about the most difficult problem ever offered to any architect or body of architects to solve from the days of Babel downwards."[79] Popular opinion was formed around simpler issues.

The most easily apprehended feature of the designs as a whole was the fact that all of the competitors chose to work in Gothic, including the predicted classicists, Barry and Garling. The latter did prepare a Renaissance version of his entry, but it went virtually unmentioned and no visual record of it has been preserved. Thus, the competition was celebrated as the victory for which progressive architects had striven for two decades: the complete acceptance of medievalism in the contest for an urban, secular building. The achievement of this important High Victorian objective was made more remarkable by the fact that the competitors had received no specific instructions as to style. The *Ecclesiologist* understandably called the success "a matter of much congratulation to us, and those who think with us."[80] A. J. Beresford-Hope's *Saturday Review* and the *Spectator* agreed, and even the often unsympathetic *Times* doubted that classical designs could have been more successful.[81]

However, a few significant voices did protest the prominence of Gothic in the law courts competition, and the future turned out to be on their side. Far from inaugurating an age of confident medievalism, as the statistics of the competition seemed to predict, the law courts became the last great, contradiction-ridden monument of the High Victorian Gothic revival.

The critics of Gothic belonged to two schools whose complaints had been heard for at least twenty years. First were those who scorned Gothic out of a general contempt for historicism. The *Builder* had perennially championed this view, and, confronted with eleven medieval designs for the law courts, its tone was initially resigned: "It appears to have been understood from the beginning that the Law Courts were to be in the Gothic style, and Gothic they, doubtless, will be. Probably, indeed, such has been the course of study in England, we shall thus get a more agreeable building, for the time, than might have been the case had another style been worked on." "But," they went on to warn, resuming their usual argument, "we should belie often-expressed opinions if we admitted that it is thus that the century is likely to arrive at the possession of a noble vernacular architecture of its own."[82]

The views of James Fergusson, another persistent foe of historicist copyism, were very similar. He lamented that architecture, alone among the arts and sciences, was "retrogressive," and he called the Gothic designs hung in New Square a "masquerade of Mediaevalism."[83] These ideas also infused the petulant essay prepared by Philip Smith and J. T. Emmett for the *Quarterly Review*. "The simple sad truth is, that Architecture in England is dead," they concluded, adding, "To ourselves, we candidly confess, after years of sympathy with the Gothic revival, this discovery has come while studying the designs exhibited in New Square. . . . The works of our modern architects are composed in a foreign language."[84]

While such radical critics claimed to oppose all historicism, a preference for classicism underlay much of their displeasure. This taste was undisguised in the comments of a second school of disgruntled observers, including Cavendish Bentinck, who introduced the matter in the House of Commons. Bentinck charged: "The designs exhibited are very curious . . . as illustrations of Gothic cathedrals, feudal castles, and other medieval monuments, but they were most extravagant in their character, costly in their estimates, and barbarous in their details." Beresford-Hope, speaking for the medievalist majority of the day, replied that "English Law Courts, built in English architecture, was what English common sense dictated."[85]

The Gothic majority was not swayed by the repetition of old arguments, but other forces guaranteed that it would not prevail for long. The stylistic uniformity of the law courts competition is best explained as the fortuitous combination of many factors, all of them temporary. As this combination dissolved, so did the imagined triumph of High Victorian medievalism.

The first temporary contributor to the cause of Gothic architecture in 1866–67 was demographic: the greatest architects of the day were Goths. As Robert Kerr, no friend of their movement, later observed: "The Classic leaders . . . were neither many nor strong; all the real artistic vigour was now Gothic—romantic."[86] This had not come about by the conversion of the older generation of architects to a new creed, but by the progress of a new generation, with new ideas, up the ladder of professional seniority. Because the Goths succeeded by seniority rather than by the victory of their ideas, their triumph was limited by their longevity. At the peak of their powers at the time of the competition, seven of the eleven entrants would be dead before the law courts were completed in 1882.

The choice of style was also, as always in public commissions, a function of politics, and in the case of the law courts the composition of the jury and the predilections of William Ewart Gladstone were influences favorable to Gothic. But as political power was impermanent, so were these forces. When the jury was disbanded and Gladstone rose from the position of chancellor of the Exchequer to the artistically remoter post of prime minister, Gothic architecture was no longer so securely placed.

Other factors which helped to marshal opinion toward a Gothic consensus were similarly specific to this particular project. For example, the irregularity of the chosen site argued for the employment of a picturesque architectural vocabulary, and the location of the old courts at Westminster Hall provided an associational justification for the use of Gothic.

The impermanence of these fostering conditions was not, however, the sole agent in determining that the law courts would be the last major monument of nineteenth-century Gothicism. The ideological structure of the Gothic movement was already disintegrating, and the competitors were an enormously diverse group—not at all the united phalanx of Goths that the public perceived them to be. Despite the uniformity imposed by broadly similar decorative vocabularies and by planning principles established by years of preliminary study, this diversity can be detected in the designs for the law courts. It reflects the disruptive internal stresses of a terminal, not a victorious, episode.

These stresses were seen in the manner in which each of the competitors faced the intractable dilemma of High Victorian architecture—the confusing quest for Ruskin's "central building of the world" and for Street's combination of "the verticality of Pointed with the repose of Classic architecture."[87] The High Victorian challenge was to create an embracing architectural language for the nineteenth-century city that resolved the "Battle of the Styles," and almost all of the competition designs, despite their nominal Gothicism, can be analyzed as efforts to unite the picturesque capabilities of medieval architecture with the stateliness and dignity that were considered classical. The irregular, hemmed-in site called for the former, while the latter was a programmatic requirement for a great public building.

But rarely were these two elements—what Street summarized as "verticality" and "repose"—perfectly balanced in the designs, and the demise of the High Victorian dream was foretold in this failure of most of the competitors to achieve the equilibrium so important to the theorists. In preference to the middle way, most architects and critics of the law courts rallied to the poles, the reconciliation of which was now abandoned. The majority of entries either exaggerated the picturesque or adopted a kind of quasi-classicism. This fragmented the Gothic movement, and in the rekindled, somewhat gentler "Battle of the Styles" that ensued, the brave promise of a single architectural idiom—a "central building of the world"—was lost. For generations to come, churches would be Gothic, public buildings would be explicitly classical, and houses would be that pretty mongrel, the Queen Anne, whose mild conflation of medieval and Renaissance was the only long-lived product of the heroic posturings of mid-century.

Polarized Taste

THIS POLARIZATION of the architectural community was apparent both in the designs submitted to the law courts competition and in the criticism that was devoted to them. The designs themselves fell quite clearly into two categories which foreshadowed the divided tastes of the next generations. Although all were superficially Gothic, some emphasized irregular composition, with its stronger medieval connotations, while others stressed such classical qualities as regularity and symmetry. The critics eagerly took sides in this confrontation of tastes, with a majority preferring the picturesque designs and thereby contributing further to what was presumed to be the triumph of Gothic. Only a few architects with ideological roots firmly in the 1850s, notably G. G. Scott and G. E. Street, still attempted synthesizing designs of the High Victorian type.

Whichever solution was chosen, each architect faced the same fundamental design problems. First, he had to determine how best to utilize the rather flexibly defined Carey Street site. This property rose quite sharply to the north, where it was thrust up against large tracts of poor, crowded housing, not unlike that which had been demolished for the new building. On the south it fronted on the Strand, the overworked main artery that linked Westminster and the City of London. The roadway was not wide enough to begin with, and in front of the site for the law courts it was further constricted. Christopher Wren's Temple Bar, a gate of the City of London, spanned the roadway near the east boundary of the site, and the church of St. Clement Danes, begun by Wren and given its steeple by James Gibbs, sat on an island in the middle of the roadway to the west.

Upon this difficult terrain, the architect had to fulfill the difficult program outlined by the Royal Commission. This involved providing courtrooms and offices for both major judicial branches, equity and common law, as well as for the Admiralty court and for the new, specialized courts for probate and divorce cases. Facilities for several purely administrative departments were also to be included. The space requirements were set forth exhaustively in the table appended to the instructions, which specified a minimum total floor area of 683,000 square feet. Twenty-three courtrooms were mandated, and it was suggested that those designated for the equity courts should be placed to the north, near Lincoln's Inn and its concentration of equity practitioners. Common law courts were to be located to the south, close to the Temples, the inns traditionally favored by common law specialists. The competitors were asked to connect the new building to the Temples by means of a bridge across the Strand on the site of Temple Bar, and to Lincoln's Inn by a bridge across Carey Street. Substantial record storage facilities were to be provided for the probate department.

The instructions stressed the need for efficient planning, which was to override all other considerations. This proviso was coupled with a set of daunting requirements, evolved during the long period of preliminary consideration of the new courts. Quiet, good natural light, and efficient ventilation were essential, but none of these was easily provided on the crowded urban site. And the architect was strongly enjoined to see that his circulation system separated the various types of people who would come to the building. Most important of all, he was to insure that mere spectators never crossed the path of those who were occupied with legal business. Their entrances and corridors were to be clearly partitioned from the working parts of the building, and they were to be denied admission to its largest spaces. For achieving these difficult objectives the commission made few concrete recommendations, but, given the now well-established principle of concentric organization, most of the competitors offered similar solutions.

The format for the submission of the designs was left largely to the taste of the competitors. The only required drawings were plans of each floor (at a scale of one inch to sixteen feet), a transverse and longitudinal section, elevations of each façade, and one perspective or bird's-eye view. To these the architects might add an unlimited number of additional detail drawings, renderings, and even alternative solutions. Models would also be accepted. The elevations could be colored with only one tint of sepia, with no foreground or sky to be shown. The plans could be color coded to show different departments, and the perspectives, in which foreground and sky were permitted, were restricted in media to sepia, Indian ink wash, and pen and ink. A written description was required.

Of the designs that sought to fulfill these conditions, the most popular among reviewers was the castellated fantasy submitted by William Burges (Fig. 26). His was the most irregular of all the picturesque entries, with its powerful asymmetries accentuated by a bird's-eye view which placed the 460-foot record tower in the foreground. Overall, seven of the sixteen publications known to have rated the entries preferred Burges's, which was always referred to as the favorite of artists and architects.[88] This acclaim has been little noted by modern art historians, although it is a critical milestone in the evolution of architectural taste in the nineteenth century, marking the polarization that swept away what Street and Ruskin had worked for in the preceding decades.

26 William Burges. Competition design. 1866–67. Bird's-eye view by Axel Herman Haig. (Photograph at NMR.)

Although Burges's description of his design claimed that one of his objectives had been "breadth and unity," this was something very different from the kind of semiclassicism with which the other group of competitors infused their designs.[89] While Burges provided an axial focus for his composition at the entrance and created long lines of unbroken roof ridges, the major component of his "breadth and unity" was the asymmetrical but balanced juxtaposition of large, uncomplicated masses. In this way he adapted his design to the artistic exigencies of the difficult site with greater success than any other architect. His mighty forms responded flexibly to the tight urban space that lay before them to the south, defined on the east by his new bridge across the Strand and on the west by St. Clement Danes. Significantly, Burges was alone in showing the church in his rendering of the Strand front. He did so because St. Clement provided the rationale for his dynamic façade, absolutely precluding an unobstructed view of the entire building as one approached from the southwest and Westminster, the direction from which it was presumed that most traffic would come to the law courts. Burges placed his great record tower to greet visitors who passed in front of the church, while the main entrance, with its two towers, was aligned with the roadway that passed around the chancel. Those who submitted more placid, symmetrical designs, which had to be seen in their totality in order to be appreciated, were careful to exclude the church from their drawings.

Burges lived up to his reputation as a leader of the Early French school. He admitted that he had been "driven by the exigencies of the case"—a large secular building in a dirty nineteenth-century city—"to the broad details of French work," and away from the multiplicity of finer ornament that was characteristic of English Gothic.[90] With its high-peaked roofs, enormous towers, and abundance of smooth masonry, his design owed much to the illustrations of medieval fortifications published by Eugène Emmanuel Viollet-le-Duc and to his restorations at Carcassonne and Pierrefonds. However, the specifically French appearance of Burges's building is even more convincingly demonstrated when it is compared with the Conciergerie façade of the Palais de Justice in Paris, whose reconstruction by Louis Duc was then nearing completion. Burges virtually quoted the compositional relationship between the tall corner tower and a pair of smaller, round towers at the center from that most relevant Parisian prototype (Fig. 27).

To all of this the *Ecclesiologist* responded enthusiastically. The editors had long ago abandoned the narrow preference for English Gothic they had espoused in the early and middle forties, and were now prepared to embrace this most advanced foreign experimentation. They wrote:

> It is quite refreshing to turn to the exquisite and pure art of Mr. Burges' charming drawings. We have no slovenly half-thought-out work here; no attempt at effect by quaint notching or irregular arrangement; none of the patchwork and piecing—too often ill matching—which we have felt bound to reprobate in other works. The architect, both in design and plan, has shown a thorough mastery over his subject. There is no design in the whole building so perfectly congruous in all its parts, that so surely proclaims that it is the work of a master mind, an original work of an accomplished artist, who had so thoroughly learned the style that he was working in as to make it truly express his own thoughts and intentions.[91]

27 *Palais de Justice, Paris. Conciergerie façade. Restored by Louis Duc, 1852–69. (Fine Arts Library, Harvard University.)*

The owner of the *Saturday Review* was the Ecclesiologically minded A. J. Beresford-Hope, a friend of Burges, and his journal responded similarly. Burges's work was called "a very original composition of great breadth and balance, of palatial dignity and scholastic repose, carried out with details as right in their proportions as they are rich and beautiful in their effect."[92] The *Building News*, then very much the journal of the Early French forces, concurred, reporting that his entry was "by far the most deserving of careful criticism."[93] Even the *Civil Engineer and Architect's Journal*, in whose generally unexciting pages young architects sometimes found the recognition that was denied elsewhere, noted Burges's success. "Of Mr. Burges' design, architecturally considered," the editors wrote, "it is not too much to say that it is certainly the most original and, in many respects, the most beautiful in the collection."[94] Among the dailies, the *Standard*, after an early enthusiasm for Scott, also joined the admirers of this powerful work, praising its "true artistic feeling and refined architecture, as pure as anything Greece produced, and as original as if it had actually been built in the middle ages."[95]

Nor was praise restricted to the beauty of Burges's external arrangement. Although admitting that ingenious planning had not been expected of an artist who was best known for his romantic vision, the *Building News* judged that he had been the most successful in solving the complex problems posed by the instructions.[96] And the most unexpected testimony to this success came from the *Law Times*, which overcame the prejudice most lawyers felt in favor of Waterhouse, on account of his success at Manchester, and praised Burges's "wonderfully simple" plan (Fig. 28). It went on to join the artistic press in agreeing, "In point of architecture it is the only one which would be creditable to our art knowledge."[97]

Indeed, despite his deserved reputation as an "art architect," planning was so important to Burges that, as he explained in his *Report*, he had devoted most of the available time to the problems of organization and had made no effort to prepare a large number of perspective drawings.[98] There are, in fact, only five perspectives of which some record survives, and most of these were made by Axel Herman Haig, an architectural draftsman and renderer.[99] Edward W. Godwin and Richard Phené Spiers are known to have assisted with the drawings as well.[100]

Burges's greatly admired plan was the most unusual as well as one of the most successful in the competition. It dramatically inverted the concentric circle paradigm adopted by most of the other architects, and its discussion here, in advance of any of the more standard type, can only be justified on the basis of the wide favor that it found.

Like the other competitors, Burges began by shaping an outer enceinte of offices to create the desired external aspect of the building, just as Barry had done at the Houses of Parliament. But he differed from his colleagues in the organization of the building within this shell. Rather than arrange the interior in circles around a central hall, or in any of the variations of this scheme that used "streets" on either side of a

28 Burges. Competition design. 1866–67. Plan at courtroom level. (Burges. Law Courts Commission: Report to the Courts of Justice Commission. *London: George Edward Eyre and William Spottiswoode, 1867.)*

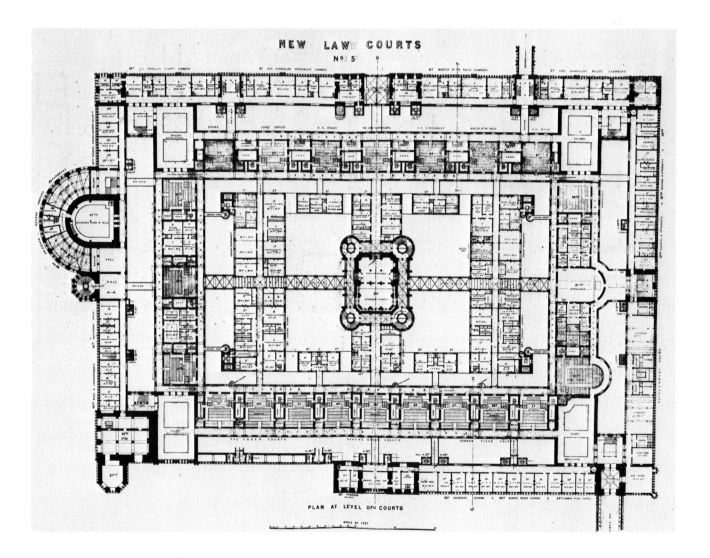

W Burges

central "avenue" or repeated the concentric arrangement in several smaller zones, Burges realized that all of these possible arrangements brazenly violated the most important condition of the instructions: that the general public should be excluded from all of the building save the galleries of the courts. He saw that a central hall or street would inevitably draw the public into the midst of the activities from which they were meant to be segregated.

To solve this dilemma, Burges retained only the skeleton of the concentric scheme while rearranging its components. At the center were placed judges' offices and their own private hall, not a "great hall"; the courtrooms lay in the intermediate circle; and an outer boundary was composed of offices. Circulation, rather than being drawn to the center, was held at the perimeter of the plan. Lawyers and clients would assemble in four halls at the corners of the building, not at the center, and pass through corridors to the courts (Fig. 29). The public at large would enter by means of a large number of stairs in the outer circle of offices that were connected directly and solely to the galleries of the courts by bridges that spanned the interior courtyards. In no way could the public penetrate further into the building. Thus Burges overcame the curious predicament fostered by the orthodox concentric circle plan, in which the public was tempted to pass into the center of the building, while the judges' chambers were pressed toward its outer shell. He alone instituted this significant rationalization, while the other contestants remained fixated by the concentric circle model evolved by Soane, Barry, Abraham, and Pennethorne, and codified by Thomas Webster. Burges's plan, as the *Ecclesiologist* noted admiringly, was "all his own."[101]

Burges did have critics, however, and they questioned the appropriateness of his romantic, castellated, and explicitly medieval architecture for modern courts of law. As the *Athenaeum* observed, "Delight in picturesque effects and minor beauties has mastered this architect's sense of fitness for the general character of the proposed structure." This was to be regretted, they continued, for his work might have rivaled the best of the designs "if he had avoided the whimsical in proposing a work so 'uncivil' in its character."[102] The *Spectator* also questioned the suitability of the military or "castellated character" of the Burges design, and similar doubts were expressed in the *Quarterly Review, Belgravia,* and the *Times.*[103] Theirs was a minority opinion for the moment, but late Victorian taste would agree with them.

Besides Burges, five other competitors submitted designs with irregular massing. The most highly esteemed of these and the second most popular of all the entries was that prepared by Alfred Waterhouse, who, like Burges, combined a picturesque elevation with ingenious, if somewhat unorthodox planning (Figs. 30–32). In particular, critics praised the plan in Waterhouse's design, and this was to be expected, for he had been invited to join the law courts competition on the strength of his new assize courts in Manchester. The successful planning of this building made him the favorite entrant among a large segment of the legal community, and he had the further advantage of a close association with the Royal Commission, serving as its clerk while the instructions were being drafted. With this combination of experience and inside knowledge, it was no wonder that Waterhouse produced a design which the *Times* predicted would win. Even the otherwise unappreciative *Civil Engineer and Architect's Journal* admitted to "the cleverness of some peculiar arrangements in the plan."[104]

29 Burges. Competition design. 1866–67. One of the barristers' halls, signed by Burges. (Victoria and Albert Museum. Crown copyright.)

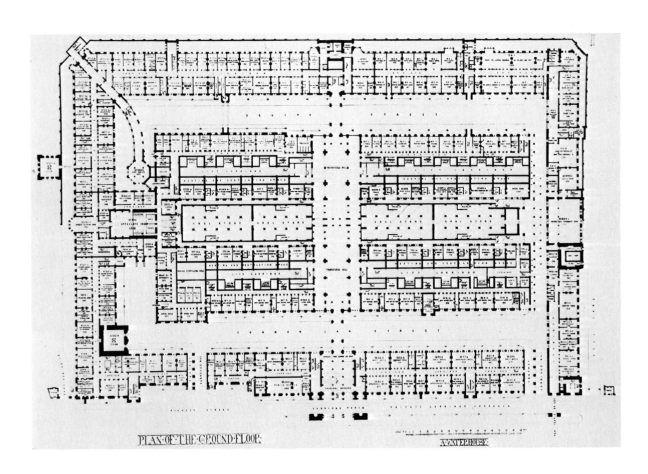

PLAN·OF·THE·GROUND·FLOOR:　　　　　　　　　　　　WATERHOUSE

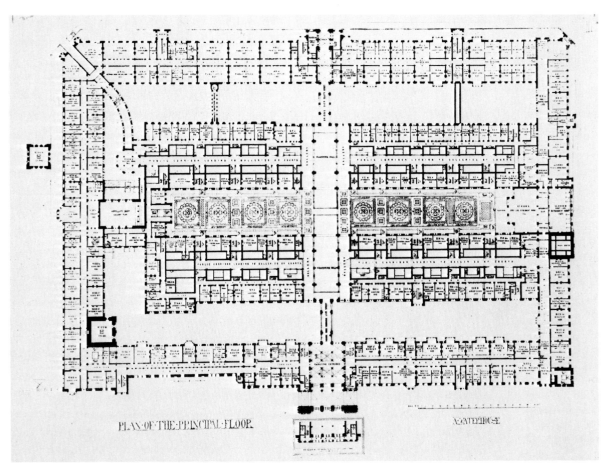

PLAN·OF·THE·PRINCIPAL·FLOOR　　　　　　　　　　　WATERHOUSE

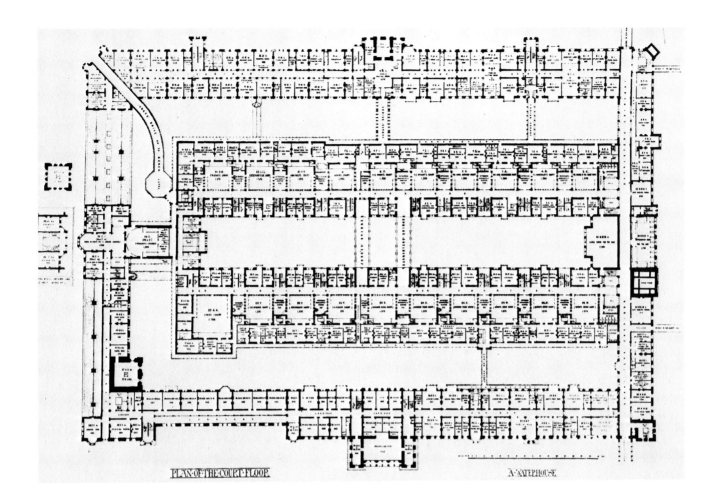

PLAN·OF·THE·COURT·FLOOR   A·WATERHOUSE

30 *Alfred Waterhouse. Competition design. 1866–67. Plan at Strand level. (Waterhouse. Courts of Justice Competition: General Description of Design. London: George Edward Eyre and William Spottiswoode, 1867. Courtesy of University of Kentucky Libraries, Lexington.)*

31 *Waterhouse. Competition design. 1866–67. Plan of principal floor. (Waterhouse. Courts of Justice Competition. Courtesy of University of Kentucky Libraries, Lexington.)*

32 *Waterhouse. Competition design. 1866–67. Plan at courtroom level. (Waterhouse. Courts of Justice Competition. Courtesy of University of Kentucky Libraries, Lexington.)*

What Waterhouse achieved was a coherent adaptation of the basic concentric circle formula that, like Burges's more radical solution, overcame the problem of public admission. In effect, he designed two central halls, whereas Burges had effectively omitted the central hall altogether. In Waterhouse's scheme, the public was admitted only to a lower, north–south hall (what he called the "Transverse Halls"), from which stairs and minor corridors beneath the courts led to the spectator galleries (Fig. 30). The larger, east–west hall crossed the Transverse Halls at a higher level in the center of the building, spanning them with a single narrow bridge (Fig. 31). This vast concourse (478 by 60 feet) was reserved for lawyers and the parties to cases, and the courts were arranged in a very simple pattern along either side of it, one story above the level of the hall floor (Fig. 32). With its iron-and-glass roof and façadelike interior elevations, the hall closely resembled contemporary Continental shopping galleries (Fig. 33). The courtrooms themselves were served by several systems of circulation, each reserved exclusively for a single type of visitor.

The exterior of Waterhouse's design was illustrated by numerous perspective renderings, all by his own hand and all of superlative quality. The *Building News* suggested that they merited hanging as watercolors in their own right, and questioned whether their beauty might not mislead some of the judges.[105] Indeed, with their blue-tinted water and sky, Waterhouse's perspectives apparently violated the injunction in the instructions that "sepia, indian ink, or pen and ink only is to be used."[106] But no official complaint was made against them.

The design illustrated by these drawings, like that of William Burges, emphasized elements of picturesque irregularity and a relationship to the tight urban setting. Like Burges's, the main façade stepped back to accommodate Pickett Street as it swept around St. Clement's, and Waterhouse portrayed the building in a fairly realistic, close perspective, although he chose not to show the church itself (Fig. 34). Waterhouse also composed a breathtakingly dramatic skyline with four major towers devoted to ventilation and record storage, the tallest of which was to reach 354 feet. This silhouette would have been seen to particularly good effect from the far side of the Thames, as suggested in what must have been the most beautiful drawing in the exhibition (Fig. 35). But while these qualities indicate that Waterhouse had been studying the strong picturesque of the Early French with interest, his design retained a thin and flinty angularity that set it apart. He had rejected the somewhat staid symmetry of the Manchester Assize Courts, but he was still marked as a Northerner (i.e., from the north of England) and an outsider. Rather naively, Waterhouse claimed that he had adopted early thirteenth-century Gothic for his entry, close to the favored period of Burges and his admirers, and that he had sought to "avoid any extreme delicacy in the detail of the exterior."[107] But while this was up-to-date rhetoric, the design, with its often busy surfaces and linearity, lagged behind.

34 *Waterhouse. Competition design. 1866–67. Perspective in the Strand,*
by Waterhouse. (BAL)

35 *Waterhouse. Competition design. 1866–67. Perspective across the Thames,*
by Waterhouse. (BAL)

Although some critics, like that of the *Spectator,* did admire the design's "genuine civilized and civic Gothic" (a slap at Burges's quasi-military taste), many others found its elevations rather weak.[108] The *Building News,* which had admired Burges's entry, deplored the absence of a "leading feature" and of "unity and fair proportion of mass," and called Waterhouse's claim to have adopted early thirteenth-century prototypes a "libel" against the best medieval architects.[109] But it was the *Athenaeum,* whose critic was also pleased with the work of Burges, that delivered the most scathing criticism. The lean detail of Waterhouse's law courts was "somewhat effeminate," and the clock tower was "a little thin." "What is wanting . . . is Gothic expressiveness, even rudeness," the *Athenaeum* suggested, but the design offered only "the best examples of drawing-room Gothic we have seen."[110] This was a fine summation of the Early French critical perspective.

The central hall, with its glass roof and bridges, was almost universally condemned (see Fig. 33). Even the *Engineer* and the *Civil Engineer and Architect's Journal* doubted the propriety for the law courts of a form so closely related to railway stations and exhibition halls.[111] Other critics argued that the hall was excessively large, that it would be difficult to heat and cool, and that the plan to light some of the rooms by means of windows looking into the hall was inadequate.[112] Thus, although Waterhouse obtained broad acclaim for what the *Building News* called his "dexterity of plan," and although his design was always considered a front-runner, the more sophisticated art critics were never satisfied with his elevations and details.[113] He did, however, have the satisfaction of realizing part of his design for both the central hall and the main façade in the Natural History Museum at South Kensington (1873–81).

The large number of reviewers who admired the work of William Burges were also generally impressed by the artistry of John Seddon (Fig. 36). His design was a second powerful example of Early French thinking, although, probably for political reasons, Seddon called it "pure English Gothic."[114] It alone was represented in the competition exhibition by a model, now known only through photographs, that admirably demonstrated its vigorous massing.[115] The *Athenaeum,* critical of the femininity of Waterhouse's elevations, was pleased by Seddon's "extreme simplicity and breadth," and reported: "This is an intensely honest and thorough Gothic design, rude, and even uncouth in some of its parts." It called the great record depository "the *beau-ideal* of a tower proper."[116] The *Building News,* a champion of Burges, praised the "simplicity and breadth of grouping" and the "general balance of parts."[117]

However, less adventuresome tastes, especially those who preferred more regularity in composition, were not inclined to admire Seddon. His Strand façade, with its very long rank of small gables, was called excessively domestic, although its centerpiece was related to the Continental town hall types that E. W. Godwin, Burges's collaborator and friend, had adopted for his town halls at Congleton and Northampton. For all its picturesque attributes, the very straight, symmetrical main front was unresponsive to the particulars of the crowded site when compared to Burges's work, and the rather poorly related tower seemed to be entirely out of scale with the rest of the building. These idiosyncrasies interested some critics, but worried others, including those who appreciated the milder elevations of Waterhouse. The *Times* deplored the attempt to impress "by mere size and mass," and the *Spectator*

36 John P. Seddon. Competition design. 1866–67. Perspective by E. S. Cole. (Photograph at BAL.)

called the record tower "uncouth and one-sided"—and, unlike the *Athenaeum*, the *Spectator* did not mean "uncouth" as a compliment.[118] The antihistoricist *Builder* was offended by Seddon's gleeful romanticism and commented archly, "We might fairly praise Mr. Seddon for the cleverness with which he has given an archaic aspect to his elevations."[119]

Even the admirers of Seddon were hard pressed to explain the two glaring weaknesses of his proposal: its prodigious estimated cost and its weak planning. Like all the competitors, convinced by the tone of the Royal Commission's instructions that extra funds would be available, Seddon calculated that his design would exceed the ceiling of £750,000. But Seddon's design was the costliest of all, estimated by its author at £2,046,644, compared to the next highest calculation, Burges's for £1,584,589, and the lowest, Deane's for £1,074,278. Such a sum was politically impossible.

Moreover, this most expensive plan was seriously defective (Figs. 37, 38). Superficially it resembled Waterhouse's scheme, with another gigantic central hall lined by courtrooms. But because Seddon, alone among the competitors, felt compelled to be thrifty in the use of land, the layout was a confusingly dense grid of inadequately lit repetitive units. Rather than generous internal "streets," Seddon provided only narrow areas for light and air. The *Solicitors' Journal* complained that he had shown "no pity" in arranging the building, placing the bar library four floors above the courtrooms, or six above the Strand.[120] The refreshment rooms, by contrast, were placed below the central hall, where they had to be lighted by great glass

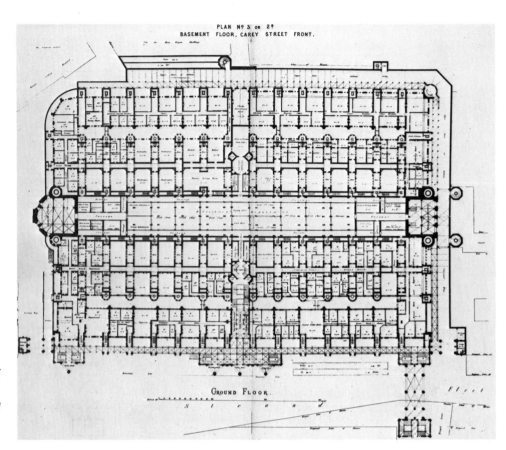

37 *Seddon. Competition design. 1866–67. Plan at Strand level. (Seddon. New Courts of Justice: Design Submitted by John P. Seddon. London: Day and Son, 1867. PRO Works 6/123.)*

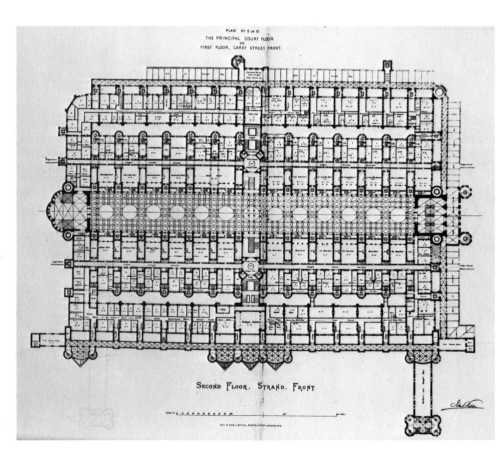

38 *Seddon. Competition design. 1866–67. Plan at courtroom level. (Seddon. New Courts of Justice. PRO Works 6/123.)*

39 *Seddon. Competition design. 1866–67. Interior of the great hall, by E. S. Cole. (Photograph in Seddon. New Law Courts: Description of Design. London: George Edward Eyre and William Spottiswoode, 1867. Courtesy of the Property Services Agency, Department of the Environment.)*

domes set in the floor of the hall. The realization that this unusual provision would be necessary seems to have struck the architect rather late, for they are not shown in his large perspective of the interior (Fig. 39).

However, the greatest failing of Seddon's plan was his admission of casual visitors to the central hall, where they could disrupt the conduct of official business. He rather lamely sought to justify this grave divergence from the instructions:

> The general public can enter the Great Hall by the four principal entrances in the centre of the four sides of the building, and by the recesses in front of each Court to the spaces allotted to the public under the gallery in the Court. . . . It appears to me that such provision as I have made for the public in the shape of the Central Hall is essential to maintain the dignity of a Palace of Justice, which should be impressive equally by its internal as by its external effect. I believe that no inconvenience need arise from its use, and that it is not necessary that the public entrances to each Court should be separate and direct from the street.[121]

It is unlikely that such an explanation satisfied those who had drafted the instructions, and Seddon's flagrant violation of what was probably their most absolute stricture seems like an act of defiance, like much else in his flamboyant design.

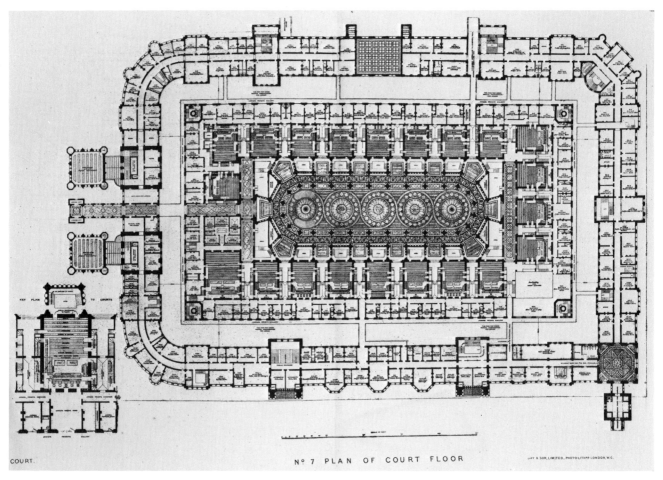

COURT.   Nº 7 PLAN OF COURT FLOOR   DAY & SON, LIMITED, PHOTO-LITHRS LONDON, W.C.

40 *Raphael Brandon. Competition design. 1866–67. Perspective. (Photograph at BAL.)*

41 *Brandon. Competition design. 1866–67. Plan at court-room level. (Brandon. New Courts of Justice: Design Submitted by Raphael Brandon. London: Day and Son, 1867. PRO Works 6/123.)*

42 *Brandon. Competition design. 1866–67. Interior of great hall. (Photograph at BAL.)*

In three further entries—those of Brandon, Deane, and Abraham—the pictur-esque elements predominated. Of substantially less interest, most reviewers dismissed them at the time of the competition. They do, however, provide further evidence of the popularity of irregular composition among architects of the day.

Raphael Brandon's design, with its traceried towers and 200-foot-high central hall, astonished the naive but found little informed approval (Figs. 40–42). The *Engineer*, before settling on the very safe conclusion that the choice lay among Waterhouse, Scott, and Lockwood, confessed that Brandon's law courts were "the most magnificent."[122] And the sarcastic critics of the *Quarterly Review*, on their way to concluding that they liked none of the designs at all, admitted that his had "more variety and independent thought than any other in the room." [123] But the general opinion of the design was very low. After examining the twin spires that flanked the western, state entrance, and the double apse-ended central hall, with its tripartite elevation, aisles, and flèche, critics were almost unanimous in concluding that the Brandon design was excessively ecclesiastical. While Burges's law courts were too

43 *Thomas N. Deane. Competition design. 1866–67. Perspective.* (Building News, 28 June 1867.)

44 *Deane. Competition design. 1866–67. Plan at Strand level.* (*Deane.* New Courts of Justice: Design Submitted by Mr. T. Newenham Deane. *London: Day and Son, 1867.*)

45 *Deane. Competition design. 1866–67. Plan at courtroom level.* (*Deane.* New Courts of Justice.*)

much like a fortress, this design resembled Westminster Abbey too much within and the Ste. Chapelle without. "How Mr. Brandon can have so much mistaken the spirit of the building on which he was engaged as to offer such a hall is past comprehension," puzzled the *Saturday Review*.[124] The *Chronicle* called his entry "one of the greatest mistakes ever committed by a really clever architect."[125]

What Brandon had intended is only dimly hinted at by his avowal that he had "allow[ed] no mere reproduction to creep in, but endeavour[ed] to deal with the whole as I believe the old architects would have done if it had been built in their day."[126] While this sounded like the philosophy espoused by most of the leading High Victorian medievalists, in Brandon's case it seems to have had a different meaning. The "mere reproduction" that was to be avoided concerned only the copying of entire monuments, and in place of this Brandon permitted himself a rather old-fashioned, wide-ranging eclecticism. As Sir John Summerson has pointed out, Brandon's design, with its borrowings from identifiable ancient sources, was "the kind of 'copyist' romancing that the Gothic Revival is often supposed to be but so rarely is."[127] In plan, he adopted the usual concentric scheme, complicated only by the addition of a major western entrance, which gave his design two major façades. The ceremonial emphasis of the longitudinal entrance was perhaps a reflection of Brandon's Parisian training.

The plan proposed by Thomas N. Deane was far more innovative, but it won for him very few admirers (Figs. 43–45). He evidently took as his model Pennethorne's design of 1865, in which the building was divided into two blocks. In fact Deane cut his building into four separate divisions, each with its own small version of the concentric plan. The common law courts were placed in a large southern block, with their own central hall and a separate building to the east for offices. Equity, divorce, and probate shared a long block across the back of the site, and the appellate and Admiralty courts were housed in two small buildings to the southwest.

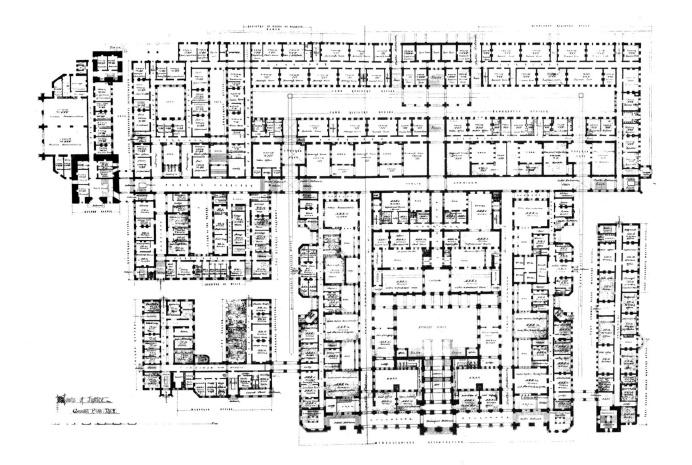

Courts of Justice
Ground Plan No. 1

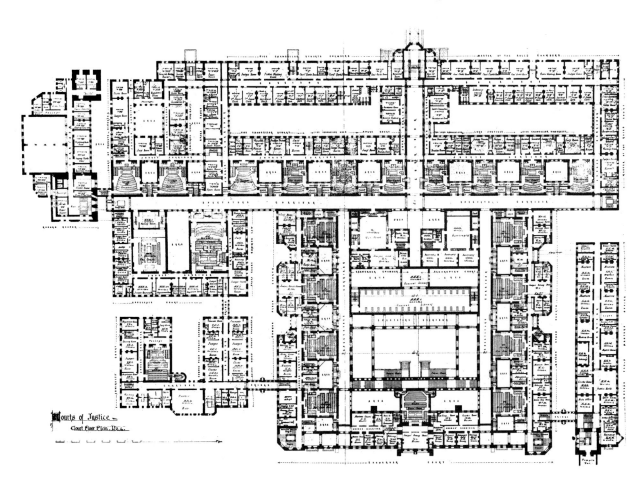

Courts of Justice
Court Floor Plan No. 2

The practical effect of this subdivision would hardly be the promotion of fusion, and Deane's unfamiliarity with the wishes of the legal profession was also reflected in his imperfect exclusion of the public from the common law central hall, the largest space in his building. He covered this hall with a peculiar hammerbeam roof, constructed of masonry.

Although the fragmentation of the building allowed Deane to adapt it well to the irregular site, adjusting its small-scale components to the manner in which they might actually be seen, he did not exploit the opportunity to make a dynamically composed composition. Instead, Deane proposed a rather staid, slack treatment which permitted him to submit the lowest of all the construction estimates. Stylistically, his solution returned to the polychromatic Italian Gothic of his late partner's design for the government offices competition, now hopelessly outdated. The massing of the largest, common law block was a sort of medieval translation of the mansarded designs that had won that contest but were also anachronistic. A still earlier prototype, Charles Barry's Big Ben, was reflected in the design for the clock tower.

Even the journals that were most enthusiastic about picturesque composition found little to like in Deane's law courts, lacking, as they did, all drama and vigor. The *Saturday Review* had been charmed by Burges, but declared that Deane's disjointed façade "more resembles a mediaeval town than a public building."[128] And the *Building News,* another Burges admirer, declared that the design was "straggling and irregular."[129] Only the mercurial *Belgravia,* which ultimately favored a quasi-classical entry, had praise for the flimsy ensemble, noting especially "the marvelous picturesqueness which gives the *timbre* to this beautiful composition," a compliment that must have baffled most observers.[130]

By contrast, poor Henry R. Abraham, the eldest competitor and the only one to have prepared a preliminary design for the entire program, was himself clearly baffled by the competition (Fig. 46). Most journals failed to discuss his design at all, or assigned it only a short epitaph. *Belgravia* concluded: "We can only regard Mr. Abraham's efforts as evidence of a race in which he was hopelessly outweighted. This is the kindest remark that can be made."[131]

Ironically, for his competition plan, Abraham abandoned the regular concentric system that he had adopted in 1860–61 and that many of the competitors had emulated. He explained in his odd, third-person descriptive text, that "a new and original design was due from Mr. Abraham under his present engagement."[132] Like Deane's design, Abraham's system was perhaps inspired by the Pennethorne pilot project, for it consisted of four separate blocks of courtrooms and a central domed structure. No image of the elevation has been preserved, but the dome, in which records were to be stored, was to reach a height of 310 feet, and a clock tower was placed at the southeast corner of the complex. The style was Gothic, but it was what the *Civil Engineer and Architect's Journal* called "the Gothic of Wyattville at Windsor Castle," lacking, as the *Saturday Review* agreed, "every feature or detail which makes a Gothic building of 1867 superior to one of Hopper or Wilkins."[133] Some of this criticism must have been journalistic hyperbole, for Abraham's Middle Temple Library was a building of substantial medieval conviction (see Fig. 23).

In contrast to all of these designs—in which a degree of picturesque imbalance was cultivated—stood the group of competition entries that embraced formal symmetry. These represented, in effect, the other half of the hoped-for High Victorian solution to the problem of urban secular architecture. Such work hinted strongly in the direction of classical models, and although this was far less popular among the critics of 1867, it represented a trend that would dominate architecture before the end of the century.

Among the symmetrical designs, the public most admired that of Henry Lockwood, and his alcove, filled with many large perspectives, was always crowded (Figs. 47–49).[134] His extremely simple and logical plan, perhaps the most straightforward embodiment of the concentric formula, contributed to the success of his work, and, like Waterhouse's very clear plan, it paid tribute to Northern architectural training, or at least to Northern common sense. His only innovation was the division of the central hall into thirds in order to serve the separate divisions of the legal system. Around the halls the courtrooms were arrayed in a very regular pattern, save for the bankruptcy courts and a large spare court which it was found convenient to place in

46 Henry R. Abraham. Competition design. 1866–67. Plan at courtroom level. (Abraham. New Courts of Justice: Design Submitted by Henry Robert Abraham. London: Day and Son, 1867. PRO Works 6/123.)

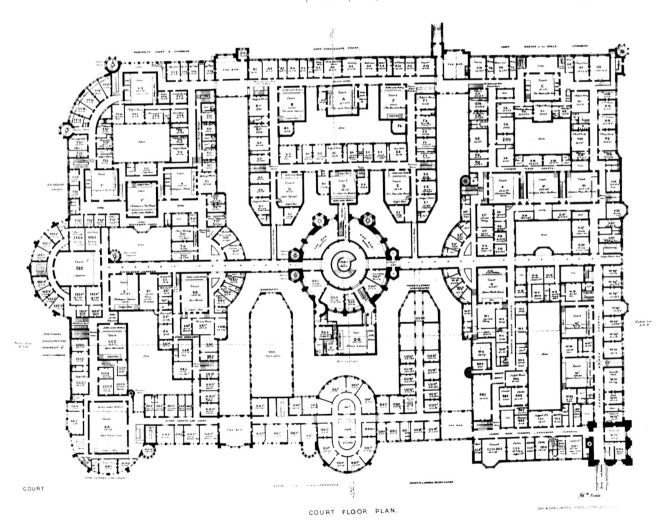

· NEW·LAW·COURTS ·

COURT FLOOR PLAN.

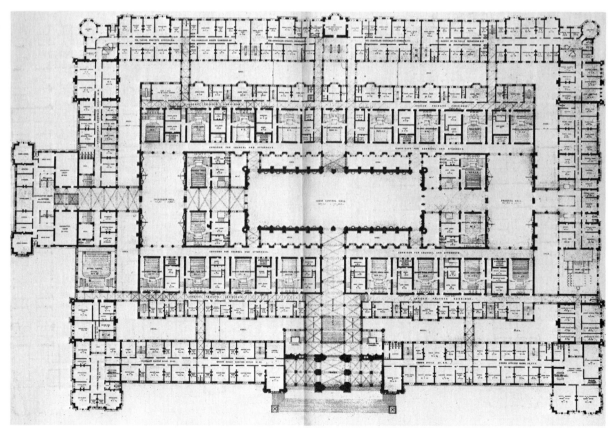

47 *Henry F. Lockwood. Competition design. 1866–67. Perspective. (Photograph in* Lockwood. Design for the Concentration of the Law Courts. *n.p. [1867].)*

48 *Lockwood. Competition design. 1866–67. Plan at courtroom level. (Lockwood.* Design.*)*

49 *Lockwood. Competition design. 1866–67. Interior of great hall. (Lockwood.* Design.*)*

the western wing. The courts were served by the usual battery of corridors, each restricted to a different type of visitor, with the public corridor in this case at ground level, linked by a separate stairway to the gallery of each court. Evidently impressed by the care which Lockwood devoted to such provisions, the *Engineer* picked his design as one of those most likely to be selected.[135]

The rather dry symmetry of Lockwood's elevations, the version of Big Ben that he called the "Albert Tower," and, inside, his re-creation of Westminster Hall, also found some friends. The source of his exterior conceit was Scott's entry in the Hamburg Rathaus competition of 1854. But while the Scott design was a brazen, High Victorian rejection of picturesque triviality, Lockwood reduced this to a mechanical formula. His perfectly balanced façade was wholly unresponsive to its position on the Strand, and it could only be appreciated from an entirely artificial point of view. Nevertheless, insofar as his solution provided regularity and continuous horizontals, critics with classical leanings warmly applauded it. The *Builder*, whose antihistoricist position sheltered a kind of closet classicism, had been noncommittally curt about Burges, but was almost effusive about the "unity and harmony" of Lockwood's "decidedly municipal" composition.[136]

The *Builder* did not stand with a large company of fellow admirers, however, for monotonous regularity bored that majority of the reviewers who had been charmed by Burges's design. The *Civil Engineer and Architect's Journal,* after praising Burges, complained that Lockwood's law courts were not really Gothic, as that style was now understood: "The prevailing features and character throughout are of an age gone by; the age which glorified Eaton Hall and Hopper's designs for the Houses of Parliament, and which attended more value to showy florid ornament than genuine Gothic leading forms. . . . And we question, moreover, whether Mr. Lockwood would not have felt more at home giving a Classic rather than a Gothic version to his building."[137] The *Saturday Review* agreed: "The true Gothic spirit is the one thing wanting; the composition is stilted, and the details bookwork."[138]

Most critics were even less sympathetic toward Henry B. Garling's design, whose underlying classicism was virtually undisguised (Figs. 50–53). Garling alone dared to submit a Renaissance alternate elevation for his entry, and his true preference was not difficult to discern in even his Gothic version. Beneath the buttresses and tracery, the mansards and pavilions of the Second Empire design with which he won the War Office competition were easily recognized (see Fig. 22). As the *Building News* acutely observed, Garling seemed to believe that "the fine art we call architecture is only a skin deep affair."[139] Like Lockwood, he had to portray his symmetrical design as if the Strand were a vast, unobstructed parade ground.

Even those critics naturally disposed to prefer the more regular designs were unexcited by Garling's work. The François Ier classicism of his alternate design was just as old-fashioned as his Gothic, and only an unimpressive group of reviewers came to his defense. The unpredictable *Belgravia* actually preferred his entry, praising it for "a repose which distinguishes it from all the others" and for its lack of "fussy pinnacles." "It is picturesque," the editors concluded obscurely, "without a trace of whimsicality, and original without being extravagant."[140] Similarly, the often anti-Gothic *Illustrated London News* admired Garling's unbroken skyline, which "satisfies the eye at first glance," and the Continental press also gave their expected approval to his lonely advocacy of classicism.[141]

50 Henry B. Garling. Competition design. 1866–67. Perspective. (Photograph in Garling. New Courts of Justice: Design Submitted by Mr. Henry B. Garling. Augmented edition. London: Day and Son, 1867. BAL.)

51 Garling. Competition design. 1866–67. Interior of the "Central Corridor." (Photograph in Garling. New Courts of Justice. Augmented edition. BAL.)

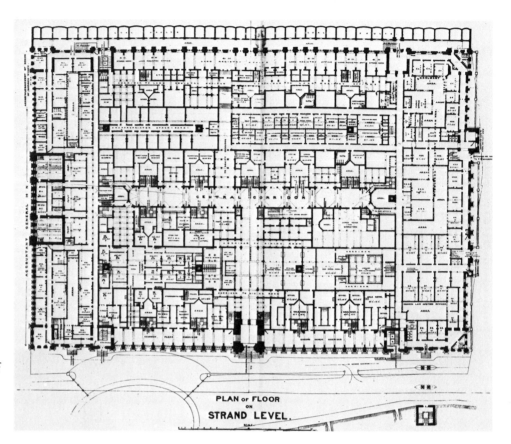

52 *Garling. Competition design. 1866–67. Plan at Strand level. (Garling.* New Courts of Justice: Design Submitted by Mr. Henry B. Garling. *London: Day and Son, 1867. PRO Works 6/123.)*

PLAN of FLOOR
ON
STRAND LEVEL.

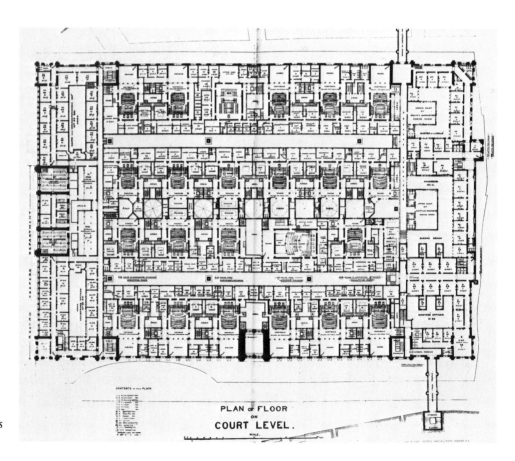

53 *Garling. Competition design. 1866–67. Plan at court-room level. (Garling.* New Courts of Justice. *PRO Works 6/123.)*

PLAN of FLOOR
ON
COURT LEVEL.

Garling's plan also reflected his independence, for he confronted the dilemma of the central hall with nearly the Draconian ruthlessness of Burges, although with less success. He began by demonstrating, in the printed explanation of his design, that the site was too small to accommodate the optimum realization of the concentric paradigm: a circular building with a round central hall and twenty-three radiating courtrooms.[142] This utopian arrangement was surely inspired by Abraham's earlier experiment with a Colosseum-shaped building. Garling then explored the general weaknesses of the concentric plan and arrived at the same conclusion as Burges, that "a central hall, in fact, would be scarcely used except by loungers and that class whose exclusion from the building is especially aimed at in the instructions."[143] Like Burges, Garling accordingly did away with—or claimed to do away with—the hall altogether, replacing it with three great east-west corridors that would be less attractive to idlers. One of these corridors ran across the Strand front at street level, the second ran behind the north façade at the higher street level there, and the third, "Central Corridor," cut through the center of the building (see Fig. 51). The courtrooms were arranged in four rows between these hallways. But for all its logic, Garling's plan was even more dense than that of Seddon. Moreover, the generously proportioned central corridor, which had to be lit by lanterns pushed up through the upper floors of the building, was not very different from the great central halls of most of the other architects.

Another inherently classical design, and a better one, was prepared by Edward M. Barry (Fig. 54). At heart a classicist like Garling, Barry offered an even more frankly un-Gothic proposal for the law courts, one that was unnervingly similar to the overtly classical design that he submitted in the National Gallery competition (Fig. 55). In the latter, the ideas of an architect who considered the Renaissance "a protest against the austerity and dogmatic intolerance of Mediaevalism" appeared in their natural garb, and in this pure form they had considerable merit.[144] Even the unfriendly *Building News*, reviewing the National Gallery designs, reported, "Mr. Barry's perspective is unquestionably *the* drawing of the whole exhibition."[145] Few were surprised when his entry, with its unsubtle panache, was judged the best in the relatively weak field of that competition.

However, Barry's ideas had far less merit for the law courts, where they were thinly resheathed with what the *Building News* called "that kind of Gothic in which Batty Langley and Horace Walpole delighted."[146] The *Civil Engineer and Architect's Journal* accurately observed, "The composition is essentially classic in its masses, but overlaid with Gothic detail, not always of the purest kind."[147] The *Times* noted more succinctly of Barry: "It seems as if he could not get St. Paul's Cathedral out of his head."[148] Other elements of his pastiche included his father's clock tower at Westminster (the third recollection of this already famous landmark among the designs) and his own fussy, high-roofed façades for the railway hotels at Cannon Street and Charing Cross, which had much in common with the central feature of his law courts elevation. Barry's compilation of these largely classical motifs under the rubric of Gothic was architectural transvestitism rather than the stylistic fusion of which the High Victorian generation had dreamed.

Like the other quasi-classical designs, Barry's had to be viewed as though the Strand were a broad and uncluttered thoroughfare. His perspective showed the site fronting on an open area the size of Trafalgar Square.

54 Edward M. Barry. Competition design. 1866–67. Perspective. (Builder, 18 March 1867.)

55 Barry. National Gallery competition, London. 1866. (Builder, 25 May 1867.)

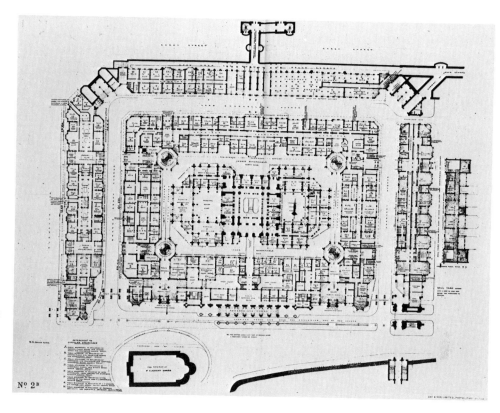

56 Barry. Competition design.
1866–67. Plan at Strand level.
(Barry. New Courts of Justice:
Design Submitted by Mr.
Edward Middleton Barry,
A.R.A. London: Day and
Son, 1867. PRO Works
6/123.)

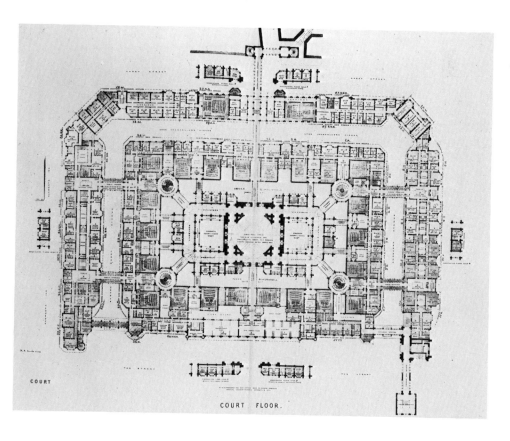

57 Barry. Competition design.
1866–67. Plan at courtroom
level. (Barry. New Courts of
Justice. PRO Works 6/123.)

58 George Gilbert Scott.
Competition design. 1866–67.
Perspective by Thomas Allom.
(Royal Courts of Justice. Photograph in Scott. Design for
the New Law Courts. [Lon-
don: 1867].)

However, for those weary of the storm and stress of High Victorian medievalism, Barry's design offered an attractive alternative. Moreover, its more accessible
style was complemented by what many judged to be an excellent plan (Figs. 56, 57).
The *Builder*, with its utilitarian, antihistoricist, and specifically anti-Gothic bias, led
those who admired his work. Although their views were not at first explicit, in an
early, relatively nonjudgmental review the journal praised Barry's solution for the
public circulation problem. His planning was declared to be his "strong point," with
the observation, later proven correct, that this strength would "count for much
when the weighing of merits comes."[149] When the Barry entry later received the
favorable consideration of the judges, the *Builder* was pleased to report that this
"confirms the good opinion that we arrived at."[150]

The plan that earned this admiration was another modification of the concentric format, adapted to reduce the temptation for loitering in the central hall. Barry
accomplished this by shrinking the hall to a small chamber beneath the dome and
by devoting most of the contiguous space to the probate department. This inner
block was encircled by a belt of corridors that serviced the courtrooms, most of
which were distributed around the middle ring of the building's concentric configu-
ration. The courts were provided with a clear arrangement of separate circulation
systems, and the troublesome spectators were restricted to four double-helix stairways
in the corners of the building. The outermost circle of building was devoted to
offices, as was usual in the concentric plans, but it was cut away on the south side
to present the main block of the building to the Strand.

George Gilbert Scott's lavishly illustrated design was superficially similar to
Barry's entry (Figs. 58, 59). But in Scott's work something of the High Victorian
stylistic equilibrium survived, with general symmetry balanced by the picturesque
accent of the western record towers, and classical repose set off against medieval
vigor. Thus Scott's dome was not simply a thinly disguised classical borrowing, such
as Barry's theft from St. Paul's. With its pointed profile and Byzantine encrustation
of mosaics—complete with an image of the Pantocrator—it aspired to being medieval while contributing classical order and focus to the composition (Fig. 60). Such
a dome, associating features of classical and medieval architecture, was one of the
great symbols of High Victorianism, and Scott had spoken and written about it
eloquently.[151]

59 Scott. Competition design.
1866–67. Bird's-eye view.
(Scott. Design.)

60 Scott. Competition design.
1866–67. Interior of domed
central hall, by Thomas Allom.
(Scott. Design.)

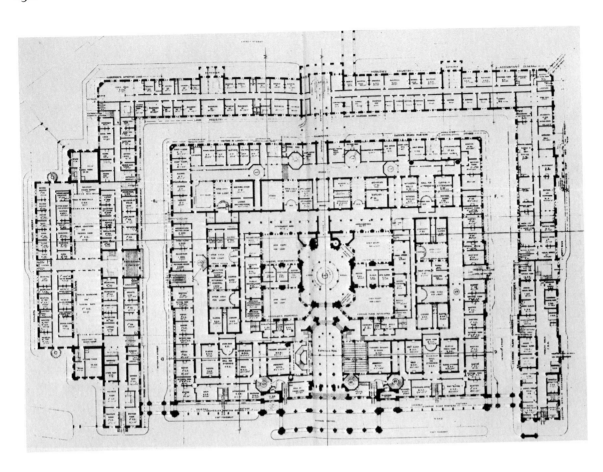

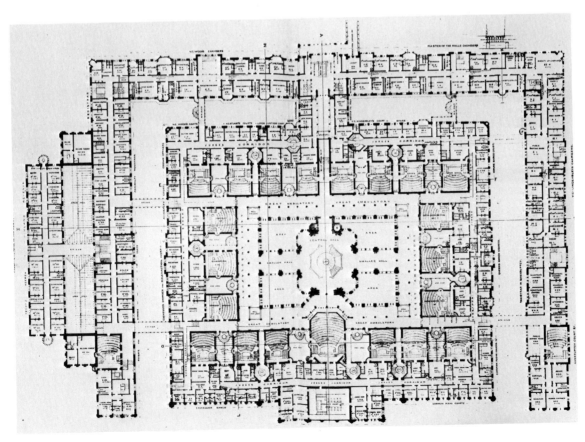

But High Victorian intentions were little appreciated in the polarized setting of the law courts competition. Despite general respect for Scott's professional standing, his effort at stylistic mediation was caught in the crossfire between the opposing camps. The dominant Early French enthusiasts were appalled by the fundamental monotony of his design, which paid little heed to the confined site. The *Athenaeum* decried the façade in which "bay after bay repeats itself . . . to the destruction of our sense of richness and artistic freedom."[152] The *Civil Engineer and Architect's Journal* regretfully concluded that Scott's entry had "more of staid orthodox correctness than of advanced vigour," and the *Building News* found only "nervousness and restless anxiety" and, ultimately, "baldness."[153] But on the other hand, those with more overtly classical tastes preferred the more openly classical designs, like those of Garling and Barry, and they, too, had little praise for Scott. *Belgravia*, however, did have a kind word for his "noble proportions."[154]

That Scott was at least partly aware of the drift of the majority opinion is clear from his design the preceding year for the Midland Hotel at St. Pancras Station. The bold asymmetry of that project was only slightly justified by the small irregularities of the site. But for the law courts competition Scott clearly felt constrained to attempt again what he had failed to achieve in the Foreign Office fiasco: the erection of a public building whose classically tempered Gothic would embody the theoretical position of the High Victorian generation.

To be sure, disapproval of Scott's entry was not all-encompassing. Drawing on years of professional experience, he had developed a plan that was generally well-regarded, based on the usual concentric model (Figs. 61, 62). Although he cited Thomas Webster in his descriptive text, Scott amended the Webster pattern in ways similar to Barry. Most importantly, he reduced the central hall to a kind of domed vestibule, set in the middle of a large interior courtyard and connected by covered passages to an encircling two-story "ambulatory" which connected the courtrooms. This smaller hall was a more realistic accommodation for the limited number of people who might properly be admitted. Those with legal business would be served by the upper passageway of the ambulatory, while spectators might reach the courts from its lower passage, which provided no access to the rest of the building. Scott also proposed an alternate version, however, in which the entire central courtyard was converted into a much larger hall (Fig. 63), covered by a glass roof whose pointed silhouette was derived from Barlow's great train shed at St. Pancras, where the shape had supposedly been generated by structural requirements rather than by historicism. Scott, who had probably thought more about the demands of public architecture than any other competitor, with the possible exception of Waterhouse, provided an unusually large entrance hall to the south (see Fig. 61), which possessed an almost Baroque spatial relationship with the central, domed space.

Like Barry, Scott departed from the Webster formula by removing the southern portion of the outer circle and moving the main block of the building out to the Strand façade. Unfortunately this placed the appeals court, located over the main entrance, in close contact with the noisy roadway (see Fig. 62). However, the other courtrooms were conveniently placed within the main block or adjacent to their departments, and they were provided with the usual multiple circulation systems.

Proud as he was of his efficient planning, Scott was unable to refrain from confessing, "I could not have kept myself up to this pitch of virtue had I not the

61 Scott. Competition design. 1866–67. Plan at Strand level. (Scott. Design.)

62 Scott. Competition design. 1866–67. Plan at courtroom level. (Scott. Design.)

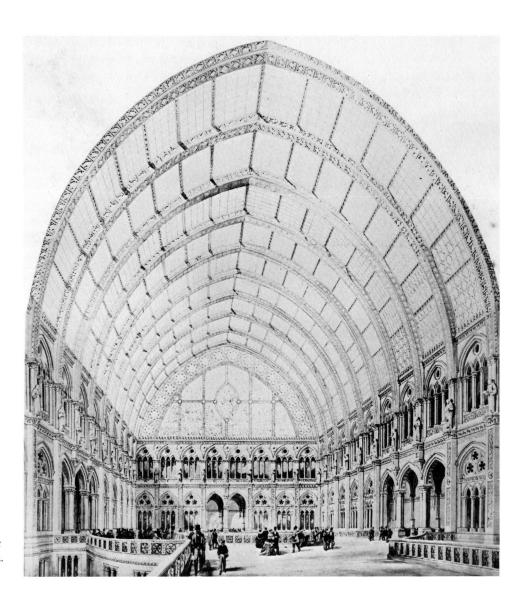

63 *Scott. Competition design. 1866–67. Interior of alternate central hall, by Thomas Allom. (Scott. Design.)*

prospect before me of at length clothing my work in a sightly garb, and rewarding myself at last by the application of art to that which had hitherto been merely contrivance."[155] Perhaps this denial of the organic wholeness of plan and elevation prevented Scott's law courts from winning any strong proponents. A professional architectural renderer, Thomas Allom (1804–72), was responsible for the vast number of beautiful perspectives that illustrated the entry, and public knowledge of this further damaged Scott's reputation. The *Athenaeum* suggested caustically that Allom might have succeeded as well on his own.[156]

Street's Design

IN MANY respects the design submitted by George Edmund Street was the ideological ally of Scott's, but it possessed far greater unity and power. Like Scott's, his law courts were a final expression of faith in the possibility of High Victorian stylistic mediation (Fig. 64). The long regular façades, with their central and terminal climaxes and unbroken rooflines, bespoke the "horizontality" and "repose" that Street had long championed for urban secular architecture. Against this were contrasted the bold verticals of asymmetrically placed towers. He himself explained his effort as a compromise:

> I have taken occasion, so far as was reasonable, to make all my façades tolerably regular in arrangement. So I have made distinct centres to the north and south fronts, and have also made the other main fronts equally uniform in their general character. With all this uniformity there are, however, very often, of necessity, features where uniformity was unnecessary, and irregularity a virtue, and I have gladly availed myself of them in all cases. So that I hope my design has sufficient picturesqueness not to be tamely uniform, and yet enough uniformity to prevent the building looking trivial or frittered away.[157]

64 George Edmund Street. Competition design. 1866–67. Bird's-eye view by Street. (Architectural Association. NMR photograph.)

The uniformity which was part of this compromise marked a substantial departure from Street's previous practice. Although his rhetoric had always supported the incorporation of classicizing properties in contemporary architecture, he had heretofore designed little that conformed with this theoretical position. He had excused

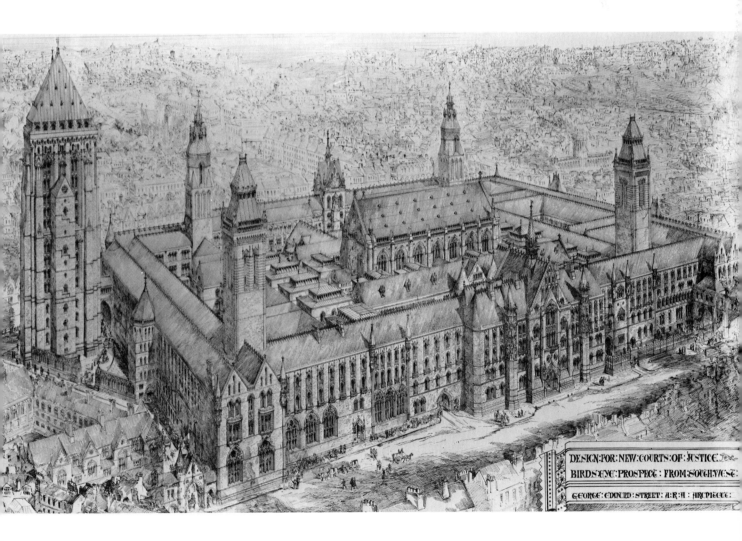

DESIGN·FOR·NEW·COURTS·OF·JUSTICE
BIRDS·EYE·PROSPECT·FROM·SOUTH·WEST
GEORGE·EDMUND·STREET·A·R·A·ARCHITECT

140

65 *Street. Competition design.
1866–67. Perspective of eastern part of Strand façade and
Strand bridge, by Street. (Photograph in GES.* Explanation
and Illustrations of His Design for the Proposed New
Courts of Justice. *London:
J. E. Taylor and Company,
1867.)*

66 *Street. Competition design.
1866–67. Perspective of record
tower, by Street. (Photograph
in GES.* Explanation and
Illustrations.)

67 *Street. Competition design.
1866–67. Perspective of alternate record tower, by Street.
(Photograph in GES.* Explanation and Illustrations.)*

View of RECORD TOWER from Clement's Inn

View of Alternative design for RECORD TOWER from Clement's Inn

the irregularity of his entry in the government offices competition on the basis of the irregularity of the site and the proximity of St. James's Park, while the picturesque properties of his other large planning exercise, the convent at East Grinstead, could be justified on the grounds of its rural setting (see Figs. 5, 8).[158] In the late fifties and sixties, Street, nearly as much as Burges, was identified with the powerful picturesque of the Early French, but now, with the law courts, he had at last resolved to put theory to practice.

Nevertheless, to counterbalance the apparent symmetry and insistent horizontals of the main body of the building, Street provided a number of picturesque accents. The most dramatic of these was the soul-stirring record tower, which he called his "one grand feature."[159] The four ventilation stacks were also placed without exact symmetry, and the fenestration patterns on each side of the main entrance were significantly different. Varied groupings of small pinnacles punctuated the roofline. Moreover, the proposed bridge across the Strand on the site of Temple Bar blocked from view the pair of eastern gables, obscuring the symmetry of the main façade (Fig. 65).

These picturesque elements were demanded by the nature of the Carey Street site. Although Street submitted a bird's-eye view of the entire building which did not show the church of St. Clement Danes, he also prepared a number of smaller, close-up perspectives which demonstrated that he understood that passersby would see only fragments of his façades. This realistic outlook shaped Street's work.

Street's chosen architectural vocabulary, employing a variety of picturesque forms, complemented this dynamic composition. Much of his vocabulary derived from his earlier experiments with the forceful massing of the Early French, as seen in his churches at Howsham (1859–60) and Denstone (1860–62), and in the executed version of the Crimean War Memorial Church (1863–68) (see Fig. 7). His enthusiasm for these strongly picturesque forms had been responsible for delaying until now the realization of the more even and regular composition that he advocated in theory, and this enthusiasm continued in the law courts' vigorous massing, reticent surfaces, steep-pitched roof, and in the asymmetrical placement of the record tower—especially in its more economical alternate version (Figs. 66, 67). The same feeling prevailed in the numerous round, conically roofed stair towers, in the chamfered corners of the central Strand pavilion, and in the general wide spacing of windows.

The unbalancing effects of the Early French were partially offset by a strong recollection of Italian Gothic in other parts of the design, particularly in the two, campanile-like ventilation towers at the southeast and southwest. With their strong cornices and horizontal striping, they harkened back to the towers Street had designed in the fifties for the government offices (1856) and St. Dionis Backchurch (1857), when his interest in Italy had been at its peak. As recently as 1864, in his design for All Saints, Clifton, he had adopted a partially Italian vocabulary for an urban setting. It may have been this consideration which brought Italian models into use once more at the law courts, for the urban applications of Italian Gothic, with its strong classical survivals, had first attracted him to its study. But although the Italian towers of the law courts contributed an element of repose to the design, they were grouped in a picturesque pattern, and their overall effect remained rather informal.

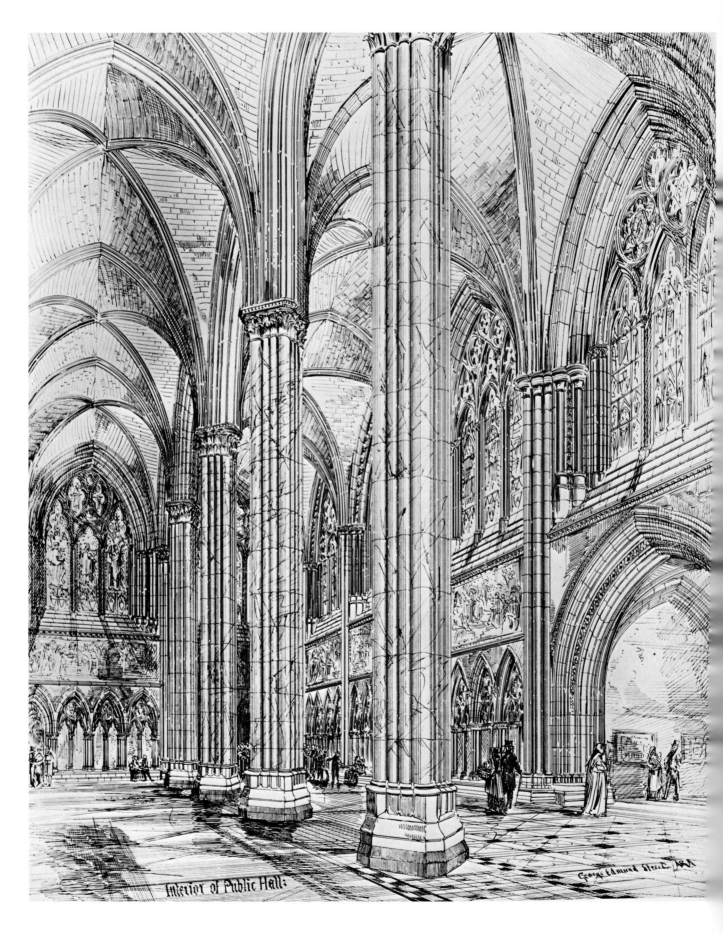

Interior of Public Hall

George Edmund Street

The final ingredient in Street's picturesque stylistic mix was English Decorated Gothic. Of course, English precedents remained only one part of his encyclopedia of sources, but their presence was important, signaling his desire to temper the unbridled power of the Early French. In his competition design, Street gave up the plate tracery and softened the almost brutal plainness of what had long been his preferred style, introducing more Decorated tracery and richer moldings than in any project since his sketch for the Oxford Museum in 1853 (see Fig. 3). He rejected characteristically squat Early French columns in favor of the tall, multiple shafts with which he supported the vaults of his central hall, a chamber whose refectory-like plan was intended to create a secular appearance without copying the hammer-beam roof of Westminster Hall (Fig. 68).[160]

The return to later and English precedents was part of a general tendency among architects of the time. In 1864, G. G. Scott observed that this shift in taste was taking place "at the present moment," and recent scholarship has proposed that the revision by G. F. Bodley of his design for the church of All Saints, Cambridge, between 1861 and 1863, was the first important evidence of the new nationalism.[161] Street's interest in later English architecture was rekindled at least as rapidly, as demonstrated by his All Saints church of 1862–63 at Brightwalton, Berkshire.[162] But he only faced nationalism as a theoretical issue in two essays written in the spring of 1866, the year in which he worked on his designs for the National Gallery and the law courts. The first, "The Study of Foreign Gothic Architecture," was published in an anthology of essays dated April 1, while the second, "Architecture in the Thirteenth Century," was first given as a series of lectures in Dublin in April and May.[163] In both Street discussed the fundamental differences between French and English medieval architecture, but while the earlier essay was a full-blooded endorsement of foreign studies, of the type to be expected from the author who had added a recent book on the Gothic architecture of Spain to previous writings on Germany, Italy, and France, the second was far more circumspect in its recommendations, and an undercurrent of antiforeign sentiment could be detected.

Both essays offered a novel explanation for the differences between English and French Gothic, based on an extrapolation of the observed differences in the capital types of the two national styles. The French had shown a historic preference for square capitals, while the English preferred round ones, and from this Street argued that there evolved correspondingly simple and severe molding profiles in France and softer, less pronounced forms in England. Throughout entire buildings he could trace the effects of this basic difference: "And just as the French system of moulding led naturally to an equally bold system of design in window tracery and other details generally, so in England the delicacy of eye and feeling which was accidentally fostered by the round abacus and its accompanying mouldings, produced, equally naturally, a more delicate design in every other part of the fabric."[164]

In the earlier essay, Street, still clearly a full proponent of the Early French picturesque, proceeded from this analysis to lament the "lack of vigour and majesty about English work" and to exhort, "it is certainly our duty, to do our best to develope by degrees beyond the point to which our forefathers reached, and to some extent by means of foreign examples."[165] But in the later lectures in Dublin, although Street still recommended a broad understanding of foreign architecture, his assessment of the relative merits of English and French prototypes had begun to change.

68 Street. Competition design. 1866–67. Interior of the "Public Hall," by Street. (Photograph in GES. Explanation and Illustrations.)

English architects, he told his audience, were "the more truly poetical in their work, [and] more essentially possessed of the feelings of artists."[166] He had begun to esteem poetry as well as vigor, and perhaps he recognized, too, that his enthusiasm for the Early French had kept his work more powerfully picturesque than was desirable.

Street's taste for English Gothic subsequently deepened and grew. When he replaced the ailing Gilbert Scott in presenting two of the Royal Academy architecture lectures in 1871, his position had become more plain. He advised his listeners,

> I feel myself unable too strongly to express my hope that not one of you students of the Academy will ever allow yourselves to be seduced from what is at once the most natural, the most useful, and, fortunately, the most easy course of study which you can take up—that, namely, of the ancient buildings in your own country. . . . No one, I believe, values foreign study or foreign Art more than I do. But there ought to be proportion in all things.[167]

By 1879 Street was even more forthright, telling a meeting of the St. Paul's Ecclesiological Society, "I confine myself to-night almost entirely to English architecture for several reasons:—1st. It is ample for our time. 2nd. It is, I think, the best architecture of [the thirteenth century]."[168]

This growing artistic nationalism—perhaps a reaction against a perceived military threat from Second Empire France—suppressed the impetus that had sent Ruskin, Street, and other High Victorian theorists to the Continent. A new architectural ideology was emerging. Street now found himself linked with a large group of younger architects, many of whom had first learned to admire the picturesque quality of French Gothic but later discovered a gentler, more flexible architecture at home. Richard Norman Shaw, Street's own chief assistant five years earlier, was a leader of this movement. Shaw's early work, like the competition design for the Bradford Exchange (1864), was in the Early French manner, but he made his enduring reputation with virtuoso adaptations of English vernacular architecture, beginning in the middle sixties. The fruitful interaction of Street with the architects of this younger generation continued to be an important part of the story of his design for the law courts.

However, at the time of the competition, those who admired Street's work were largely blind to his partial reaction against the Early French. They approved of his design because it contained an element of the powerful irregularity found in those of Burges and Seddon. The *Athenaeum*, whose critic liked Street's entry best of all, specifically associated it with the designs of those two architects. Oblivious to the substantial amount of surface detail and tracery with which Street had enriched his building—covering even the upper parts of the preferred version of the record tower—the reviewer noted: "Mr. Street has sought effect, not by placing ornaments over the whole of his fronts, but by skilfully grouping the masses of his building into a composition."[169] While such a description was not entirely inapplicable to the law courts, it would have been more appropriately attached to a slightly earlier work, like the Crimean Memorial Church. But it was for what remained of such Early French qualities in his elevations that he received a generally favorable reception, ranking third in the esteem of critics after the entries of Burges and Waterhouse. Street's work even garnered the most positive evaluation offered by the cynical *Quarterly Review.*[170]

Street executed all of his own perspectives, and his extraordinary drawing ability certainly contributed to the popularity of his design. Alone among the entrants, he restricted himself to simple pen and ink, but this was a medium of which he was an undisputed master. From his office, through Shaw, the wonderfully evocative drawing technique of the Queen Anne generation was disseminated, and his perspectives must have thrilled the visitors to the exhibition in New Square. "See what can be done with only three strokes," the *Builder's* critic overheard an admirer say of his drawings.[171]

The reviewers who were dissatisfied with Street's design, like his admirers, were somewhat confused about his intentions, failing to note his efforts to moderate the massive picturesque quality of his earlier work. Only the perspicacious writer for the *Building News* recognized his significant return to an English architectural vocabulary, but, because he preferred Burges's Early French, he doubted whether the gentler picturesque of English Gothic was "strong enough" to give the needed "dignity and unity" to a large public building.[172] In the same way, the *Chronicle's* enthusiasm for Burges led it to complain that Street's elevation was "rather flat and monotonous."[173] But most detractors found the work too irregular, like the *Ecclesiologist,* which complained that "the whole design is to our mind wanting in unity and strength."[174] With this the *Saturday Review* and the *Civil Engineer and Architect's Journal* agreed, and the *Belgravia* critic, who had favored Garling's ill-disguised classicism, argued that the façade was more like a "college on a high street" than a monumental public buiding.[175] The *Builder,* the champion of Barry, did not even discuss or illustrate Street's exterior until the design had won an award, and its later assessment was predictably negative.

This failure to appreciate the classical monumentality of his elevations surely dismayed Street, but even more troubling was the almost universal condemnation of his planning (Figs. 69, 70). In this area, several other competitors had a clear advantage. While Street adopted the usual concentric layout, he produced neither a logical realization of that system, such as Waterhouse and Lockwood had developed, nor an ingenious modification like Burges's. His solution did not even equal the less brilliant variants prepared by Barry and Scott. Street muddled the logic of the concentric arrangement by so reducing his central hall that it was impossible to align all of the courtrooms adjacent to it, as most of the other contestants had managed. Instead, he was compelled to locate more than half of his courts on secondary corridors, and their less concentrated placement made it very difficult to provide the necessary separate routes of access for different types of visitors. To provide a private passage for lawyers between the lobbies at the rear of the courtrooms, he was forced to throw iron catwalks across the intervening light wells (Fig. 71), creating the unfortunate necessity of roofing the light wells with glass in order to protect the lawyers from inclement weather. Street compounded these general deficiencies by an inexplicably careless error with respect to the commission's most important requirement—the careful restriction of public access to the building. Several of the competitors entirely reordered their plans to provide for this one necessity, and Street, coming from a legal family, must have understood the general objective. His published description of the design did include a strenuous statement about spectators: "There can be no necessity for admitting large numbers of curious visitors to any Court. All that is required is that there shall be just so much

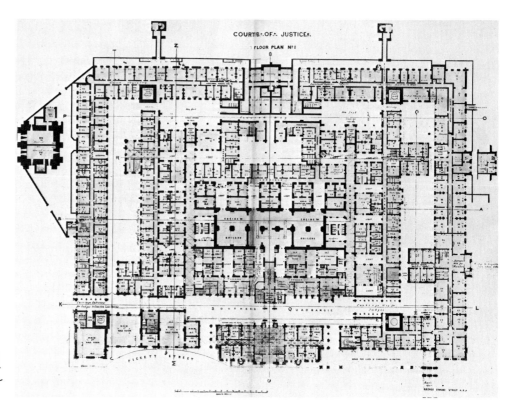

69 Street. Competition design.
1866–67. Plan at Strand level.
(GES. Explanation and Illustrations.)

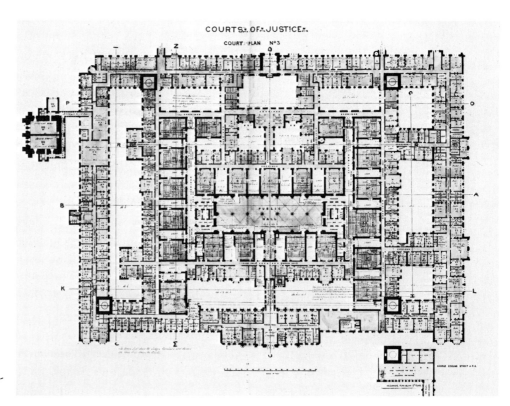

70 Street. Competition design.
1866–67. Plan at courtroom
level, two floors above Strand.
(GES. Explanation and Illustrations.)

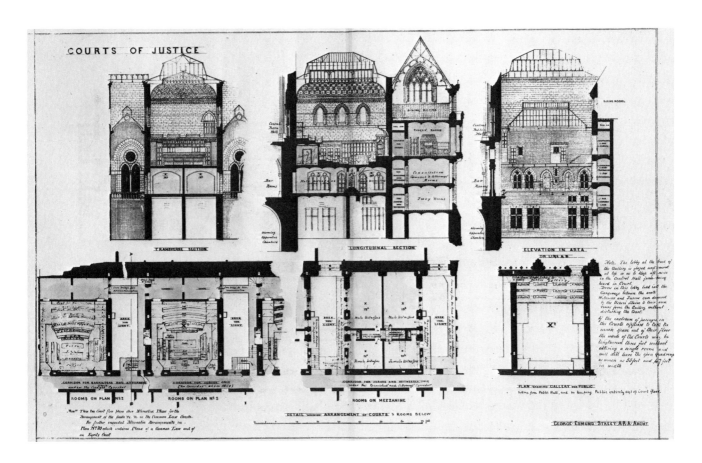

71 Street. Competition design. 1866–67. Plans and sections of courtrooms, showing access arrangements. (GES. Explanation and Illustrations.)

accommodation for them as shall make the proceedings of the Courts public."[176] But despite this, Street somehow began with the intention of admitting the public to the central hall, from which they could pass into the galleries of the courts. This clearly jeopardized any scheme to limit public admission. On his drawings, he labeled this space the "public" hall, and located it on the level of the spectator galleries, where only the general public was likely to venture (see Figs. 68, 70).

Fortunately, he detected this error at the last minute, and made a make-shift correction by adding railings to confine the public to the corners of the hall. But the noisy throng could still disturb the atmosphere of the great concourse, and, as the *Builder* pointed out, the railings cut off all public entry to the lord chancellor's court.[177] The haste with which the design was revised as the deadline approached is reflected in the fact that a few of the labels on the plans were added in a rapid, ordinary script, and a number of the carefully lettered labels were crossed out and altered. There must have been a burst of feverish activity in Street's office when it was discovered that the plan violated the chief stipulation of the instructions.

Street's scheme for dealing with public circulation was also faulty in another important respect. In order to prevent loungers from drifting from courtroom to courtroom, the program had specifically called for separate outside public entrances to each court. However, Street funneled the public from ground floor entrances up to the level of the galleries in two large groups, each of which might be admitted easily to ten or eleven courts. He argued in his description that the commission's requirement was "an impossible arrangement without vast loss of space and great expense, and therefore an impossible arrangement in so restricted a site."[178] But to this the *Builder* replied sarcastically, "that the arrangement denied is not actually 'impossible,' is shown conclusively by more than one of the competitors."[179] Barry, the *Builder's* choice, had accomplished at least a part of the task by subdividing the flow of spectators with eight nonconnecting stairs, while Burges had provided precisely the separate external entrances which were recommended. Several other competitors, including Waterhouse, at least provided separate stairs to each court from the basement level.

On the whole, Street's plan must be ranked in the bottom half of the competition field, and this failure is not altogether surprising. He had had little experience in planning large buildings, and a glance at the great warren of rooms strung along ill-lit corridors which he had devised for the convent at East Grinstead (begun in 1864) suggests that he had achieved little sophistication (see Fig. 8). Nor was Street unaware of his shortcomings. In a letter written to the Royal Commission shortly after the designs were submitted, he urged its members not to devote too much attention to aspects of planning and too little to the "architectural character of the elevation."[180] Contrary to the avowed priorities of Burges and Scott, and to the expected procedure of most architects, Street devoted the more important part of his efforts to the latter concern. Street believed that it was in the outward aspect of the building that he might at last give concrete form to what had for so long been only a potent theory, and, fortunately, the years ahead afforded many opportunities to refine his plan in accordance with the advice of its critics.

During those years Street also revised his elevations, and in that work the critics again played an important role. Their enthusiasm for Burges's extraordinary design encouraged Street to abandon his experiment with the classicization of Gothic, just as it was bearing fruit. The future seemed to lie with an almost undiluted picturesque, and Street—long an Early French devotee—needed little convincing to redirect his energies. Indeed, a comparison of the law courts design with his slightly earlier competition design for the rebuilding of the National Gallery suggests that Street had begun to revert to his picturesque habits before hearing a word of this most recent praise of Burges (Fig. 72).

Street had made a sketch for the National Gallery by the time he returned from his tour of Continental museums in March 1866, when the instructions for the law courts had not yet been issued.[181] His gallery design, even more than the law courts, imposed classical regularity upon medieval structural principles, specifically adapted to its formal, unobstructed site on Trafalgar Square. For that location, Street created a virtually symmetrical façade, whose repetition of gables recalled the composition of a Roman basilica or bath, and at the center he raised a medieval dome to symbolize the Gothic and classic congruity he was seeking. Derived from the Byzantine-inspired domes of southern France, it linked the design to the Romano–Byzantine style practiced by some contemporary French architects, and, specifically, to Léon Vaudoyer's Marseille cathedral (begun in 1852). Like his Continental colleagues, Street evidently turned to Byzantine precedents because they were the most classical form of medieval architecture, and he wrote boldly about these intentions: "I have attempted to give [the design] so much simplicity, dignity, and classicality of

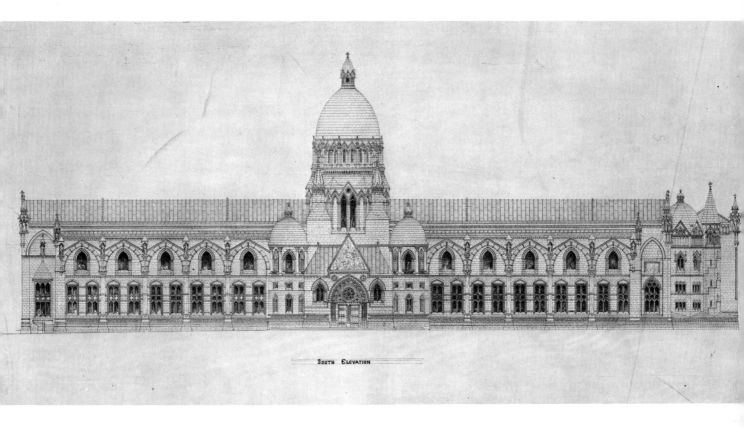

SOUTH ELEVATION

72 *Street. National Gallery competition, London. 1866. South elevation. (Victoria and Albert Museum. Crown copyright.)*

effect, as will ensure its having a sufficiently grave and monumental character."[182] No more daring word than "classicality" could have been spoken by a convinced medievalist. Street's design for the National Gallery was the most audacious of his career and the fullest expression of the High Victorian creed.

However, the same critics who favored the Early French entries in the law courts competition also reviewed the National Gallery contest, and they were very critical of the classicality that Street had so forthrightly adopted. The *Building News* was representative of such opinion: "The composition is slight and not even picturesque. The front shows a long uninteresting straight building of two stories, divided on each side into five arched compartments, with a single doorway in the centre."[183] In reconsidering this as he commenced the design for the law courts, Street evidently reached the same conclusion. With impressive critical detachment, he decided that his best work had depended upon the telling juxtaposition of powerful masses rather than the imposition of linear order, and that classic and medieval could not be mixed as evenly as his theory had postulated without losing the qualities with which he felt most comfortable as a Gothicist. And so in the law courts Street contrived to shift the balance of regular and irregular features more in the direction of the picturesque. This reflected a new, general sensibility and was not merely a reaction to the nature of the confined Carey Street site.

Moreover, in the descriptive text Street prepared after the drawings were complete, he gave a sure indication that his thinking was continuing to evolve along the same lines. He wrote that he would have preferred to break up the long rooflines, which gave so much regularity to the building shown in the bird's-eye view, by hipping the roof at short intervals. He only apologized lamely for this last-minute alteration: "I regret very much that any of the drawings should not illustrate my exact intention; but it was impossible, I found, to alter the drawings without, in point of fact, redrawing them, and for this I had not time."[184] Street could not ignore the instinctive artistic imperative that now seized him, although in yielding he had to begin to retreat from his theoretical ideal: the perfect equilibrium of classical regularity and the picturesque of Gothic.

The Decision of the Judges

BETWEEN FEBRUARY and July 1867, the competition judges evaluated these eleven designs. During the spring and early summer, many members of the jury were also involved in the new Reform Bill debate, but because the Conservatives had exploited the Adullamite revolt to return themselves to power, the judges—except for Stirling-Maxwell, the sole Tory among them—now found themselves on the Opposition side of the question. Only because the Liberals had been appointed as jury members by name (rather than *ex officio*) did they retain their responsibilities with regard to the law courts. Gladstone's diary tersely records their activity as architecture critics during that turbulent political season: (February 7) "Visited the Law Courts as a Judge 3–4"; (May 29) "Conclave of Judges Law Courts Designs 4 pm"; (July 19) "3–5½ Lincoln's Inn: Meeting of Judges of Law Courts' Designs"; (July 24) "Meeting on Law Courts Designs 4–5¼"; and (July 29) "Law Courts' Meeting 3½–4½. We chose Street for Elevation and Barry for plan."[185]

To flesh out this skeletal record and to explain the awkward joint award with which it concluded, it is necessary to rely to some extent upon conjecture. But a credible reconstruction of the law courts decision can be based on an analysis of the architectural tastes of the judges, the prevalent rumors attending the judging, the known opinions of informed observers of the competition—most notably the press—and the advice which the jury is known to have received.

The prejudices with which each of the judges approached his work have been discussed. Next to these, the rumors provide the most tantalizing hints about the thinking of the judges, even though none of the preliminary gossip properly predicted the rather surprising shared victory of Barry and Street. Rather, Waterhouse and Burges were the subjects of the most persistent speculation, even before the competition was fully under way.

As early as March 22, 1866, in his comprehensive attack on the conduct of the contest, Cavendish Bentinck reported but discounted a rumor that the Royal Commission had already made up their minds in favor of the architect of the Manchester Assize Courts.[186] This report was given some plausibility by Waterhouse's brief service as the commission's architectural clerk, even though he resigned that position on December 1, 1865, lest it jeopardize his opportunity to compete. Waterhouse was also known to be a friend of Edwin Wilkins Field, the secretary and true driving force of the commission. It was Field who had nominated him to serve as the architectural clerk, citing his "special knowledge [of law courts] which certainly no other architect can have," and the two men maintained a friendly correspondence throughout the competition.[187] Field betrayed his friendship by indiscreetly pressing his opinion on those who visited the designs when they were hung in New Square. A correspondent to the *Builder* charged him with "acting neither wisely nor well" and went on to allege, "I could tell instances by the score, and will, publicly and by affadavit, if this note should have no effect, of his endeavours to bias persons in favor of one particular set of designs and against others. In fact it is going on all day."[188] Several other letters repeated the accusation, and the *Builder* was moved to regret Field's "excess of zeal."[189] Waterhouse learned of Field's activities when he attended the House of Commons on February 22 and heard Francis S. Powell allude to the secretary's lobbying. He promptly wrote to Field and Powell, and the charges of favoritism gradually died away.[190] Another, unsubstantiated rumor alleged that Dr. John Percy, the heating and ventilation consultant of the commission, was personally prejudiced in favor of Waterhouse and that he had kept his advisory position even after privately notifying Field of this predilection.[191]

The impression that Waterhouse enjoyed special advantages was not diminished by the fact that he was anything but shy about promoting his own interests. Early in 1865 he was already corresponding with members of Parliament about his hopes for the competition, and he later campaigned concertedly to bring his design to the attention of the judges and the public.[192] A correspondent to the *Builder* reported that he circulated a private memorandum in support of his entry to certain members of the Royal Commission.[193] And it was Waterhouse who initiated the idea of preparing a portfolio of photographs of presentation drawings to supplement the official set of plans lithographed for the jury. By November he had already hired a photographer, and in early February, he began to distribute his portfolios to commissioners and judges.[194] However, the other competitors learned of his strategy and prevailed upon him to wait until they could publish similar volumes. William Burges was particularly concerned, but Waterhouse assured Field that he did not wish to be seen as "stealing a march" on his colleagues.[195] Later in the spring, Waterhouse prepared a printed letter that touted certain features of his plan in such a way that Burges replied in his own letter to the Royal Commission on June 8.[196]

Burges was the other competitor most often mentioned in the early reports of favorites, but these rumors were generally less substantial than those concerning Waterhouse. The Burges reports originated for the most part from E. W. Pugin, the seemingly ever-petulant son of the author of *Contrasts*. Pugin later wrote that in the spring of 1867 he had learned that "in spite of castles, towers, and every other incongruity, Mr. Burgess's [*sic*] design was booked for the first premium."[197] Outraged by this news, he had responded in the London *Standard* with a general critique of the competition designs whose disparaging discussion of "medieval castles" and "dungeon keeps" could be read as a specific attack on Burges.[198] Pugin later claimed that he had mobilized his friends to support Street and Waterhouse, thus altering the outcome of the competition. He did at least inspire a like-minded, explicit attack on Burges in the *Westminster Gazette*.[199] A partial confirmation of Pugin's tale came in 1871 from the *Architect*, which, looking back on the competition, suggested that the judges had been prejudiced in favor of Early French muscularity. In support of this hypothesis, it alleged that A. J. Beresford-Hope had been a special advisor to Cowper, the chairman of the judges.[200] When this story is coupled with the knowledge that the *Saturday Review*, of which Beresford-Hope was the proprietor, had endorsed Burges, Pugin's assertion becomes more plausible. But within this scenario it is difficult to explain why Burges was one of the last competitors to receive an invitation, and it is safer to assume that whatever chance his design may have had with the judges was based on its own merits, which were many and widely recognized.

Ultimately, the most convincing support for these rumors is the fact that the designs of Burges and Waterhouse were also the most popular among the journalistic critics. When their entries are added to the two other designs that received important endorsements, those of Street (from the *Athenaeum* and the *Quarterly Review*) and Barry (from the *Builder*), a group of four is assembled that seems to have been the short list considered by the judges. This correspondence between the likely reasoning of the judges and that of a cross-section of the general press is what might be expected with a jury of amateurs, whose views would parallel those of other intelligent but not necessarily art-minded observers. Although the prejudices of the judges were undoubtedly an important factor, it is unnecessary to assume, as the rumors suggest, that special favors were being conferred. In selecting the likeliest entrants, the opinion of the judges differed little from public opinion at large.

The ranking of these four favorites was, however, influenced by the welter of further information provided to the judges by specialists and experts, and this material was not immediately made public. The Royal Commission, sensitive to the amateur status of the jury, had gone to considerable lengths to insure that they would receive a great deal of such expert advice, and the most important of this came from two special architectural assessors appointed by the commission in December 1865. Although their powers quickly grew, their appointment began with the simple request by the architectural clerk, William Burnet, that George Pownall be employed to prepare a comparative statistical study of the competition designs. Pownall asked to be associated in this with John Shaw.[201]

George Pownall (1808–93), who was already the government surveyor for the acquisition of the law courts site, had previously served as a professional assessor in the competition for the War and Foreign Offices. As an architect, he had designed the block of "Jacobethan" chambers at Staple Inn (1842–43) with his partner Francis Wigg, and in 1852 he had been associated with an architect named Baly in designing the rather Wrenian St. Giles and Bloomsbury Public Baths. In addition, he served as the surveyor for the Eton College Estate at Chalk Farm, London, where his talents were displayed in dreary amplitude. John Shaw (1803–70) was a more important architect whose similar interest in Wren's classicism may have been his link to Pownall. Shaw's work in that mode, the Royal Naval College, Deptford (1843–45), and Wellington College, Sandhurst (1856–59), are monuments of some interest, for they are perhaps legitimate precursors of the neo-Georgian phase of the Queen Anne. However, neither Pownall nor Shaw was an architect of great standing, as their modest joint fee of £210 confirms.

Although first asked merely to compile statistics, at a meeting with the commission on March 23, they agreed to report additionally on which design best fulfilled each point of the instructions. They strictly understood, however, that their evaluation would ignore all "aesthetical considerations."[202] It was not until May 13 that they were able to make their report, but the judges had met only once before that date. Shaw and Pownall's findings turned out to be an overwhelming endorsement of Barry, whom they adjudged to have provided the best solutions to forty-one of the eighty-eight problems that they measured. He was followed by Scott (twenty-five), Lockwood (nine), Waterhouse (six), Burges (five), Brandon (four), Seddon (four), Street (three), Deane (two), Garling (one), and Abraham (one).[203] While their system of accounting tended to skew the results by counting only first place points in each area and by concentrating on particulars rather than overall clarity, the triumph that their report represented for Barry's design and for the very similar design submitted by Scott is difficult to lessen.

The importance of Shaw and Pownall's report was magnified greatly because they were added to the panel of five judges during its compilation. Their appointment came after a long struggle. As early as March 1866, when Bentinck had questioned the qualifications of the judges in Parliament, Beresford-Hope had recommended "a larger infusion of the artistic element in the shape of architects."[204] He renewed this request on behalf of the R.I.B.A. when the drawings were submitted in January of the next year, but the Treasury rejected his argument.[205] Nevertheless, the debate continued, and ten of the competitors voted on February 22 to ask that Shaw and Pownall be added to the jury. In addition, they requested that a third architect of their own choosing also be made a judge, no doubt wary of the tastes of the undistinguished professional assessors. The R.I.B.A. Council passed a resolution in support of these requests which was forwarded to the Treasury, but the reply was again negative.[206] However, Beresford-Hope had kept the question alive in Parliament, and when the matter was once more brought up for discussion on May 3, the Government at last withdrew its opposition, and William Cowper, the chairman of the judges, rose to express his willingness to accept the two architects.[207]

In addition to the report prepared by the two assessors-turned-judges, the jury was also given a report prepared by a subcommittee of the commission composed of barristers and solicitors, a survey of opinions among the chief officers of the legal departments, and special evaluations from experts on firefighting and ventilation. The first two were the most significant, for it was stipulated that they were to provide the basis on which the successful competitor would be asked to make final revisions in his design.

Not surprisingly, the bar and solicitors committee report on June 5 reflected the common attitude of lawyers and recommended acceptance of the plans prepared by Waterhouse.[208] Their most important conclusion was that a central hall was necessary and that it should be located one level below the courts. This decision entirely eliminated from consideration the schemes of Burges and Garling, and perhaps also those of Barry and Scott, with their small halls, while Waterhouse alone was found to have located the hall at the preferred level.

The survey of law officers, which was attached to the bar and solicitors report, was difficult to summarize, but it concurred generally with the findings in favor of Waterhouse, with some good words for Scott as well.[209] One critical point on which the two evaluations fully agreed was that the probate offices, the largest legal department and one with numerous daily visitors, should not be located at the center of the building, where Barry, the favorite of Shaw and Pownall, had placed it.

On May 27, Captain Eyre Massey Shaw, chief officer of the Metropolitan Fire Brigade, submitted another advisory report.[210] He had unhelpful praise for Deane's plan, with its fire-conscious subdivision of the building. However, Shaw was scathingly critical of Scott, who, he said, "does not appear to have made the smallest attempt to master the subject"—an unexpected charge against an architect with so enormous and varied a practice. On most of the other designs he was noncommittal.

And finally there was Dr. John Percy's report of June 8 on heating and ventilating, that vexed issue in public architecture that had grown into a storm of controversy at the Houses of Parliament. Percy, in fact, had just completed a report on the unsatisfactory arrangements in that building, and the commission was anxious to have his expert advice about the law courts before a design was selected.[211] Like most specialists in his field, Percy proved difficult to get along with, and his report seems to have been little heeded. He was most impressed by the plans submitted by Scott and Seddon, which received no great attention from the judges, while he disapproved of those of Barry and Street, their eventual choices. Of the last, with its combined use of hot air and hot water, he warned, "I should advise the Commissioners to hesitate long before they accept this proposal."[212]

As these reports were published or leaked late in the spring, the fortunes of Barry and Waterhouse were perceived to rise, and tensions noticeably increased. From the entrants came a flurry of rebuttals and rejoinders. No established procedure existed for such responses, but in January Street and Garling had asked that the architects be allowed to explain any confusing details of their designs to the judges.[213] This request had been refused, and the dissatisfied now resorted to plaintive letters to the Royal Commission.[214] Nothing eventually depended on the small points argued back and forth in this war of claims and counterclaims.

Meanwhile, the judges were meeting. On May 29 they assembled for the first time since February, probably to consider the newly submitted report of Shaw and Pownall. They did not meet again until after the Reform Bill received its third reading in the Commons on July 15. Thereafter, they pushed rapidly toward a decision, meeting on July 19 and 24, with several meetings with individual judges recorded in Gladstone's diary as well. Finally, at their fifth session on July 29, they reached the split decision that Gladstone duly noted in his diary, and on the next day William Cowper wrote to the Treasury that

> The Judges of Designs . . . have been unable to select any one of the designs as best in all respects; but they are of the opinion that the design of Mr. Barry is best in regard to plan and distribution of the interior, and that the design of Mr. Street is the best in regard to merit as an architectural composition; and they recommend that an offer be made to those two architects to act conjointly in the preparation of the final plan to be executed.[215]

Government dissatisfaction with this awkward suggestion was such that it was never reported to the architects, but news of the recommended appointment of Street and Barry escaped and was reported curtly by the *Builder* on August 10.[216]

With the proposal of such an impossible joint commission to be shared by men of incompatible temperaments, the law courts competition joined the great list of past competition failures and perpetuated their ignoble tradition. The contest judges themselves were aware of their failure. A year later Gladstone expressed his regret that "he and those who acted with him had so entirely failed in rendering effective aid to the Government in this matter."[217] On the same occasion, Palmer spoke of his "misfortune to be one of the Judges of these designs."[218] Cowper, too, later admitted the awkwardness of their decision.[219] But the judges had simply been unable to sort out the divergent evidence and preferences that pulled them toward several of the architects, and, under the circumstances, they had probably been relieved to narrow the field to just two.

Two extant contemporary accounts explain the judges' split decision, and with these and an understanding of their predilections, the rumors, the other opinions, and the advice they received, a reconstruction of their thinking can be proposed. The first explanation was offered by Henry S. Winterbotham (1837–73), the irregular Liberal M.P. for Stroud, Gloucestershire, and the leader of the nonconformists in the House of Commons. In a later debate over the dilemma of the law courts competition, he suggested that

> The confusion that had arisen was entirely owing to the circumstances that Messrs. Shaw and Pownall had been raised from the position of assistant architectural clerks to that of Judges. This step had been taken in deference to the Trades' Union feeling of the London architects, who anticipated that this addition to the number of the judges would neutralize the chance of the competitor from Manchester [Waterhouse] being successful. The result of this increase in the number of Judges was that the two Judges who were in favour of Mr. Barry united with the two who were in favour of Mr. Street against the three who were in favour of Mr. Waterhouse, who had succeeded so admirably with regard to the Manchester Law Courts.[220]

Winterbotham's analysis of three parties within the jury is entirely acceptable. Given what is known about the feelings of lawyers—and two of the judges, Cockburn and Palmer, were lawyers—and the bar and solicitors report, some feeling in favor of Waterhouse was logical. Shaw and Pownall's approval of Barry establishes a *prima facie* case for his clique as well. And the sentiment which Gladstone and perhaps Stirling-Maxwell could have felt for Street explains the third division among the judges. What Winterbotham said about the conspiracy of Londoners against Waterhouse is less likely, however, for the agitation to add the professional assessors to the judges began long before their opinions could have been known. Also, his hypothesis fails to account for the rumors that were circulated about Burges.

The main elements of Winterbotham's story were repeated in the cryptic explanation that was proposed by the *Architect* some years after the competition was over. After suggesting that the judges had invited architects from whom "muscular" or Early French designs could be expected, namely, Burges, Street, Deane, Brandon, Waterhouse, and Seddon (this was the *Architect's* own idiosyncratic list), they proposed,

> Accordingly, when, after a vast amount of structural investigation of the designs, it came to be apparent that the balance of preference would on this ground lean towards either the altogether unexpected Mr. Barry or one of the above-named competitors who had not come up to the expected mark of muscularity . . ., some one in authority was said to have intervened (the name of Mr. Gladstone, in fact, was personally mentioned), and suddenly and surprisingly the selection fell upon Mr. Street.[221]

The *Architect* story confirms Winterbotham's suggestion that the choice fell among three competitors. If the unnamed third architect who "had not come up to the expected mark of muscularity" was not Burges—and, reasonably, it could not have been—then most likely it was Waterhouse. The stories thus coincide in identifying the same three front runners, and an important confirmation is obtained for the hypothetical support of Gladstone for Street.

On these bases, the decision-making process of the judges may be sketched tentatively. Shaw and Pownall, both predominantly classical architects in their own practices and concerned principally with planning in their work for the commission, were clearly the locus of support for Barry. Their report, of course, confirms this. Although Waterhouse was unmentioned in the final decision, evidence reveals that he, too, had several proponents. His design was generally popular, and lawyers, including the members of the subcommittee of solicitors and barristers, especially admired it. The lawyers on the jury, Cockburn and Palmer, may have been naturally predisposed to favor him, and the latter had commissioned him to design a house. Perhaps, at least initially, Gladstone was also a supporter of his South Lancashire constituent.

However, Street's design was the ultimate recipient of Gladstone's support. The casual contacts made during the preceding decade and the striking affinities of the two men do not alone prove this assertion. But the further story of Street's commission for the law courts is so full of instances in which he turned to Gladstone as a natural supporter that his help at the time of the competition seems almost certain.[222] This theory is further confirmed by the conjecture of the *Architect.* With Gladstone may have voted Stirling-Maxwell, linked to Street as a fellow Spanish scholar, and, as a real art critic, aware that the work of Barry and Waterhouse was of substantially less artistic significance than that of Street.

Although neglected in the explanations of the judging offered by Winterbotham and the *Architect,* the very popular design submitted by Burges probably had some support among the judges as well. Despite being a late invitee, Burges may have been championed by William Cowper, acting on the advice of Beresford-Hope. Thus supporters may be identified for at least three, and possibly four of the competitors—the probable "finalists."

How these parties ultimately regrouped themselves to vote for a joint award to Barry and Street is more difficult to reconstruct. No evidence, however indirect, can be found. Perhaps it was the pragmatic lawyers, Palmer and Cockburn, who chose to transfer their allegiance to Barry, increasing his supporters to four in an effort to break the deadlock. They would not have been attracted to Street's design, with its terrible planning, nor to Burges's, which, while well planned, was the work of an architect with no great reputation for completing major commissions. Perhaps Cowper, seeing the thinness of support for his presumed favorite, Burges, shifted his vote to Street, bringing his party up to three in number. He would have recognized that Street came closest to equaling Burges's power among the architects under active consideration. Thus, Shaw, Pownall, Cockburn, and Palmer, interested chiefly in convenience of plan, may have voted for Barry, while Gladstone, Stirling-Maxwell, and Cowper voted for Street and for art.[223]

The Decision Is Abandoned

DISSATISFACTION with the judges' recommendation was enormous, and immediate steps were taken to overturn it. Without waiting for what they correctly predicted would be a hostile public reaction, the Treasury drafted a minute asking the judges to reconsider their decision.[224] The Treasury argued that the instructions had specified the appointment of a single architect and that the jury had reached its conclusions without consulting the last of the reports of the special advisers, an estimate of comparative costs submitted by W. J. Gardiner on August 3, after the joint award had been suggested.[225]

Gardiner had tested the estimates prepared by the architects themselves by making an independent survey of their designs, and his figures did provide an additional standard of comparison in general, and further evidence in support of Waterhouse in particular. While all of the already costly designs were found to have been underestimated by their authors, Gardiner determined that Waterhouse's entry would cost only 0.1 percent more than the architect had calculated. At £1,421,430 it was, in fact, the second least costly of all the designs. In contrast, Street's plan would cost 14 percent more than he estimated, or £1,523,273, and Barry's, 26 percent more, or £1,610,966. The least reliable estimate was that submitted by Garling, whose design would cost 55 percent more than he had claimed, or £1,688,458.[226] Given these figures, it is not surprising that on August 9, J. W. Pease, M.P., a relative of Waterhouse, asked in the House of Commons whether the judges had reached their decision prior to consulting Gardiner's report.[227]

The judges, having struggled to reduce the favorites to two, must have been dismayed to have the Treasury return the matter to them for reconsideration. Moreover, the impending Long Vacation prevented any swift resolution of the problem. Gladstone wrote to Cockburn on August 19 and to Cowper on September 7, but no reply survives from Cowper, who was in Ireland, and Cockburn only replied on October 4, after Gladstone's letter caught up with his yacht at Stornoway.[228] Cockburn held out no hope that the judges would be able to settle their differences: "Not, indeed that as it appears to me, we can do anything more. We have given the subject our fullest consideration and cannot agree in selecting any one of the competing architects, and, therefore, as the next best thing, suggest that the execution of the work shall be committed to two."[229] The tone of the reply indicates that Gladstone and he had supported different architects, as hypothesized, and that neither was willing to give in.

Accordingly, when the judges reassembled in London on November 22, they could not revise their previous award. The evidence of the Gardiner report in favor of the very efficient Waterhouse could not dislodge the supporters of either Barry or Street, and on November 28, Cowper reported ruefully to the Treasury, "On reviewing our proceedings, no course appears to have been open to us better than that we have taken, but whether we judged rightly or not, it is clear that we have now no power to render further assistance in this matter."[230]

But although reconfirmed, the decision was not rendered any more palatable, and the other competitors were among the first to protest. Waterhouse, perhaps sensing that the prize had nearly been his, was especially implacable. He published a letter which he had written to Cowper on November 13, calling attention to the favorable reports made on his design by the court officers and by the committees of lawyers. He further charged, correctly, that Shaw and Pownall had made up their minds in favor of Barry even before they were appointed judges.[231] He followed this with a letter to the Treasury on November 28—perhaps written with knowledge of the judges' reconfirmation of their decision on that date—which repeated much of the same argument and demanded a single award.[232]

G. G. Scott was less persistent, although he too believed to the last that a single architect should have been chosen and that he deserved to be that man.[233] He protested the award when it was first revealed in August, questioning "the justice . . . of . . . clubbing together the merits of different competitors" against the un-combined merits of the rest.[234] But his friend Street appealed to him to withhold his criticism, and Scott subsequently wrote to the Government offering to accept the decision if the judges should reconfirm it.[235] After the judges did so, Scott gracefully retracted his complaint on December 18: "I feel bound in all honour, not only to submit to the decision and to express my earnest desire that it may be fully acted on, but further to state that, if under the circumstances the appointment were offered to myself I should feel that I had no right to accept it, nor if the competition were in any way re-opened should I deem it right to re-enter it."[236] He also expressed his confidence that Street and Barry would be able to collaborate successfully.

Some of the other competitors emulated their tactful chairman. On December 13, Seddon wrote to the Royal Commission deploring the complaints made about the judging and urging that the decision be upheld.[237] A month later, Deane advised the Treasury that he concurred with the award.[238]

The opinions of Street and Barry were, of course, tinged by different sentiments than those of their colleagues. For them this was surely a period of agonizing suspense, for their appointment was not yet formally announced and the majority of feeling was set against it. For five months neither dared to express any view, but after the judges had reconsidered their decision, both wrote to the Royal Commission for confirmation of their joint appointment. Street later recalled that they had been in "constant friendly communication" at this time, and their letter writing was coordinated.[239]

Both worried that the judges might be swayed by the arguments that were now brought forward on behalf of the other competitors and against the split commission. Street wrote on December 12 to defend them against this threat: "The eleven competing architects all agreed to accept the decisions of the Judges of Design, and this being so, these supplementary criticisms of the judgment after it is given ought not, I venture to think, be admitted or entertained by the Commission."[240] Barry wrote in the same vein on December 13: "I do not . . . suppose that at this late period, after the award of the judges has been made and published, the Commission will entertain any representations by competitors in their own favour, based upon ex parte statements of facts and figures, the accuracy of which is not admitted."[241]

They followed the letters to the commission with direct appeals to Lord Derby, the Tory prime minister, on January 20. In this further allied effort, Street and Barry stressed that the instructions had specified that the decision of the judges was to be final. Each emphasized his willingness to work with the other. Barry pledged: "Our intimate acquaintance, and (I think I may add) mutual respect and esteem, will be a guarantee for our working harmoniously together."[242] Street concurred: "I have always been on the best terms with Mr. E. M. Barry, and . . . neither of us see any difficulty about working together harmoniously in the execution of [our] respective portions of the work."[243]

Why, exactly, the two were so anxious to join in what promised to be a most difficult partnership may only be guessed. It is likeliest that Street and Barry recognized that because of their respective deficiencies in planning and composition, their only hope of receiving the commission at all was a joint appointment. Judged on their individual merits, their designs would both lose to that of Waterhouse, and perhaps to Burges's as well. So eager were they to have some part of the great prize that they were willing to ignore the professional embarrassment caused by the joint award and to attempt to work around their profound artistic and temperamental differences. Like Scott, who had persisted in revising the Foreign Office design to meet the requirements of Palmerston because "to resign would be to give up a sort of property that Providence had placed in the hands of my family," Street and Barry were willing to accept a great hardship in pursuit of a greater glory.[244]

But they, together with a very few of their colleagues, were nearly alone in their confidence that a joint appointment would be successful. Just at this time, the controversy over the relative shares of Charles Barry and A. W. N. Pugin in the design of the Houses of Parliament was made a public issue, and this encouraged doubts about shared responsibility. Criticism of the award began to appear in the press in the fall, and it intensified after the decision was reaffirmed. On November 19 the *Times* argued that great art could not be collaborative and that "such works require an incubation, which is a solitary process." The only acceptable solution was a new competition.[245] The *Ecclesiologist*, too, supported a rejudging, if not an entirely fresh competition, to break the deadlock. It was confident that if a single award were demanded, Burges would emerge victorious, and its reviewer now called his entry "in many respects the very best architectural work we have seen since the commencement of the Gothic revival."[246] The *Building News*, another Burges admirer, took precisely the same position on December 6, calling on the Treasury to exercise its final authority and select the single design that was the best.[247]

The *Builder* joined the slim company that endorsed the joint decision. Perhaps it feared that the design of its favorite, Barry, would have no chance by itself. In any case, the support did not reflect any fondness for Street, for in the December 28 article accepting the reaffirmation of the judges' decision, the editorialist admitted, "Candidly, we shall never be contented with Mr. Street's elevations, nor will the public be. We should prefer that Mr. Barry's design be carried out in its integrity."[248] This antipathy of the *Builder* toward Street had not been especially obvious before the decision of the judges became known, although the journal had failed to publish his perspective. However, the editors now began a campaign against his work that lasted through all the difficult early years of his association with the law courts.

The *Builder*'s assault had actually begun three weeks earlier with a signed review by William Watkiss Lloyd (1813–93), a well-respected scholar of classical art and letters. Lloyd had attacked Street's design from the point of view of a classicist in search of uniformity and order. Ferociously, he charged that Street's law courts would be a "deformity and an eyesore for all time," and he continued, "Anarchy reigns— section after section seems to do what seems good in its own eyes. Architect and clerk of the works must have been spirited away to Dreamland; and the masons, tired of waiting for them, have evidently got the working drawings into confusion and finished the undertaking somehow—anyhow."[249] George Godwin, the editor of the *Builder*, adopted this position in his later criticism.

Dissatisfaction with the decision and with the victorious designs also spilled into the letter columns, particularly that of the *Times*. On August 15, E. W. Pugin had the honor of publishing there the first criticism of the newly selected architects. Although he was thankful that the judges had abandoned their rumored early preference for Burges, against whom he had fought, Pugin labeled the joint award "a forced and uncongenial partnership, in which every possible element of success is conspicuously absent, and every ingredient of combustion and speedy dissolution glaringly palpable." Neither of the winners had much to recommend him, he reasoned. Disagreeing with Shaw and Pownall, he judged that Barry had only a "moderately good plan," while of Street's façade he wrote, "My reason for coming to this conclusion [that the design was inappropriate for its purpose] is the ostensible poverty, not to say meanness of his Strand front, arising from two distinct causes—first, the absence of consecutiveness, which gives it the appearance of eight distinct detached buildings tacked together; second, an utter want of dignity in any part except in the entrance."[250] This might have been the complaint of a classicist, but the remarks of the fiery younger Pugin always defy easy interpretation.

Pugin's assault was applauded five days later by a letter to the *Times* from "W. E. G.," who accused the victorious architects of paying off the losers at the rate of £1,000 apiece.[251] This absurd libel was only denied by Street on September 4, for he was then in Venice and the allegation was slow in reaching him. "I have made no such bargain, and nothing would have induced me to do so," he replied icily.[252]

E. W. Godwin, who had not received an invitation to compete and who had therefore assisted Burges, also wrote to the *Times* that architects were generally unhappy with the judges' decision.[253] But amid this great outcry against the joint award in general and Barry's planning and Street's designing in particular, Matthew Digby Wyatt could still write to the *Times* with enthusiasm for the dual appointment. Based on his own experience in collaborating with Scott at the Foreign and India Offices, he was able to assure readers that such an arrangement was workable.[254]

The cacaphony of displeasure resounded throughout the late summer and autumn of 1867, and when Parliament reassembled that winter the law courts were an inevitable topic of debate. Needling questions were asked of the Government on November 29 and again on February 14.[255] However, this approach made no headway, and on May 12, 1868, Lord Denman, long a foe of concentration, urged the Peers to end the present state of confusion by giving up the plan for a new building altogether.[256] Two days later Cavendish Bentinck resumed his almost equally drastic criticism of the competition in the Commons. Alluding to his earlier warnings, he likened the recent complaints about the decision of the judges to "locking the stable door after the animal had been abstracted."[257]

At last the matter was brought to a full debate on May 15. The disastrous effect of the long indecision on the inhabitants of the area surrounding the intended site and the ever-growing need for new courts were detailed. Cowper and Gladstone, speaking for the judges and the Opposition, called on the Government to decide the issue quickly.[258] Derby had retired in February, and Benjamin Disraeli was now the prime minister.

The Government committed itself to no definite course of action, and this apparent hesitation encouraged a renewal of the campaign, begun three years earlier, to transfer the entire project to a new site on the Thames Embankment. Proposed during the debates of the spring of 1868, this culminated in an important discussion in the Commons on May 29. Baillie Cochrane (1816–90), the Conservative M.P. for Honiton, led the fight, rising to recommend the abandonment of Carey Street with the awkward assertion that "nothing could well be finer as a building site in

European capitals than the banks of the Thames."[259] But both William Cowper, the late first commissioner of works and the chairman of the jury, and Lord John Manners, the present commissioner, replied strongly. Both predicted added expense and further delay if the site were now changed. And they saw in the proposal a risk to the entire scheme. As Manners said, "This question [of site] had been decided years ago."[260] Such bipartisan cooperation, aimed at keeping the threatened project on course, was of immense importance as the process of selecting an architect entered its final, dramatic stages.

While debate and criticism of the law courts competition grew, the Tory administration had not been as inactive as the public record seemed to show, but its activities had not yet borne fruit. In the wake of the reaffirmation of the award by the judges on November 28, 1867, the Treasury asked the Royal Commission for advice on how to proceed. Recognizing that the joint decision was unacceptable, the commission met on December 13 and recommended that the matter be referred to the attorney general, whom the instructions named as the referee of all disputes.[261] He could decide whether the dual award was legally binding. The Treasury adopted this course, submitting a brief to Attorney General John B. Karslake on February 15, 1868. He was asked to rule on three questions: (1) whether a decision made by the judges without reference to cost was valid (a seemingly pointless query since the judges had reaffirmed their selection after considering Gardiner's report), (2) whether Barry and Street could sustain any legal right to be employed, and (3) whether any other competitor could compel the judges to alter the form of their decision.[262]

The competitors were invited to inspect the Treasury's brief to the attorney general, and Street and Barry both did so and submitted their own arguments. Street's submission, prepared by his brother Thomas, a solicitor, has not survived.[263] Barry's letter of February 26 has, and it reflects a marked change in the joint strategy that he had pursued heretofore in cooperation with Street.[264] The case submitted by the Government cited Street and Barry's earlier support for the tandem award, but Barry now protested: "I cannot, in justice to myself, limit my claims to our joint employment." He then outlined what would be his usual argument in the long ensuing debate, an argument that rested largely on a single passage of the instructions: "The chief points to be kept constantly in view, and to be treated as superseding, so far as they may conflict, all considerations of architectural effect, are the accommodations to be provided and the arrangements to be adopted so as in the greatest degree to facilitate the despatch and accurate transaction of the law business of the country." This, Barry suggested, when coupled with the findings of Shaw and Pownall and of the judges as a group in favor of his planning, gave him a claim to the whole commission. Whether a quarrel between the two architects led to this change of position is not known. Perhaps Barry was merely encouraged by the increasingly hostile reception of Street's design to assert his own claims more confidently.

Karslake reported his decision on May 14, the day before the major debate on the appointment in the Commons. He ruled that the joint award could not be binding on the Treasury, although it was the failure of the judges to reach a decision in accord with the instructions and not their initial failure to consider the Gardiner report that rendered the award invalid. Hence Street and Barry could not claim any right to be employed, but Karslake also ruled that neither could the other competitors force their ouster.[265] A few days were required to interpret this interpretation.

IN THE END, the Treasury recognized that Karslake's decision gave it the power to break the impasse. After analyzing the new position in a minute on May 22, the Treasury explained its conclusions to the commission on May 25: "My Lords now consider themselves free to make any appointment they may think proper, and . . . they will forthwith proceed to consider what appointment should be made."[266] Just four days later, on the day that the Embankment debate went forward in ignorance of the Government's new initiative, George Ward Hunt, Disraeli's chancellor of the Exchequer, directed the drafting of a second minute. It was promulgated on May 30:

> The First Lord of the Treasury and the Chancellor of the Exchequer state to the Board that after the decision which my Lords have come to, as expressed in their Minute of 22nd May, to the effect that they considered themselves free to appoint any architect for the new Courts of Justice Buildings, and after consultation with the First Commissioner of Works, they recommend that Mr. G. E. Street should be appointed the architect. My Lords approve.[267]

The explanation of this surprising triumph for Street is a difficult problem, for little is known about the architectural tastes of two of the three officials named in the minute. The first lord of the Treasury (that is Prime Minister Benjamin Disraeli) was not the intimate of architects that Gladstone was. His Young England Toryism, however, did have an architectural component in its vision of a paternalistic, well cared for society, and in his novel *Sybil*, Disraeli had written of a model factory covered with roofs of iron and glass. He had also had his own home, Hughenden, remodeled by E. B. Lamb in 1862, but neither an interest in iron and glass nor an appreciation of Lamb's old-fashioned "rogue" architecture was likely to have led the prime minister in the direction of Street. However, as chancellor of the Exchequer Disraeli had approved the appointment of a Goth, G. G. Scott, to design the government offices in 1858, and perhaps his notorious anxiety to establish his credentials as an impeccable Christian gentleman inclined his thinking toward a High Church architect for the law courts.

Of George Ward Hunt (1825–77) much less can be postulated. Under Derby he had served as the financial secretary of the Treasury, and when Disraeli became prime minister, just three months earlier, he was elevated to the chancellorship. His brief tenure ended in December when the Government fell, and nothing is known of his artistic preferences.

However, the predilections of Lord John Manners (1818–1906) are quite well understood, for he had a long record as first commissioner of works, serving several Governments of the 1850s before his last tenure of that office under Derby and Disraeli. He was known as a High Churchman and a friend of Gothic architects, having been active in the Camden Society while at Cambridge, and under his administration Scott had received the Foreign Office commission and encouragement for his Gothic design. In the choice between Street and Barry, at least Manners's preference can be counted on the side of the former.

By contrast, almost no support can be adduced for Barry. The sole voice to speak on his behalf was that of William Baxter, the financial secretary of the Treasury, who wrote a memo on May 22 on the back of a copy of Karslake's decision, proposing that the award should go to Barry, without elaboration.[268] Several other memos on the same document note simply that the Treasury might choose whom it liked, and the absence of any evidence of a major internal disagreement at the Treasury—with the exchange of hostile arguments—suggests that Street's selection was rather mysteriously unanimous.

Several factors might have contributed to this consensus. First, the glaring deficiencies of Street's plan may have been overshadowed by the serious complaints made about Barry's design. The most telling of these came from the probate department, whose original report, critical of Barry, had carried little weight with the judges. After the confirmation of the joint award, the department submitted a petition against his plan to the Royal Commission on January 18, 1868, and its views seem to have been more influential on second hearing.[269] The probate officers again criticized Barry's intention to place their huge complex of rooms in the center of the building, a "position we cannot but consider the most detrimental to the due performance of our public duties which could easily have been selected." They complained that his placement of the record depositories several levels above the reading room would "tell severely upon the accuracy and despatch of the business throughout the Registry." Moreover, in the event of fire, they feared that their records "would probably be entirely destroyed in the position Mr. Barry assigns them."

Another major complaint was the expense of Barry's design. Gardiner's report had shown that his entry was both more expensive and less accurately estimated than that submitted by Street. This information had had little impact on the judges, but it may have helped to turn the opinion of the Treasury toward Street.

Those who were concerned by these criticisms, but who believed that Barry had at least some moral claim to part of the commission, may have had their consciences salved by the knowledge that he had only recently received another prestigious public appointment. On May 8, even before the attorney general's decision had been prepared, the commission for the rebuilding of the National Gallery had been awarded to Barry, following another controversial competition. His entry had been adjudged the best of a poor lot, but the original jury had declined to recommend that it be carried out, and the circumstances of his eventual appointment have yet to be decoded. Perhaps, as many speculated at the time, the National Gallery job (which was never executed) was given to Barry as a consolation for what the Treasury already intended to do with the law courts commission. But this interpretation implies that they had some advance report of Karslake's ruling, which freed them to give the law courts to Street.

Finally, and probably most importantly, the award must be analyzed in its political context, for the month of May 1868 was a peculiar period of transition. The Conservative Government which appointed Street had, in fact, been defeated on April 30 over the disestablishment of the Irish Church, and it had only remained in power at the behest of the Queen, who was perhaps manipulated by Disraeli. This was obviously a temporary situation and the Liberals and Gladstone were expected to return to office following the November elections, the first held under the expanded franchise of the Second Reform Bill. In the meantime the Tories continued in a twilight of insubstantial power.

The peculiarity of this situation perhaps helped to shape the law courts decision. The bipartisan alliance which defeated the proposed move to the Embankment on the very day when the Treasury drafted its minute of appointment has already been noted, and a similar alliance overcame subsequent opposition to the selection of Street. Perhaps in this interregnum, such bipartisanship extended to the matter of the appointment itself, particularly in the case of a project fostered and judged by members of the Opposition. A direct consultation between Disraeli and Gladstone need not be postulated, for the architectural tastes of the most powerful of the competition judges and the apparent next prime minister may well have been known in official circles. Nor need any feelings of good will between the two leaders be assumed. The Tories may have been perfectly satisfied to let the Liberals have their own way in the matter of a competition that was evidently headed toward disaster.

Whatever the explanation of the award, Street had to spend some time in suspense while waiting for formal notification, for nine days elapsed between the May 30 Treasury minute and the forwarding of a copy to the successful architect.[270] By then the news of his appointment had already been widely circulated by informal means, and Street later recalled, "I first heard on the 3rd of June, 1868, from a . . . friend, an architect, a rumour that I was to be appointed, and I received the first official notice of the fact on the . . . 9th of June. Between these two dates the *Builder* published the rumour."[271] Thus he learned that he was to receive the largest commission of his career.

After the rumors had begun to circulate, but while still awaiting the arrival of the formal confirmation, Street received two letters from E. M. Barry, dated June 5 and 6, which he characterized as "very kindly" in tone. To these he wrote two replies.[272] "The letters were full, friendly, and kind on both sides," according to Street's account, and he maintained that Barry "congratulated me, and wished me success in the work."[273] On another occasion he quoted one of Barry's letters, in which his colleague had conceded: "I can fully sympathise with your natural joy at being independent and have no doubt of the result being a worthy building."[274] But Barry was later unable to recall this cordiality.[275]

Street realized that his good fortune entailed a moral dilemma, for, in good faith, he had pledged to carry out the design in partnership with Barry. He therefore sought advice:

> I at once consulted one of the most eminent of my brethren as to whether or not I should accept it without Mr. Barry. He pointed out to me, with obvious force, that the Attorney-General had decided the joint award in favour of myself and Mr. Barry to be invalid, and that if the judges could not name one of us, as being superior to the other, nothing was left but for the Treasury to do so; and he advised me that I should do no good, to either Mr. Barry or myself, by making another protest.[276]

Street's "eminent" adviser was most likely his old employer, G. G. Scott, and his counsel to persist, despite the claims of others to the commission, had the precedent of his own conduct in the case of the Foreign Office. Street must have been grateful that his advice was so easy to follow, and, probably without an excess of qualms, he accepted the single appointment on June 10.[277]

Unfortunately, E. M. Barry had already launched himself on a course that would ultimately magnify his professional setback in this competition into a career-shattering defeat. He commenced an unceasing battle against Street's selection which irrevocably tarnished his own reputation and caused untold embarrassment and difficulty for his successful rival. Some foretaste of his hardening attitude was evident in his comments on the case submitted to the attorney general by the Treasury, yet after Street's appointment he only warned that "I may probably put on record my view that I have not been well used at the Law Courts, and then you will hear no more of me in connection with the matter."[278] In fact, his all-out effort to upset the commission began even before Street accepted the award.

On June 8 Barry wrote a long protest to the Treasury in which he again cited arguments from his February letter to the attorney general. If a single award was to be made, he reasoned, it ought to be his, for his plans had been judged best in solving the practical problems which the instructions had said should be the principal concern of the competitors. The plan submitted by Street would have to be revised in order to meet the requirements of the commission, and, hence, Street had been selected "for *what he may yet do*" while Barry deserved proper consideration "for *what I have done*."[279] A copy of this letter was also sent to the Office of Works, and it was submitted to a number of journals and was widely printed, appearing in the *Times* on June 15.[280]

Barry dispatched a short addendum to the Treasury on June 13, but he also turned his attention to rallying support for his cause in Parliament.[281] In this he achieved a swift and notable success when the House of Lords discussed his situation sympathetically on June 19. The marquess of Salisbury outlined Barry's argument in detail and tabled a question to the Government. It asked, "If it is true that the Government has rejected the Design which was recommended by the professional Judges and the Judges of Designs as the best for Plan and internal Arrangements, and has adopted the Design which was recommended for Elevation only; and, further, if the Competitors were instructed that Utility and convenient Arrangement were to be preferred to architectural Effect?"[282] Supportive statements were made by several Peers. Lord Cranworth, who had signed the architectural instructions as lord chancellor in 1866, admitted that the architects had been asked to "attend, not perhaps exclusively, but mainly, to matters of internal accommodation, convenience, and arrangement."[283] However, because of the decision of the attorney general, Cranworth concluded that the Government was free to appoint Street if it desired. Replying to this broad assault on behalf of the administration, Chelmsford, Disraeli's lord chancellor, could make only the rather weak argument that Street's plan, with its admitted deficiencies, would be revised to take into account the lessons learned from all the other competition entries.[284]

After this success, Barry prepared his case for a debate in the Commons. To introduce his petition he secured the services of Robert Lowe, the great orator of the Cave of Adullam and the man whom Gladstone would choose as chancellor of the Exchequer when he formed the new Government in December. Barry also obtained the support of Sir Francis Goldsmid, active before in the law courts debate, who was to introduce a motion for a select committee to investigate the appointment.

Street, realizing that Barry's amiability had evaporated, was now driven to make an enormous defensive exertion, and he prepared his own long memorandum which was forwarded to the Treasury on June 22.[285] He argued that the decision of the judges had been shaped by a number of advisory reports in addition to that of Shaw and Pownall, which Barry had emphasized because it was favorable to his claims.

Street noted that the bar and solicitors' committee and the officials of the legal departments had all been highly critical of Barry's plan and that Gardiner had reported that Street's design was £87,000 cheaper.

Street sent a copy of this memorandum to Austen H. Layard, M.P., on June 24.[286] Layard was an Assyrian archeologist and an art critic, and he would soon be appointed Gladstone's first commissioner of works, a position that would bring him into steady and cordial contact with the architect of the law courts. But this future relationship could scarcely have been foreseen, and the surviving letter from Street is probably one of many which he sent to art-conscious M.P.'s in preparing his defense against Barry. Apparently suspecting that Layard, who had lived for a long time in Italy, was classical in his architectural tastes, Street reassured him in a covering note that "Barry's design is more violently Gothic than mine—covered in all directions with traceries crockets and pinnacles. Whereas mine was a comparatively simple straightforward work as is proved by the Government Surveyor's estimate of costs." His memorandum appeared as well in the correspondence column of the Solicitors' Journal under a supportive letter from his brother Thomas.[287]

Most importantly, on June 29 Street openly solicited the assistance of Gladstone.[288] This nearly confirms the theory that Gladstone supported him in the competition, although Street emphasized that he had asked no favors until now, feeling, as he said, "a certain delicacy about claiming any acquaintance with [one] who had so much to do with the decision." It was only after one of Gladstone's "followers" had urged Street to overcome his scruples that, faced with the serious challenge from Barry, he felt free to act. In a letter to Gladstone he relied on the same argument he had presented in his memorandum, but concluded by stressing the importance to him of Liberal support, and Gladstone's in particular. Noting his own wonder that he had been so well treated by the Conservatives, he asked,

> I venture to hope therefore that you will lend the just weight of your authority to support my appointment. I venture to say that there never was one made which was more entirely free from personal bias. I have absolutely no speaking acquaintance even with any member of the present Government (except a very slight one with the Duke of Buckingham), whereas it is notorious to those who know much of me or my writings in how much respect I hold your person and proceedings as a public man. It is not open to any one to say, therefore, that any political bias has the least degree affected my appointment.

If Street did have political differences with the future prime minister, he recognized that this was not an opportune time to air them.

Street's defense succeeded. With the support of both Liberals and Tories the challenges brought by Lowe and Goldsmid were beaten back in the House of Commons on the evening of June 29, the very day that Street had appealed to Gladstone. In the debate, which centered on the motion for a select committee "to inquire into the recent appointment of Architects for the New Public Buildings in the Metropolis," Gladstone was the first to speak in opposition.[289] Although he felt that his role as a competition judge disqualified him from voting on the motion, he believed that

> Upon the whole, the Government had come to a recommendation which the House would do no good in endeavouring to disturb. The House in this matter was, if he might so speak, a rude instrument for a delicate process. To

appoint a Committee upon this subject would be to re-open from the beginning an operation which had been found to be extremely laborious and complicated, and to re-commence the labour with even less chance of arriving at a satisfactory conclusion than they had when the matter was first started.[290]

Roundell Palmer, another Liberal competition judge, also spoke in support of the decision made by the Conservative Government. He argued against Barry's claims, observing that "it was never considered that the competition was to be decided by reference to internal matters only." Moreover, Palmer reported, "It was not the opinion of the judges that Mr. Barry had by his internal arrangement placed himself upon such a pinnacle, that they, without taking into consideration other things, could recommend him."[291] Further arguments were added by Beresford-Hope, a Tory, and the Tory commissioner of works, Lord John Manners, concluded the case against Goldsmid's motion. Manners reviewed the award from the point of view of the Government, citing, as Street had done in his memorandum, the reports critical of Barry's planning:

> After considering all the circumstances they had appointed Mr. Street to build the new Law Courts, and in so doing they believed they had taken the wisest course open to them. . . . If the Government had appointed Mr. Barry to be architect of the interior and Mr. Street to be architect of the exterior this result would have followed—Mr. Street would have been able to carry out his part of the design, while Mr. Barry would have had the mortification of finding that his plan for the interior would have to be materially altered before it would give satisfaction to one important branch of those using the new Courts [the probate department].[292]

Support for the select committee motion came from several members, including William Tite, the president of the R.I.B.A., who called for the joint award to be upheld. But in the vote, the Liberal leadership allied themselves with the Government and the Government made the issue a ministerial question. This insured the defeat of the motion, which was accomplished by a margin of 90–45.[293] Thereafter, the law courts commission belonged securely to Street.

The substantial margin of the division, however, did not dissuade Barry from pursuing his increasingly pathetic campaign. On the day of the debate he replied briefly to Street's memorandum in a letter to the Treasury, asking that the letters written on January 20 by the two architects, in which both accepted the joint appointment, be included in the materials that were being published by order of Parliament.[294] This request was sent to the newspapers and was widely printed.[295] Three days after the vote he wrote to the *Times* that his purpose was not to prolong the debate, but he was unable to restrain himself for long.[296]

Complaining that he had received no reply to his earlier letters, Barry again addressed the Treasury on July 21.[297] He cited Lord Cranworth's description in the Lords of the requirements stated in the instructions, and he repeated once more his usual argument against the single appointment of Street. Barry concluded, "I had hoped the Government would have hesitated to pursue a course which has turned my success in the competition into a serious misfortune, or at least would have furnished me with some satisfactory explanation of the reasons which have induced them to inflict upon me so great an injury." The *Law Times* published this painful document, which was thoroughly summarized in a further letter from Barry to the *Times*, but the *Solicitors' Journal* declined to print a repetition of his previous statements, noting that the text was "extremely long."[298] At the Treasury, Barry's letter was read by Sir William H. Clerke, a principal clerk, who observed in a memo, "this hardly requires an answer."[299]

Consciously or unconsciously emulating his successful rival, late that year Barry also appealed to Gladstone. The new prime minister took several weeks to reply and then carefully avoided making any promises. While expressing his hope that the effects on Barry's career would not be as unfavorable as the architect had predicted, Gladstone firmly explained that "as one of the 'Judges' I think my duties have terminated and could not be revived."[300]

With no political support for his cause, on December 21 Barry again repeated his complaint to the Treasury.[301] Clerke was nearly incredulous, and he wrote, "it is so long since we have heard from Mr. Barry that I thought that he had accepted the decision of the Treasury in favor of Mr. Street's appointment."[302] He recommended that the letter only be acknowledged. Poor Barry simply lacked the resiliency necessary to do business in the Victorian political world. Although an architect of middling talent, he had the touchy disposition of a prima donna.

Understandably, the press and public opinion, both critical of the proposed tandem commission, were pleased that the Government had extricated itself from a difficult position. Some, however, remained on Barry's side in his quixotic endeavor. The writers of the *Builder*, who had been so entirely repelled by Street's design, were Barry's best allies, and they predicted that the decision would have "a fatal effect on future competitions." They explained,

> If Mr. Street be appointed sole architect of the Law Courts, and Mr. Barry be refused connexion with the work, it will be an act of injustice that, like other acts of injustice, will bring disaster in its train. Mr. Street's plan is altogether out of the question; no competent judge, so far as we know, ventures for a moment to assert that it might be adopted; and as to his design for the exterior, we consider it to be, with the exception of a few portions, altogether unworthy of Mr. Street's reputation.[303]

Even after the Commons rejected the motion for a select committee, the *Builder* queried, "Is it yet too late to obtain justice?"[304] And on November 2, in his presidential address at the first meeting of the R.I.B.A. winter session, William Tite endorsed the *Builder*'s editorial position and, as he had in the Parliamentary debate, called for the division of the award between the two architects. Perhaps separate buildings for the common law and equity courts could be built, he suggested.[305]

Some of the law journals, conceivably impressed by the niceties of Barry's argument, also briefly tendered him their support. The *Law Times* was surprised at the award to Street and could not see "how that appointment can be justified."[306] The editors concluded that the motion for a select committee placed the Government in "a very awkward dilemma," and even after the defeat of that motion they called for a new competition for an even larger building.[307] The *Solicitors' Journal* merely wished to see the joint award upheld, but neither of these publications was willing to stand with Barry as he continued, even in later years, to press his case.[308]

The *Times* maintained a more common and more pragmatic position, although admitting that, in choosing between Barry and Street, its first sympathies had been with the former. The journal urged readers not to commit themselves to either architect and to remember that fairness to the competitors was not more important than fairness to the nation. The serious criticisms of Barry's plan were carefully reported.[309]

Other journals were less fainthearted in welcoming Street's appointment. The *Building News* observed that "Mr. Street and Mr. E. M. Barry were scarcely the two men to be yoked together," and in the manipulation of the two commissions—for the National Gallery and the law courts—a "happy stroke of diplomacy was achieved."[310] Its critics doubted that Barry would gain anything even if he did secure the appointment of a select committee, and when Goldsmid's motion was defeated, the *Building News* noted with relief that it would be "useless for Mr. Barry or for anyone else to disturb the arrangement." Perceptively, it concluded that Street had been selected "not because his plan is best, but because . . . he is the best architect for the purpose."[311]

Architects rallied to Street as well. In a letter to the *Times*, Scott, who had, albeit unwillingly, accepted the tandem award and who was not quite ready to concede that his own plan was not the best of all, nevertheless renewed his pledge to keep his own name out of the contest. He applauded Street's victory as well, noting, "whether or not the final decision be logically correct, I cannot but rejoice that this great work has fallen into the hands of an architect of the highest class of talent."[312] Such was the self-indulgent praise of Street's former employer and, perhaps, his present adviser.

Satisfaction was also expressed in an altogether unexpected quarter, when E. W. Pugin joined with those who supported the award going to Street. In another letter to the *Times* he drew back from his previous criticism of both designs and registered his decided preference for that of Street.[313] While he suspected that Barry would have an "incapacity for mending his elevations," which he called a "giddy, puerile, and firework sort of design," he now maintained that Street's façades "evince a power which, when coupled with a sense of the responsibility and grandeur of his position, will enable him to rise far above the comparative mediocrity of his present design." As for the argument that the selection should have been decided on the basis of convenient planning, Pugin offered perhaps the most sensible comment of his life: "A camel is a very conveniently arranged animal, and its 'internal accommodation' appears to be remarkably well adapted to the countries wherein it flourishes, but I suppose people would not generally prefer a camel if they could procure the same advantages in an animal of less ungainly exterior." In the final analysis, the successful interpretation of the decision to appoint Street need account for no more than the unwillingness of any public official to erect a great camel of a building on the Strand. For a camel was what Barry's design undoubtedly was.

And so George Edmund Street won what Barry called "the greatest architectural prize in this generation."[314] But his troublous initiation foretold a long and difficult task ahead, which ended with his death a year before the great building opened. Scott remarked a few years after the award, "It is well this . . . load of persecution has fallen upon a man of spirit and nerve calculated to bear it. I heartily wish him the highest success."[315]

Chapter 4

Revised Plans

GEORGE EDMUND STREET promptly showed his mettle, preparing three new plans for the law courts within the first year of his appointment. Because of the weaknesses in his competition entry, the Royal Commission requested a thoroughly revised design as soon as he was awarded the commission, and this revision was barely completed when a new Government took up the proposal to relocate the entire project on the Thames Embankment, requiring two further designs from Street. These new designs demonstrated that he had learned the lessons taught by the successful and popular competition entries of Burges and Waterhouse. Street adopted the extraordinary effectiveness of Burges's picturesque composition, and he dramatically clarified his plan under the influence of Waterhouse's example. But while these alterations increased the visual and functional success of his design, they also marked a retreat from the more purely cerebral power of his competition entry. High Victorianism was waning, and a new agenda for architecture was being composed.

The Great Plan

ALERTED to the deficiencies of his planning by the public criticism of his competition design, Street actually began to work on his first revised scheme a week before he was officially appointed on June 9, and before the defeat of Barry's efforts to oust him. When he appealed to Austen H. Layard for support against Barry in the Commons on June 24, he could already report: "For the last three weeks I have been working night and day on my final plans."[1]

In response to the formal notification of his appointment, Street asked to call at the Treasury on June 10 to obtain official directions.[2] In a minute dated June 15, the Treasury authorized the architect to proceed with ground plans and sections for a revised scheme, to be prepared in consultation with William Burnet and the Royal Commission. The minute added that £800,000 had already been spent on acquiring the site, and only £700,000 remained out of the original appropriation for the building. But, like the financial stipulation contained in the instructions, the warning implied in these figures was destined to be ignored.[3]

Edwin W. Field, secretary of the Royal Commission, was eager to advance the work as rapidly as possible now that the Government had finally resolved the dilemma posed by the judges' decision. The commission also had to advise as to the final plan, for which the selection of the architect was only the first step. Accordingly, Field and Burnet contacted Street soon after he was appointed—even while the controversy over his selection still raged.[4] They provided the architect with offices in John Soane's old Insolvent Debtors' Court at 33 Lincoln's Inn Fields, where the commission was housed. Street first inspected his rooms on June 23. They were in the rear, with a door at 5a Portugal Street, and although he paid no rent, the Treasury required him to furnish and heat the rooms at his own expense.[5] Street attended the general meeting of the commission on June 29, when this housekeeping arrangement was approved, and a committee was set up to confer with him.[6] That evening the motion by Goldsmid for a select committee to investigate the appointment was defeated in the Commons.

The "Committee as to Final Plan" of the Royal Commission first met with Street on July 2.[7] Well aware of the critical report of the bar and solicitors' committee, all realized that the architect first had to clarify his plan. As part of the process of revision, the new committee also listened sympathetically to his request to reduce and consolidate some of the accommodations listed in the competition program. It was now apparent to Street that the legal officers had treated the commission's questionnaire as an invitation for utopian planning, or, as he later reported more diplomatically, that "many of the heads of departments had asked for more space than was absolutely required."[8] A smaller subcommittee was accordingly created to assist in paring away the needless provisions, with the vain hope of reducing the huge program to the level of the stated budget.

When the subcommittee met the next day, Street already had "sketch plans" for the members to inspect, the products of one month of concerted labor. These drawings, now lost, were the first version of what would come to be called the "great plan" for the law courts.[9] They were approved by the subcommittee at its next meeting on July 13, approved by the full committee as to final plan on July 15, and approved and forwarded to the Treasury by the commission on July 23.[10] The subcommittee met with Street twice more before the Long Vacation, and then he was left on his own to refine the design. July 1868, with its chorus after chorus of approval for his work, must have been one of the most encouraging months of his life.

After an early autumn holiday in Italy with his wife and son, Street began intensive negotiations with the various legal departments to fix their accommodation in the new plan. In October these details had been sufficiently determined to permit him to publish a lithographed portfolio of small-scale plans and sections, based on the sketch plans; these were circulated for discussion and comment (Figs. 73–75).[11] Only one of the original drawings for the portfolio is preserved, and it is the oldest drawing by Street's office for the law courts to survive from the period after the competition (Fig. 76).[12]

The great plan was an enormous achievement for Street, for in it he corrected the planning deficiencies of his competition design and also responded to the artistic criticism to which the competitors had been subjected. It was no simple amendment of the plans that he had drafted in 1866, but an entirely new building, related more closely to the designs of some of the other competitors than to his own. The great plan reflected his astounding ability to begin anew, with fresh ideas, even when he had already devoted nearly a year of effort to the project. Street prepared not merely block plans and sections and detailed study plans for all the departments, he also began to make elevations and even working drawings, although the latter were never inked.[13] He later reported: "I have got, I am afraid to say how many rolls of drawings, all prepared in pencil to a building scale for the approved plan."[14]

In creating the great plan, Street turned first to the design of an efficient layout.

73 *Street. The great plan.*
1868. Plan at Strand level,
October 1868. (GES. New
Law Courts: Block Plans and
Sections Prepared by George
Edmund Street, A.R.A., the
Architect to the New
Courts, and Approved by the
Courts of Justice Commis-
sion, 23rd July 1868; Details
Added, October 1868. Lon-
don: Kell Brothers, 1868. PRO
Works 6/123.)

74 *Street. The great plan.*
1868. Plan at courtroom level.
October 1868. (GES. New
Law Courts. PRO Works 6/
123.)

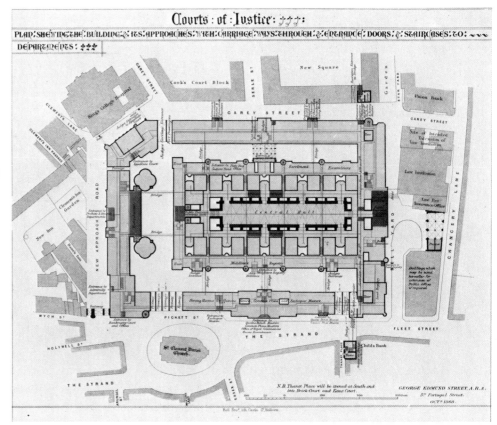

75 *Street. The great plan.*
1868. Transverse and partial
longitudinal sections, October
1868. (GES. New Law
Courts. PRO Works 6/123.)

76 *Street. The great plan.*
1868. Plans and sections of a
courtroom, c. October 1868.
(PRO Works 30/2235.)

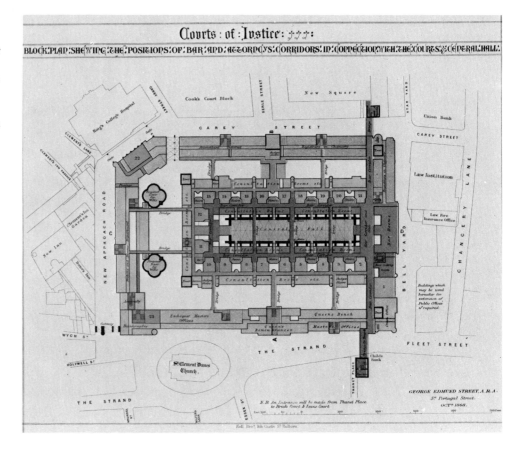

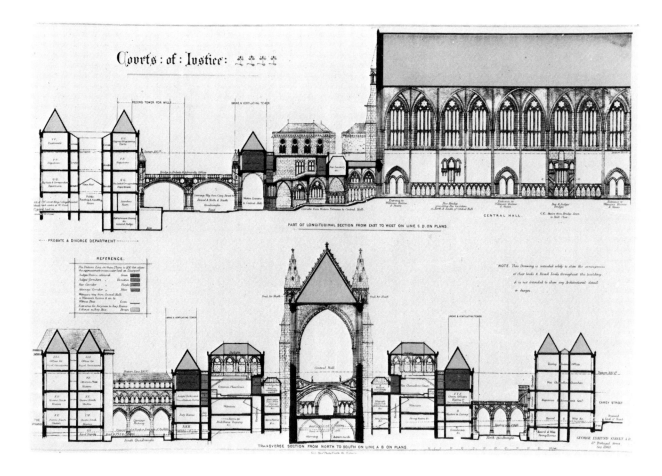

Courts : of : Justice :

RECORD TOWER FOR WILLS   SMOKE & VENTILATING TOWER

CENTRAL HALL.

PART OF LONGITUDINAL SECTION FROM EAST TO WEST ON LINE C.D. ON PLANS

PROBATE & DIVORCE DEPARTMENT

REFERENCE.

NOTE. This Drawing is intended solely to shew the arrangement of Clear Levels & Bench Levels throughout the building & is not intended to shew any Architectural detail or design.

Central Hall

TRANSVERSE SECTION FROM NORTH TO SOUTH ON LINE A.B. ON PLANS

GEORGE EDMUND STREET A.R.
6th Portugal Street
Oct 1868.

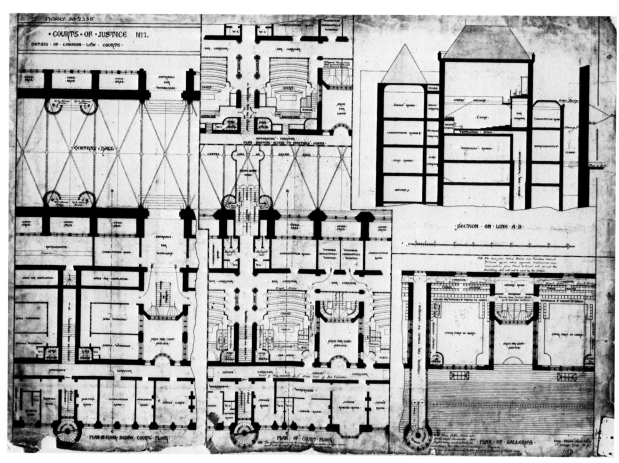

WORKS. 30/2235

• COURTS • OF • JUSTICE •   No 7.

DETAILS • OF • COMMON • LAW • COURTS •

CENTRAL HALL

SECTION • ON • LINE • A·B·

PLAN OF FLOOR BELOW COURTS FLOOR   PLAN OF COURTS FLOOR   PLAN OF GALLERIES

Artistic effect was not even discussed in principle in the full report that he submitted to the Royal Commission on January 11, 1869, and the cross-section that was included in the published portfolio carried the warning: "This Drawing is intended solely to shew the arrangement of floor levels & Road levels throughout the building & is not intended to shew any Architectural detail or design" (see Fig. 75). In part, this caution was inspired by the directions of the Treasury, which authorized Street to prepare only plans and sections, but there was probably a kind of self-discipline as well. He did not wish to experience again an embarrassment like that caused by his ill-conceived arrangement of public access to the central hall in the competition design. So, in his report, he stressed his detailed consultations with the various legal departments while reordering their accommodations. He reported proudly, "In almost all the reductions in size which have been made, we have had the active concurrence of the officers who represented the departments affected, whilst in every case we have invited statements of objections and criticisms, and have as far as possible, and, I believe, in nearly every case satisfied them."[15]

The reductions which Street achieved were substantial, totaling 37,000 square feet. They included a major simplification of the chambers of the common law judges, a consolidation of the multiple facilities for witnesses, and the elimination of some of the redundant amenities provided for lawyers.

However, more important than this trimming was Street's reorganization of the entire plan according to a clear and regular system, freed of his earlier mistakes. This was certainly a higher priority for the Royal Commission than the lessening of expense. The courtrooms were now grouped in pairs, sharing certain facilities, and all except the appeals and bankruptcy courts were aligned on either side of the central hall. None was relegated to a secondary passage, as in the competition plan, but the price of this regularity was a much longer central hall, lengthened from 190 to 322 feet. The row of central columns of the earlier hall was not retained in this elongated and narrowed format. General access to the hall was entirely rethought, and no admission at all was provided for those whom Street, with his later, better informed understanding, came to call the "dirty public."[16] Spectators were funneled into the galleries of the courts by small circular stairs, each of which served only two or three courtrooms and led only to the outside. The central hall itself was lowered to the level of Carey Street, one floor below the courts, where the bar and solicitors' committee and the recent subcommittee had agreed that it should be placed. He also eliminated other makeshift arrangements in the competition entry, most notably the iron catwalks and the glass roofs they had required in the areas between the courtrooms. Street's only admitted failure was in providing spacious courtyards within the building, but this was blamed on the dimensions of the site.

It is hardly possible to credit Street with great originality in working out the problems of his plan in this way. He had available all of the ideas generated by the other ten competitors, and he was not shy about borrowing. In particular, Street's replanning owed a great deal to the design that had been most highly favored in the legal community, Alfred Waterhouse's elegant realization of the concentric zone model. The great plan incorporated Waterhouse's clearly defined and nearly uninter-rupted north and south streets, crossed at intervals by bridges, and his long central hall—a central street really—with its own bridges for lawyers and judges (see Figs. 30, 31, 33). Because the lengthened main block of the building, with its long hall and contiguous courts, ran nearly the entire length of the site, Street slid it against the eastern perimeter of offices, just as Waterhouse had done, in order to open up a courtyard to the west. Only in pairing the courts and giving up the idea of "transverse halls" in favor of direct exterior entrances to the public stairs, did Street's design differ markedly, and the latter feature may have been borrowed from Burges.

Street offered other indications of his admiration for Waterhouse's planning ability. In 1868, while waiting for the commission for the law courts to be resolved, he and Professor Thomas Donaldson had served as the judges in the second stage of the Manchester Town Hall competition, which Waterhouse won on the strength of his plan.[17] Street was also impressed by Waterhouse's artistic ability, for when he explained his great plan to a public meeting in March 1869, he worked up a perspective study of the building as it would appear from Waterloo Bridge—precisely the vantage of Waterhouse's celebrated view of his competition entry (see Fig. 35).[18]

The picturesque effects which such a drawing emphasized, like the improved planning, were evidence that the great plan had been made with an eye to the more successful competition designs. In particular, the warm reception accorded William Burges by the *Ecclesiologist,* the *Building News,* and the *Saturday Review* must have convinced Street that his last-minute decision to break up the roofline of his own entry had been a step in the proper direction. A. J. Beresford-Hope recalled that the architect had openly admired Burges's design, gesturing at his drawings in the exhibition building and professing: "I would not mind being beaten by those!"[19] At nearly the same time, Street also expressed his admiration in a more tangible way, for in fulfilling his duties as the assessor in the third Bristol Assize Courts competition in 1867, he awarded a second prize to Edward Godwin, Burges's friend, helper, and artistic ally. Godwin's design was another example of Early French solidity, like his earlier town halls for Congleton and Northampton.[20] Street again awarded a prize to Godwin in 1871, placing his Burges-like design first in the competition for the Leicester Town Hall (Fig. 77). (Godwin's design was not executed.)

Street's increased conviction that a careful balance between irregularity and symmetry was unnecessary can be detected in the surviving illustrations of the great plan, even though they include no elevations. With the main block of the building pushed eastward, the counterbalancing role of the two massive, quatrefoil-plan record towers to the west is very pronounced.[21] The four secondary towers (for ventilation) were related to these in a syncopated pattern, and the south façade was broken back asymmetrically in response to the site, particularly the northward arc of Pickett Street.

All of this bespoke a sympathetic study of Burges's design, but other influences were also at work. While the plans of the record towers suggest a solidity of form similar to that of the Early French, the section of the great hall showed a profusion of English Decorated tracery in the windows (see Fig. 75). In this respect, Street's mix of precedents remained that of the competition design. Although he was now converted to the desirability of more irregular massing, he had resolved not to limit himself exclusively to the tough muscularity of the Early French.

Despite its technical and artistic achievements, the great plan faced an uncer-

77 Edward W. Godwin. Leicester Town Hall competition. 1871. (Architect, 6 January 1872.)

tain future in the hands of its official patrons. The printed plans were distributed to the members of the commission, to the legal professional societies, and to the officers of the law departments on December 19 and 21, 1868. Field also forwarded a copy to the Treasury, which, ominously, had not yet responded to the plans submitted in July. Street was anxious to proceed with the elevations for the building, and the Treasury, which shared responsibility for approving the plans with the commission, was asked to provide further instructions.[22]

The situation was further confused by a new Government, formed after the general election of November 23, in which the Liberals had won their expected victory from an enlarged electorate. Gladstone became prime minister, and, friend of Street or not, under his economical regime the cautious silence with which Disraeli's Treasury had dealt with the law courts was firmed into more active resistance against what still seemed to be unchecked expenditure.

However, Street chose to ignore this gloomy prospect and submitted his full report on the great plan on January 11, 1869, asking for permission to advance beyond the plans and sections authorized the previous summer.[23] Already at work on the elevations, he felt that if allowed to proceed, the first stone could be laid in the summer of 1869. On January 15, the commission read this report, inspected Street's more detailed "volume of Plans of Departments," and empowered Field to ask once more for a response from the Treasury.[24]

The Treasury finally recognized the existence of the great plan on January 25, by asking Burnet to prepare a summary of the alterations.[25] These were duly calculated and submitted to the Treasury on February 2, accompanied by a resolution passed by the Royal Commission on the previous day: "That this Commission do approve the detailed plans submitted by the Architect in accordance with the block plans already approved by the Commission . . . , subject to such modifications in matters of detail as the Commission may hereafter approve."[26] Rather than deal with them directly, the Treasury transferred these materials to the Office of Works, where the puzzled chief secretary, George Russell, replied on February 5, asking what was to be done with them.[27] No answer appears to have been given. The Treasury, anxious about costs, was then quietly preparing its own, alternate proposal for the law courts, and was little interested in the scheme that Street had designed for the Royal Commission.

The great plan was thus destined to be abandoned. It had the misfortune of being prepared in the uncertain climate of an election year and in ignorance of the deeper concerns of the new Liberal Treasury. But in the great plan, the fruits of Street's admiration for Waterhouse's planning and for Burges's picturesque composition first coalesced. These lessons from the competition also shaped all of Street's subsequent designs for the law courts, and the pragmatic and visual criteria that they reflected became the standards for late Victorian architecture.

Spiraling Costs

THE DEMISE of the great plan was a result of the difficulties encountered in providing funds for a building and a site that had been enlarged by the enthusiastic law reformers of the Royal Commission well beyond the limits set by the enabling legislation of 1865. Despite Street's parings, the site had grown from $7\frac{1}{2}$ to $13\frac{1}{4}$ acres. The total cost was now estimated at £3.25 million, more than twice the approved ceiling of £1.5 million. Even the Conservatives, who remained in power as lame ducks until December 1868, were not eager to assume this financial burden. They reserved the matter for consideration by the new Government, while they closely monitored the gloomy financial outlook for the project.

Some of the financial difficulty lay with acquisition of the original $7\frac{1}{2}$-acre site, which had been almost entirely cleared when Street's appointment was announced. In fact, demolition had commenced while the competition designs were on display in New Square in 1867. The total acquisition cost had been £765,441, which corresponded with the original £750,000 estimate, when the £17,000 paid for an additional house in Fleet Street was subtracted.[28] However, the Office of Works spent an additional £28,000 on an accountant, a firm of wreckers and valuers, and auctioneers to sell salvaged materials. Moreover, the law firm of Field, Roscoe, and

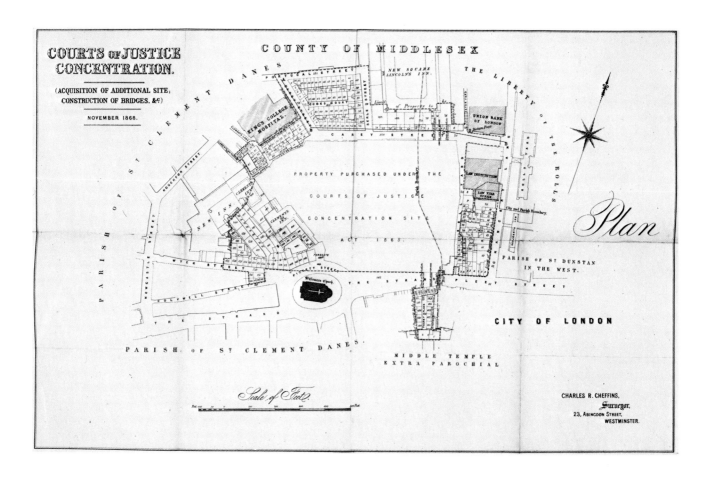

78 *Charles R. Cheffins. Carey Street site. Plan of proposed enlargement, November 1868. (PRO Works 12/36/2 f.112.)*

Company, charged almost £400 to untangle the complex ownership of some of the houses. As Edwin W. Field, the secretary of the Royal Commission, was a partner in this firm, Parliament later questioned the propriety of their employment, although no particular wrongdoing was alleged.[29]

In addition, the original site, although expensive, could accommodate neither the grandiose competition designs nor the great plan, whose foundations alone would have covered eight acres. As a result, the same committees that met with Street after his appointment to discuss his plan also discussed the site, and they approved his proposal for an enlargement of the purchased land. The commission accepted these purchases, which expanded the site to 13¼ acres, in July 1868, at the same meeting at which the great plan itself was first approved. Like the plan, the request for an expanded site was forwarded to the Treasury, accompanied by George Pownall's calculation that the enlargement would cost an additional £668,000.[30]

This estimate may have discouraged the Conservative chancellor of the Exchequer, George Ward Hunt, from giving serious consideration to the great plan, but he did go through the motion of ordering the Office of Works to draft a bill for the acquisition of the larger site on August 13.[31] Charles R. Cheffins, the surveyor employed in 1866, again prepared the plan and books of reference needed for the provisional legislation.[32] His final site plan of November showed the acquisition of all lands as far east as Chancery Lane (excluding the building of the Law Society) for the purposes of an improved eastern approach, although some of that land could be resold later (Fig. 78). The purchase of the houses in Thanet Place, to the south of the Strand, would permit a bridge to be built to the Temples. To the southwest, Danes Inn and Clements Inn were to be bought, with the understanding that the latter would rebuild on the site of the former. In the northwest corner, the squalid buildings adjacent to King's College Hospital were to be acquired. The entire north side of Carey Street was also to be obtained to permit the northward expansion of the site. Included in this last area was the large Cook's Court property, on which a private group of Manchester investors erected several office blocks based on Waterhouse's design. The Government gave official notice of its intention to introduce the new bill, but Cheffins's supporting documents were not deposited until November 30, one week after the general election and just three days before Gladstone accepted the premiership.[33]

The Royal Commission had not proposed the vast expenditure required by this bill, and by the still enormous scale of its building program, without having prepared its own, audacious financial plan. This was drafted in July and sent off to the Treasury with the sketches of the great plan and the additional site request.[34] Based on Pownall's July estimate for the site, and on the assumption that the great plan could be built for the sum that Gardiner had assigned to Street's competition entry, the commissioners admitted that the total cost of the law courts would be £3,250,000 rather than the legislated £1,500,000.[35] To make up this deficit of £1,750,000, they proposed that an additional £754,850 be obtained from some of the other surplus legal fee funds held by the courts, and that the remaining £995,150 might come as an additional advance from the general budget, to be repaid by levying higher taxes on the suitors.

Skeptical of this scheme, the Treasury prepared its own internal study in October.[36] The findings were disturbing. Income from the other fee funds that the commission had proposed to tap was already fully committed to paying court expenses, and so the entire burden of the increased expenditure for the law courts would have to be borne by the Treasury. This could be relieved only if the unpopular court taxes were enormously increased.

However, the doubts in Hunt's mind that were strengthened by this report were never tested, for he left office shortly thereafter, in the wake of the Conservative election defeat on November 23. Gladstone's new Government was even more likely to question large public outlays, and its members also had new ideas about the site for the law courts. This unlikely conjunction of thrift and sensitivity to the artistic issues of siting inspired a final, climactic debate over the cost and location of the new building. In the course of this discussion, Street prepared two further designs. What was promptly christened the "Battle of the Sites" saw attention focused once more on the attractions of the Thames Embankment.

The Embankment

THE THAMES-SIDE alternative had been a persistent subcurrent in the law courts discussion ever since a royal commission in 1861 had recommended the construction of quays along both banks. Legislation authorizing this enormous project, engineered by Joseph Bazalgette, was enacted in 1862 and 1863. As work progressed, numerous plans were prepared for the construction of public buildings along the

79 Austen H. Layard, by G. F. Watts. (National Portrait Gallery.)

river, including the Royal Courts of Justice. However, opponents of the law courts concentration project had also used the Embankment as a red herring. Such was Frederick Lygon's intention when he moved that the 1865 legislation be recommitted to a select committee to study the site question. Baillie Cochrane's appeal for a change of site while the appointment of the architect was being discussed in 1868 was interpreted at first in the same way.

But in July 1868 work began on the last portion of the northern or Victoria Embankment, and as the attractiveness of the riverfront increased, Baillie Cochrane's proposal began to seem more constructive. That month, as Street worked out the preliminaries of the great plan with the Royal Commission, the *Law Times* endorsed the "new site [on the Thames] which invites the Palace of the Law." They spoke rhapsodically of "spacious halls, and airy terrace walks, and cool fountains on July evenings, with a breadth of a quarter-mile of tidal water at [our] feet."[37] Only a few days earlier the *Times* had also, more prosaically, endorsed the Embankment as a site for the law courts, briefly refuting the three arguments that would be employed against the proposal: first, that the new site was not at the center of the legal district; second, that added expense would be involved; and, third, that a change in location would delay the completion of the project.[38] When the R.I.B.A. opened its new session on November 2, President William Tite reiterated the suggestion he had made in the Commons in June for splitting the building into two parts, with one unit to be built on the river. One of Barry's sympathizers, Tite hoped that one of the new buildings might be awarded to that architect.[39]

Austen H. Layard, M.P., was also present at the R.I.B.A. opening night, and he too spoke of the great opportunity that the new Embankment provided for siting public buildings.[40] His endorsement was most significant, for five weeks later he was named to serve as Gladstone's first commissioner of works. Allied with Robert Lowe, the new chancellor of the Exchequer, Layard would see that a reconsideration of the site for the law courts was made a part of official policy.

Layard (1817–94) and Lowe (1811–92) were the reflections of the opposite sides of Gladstone's character, and they represented the divergent artistic and economic motives with which the new administration took up the banner of the Embankment site. The new first commissioner was an acknowledged connoisseur of art and an archeologist of international reputation (Fig. 79).[41] Raised in Florence, where his parents rented a floor of Alberti's Palazzo Rucellai, Layard had set off in 1839 to practice law in Ceylon. En route, he was seduced by the romantic ruins of Assyria, and he never reached his destination. He spent much of the forties in the Near East, excavating what he followed Sir Henry Rawlinson in believing to be Nineveh, but was actually Nimrud.[42] A vast quantity of the excavated material was sent back to the British Museum, and when Layard himself returned he was appointed to a secretaryship in the Foreign Office. Shortly thereafter he was elected to Parliament as a radical Liberal. An active consultant to the national art collections, he frequently published essays on art and foreign affairs. Layard had the best credentials as an art critic of any Victorian first commissioner, and his appointment was a symbol of the idealism and the sensitivity to artistic matters with which Gladstone began his first administration. Layard, for his own part, assumed that his chief responsibility was the creation of a worthy capital city for Victoria's empire. He aspired to be the Georges-Eugène Haussmann of London.

In contrast, Gladstone selected Robert Lowe to represent the harsher, economical side which he had displayed during his own chancellorships.[43] Indeed, Gladstone said that he had chosen Lowe on the basis of an essay in which Lowe had defined the duty of the chancellor as the defense of "the pockets of the people against the attacks of their representatives."[44] This congenial economic philosophy outweighed the aversion that the prime minister probably felt for some of the other views of his new appointee, for Lowe had been a leader of the Cave of Adullam in 1866 and had contributed to the defeat of the Russell–Gladstone Government over the Representation of the People Bill. His fear that democracy must inevitably turn to mob rule was born of his long experience with politics in Australia, where doctors had exiled him as a young man on the erroneous assumption that the southern climate would decrease the discomfort of his albinism. A brilliant economist—nearly the equal of Gladstone—Lowe prepared a first budget in April 1869 that astounded Parliament by closing a projected deficit with the simple but previously untried expedient of collecting annual taxes three months in advance. But he was also a man of difficult disposition, and this combined with his strong financial opinions to steer him to the center of many controversies, including that of the law courts.

These two officers, with entirely different objectives, joined forces to thwart the execution of Street's great plan and to block the intentions of the Royal Commission. Lowe, like his Tory predecessors, dreaded the proposal to double the authorized expenditure. Layard took advantage of his colleague's economizing by suggesting that a fresh design be prepared for the law courts. The courts were to join the Houses of Parliament and an enfilade of new public buildings erected along the north bank of the Thames. At the same time, he instructed Waterhouse to redesign the Natural History Museum for placement between the Waterloo and Hungerford bridges (Fig. 80).[45] The construction of monumental buildings along the Thames, on the model of the Seine in Paris or, perhaps more significantly, the Tigris in the cities of ancient Assyria, was the cornerstone of Layard's plans for London.

Lowe's and Layard's greatest foe in making any financial or geographic change in the scheme for the law courts was the Royal Commission, which had invested more than three years in preparing the present plan. The new ministers did not announce their intentions to the commissioners themselves, but they quickly tried to win Street's support. Just five days after taking office, on December 14, Layard arranged to meet with the architect. Street already knew Layard's publicly stated position on the Embankment as a site for public buildings in general, but he must have learned at this meeting that the plan included the law courts.[46] Quite naturally, having already designed two buildings for the Carey Street site, he was opposed to the suggested location between the Temple and Somerset House, with a northern boundary on the Strand. In a memorandum on their meeting, Street summarized his objections.[47] First, and probably most important, given the Government's financial motives for undertaking the change, he argued that the relocation would further raise the cost of the project. Pownall had recently calculated that £500,000 would be lost if the Carey Street property were resold. Because the riverside site was covered with better houses and was more steeply inclined, purchase and construction would also be more costly than on the present site. In all, Street estimated that a further expenditure of £1 or £1.25 million would be required, and there were other, nonfinancial reasons for supporting Carey Street as well. The northern site could be easily expanded if need later arose, because it was surrounded by a poor district, while the southern site would be fixed for all time, locked in between the Temple and Somerset House. Moreover, the Embankment location invited the annoying use of the new building as a public thoroughfare from the river to the Strand, and, because it comprised low-lying land, it would be difficult to arrange the needed pedestrian bridges to connect it with the inns north of the Strand. Even with proper bridges, the Embankment site could not serve the legal profession as conveniently as the present one, which was located directly in the center of the legal quarter. Surprisingly, Street also maintained that the Embankment offered no great artistic advantage. "A fine building may be designed for either site," he wrote. "I think the building itself would not gain very much (if at all) by having a front towards the River."

Unable to persuade Street to change his thinking, Lowe and Layard were compelled to move more directly to stop work on the great plan. On January 4, Layard's private secretary wrote to the architect: "Mr. Layard desires me to send you a line requesting that you will not proceed further with the preparation of your plans

80 *Alfred Waterhouse. Natural History Museum, London. Sketch of Embankment design, 1869. (BAL)*

at present, but will wait till you hear from him again."[48] Street acceded the next day, and his reply shows that he had begun to reconsider his position: "Fortunately for me, if the change of site is decided on my work will not all be thrown away as the details of arrangements of the various Courts and Departments (all of which are pretty nearly decided on) can no doubt be transferred to the other plans which I shall have to make."[49] However, the ministers lacked the authority to stop Street in this way. Layard's staff reviewed the situation and advised him that the Government could not impede the architect, as he explained to Lowe on January 6: "I learn . . . that even the Treasury has no power to control Mr. Street, and that until the Royal Commission has made its Report no department can in any way interfere in the matter of the Law Courts."[50] Accordingly, Layard met with Street that day and withdrew the impotent order.[51]

Their subordination to the commission was an embarrassing nuisance to Lowe and Layard, and the latter was angered when Street went ahead with his full report on the great plan, submitted on January 11. This included, as Layard explained to Lowe, the audacious proposal to "commence proceedings at once, even to laying the first stone, and this without the necessary final approval of the plans having been obtained and without any communication to Parliament, which has been induced to sanction a scheme upon statements and estimates which have proved altogether fallacious."[52] Layard was even more upset when the agenda for the January 15 meeting of the Royal Commission included a report of his private order for Street to stop work on the great plan. He protested this leak to the architect on January 20, but he was mollified when Street explained that Field had published the information without permission.[53] Now, however, the antagonism of the Government toward the Royal Commission was public knowledge.

T HE CONTROVERSY intensified as an open debate started in the press. This was heralded by a letter in the *Law Journal* on New Year's Day which commented favorably on the rumor that a committee would be formed to study the Embankment site for the law courts.[54] This seems to have been the first public indication that the Government was contemplating a change such as the *Times* and the *Law Times* had suggested the previous summer.

The *Times* now led the renewed debate, publishing on January 5 the first of what was to be a long series of pro-Embankment letters from Sir Charles Trevelyan (1807–86), a Liberal reformer who had returned to England a few years earlier after a successful but controversial career in Indian government. Trevelyan became identified with the Embankment cause, and while he may not have begun his efforts in consultation with the Government, by the end of the month he was corresponding with the first commissioner as an established ally.[55]

The first letter dealt quickly with the objections that, six months earlier, the *Times* had predicted would stand in the way of the transfer of the building to the new site.[56] To answer the complaints of barristers from Lincoln's Inn that the Embankment was farther away from their chambers, Trevelyan proposed that their entire inn be moved into Somerset House, adjacent to the new site, thus abandoning the old buildings which he said were due for replacement. To those who argued on the grounds of expense, he replied that the Carey Street site, when expanded as much as the Royal Commission now proposed, would cost the nation £1.5 million, which happened to be just the sum needed to acquire the 9½ acres that lay between the Embankment and the Strand. (The area of the site was later calculated at just under 10½ acres.) To concerns about delay, Trevelyan answered emphatically: "It would be better that we should wait for ten years than that our descendants should reproach us for hundreds of years to come." He went on to contrast the advantages of the Embankment with those of the Carey Street site, citing the better light and air and the triple provisions for transport (the new Embankment road, the new Metropolitan Railway, and the popular river steamers) afforded by the former. But for Trevelyan, the argument hinged on the artistic potential of the proposal, and he asserted: "Without exaggeration, the Thames Embankment is the finest site in Europe—perhaps, all the circumstances considered, in the world."

The *Times*, where Lowe had served as an editorial writer until the press of other work forced his resignation just eight months before, promptly resumed its editorial support of the Embankment. In a leading article one day after Trevelyan's letter appeared, it endorsed his plan as one that would make the law courts "do the greatest possible credit to the nation."[57] Trevelyan continued to provide the editors with fresh arguments, contributing five more letters to the paper over the next two months.[58]

Trevelyan's letters were answered, of course, by a variety of opponents to the Embankment site. In addition to arguing again the points addressed by Trevelyan in his first letter, these laid particular stress on the fear that the riverfront location was either too small or that it denied the possibility for future expansion. A succession of writers measured and remeasured the available land.[59] Street himself wrote to the *Times* in late January to defend his plans for Carey Street, and in early February, Trevelyan arranged to have all of the correspondence to date published as a pamphlet, with two maps illustrating his proposal.[60]

The other journals began to take sides. The leading general periodicals with strong artistic interests, the *Saturday Review* and the *Athenaeum*, split on the issue. The latter, which had doubted the practicality of Baillie Cochrane's proposal in 1868, now predicted victory for those who sought to move the building to "the noblest site in the world."[61] But the *Saturday Review* rejected the proposed change on both aesthetic and practical grounds, allowing, however, that it would like to see a broad esplanade between the Carey Street site and the river.[62]

The legal journals generally opposed any displacement of the building from the very center of the Inns of Court, a most important consideration for many lawyers. Only the relatively unimportant *Law Journal* warmed from neutrality to faithful support of the Embankment.[63] The *Solicitors' Journal* was a dogged opponent of any change of site, and the *Law Times*, which had endorsed Baillie Cochrane's proposal in 1868, now admitted: "We have not been sufficiently prosaic," and shifted its support back to Carey Street.[64]

The architectural magazines were divided on the question. The *Builder* supported William Tite's proposed division of the building between two sites at first, but its enthusiasm waned as the debate progressed, and the *Building News* was skeptical about the Embankment from the outset.[65] Fearing that Trevelyan's grandiose project would get out of hand and that a loss would be sustained in reselling the Carey Street property, the latter journal warned ominously: "It would be well for correspondents and architects to bear in mind that we are year after year closer and closer to grave economical questions, which will test to the utmost the abilities of our statesmen. With all our boasted wealth and material progress, pauperism increases more rapidly in proportion than our population."[66] The editors trusted that Gladstone's "strong Government pledged to economy" would not succumb to what might have tempted Disraeli. Only the *Architect,* perhaps seeking to make a name for itself in its first year of publication, consistently spoke in favor of the riverside site.[67] Its weak voice was not very influential, however. In general, the architectural press was forced to play a secondary role as the site question was settled in the arena of national opinion.

The dividing lines of the debate were drawn most clearly in the March discussions conducted by a special committee of the Society of Arts. The committee, formed at the request of Henry Cole, secretary of the department of practical art at South Kensington, included Trevelyan, Field, and Street, whose testimony dominated the hearings. Lord Elcho (Francis Wemyss-Charteris-Douglas) was the chairman. They met for three days in March, and on April 8 voted to publish their minutes; but they issued no formal recommendation, probably because no agreement could be reached.[68]

The first clear division among the participants in the discussion, and the most important one, lay between the supporters of the Royal Commission and those of the Government. The proceedings began with Trevelyan's lengthy presentation of the scheme that he had outlined in the *Times.* Although this was no longer exactly the Government's plan, his testimony was generally accepted as a statement of administration policy. In his almost equally lengthy response, Field, the secretary of the Royal Commission, defended the great plan. So the battle was joined. Notably, both Trevelyan and Field were Liberals, underscoring the fact that the law courts debate was rarely argued along strict party lines.

Secondly, the two camps were clearly defined according to membership in the

Inns of Court. Benchers of Lincoln's Inn by and large favored the closer Carey Street site, christened by Field "the very Acropolis of the law" on account of its centrality, while the Templars supported a move to the river.[69] These prejudices were not shaped merely by the issue of convenient location, however, for the members of the inns held substantial financial interests in their inns and in surrounding real estate. As Trevelyan wrote to Layard on February 5: "The two Treasurers of the Inner and Middle Temple are warm in the cause [of the Embankment site]—*and well they may be,* for it will increase the value of the Temple estate by 2 or 3 hundred thousand pounds."[70] In supporting Carey Street, Lincoln's Inn was joined by the Law Society, the organization of solicitors whose members generally maintained chambers in the northern precincts of the legal district and whose clubhouse was adjacent to the original site. This self-interested involvement of the inns and the Law Society in the debate enraged the pro-Embankment *Architect,* which characterized the argument as a match of "Lincoln's Inn against all England."[71]

A third division was evident between equity and common law barristers. The former were in the main members of Lincoln's Inn, while the latter traditionally massed in the Temples, with a natural inclination for Carey Street and the Embankment, respectively.

Finally, a bitter split existed between artists and utilitarians—between those who valued the artistic potential of the Embankment and those who were convinced that the law courts must be placed in the most efficient, central location if the thirty-year campaign for their construction was to be successfully concluded. Field thus scorned the adherents of the riverfront site as "dilettanti" and preached that "the highest art was the highest utility nobly clothed."[72]

Street's contribution to the discussion at the Society of Arts unexpectedly showed him to be on the side of the utilitarians. He was still an ally of Field and the Royal Commission. Although he now admitted that "he did not know whether, if both sites had been open to him, he should not, on architectural grounds, have selected the Embankment," the matter had been decided for him when it was determined that the Carey Street site was "the most convenient."[73] And he gave a long and glowing account of the artistic capabilities that the northern site did possess. Street showed the committee his perspective sketch of the great plan seen from Waterloo Bridge, and he explained:

> I cannot help but think that the Carey-street site has been most unnecessarily disparaged. It appears to me to have some very great advantages, which may be allowed without the slightest disparagement of the Embankment site. The ground on which it stands is so well raised above the river, that any large and lofty building erected on it ought to add enormously to the architectural effect of London in all distant views, and even in all views from the bridges. . . . If my plan is carried out in its integrity, the upper part of the great central hall would be well seen as is the upper part of the western front of St. Paul's, and it would be seen not only from the south, but generally also from the north.[74]

Outside the meetings of the Society of Arts, the divisions of the debate were also becoming increasingly evident. The Law Society emerged as the most forceful agent on behalf of the Carey Street site, launching its campaign with a pamphlet in early February which lashed out at those "persons who have no connection with the administration of the law in this country, and are not conversant with its requirements." Locating the building on the Embankment would cause "miles and miles of wasteful traversing" by lawyers and "weeks and months of delay." Moreover, half a million pounds would be lost if the Carey Street site were resold, while it might be successfully utilized for the courts, even without the purchase of the additional land requested by the Royal Commission.[75] The society also sent a deputation to discuss the matter with Robert Lowe on March 1, and it circulated a petition against the change in site among lawyers generally.[76]

Perhaps prompted by the action of the Law Society, the Articled Clerks' Society passed its own resolution against the Embankment site on February 17, calling the change "both unnecessary and undesirable."[77] And the Metropolitan and Provincial Law Association quoted the Law Society in the printed letter, dated March 17, which it circulated. Provocatively entitled *The So-called "Embellishment" of London at the Expense of the Suitors,* it asked rhetorically: "Will a building on an unfit and inconvenient site be more decorative to the Metropolis than one on a site eminently fit and convenient?"[78]

Against this opposition Lowe and Layard sought to rally their own forces. Before February, no evidence exists that they had begun to formulate their own specific plan for the use of the Embankment site, preferring to give quasi-official support to Trevelyan and his proposal. But on February 19, 1869, William H. Gregory (1817–92), the Liberal M.P. for Galway and a close friend of Layard, announced that he would introduce a motion for the new site on March 3. Gregory apparently warned the Government, which began to draft the needed legislation. The intended bill was based on a scheme whose details differed from those of Trevelyan's plan, and to give them time to complete this new proposal, Layard prevailed on Gregory to postpone his motion until April 20.[79]

The Government was constrained to be thrifty as well as artistic, and its studies were based on a smaller parcel of just 7½ acres, rather than the 10½ acres staked out for the new building by Trevelyan. F. W. Shields, an expert on ironwork whom Lowe had once supported in a claim against the government, was asked by the chancellor to prepare a comparative study of this new proposal and Carey Street.[80] On February 17, just two days after he was appointed, Shields submitted a contradictory and confusing report which cast some doubt on the affordability of the Embankment site and moved the government yet further from Trevelyan's proposal.

Shields concluded that on economic grounds the courts should remain north of the Strand, although he conceded that the artistic "superiority of the river frontage is obvious" and that the Embankment site also had "great advantage" with respect to accessibility.[81] He quoted calculations showing that £400,000 would be lost in the resale of the Carey Street site, and that the 7½ acres on the Embankment (equal in size to the acquired site) would cost an additional £1,125,000. Since about £800,000 had already been spent on Carey Street, the substitution of the same amount of land on the river would be £725,000 more expensive.[82]

On the other hand, Shields also emphasized that the approach roads to the Carey Street site would have to be improved. He appended a detailed proposal for this to his report, including plans for the construction of a combined roadway and underground railroad from the West End. Even according to his own optimistic figures, this project would cost an additional £1,200,000, surely enough to offset his argument that Carey Street was inherently cheaper.[83]

Distressed by Shields's high estimates and perhaps baffled by his ambiguous recommendation, Layard asked for a second estimate from Henry A. Hunt, the surveyor of the Office of Works. In the hope of reducing the cost of the Embankment site to a reasonable level, he asked Hunt to survey an even smaller property lying between the Temple and Somerset House but extending no further north than Howard Street (see Fig. 82). On February 24, he reported that the 6½ acres could be acquired for just £600,000—a much more encouraging estimate for the ministerial planners.[84] Layard later told Parliament that it had been his own idea to reduce the site in this way.[85]

This proposal became the basis of the Government's legislation, and the organization of its support now also began. In this Trevelyan collaborated, lining up endorsements from the Inner and Middle Temples and overseeing the distribution of a large pro-Embankment petition which was presented to Parliament.[86] The support of judges was also solicited, and on April 19, Sir Fitzroy Kelly, the lord chief baron of the court of Exchequer, reported to Layard the good news that "I and all of the Judges with whom I have been able to communicate (with a single exception, and that of one who only thinks that the proximity of Lincoln's Inn is essential) are as I am strongly and decidedly of the opinion that upon every ground as regards the Bench, the Bar, the Solicitors, the Suitors and the Public, the Thames Embankment should be preferred."[87]

The Howard Street Site

IN EARLY March, Gladstone himself studied the site question, and on March 9, he prepared a memo setting forth his administration's nearly incompatible twin goals for the law courts: metropolitan beautification and concomitant economy.[88] On the first score, he agreed that the Embankment had "some great advantages not possessed by the site already obtained." With respect to economy, he was willing to approve the new reduced version of the riverside site, even though he believed that the absolutely cheapest solution would be to build a simple building on the acquired site. Gladstone argued that "some vigorous effort is needed to arrest the plan of the Commission as it stands, and give a new direction to the general scheme," and he saw the Embankment plan as such a therapeutic shock. He allowed Lowe and Layard to proceed.

With their plan for a smaller Embankment site in hand, the two ministers awaited Gregory's motion on April 20, knowing that the Government's revised position would entirely change the thrust of the debate. Gregory himself does not seem to have been advised of the new official plan, and he opened the discussion with what was by now a routine explication of the Trevelyan proposal for a site stretching from the Thames up to the Strand. In its support he presented a petition with 7460 signatures, and he concluded by moving: "That, in the opinion of this House, it is desirable to reconsider the question of Carey Street as the site of the New Law Courts, inasmuch as the Thames Embankment, between the Temple and Somerset House, now offers many advantages for the erection of such buildings."[89]

Roundell Palmer rose to reply. As attorney general he had shared the responsibility for the legislation of 1865, and he had served as a member of the Royal Commission as well as a competition judge. He was now understandably distressed to see so much of the planning in which he had participated placed at risk. Although a Liberal, he became the leader in Parliament of opposition to the Liberal Government's plan to change sites, just as Field had done at the Society of Arts. Palmer scathingly contrasted the *"dilettanti* gentlemen" who preferred the Embankment with "the practical and prosaic solicitors, whose main business it was to deal with the administration of the law, and who know what its wants were."[90] He also spoke apprehensively of what he called "this demon of good taste" which threatened the most sensible and efficient siting of the courts.[91] Two other commission members, William Cowper, a Liberal, and Lord John Manners, a Conservative, also defended the Carey Street site. Their work seemed to be on trial.

Robert Lowe did not begin to speak until late in the evening, but what he said entirely reshaped the discussion. He began by explaining that his chief concern was for the British taxpayer and how, from the day he had entered office, he had been troubled by the financial features of the great plan. Lowe then enumerated the various additional land purchases required by the Carey Street site and the cost of the enormous building proposed by the Royal Commission. He ended with the frightening prediction that the total expense would approach £4 million.[92] This he attributed to the excessive zeal of the commission in seeking to bring so much more together under one roof than the enabling legislation had specified. "Why, we have been seized with what I may call a frenzy of concentration. . . . We have set ourselves to build a sort of Tower of Babel," he said.[93] But if a Babel was contemplated for Carey Street, he went on, the Trevelyan plan for the Embankment was no more fiscally responsible. Lowe calculated that the site alone would cost £2 million, and he strongly advised against "such an extravagance as that."[94]

His audience must by now have been feverish with anticipation, remembering his budget speech of less than two weeks earlier in which he had concluded a long and gloomy financial survey with a piece of legerdemain that turned a potential deficit into a surplus. They were not disappointed, for having demolished the rival schemes for the law courts, Lowe now advanced the new Government proposal, the details of which had been sketched out at the Office of Works during the preceding month. "There is a street called Howard Street," he began, and so his plan came to be named after that northern border of the intended site.[95] He cited Hunt's estimate that this smaller property would cost £600,000, and, allowing £1 million more for a reduced building, Lowe reported that the new plan could be executed for only slightly more than the £1.5 million that was originally authorized.[96] The project would be guaranteed against another escalation of costs, because Lowe intended to abolish the Royal Commission and bring the law courts under the direct control of the Office of Works and the Treasury.[97]

At this point, Parliament adjourned the debate to allow the thorough consideration of the new particulars. The *Times* aptly summarized the chancellor's astonishing reformulation of the issue in a leading article: "The lawyers wanted a convenient monster, the artists a picturesque monster, but Mr. Lowe stoutly maintained that monstrosity was out of place altogether."[98] As a prominent proponent of the larger Embankment site, the *Times* had editorialized in support of Gregory's motion, but in the wake of Lowe's speech, the editors began to accept the idea that the cost should be "less absolutely outrageous."[99] Trevelyan himself endorsed the reduced site.

Street's Plans of 1869

GEORGE EDMUND STREET was now asked to provide the architectural component of the Government's plan. In his last words to the House of Commons on April 20, Robert Lowe had accepted "the duty of making, with as little delay as possible, some definite proposal upon this subject."[100] Very shortly thereafter, Layard sidestepped the Royal Commission and contacted Street directly.[101] He was able to convince him to prepare a design for the Howard Street site, even though Street had expressed no change of heart on the site issue as recently as April 8.[102] To protect a possible route for strategic retreat, on May 13 Street was also ordered to draft plans for a building which could be accommodated on the unenlarged Carey Street site.[103] Within a week of the first request, Street had ready for the Embankment "a rough plan showing the sort of arrangement which I propose to work out."[104] The plan for Carey Street took no longer, and on May 24 he submitted an illustrated report on the two, his third and fourth designs for the law courts.[105] His latest work demonstrated that while the question of site had become more uncertain, Street's attitude toward the visual and practical requirements of the commission had become increasingly sure.

More and more confident of his own conclusions, Street must have been alarmed by some of the first indications of what his official patrons would demand. Robert Lowe, once a supporter of E. M. Barry's claims, had already proposed to Layard that the Embankment site would require a classical building, in harmony with Somerset House, rather than Street's "Gothic Temple."[106] He had made his views known in the Commons, where he had advanced the more specific suggestion that the unexecuted design made by Inigo Jones for the Palace of Whitehall might be adapted for the courts.[107] The *Building News* justifiably labeled this proposal "too crude and spasmodic to be reduced to practice."[108] Also of concern to Street was Layard's appointment of James Fergusson as secretary of works and buildings. Layard and Fergusson had long shared an interest in eastern archeology, and they had conferred when Fergusson was writing his *Palaces of Nineveh and Persepolis Restored* (1851). But although Fergusson was learned, he was also a keen foe of the Gothic Revival, as shown in his critique of the competition designs in the *Builder*. Layard himself, at the meeting of the R.I.B.A. when he had praised the Embankment site, had also lashed out at all types of historicism, both medieval and classical, and called for the development of a "true English style."[109]

Fortunately, none of these ill omens was realized. Layard stood up to Lowe from the start, telling Parliament in the aftermath of the chancellor's speech that "it would be unfair to Mr. Street, who was essentially a Gothic architect, to impose upon him a style of architecture which he had not made the subject of special study."[110] And Fergusson's employment at the Office of Works was chiefly in the capacity of financial watchdog.[111] When Layard contacted Street to ask him to prepare a design for the Howard Street site, he made no stylistic stipulation.

The aesthetic potentials of the two sites were very different, but Street created picturesque compositions for both. He had learned an enduring lesson from the competition, to which he adhered despite the fact that his recent picturesque work had attracted criticism. E. W. Pugin and the *Builder* had already attacked the competition design for being too irregular. Likewise, the great plan, while praised by the *Building News* for its "varied and picturesque treatment," had also earned a warning from that journal. The editors advised Street "not [to] luxuriate too much in the irregularities which, to a great extent, are forced upon him."[112] However, he recognized that Waterhouse and Burges had been able to please the critics of the competition with even less regular compositions, and he evidently concluded that a picturesque design could escape rebuke if it was sufficiently dramatic and compelling.

For the Embankment location, Street displayed particular confidence in this line of reasoning (Figs. 81–83). Rather than exploit the unobstructed sightlines that stretched across the river and contrive a symmetrical façade as William Chambers had done at Somerset House, he wrung the utmost from the irregularities of the site. His perspective gave a clear indication of his new artistic intention for the law courts, inspired at least in part by the success of Waterhouse's great perspective of the building as seen across the Thames from the same vantage (see Fig. 35).[113] Also influential was the irregular silhouette of the Houses of Parliament only a short distance upstream from the intended site. Street may have had in mind as well the reconstruction of Assurnasupal's palace on the banks of the Tigris at Nimrud, drawn by James Fergusson for Layard (Fig. 84).[114]

Street's concept of the appropriate architecture for the Embankment site had already been formed at the time of his testimony before the Society of Arts. Then, although preferring Carey Street, he had argued that a large building on the river would be "very tame and monotonous" if it were composed as "a continuous line . . . with no break." In Street's view, the only acceptable type of design would have to be very different: "It ought to have some grand recesses, shewing something of the internal quadrangles of the building from the river, and so giving some opportunity of obtaining striking light and shade, and good architectural effect."[115]

His submitted Embankment design realized this objective, with its telling juxtaposition of the major mass of building to the west and a smaller but tower-topped office block to the east. Ventilation towers, derived from the rear towers in the competition design, pushed up at the ends of the hall, and the rooflines of the encircling offices were repeatedly broken, as Street had said he had intended in the description of that earlier project. Because of the elimination of the probate department, the principal tower was no longer used as a record depository, but it was brought up to the façade of the building to play a more active role in the composition. As he had proposed at the Society of Arts, he offered an oblique glance into the courtyard of the building through a semicircular colonnade. Its Italian character was perhaps related to the taste for Venetian Gothic that Layard had professed in the House of Commons on May 10.[116] Much of the rest of the exterior was richly embroidered with Decorated ornament.

The whole of the building was united, not by the imposed regularity of the competition design, but by the organic cohesion of many small parts, clustered beneath the dominating roof of the central hall. As Street said of his perspective sketch:

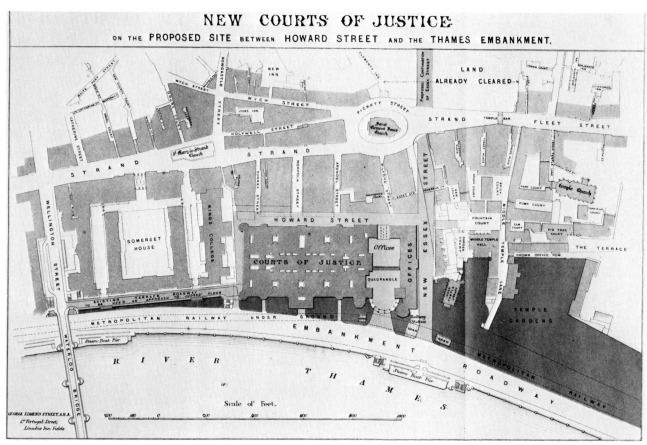

NEW COURTS OF JUSTICE
ON THE PROPOSED SITE BETWEEN HOWARD STREET AND THE THAMES EMBANKMENT.

Scale of Feet.

GEORGE EDMUND STREET, A.R.A.
8, Portugal Street,
Lincoln's Inn Fields.

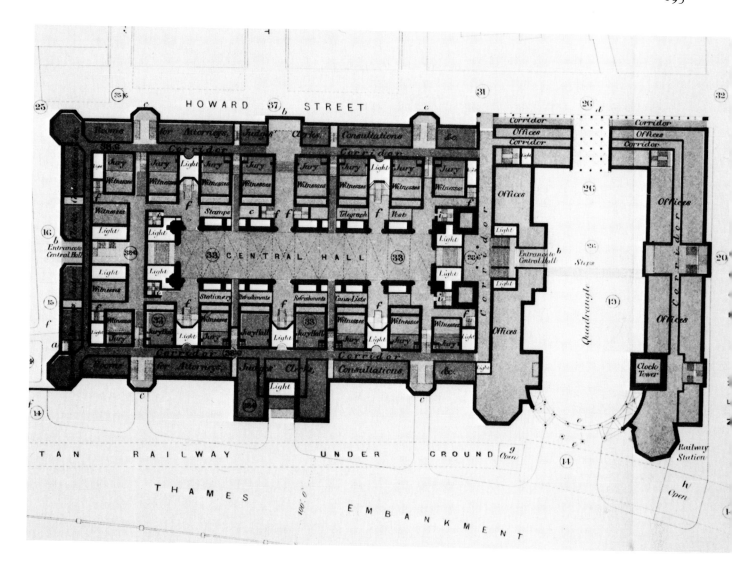

81 Embankment design. April–
May 1869. Perspective by
Street, May 1869. (Building
News, 28 April 1871.)

82 Embankment design. April–
May 1869. Site plan, May
1869. (BPP, Volume 47 in
1868–1869.)

83 Embankment design. April–
May 1869. Plan at courtroom
level, May 1869. (BPP, Volume 47 in 1868–1869.)

84 James Fergusson. Palace of
Assurnasupal, Nimrud. Recon-
struction prepared for A. H.
Layard, 1853. (Layard. The
Monuments of Nineveh, 2s,
London: John Murray, 1853.)

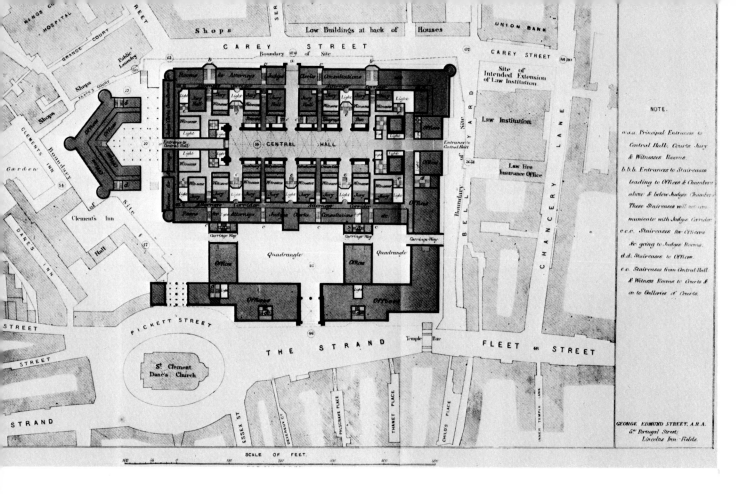

The following labels appear within the plan:

KINGS CO HOSPITAL · GRANGE COURT · FEET · SER · UNION BANK

Shops · Low Buildings at back of · Houses

CAREY STREET

Public Laundry · Boundary of Site · CAREY STREET

TEATE'S COURT · Shops · Offices · Rooms for Attorneys · Judges · Clerks · Consultations · Site of Intended Extension of Law Institution

Garden · Shops · Light · Witness · Light · Light · Witness · Light · Law Institution

CLEMENTS INN · Boundary · Site · CENTRAL HALL · Entrance to Central Hall · Entrance to Central Hall · Law Fire Insurance Office

Clement's Inn · Light · Witness · Office

DANES INN · Hall · Corridor · Witness · Jury · Light · Light · Witness · Corridor · Attorneys · Judges · Clerks · Consultations · Office · BELL YARD · Boundary of Site · CHANCERY LANE

Carriage Way · Carriage Way · Carriage Way · Carriage Way

Quadrangle · Offices · Offices · Quadrangle

Offices · Offices · Offices

PICKETT STREET · THE STRAND · Temple Bar · FLEET STREET

STREET · St Clement Dane's Church · STRAND

STREET · ESSEX ST · DEVERAUX CT · PILSGRAVE PLACE · THANET PLACE · CHILD'S PLACE · INNER TEMPLE LANE

STRAND

SCALE OF FEET.

NOTE.

a.a.a. Principal Entrance to Central Hall, Courts Jury & Witnesses Rooms.

b.b.b. Entrances to Staircases leading to Offices & Chambers above & below Judges Chambers. These Staircases will not communicate with Judges Corridor.

c.c.c. Staircases for Officers &c going to Judges Rooms.

d.d. Staircases to Offices.

e.e. Staircases from Central Hall & Witness Rooms to Courts & on to Galleries of Courts.

GEORGE EDMUND STREET, A.R.A.
5th Portugal Street,
Lincoln's Inn Fields.

85 Reduced Carey Street design. May 1869. Plan at Strand level, May 1869. (BPP, Volume 47 in 1868–1869.)

From Waterloo Bridge . . . I find the view will be most admirable, because not only will the whole front be seen, but owing to the height of the bridge above the Embankment, the central hall rising above and behind will also be well seen, and will have the most important effect in binding together and combining the general features of the composition. Again, any one who goes to Hungerford or Westminster Bridges, and notices the gap between Somerset House and the Temple, will see at once how much such a space will be beautified by the occurrence of a succession of bold vertical lines, forming a varied skyline, an effect which I think the disposition of my plan will give very completely.[117]

Street now made no mention of the judicious High Victorian mixture of verticality and horizontality and of irregularity and repose.

To a lesser extent, the same characteristics can be identified in the alternative plan for the Carey Street site, even in the absence of elevation studies (Figs. 85, 86). Although the Strand façade of this hastily prepared scheme, with its central clock tower, is rather dully symmetrical, a few more interesting and piquant aspects of the work can be noted. These include an asymmetrical recession of the façade above Pickett Street and, most striking of all, a bastionlike western office annex with few outward-facing windows. Street called the latter "an ingenious termination of my building."[118] Like the round towers indicated at three corners of the main block, it was perhaps a recollection of the quasi-martial features of Burges's heavily massed competition entry.

The planning devised for these two projects was based on a reduced program

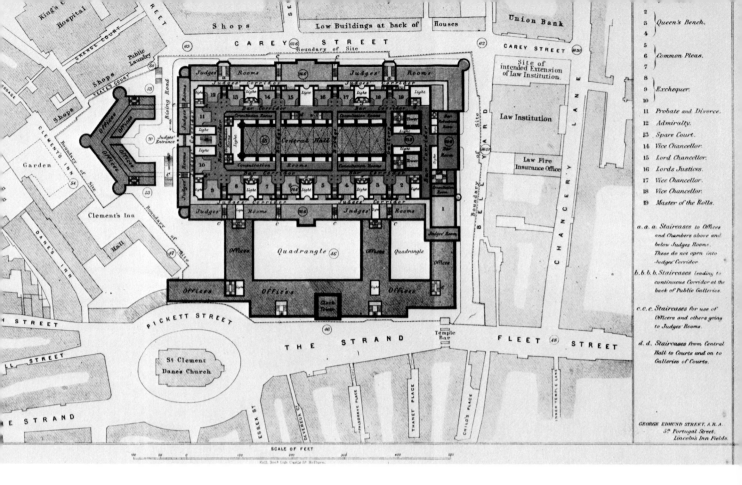

86 *Reduced Carey Street design. May 1869. Plan at courtroom level, May 1869. (BPP, Volume 47 in 1868–1869.)*

for the building which Lowe's economizing had mandated. Only eighteen courts were provided and numerous departments were altogether eliminated. The largest of these was the probate department, with its requirements for a record tower, and also canceled were plans for the divorce department, the Appellate Court, the bankruptcy department, the Admiralty offices, the land registry, and the Middlesex registry.

Although the two sites differed in shape, Street was asked to make the same planning provisions in both designs, so that they might be compared impartially. To this end, he fitted nearly identical central blocks into both, with courtrooms coherently arrayed around a central hall, as in the great plan. Again, the lessons of the competition were borne in mind, and Street was directed to attend first to the exigencies of organization. However, the smaller sites required the elimination of the multitude of separate public stairs leading to the courts that had been possible in the great plan, as well as other concessions.

The architect faced his greatest challenge in providing the necessary office accommodations, and the differences in the two sites resulted in different solutions for each. Neither plan adopted the paradigmatic concentric outer ring of offices used in both Street's competition design and the great plan. For the Howard Street site, which was shallow but relatively wide, Street concentrated most of the necessary offices around a single eastern quadrangle (see Fig. 83). Additional office space was provided in the main block on upper floors, reached by special stairs that connected neither to the courtrooms nor their immediate adjuncts. At the irregular Carey Street site, with its maximum width located near the northern boundary, the main block was placed quite far from the Strand (see Fig. 86). The southern portion of the site was devoted to a large wing of offices that could screen the courts from street noises. Further accommodation was provided by the bastion-shaped block placed in the awkward triangle of land on the west side of the site, north of Clement's Inn.

Both plans provided for a roadway to bring judges to the building at the level of their offices. On the Embankment, Street used the existing terrace of Somerset House for this purpose, while at Carey Street he designed an elevated carriageway at the northeast. Waterhouse had included a similar feature in his competition entry.

Having designed buildings for both sites, Street now revised his assessment of their relative merits. By early May, Layard could report to the House of Commons that "he had gone fully into the whole plan with Mr. Street, who had met him most honourably, and though at first in favour of the Carey Street site, and anxious to carry out that plan, now approved of the new proposal."[119] Street's dramatic change of opinion occurred because it became apparent that the Liberals would not pay for the great plan and a concomitant enlargement of the original site. He explained his reasoning in the official report:

> In previous expressions of my opinion on this subject, I have spoken strongly of the effect of a great building crowning this eminence [north of the Strand]. I had in my mind when I did so the vast extent of my plan as approved by the Courts of Justice Commission, including not only the central hall and Courts, but the great Probate Department, with its towers for the reception of wills, which, grouping with the other towers and lofty roofs of the building, would have given scope for great architectural effect. The reduction of the scale of the building, the omission of the towers for wills, and the apparent certainty that the surrounding buildings will all be mean and unworthy of their position, if no more land is purchased, seem to me to make a vast difference in the view I am compelled to take, and deprive this site of the claims I considered it had to be very nearly on a par with the other, in regard to the opportunities it afforded for erecting a building which should be a great architectural success and an ornament to the Capital.[120]

In addition to these artistic considerations, Street emphasized the other advantages of the Embankment site, concluding that it possessed better approaches, more light and air and quiet, and was better suited to efficient planning. There were financial advantages as well, he calculated, and this must have delighted Gladstone and Lowe. Either building, Street reported, could be built for £900,000—rather less than Hunt had estimated. Although foundations on the steeper riverside site would be more costly, compensating savings could be made by transporting the materials by water.[121] And while the buildings themselves were of equal cost, the Embankment location was cheaper. Even with the reduced program, Street would permit "very little" reduction in the purchase of land for access roads and ventilation that he and the Royal Commission had recommended for Carey Street. But Howard Street might be used just as the Government proposed, without any enlargement. He assumed, however, that Essex Street would be improved by private investment to provide a thoroughfare leading to the northern inns, perhaps lined by covered walkways like the "rows" of Chester.[122]

Street was enthusiastic about these new opportunities. On May 19 he explained to Layard: "I am really delighted with the way in which my plan [for the Embankment] is working out." However, he recognized that the question of site was still unresolved, for he added, "[I] hope that it may live through the threatened opposition."[123] As it happened, that opposition gained new strength just as Street defected to the Embankment and the side of the Government, abandoning Carey Street and the Royal Commission.

Defeat

PROSPECTS for the Embankment proposal darkened as soon as the Howard Street site was thoroughly explained. Led by the *Times*, many who had supported Trevelyan's plan withdrew their endorsements following Layard's introduction of the authorizing legislation on May 10. Although the *Times* had been impressed by Lowe's economic argument, it finally concluded: "If . . . the New Law Courts need not be on the extensive scale suggested by the Commission, the Thames Embankment site . . . loses its principal charm for us."[124] The *Builder*, a supporter of Tite's version of the Embankment scheme, was similarly disenchanted. Even artistically, the smaller Howard Street site was not favored, since a building there would have no important northern façade and would lie "buried behind the houses on the south side of the Strand."[125] In response to these criticisms, the Government had asked Street to sketch a reduced plan for Carey Street in addition to his Embankment design.

Layard recognized that the strategic situation was difficult, but he was exhilarated by the challenge of the Parliamentary contest. On May 13, he wrote to his friend Gregory:

> We shall have a heavy fight with the Embankment site, but I think that we shall carry it. Elcho [chairman of the Society of Arts committee] has been this morning with Dizzy [Disraeli], and has shown him all the plans. He expressed himself on the whole favourably. A good number of men of the Conservative side will go with us. The chief opposition, curiously enough, comes from our own side, from below the gangway. It is most important to get the Irish right. Palmer was furious, stamped on the ground and clenched his fist, to the amusement of the House. The attorneys of the Law Institution will move heaven and earth against us, so we must be prepared. Unfortunately they have great influence in the Press.[126]

This was a realistic analysis of the line of battle, cutting across party loyalties, and of the powerful position held by the Law Society.

The Law Society now led the fight for Carey Street, lobbying strenuously in anticipation of a great debate when Layard's bill was presented for second reading. Lithographed letters from the president were circulated on May 12 and May 26, and, more insidiously, lithographed form letters were provided in large numbers to solicitors, who could address them to M.P.'s and sign them to give the appearance of a multitude of personal appeals.[127] A deputation of the society joined Roundell Palmer in meeting with Lowe and Layard on May 27, and their influence can probably also be detected in the actions of some of the provincial law associations.[128]

The boldest efforts of the Law Society were made in a quasi-alliance with the Royal Commission, the other leading foe of the Embankment. In May, the commissioners asked William Burnet, the commission clerk, and George Pownall, a professional assessor and competition judge, to prepare documents in support of the Carey Street site. Before the end of the month Burnet produced a map that purported to show the two locations, and Pownall submitted an estimate for the purchase of the Howard Street site and for the resale value of Carey Street.[129] Both men aimed to damage the Embankment cause. Burnet contended that the law courts could be accommodated with ease on the acquired site, thus avoiding any risk of resale loss. And Pownall argued that the Howard Street site could be used only if Essex Street were also purchased, thereby requiring an expenditure of £812,415 instead of the £600,000 estimated by Henry Hunt. Pownall also projected that the resale of the land already acquired would net only £364,320.

Even more damaging, but decidedly unscrupulous, was the building plan that Burnet devised to bolster these arguments. This attempted to show that the bulk of the great plan could be wedged onto the acquired site. Burnet ingenuously called this "a mere suggestion which I offered to Mr. Field . . . to help in the work of the Commission," and Field said, "It was . . . done . . . to see how far the Chinese puzzle could be put into the box."[130] But its true intention was to discredit Street and the Government, which maintained that the existing site was too small to contain any but an entirely reorganized version of the building. Burnet tried to prove that the Royal Commission's plan could be salvaged, complete with what Field now called the full "quadrilateral system"—in essence, Webster's concentric circles. He published a table of figures which seemed to show that his plan provided more and better accommodation than either of Street's reduced designs, while requiring the same amount of land. All this was done without consulting the appointed architect, for Burnet complained that "Mr. Street has kept his doors locked since he began to prepare plans for the Howard-street scheme."[131]

The Law Society used this information to rally Parliamentary opposition to the Government proposal, and on June 4, Burnet's and Pownall's figures were laid before the Royal Commission. On the basis of their evidence, Roundell Palmer introduced an anti-Embankment resolution, but others questioned the accuracy of the new evidence, referring it to a special committee for evaluation.[132] Although that committee found numerous errors, the commissioners as a whole felt that the merits of the argument had not been altered. They voted on June 23 to approve Palmer's motion: "That in the judgment of this Commission the substitution of the proposed Howard Street site for the Parliamentary Carey Street site would be an obstacle to the attainment of the advantages contemplated . . . , and in particular that great loss of time and inconvenience would arise to the barristers and others practising in the Courts of Equity by the removal of the Courts in which they practise to so great a distance."[133]

Against this concerted onslaught, backed by a swing in public opinion, the Government marshaled its defenses. Street strove to blunt that part of the offensive launched on the strength of Burnet's site map, which he called "worse than misleading" in his own report on the two sites. As also noted by the committee of the Royal Commission, it effectively increased the apparent area of the Carey Street site while shrinking that of Howard Street. Street later observed to Layard: "Whoever did it must have known what he was doing. It is not the sort of thing that happens accidentally."[134] When Burnet was confronted with his errors at a select committee hearing, he meekly explained that he had "never intended" the map to be metrically accurate.[135]

At Layard's request, Street also prepared a full report on Burnet's attempt to shrink the great plan to a size that would fit onto the acquired site.[136] Street took this opportunity to lash out at the crude attempt which had been made to adapt his own work without consultation.[137] In particular, Street criticized Burnet for reducing the size of all the interior areas, courtyards, and streets of the building, while adding an extra story. He complained, "These two alterations, or either of them, would, in my opinion, damage most seriously the convenience and usefulness of my plan for the building, whilst they would cause its arrangements to be a constant ground of complaint, in first place on the part of all the permanent officers of departments, and in second of those who have from time to time to attend to the offices and the courts." Obviously, Street was also annoyed that a man of Burnet's status should attempt to improve on his work. "I have . . . a greater knowledge than anyone else can possibly have of the space which is really required," he asserted.

At the same time, Henry A. Hunt prepared a new estimate to refute Pownall's figures. He published an up-to-date version of the calculations used by the Government, reaffirming his estimate of £600,000 for the Howard Street site.[138] The expense of erecting the reduced building was now set at £800,000, although the new bill would allow £1 million. Hunt was also sharply critical of Burnet's work, noting that "statements of this sort ought not, I think, to have been laid before the Courts of Justice Commission without previous consultation with Mr. Street."

While these reports were being assembled, the Government was anxiously enlisting supporters. Trevelyan had been completely won over to the smaller, Howard Street plan, writing to Layard on May 20: "Today I have seen Mr. Street's Design for the Embankment site, *and I am delighted with it.*"[139] He campaigned energetically for the bill, paying particular attention to the circulation of petitions and to securing the support of judges.[140] In the latter effort he was most successful, but it was hard to convince judges to make their opinions public.

In response to the Law Society, a group of solicitors who supported the Embankment, drawn chiefly from the City, Westminster, and the West End, was organized. They called on Lowe and Layard on June 18, and they argued that the Carey-ites were "a clique, who were privately and personally interested in the question."[141]

The Office of Works commissioned the South Kensington Museum to build a model of the Embankment site to illustrate the Government plan.[142] Apparently at Gladstone's suggestion, copies of Street's plans were even sent to Queen Victoria at Balmoral, where she viewed them on June 9.[143]

Probably the most curious tangential effect of this renewed site debate was E. M. Barry's attempt to exploit the fresh uncertainty by reopening the entire question of the appointment. In June, he wrote again to the *Times* to ask for the publication of the letters that he and Street had written to Derby in January 1868.[144] These letters were now made public in a blue book.[145]

Despite the best efforts of Lowe, Layard, Street, Hunt, and Trevelyan, the Howard Street proposal had become so controversial that Gladstone decided not to risk the prestige of the Government in its support. Ferocious opposition from within the party, headed by Roundell Palmer, insured the divisiveness of the issue, although an unsuccessful attempt was reportedly made, under the mediation of a Conservative, to heal the rift between Lowe and Palmer.[146] On June 22, rather than bring the beleaguered bill to the Commons for a second reading, Gladstone moved that the matter be committed to a select committee.[147] Pointing to the lateness of the session and to the newness of the Howard Street plan, he argued that the complex issues could not be debated adequately in the busy House of Commons. The motion was agreed to, and a committee under the chairmanship of Lord Stanley was appointed. They reported on July 30.

Trevelyan once again assisted Layard in recruiting the strongest possible witnesses to testify before the committee. For a time, Scott and even Barry were to testify for the Embankment plan.[148] Street and Hunt carried the bulk of the argument, however, largely reiterating the points made in their published reports. Hunt was impressive, with his prediction that Carey Street, with all the necessary additional land, would cost £1 million more than Howard Street. Several lawyers presented statistics proving the Thames-side location to be more convenient for the majority of their profession who did not have chambers in the legal district itself.[149] Field, Palmer (who gave evidence but did not serve on the committee), P. C. Hardwick (the architect of the Law Society), Burnet, and Pownall led the opposition. They made the usual strong case against risking possible loss by the resale of the Carey Street site and in favor of the most central possible location. Palmer argued reassuringly that the Carey Street site was sufficient "strictly as it stands."[150] Moreover, Street's design for the Embankment was humiliatingly criticized by George Pownall, the last witness to be heard. Pownall said that he had conferred with John Shaw, his fellow professional assessor and competition judge, and that the two had agreed that the law courts should not project beyond Somerset House, as Street proposed.[151] Street must have wondered if he would ever escape such harassment.

Street probably expressed some of his anxiety about the select committee hearings to Gladstone at breakfast on July 22.[152] But having called for the appointment of the committee, the prime minister's hands were now tied. On July 30, Lowe presented a draft report in favor of the Howard Street site, but the members declined to consider it by a vote of 8–5. A pro-Carey Street report drafted by Gabriel Goldney, M.P. for Chippenham, was considered instead and adopted, after paragraphs asserting the artistic superiority of the original site were deleted on narrow votes.[153] The approved report concluded: "The Carey-street site, upon the whole, affords the best opportunity of concentrating the courts and offices in the centre of the great legal district." It advised that the property already purchased would provide adequate access "for all ordinary purposes."[154]

This decision effectively ended all hope for the Howard Street site. On August 10, Gladstone replied to a questioner in the Commons that it was too late that year to apply for either a bill to purchase a new site or for money to build on the present one.[155] Little serious consideration was given again to the riverfront location, although Street may have continued to tinker with the Embankment plan until the fall.[156] The defeat was the product of several factors. First, the abandonment of Trevelyan's grandiose but costly scheme lost for the Government the support of those most eager to improve the appearance of the city. As S. B. Robertson, a Temple bencher, wrote to Layard after the select committee vote: "Many . . . would have been prepared to sacrifice some amount of personal convenience to a really Grand National Work, who opposed an incomplete design like the substituted plan, and who objected that after all said in its favour, the principle [north] front of the Building would be hidden from view by a screen of inferior houses."[157] Then too, there was the damaging economic argument against moving the entire project to a different site after four years of work and investment. Finally, there was the issue of centrality within the legal district—a point concerning which the Law Society and Lincoln's Inn, both adept from years of lobbying for the law courts, were willing to offer every possible resistance. As Lowe observed to Layard in the midst of the struggle: "It is very hard to fight with the lawyers."[158]

For Layard, the loss of Howard Street was a personal defeat which he saw as the end of his effective role at the Office of Works. He felt that his idealistic goals of metropolitan beautification could not be achieved within the constraints of Liberal economic policy. Aware of Layard's feelings, Earl Granville, his old colleague at the Foreign Office, advised him nine days after the select committee report that the governorship of the Cape Colony would soon be vacant, should he wish to escape from London.[159] He turned down this kind offer, but when the foreign secretary asked him to be ambassador to Madrid on October 4, Layard accepted.[160] On October 12, he sent his resignation to Gladstone. The letter was full of bitterness and disappointment, directed particularly against the subjugation of his department by the Treasury, despite the fact that he had been on polite, if never intimate terms, with Robert Lowe himself. Layard wrote,

> I am convinced that the relations between the Department of Works and the Treasury have now become such that no man who has a proper sense of self respect and who takes the view that I take of the duties of a First Commissioner can hold the office as it is at present constituted. . . . Now that I find that the office is little better than that of a Clerk in the Treasury, and that I am responsible to Parliament and country without having any independent action of my own, I feel that I cannot hold it any longer.[161]

Layard's complaint lay chiefly with the lesser officials of the Treasury, among whom the most bothersome was the financial secretary, Acton Smee Ayrton, the radical M.P. for the Tower Hamlets.[162] Ironically, Ayrton, who was much admired by Gladstone because of his strict economic views, was also considered a nuisance by Lowe, who often found that his subordinate obstructed the type of direct control he wished to assume over every function of his department.[163] Moreover, Ayrton's populism must have sorely tried the old Adullamite. And so, given Layard's resignation and the desirability of separating Lowe and Ayrton, Gladstone adopted the peculiar stratagem of moving Ayrton into Layard's old place at the Office of Works.

When he learned of the new arrangements, Street wrote to Layard: "I . . . can only hope that I may find some of the pleasure in working with your successor that I had in doing so with you."[164] But there was little chance of this with Acton Ayrton, whose personality was already well known. As Lord Elcho spouted to Layard soon afterward:

> I am *aghast!* at what I have seen in the papers. Can it really be true! You gone from the Board of Works. Ayrton your successor! The only fit man in the Government replaced by the most unfit.[165]

Chapter 5

The Final Plan

"To Agree Would Be to Commit
an Act of Artistic Suicide."
—George Edmund Street, May 1, 1869

IN APPOINTING Acton Smee Ayrton (1816–86) to the Office of Works, Gladstone cured the schizophrenia that had split his Government between the divergent objectives of economy and art (Fig. 87). But for George Edmund Street this remedy was to prove far worse than the previous illness. While Layard's efforts to transfer the law courts to the Embankment had required the preparation of plans that were ultimately rejected, at least Street's art had been allowed to develop in the process. The parsimony of Ayrton was not productive of so much artistic limbering, although it did test Street's new convictions as he readied the final design between 1869 and 1873. Unfortunately, not only did he have to fight against the will of the first commissioner, his plans were now subjected to a great wave of adverse public opinion. The law courts remained a strenuous testing ground for Street as the seventies began and High Victorian Gothic was supplanted by the Queen Anne.

Ayrton and the Office of Works

AYRTON sat in the House of Commons as the radical Liberal representative of the Tower Hamlets, a slum district in East London. Fiscal conservatism was a prerequisite of his radical politics, and so Gladstone considered him an obvious candidate for a Treasury secretaryship under Lowe in 1868. But Ayrton became deeply dissatisfied with his chief's unwillingness to delegate responsibility, and he complained several times to the prime minister about the discomfort of his position. Gladstone alluded to these difficulties on October 13, 1869, when he offered Ayrton the post now vacated by Layard. "A close and cordial union of the principal persons is to be desired . . . in the Treasury," the prime minister suggested, and the present less than cordial situation might be improved if Ayrton were willing to "advance" to the Office of Works. With ominous import for the artists and architects then employed by the government, Gladstone added, "In the details of its expenditure you will I am confident find ample opportunity for rendering valuable service to the state and to the cause of economy, even while paying every regard to the susceptibilities of the London public and local communities."[1] Ayrton accepted on October 15.[2]

Public response to the appointment was extremely unfavorable, generally agreeing with Lord Elcho's judgment that a supremely well-qualified minister was being displaced by one with no apparent aptitude for the job. The contrast between the new and retiring first commissioners was dramatically demonstrated by speeches the two men gave shortly after the transfer of office took place. Before a gathering of his dockyard constituents, Ayrton sneered at "people who had been at public schools and universities" and those who were "fond of what is called art." He complained of the drain on the public purse by those he classified as "painters, sculpturers, architects and market-gardeners."[3] A little later Layard gave a charity fund-raising lecture at the Metropolitan Tabernacle on the subject of Pompeii, attended by many of his Southwark constituents. He replied directly to what he called Ayrton's "false econ-omy," and, with the insight of an archeologist, he reminded his listeners that what was known of ancient civilizations was largely learned from the great public monu-ments that they had erected. Ayrton, he feared, would forfeit the opportunity of rescuing London from the disgrace of being the ugliest capital city in the civilized world.[4] *Punch* offered the best, succinct characterization of the new commissioner:

> A stands for Architect, Artist, and Ass.
> A stands for Ayrton. A stands for Alas!
> He boasts he's no Artist, an Architect not.
> Then Alliteration makes Ayrton out—What?
> An Edile he said he was glad he was none.
> Then why was he raised to the office of one?
> O Gladstone, your reason? Speak, Premier, and say
> An Edile what moved you to make such an A?[5]

87 Acton Smee Ayrton. (Illus-trated London News, 16 May 1857.)

Ayrton soon reshaped the Office of Works to reflect his economical views. Even Fergusson, no friend of contemporary architects, felt uncomfortable under his anti-art regime, and soon resigned. The position invented for him by Layard was abolished, and a director of works was appointed to deal with the architectural work of the department.[6] This post was filled by Douglas Galton (1822–99), a former captain in the Royal Engineers, apparently at the insistence of Gladstone and Lowe.[7] Despite their awkward introduction, Galton and Ayrton were united quickly by similar objectives.

Galton was no artist, but he had had substantial experience in architectural design and construction. Although he had come to the Office of Works after eight years as the assistant undersecretary of state for war responsible for Army finances, in his previous service with the engineers he had built fortifications at Malta and Gibraltar, with adjunct service as the secretary of the railway department of the Board of Trade. In 1859, he had been named assistant inspector of fortifications, with a special charge to improve military hospitals in light of the terrible lessons taught by the Crimean War. Galton's principal architectural work was the enormous, meagerly classical Herbert Hospital at Woolwich, erected in 1859–60—the first large pavilion system hospital in England.[8] He also developed a successful ventilating fireplace and wrote substantially on the design of healthful buildings.[9] Ayrton must have viewed him as a safe architectural adviser—uninterested in costly ornamental features and oblivious to stylistic controversy.

The other architectural adviser in Ayrton's office was a man of longer standing with the department, Henry A. Hunt (1810–89), who had served as the surveyor of works and public buildings since 1856. Although Hunt provided the office with a great reservoir of common sense and experience, he was no artist either, and he had no aversion in principle to the tight economy advocated by the new, politically appointed head of the department. A professional surveyor, Hunt had an unusual civil service position that allowed him to maintain his lucrative partnership in the private surveying firm of Hunt, Stephenson, and Jones.

George Russell, the administrative secretary of works, was also inclined to accept the philosophy of the new regime. He had been advanced from the post of assistant secretary by Layard and was said to be "very highly connected" in social circles.[10] Indeed, Lowe characterized him as almost "too great a swell" for the job.[11]

The first dramatic evidence of the new attitude at the Office of Works was the handling of the design for a new block of offices at the General Post Office. In fact, James Williams, an official of the department, had already prepared a design for the new building on the authority of Layard. But Ayrton claimed the project as his own, determined to publicize as much as possible this decision to function without the services of a private architect. At the cornerstone ceremony on December 16, 1870, he preached on the themes of economy and utility in public architecture.[12] This was rightly construed as a threat to give all Government design work to civil servants, and to tighten the controls over every architect already working on a public building.

George Gilbert Scott, who had been commissioned in 1869 to build the new Home and Colonial Offices adjacent to his Foreign and India Offices, was one who suffered at the hands of the new commissioner. Ayrton ordered him to eliminate the corner towers of the Whitehall façade of his building in order to save money. Scott complained that his "scheme ha[d] been greatly impoverished for economy's sake," but, despite continued efforts, he was unable to reinstate the original design.[13]

Alfred Waterhouse was more successful in undoing Ayrton's harm to his plans for the Natural History Museum. When the building tenders were received in September 1872, all exceeded the two-year-old estimate of £300,000, and Ayrton demanded reductions to meet that expenditure ceiling. The Treasury interceded and worked out a compromise of £330,000, but substantial alterations in materials and ornamental work were still required. Waterhouse's intended towers on either side of the main entrance were replaced by short spires, but the original towers were restored by the Conservatives in 1878 after a campaign on their behalf by the architect.[14]

Ayrton reserved the worst for E. M. Barry, whose commission to rebuild the National Gallery never amounted to more than the construction of a few new rooms and the refitting of some others. Moreover, in January 1870, the Office of Works abruptly severed his connection with the Houses of Parliament, where he had directed work since the death of his father. He was curtly ordered to hand over all construction plans and other drawings in a letter which one M. P. said "no gentleman would send to his butler."[15] Barry protested his treatment to Gladstone, who referred the matter to Robert Lowe with the sympathetic observation that the architect had "suffered severely and most undeservedly though unavoidably from the course which things ultimately took in regard to the competition for the designs of the new Law Courts."[16] But Lowe did not interfere in Ayrton's business, and although Barry wrote again to Gladstone to press his complaint in April, the prime minister only expressed his regret for his "inconvenience."[17] This melancholy sequel to Barry's misfortune in the law courts contest marked the effective end of his career, although he served as the architectural professor of the Royal Academy from 1873 until his death in 1880.

Fortunately, Street was not similarly humiliated. Ayrton subjected his design for the law courts to the same kind of economic reductions imposed on the government offices and the Natural History Museum, but his resistance was staunch and his friends were powerful. Like Waterhouse, he was able to have some of the lost features restored after a change of Government. His relationship with Ayrton was not happy, however.

Fresh Designs for Carey Street

ACTON AYRTON officially took office on October 26, 1869, but he does not seem to have contacted Street about the law courts until the end of the year. He was not eager to pursue any program requiring expenditure. His correspondence with Roundell Palmer in November, however, suggests that he had already decided against the Embankment site.[18] In the meantime, the Royal Commission and Street left their quarters in Lincoln's Inn Fields and Portugal Street. The commission moved to 7 Lancaster Place, while Street established a special law courts office in a temporary building on the acquired site, just behind the Carey Street hoarding. Here he assembled a separate staff to work on his single largest commission.

When Ayrton met with Street on December 31, 1869, he chose to instruct him directly, as Layard had done, rather than accept the intermediation of the Royal Commission. As this left nothing at all for the commission to do, it did not meet

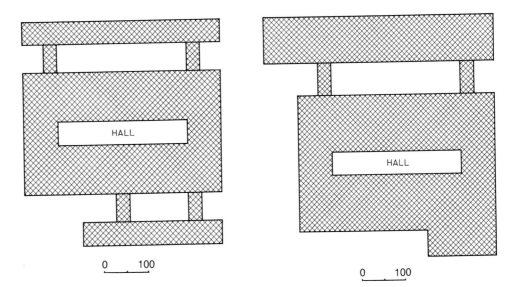

88 Reduced Carey Street design, submitted 25 March 1870. Reconstructed block plan. (Daniel McCoubrey.)

89 Reduced Carey Street design, submitted 17 June 1870. Reconstructed block plan. (Daniel McCoubrey.)

between June 1869 and June 1870, when the members considered the new design that Street had devised during the first half of 1870, in response to Ayrton's instructions to prepare a proposal for the unenlarged Carey Street site. Although he had already made one such design in May 1869 (see Figs. 85, 86), Street maintained that Ayrton's instructions required "an entirely fresh plan in every particular."[19] In fact, before presenting his work to the Royal Commission, Street made three fresh block plans for Ayrton, the last of which, his seventh scheme for the law courts, became the basis of the executed design. No visual record of the first two plans of 1870 survives, although their general outlines may be reconstructed on the evidence of written descriptions.

Ayrton told the House of Commons on February 11 that Street was at work "drawing up plans for the construction of the courts within the limits of the site prescribed by the Act passed in 1865, also within the limits of the funds which were provided by the Act passed in the same year."[20] Ten days later he examined the first fruits of Street's renewed labor. Ayrton expressed some doubts about the effect of the Strand façade, but he allowed himself to be reassured by Street. He reiterated the funding ceiling of £750,000, and he explained that, after the subtraction of Street's commission, only £710,000 was left for construction.[21]

On March 25, Street submitted a long report and his first new plan, designed to meet Ayrton's requirements (Fig. 88).[22] While the program remained that of the reduced designs of 1869, he sought to restore the full "quadrilateral" or concentric system of the great plan. Indeed, he now attempted what Burnet had proposed: a modification of the great plan to fit the acquired site. Accordingly, the plan provided for both north and south office blocks, separated from the central building by two internal streets. At the center lay a great hall, 290 by 50 feet, and around it were gathered the eighteen courtrooms. The simpler public access pattern of the plans of 1869 was retained, with only four stairs for spectators leading to the galleries of all courts. Unfortunately, because of the limited north–south dimensions of the property, this symmetrical solution could only be achieved with a compact central block, some 20 feet narrower and 70 feet shorter than those of the previous year. Within this adequate openings for light and ventilation proved impossible.

Despite the compression of the central block, the design required some adjustment of the western boundary of the site. Street suggested exchanging property with Clement's Inn and purchasing some additional land in order to provide a rectangular building plot. He also recommended the demolition of St. Clement Danes, which would "entirely fail to harmonize" with the new Gothic building, and vaguely proposed to build a replacement west of the courts. But if this removal could not be accomplished, he had contingency plans to tuck back the southwest corner of the building, opening the space between it and the existing church and providing a courtyard for carriages. In the now familiar manner of these experimental block plans, Street had been instructed to prepare no elevations, and his report made few allusions to the artistic considerations of the design. But he did plead for the acquisition and preservation of as much open ground as possible around the building, and he noted that the roof of the hall would be visible above the surrounding offices and courts. Because of the reduced budget, Street reported that "very decorative work" would be ruled out, although, he wrote: "It will be possible, I hope, to build solidly, and with due regard to the Architectural effect of the building." From the start he seemed committed to the simple, weighty massing of the Early French in his work for Ayrton.

Ayrton asked Galton and Hunt to report on this plan, and they evidently criticized the modest provision for spectators.[23] On April 19, Street submitted revised plans which restored separate public stairs for each pair of courts.[24] But Hunt and Galton made more sweeping complaints, later described as "objections . . . to the crowded position of the courts and their accessories around the Central Hall," and Street was asked to reconsider his proposal more thoroughly.[25]

When Street submitted a report and his second set of block plans of 1870 on June 17, he admitted that he had again been compelled to give up the "main feature" of the plan approved by the Royal Commission, namely, the "quadrilateral" arrangement of courts and offices in a concentric pattern around the central hall (Fig. 89).[26] He had widened the main block by 30 feet to provide better light and ventilation, but this involved sacrificing all but a fragment of the southern wing. To replace the lost office space, Street lengthened, widened, and increased the height of the corresponding northern wing. With its remaining single block on the north side of the site, the design was now the mirror image of his Carey Street design of May 1869, which had one range of offices to the south. The reversed orientation permitted Street to create a forecourt, 55 feet deep, between the main block and the Strand, and he argued that this feature would be "very advantageous to the effect of the building on the side on which it will be most seen, and where the effects of light and shade will always be the best."[27] Evidently he sought to recreate the type of open setting that he had come to appreciate on the Embankment. Immersed in this incessant work of revision, Street began to find it easier to set aside theory and allow his work to be shaped by the interaction between such visual considerations and the remorseless practicalities of the program.

In the end, Galton and Hunt gave this design their lukewarm endorsement, advising Ayrton that "the revised plan is an improvement upon the previous plan; but the buildings are still somewhat crowded around and overshadowed by the Central Hall."[28] They stressed the need for additional land, the cost of which they estimated at £53,000, but they concluded that the building itself could be erected for the statutory amount. This was sufficient approval for the first commissioner, who forwarded the plans to the Treasury on July 2.[29] However, in an accompanying letter, Ayrton warned that it would be necessary to acquire additional land to the west, as Street had requested. Ashamed at this suggestion of increased expense, he sweetened the bad news with the troubling observation that Street's design included "some architectural features of an extremely expensive character which do not in the least affect the purposes for which the buildings are to be erected and which it may be found desirable to modify or dispense with altogether."[30]

Naturally, this financial aside alarmed the officials of the Treasury, and on July 7, Robert Lowe drafted a minute in which he declined to approve the plans.[31] Gladstone had placed the chancellor under relentless pressure to economize, and he was determined not to allow his annoying former assistant to upset his strict budget.[32] As a result, Lowe reviewed the design in harsh financial terms. He flatly refused the requested expenditure for additional land, and he seized Ayrton's suggestion and criticized some of the seemingly extravagant architectural details. Lowe's recommendations were specific and provocative: "The Central Hall is unnecessarily large, both in respect to its height and to its width, and . . . by lowering it a large amount of additional accommodation might be secured, while by narrowing it even more room might be gained either for more buildings or for more light." Similarly, he questioned the generous provisions made for retiring rooms, waiting rooms, and even entire departments. The need to separate classes of visitors, the keystone of the instructions of the Royal Commission, was itself cast into doubt, and the creation of the large forecourt was judged wasteful when land was at a premium. Finally, Lowe disagreed with the estimated budget of £750,000, predicting an ultimate outlay of £1 million. The Treasury, he asserted, "would prefer to wait another year rather than involve the Government in the indefinite expenditure which these papers disclose."[33]

Curiously, this rejection temporarily allied Ayrton and Street. The first commissioner asked for the Royal Commission to be reconvened to consider the Treasury proposals for the further reduction of the program.[34] And in answer to the Treasury's criticisms, Street adopted a now characteristic response: he redoubled his efforts to solve the planning problems posed by the small, irregular site, but defended the artistic character of his design with increasing vigor.

A breakthrough came on July 14, only six days after the Treasury minute was communicated to the Office of Works. On that day Street completed his third new proposal of 1870, brilliantly cutting the Gordian knot that had so long encumbered the Carey Street site and all the solutions proposed for it.[35] The fundamental problem had been the shallowness of the site, and efforts to compress the entire concentric plan onto the existing parcel, like Burnet's proposal of 1869 and Street's first plan of 1870, had been unsuccessful. Now, on his seventh attempt to solve the law courts puzzle, Street overcame these difficulties by rejecting the fundamental premise of all his previous designs, and of most of the other ten competition entries as well. He simply rotated the entire plan ninety degrees until the hall ran north–south, utilizing the greater east–west dimension of the site for enlarged courtyards and light wells. The gable of the great hall was turned toward the Strand for the first time.

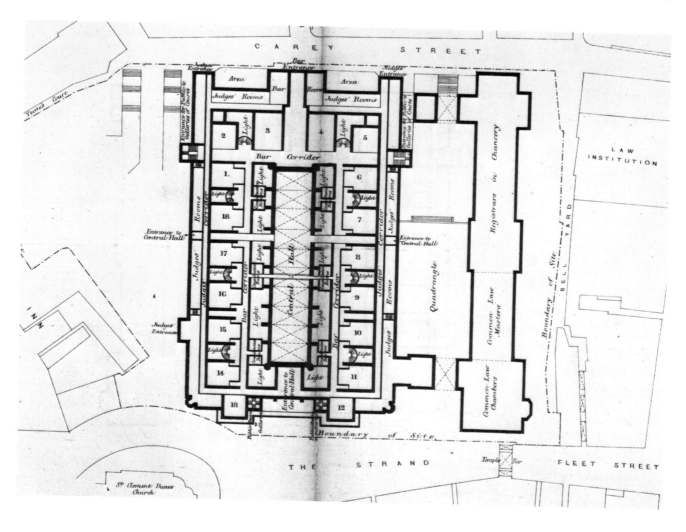

90 *Adopted design. Block plan at courtroom level, 27 July 1870. (PRO MP 1/9.)*

On July 14, the date of his report on this new plan, Street displayed a drawing to the "Committee as to Final Plan" of the Royal Commission.[36] No copy is preserved of that first draft of the design, but it is known that Street provided blocks of offices on both the east and west sides of the building, a generous arrangement that he altered six days later in an addendum to his report.[37] A lithographed representation of this later version of the plan, shorn of the western offices, is extant (Fig. 90). Dated July 27, Street clearly prepared it for the general meeting of the Royal Commission, which met that day to discuss the Treasury minute and to consider Street's design and report.

In his report, Street explained that the main block of the new design would preserve the lessons in planning he had learned so painfully. The hall had to be shortened slightly to 240 feet—50 feet less than the halls of his earlier plans of that year and 80 feet less than the hall of the great plan, but still 50 feet longer than the hall of his competition entry. He carefully exploited the slope of the site, providing ground level entrances both to the main hall from the Strand and to the level of the courts, one floor higher, from Carey Street. Public access to the courtrooms reverted to the simpler scheme employed in most of the reduced plans, utilizing only four stairways. All offices were in the eastern wing or in the main block, although the first draft of the report made mention of the short-lived western wing as well. This would have had to be dovetailed into the irregular northwestern corner of the site, for no additional purchases of land were required.

Having wrought this strikingly successful transformation of his design, Street made certain to include a strong argument against any further economizing, responding specifically to the criticism leveled by the Treasury at the alleged extravagance of the central hall. He wrote, explaining his artistic intentions, "I must plead earnestly to be allowed to make a fine Hall in the centre of this Building—I am sure the funds are sufficient to enable me to do so, and I have no kind of desire to be extravagant in the decoration of this, or any part of the Building. I hope to shew that solidity and good arrangement of outline, are of much more importance than an excess of rich and costly architectural detail."[38]

Despite this exhortation and characteristic description of simple masses and active outlines, the royal commissioners were rather impressed by the contrary economic arguments put forward by Lowe. At last they seem to have developed financial scruples of their own, and, after discussing the design on July 27, they passed an ominous final resolution:

> The Commission are desirous that the Building, considering its situation, its national character, and importance, should not be imperfect in respect of its architectural character, but they are decidedly of the opinion that it is undesirable, if the funds at the disposal of the Government for the purpose are so limited as to render any change necessary, to sacrifice the complete usefulness of the building to architectural ornament. If this completion cannot be accomplished by any other means so effectually as by a change in the architecture of the Central Hall, the Commission, though with reluctance, express their opinion that such a change should be made.[39]

Having issued this proviso and placed Street's central hall in jeopardy, at their next and last meeting on August 3, the commissioners were willing to approve his plan, now formally presented for their consideration by the Treasury.[40] This design incorporated a further slight revision, effected after some of the commissioners had objected to the location of two courtrooms directly adjacent to the noisy Strand (Rooms 12 and 13 on Fig. 90). Street had pulled these rooms back into the body of the building and screened them from the street with larger public stair towers (Fig. 91). This plan, published subsequently in the *Builder,* was signed by the chairman of the commission, Lord Chancellor Hatherley, and returned to the Treasury. On August 13, the Treasury, apparently also satisfied that sufficient safeguards against extravagance had been provided, directed Ayrton to obtain tenders for the plan upon which they and the Royal Commission, the joint statutory authorities, had at last agreed. The commission now passed out of existence, and on August 15 the Office of Works notified Street that he might proceed.[41]

Toward the Final Plan

THE FRANCO-PRUSSIAN WAR deprived Street of his usual late summer trip to the Continent in 1870, and so after a holiday in Scotland, he returned to London in September to begin to flesh out the approved block plan. Most of the

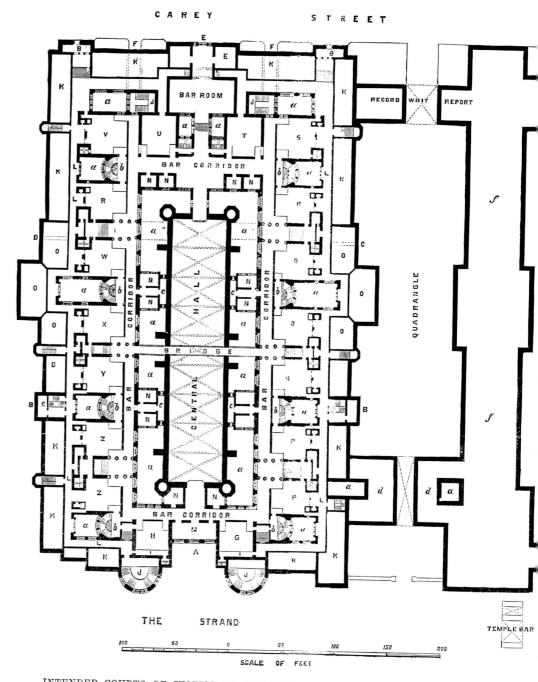

INTENDED COURTS OF JUSTICE IN THE STRAND.—Mr. G. E. Street, A.R.A., Architect.
Plan of Court Floor.

91 *Adopted design. Block plan at courtroom level, August 1870. (Builder, 20 August 1870.)*

REFERENCES.

A. Position of Strand Entrance to Central Hall.
B. Judges' Entrance.
C. Eastern Entrance to Central Hall.
D. Western Entrance to Central Hall.
E. Bar Entrance and Bar Robing-room.
F. Entrance to Public Galleries.
G. Court of Common Pleas.
H. Court of Exchequer.
I. Juries.
J. Public Stairs to Galleries of Courts.
K. Judges' Rooms.
L. Judges' Corridors.
M. Bar or Consultation Rooms.
N. Consultation Rooms.
O. Vice-Chancellor's Chambers, over
P. Court of Common Pleas.

Q. Queen's Bench.
R. Vice-Chancellor's Court.
S. Vice-Chancellor's, or Appeal Court.
T. Lord Justices.
U. Lord Chancellor.
V. Master of the Rolls, or Appeal Court.
W. Bankruptcy Court.
X. Admiralty Court.
Y. Divorce Court.
Z. Exchequer Court.
a. Area for Light.
b. Witnesses' Stairs.
c. Bar Water-closets.
d. Admiralty and Probate Registrars here, or over Vice-Chancellors' Chambers.
e. Messenger.

f. Second floor above Courts, Stationers' Department, Taxing Masters.
Floor above Courts.
Exchequer Masters, Queen's Remembrancer, Registrars in Chancery.
Court Floor.
Common Law Judges' Chambers, Common Law Writs, Appearance and Judgments, Queen's Bench Masters, Registrars in Chancery.
Floor below Court.
Common Law Judges' Chambers, Common Law Writs, Appearances and Judgments, Common Pleas Masters, Accountant-General, Record Writ and Report.

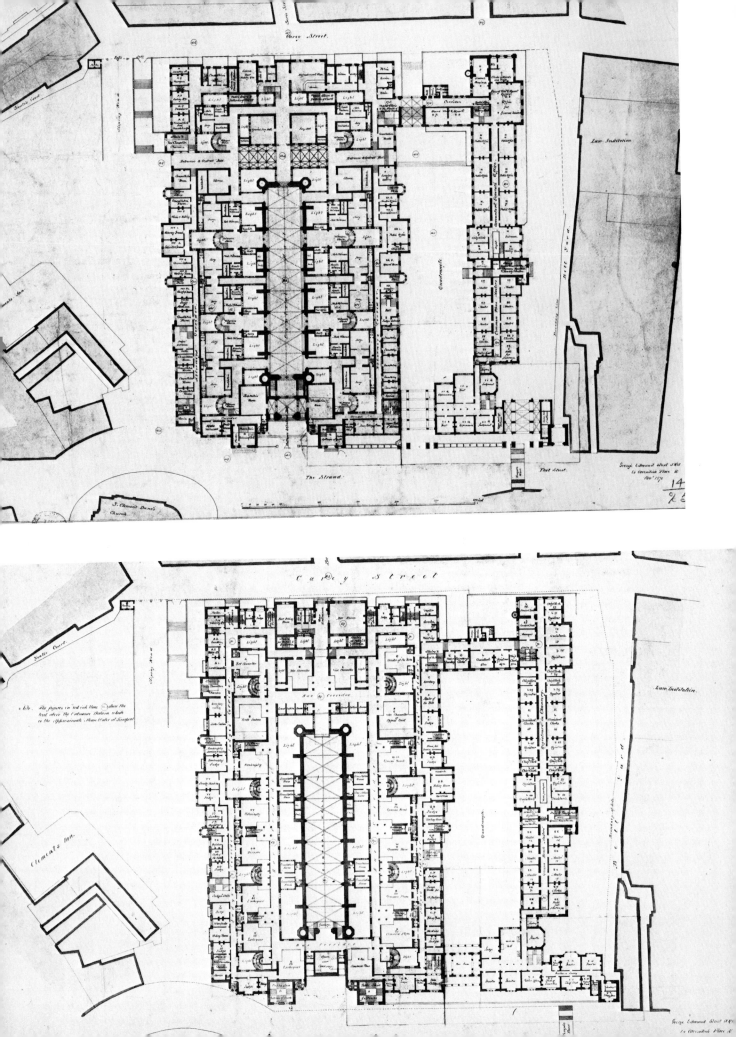

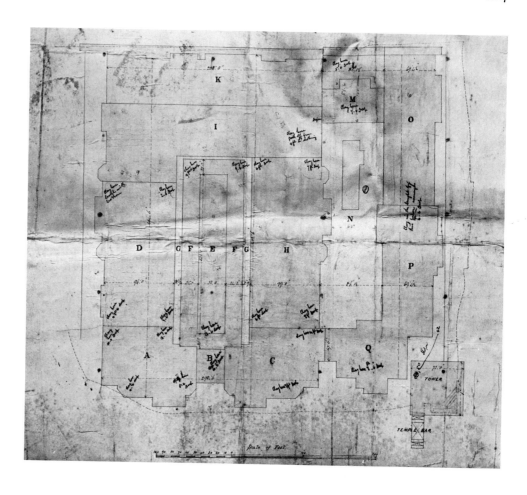

92 *Plan at Strand level. November 1870. With laminate at lower right, January 1871. (PRO Works 30/1280.)*

93 *Plan at courtroom level. November 1870. With laminate at lower right, January 1871. (PRO Works 30/1281.)*

94 *Foundation plan, showing great clock tower. Late 1870. (BAL)*

nine small-scale drawings which he prepared in November and December have been preserved, although these do not include the Strand elevation, which was later extensively revised. The plans in this set were altered by pasted laminations at the southeast corner, indicating these later changes (Figs. 92, 93). Street showed these drawings in their original form to Ayrton late in December.[42]

The design created during the latter half of 1870 was Street's most practical and visually astute response to what were now the familiar challenges of the law courts program and the Carey Street site. Although it had lost its ideological purity during its complicated genesis, it was a work of great conviction.

The visual character of the principal façade was not defined by a single ordering system, but by a dialogue between two powerful features—the gable of the great hall, now turned toward the Strand, and a mighty, freestanding clock tower at the southeast corner. Because of the subsequent alteration of drawings, only a foundation plan survives to show this tower—the last, almost uncompromising descendant of the record depository in Street's competition design (Fig. 94). The adjacent block of offices shrank away from this dominant neighbor, whose individuality demonstrated a continuing belief in active composition. As Street later wrote: "I introduced a Clock tower of Grand proportions near the South East angle of the building, because I thought that in so large a building some striking break in the general horizontal line of the building would not only be effective, but was indeed urgently required."[43]

95 William Burges. Cardiff Castle. 1866–1928. Perspective of clock tower, built 1869–73. (Building News, 9 December 1870.)

A persistent Early French enthusiasm echoes in this explanation, and the influence of William Burges himself was not far away. Although no confirming elevation of Street's tower now exists, he almost surely conceived its design in full knowledge of Burges's most recent work for the marquess of Bute at Cardiff Castle. The clock tower at Cardiff was then under construction, and Burges had illustrated it with an evocative perspective in the spring exhibition of the Royal Academy in 1870, just as Street was devising his final arrangement for the law courts (Fig. 95). The Cardiff tower can be accepted as a surrogate for the unrecorded tower of the law courts, positioned with martial assurance at the very corner.

However, the muscularity of the Early French was not the only stylistic determinant of the Strand façade. The noble gable of the central hall, framed by stair towers, was an allusion to English rather than Continental precedents, paying par-

ticular homage to the north face of Westminster Hall (see Fig. 9). This may be seen
in a later elevation by Street which follows the basic outline of the design of late
1870 (see Fig. 101). During Street's lifetime, Westminster Hall served as the *salle
des pas perdus* for the adjoining courtrooms built by John Soane, and its north door
was the principal entrance. The appropriateness of making an allusion to this ancient locus of English law in the design of its new home surely captured Street's
imagination, even though he was not an especially sentimental man, and this
lessened the drudgery of remaking his plan around a realigned axis. His great portal
differed in detail from that at Westminster, but its similar massing could not have
been conceived unthinkingly. The relationship between Soane's courts and the
medieval hall may have even inspired Street's definition of the relationship between
the main block and east wing in his own design. Such nationalist sensitivity was
now a firmly re-established component of his work.

Street employed the contrasting strengths of the hall façade and the tower to
assert the importance of his building in its crowded environment. The composition
was adjusted with the expectation that most visitors would approach the building
along the Strand from the west, en route from Whitehall and the Houses of Parliament. Even before passing the church of St. Mary-le-Strand, such travelers would
glimpse the great clock tower, and it would loom ever larger as they neared the
courts. Then, passing south of St. Clement Danes (a clear thoroughfare north of
the church was not created until later), they would swing around its apse to be
confronted suddenly by the formal symmetry of the principal entrance (see Fig.
112). To the east, the clock tower still proclaimed its solitary counterpoint, marking
the furthest extent of the building.

Before the south façade lay a relatively wide portion of the Strand, roughly
triangular in shape, and Street attuned his composition to this lopsided frontage.
The great portal looked across the broadest expanse of the triangle, adjacent to its
base at the west, where formality could be best appreciated. The base itself was
occupied by St. Clement's church, while the tower of the law courts rose at the
narrow eastern apex. Street had contrived a similar two-part composition to fit the
curve of the Embankment site, with the main block of the building set off against a
large eastern tower, but on the Strand the solution responded to more readily identifiable requirements. The main entrance and the clock tower, although separated
by only about three hundred feet, confronted very different environments. Indeed,
so confined was the site for the Royal Courts of Justice that the two great features of
the façade could rarely be seen at the same time.

Drawing on a lengthening experience in devising picturesque designs for this
building, Street had now simplified his vocabulary. Compared with the Embankment
project, the new elevation was assembled from fewer and more generously scaled
units. Most notably, the fundamental contrast between the tower and the portal had
been reduced to an almost elemental confrontation. Set back in shadow and bol-
stered symmetrically within the most horizontal portion of the composition, the
entrance remained detached and rather introspective. But it was answered to the
east by a tower that stood forward in the sun, accenting the façade with an exuberant
vertical at its point of minimum equilibrium. Power and simplicity were the complementary colors of Street's compositional palette.

Street pursued these effects despite growing criticism of his judgment. Having already complained about the irregularity of the great plan, even the generally friendly *Building News* lamented that his Embankment design "lacks . . . breadth and consequent repose."[44] The overtly hostile *Builder* observed more predictably, "A far greater repose and length of unbroken line would indeed have been our choice for a long river front."[45] With supreme confidence, but at his own peril, Street chose to ignore this evidence that architectural taste had evolved since the evaluation of the competition designs in 1867.

The north façade, which is alone represented in an extant drawing from 1870, was a more understated but no less irregular design (Fig. 96). As in the Strand front, the relationship between the main block and the eastern office wing defined the entire composition, but this was achieved with a more gently syncopated vocabulary. This solution was no doubt prompted by the residential scale of the architecture on the north side of Carey Street.

The western portion of the Carey Street façade was centered on the barristers' entrance and the barely visible northern gable of the central hall. Its symmetry was disturbed only slightly by the bar room, just east of the barristers' door, whose large windows were not repeated to the west. As on the south front, the eastern wing contrasted markedly with this regularity, accented by a 130-foot tower and by a cluster of spikey gables and tall roofs. Much of this evinced a clearly French flavor, especially the pavilion which lifted its mountainous roof over the gateway into the

*96 North elevation.
c. December 1870. (PRO Works 30/1286.)*

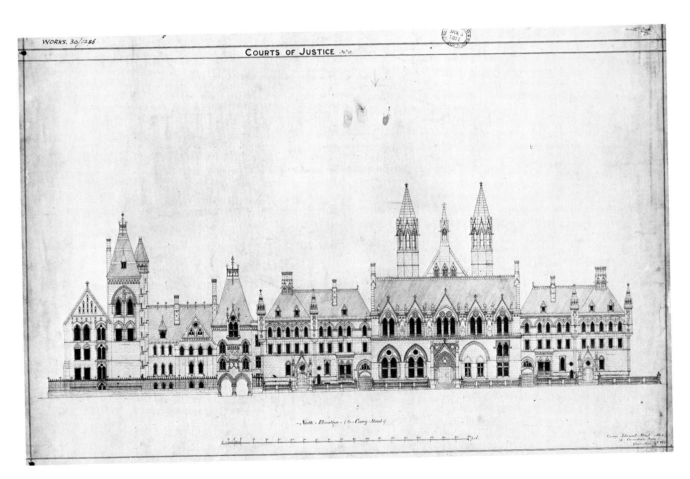

North · Elevation · (to · Carey · Street ·)

internal courtyard. Portions of the lost Strand elevations probably possessed the same character.

The northeast tower was sensitively sited just opposite the southern entrance to Lincoln's Inn, with its top visible almost anywhere in New Square. In a similar way, the clock tower at the southeast corner was placed on the axis of the longest and straightest part of Middle Temple Lane, which led from the Temples up to the Strand. It too would be seen from many of the courtyards where barristers had their offices.

Complementing the growing simplicity of his conception for the exterior was Street's treatment of the central hall, where the traceried windows of his earlier designs were now replaced by paired lancets (Fig. 97). Beneath the clerestory stretched a broad expanse of uncarved walling, while nine bays of quadripartite vaulting spread overhead. The whole possessed a suitably "Early," early thirteenth-century character. Rather richer tracery was reserved for the public stair towers of the main façade, shown in the same section. Those towers were now square in plan.

The general arrangement of the building as a whole was very much like that approved by the Royal Commission and published in August by the *Builder* (see Figs. 91–93). The reoriented central hall had only one significant negative effect on the plan, rendering impossible the logical distribution of all equity courts north of the hall (adjacent to Lincoln's Inn and the chambers of most equity barristers) and all common law courts to the south (near the Temples and the quarters of the majority

97 Section through central hall. December 1870. (PRO Works 30/1322.)

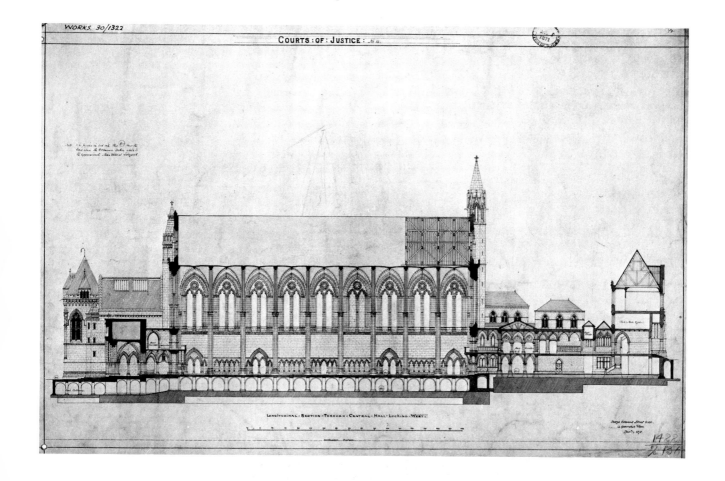

of common law barristers). This arrangement had been suggested in the competition instructions, perhaps accounting for the long preference for east–west axes.

How Street at last saw that a realignment would solve more problems than it would create cannot be determined precisely, but it is likely that both visual and practical matters engaged his attention. The almost countless revisions of the plan had ultimately made him a more pragmatic thinker, and he thus looked afresh at the much studied practical problems of light and air. Moreover, the wandering of the project away from the Strand and then back again had opened his eyes to the real visual character of the site. Street's insights led him to rotate the central hall, not only to simplify the plan, but also to rid the façade of a static, horizontal roofline. In its place he created a dynamic balance between the major western block and the office wing.

Other lesser factors certainly influenced his decision. The expectation that equity and common law would ultimately be "fused" had reduced the rationale for a geographic distribution of the courtrooms. Street may also have recalled that even before this legal reform had won many supporters, Charles Barry and James Pennethorne had made designs for Carey Street with north–south halls. Medieval precedent, too, supported the placement of the main entrance on the long axis, and the most relevant such precedent was Westminster Hall, with its strong legal associations. Street may have received some advice as well, although no documents support Ayrton's offhand claim that the reorganization had been his idea.[46]

Perhaps surprisingly, the reorientation of the entire plan did not substantially upset the long canonical concentric formula for the main block. Eighteen courtrooms were gathered around the central hall, one level above the Strand and the hall floor. Two larger courts, numbers four and eighteen, were originally set aside for spectacular trials and appeals. The courtrooms were separated by the now enlarged light areas, and further light areas lay between them and the great hall.

The building was served by four systems of circulation, each restricted to a single type of visitor. (These are most clearly shown in a later section, Fig. 98.) A private corridor for the bar circled the building between the courts and the central hall. Barristers might enter the building from their own door in the center of the northern façade of the main block, or they might enter through the main Strand doors and reach their corridor by means of staircases located along the sides of the central hall. Immediately adjacent to the northern entrance was a bar room. Judges were similarly provided with their own exclusive circuit of corridor, one-half level higher than that of the bar. This ran behind the courtrooms and gave direct access on one side to the raised daises on which the judges sat in the courts, and, on the other side, to their offices. The judges had their own entrances as well: two doorways at the northeast and northwest corners of the main block opened directly from their corridor onto Carey Street, and lower level entrances on the east and west side of the main block were connected to their corridor by private stairs. Attorneys were accommodated by a circumferential corridor running just under that of the judges, with its own doorways into the courts but no private entrances from the outside.

The troublesome public were treated with special care. They were segregated in their own corridor, above the bar corridor, which connected only to the upper galleries of the courts. Under normal circumstances their corridor could be reached

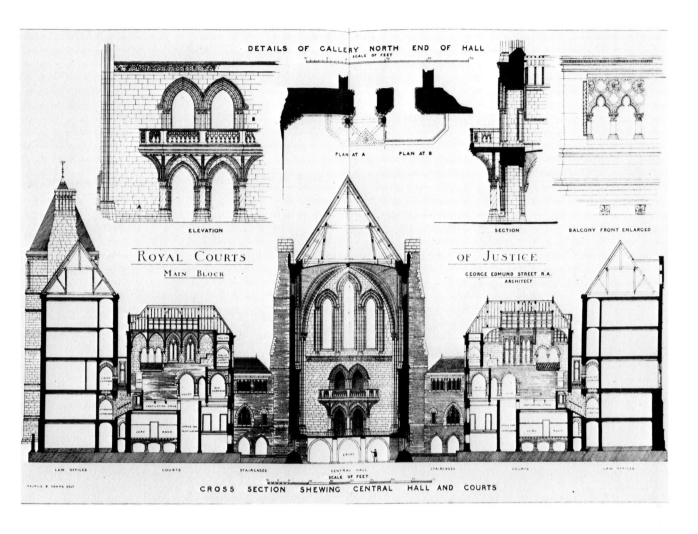

DETAILS OF GALLERY NORTH END OF HALL
SCALE OF FEET

ELEVATION

PLAN AT A   PLAN AT B

SECTION   BALCONY FRONT ENLARGED

ROYAL COURTS
MAIN BLOCK

OF JUSTICE
GEORGE EDMUND STREET R.A.
ARCHITECT

LAW OFFICES   COURTS   STAIRCASES   CENTRAL HALL   STAIRCASES   COURTS   LAW OFFICES
SCALE OF FEET

CROSS SECTION SHEWING CENTRAL HALL AND COURTS

98 Transverse section. Re-drawn from contract drawing for publication by Maurice B. Adams, 1882. (Building News, 4 August 1882.)

by only four stairs, two of which were contained by the large towers flanking the Strand entrance. The other two stairways were located just north of the great hall, and all four communicated directly and solely with the outside.

This elaborate circulation system guaranteed that the great hall would be reserved as a concourse for those who were already inside the building on official business. Moreover, the plethora of specialized entrances insured that few visitors would enter the hall through the large doorway set between stair towers in the south façade. On ceremonial occasions, like the commencement of the judicial year, processional use was made of that portal, but dignitaries were compelled to traverse a low, dark vestibule which provided the sole passageway between it and the central hall. No direct connection of any kind was provided between the hall and the central northern door, which was intended for barristers. Such was the pragmatic imperiousness of Street's seventh design.

The courts were provided with a full set of service rooms. A large number of consultation rooms for conferences between counsel and clients opened off the bar corridor, and two spacious arbitration chambers were provided south of the central hall at ground level. Also at that lower level were the jury rooms and the waiting rooms for male and female witnesses, located directly beneath the courtrooms. Separate stairs to the courts were provided for jurors and witnesses. The north end of that floor, which was the basement level at the Carey Street façade, was devoted to refreshment rooms.

The main block contained four floors of additional office space, located above and below the chambers of the judges. These rooms were designated for the judges' personal staffs and for services closely connected with the daily functioning of the courts. Administrative departments which were less directly involved in litigation were housed on the five floors of the separate eastern wing of offices. This block, only a fragment of the circumferential offices of the great plan, was joined to the main body of the building by short wings at the north and south which bridged the passages leading into the quadrangle.

Resistance and Revision

ON JANUARY 2, 1871, Street submitted the drawings of this remarkable design to the Office of Works, where their consideration was made hostage to the personal dispute between Acton Ayrton and Robert Lowe.[47] By the end of 1870, the first commissioner and the chancellor of the Exchequer no longer communicated directly, locked as they were in a bitter contest to determine who was the better guardian of the Nation's purse.[48] Street soon found that his only route of escape from this bureaucratic wilderness lay outside the ordinary channels of authority.

After the dissolution of the Royal Commission, Ayrton had acted swiftly to place the law courts under his personal control. Street was required to sign a contract with the Office of Works in September 1870, the severe terms of which became the subject of a controversy among the architectural profession at large.[49] When the first new drawings arrived at his office, Ayrton turned his attention to the design itself.

Economy was, from the start, the chief concern of the first commissioner, but his policy had inevitable artistic consequences. These were immediately apparent in the review of Street's design prepared by Douglas Galton and Henry Hunt, who suggested that Ayrton might choose "not to sanction the erection of [the great tower]—as it does not appear to provide any useful accommodation."[50] Persuaded by this frugal logic, Ayrton wrote to Street on January 14 that he approved "generally" of the design, but that "it would not be in accordance with the spirit of the Report of the Royal Commission to devote a large space and a considerable expense to the erection of the proposed Clock Tower and [the first commissioner] therefore requests that the tower and its foundations may be omitted."[51] In its place, he directed the placement of a larger block of offices, accommodating a second bar room and, with unconscious irony, the offices of the lunacy department.

Street responded without rancor, drawing on a nearly depleted reserve of patience, and one week later he returned his drawings with alterations shown on pasted laminations (see Figs. 92, 93). Again, the Strand elevation that accompanied these plans has been lost. The revised design showed the insertion of a block of offices in place of the great tower at the southeast, but Street had retained a very small tower, moved outward as far as possible to achieve by prominence what it could not by scale. This largely satisfied Ayrton, who dispatched the drawings to the Treasury on February 13. However, in view of the earlier reservations expressed by the Treasury and the Royal Commission about the central hall, the first commissioner suggested that approval for the vaulted roof be postponed. Ayrton wished to subject this costly feature to further scrutiny.[52]

More than a month passed before the Treasury replied, asking Douglas Galton to submit a report on Street's plans.[53] In the report, ready on March 28, Galton also questioned the vaulting of the central hall.[54] He doubted, with the common sense of an engineer, the necessity of covering in stone a chamber that was to have an exterior wooden roof anyway. But Galton also turned his attention to the aesthetic merits of the Strand elevation, and, with this, the relationship between Street and the Office of Works took on a new character. Galton found the same defects in the new design that some press reviewers had noted in both the great plan and the study for the Howard Street site: "The Elevations are broken up into many parts, so as almost to convey the idea that the structure is composed of a group of buildings not necessarily dependent on each other, and the roofs assume an unusual variety of forms." Galton's opinion evidently carried great weight at the Treasury, which declined to approve the plans.[55] The Treasury noted with regret the "failure to secure an adequate architectural effect in the Strand front" and predicted that "great and just disappointment will be experienced by the Public if the elevation fronting the Strand is executed according to the present design." Street was ordered to "reconsider his plan for the Strand front so as to render it more worthy of the importance of the Building and of its position in the Metropolis." This placed the Government squarely in opposition to the artistic direction in which their architect had been working for a half dozen years.

The complaints were sent on to Street, who, on the basis of the general approval given to the drawings submitted on January 2, had been preparing contract plans on a larger scale. These showed some further modifications of his own making, and so he was not terribly dismayed by the latest objections. In sending thirty-four of the new drawings to the Office of Works on April 22, he observed that the paste-over design rejected by the Treasury was "a very hasty one and I had long since revised it both in plan and elevation; and another drawing shall be sent to you in a day or two."[56] The additional drawing, another small-scale elevation delivered to the Office of Works on May 2, unfortunately has not survived.[57] However, the extant contract drawings, which had been prepared after January 2, show that the most striking element of this revision was a large, crocketed spire placed at the middle of the central hall and flanked by two thick-set ventilation stacks (Figs. 99, 100). These vertical accents were probably meant to compensate in part for the loss of the great clock tower, although they were located at the other end of the building and focused attention on the main entrance.

The overall effect of the Strand front apparently differed very little from that of the prior design, but the added panache of the new stacks and turret apparently impressed Ayrton. He submitted the newest plans to the Treasury on May 5, alluding in his letter to Street's professed haste in making the first design and pointing out that Galton, whose opinions had been cited by the Treasury, had not been hired as an artistic counselor. Again ironically allied with the architect against his old chief Lowe, Ayrton asserted: "The only professional adviser of the office respecting the new Courts of Justice is Mr. Street."[58]

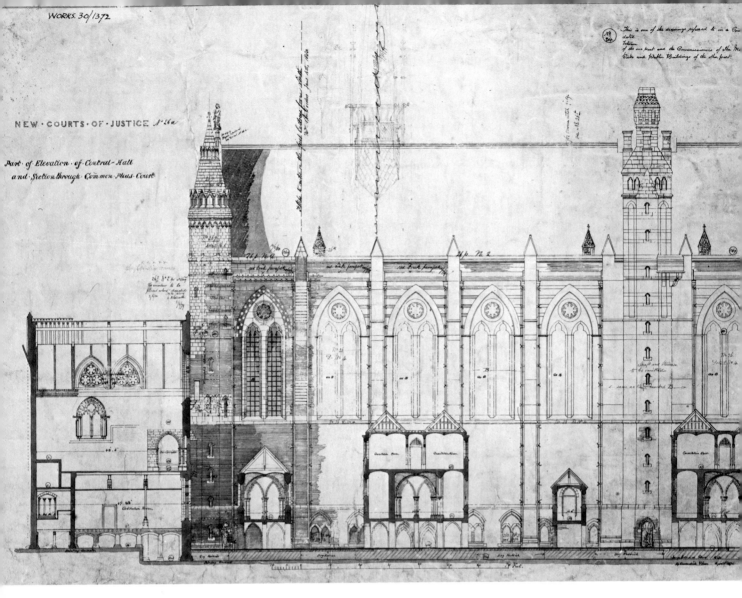

NEW·COURTS·OF·JUSTICE Nᵒ 26a

Part·of·Elevation·of·Central·Hall
and·Section·through·Common·Pleas·Court

99 *East elevation of central
hall, southern half. Lithographed contract drawing, April
1871. Ventilation turret later
omitted and brickwork introduced. Sketching shows two locations for flèche, introduced in
1879–80. (PRO Works 30/
1372.)*

The Treasury, however, declined to approve the new elevation in spite of Ayrton's defense. The first commissioner was advised in a letter drafted by Lowe that
"My Lords admit that the altered design is free from some of the defects of the former
plan, and is generally an improvement on that plan; but they do not consider that,
even thus improved, it presents an appearance worthy of the principal front of so
important and costly a building."[59] This was not a surprising verdict, for the new
stacks and turret had actually increased the irregularity against which the Treasury
had protested in the first place.

The bad news was immediately relayed to Street, whose relatively complacent
acceptance of earlier criticism now came to an end. He replied with his fullest
analysis and justification of the lively elevation, keyed to the crowded nature of the
Carey Street site:

I feel very sure that seen in perspective it will be an effective and fine front,
quite worthy of the building. I have intentionally made it comparatively simple in detail, but in London I hold that the effect which is best worth obtaining is that which is produced by sunlight and shade, and by effective distribution of the masses of the building. And it is this sort of effect which my design

100 *Intended turret for central hall. Lithographed contract drawing, spring 1871.*
Plans, sections, and elevations. (PRO Works 30/1330.)

proposes. Of course it would be very easy to add much ornamental detail, if the examples of all the best buildings in the world did not prove that this is not the way in which really good architectural effects are produced.[60]

Street concluded his argument with a plea for the restoration of his original clock tower.

However, the architect now recognized that no artistic argument alone, be it ever so compelling, could rescue his design from the endless sparring of Ayrton and Lowe. As their criticisms became artistic, his defense accordingly became more political. He shrewdly concluded that it was more important to satisfy Lowe than Ayrton, and so he complained to the Office of Works: "You request me to amend the design in accordance with the views of the Treasury, but you have given me no means of knowing what their views are. May I, therefore, ask you as speedily as may be, to put me in communication with the professional or artistic adviser of their Lordships [the lords of the Treasury], in order that I may ascertain what they are." Street triumphed in this first test of his political acumen, for the Treasury agreed to consult with him directly. The complexion of his relationship with his official clients was changed forever, and Ayrton was left to sniff that he had no "functions to perform except being a channel of communication."[61]

Circumventing Ayrton; Final Revisons

STREET now undertook to win Treasury approval for his design. He began by supplying them with thirty-seven drawings, including perspectives of the Strand façade and the courtyard and a two-part elevation of the south front, now drawn to a larger scale, photographed, and assembled on one sheet.[62] Many of the working details were preserved as final contract drawings, but the perspectives and new elevation are among the many missing drawings from this period. A drawing of 1872, however, probably resembles the courtyard perspective, and the massing of the Strand front, if not its details, was not dissimilar to that recorded in a view of some months later (see Figs. 107, 105). The contours of the main façade were simplified in these drawings, and, in particular, the notched southwest corner was filled in, an improvement tested in pencil on an earlier plan (see Fig. 93). But, once more, the changes were not sweeping, and Street probably counted on his own personal lobbying and the effectiveness of his powerful perspectives to change the opinion of the Treasury in his favor. His gambit was successful, and the Treasury communicated its approval to Ayrton on August 4.[63]

Thoroughly annoyed by his progressive exclusion from the decision-making process, the first commissioner protested that the Treasury had "without further reference to this office . . . approved the plans, and . . . taken the matter into your own hands."[64] But when his letter reached the Treasury, someone annotated this passage with pencil in the margin: "This is fortunate because if the 1st Commissioner's advice had been taken a worse design would have been approved."[65] Street had successfully played on the growing antipathy between the two departments to win acceptance for his design. Despite his reputation for parsimony, Robert Lowe turned out to be sensitive to artistic feelings, and Street was not the only artist whom he rescued from Ayrton's clutches at this time. On July 20, Ayrton fired the sculptor Alfred Stevens, then at work on the Wellington Monument for St. Paul's, for delays and cost overruns. But Lowe paid a dramatic visit to the artist's studio and ordered that money be found to continue his commission.[66]

Street was not content to rely solely on the judgment of Lowe, perhaps remembering his suggestion to resurrect Inigo Jones's design for the Palace of Whitehall. He also appealed to Gladstone for support. The prime minister had only recently offered to subscribe toward the stained glass of Christ Church Cathedral, Dublin, which Street was rebuilding, and on July 11, the architect wrote to accept Gladstone's standing invitation to breakfast.[67] He accompanied his note with "some photographs of my drawings for the Law Courts which I hope will please and satisfy you."[68] By this date he surely believed that his work would please the premier and that he could thus cut off Ayrton's only course of appeal against Lowe's decision. He was developing the acute political sense necessary in Government service.

With the approval of the Treasury and reinforced political defenses, Street must have embarked on his summer travels in 1871 feeling that he had weathered the worst of his difficulties. This was hardly true, although two years passed before another crisis arose in his relationship with his official masters. But despite its happy prospects, his vacation was not tranquil. While traveling with his wife and son in Switzerland he met with a serious accident during a nighttime carriage journey. Arthur Edmund Street later recalled:

> We were run away with in the dark on the Weissenstein, a mountain above Solothurn, the horses dashed up a bank, and we were thrown out amid the debris of the carriage. Luckily we were only some few hundred yards from the hotel, and within sight of its lights. My father suffered so much pain in his left—happily his left—arm, that it was clear it was either dislocated or broken, and apparently the former. As the Weissenstein hotel is three or four hours above Solothurn, there was nothing to be done that night, and he had to grin and bear it. The doctor did not put in an appearance next day until late in the afternoon—about eighteen hours after the event. He found the arm to be dislocated, and so firmly fixed had it become that the services of several waiters had to be enlisted to pull it in again. The innkeeper from whom we had hired the carriage demanded compensation; but our landlord with great kindness took the whole thing into his own hands, and we heard no more of the claim. The effects of the accident were lasting; whenever my father used his hand he felt a sensation of cramp, which would have been enough to stop his drawing entirely if it had been in the other hand.[69]

It was thus with an aching shoulder that Street set about making the final revisions of his design in the fall of 1871.

The changes which he now wrought strengthened the established character of the building (Figs. 101–104). On October 13 the *Building News*, whose critic was given access to the drawings in the architect's office, reported that the square public stair towers had been made polygonal in plan, like the pavilions of his Embankment project (see Fig. 81).[70] The fuller, rounder profile of the towers was also reminiscent of the semicircular stair towers of the block plan approved by the Royal Commission, and their general appearance was more in keeping with the broad, massive effect which Street sought (see Fig. 91).

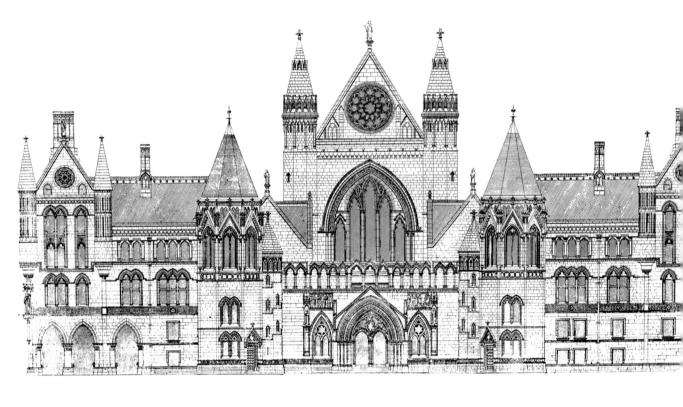

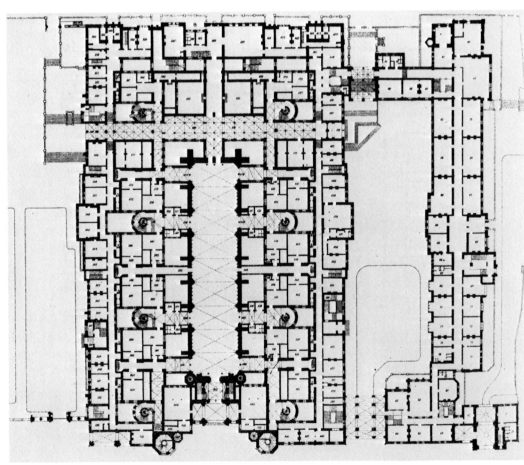

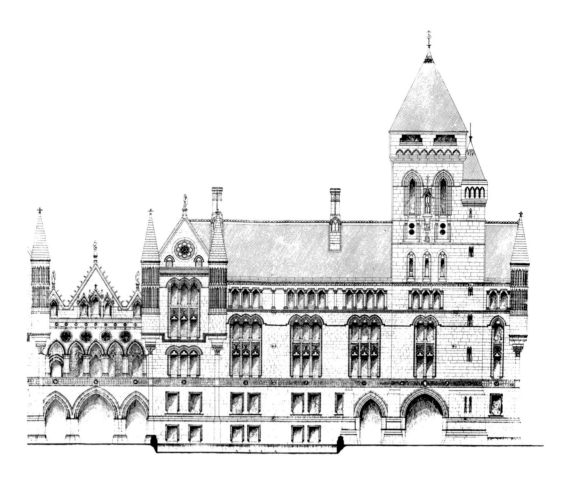

101 Strand elevation, western portion. Published from contract drawing, October–November 1871. (Building News, 17 November 1871.)

102 Strand elevation, eastern portion. Published from contract drawing, October–November 1871. (Building News, 8 December 1871.)

103 Plan at Strand level, as built. (Building News, 27 October 1882.)

104 Plan at courtroom level, as built. (Building News, 27 October 1882.)

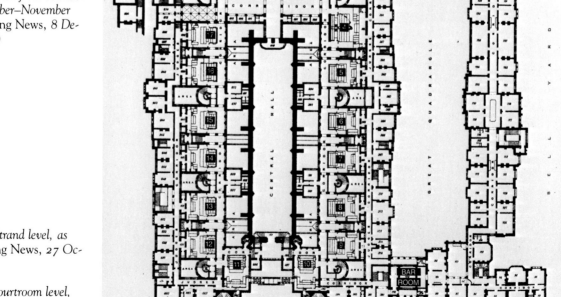

The clock tower was also revised. Although the Treasury had approved a design with the small tower of the paste-over plans, as late as November 3, Street was reportedly still working out the details of the large, freestanding version that Ayrton had proscribed.[71] At the same time, he had prepared a compromise proposal which was at once more economical than the original design and more impressive than the straitened variant accepted by the Treasury. By reinforcing some of the internal walls of the new southeast wing it was possible to build a broad tower that sprang from within the body of the building and so required no expensive, separate foundations. This powerful but affordable design was presented to the public in the architectural magazines of November and December 1871.[72]

In addition to releasing a number of the contract drawings to the press, Street also prepared several special perspective views of the design, with the intention of publicizing its merits. In the midst of the acrimonious debate of the previous spring, he had at last been elected a full member of the Royal Academy, and for his "diploma drawing," which was made in December, he chose to represent the main entrance of the law courts (Fig. 105). In keeping with his understanding of the hemmed-in site, the view was a realistic one which showed only that part of the main front facing the widest part of the Strand. This limitation also allowed Street to avoid any representation of the clock tower, whose compromised design he must have regarded as less than ideal. In a similar way, Gilbert Scott had submitted for his diploma drawing a view of the Foreign Office in a re-Gothicized form. Both architects exploited their Royal Academy submissions to present an edited image of designs that had been altered by Government interference.

105 Perspective of the main entrance. Royal Academy diploma drawing, by Street, December 1871. (Royal Academy of Arts, London.)

Street provided a fuller view of his work, tower and all, in the perspective which he apparently authorized the *Illustrated London News* to publish on January 20, 1872 (Fig. 106).[73] In preparation for the May exhibition of the Royal Academy, he also drew a large perspective of the main courtyard and commissioned a bird's-eye watercolor of the building seen from the northeast from the celebrated renderer and illustrator, H. W. Brewer (Fig. 107).[74]

So confident was Street in his new, more direct relationship with the Treasury, that he neglected to discuss these final revisions with the Office of Works until they were published. Understandably, his report of November 30, explaining the altered foundation requirements of his new tower, was received sourly.[75] Street was stiffly advised that he should seek formal approval for all contemplated revisions, and so on January 16, the day after he delivered sixty-nine additional contract drawings to the Office of Works, he officially presented these last alterations.[76] Ayrton forwarded the request to the Treasury on January 27 with a typically graceless explanation: "The plan as approved of by your Lordships having been received by your Lordships direct from Mr. Street, and this Board not having been informed of the grounds on which the plan and elevations were approved of, I can only forward to your Lordships the plan and elevation now prepared."[77] But Street had properly judged the attitude of Robert Lowe, who accepted the revisions without comment on February 5.[78]

Street was not successful, however, in winning approval for his controversial plan to demolish St. Clement Danes in order to improve the visibility of his design in the crowded Strand. On August 7, 1871, just three days after the Treasury approved his design, he obtained Robert Lowe's support for the elimination of the old church, the work of Christopher Wren and James Gibbs.[79] However, sentiment for Renaissance and Baroque architecture was on the rise. The proposal was attacked from almost every quarter, and the Metropolitan Board of Works declined to approve the demolition.[80]

By the end of 1871 Street had completed the vast majority of the contract drawings, and these, together with his latest perspectives, provide a very complete representation of the design. The plan of the building now differed very little from that shown on the small-scale drawings of November and December 1870. Indeed, construction of the foundations was allowed to begin in February 1871, and surveyors had been at work since May 1871 taking out quantities for the main contract based on the earlier plans. However, the Strand elevation had been much revised, and the ornament for the building as a whole had been worked out in greater detail. These were the last substantial changes and additions made in the design before the superstructure was put out for bids.

The Strand elevation had undoubtedly benefited from the long process of reconsideration, and Street had begun to pay at least some heed to those who complained against the irregularity of his work. Although the abandoned free-standing tower might have established the identity of the building more effectively from afar, the integral clock tower of the final design made a better coordinated contribution to the difficult composition (Fig. 108). Welling upward for 160 feet in a nearly unpunctured surge of blunt masonry, and tightly capped by a pyramidal roof, the tower certainly reflected the continuing influence of Burges. But the design was not Early French alone, and muscularity was tempered by other considerations and harnessed to the shared responsibilitites of the Strand elevation.

107 *Perspective inside the courtyard, looking north; by Street, February 1871. (Building News, 21 July 1882.)*

108 *The clock tower.*

Chief among the tempering elements was the influence of the Queen Anne, the new, gentler picturesque architecture of the seventies. Of the leaders of that movement—Richard Norman Shaw, Philip Webb, and William Eden Nesfield—the first two had been Street's assistants, and he had followed their work and their growing success with interest. Webb had allied himself with William Morris, whose firm was now receiving important commissions, while Shaw's career had already commenced a meteoric ascent. In 1870 Shaw had made his brilliant debut at the Royal Academy annual exhibition, the same show in which Burges's Cardiff Castle was hung and at which Street undoubtedly spent some hours on the eve of reorienting the block plan for the Royal Courts of Justice. Shaw had shown his drawings for Leyswood, the great "Old English" country house on which he had been at work since 1866, and their unveiling occasioned the first public acclamation for Queen Anne architecture (Fig. 109).

The precocious sophistication of Leyswood largely concealed its complex artistic origins, but Street would have recognized its underlying nuances. On the one hand, the design betrayed a continuing interest in Burges's—and Street's—Early French, most apparent in the compact masonry of the entrance tower. This was not unexpected, for most of the young Queen Anne architects had begun their careers in the thralldom of Gallic toughness, as seen undiluted in Shaw's earlier entry in the Bradford Exchange competition (1864) and in his All Saints, Bingley, Yorkshire (1867–71). However, the muscular Early French features of Leyswood were wedded with Shaw's new interest in picturesque half-timbering, and the resulting whole was milder and more English in character than his previous work. Although the component units were conceived with great care and discipline, their individual power was reduced in the interests of the pretty composition.

Sharing Shaw's awareness that muscularity was beginning to achieve diminish-

109 Richard Norman Shaw. Leyswood, Groombridge, Sussex. 1866–69. Bird's-eye view by Shaw, 1870. (Building News, 31 March 1871.)

110 The Strand façade, from the great portal to the clock tower.

111 The frieze of emblematic plants on the face of the clock tower.

ing returns, or perhaps inspired to direct emulation, Street created a final façade for the law courts which resembled Leyswood in many respects. The clock tower, while undoubtedly still designed with Burges's work at Cardiff in mind, was detailed with a kind of crisp precision that was alien to Burges, and Street stretched its surfaces much more tautly over the implicit bones of the building than Burges would have done. Shaw's reconsidered Early French, as seen in the gate tower at Leyswood, was much closer in feeling to what Street now intended.

Moreover, the tower of the law courts, like Shaw's, was nestled in the body of the building, and many features were calculated to restrain its individualism and to unify the entire façade. The division of the building into two major blocks was itself carefully disguised at the point of contact, the gateway into the courtyard, by the repetition of similar gables and tourelles on both sides of the dividing line (see Figs. 101, 102). Similarly, although the surfaces of the clock tower were notably free of ornament and offered a refreshing contrast to the lush floral carving concentrated around the principal entrance, a linking frieze of the emblematic plants of the British Isles was wrapped around its midriff before being unspooled across the long face of the building (Figs. 110, 111).

The national character of the Queen Anne must have interested Street as well, for he had already begun to invest the law courts with English references, like the allusion to Westminster Hall made by the composition of the entrance. The richer carving of the portal, including an almost veil-like screening arcade above the door-way, also betrayed a sensibility more English than French (Fig. 112). Inside the great hall, the massy balconies under the north and south windows recalled Gallic muscularity, but, with its Purbeck marble shafting and richly diapered tympana, the overall effect of the hall was much like English work of about 1250 (Figs. 113–115).[81] Street intended that the upper walls would be covered by mosaics.

238

112 *The great portal.*

113 *Supporting corbels under the south balcony in the central hall. (NMR)*

114 *Doorway leading to witness and jury rooms from the central hall. (NMR)*

115 *The central hall, looking south. (Archives Department, Westminster City Libraries. M.D. Trace photograph.)*

116 *Carey Street elevation,
eastern portion. Lithographed
contract drawing, 1871.* (PRO
Works 30/1991.)

117 *Carey Street elevation,
western portion. Lithographed
contract drawing, 1871.* (PRO
Works 30/1990.)

118 *The west façade.*

The north elevations which Street drew for the building show fewer changes, although his refinements emphasized simplicity and order in a comparable way (Figs. 116, 117). The fenestration pattern and the eaves-line of the central block were made less complex, and the center of the block was dramatized by a larger gable.

The flank elevations, unlike the north and south façades, did not have to define the relationship between the two blocks of the building. The western flank fronted on cleared land where Street did not intend to build, and so it was the only façade that might be seen in one glance (Fig. 118). Street contrived for it a generally symmetrical composition whose central feature was a high-roofed pavilion. This was set in a rather dull middle block, with stair towers at each end. The larger, southern stairs were designated for the use of judges. Beyond these a less restrained composition of office windows ran north and south to the corners of the building. The fenestration pattern clearly reflected the internal organization, the judges' chambers being identified by the tallest windows.

The eastern façade presented a more active face to Bell Yard, with two pairs of gables and a stair turret punctuating the interval between the building's principal northeast and southeast towers (Fig. 119). An irregular fenestration pattern reflected the division of the interior into a vast number of small rooms. The liveliness of this composition was intensified by the decision to build most of the east wing of brick, coursed with brilliantly contrasting bands and moldings of Portland stone.

Each of the four principal elevations could be seen, for the most part, only in

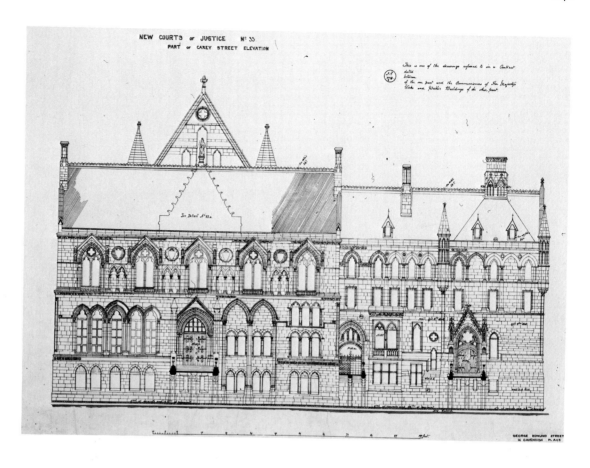

119 The east façade.

isolation from the others, and so each was imbued with a slightly different character. The brick-faced east façade was crowded with windows but sparsely ornamented. The west façade was composed of slightly larger units, and its leading features were considerably enriched with carved ornament. The north façade had two personalities, reflecting its division between the two main blocks of the building. To the west it presented a formal and grave aspect, with little that broke forward of the wall plane, but to the east there was an almost straggling concentration of tower and gabled bays. The scale of the Strand façade was the largest of all, and it contained the greatest contrast in detailing as well. The main entrance, set back in shadow and flanked by the richly traceried stair towers, was pitted against the simple masonry and unembellished openings of the clock tower.

The ingenious plan and forceful aspect of the law courts had evolved through a long series of circumstantial decisions rather than springing from a set of pre-established determinants. The pragmatic eclecticism of this process of design was not unfamiliar to Street, although he had abandoned its familiarity to pursue what seemed to be the more vital but theoretical objectives of High Victorian architecture. Restored to his accustomed practices as an artist, refreshed by the visual excitement of the Early French and Queen Anne, and goaded by the relentless practicality of the Office of Works, Street had produced a very up-to-date design for a middle-aged architect.

Public Controversy

DESPITE the contemporaneity of Street's thinking, and despite his success in securing the approval of the Government, his plans for the Royal Courts of Justice became the object of an extraordinary public assault. From the summer of 1871 through the fall, as he worked out the final details of the Strand elevation, his design was publicly abused and ridiculed. Edward J. Tarver illustrated this traumatic episode for the program cover of the 1872 soirée of the Architectural Association (Fig. 120). Street is shown seated behind a model of his design while his tormentors

120 Edward J. Tarver. The critics and the law courts. Architectural Association soirée program, 9 February 1872. (Architectural Association.)

fling missiles and squirt acid in its direction. A large body of his colleagues stands in the background, blindfolded.

The brunt of the criticism was directed at Street's picturesque Strand façade. In part, the complaints were antimedieval in spirit and reflected the resurgence of classicism in the last quarter of the nineteenth century, but other critics would have been satisfied with the kind of classicized Gothic that Street had now abandoned. The painful irony of this negative reaction was that he had begun to work on the law courts with his own strong, High Victorian reservations about the appropriateness of a picturesque solution. The successes enjoyed by the Early French and more recently by the Queen Anne had helped to overcome these doubts, but he now discovered that the picturesque was not as popular as he had imagined.

The dissatisfaction began rather quietly in Parliament, and at first the matter seemed containable. Questions had been raised for at least a year about the long delay in starting construction, and to satisfy these the drawings that Street had sent to the Treasury were also exhibited in the library of the House of Commons in July 1871.[82] The pressing business of the Ballot Bill kept them from being fully debated, but Cavendish Bentinck did inquire, skeptically, whether the plans had been approved, and he was satisfied by Lowe's explanation that they had only been put on display to encourage discussion.[83] The Treasury officially approved the design in August, but the decision was not made public.

It was James Fergusson, the turbaned acid-squirter of Tarver's cartoon, who stirred this matter into a tempest. The former secretary of works published an essay on the courts in the July 1 *Builder*, opening the debate that filled the press for the next eight months.[84] His complaint was, not surprisingly, very much like that voiced privately by Douglas Galton a few months earlier, for Fergusson and Galton were men of similar taste. Both saw the solution to the nineteenth-century architectural dilemma in a hard-headed analysis of contemporary material needs and capabilities. Although neither admitted to taking sides in the "Battle of the Styles," both chose Renaissance classicism for their own work. Fergusson, like Galton, now railed against the central hall because it was powerfully and extravagantly medieval and against the Strand elevation because it was picturesque. The groined roof of the hall he labeled an "imperforate, gloomy, solid vault," and he complained about both its expense and its effect on lighting. The new Strand façade, which Fergusson had seen "the other day," perhaps at the House of Commons, was called "the meanest design for the principal front of so important and pretentious a building which has been proposed in our day." He unhappily predicted that Street would "force his crotchet on his unwilling clients in spite of their wishes or interests." His review set the anti-Gothic tone of the many articles that followed.

George Godwin, the editor of the *Builder* who published Fergusson's piece, became one of the most dogged foes of the design. From the beginning he had preferred the classicism of Barry over Street's work, and he now launched a last, extraordinarily vicious campaign against the appointed architect. After the publication of illustrations of the design later in the year, the Strand façade became the *Builder*'s favorite target for abuse:

The overhanging turrets of the two extremities (the details of which, moreover, are so poorly designed, that they would not pass muster in a suburban villa); the overhanging pinnacles of the staircase turrets; the meanness and insufficiency of the main entrance; the ugliness of the great window; and the feeble treatment of the gable of the central hall, are amongst the weaknesses which will strike most critical observers. The great objection to the design, however, is utter want of unity and of anything like the dignity which should mark an important public building.[85]

Street, it concluded, should start over. Godwin published several other hostile descriptions and numerous caustic letters in the effort to unseat what he decried as "a lasting discredit to the age and the architect" and an "eyesore."[86]

Fergusson and Godwin quickly won the important support of the *Times*, which printed a scathing review on August 19 of the design shown to the House of Commons. The article, according to the custom of the *Times*, was probably written by a regular reporter rather than by the art critic, Thomas Taylor, and it warned that Street's project was "absolutely wanting in the essentials of a great public building."[87] The reviewer went on: "The best that can be said of Mr. Street's design as a whole is that it has a certain picturesqueness. . . . But we want much more than this in a building devoted to a great purpose, a building which is intended to stand forever, in the centre of a metropolitan city, as a chief credential of its empire and pre-eminence. We require pure and noble form, exalted dignity, entire unity." Instead, the Strand façade was found to resemble "some street in a college town" complete with "some goodly houses, a church, and town hall." One of the great symmetrical town halls of northern Europe, taken by itself, was recommended as the proper model for the law courts. The critic did not believe that Street would be able to mend his design and called for a new competition.

Significantly, an editorial in the *Times* repeated these criticisms three weeks later, complaining against the "broken outline, bound together by no visible dominant conception."[88] The recommendation of a Continental town hall model, and of the Cloth Hall at Ypres in particular, was reiterated, but it was now hoped that Street might be "liberally dealt with" and that he could revise his work himself. However, the *Times* was unimpressed when the slightly altered elevations were published in November and December, and a second review savagely attacked "that admired disorder which seems to be the sole and coveted ambition of a style of architecture which may be termed the promiscuous Gothic."[89] Street had proved himself unequal to the challenge, and the critic now recommended: "Sooner than show the world such buildings as these we now reject, buildings in which the meanness of a mass of jumbled detail is only relieved by the monstrosity of a huge false gable, and the studied deformity of a misplaced and mis-shapened tower, we would prefer to commission some contractor to copy one of the continental cloth-halls stone by stone." No wonder Tarver portrayed the *Times* as the large bucket of acid from which Fergusson replenished his syringe.

The *Times* was enormously influential, and the views expressed by its writers were closely imitated in the critical articles of the two big illustrated weeklies, the *Illustrated London News* and the *Graphic*. The former repeated the analysis of the Strand façade as a compilation of "separate buildings, each treated differently" with "here a hall, there a church, next a school, then a house or convent."[90] And it also joined the *Times* in recommending the adoption of a Belgian town hall as a prototype. The *Graphic* was even more literal in seizing this suggestion from the *Times*. Decrying the "entire absense of unity" in Street's design, it published illustrations of the civic halls of Ypres, Louvain, Oudenarde, and Brussels for inspiration in remaking the law courts.[91]

This criticism encouraged a great surge of letter writing. More than forty letters appeared in the *Times* during the eight months that the controversy raged, and these were almost entirely hostile. Almost every other architectural, legal, and general periodical printed similar correspondence or reprinted the letters that appeared in the *Times*. In general, the writers took up the antipicturesque prejudices voiced by the leading journals. One prominent correspondent was Edmund B. Denison, later Lord Grimthorpe (1816–1905), who found in the design "but one tone of fussiness and overdoing and want of repose everywhere," and condemned it for being "Streetian" rather than Gothic.[92] In gentler times, his latter comment might have passed for a compliment. The controversial younger Pugin, whom Tarver depicted wearing his father's overlarge mantle, with a supply of rocks for hurling at the design piled at his feet, was also a persistent critic, despite his lukewarm endorsement of the appointment of Street in 1868. The last of his incredibly vituperative letters to the *Times* claimed that Street's law courts "brought to a focus all that is un-Gothic in feeling, confused in arrangement, and unsightly. In fact, the whole design is irrational."[93] Pugin called on Parliament to "rescue the nation from an unparalleled degradation." A large number of letters received by the *Times* were written by unabashed classicists. "Anti-Gothic" wrote several times, and Sydney Smirke wrote once to recommend a closer study of the Colosseum and the Palazzo Medici.[94] "F.R.I.B.A." renewed Lowe's suggestion that the design might be based on Inigo Jones's Palace of Whitehall.[95] Street could not have followed all of this contradictory advice even if he had agreed with it.

Although the criticism was loud and widespread, the architect did find some welcome support, especially from magazines particularly interested in art. The *Athenaeum*, which had preferred Street's competition design, remained loyally at his side, perhaps through the continued support of its art critic, F. G. Stephens.[96] In July 1871, before the torrent of protest had gathered much headway, the *Athenaeum* paeaned: "It would not be easy to conceive greater elegance than appears in the details of this work, or combined masses finer than those it exhibits."[97] It reiterated its support after the mudslinging had begun.[98] A. J. Beresford-Hope's *Saturday Review* also joined the fray on the side of Street, deploring the "Donnybrook style of criticism" to which he had been subjected. It protested: "We should, in the present aspect of the question, regard it as an equal misfortune to law and to art if Mr. Street were to be shaken in a position he is so competent to fill."[99] Having favored the competition entry of Burges, it was reasonable that the *Saturday Review* should approve of Street's revised plans.

Perhaps most comforting to Street was the support he received from two architectural journals, the *Building News* and the *Architect*. Both initially followed the lead of the *Builder* in criticizing his design, but both later reversed their positions. In each case the change seems to have been effected by the intervention of the architect Edward Godwin, no kin of George Godwin of the *Builder,* whose own Early French predilections disposed him favorably toward the final design for the law courts. Perhaps significant was the fact that Godwin's Leicester Town Hall competition design had only recently received the highest award from Street, the contest assessor.

The *Building News* began inauspiciously by reprinting Fergusson's article from the *Builder.*[100] But on July 28, it published an article by Godwin, who was doing a good deal of journalistic work at that time. He carefully refuted Fergusson's criticism of the lighting of the central hall, and he called that great chamber "one of Mr. Street's very happiest efforts."[101] Indeed, Godwin judged the design overall to be better than any of Street's prior work, although he lamented the loss of the intended, larger clock tower and objected that, in a few places in the Strand front, "the temperance of horizontal lines so admirably introduced in the other elevations is wanting." Godwin's essay did not immediately change the editorial policy of the *Building News,* but in October and November, it published a series of four unsigned articles which discussed the design as revised by Street in exhaustive and favorable detail.[102] The effect of these articles was marked, and thereafter, although the *Building News* continued to reprint hostile criticism from other sources, its own remarks were friendlier.[103] The new tone was established by the anonymous reviewer of Street's elevations:

> Nothing could be happier than the varied yet always harmonious balance of parts that pervades all these fronts, and contributes in so high a degree to the effectiveness of each one of them; and equally happy also is that subordinate balance of parts that invests with a peculiar value and dignity the principal component members of each front. When studied in succession, and due attention is given both to the palpable evidence of unity of principle and to the recurrence of familiar details, all the fronts are seen to belong to each other and to the same edifice, as with equal impressiveness each front declares its own completeness as being in itself an independent composition.[104]

Street must have been relieved to read such a sympathetic analysis of his work. The *Building News* quixotically announced several weeks later that it had championed his design from the outset, and its first leading article of 1872 was a long refutation of his critics entitled "Damnatory Art Criticism."[105] As in the case of the *Saturday Review,* it seems that an earlier enthusiasm for Burges's competition entry could be converted into approval for Street's revised design.

The *Architect* also began with little that could comfort Street. The first discussion of his façade in July 1871 argued that Gothic need not be "antagonistic to grace" or characterized by "beggarly severity," the qualities the journal saw in his work.[106] The next notice concluded that the architect should alter his elevations to make them "less pretentiously inelegant; unless indeed he were seriously minded to make himself a martyr to the ungainly cause of exaggerated muscularity," and in mid-September it advised him to "begin again *de novo,* and . . . compose a noble symmetrical façade for the whole 500 feet."[107] But on September 30, the *Architect* printed its own article by Godwin, who aptly characterized the bulk of the unfriendly criticism as inherently anti-medieval.[108] He defended the much-maligned Strand façade in sympathetically Gothic terms, like those used by the anonymous critic of the *Building News:*

> The perfect balance of parts shows unity of plan. The absence of all small features and the fewness of large ones shows simplicity of form or composition, whilst the dimensions alone of the great gable will show whether it is mean or imposing in its mass. The eastern part of the Strand front looks just what it is—five storeys of offices *attached* to the Law Courts. No doubt the *Times* would like to see the windows in a frontage of 507 feet all of uniform shape and size. This possibility is the only idea of architectural unity which our amateurs possess—closet and council chamber, court and corridor, all lit by a regulation pattern window.

Godwin's rebuttal applied with nearly equal effect to the criticism voiced by the writers of the *Architect* themselves, and, suitably chastened, they treated Street much more favorably thereafter. In December, they quoted Godwin in replying to the further attack launched by the *Times,* and their publication of illustrations of the new design was accompanied by an appreciative description.[109] On January 6, the *Architect* recommended Street's plan as a "fine example of pure Gothic detail," and a month later the editors sharply rebuked Fergusson for his "querulous dogmatisms."[110] Edward Godwin had worked the same magic with T. Roger Smith, the editor of the *Architect,* that he had with the proprietor of the *Building News,* the philanthropist Passmore Edwards.

A similarly heartening change of attitude was recorded in the one legal journal which followed the design controversy closely, and in this Street's own intervention was instrumental. The *Law Journal* had reprinted the first review from the *Times* in late August, and had agreed that the design should be submitted to "searching criticism."[111] Shortly afterward its writers predicted that the Government would subject Street's work to a "competent tribunal or to a public competition."[112] But in early October the *Journal* abruptly reversed this position. At the invitation of Street, the editors had examined the drawings on which he was then making the final revisions, and, expressly limiting their remarks to utilitarian questions, they concluded: "After a careful inspection of the plans, and after the full and lucid explanations of Mr. Street, we are able to state that, so far as the business capacity and accommodation of the New Law Courts are concerned, the most exacting critic must be thoroughly satisfied. . . . In respect to convenience the plans of Mr. Street leave nothing to be desired."[113] The *Law Journal* supported Street faithfully after being thus flattered by personal lobbying, and the next year it extended its approval beyond the narrow realm of practicality.[114] "In his style—the Gothic," the editors wrote, "Mr. Street is the foremost architect of the age."[115]

Street felt that others might be similarly converted if given the opportunity to study his drawings, and so he admitted the writer of the *Building News* to his office. On December 23, he extended his campaign by holding an afternoon open house for the members of the R.I.B.A. in the temporary building that housed his staff on the site.[116] The cartoonist Edward J. Tarver accepted the invitation, and came away convinced of the high quality of the design.[117] Finally, other architects began to come to Street's defense in the correspondence columns. In particular, John P.

Seddon took Street's critics to task in several letters to the *Times* in December. Seddon, like Godwin, had every reason to approve the artistic character of the new design, which approached the spirit of his own Burges-like work. He also reproved Fergusson for "his persistent misrepresentation" of the lighting of the central hall—which that critic had called gloomy—and termed his entire critique of the law courts a "farrago of windy nonsense."[118] Seddon appealed to the medievalist Edmund Sharpe to lend his opinion to the controversy surrounding the hall, eliciting one of the most impressive defenses of the design ever written. Sharpe wrote from the French Pyrénées to give his warm endorsement to the entire design, but especially to the vaulted hall. If erected, he predicted that London would acquire "the finest hall of the kind, without any exception, that has ever been constructed in any country, or in any age up to the present time."[119]

Thomas H. Wyatt, the R.I.B.A. president, also intended to defend Street in his address to the first meeting of the 1871–72 session of the institute on November 6. Of the published complaints he observed: "A more painful bewildering array of criticism I cannot conceive, or one more likely to paralyse and destroy the powers of the architect," and he particularly questioned the "tone and severity" of Fergusson's comments and Pugin's "tirade of self-sufficient abuse."[120] But, warming to the subject, Wyatt went on to say, "I claim the right personally to criticise Mr. Street's design, and to express regret that the Strand front is so broken up into various and perhaps disjoined parts, so long as I do so without personality or violence." Unfortunately, these negative comments were widely quoted as the gist of his talk, even though Wyatt wrote to the *Times* to explain that he had "no wish to see the general character of Mr. Street's design altered."[121]

The debate reached a final crescendo of ill will when James Fergusson reiterated his earlier criticisms in a long essay for *Macmillan's Magazine* in January 1872. His attack on Street was searingly personal:

> According to this Joshua of architects, the sun of art stood still when Edward III. died in 1377, and has not moved forward since that time. Hence the lawyers of the nineteenth century must be content to lounge in vaulted halls, with narrow windows filled with painted glass, and so dark that they cannot see to read or write in them. They must wander through corridors whose gloom recalls the monkish seclusion of the Middle Ages. They must sit on high straight-back chairs, and be satisfied with queer shaped furniture, which it is enough to give one the rheumatism to look at; and no higher class of art must be allowed to refresh their eyes than the heraldic devices, or the crude, ungainly nightmare paintings of the Middle Ages.[122]

Fergusson also reopened the entire issue of Street's appointment, asserting, with reference to the report of Shaw and Pownall, "To Mr. Street was awarded the Law Courts, because his design was the worst—a perfectly competent tribunal having awarded him only three marks in the competition, while it had assigned Edward Barry forty-three."[123] This at last goaded Street into replying publicly to his critics.

As suggested by Tarver's cartoon—in which the cup of vitriol in Fergusson's hand is labeled "Macmillan's"—Street had so far endured the slings of his critics in silence, knowing at least that his design had received the support of the Government. But the possibility that his appointment might be reconsidered evidently alarmed him, and he rushed his reply to Fergusson into print. In a pamphlet dated January 1, 1872, Street explained his feelings:

> For six months I have held my tongue under great provocation; and if I now speak, it is only because when one, who is "proud to call me his friend" [as Fergusson had asserted], circulates persistently statements about my work and my intentions, as to which he has no knowledge whatever, and which are, in point of fact, in almost every particular contrary to the facts, it is necessary for my own credit's sake, and out of deference to those real friends who concern themselves for me, that I should at last brush away the cobwebs in which my critic is attempting—I hope in vain—to entangle me.[124]

To this end Street explained the care with which he had planned the building, stressing that complete practicality, not cranky medievalism, was its most salient quality. To the charge of blind historicism he replied: "If Mr. Fergusson, or any one else, can find any feature in my design which is copied from any thing else any where, I shall be happy to change it."[125] He defended his Strand elevation on the ground that it would have to be seen "bit by bit, or in a very fore-shortened perspective," but he noted that the west front, which would look onto a large piece of cleared ground, was "treated in a very regular and uniform fashion."[126] Street complained that the misapprehensions of Fergusson were caused by his lack of detailed knowledge of the design, and that he had missed the opportunity to remedy his ignorance afforded by the office open house on December 23. Even George Godwin of the *Builder* had been present on that occasion, although he stayed only fifteen minutes.[127] Street also made a complete restatement of the arguments with which he had defended the single appointment, noting particularly those advisory reports that reflected unfavorably on Barry.

The pamphlet made scant mention of the other critics, for Street sensed that Fergusson, whose essay in the *Builder* had struck the first blow, was his chief foe. Fergusson made only one reply, a letter to the *Athenaeum*, but it was exceptionally virulent, calling Gothic revivalists "a small clique, worshipping that peculiar fetish."[128] This was nearly the last barb cast in the controversy, although an essay in the *Quarterly Review* in April did reconsider some of the issues.[129]

The debate was effectively diffused during the first months of 1872 through two outlets. The first was a deflection of attention to the unlucky but dogged E. M. Barry, who now reasserted his claims. In September 1871, when sentiment seemed to be turning against Street, Barry had written privately to the Treasury to remind them of his contention that the original award of the judges ought to be upheld.[130] This received the usual indifferent reply, but in December he repeated his claim in a letter to the *Times*, observing that Street's elevation "does not seem likely to command general approval."[131] The renewed discussion of the competition in the exchanges between Fergusson and Street spurred him to redoubled activity, and he published a pamphlet of his own on January 22.[132] Barry complained that Street had failed to consult with him before accepting his appointment and repeated his familiar and pathetic story of near misses, frustrated hopes, and bureaucratic insensitivity.

Even the *Athenaeum* noted his pamphlet sympathetically, and Street could only reply with a second edition of his booklet, dated January 31, in which he explained in a postscript his own version of the events following the appointment.[133] Street maintained that he had corresponded cordially with Barry at that time, and although Barry argued with Street in several letters over the details of the story, it does seem that he had at first accepted the good fortune of his colleague with something like equanimity.[134]

Barry's private argument provided a distraction, but the altercation reached a more definite conclusion when the discussion was at length transferred to the House of Commons, even though that body was not required to approve the design. The controversy had begun during the long annual recess, and so it was only when Parliament reconvened in 1872 that the law courts became the subject of a brief but decisive debate. On March 23 George Cavendish Bentinck, who had questioned the merits of the design the previous July and who had himself written one letter to the *Times,* rose to call attention to the criticism which had been leveled against Street. He introduced a hostile motion: "That, in the opinion of this House, the designs prepared by Mr. Street for the New Building of the Courts of Justice are unsatisfactory, and ought not to executed."[135] The usual bipartisan coalition replied. A. J. Beresford-Hope, a Tory, led off, branding the review in the *Times* a "magnificent monument of big words piled together with reckless profusion."[136] He was followed by the Liberal Roundell Palmer, then on the eve of his appointment as lord chancellor, who confessed that he had "no taste whatever" but went on to proclaim that the confidence he had felt in Street while a competition judge was not diminished by the evidence of the revised design.[137] Others spoke in support of Street from both sides of the aisle. The costs and inconvenience of further delay were referred to, and Ayrton concluded the debate with the assertion that the motion against Street had come four years too late. In fact, no member spoke in support of the resolution after it had been seconded, and, in the end, Cavendish Bentinck withdrew it from consideration without a vote. Despite the heated discussion, Street's position remained secure, and the design that had been approved by the Treasury received what amounted to a vote of confidence from Parliament.

Street's status was reaffirmed over the next several months. In July, responding to further questions about the design from Cavendish Bentinck, Ayrton observed that "While great difference of opinion and much dissatisfaction had been expressed, there had been no such general disapproval as would render it necessary for the Office of Works to take any steps on the subject."[138] In August, when Cavendish Bentinck warned that the adoption of Street's "elaborate elevation" would be a "lasting disgrace to the art of this country" and called for the appointment of a new architect, Ayrton was again heard to speak of Street with unexpected respect. "That gentleman was singularly well qualified to carry out that style [Gothic]," he was reported to say, "and to produce a building of as much beauty as any other architect that could be named."[139] So the slow process of preparing the quantities and completing the contract drawings was allowed to proceed, and builders were finally invited to bid for the superstructure early in 1873. Their tenders were delivered on March 25.[140]

Economy

AFTER the construction tenders were received, Street learned how tenuous his position still remained. While he had been sparring recently with the Government on matters of taste—about which he might presume to be better informed than it—the subject was now economics again, and in that realm Ayrton and Lowe reigned unchallenged. As a critical correspondent had written to the *Builder* in 1872: "To get a satisfactory building for the Law Courts it may not be necessary to change the architect, but only to change his views, and the purse-bearer will do that for us in a trice."[141]

Economy now became a serious issue because the lowest tender substantially exceeded the £710,000 that remained for construction, after the payment of Street's commission. In the spring of 1873, following a year of relative peace, the architect was thus asked to alter his design once more in order to reduce its cost. This new debate revived many of the aesthetic arguments of 1871–72, and Street was again compelled to rally a political defense for his art.

Street was first warned that his work was threatened when the Office of Works notified him on March 26 that the low bidder for the main contract was Joseph Bull and Sons, with a tender of £758,816.[142] To this had to be added £31,500 which had already been expended on the foundations, as well as the cost of heating and lighting apparatus, calculated by Street at £20,000 and £8,000 respectively. The total excess over budget was thus £108,000. In his defense, Street cited the additional offices of the lunacy department which he had been required to provide and the recent steep inflation. He quoted an overall rise in builders' work of fifteen percent since he had begun to flesh out the approved block plan in 1870, and, in fact, modern economic research suggests that the inflation of building costs during this period was twenty-two percent.[143] These figures easily account for the projected overrun. The best courses he could suggest, in the interest of economy, were to eliminate £14,000 which the contractor had allowed for contingencies, to reduce the amount to be spent on stonecarving from £35,000 to £20,000, and to adopt the alternate bid, submitted by all tenderers, for the use of deal in place of oak for courtroom fittings and of Chilmark instead of Portland stone for the carcass of the building. These savings would be preferable to reducing the accommodation or altering the general outlines of the design, against which Street protested: "I really cannot see how a building which has been designed on a uniform system throughout can be largely reduced in cost without complete ruin to its character." His proposals would reduce the projected excess to approximately £50,000.

Street's suggestions did not find favor with Henry Hunt, who judiciously recommended the "employment of the best and most suitable Materials," namely, oak and Portland stone.[144] Chilmark stone had only recently come into use, having been employed by Gilbert Scott at the chapter house of Westminster Abbey, and it was not yet realized that it survived the London atmosphere better than the long-established Portland.[145] Deal—the term applied to fir and pine—was soft and wore quickly. Rather than skimp by using such materials, Hunt advised just what Street had opposed:

> If reductions are to be made, they should I venture to think be effected by omitting some of the Buildings—the Lunacy Offices for instance, by which a saving of probably £30,000 would be made—or by the entire omission of the

Central Hall, the cost of which I calculate will be according to Messrs. Bull's Estimate about £80,000. This course would in my humble judgment be far better than impoverishing a Building of National importance.

Ayrton concurred with this assessment, and on April 3, he sought approval from the Treasury to revise the design. He repeated many of the bigoted arguments that had been raised against medievalism and irregularity in the previous debate:

In my opinion, . . . the excesses on the proposed Contract is [sic] to be ascribed to the character of Mr. Street's plans and designs in the following particulars. The Central Hall, though an excellent reproduction of an ancient mode of construction, is an extravagant building unsuited to the purpose for which it is to be constructed, and prejudicial to the buildings on either side of it. In order to exhibit a part of the gable end of the Hall, which is not in the centre of the Southern Front, the Southern Elevation is broken up in an irregular and costly manner to produce a picturesque effect. But this cannot be seen on account of the narrowness of the road which is not likely to be widened. A more uniform elevation of ample grandeur would be better adapted to the side of the street, and would admit of more convenient arrangement within the building.[146]

In the context of the recent public criticism of the design and the risk of exceeding the budget, the Treasury, heretofore the ally of Street, accepted this assessment and authorized Ayrton to proceed as he liked. The elimination of the central hall—contemplated since 1870—was now specifically endorsed, and in its place the Treasury recommended "an open Court with such protection from inclement weather . . . by Cloisters or otherwise as may be desirable."[147] On April 21, Ayrton summoned Street to a meeting at which this proposition was laid before him. He was asked to begin to work out possible alterations in the hall and the main façade and to return to discuss them in the near future.

Street realized that his artistic control over the project had been placed in jeopardy. Rather than return for a second meeting at the Office of Works, he stood his ground and dispatched a lengthy written protest to Ayrton on May 1.[148] This is the most powerful document pertaining to the law courts in the correspondence files of the Office of Works. For Street the central issue was the great hall, whose vaulting Ayrton wished to replace with a roof of iron and glass. Street argued that the hall was "an absolute necessity for convenience and arrangement" and that to replace its masonry covering would be "a fatal error both to the Architectural dignity of the Building and also to its stability." The new materials were subject to "rapid decay," while no one had succeeded in making such a covering "dignified or fine." He concluded this passage with an impassioned avowal:

It would be impossible for me, feeling this as strongly as I do, to consent to such an alteration of this feature as I understand you to propose—To agree would be to commit an act of artistic suicide, and my contemporaries no less than my successors would blame me most heartily and most rightly, if, knowing that acquiescence would ruin a public building of such importance, I should on any account acquiesce in such a proposal.

Having recorded this stirring protest, Street outlined an alternative scheme of reduction that preserved the Portland stone, the oak, and the central hall, and still afforded a saving of £52,000. Its chief elements were a decrease in ornamental carving and the elimination of the contractor's allowance for extras—both previously suggested, the substitution of brick cornices and iron gutters for stone and lead in the light areas between the courtrooms, and the elimination of the turret and ventilation stacks of the central hall.

At the Office of Works, Street's passion inspired few tears, and his financial proposal, which would account for less than half the projected deficit of £108,000, convinced no member of the economical regime. On May 9, he was sent a stiff reply.[149] "It is to be regretted that you should have brought forward questions of a personal character," he was told, and the history of his employment by the government, with frequent references to the budget ceiling, was recited for his benefit. The Office of Works demanded three further alterations to bring the building within its appropriation. The first target was again the central hall, of which it was now said: "This structure with its stone vaulting is undoubtedly a fine but costly imitation of architectural works erected centuries ago but it has been questioned whether it is suited for the purposes for which the buildings are to be erected." The Strand façade was also to be cheapened and, at the same time, made "harmonious, dignified, simple, and free from redundant decorations." The third proposal, an ingenious new idea, was made with the logic of an accountant: "The Clock Tower at the South East corner is wholly unnecessary and might be dispensed with as the building will have to be provided with clocks in all parts of it." Street was asked to prepare rough sketch plans of these changes as soon as possible.

As the situation seemed to be moving very rapidly beyond his control, Street stalled by requesting details about the desired alterations. He also complained bitterly against Ayrton's demands saying: "If I am compelled to carry out the suggestions he has made the result will be a building which both in convenience and appearance will be grievously maimed and mutilated."[150] The Office of Works replied with merely the required information.[151]

On May 22 Street wrote again to report the unpromising results of his reconsideration of the design. He told Ayrton, "I regret that I do not quite see how . . . I can accomplish what you require even by the wholesale alteration of my plans which you suggest and which I have so earnestly deprecated as being destructive to their character."[152] He pointed out that any savings would be canceled by the £30,000 that he had been asked to allocate to the revised central hall and by the extra £20,000 that he estimated the alteration of the Strand façade would cost—an alteration ordered to save money. Clearly, Street was not ready to comply, although he was forced to be realistic. He found himself pitted against an enormously powerful bureaucratic agency, and if he could not stop it, he had resolved at least to retreat as slowly as possible.

In the meantime, a decision had been made that would ultimately rescue Street from his predicament. While still negotiating with the architect, Ayrton had asked the Treasury if he might sign a contract with Bull and Sons on the understanding that the amount was to be reduced to the statutory limit. On May 20, it allowed such an arrangement, but, apparently in analogy with allowance for inflation that had been permitted in the contract for the Natural History Museum, it also allowed an increase of £54,000 in the total contract sum for the law courts—an allowance Ayrton had not requested.[153] This was half the overrun of Bull's tender, leaving only £54,000 of reductions to be made, and Street had already contrived savings of nearly that amount. But the devious Ayrton chose not to advise the architect of this reprieve, granted by the characteristically more sympathetic Treasury. Perhaps he was eager to prove that he could be more economical than even his old colleagues at the Exchequer. In any case, he reaffirmed to Street the goal of cutting £108,000, hinting only obliquely at the new flexibility provided by the Treasury decision. Street was assured, "The First Commissioner does not doubt that, not merely an adequate building, but one which would do credit to you as an Architect could be constructed within these limits, but if it shall appear upon examination of the sketch which you have been directed to furnish that this could not have been accomplished, the First Commissioner will then be prepared to reconsider his opinion on the limit of cost."[154] The new Treasury policy was not mentioned, and the architect was admonished, "The First Commissioner thinks that if you had attended at this office some time ago, as requested by him, instead of writing letters, the sketch might now have been in a forward state, if not ready for a preliminary inspection."

The Fall of Ayrton

UNABLE to detect any change, Street resolved to play his last and strongest cards. On May 27, when he received his latest instructions from the Office of Works, he appealed privately to Gladstone, his old supporter, and he called on Robert Lowe, who had assisted him in his last dispute with Ayrton. The aid of Gladstone was not needed, for Street learned from Lowe the happy news that the Treasury had already reduced its demands and had directed "for the works of the New Law Courts to be proceeded with in the way proposed."[155] Thus fortified, Street again advised the Office of Works that "I find myself quite unable to make the reductions required by the First Commissioner of Works in the cost of this building."[156] However, he reported slyly that by altering some of the stonework he could increase the possible savings to just over £54,000, precisely the amount he now knew that the Treasury had approved.

Street must have been astonished when the Office of Works, despite the instructions of the Treasury, persisted in requiring the full £108,000 reduction and curtly asked him to inform the office when his revised sketch plans would be ready.[157] He did not answer, and on June 14 the secretary of works sent him an ultimatum: "I am directed by the First Commissioner to request that you will be so obliging as to furnish the Board with a reply . . . before 12 o'clock on Monday next the 16th instant."[158] But Street had now taken the entire matter to a different authority.

On June 11, he had formally appealed to the Treasury against Ayrton's autocratic behavior. He described what the first commissioner had ordered, and he explained:

> As I believe it to be absolutely impossible to make any such alterations effect such a saving, and as I am quite sure that if I made the attempt I should only succeed in ruining my design both as regards convenience and Architectural character I am compelled much against my will to lay before your Lordships the reductions which I believe might be made without damage to my design,

and to most of which I have repeatedly and in Vain endeavored to obtain the consent of the First Commissioner of Works.[159]

He then detailed the £54,000 in cuts that Ayrton had just rejected. Although a Treasury official noted dubiously, "Do you think we have any chance of inducing the First Commissioner to fall in with our proposal?" on June 14 another letter of instructions was prepared for Ayrton.[160] He was told to accept the suggestions made by Street and to desist from requesting further alterations:

> Their Lordships [the lords of the Treasury] cannot but think, although they made a suggestion in regard to the Central Hall in a previous letter, that it is highly undesirable that in an undertaking of such magnitude as the proposed New Building, the Architect should be compelled to make reductions, which he so strongly deprecates himself; and for which, if insisted upon, and in the event of their being disapproved by the Nation, the Executive Government will be held responsible.

Apparently confident concerning his appeal to Lowe, Street sent a letter to the Office of Works just in time to meet the deadline, restating his inability to revise the design in the desired manner. He also protested the entire policy of interference in his art, "a condition of affairs which no Architect who had any respect for his work could possibly accept."[161]

Ayrton, of course, was outraged. On June 19, he vented his paranoia to the Treasury, protesting that Street "had been engaged in negotiations with . . . your Lordships to defeat my instructions, which he had carefully concealed from me."[162] If the matter were left with the Office of Works, Ayrton now proposed to be rid of the troublesome Street entirely and to place the law courts "under the supervision of an Officer of the Department." He thus intended to adopt the example of the General Post Office annex as a general principle, a gloomy possibility. Should Lowe wish to enforce his views, the Treasury, at its own risk, would have to "employ Mr. Street directly as your own Architect," and Ayrton would then accept no responsibility for the law courts.

Ayrton's refusal to cooperate made it necessary to refer the problem to the Cabinet. Apparently realizing that a major decision was imminent, Street reinforced his position in the highest circles of the Government. On June 17, he wrote to Gladstone, again accepting a standing breakfast invitation.[163] On June 18 and also, it seems, on June 26, the prime minister entertained him, and they almost surely discussed the law courts.[164]

The matter came before the Cabinet for the first time on Saturday, June 21, when Lowe explained the situation to the other ministers. As a result of their discussion, Gladstone arranged to meet with Ayrton, who was not himself a member of the Cabinet, on the following Monday.[165] Nothing seems to have come of this conference with his infuriating subordinate. Therefore, the subject was raised again at the next Saturday meeting of the Cabinet, for which both Lowe and Gladstone prepared extensive notes on the case, both favorable to Street.[166] The ministers approved Gladstone's draft of a letter to Ayrton. He was advised:

> What Her Majesty's Government desire is that the plan as it has been de-

signed and approved according to the Statute should now be put in execution in the best and most effectual manner, which as Her Majesty's Government understand is still practicable within very nearly the limits of costs prescribed by Parliament not withstanding the heavy increase of prices now prevailing. Now that the Cabinet has arrived at these conclusions we may I am sure rely on your cordial cooperation.[167]

On Tuesday, the Treasury sent a letter in the same spirit to Ayrton, and the Office of Works began to give way.[168] On Wednesday, the assistant secretary informed Street that "for reasons independent of the questions which have engaged the attention of this Board, the Lords of the Treasury have determined that the instructions desiring a reconsideration of your plans and drawings for the New Courts of Justice shall not be acted upon."[169] On the same day Gladstone patiently urged Ayrton to yield gracefully.[170]

But conciliation was not in Ayrton's character, and on July 11 he again protested to the prime minister the decision to go ahead with the largely unaltered design.[171] His letter was discussed in the Cabinet the next afternoon, and it was decided that he must be asked to withdraw his criticism. Gladstone noted, "Probably this would best be done by his own spontaneous action. I asked Mr. Glyn [George Grenfell Glyn, the majority whip] to go to Mr. Ayrton, believing that this informal intervention would be more agreeable to him than any other method of communication."[172] But the thoughtfulness of the premier went for nought; on July 19, he was compelled to rebuke Ayrton for his rudeness toward poor Glyn.[173]

Complicated by other difficulties, the law courts imbroglio was rapidly becoming a Government crisis of the first magnitude. The long and costly delay was more and more often the subject of questioning in Parliament, and of public skepticism as well.[174] The latter was recorded by Anthony Trollope in the *Prime Minister* (first published in 1875–76), which described the "neighbourhood of Portugal Street," where much had been "pulled down a dozen years ago on behalf of the law courts which are to bless some coming generation."[175] To compound this, both Lowe and Ayrton were involved in other unpopular policies. The chancellor lived forever under the shadow of his infamous budget of 1871, in which he had sought to pay for the costly reform of the army commission purchase system with a tax on matches. This inspired a heartrending demonstration by the waifs who manufactured and hawked lucifers on street corners. Amid much criticism of the cruel economy of the Government, the tax was withdrawn. Lowe had also been implicated in two scandals in 1873. In the first, it was found that he had unknowingly approved the financing of the deficits of the newly nationalized telegraph system out of the assets of the Post Office Savings Bank, and he was barely saved from censure after the report of a royal commission. In the other scandal, Lowe authorized the award of the Zanzibar mail contract without competitive bids, and a commission of inquiry on this question was appointed just as the controversy over Ayrton and the law courts reached its peak.[176] Ayrton, meanwhile, had made himself generally offensive to every official with whom he came into contact, and, perhaps most critically, he had deeply offended Queen Victoria by his handling of the reconstruction of the drainage system at Windsor Castle.[177] His relations with Lowe, the minister with whom he had the most official contact, had never even been polite, and they were certainly not improved by the law courts struggle.

The unhappy state of Gladstone's Government at this time was parodied by W. S. Gilbert in *The Happy Land,* a play that opened at the Royal Court Theatre on March 3, 1873. The satire was banned by the lord chamberlain on March 7, because of its scarcely disguised political commentary. Gilbert had portrayed the deputation of three earthly ministers, Messrs. G[ladstone], L[owe], and A[yrton], to Fairyland, where they were to instruct the inhabitants in the principles of popular government. In one very pertinent scene, Zayda, the fairies' minister of works, and Mr. A. are heard discussing the activities of her department in the light of recent criticism:

ZAYDA   Well you see what it has come to; they've been grumbling about those subterranean Law Courts again, I dare say.

Mr. A.   Subterranean! Why not subterranean?

ZAYDA   Why, it's all in the dark.

Mr. A.   Well, what of that? Isn't Justice blind? What does it matter where she sits. Listen to me. You've done *too much.* That's what you've done. You want your Law Courts? Good! You open the affair to public competition. Three hundred enthusiastic architects instantly rush to the front, and prepare designs. *Very* good again! You pin them all to a wall, shut your eyes, and pick out one of them. Now you begin business in earnest. You clear a site; you collect all the dust-carts in Europe; you go to work and bring in—

ZAYDA   Bricks and mortar by the hundredweight.

Mr. A.   No. Rubbish! All the rubbish you can lay hold of—by the ton!

ZAYDA   And the Law Courts?

Mr. A.   Never build them at all. [178]

In Gilbert's imagination, official Philistinism and Street's unpopular, picturesque design had been combined into one unfortunate medley.

The growing unpopularity of two of the chief ministers of the Government finally compelled remedial action. On August 4, Lowe tendered his resignation to Gladstone, expressing the fear that he would be a source of "weakness and embarrassment to you and our colleagues," and Gladstone decided to take on the responsibilities of the Exchequer himself. [179] On August 6, the Cabinet approved the plan submitted by the prime minister to displace Ayrton as well, moving him to the post of judge advocate general. [180] Gladstone bluntly advised the first commissioner, "recent events have convinced me of the necessity of changes in the distribution of offices, and partially in the composition of the Government. In these events you have been a sharer. I have arrived at the conclusion that there requires to be a change of hands in the Several Departments which are principally concerned." [181] Ayrton expressed his willingness to accede "for the general interest," but he also reported that he had prepared several caustic memos on Treasury policy, to which he called Gladstone's attention. This underlined the fact that he was the second successive first commissioner to leave office after a dispute with the Exchequer over the law courts. He further asked that some mark of distinction be awarded to Douglas Galton, whose services he had come to esteem and whose criticism of Street's work had been so constant.[182] William Patrick Adam (1823–81), the Liberal M.P. for Clackmannan and Kinrose and a descendant of the famous family of Scottish architects, was chosen to succeed Ayrton.

After the rearrangement of the Government, work on the law courts was allowed to proceed without official impediment. However, the builder now raised certain objections, in part occasioned by the long delay, and the contract was not signed until February 7, 1874.[183] The first brick was laid on May 1, but by that time Disraeli was again prime minister, having ousted Gladstone with the aid of those who opposed Liberal policy toward public education. Gladstone's long association with the law courts project was thus interrupted, although he did return to power in 1880, in time to attend the opening of the new building. Because of the more straightforward objectives of the Conservatives, the later years during which Street worked on his great commission were filled with less controversy, but the design forever bore the effects of Liberal management.

In the summer that construction began on the new law courts, Street turned fifty. That fall, Mariquita, his wife of nearly twenty-five years and his companion in most of his Continental travels, died after a brief illness. Suddenly, the architect for whom the law courts had promised to be the crowning achievement of young maturity had been caught up by the rush of years. The long delay and the bitter disputes had exacted their toll, and a younger generation of architects, sometimes critical of Street's values, had come to the fore. Street now stood out in contrast among the contemporaries of Norman Shaw, although his work continued, almost gamely, to reflect the new environment.

The Tide of Taste

IT WAS ironic that Street's steadfast adherence to apparently up-to-date artistic principles in designing the law courts should have earned such unpopularity. But the explanation is not far to seek. Street had been attracted away from the High Victorian ideal of a medieval–classical synthesis by the triumph of Burges's weighty, irregular design in the competition and by the subsequent success of the pretty picturesque of the Queen Anne. However, there was simultaneously a growing reaction against picturesque excesses, especially in public architecture. As early as 1868 the *Building News*, long the champion of the Early French, had begun to criticize what it later called the "stiff and ungraceful incipient French Geometrical style, with heavy round columns and windows formed merely by piercing the wall and leaving masses of brick or stone between the several lights."[184] The new, young-spirited *Architect* joined in this complaint, attacking the "crude architecture" which was characterized by "sheer muscularity and unrestraint."[185] In this critical climate, the law courts were not alone in being attacked. G. G. Scott's St. Pancras Station (1865–71), a similarly picturesque design, was the target of almost equally savage comment. John T. Emmett wrote in the *Quarterly Review* of 1872: "There is no relief or quiet in any part of the work. The eye is constantly troubled and tormented, and the mechanical patterns follow one another with such rapidity and perseverance, that the mind becomes irritated where it ought to be gratified and goaded to criticism where it should be led calmly to approve."[186]

Shaw and his contemporaries, the successful young architects of the Queen

Anne generation, were sensitive to this nuance of taste, and they indulged in the picturesque only in their domestic, nonurban work. In the countryside, they built rambling, tower-topped and half-timbered manors, but in towns they adopted the gentle Renaissance of the English seventeenth century, with its bright red brick and white sashes, typified by Shaw's New Zealand Chambers (1871–73). Gradually, their Renaissance turned into Baroque, and by the eighties the hegemony of classicism was nearly complete. For example, in the Birmingham Municipal Buildings competition, as early as 1871, four of the five selected finalist designs were classical even though the judge was Alfred Waterhouse. While Street, the old High Victorian, may have sympathized with these architects as they attempted to define a monumental urban style, as a convinced Goth he could not have approved of their methods.

This was the final break-up of High Victorian architecture. Architects abandoned the attempt to create a single, synthetic architectural vocabulary which was medieval in principle, classical in some of its effects, and universal in its application. The "Battle of the Styles" was revived. Henceforth, urban, secular architecture would be regular and classical, while the picturesque and medieval were restricted to churches and country houses. The Queen Anne, the pretty mongrel of mixed Gothic and classical parentage, reflected only dimly the aspirations of Street's generation. Many of those who had spent their entire careers in opposition to the Gothic Revival rejoiced at this partial resurrection of classicism, as did James Fergusson when he saw that the law courts design controversy had aroused a broad fellowship of antimedievalists. As Street was tormented by his critics, Fergusson gloated: "This time the shaft has hit, and hurts, and may be the beginning of the end."[187]

The law courts had been stranded by these rapidly changing tides of opinion. Defiantly picturesque, the building turned its back on the High Victorian notion of classicized medievalism that Street had helped to define, and it also failed to satisfy the new taste for overt classicism in public buildings. The law courts were a transitional monument which pleased neither younger nor older observers. The years around 1870 were a turning point in English architectural history, when High Victorianism, with its Early French foil, yielded to the Queen Anne and classical styles that prevailed until the First World War.

Keeping abreast of these changes was no easy matter, and Street did not entirely succeed, although the final design for the law courts represented a heroic effort. However, other indications show that he did come to understand the new critical climate of the seventies. An early sign of this was the lecture he gave at the R.I.B.A. in November 1869, called "On Some of the Differences of Style in Old Buildings."[188] While his subject was limited to medieval examples, he dealt with the forces which created architectural variety, perhaps casting an eye toward the pluralistic future.

More suggestive of a changed attitude was a pamphlet Street wrote in 1871, addressing the controversy that had then engulfed the proposal to decorate St. Paul's Cathedral.[189] Street opposed the plan to encrust the interior and to fill the dome with mosaics, preferring to leave Wren's work untouched and to commission only a rich baldacchino from William Burges, then the architect of the cathedral fabric. In part this may have been the predictable opinion of one who saw his own work being tampered with, but it was also a far more sympathetic attitude toward classical architecture than he had shown in his plan of 1857 to Gothicize Wren's St. Dionis

: DESIGN FOR THE PROPOSED ENGLISH CHURCH : ROME :

121 First design for All Saints English Church, Rome. Perspective and plan by Street, January 1872. (Building News, 24 May 1872.)

Backchurch and in his scheme to demolish Wren's and Gibbs's St. Clement Danes. This classical sympathy, as well as a positive response to the criticism that his design for the law courts received, could also be detected in the proposal that he made in 1872 for the English Church at Rome (Fig. 121). With its long, pronounced cornice and repetitive detail, this unbuilt scheme for an emphatically urban site showed Street again seeking to infuse his Gothic with classical order. Almost a return to his earlier ideals, it was inspired, no doubt, by the persistent recommendations that he temper the picturesque component in his work. Interestingly the trip Street made to Italy to inspect the site for this church in 1872 brought him to Rome—and shortly later to Paestum—for the first time in his life. At last he saw something of classical antiquity for himself.

Street's more conventional Gothic work of the last decade of his career also reflected the new tastes of the seventies, although they retained a personal flavor. He continued to incorporate more and more that was late and English in his buildings, as the shafted columns and tracery of St. John the Divine, Kennington (nave, 1871–74) suggest. At Erlestoke in Wiltshire he even designed a Perpendicular church, St. Saviour (1880).

Street's two most significant buildings of this period were begun in 1873: the church of St. James at Kingston, Dorset, and his own home, Holmdale, at Holmbury St. Mary in Surrey (Figs. 122, 123). They were both personal variations on themes

KINGSTONE CHURCH DORSET, NORTH WEST VIEW.
GEORGE EDMUND STREET R·A·
ARCHITECT.

KINGSTONE·CHURCH·DORSET·

PLAN·OF·CHURCH·

122 *St. James, Kingston, Dorset. 1873–80. Perspective and plan by Street, March 1874. (Building News, 4 September 1874.)*

123 *Holmdale, Holmbury St. Mary, Surrey. 1873–76. Perspective by Street, March 1874. (Building News, 14 April 1882.)*

which were then popular. At Kingston, Street designed a large, cathedral-plan church, one of his richest commissions, whose massing and general conception were clearly based on an appreciative understanding of his old friend G. F. Bodley's masterpiece, the church of the Holy Angels, Hoar Cross, Staffordshire (1872–76). But where Bodley had characteristically employed a pure English fourteenth-century vocabulary, Street had resolved to prove that the same or better could be done in the muscular style of the previous century, so long his favorite, and his design was also full of Continental features. At Holmdale Street acknowledged his debt to the ideas of his former assistant, Richard Norman Shaw, and he created a rambling old English mansion (compare Fig. 109). But with typical discipline, he saw to it that his half-timbering was real, unlike the nonstructural veneer that the younger generation applied to their façades.[190] That was his commentary on contemporary work.

Chapter 6

Architect, Client, Builder, Workmen

Central Hall.

Transverse Section
towards Staircase.

Architect: "The rattle of his T-square."
—Arthur Edmund Street, 1888

Client: "If some good fairy . . ."
—Algernon B. Mitford, 1915

Builder: "The sort . . . we have."
—George Edmund Street, 1878

Workmen: "The first masons in the world."
—*Industrial Review*, December 15, 1877

GEORGE EDMUND STREET had thrashed out the design for the law courts with the strongest political personalities of the Victorian era, and his relationship with government officials continued to shape the progress of his work. However, as construction began, new and equally powerful figures—the builders and their workmen—entered the story. For all of them—architect, client, contractor, and craftsmen—the law courts were a great contest of personal will.

Street, for his part, succeeded extraordinarily well in imposing his stamp on every detail of the work. Even on the business side, although continuously pitted against the opinion of the Government, he had his way on many important questions. His successes contrasted with the general trend in contemporary architectural practice, in which increased professionalism had spawned huge, impersonal, and artistically timid offices. This development led to the "profession or art" controversy which divided architects at the end of the century, but much of that later argument had already been aired in the discussion surrounding the law courts.

For builders and building workers, too, the law courts came at a time of changing professional attitudes. Contractors undertook the great project just as their own legal position with respect to clients was being redefined. Then, shortly after work began, the booming economy of the mid-Victorian years collapsed, with devastating effects for their trade. Building workers, for whom the boom had meant an era of growing prosperity and expanding union activity, were also severely affected, and the weaker economy fostered a new breed of trade unionism. Each of these tremors shook the law courts.

The Architect at Work

GEORGE EDMUND STREET was "the beau ideal of a perfect enthusiast," to quote Norman Shaw's description.[1] That enthusiasm, and a concomitant, almost unshakeable confidence in his own judgment, shaped the manner in which he approached his responsibilities, both in his art and his business dealings.

Street's life was organized around the requirements of his work. He rose early in order to answer his correspondence before breakfast, which he ate at nine, leaving the rest of the morning free for meetings with clients and for work at his drawing table.[2] During the law courts years, these hours were devoted to his private commissions, conducted in a separate office at home. In January 1870, Street had moved from 51 Russell Square, Bloomsbury, to Cavendish Place, really the northeast corner of Cavendish Square, in the West End. Perhaps there was some social motive in this move, but it was more likely undertaken to obtain better light than reached the north-facing windows of his Russell Square house. Cavendish Place was also closer to his church, Butterfield's All Saints, Margaret Street.

Street took lunch at one, and then, two or more afternoons a week, he set off for the office where he conducted his law courts business. This was housed first at the premises of the Royal Commission and then in a temporary building in what would be the courtyard of the new courts. The entrance was moved from Carey Street to the Strand as the work progressed.[3] Street spent several hours there before returning home at five or six occasionally with a stop at his club, the Athenaeum. Once home, he continued to write more letters and to draw, sometimes working past midnight.

For the law courts, Street maintained a distinct staff of perhaps a half dozen or ten draftsmen and clerks, headed by Augustus W. Tanner (1845–1923), who was styled his "principal assistant." It is not known when Tanner joined Street, but he came after training with a London architect named Giles, and remained until the completion of the law courts. He was elected an associate of the R.I.B.A. in 1870, established his own practice in the 1880s, and also became a district surveyor.[4] Tanner was certainly not of the caliber of Street's earlier assistants, men like Webb, Morris, Shaw, and the Seddings, but he was thoroughly competent. Nor were there many bright stars among those who worked for Street in the seventies, save for Leonard Stokes, who assisted with private commissions in 1877–80.[5] It must have become general knowledge that one received little independence while in his employ, and, besides, Street was no longer one of the architectural avant-garde.

The names of only a few of the other assistants in Street's law courts office are known. Given his manner of working, it is not surprising that his staff was smaller than Scott's. Thomas J. B. Holland appears frequently as the signatory of minor correspondence. Evidently Street's principal writing clerk and administrative aide, he signed the contract drawings for many other commissions during this period.[6] Unlike most of those who worked for Street, he worked out of both offices. The names of E. Bell and H. G. W. Drinkwater, who were apparently assistant secretaries of some kind, appear on a few letters in 1871 and 1872, respectively. Very rarely, the name of William Young is found among the correspondence. Young was the chief assistant in the Cavendish Place office, and he probably became involved with the law courts only when pressing business arose while Street was at home.[7] The names of the draftsmen, who never signed correspondence, are largely unrecorded. Only William Bartholomew, who guided a group of the Society of Engineers around the site in 1878, can be identified as "one of the chief draughtsmen."[8]

Outside the office staff proper, Street relied on a group of other assistants. His clerk of the works was A. W. Colling, who he said was "the most superior clerk of the works he ever met," and whom he had recommended to the Office of Works in 1870.[9] Street had suggested paying him 6 or 6½ guineas per week, but Hunt, Galton, and Ayrton ruled that the foundation-laying then being executed required only £4 4s. worth of supervision, and they hired Colling on those terms.[10] However, late in 1871, Street prevailed upon Ayrton to apply to the Treasury for the authority to raise Colling's salary to £6 6s.[11] Although paid by the government, Colling was responsible to the architect, and he continued as chief clerk until 1878, when he was incapacitated by illness and then died at mid-summer.[12] He was replaced by Samuel Wallis, assisted by Edward Moore, who supervised the building work until completion.[13] To insure that the builders fulfilled the requirements of the specifications, the clerks conferred constantly with Thomas Epps, the general foreman for the Bulls, with Frederick Clarke, the foreman of the masons, and with H. Margetson, the foreman of the stonecarvers.

Finally, Street was also assisted by surveyors. These he retained, in the usual fashion of the period, to meet with the surveyors appointed by those builders who were invited to tender. In conference, the surveyors would draft a "bill of quantities," which specified the precise amounts of material required to execute the design.[14] With quantities in hand, the contractors could then bid on a uniform basis, providing a lump sum or "gross" estimate for the entire building. This contrasted with the eighteenth-century bidding practice, in which the usual form of tender was a list of prices for materials and labor, calculated per unit.[15] For the foundation contract, Street employed Charles Poland as his surveyor, while James Gandy assisted him on the main contract.

After the contract was awarded, the surveyors at the law courts remained in employment, for many points about the construction were disputed by the architect and the builder, and these had to be settled by their respective surveyors, again meeting in conference. The constant controversy surrounding the main contract kept Gandy very busy into the mid-1880s. Two firms of surveyors, working in collaboration, were retained by the Bulls to confer with him. These were Hunt and Stewart (not the company of Henry Hunt) and Widnell and Trollope, the same firms whom the bidders had retained to calculate the quantities for both contracts.

An intense atmosphere prevailed in Street's office, and the temperament of the architect himself contributed more than a little to this state of affairs. Robert Kerr, who was never an admirer, puzzled after his death, "I wonder if any one ever called Street 'Georgie'?"[16] John P. Seddon wrote of Street's "constitutional feelings of reserve."[17] But his son understandably remembered him as a warm person, fond of music, of his garden, and of the long summer evenings spent with his family on the balcony overlooking Cavendish Square, cigar in hand, musing about the itinerary for that year's foreign tour.[18] There are accounts of some office high jinks during the years which Shaw and Street's other more illustrious assistants spent with him, and as this often involved music, the architect's own great passion, perhaps the master was himself sometimes caught up in the spirit of play.[19] But, as Shaw later recalled, the rewards of working with Street derived from the work itself, not from the recreational interludes:

> We worked hard—or thought we did—we had to be at the office at nine o'clock, and our hour of leaving was six o'clock—long hours—but he never encroached on our own time, and as a matter of fact I am sure I never stayed a minute past six o'clock.
>
> There were some interesting men in the office, and we were thoroughly happy. I am sure we were loyal, and believed in our master entirely, so that our work was really a pleasure; he was our master—and he let us know it,—

not by nagging or in an aggressive spirit, but by daily showing that he knew more than any of us, and could in a given time do about twice as much.[20]

In the office Street controlled all. There was none of the substantial delegation of design responsibility which he may have experienced while working for Scott, and which was certainly a feature of Scott's practice in later years.[21] Street was always in the midst of what was being done, not merely supervising, but determining the character of every detail from the outset. Unlike many of his contemporaries, he did not assign a draftsman to work out a design problem with only a rough sketch or oral instructions to guide him.[22] Shaw described his method and his virtuosity:

> When a new work appeared, his custom was to draw it out in pencil in his own room—plans, elevations, and section,—even putting in the margin lines and places where he wished the title to go; nothing was sketched in; it was *drawn*, and exactly as he wished it to be, so that really there was little to do, except to ink in his drawings, and tint and complete them.
>
> The rapidity and precision with which he drew were marvelous. I have never seen any one, not merely to equal, but to approach him and he was as accurate as he was rapid.
>
> We used to prepare for him a dozen or fifteen sheets of details—all slightly set out to a large scale with full-size mouldings, etc., and these we placed in his room of an evening. When we came in the morning we flew to our boards to find the whole carefully corrected and any amount added, both of drawing and notes. Often, in fact generally, the sheets were covered on both sides; every moulding drawn with a fine clear line, and perhaps half a dozen sheets of ironwork (in designing which he was very fertile and original) drawn full size with all the sections indicated. No wonder that we were enthusiastic with such performances going on under our eyes daily.
>
> I well remember a little *tour de force* that fairly took our breath away. He told us one morning that he was just off to measure an old church—I think in Buckinghamshire,—and he left by the ten o'clock train. About half-past four he came back and into the office for some drawing paper; he then retired into his own room, reappearing in about an hour's time with the whole of the church carefully drawn to scale, with his proposed additions to it, margin lines and title as usual, all ready to ink in and finish. Surely this was a sufficiently good day's work! two journeys, a whole church measured, plotted to scale, and new parts designed in about seven hours and a half. . . .
>
> I am certain that during the whole time I was with him I never designed one single moulding.[23]

All those who worked with Street had similar stories, and his unceasing attention to detail was not prevented even by the enormous complexity of the law courts. His chief assistant, Augustus Tanner, could recount another astonishing exploit:

> The fastest piece of work we ever remember him to have accomplished was on one occasion when he covered fourteen sheets of double elephant paper with a mass of beautifully drawn full-size mason's mouldings, with, in addition, on nearly every sheet, explanatory portions of the building, drawn to a scale of

inch or half-inch to the foot, and all within a space of two hours. All the details were written in and referenced complete, and for all practical purposes might have been given over to the builder at once; but he always allowed his subordinates the privilege—and it was a privilege very highly esteemed—to tint and ink these drawings in, and carefully finish them as it were. After such an occasion Mr. Street would walk out of his office and away, leaving his clerks to walk into his room, and with wonder and astonishment survey the work he left behind him. . . . He used a black ebony engineer's T-square, and when drawing the rattling of this square was incessant.[24]

Even the *Builder* could manage to sound impressed by Street's ability for swift, sure work. In its obituary of the architect a similar incident was related: "A clergyman whose church he was restoring having written for details that did not arrive, called at Cavendish-place, and came down from Mr. Street's room in an hour or so with a large roll of papers under his arm, and a triumphant smile, saying 'I have got them all!' "[25] And Arthur Edmund Street, too, had comparable memories of the time he spent in his father's law courts office after completing his degree at Oxford, an achievement that symbolized the rising social status and educational requirements of the architectural profession. He wrote of his father's afternoons at the site:

These visits usually lasted two or three hours, and one such visit, provided there was no interruption, would give more than enough work for the whole of the staff there. We used to hear the rattle of his T-square through the door as it dashed up and down the board, and then my father would come out of his room with a sheaf of papers, put them down, and go out. No sooner was his back turned than we would all run to see what he had done for us, making a selection, as far as I remember, according to our likings and various degrees of proficiency.[26]

These stories are alike in recording an incredible visual fluency. Street could think and draw in one nearly uninterrupted gesture, forming a complete mental image that could be transferred to paper without hesitation. For, as Shaw noted, Street did not sketch, he drew, and Tanner remembered him remarking that "no man should put his pencil to paper to begin to draw a moulding unless the entire section was visible to his mental vision, or, in other words, that the hand should be under the perfect control of the brain, and not the brain led by the hand."[27] At the Royal Academy, where he lectured in 1881, Street advised the students to "draw accurately, firmly, and, as far as may be, with a single stroke," and it is notable in this respect that his only surviving "sketchbooks" are travel diaries.[28] No sketches in the usual sense have been preserved for any of his works. Despite all that has been said about the empiricism of English design, for Street the empirical process ended before he touched his pencil, and his first marks reflected his already firmly defined visual conceits. These first ideas yielded only grudgingly to revisions, although his work on the law courts shows that very substantial changes were possible under extreme circumstances.

The sureness of Street's method was belied by the appearance of his drawings, for the evocative perspectives he showed at the Royal Academy were invariably praised for their freshness and seemingly unstudied vitality. Less admiring critics alleged that he was "fudging."[29] However, Street himself must have regarded his drawings in a different light, for those he exhibited were not sketches at all, but formal presentation renderings chosen to demonstrate his fully matured designs. These drawings were his own work, and they were invariably finished in simple pen and ink, the medium in which he recognized that he had a natural genius for rendering atmosphere.[30] Other architects usually had their perspectives rendered with watercolor or sepia, setting Street's work apart whenever it was displayed or published. Indeed, he did devote himself enthusiastically to landscape painting, a hobby he shared with many of his contemporaries, including John Ruskin.[31] But he was never satisfied with his mastery of color.[32] Street's forte was the painterly use of line, and it is evident that the characteristic drawing technique of the Queen Anne generation, and of Norman Shaw in particular, derived from an admiring study of his work.

The stories of Street's virtuosity are also alike in stressing the attention he gave to projecting his vision of the final design onto every component detail. This was nowhere more evident than in the guidance he provided for stonecarvers. He drew literally thousands of molding profiles, and he also prepared sketches of the ornamental and figural sculpture.[33] Street even made clay models of much of the carved work with his own hands, for, as he advised his Royal Academy audience, "It is impossible to direct another man properly merely by giving drawings for such work, and you must learn to give your instructions in the round."[34] Tanner recalled Street's modeling work with special vividness: "He was in his happiest mood when his thumbs were deep in the clay, and no part of his work gave him more pleasure. If anyone had a favour to ask, that was the time to apply. Then the great man unbended himself, and many a joke has the master carver heard which we, outside the modelling shed, would scarcely have thought possible."[35]

Street had also contributed to the painted decoration of at least three of his buildings, and this kind of involvement in the ornamental arts was, of course, an ideal of all "art architects" of the latter half of the nineteenth century.[36] But the degree of his personal participation and the completeness of the instructions that he gave to workers were unusual even for the time. In the part of his *Recollections* written in 1864, Gilbert Scott observed, with respect to stonecarving: "My friend Mr. Street, during this period, has been working up the pure conventional foliage, Mr. Earp [Thomas Earp, later the carving contractor for the law courts] being his handpiece, and he has done very great things. I think that his work and mine together, for the last few years or so, have been a noble development. He can lay claim to his, more personally than I can to mine, as he gives drawings, while I do my work by influence."[37] Street certainly intended that his designs should be personally his own, and not merely the products of his influence. As Shaw noted, "The charm of his work is that when looking at it you may be certain that it is entirely his own, and this applies to the smallest detail as to the general conception."[38]

It is this attention to detail that is recorded in the surviving drawings for the Royal Courts of Justice. Their most striking characteristic is their sheer quantity. There were 248 contract drawings alone—an unheard of number even for Street, who prepared only five such drawings to accompany the contract in 1867 for an entirely new nave for Bristol cathedral.[39] The particular care he lavished on the law courts was explicitly intended to prevent the type of misunderstanding that seemed

124 Witness stairs. Elevation
and sections. Lithographed contract drawing, c. 1871–72.
(PRO Works 30/1792.)

to bedevil government work. Every detail was to be fixed before work began, and when the tenders were higher than anticipated, Street was quick to assure his employers that the completeness of his drawings and specifications would insure that no expensive additions would have to be made to the contract later.[40]

Exploiting the newly popular printing technique, the contract drawings were photolithographed in order to provide the multiple copies needed by the government, the builders, and for use at the office on the site (Fig. 124; see also Figs. 98–102, 116, 117, 125, 141). The originals, presumably retained by Street, have been lost, but the copies accurately reproduce their details, and they were even hand-colored by the draftsmen.[41] For contract drawings they were extraordinarily complete, drawn to half-inch rather than the usual quarter-inch scale, and often providing full-scale molding profiles and other decorative details. Characteristically, the drawings were tightly composed, with elevations and sections juxtaposed dramatically, and conveyed a feeling of structural and ornamental unity in addition to describing the mundane specifics of construction.

But thorough as the contract drawings were, they did not nearly reflect the full measure of direction that Street provided for the builders. In the detail drawings, of which approximately 750 survive from a probably much larger number, one can truly hear the rattle of his black ebony T-square and the rustle of a stack of double elephant sheets as he deposited them in the office of his assistants. A few of these drawings, keyed by their numbering system to the contract drawings, have been preserved in pencil, showing the form in which Street's clerks received them for inking and coloring. Many more preserve traces of penciling beneath their finished treatment. Most numerous among the details were the full-scale masonry profiles, which he drew for every scrap of molding in the building. These were often ingeniously and beautifully composed to show many different profiles, coded in different colors and overlaid upon each other (see Fig. 135).

The most breath-taking drawings were lead-work details, in the design of which Shaw rightly called Street "fertile and original" (Figs. 125, 126). His ability to exploit the malleability and ductility of metals to create convincing organic forms makes one regret, as a sympathetic observer of Victorian architecture rarely does, that he did not choose to work more with the new materials of the nineteenth century.

The surviving detail drawings certainly confirm the often-repeated story that Street was personally responsible for every feature of the design—including the uniform buttons of the staff. This is eloquently proven by the humblest drawing that is preserved, a full-scale section of a gutter which Street penciled on August 7, 1879 (Fig. 127). It is an insignificant thing, but it becomes almost heroic when seen beside the great building on which Street worked from 1866 until his death in 1881, and studied in the context of Shaw's words: "I am certain that during the whole time I was with him I never designed one single moulding."

The Government as Client

STREET'S pertinacity and thoroughness produced a rare integrity in his art, but they were traits which he also allowed to influence the business side of his work. Here their effect was not always conducive to a smooth relationship with clients, and this was certainly true in the case of the law courts. Of his ordinary clients, his

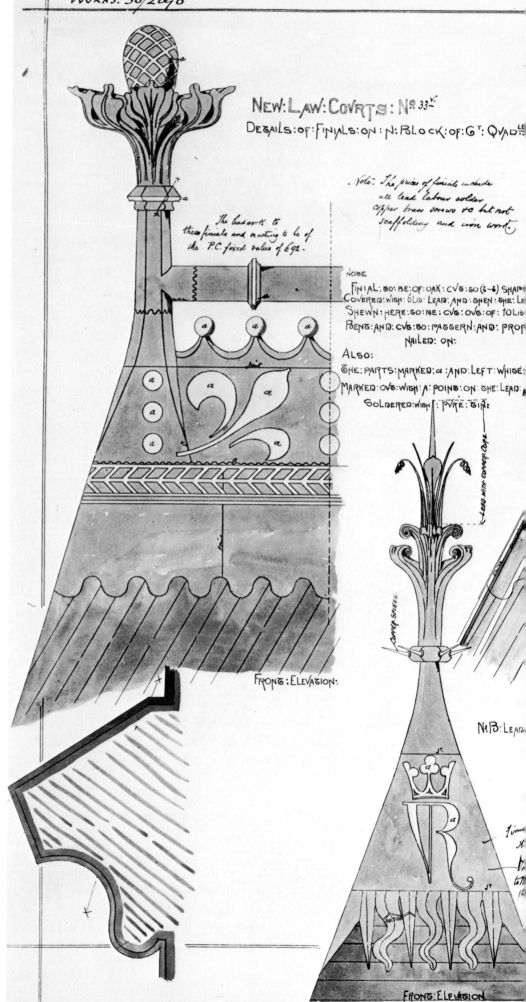

NEW: LAW: COVRTS: Nº 33ᵛ

DETAILS: OF: FINIALS: ON: N. BLOCK: OF: Gᵗ. QVADˡᵉ

*Note. The prices of finials include
all lead labour solder
copper brass screws &c but not
scaffolding and iron work.*

*The leadwork to
these finials and cresting to be of
the P.C. fixed value of £92.*

NOTE

FINIAL: TO: BE: OF: OAK: CVT: TO (⅛-⅛) SHAPᵉ
COVERED: WITH: 6Lᵇˢ: LEAD: AND: THEN: THE: Lᵉ
SHEWN: HERE: TO: BE: CVT: OVT: OF: 10Lᵇˢ
POENT: AND: CVT: TO: PATTERN: AND: PROPᵉ
NAILED: ON:

ALSO:

THE: PARTS: MARKED: *a*: AND: LEFT: WHITE
MARKED: OVT: WITH: A: POINT: ON: THE: LEAD
SOLDERED: WITH: PVRE: TIN:

FRONT: ELEVATION:

LEAD WITH COPPER CAPS.

COPPER SPIKES.

N.B: LEAD

VR

FRONT: ELEVATION.

125 Finials for the pavilion
over the north entrance to the
courtyard and finials for northeast tower (compare Fig. 116).
Lithographed contract drawing,
c. 1871–72. Altered in execution. (PRO Works 30/2096.)

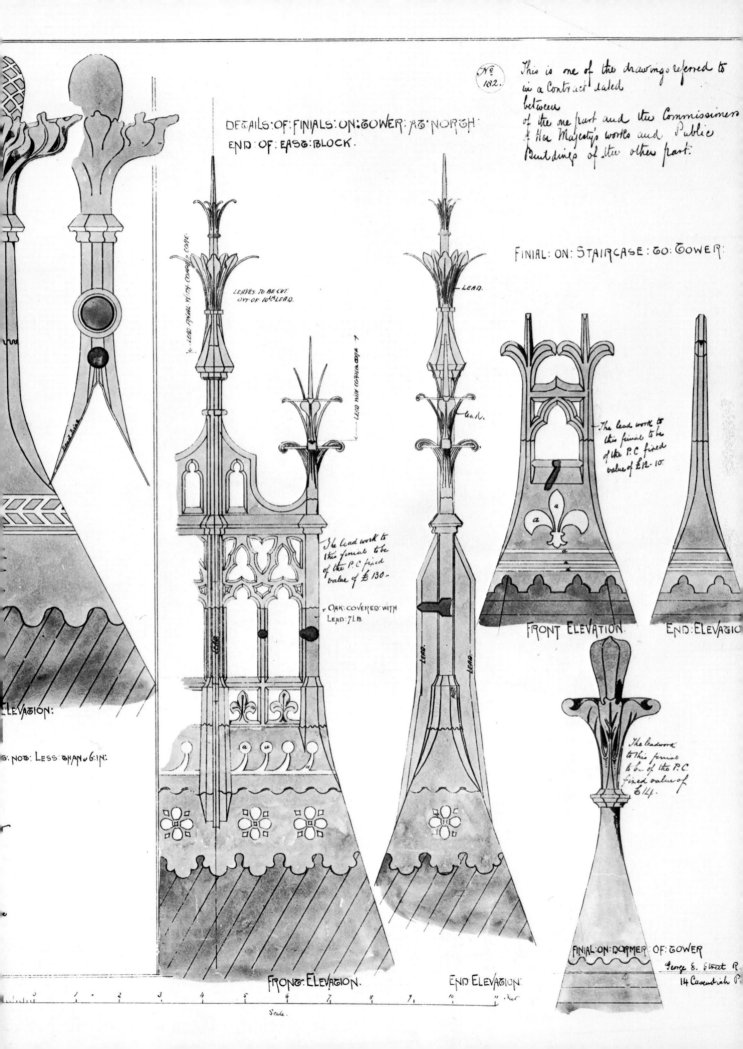

DETAILS: OF: FINIALS: ON: TOWER: AT: NORTH:
END: OF: EAST: BLOCK.

This is one of the drawings referred to
in a Contract dated
between
of the one part and the Commissioners
of Her Majesty's works and Public
Buildings of the other part.

Nº 182.

LEAVES TO BE CUT
OUT OF 10ᴸᴮ LEAD.

LEAD · FINIAL · WITH · COPPER · CORE.

LEAD · WITH · COPPER · CORE ↗

FINIAL: ON: STAIRCASE: TO: TOWER:

LEAD.

LEAD.

The lead work to
this finial to be
of the P.C fixed
value of £130.

OAK · COVERED · WITH
LEAD 7 LB.

The lead work to
this finial to be
of the P.C fixed
value of £12·10·

LEAD.

LEAD.

EVATION:

S: NOT: LESS: THAN · 6: IN:

FRONT ELEVATION.

END ELEVATION.

FRONT ELEVATION.

END: ELEVATION.

The leadwork
to this finial
to be of the P.C
fixed value of
£14.

FINIAL: ON: DORMER: OF: TOWER

George E. Street R.

14 Cavendish P.

Scale.

Rip : Finials : E : v : W : Elevation

Contract : Drawing :

hollow : copper : ball :

Nº 8 : of : these

WORKS 30 /661

Plan : of : Finial :
inch : Scale :

son reported, "Those who put themselves in his hands were generally content to do so with little restriction. His obvious self-reliance and strength of character begat a corresponding feeling of security in those for whom he worked which often became enthusiasm."[42] But Her Majesty's Government was not an ordinary client. What others might interpret as artistic vision or confidence, it was inclined to view as dilettantism and arrogance. Officials were especially worried that an architect's work might turn out to be more expensive than estimated. These legitimate concerns further strained their relationship with the architect—already soured by critical and sensitive questions related to design. Street tended to see his work, both artistic and professional, as an indivisible whole, and for him, too, the issues of professional practice were singularly important.

The lessons learned from the Houses of Parliament had substantially hardened the attitude of the public officials who dealt with the law courts. The shadows of cost overrun and artistic bickering cast by the great building at Westminster passed over all public architecture during the latter part of the nineteenth century. This was particularly true of governmental policy when Gladstone was in office, and

126 Hip finials for the east and west façades. Detail drawing, 13 November 1879. (PRO Works 30/1661.)

127 Section of gutter for witnesses' stair. Detail drawing, signed by Street, 7 August 1879. (PRO Works 30/1654.)

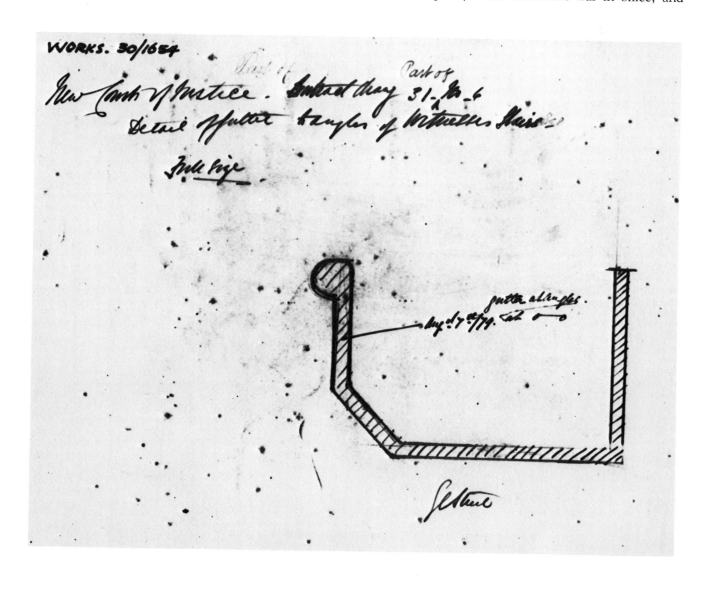

under Ayrton the distrust of artists and architects reached an icy pinnacle. Not merely an attitude with which officials undertook their daily responsibilities, it was also reflected in an attempt to restructure formally the entire system by which architects were employed by the government. Street was among the first to be subjected to the indignities of the new plan, and a long series of professional conflicts with his official clients was the result.

At the heart of the scheme devised by Ayrton was a document called the "Memorandum of the Terms of Appointment of Architects for Public Buildings," which was promulgated in the summer of 1870 in the wake of the dismissal of E. M. Barry from the Houses of Parliament.[43] This was designed to free government architecture from many of the uncertainties that plagued private construction by specifying how much the architect would be paid (and setting this at a low figure) and for how much he would be responsible (and setting this at a high level). Street, whose block plan with the reoriented hall had just been approved by the Royal Commission and the Treasury, signed the "terms" on September 23, 1870. Other architects engaged on major buildings did likewise, including Waterhouse, at work at the Natural History Museum, and Scott, at the government offices.

Ayrton's document was engineered to abrogate usual professional practice in several areas, and, indeed, one clause specifically exempted the government from compliance with the professional code published by the R.I.B.A. in 1862.[44] On the questions of fees, payment for surveyors, and drawing ownership, the terms of employment established new standards.

Whereas the R.I.B.A. had endorsed a five percent commission for architects, Ayrton now wished to replace this in government work with a flat fee. Thus, architects could not profit when projects went over budget due to inflation or unapproved additions. He based his pay scale on the five percent formula, however, so that Street was to receive £35,500 on the £710,000 allocated for the law courts. Payment would be made in three equal installments, the first when the construction contract was signed, the second when half the contract amount had been expended, and the third upon completion. This was a controversial but not unprecedented arrangement, for even Charles Barry had accepted a flat fee of £25,000 for his design for the Houses of Parliament.[45]

Coupled with this provision, Ayrton's terms also denied liability for the remuneration of any surveyors hired by the architect. The government would pay only the salary of the clerk of the works, although clients traditionally paid both clerks and surveyors.

With respect to drawing ownership, the agreement stipulated that all plans would belong to the government, contrary to yet another convention. This requirement was surely a reaction to the dispute which had arisen that spring when Ayrton had fired E. M. Barry and demanded that he turn over the drawings for the Houses of Parliament. The profession had rallied in support of the tradition of artistic property, and the commissioner wished no recurrence of that controversy. In this he was supported by a ruling of the crown law officers, issued just before Street signed the terms, which upheld the government in the Barry case. Ayrton's position was given apparently conclusive legal endorsement when the decision was reconfirmed that fall in the similar case of *Ebdy v. McGowan.*[46]

Among architects, the terms of the new agreement created widespread dissatisfaction. The *Architect* criticized Ayrton's determined rudeness toward the R.I.B.A. and asked whether those who had signed the document had acted too quickly.[47] To this last charge, Street replied as though he were personally offended, perhaps betraying his own misgivings: "I have always endeavoured in all my work to maintain, by my conduct as an architect, the claim of my profession to rank as an honorable one, to which no gentleman need object to belong. I cannot conceive how, by accepting what appear to me perfectly fair conditions, I have done less than I ought in the way of asserting this claim."[48]

In succeeding years, Street had countless opportunities to reflect on his wisdom. He partially escaped the requirement to surrender his drawings by lithographing the contract plans and retaining the originals for himself. But other questions kept him in nearly continuous dispute with the Office of Works. The most important of these related to his fee, the payment of his surveyor, and his responsibility for the design of the heating system. In none of these cases can Street be said to have acted with perfect good temper, but his provocation from the government was often severe. In most instances he was able to win important concessions.

The Architect's Pay

EVEN BEFORE Street signed the terms of employment, he was already engaged in a dispute with the Office of Works over his pay. This controversy was to last throughout the early years of his association with the law courts, colored in turn by the personalities of three first commissioners. In the end it was swallowed up by a further disagreement regarding the payment of Street's surveyors, and some questions were still unresolved at the time of the architect's death.

Street's pay first became an issue because the long debate over his appointment, the site, and the cost of the project had to be concluded before his regular payment schedule could be worked out. Like the other competitors, Street had received £800 in 1867. But although he was required to establish a separate office staff upon his appointment in 1868, and to produce the great plan and the scheme for the Embankment, he received no further remuneration during the next two years. Only his office space was provided free of rent by the Royal Commission. In November 1869, with no approved plan yet in sight, he therefore applied to the Treasury for an advance of £2000 on his yet unnegotiated fee.[49] Four months later, after lengthy consultation with the Office of Works, this was approved, but when Street applied a year later for a further £2400, his request was apparently ignored.[50] Nearly another year passed before Street again asked for an advance, complaining in January 1872 that he had paid more out in expenses than he had received from the Government.[51] At Hunt's recommendation he was promptly forwarded £1500, and two years later he received £5000 after arguing that "I have already paid away to Clerks and assistants considerably more money than you have been good enough to advance me on account of my work . . . ; so that at present I have received nothing whatever for my own constant and trying labour in this matter for some six or seven years."[52] So much was advanced to Street in this way that when the contract was finally signed in February 1874, only £2533 remained to be paid him out of the first third of his commission.

While these negotiations were proceeding, Street also attempted, with less success, to obtain some remuneration for the several designs which had been abandoned between 1867 and 1869. It was to discuss these claims that he first met with Ayrton, on December 12, 1869, and, given the economical fixation of the first commissioner, this was certainly not a propitious issue with which to begin their professional relationship.[53] The fee that Street claimed for the Embankment and Carey Street plans, a mere £750, was never disputed, and the Treasury approved it a few months later.[54] But his claim for the great plan, for which he had ultimately completed all of the working drawings in pencil, was far larger and much more controversial.

Ayrton concluded that the great plan had been an extravagant waste, and he was not eager to reward its architect for acceding to what he considered to have been the inflated requirements of the Royal Commission. He could not agree with Street, who first claimed a five percent commission on the full estimated cost of £1,523,000 for the abandoned project, or, at the very least, a three-quarter percent commission, amounting to £11,423. The architect finally offered to accept a flat payment of only £3000 or the referral of the subject to Henry Hunt for informal arbitration, but Ayrton would not be moved.[55] At a second meeting on December 31, Street again failed to convince the first commissioner, and Ayrton then wrote to the Treasury to recommend that allowing the architect to keep his competitor's honorarium of £800 (which the victor had been expected to deduct from his pay) was sufficient compensation for the "larger schemes entertained by the Commission."[56] At the Treasury, Robert Lowe chose not to address this question at all until a final design was accepted.[57]

One year later, after he had become a signatory of Ayrton's new terms of employment, Street again pressed his claims for the great plan. By establishing a fixed architectural fee, the terms were intended to prevent such disputes as that in which Street and the Office of Works were now locked. But the new provisions could not be applied to work Street had done before signing. Thus, in November 1870, although the arithmetic of his demands was somewhat different, he again asked for basically the same settlement: £3000 in lieu of the minimum of £10,000 to which he felt legally entitled, or referral of the matter to Henry Hunt.[58] But this time, sensing that he must circumvent the first commissioner, Street applied directly to the Treasury. It referred the matter back to Ayrton, however, who repeated his judgment that the £800 honorarium was sufficient compensation for the great plan. He argued falsely that the "larger design" was "for the most part embraced in the premiated plans" and that it was "not, therefore, to be regarded as involving the thought and trouble of original work."[59] He had chosen to ignore the drastic and successful revision Street had undertaken in response to the criticism leveled at the planning defects of his competition entry.

As it did later, the Treasury now exhibited greater sympathy for Street's position, directing Ayrton to obtain a report from Hunt and Galton. Accordingly, those officers met with the architect on January 12, 1871.[60] He had just submitted the plans that included the large southeast clock tower, and he clearly believed that he had been granted the requested arbitration. Ayrton did not share that view, and, in any case, Hunt and Galton were unable to agree on a recommendation. Hunt, whom Street seems to have properly judged would be an understanding mediator, proposed a compromise payment of £2100 for the great plan. But Galton, whose feelings were closer to those of Ayrton, argued that Street should have known better than to prepare plans according to the extravagant requirements of the Royal Commission. He reasoned that £800 was adequate recompense for such ill-advised labor.[61] The first commissioner submitted these contradictory opinions to the Treasury in late March, and in May he again proposed that £800 be offered to Street.[62] The Treasury now approved this meager fee, and Street was informed of the decision on June 6.[63] The architect could not believe that the offer reflected the report made by Hunt, whom he assumed had been appointed the arbitrator of the dispute. "Unless the Referee by whose award I agreed to abide had fixed this amount," he wrote, "I cannot consent to accept it."[64] But Ayrton was convinced that the matter was closed, and he advised Street that no arbitration process had ever been instituted.[65]

This exchange occurred shortly after Street had won the right to consult directly with the Treasury, an arrangement that offended Ayrton deeply. The first commissioner's resentment continued to grow, but Street, recognizing that he could now outflank his supervisor, continued to press his case. In November 1872, after his design had weathered the storm of public criticism which raged during the last half of 1871 and the first months of 1872, he renewed his argument with the Office of Works. He wrote, "The amount you have offered me (£800) is so entirely inadequate to repay me for wasted time and skill, and for expenses out of pocket that I feel sure the First Commissioner will reconsider his offer unless indeed it agrees with Mr. Hunt's recommendation, which I can hardly suppose to be the fact."[66] This letter, which betrayed more than an intuitive understanding of the report prepared by Henry Hunt, went unanswered, and Street waited until July 30, 1873, before he protested again. By then he had once more bested Ayrton in the final crisis over amending the design to reduce costs, having appealed over his head to obtain approval for his plans. It is easy to imagine the first commissioner's feelings toward the artist who had brought the Office of Works to heel with the help of the Treasury, the prime minister, and the Cabinet.

Street did not count on tact to win his claim, demanding that Hunt's report be made public or the matter submitted to the kind of formal and binding arbitration specified in the terms of employment.[67] Hunt drafted a largely favorable memorandum, proposing a generous advance of £5000 (later approved), but Galton was incredulous that Street should still claim that Hunt's report was an arbitration document.[68] An official reply to the architect was dispatched on August 11, following the outline of Galton's memo, but Street must have opened the letter with a knowing smile.[69] Gladstone had dismissed Ayrton on August 6, and by August 11 it was already known that his successor would be William Patrick Adam. Street's uncompromising strategy had been vindicated.

Adam, a genial Scottish M.P., had no particular aptitude for art despite his descent from the family of famous architects. But his brief tenure as first commissioner, which ended when Disraeli resumed office the following February, was a period of tranquility and gentlemanly conduct that contrasted happily with Ayrton's four-year autocracy. Unlike his predecessor, Adam was distressed by controversy, and a later subordinate attested, "If some good fairy were to ask me to choose a gift with which to enter the world, I should ask for tact, and I should wish it to be just such tact as possessed by . . . Mr. Adam."[70] He succeeded in soothing even Street's outraged sensitivities.

Street waited until late September before bringing his claim to the attention of the new first commissioner by officially petitioning for arbitration.[71] Although he spent several anxious months waiting for a reply, Adam, in fact, took his case under consideration immediately.[72] On September 30, noting that he was "very anxious not to prolong the misunderstandings which have arisen on this subject," Adam directed Hunt and Galton to prepare a joint report on Street's claims. He also asked that Street be advised that the matter was under review.[73] However, that letter was never written, and the report of the surveyor and director of works, submitted in November, showed that they were still unable to agree on the proper fee for the great plan. Hunt repeated his recommendation of £2100 and Galton his of £800.[74] Adam was at home in Scotland for the autumnal Parliamentary recess by the time he received this unhelpful advice, and his absence contributed to further delay. He finally replied to the increasingly agitated Street from Blair Adam on February 10, but his letter was worth the long wait. Adam, ever eager to avoid open conflict, explained to Street:

> I had purposely detained the papers in your case as to the appointment of an arbitrator till I came to town and had an opportunity of seeing Mr. Gladstone on the subject hoping that by his assistance we might be able to settle the matter and avoid a reference [to arbitration] altogether, as I am most anxious for an amicable and satisfactory adjustment of all matters in dispute between you and this Department. . . . I am very sorry there should have been any delay on the subject and if you have suffered any inconvenience I shall regret it much. The blame, however, must be attributed entirely to me acting under a sincere desire to avoid any further dispute.[75]

Street must have scarcely believed that he was still in the same world as he read these words, and he replied, thanking the first commissioner for his "polite letter" and suggesting, "I cannot but think that you [will] find that the principle of my claims is just, and the adjustment of the amounts, if the principle is admitted, need not give much trouble."[76]

Adam had explained that due to "present circumstances"—a reference to the impending fall of the Government—he would be unable to refer the matter to Gladstone. Still, he had promised to attend to the question immediately, and on February 21, he drafted a proposal that would refer the great plan dispute to "some impartial gentleman of standing."[77] But Adam must have prepared this memorandum for the files, dated as it was the day after Disraeli agreed to form a new Cabinet.

Lord Henry Lennox (1821–86) became first commissioner nearly a month later, and he treated Street with similar decency. He must have been grateful to find the law courts in far better shape than they had been under Ayrton, with the main contract signed and the architect won over by Adam's conciliatory behavior, for he was soon beset by personal misfortunes. In his first month on the job Lennox's mother died, and he suffered a nervous collapse as a result. Indeed, he seems to have been entirely well only rarely during his term as first commissioner. His correspondence with Disraeli records an unending chain of nervous weakness, colds, coughs, bilious attacks, and a broken ankle.[78] Moreover, as Algernon B. Mitford, the new secretary of works, remembered, Lennox took up his position embittered by Disraeli's failure to make him first lord of the Admiralty. He was unhappy at the Office of Works, and Mitford maintained that "Lord Henry took very little interest in the business of the office, and it was not an easy matter to get him even to pay attention to the Estimates which it was his duty to defend in the House of Commons."[79] Lennox was also somewhat reckless in managing his personal finances, and his association with the rather shady Lisbon Tramway Company forced his resignation, at the request of the Cabinet, in August 1876.[80]

Despite these troubles, Lennox treated Street liberally. The Conservatives facilitated this by their more generous fiscal policy and by changes in the permanent staff of the Office of Works. Douglas Galton now customarily absented himself, and he finally retired in 1875.[81] The new secretary, "Bertie" Mitford (1837–1916), had been appointed by Disraeli to replace George Russell with the instructions that the Office of Works "was an Augean stable and must be swept out."[82] Mitford had spent many years in Japan and China with the foreign service, and he had made himself something of an Eastern scholar.[83] In the twelve years that he served in his new position, he imbued the dealings of the department with what, after the years of Ayrton, seemed like oriental politeness and serenity.

Lennox felt free to adopt the larger commission for the great plan as recommended by Hunt, and on July 22 he asked the Treasury to authorize £2100.[84] This was approved without complaint three weeks later, but something—perhaps the Parliamentary recess or another bout of some illness—delayed the announcement of this decision to Street.[85] Finally, in December and again on January 15, 1875, Lennox met with the architect, now mourning the loss of his wife, and explained his proposal. Street was then first officially informed that Henry Hunt had recommended a payment of £2100 nearly four years earlier.[86]

On January 27, the offer was made in writing.[87] Conscious of the difference in attitude that now prevailed at the department, Street noted his gratitude to Lennox in particular: "I beg to be allowed to express my thanks to the First Commissioner of Works for the extremely kind and courteous way in which he conveyed the decision of the Chancellor of the Exchequer to me." But with what was unconscious tactlessness, Street also took the occasion of this letter to reaffirm his claim for compensation for his surveyor, first made while Adam was first commissioner, and with that the pay dispute was reopened.

Pay for Surveyors

THE NEW question centered first on the sum of £109 owed to Charles Poland, the surveyor whom Street had retained to measure the alterations in the foundation contract and to establish by how much the amount paid to the builder should be adjusted. The architect based his claim on the legal judgment that Dove Brothers, the contractor for the foundations, had obtained against the government with respect to the payment of a like sum of £109 to their surveyor. The final report on the Dove case ordered the government to pay both the surveyor hired by the builder and that hired by the architect. This was an important ruling, for the agreement Street had signed with the Office of Works denied the government's liability for such payments. Judging that the terms of employment were now open to question, the architect gladly accepted the £109 for Poland's services, but he also demanded that the government accept this decision as a precedent and undertake to pay for all future surveying.

Even under the more generous Tory regime of Sir Henry Lennox, the Office of Works did not eagerly accept this new liability. The opinion of the solicitor was obtained, and in early February Street was told that the department did not consider that the Dove case provided a universal precedent.[88] Street replied immediately in an offended and lugubrious tone.[89] If the government refused to abide by what seemed to be a clear legal obligation, he explained, he must again request that the entire matter, including the commission for the great plan, be submitted to formal arbitration. He added wearily,

> My experience as an Architect is, I am sorry to say, becoming rather a long one, and I have never yet had to pay or been asked to pay any charges of Surveyors for measuring extras and omissions. Architects who take out their own quantities always make a charge for this work in addition to their charge for their plans, and speaking generally, it is felt by the higher class of Architects that those who do so are wrong in undertaking work which is likely to be better done by men who confine themselves to it.

Street thus supported his claim by reference to the traditional practice, which Ayrton had sought to upset.

As wary as they were of risking unlimited further expense, the Tories were amenable to appeals to precedent. On March 13, Henry Hunt, himself a professional surveyor, prepared a long memorandum addressing the surveying controversy as it applied to Street. He also referred to Waterhouse, who had made similar claims for his work at the Natural History Museum.[90] Hunt began with an attack on the decision in the Dove case, but concluded with an argument for conciliation. "It is desirable no doubt," he wrote, "to avoid if possible further contention with these two gentlemen, both eminent in their profession and each engaged upon Public works of magnitude and importance." In this light he advised that it would be "wise and even fair" to yield to the architects' demands. P. H. Lawrence, the solicitor of works, added a seconding memorandum which summarized the new attitude of the department: "I can hardly express too strongly the view I take as to the expediency of removing all causes of difference (whether real or imaginary) between the department and officers such as the Architects in question whose interests ought to be identical with those of the Government, if their best services are to be devoted to the work entrusted to them."[91]

For some reason, perhaps the further illness of Lennox, it was not until June 1 that a letter quoting Hunt's generous recommendation of March was dispatched to Street.[92] During the long interval, Street protested and again requested arbitration, and even after receiving the delayed letter he continued to be suspicious.[93] Throughout the summer Street argued with the Office of Works about the magnitude of alterations for which official approval was to be required, and in October, the architect again requested that all disputed questions be resolved by an arbiter.[94]

With admirable forbearance, Hunt, Mitford, and Lennox agreed that the matter should be discussed informally with their understandably sensitive architect, and by mid-December Street had been convinced to accept the terms which had been offered six months earlier.[95] On October 17, he was sent an order for £2100 and the written assurance that the Office of Works would pay for the surveying of approved changes.[96] Street replied, "I am very glad that the questions between myself and the First Commissioner of Her Majesty's Works . . . are now finally settled after long delays."[97] Six years had passed since he had first discussed payment of the great plan with Ayrton.

This agreement prevailed throughout the construction of the law courts, but another question pertaining to the remuneration of surveyors arose in the course of the work as a result of the poor performance of Bull and Sons, the main contractor. Because of continuous disputes with them over the quality of the construction and the amount completed, it became necessary to measure the work formally every time Street issued a "certificate"—the document which authorized payment to the contractors on the basis of work accomplished. For this purpose, both Street and the contractors had to hire surveyors to confer and establish the amount to be included in each certificate. This was a highly unusual practice, and in November 1878, Street asked the Office of Works to pay for the additional surveying: "This I ask on the ground that the work done has been entirely beyond the ordinary duty or work of an architect, and such as would never have been required if we had employed a builder more able to grapple with so large a work."[98] Hunt, now Sir Henry, having been knighted at Osborne on July 21, 1876, withheld judgment at first.[99] But when the claims of James Gandy, Street's surveyor for the main contract, were presented in 1884, after the death of the architect, he allowed a payment of £1500 for these expenses.[100] In the end Street and his estate were reimbursed both for preparing the abandoned plans and for much of the surveying.

Responsibility for the Heating System

PAYMENT of the architect and his assistants was not the only matter disputed between Street and the Office of Works. Another long controversy—over the responsibility for the design of the heating and ventilating system—began in 1871 and continued after the architect's death. Here again, the Government's attitude was colored by the lessons learned in building the Houses of Parliament, and officials sought to impose conditions contrary to those prevalent in ordinary architectural practice. Once more Street discovered that, while he had powerful friends among the leadership of the Liberal party, it was often easier to do business with the Tories.

The subject of heating was first introduced in December 1871, when the final design had been published and Street was hard at work on the contract drawings. Ayrton was then first commissioner, and Street inquired of him how he wished the plans for the heating system to be worked out. He was apparently told to make the design himself and then advertise for tenders. On December 19, he protested that he would prefer to consult with several heating contractors first, outline a plan in discussion with them, and then offer the contract to them in a very limited competition.[101] This seems to have been Street's usual practice, and at St. Pancras Station G. G. Scott had also engaged a contractor as a heating consultant, later hiring him to make the installation as well.[102] However, the Office of Works was highly skeptical of divided responsibilities. They had had enormous difficulties with the independently designed heating and ventilating of the Houses of Parliament, and refused to entertain a proposal that might lead to a similar problem.[103]

Accordingly, Hunt prepared a strongly worded memorandum in which he asserted: "It [is] the duty of an Architect to devise and propose such a scheme for Warming and Ventilating a building designed by him, as he may think best adapted for the purpose."[104] He suggested that Street might wish to consult with Dr. John Percy, who had finally installed a satisfactory system in the Houses of Parliament and who had advised the Royal Commission at the time of the law courts competition, but the architect would have to pay for this advice himself. Finally, Hunt warned darkly, "If [Mr. Street] should be unable and unwilling to propose a scheme of his own, the First Commissioner can then seek the advice and assistance of Dr. Percy or some other experienced person, at Mr. Street's expense." A letter in this vein was dispatched to Street, who made no further protest.[105] Heating was not included in the main contract, and so the matter did not require urgent discussion. It was only in August 1874, when construction had already begun, that Street finally submitted a proposal, apparently his own work.[106] His plans were briefly discussed, but since there was no intention to invite tenders in the near future, the subject was again allowed to drop.

In 1877, time had come to effect some heating plan, but even then a design was only needed for the eastern wing of offices, which was due to be completed first. Street's relationship with the Office of Works had improved substantially, and he was able to proceed as he had intended in 1871. First, he consulted with two heating contractors, Rosser and Russell (46 Charing Cross Road) and G. N. Haden and Son (of Trowbridge, Wiltshire, but with offices at 123 Cromer Street, Gray's Inn Road). With their assistance, he drafted plans and specifications which were submitted to the Office of Works on April 12, and he suggested that Haden and Son and Rosser and Russell be invited to a limited competition.[107] With the specter of the Houses of Parliament having retreated somewhat, and with a more generous Conservative administration in power, Hunt was willing to approve these arrangements.[108] Tenders were invited for May 1, and a contract was signed shortly thereafter with Haden for £1244, with £525 added to Bull's contract for additional construction work.[109] Street, who had employed Haden previously, was pleased to see this outcome. "I have every confidence in their executing whatever is entrusted to them in the best manner," he assured Mitford.[110]

It seemed at first that Street's proposal for heating the main block of the building would proceed almost as smoothly, but the issue of responsibility for this much more complicated design problem surfaced quickly. Street began to consider the details of this part of the heating system during the summer and fall of 1878, and, at the recommendation of Algernon Mitford, he met several times with Dr. Percy to review his 1874 plans.[111] However, the architect assumed that Percy would be willing to accept all liability for the success of the system, and this he refused to do. Street thereupon recommended simply awarding the entire design and construction job to "some manufacturer of warming apparatus, such as Messrs. Haden or Messrs. Rosser," the two bidders for the east wing contract, and Percy rejoined by objecting "most strongly" to a number of features of the design. The specialist also complained, "I much regret that, as you wish me to assist in this matter, I was not asked *before* the work had proceeded so far."[112] Percy displayed that combination of messianic arrogance and volatility common in his profession in the mid-nineteenth century, and the Office of Works wisely chose to seek other counsel. However, rather than follow Street's advice precisely, it retained the services of Charles Hood, a heating engineer of more even temperament, who agreed on December 6 to submit a plan.[113] Although not entirely to Street's liking, the Office of Works had at least retreated from its previous, adamant demand that Street make his own design or pay someone else to do the work.

Street must have been satisfied with his partial success until he received Hood's plans on April 1, 1879, and found they were unacceptable.[114] Although Percy, when asked to comment on his colleague's scheme, judged that it was "on the whole satisfactory," he warned that any heating design was "more or less experimental."[115] Street's opinion was characteristically less equivocal. While he was glad to see that some parts of Hood's scheme coincided with his own proposals of 1874, he distrusted the plan to heat and ventilate the entire building by means of one enormous, central system, the cost of which he estimated at £110,000. He preferred to divide the building services into several smaller units, creating a "somewhat ruder and much simpler system" that would cost much less.[116]

Mitford, who had taken on substantially increased duties now that Galton was no longer at the Office of Works, was understandably annoyed by Street's rejection of the expensive advice that had been procured for him, but he conceded that the law courts could probably get by with a simpler system than that proposed by the experts.[117] Hunt concurred and proposed that Street should now be allowed to consult with whomever he wished, including Haden or Rosser and Russell, and then prepare his own plan. Sir Henry expressed his own preference for a scheme that was simple, cheap, and the responsibility of the architect alone: "I prefer experimenting with £25,000 with one responsible adviser, to a like operation costing £110,000 or more without any responsible adviser at all or rather with two irresponsible advisers."[118] Street met on May 12 with Gerald James Noel, Lennox's successor as first commissioner, and a few days later he was given full authority to proceed as he wished.[119]

Having nudged the Office of Works to accept his plan of action, on July 12 Street once more proposed to obtain expert advice from heating contractors. But whereas he had conferred with two firms in planning for the east wing, he now suggested a consultation with only Haden and Son, who had submitted the lower tender for the eastern block and whose "experience in works of exactly the same kind is far more extensive than that of any other firm."[120] Street wished to hire Haden's Manchester manager, Frederick Blake, at ten guineas per week as an assistant in completing the plans, and he proposed then to open the contract to Haden for tender, although not guaranteeing that their bid would be accepted. In a memo, Hunt agreed that Haden and Son were "undoubtedly the most skillful and experienced tradesmen" and that they might properly be employed.[121] He also approved the hiring of Blake, which was accepted by the Treasury, even though it was disgruntled at having to pay for yet another heating expert.[122]

On December 8, 1879, Street submitted a plan worked out with Blake and estimated to cost £38,713.[123] He recommended that Haden should now be given the contract, but while Hunt advised the first commissioner that it was "not improbable" that the job would go to Haden, he suggested that full specifications should be prepared first.[124] Haden and Son were then asked to draft specifications, with the understanding that their employment could not yet be completely guaranteed.[125] These were completed on March 30.[126]

However, on April 23, William Ewart Gladstone returned to 10 Downing Street, and all government work was once more subject to the more vigilant financial scrutiny of the Liberal party. At the law courts, this meant that for a time Street's long and rather tactful campaign to assert his own will over the provisions for heating appeared to have been pointless. The tone of his correspondence with his official clients warmed noticeably.

On May 3, 1879, the very day that William P. Adam resumed his position as first commissioner, Henry Hunt wrote to Mitford that he had changed his mind and decided that the contract would have to be opened to competitive bidding after all. Street was asked to suggest additional firms which might be invited to tender.[127] Alarmed by this reversal of policy, Street protested that he had only accepted the responsibility for devising a heating and ventilating system "on the distinct condition that I was able to select the men to carry out the work."[128] Street had full confidence in Haden and Son, he said, and the firm had assured him that Blake, whom he praised as a "very valuable and well informed assistant engineer," would be assigned to supervise the work at the law courts. As far as other possible contractors were concerned, Street professed that he was unable to name any who would be able to complete the job reliably according to the specifications that had been drawn up by Haden. Nor could he suggest any firms with Haden's thirty years of successful experience in heating such buildings as the National Gallery, the British Museum, and several provincial courts of law. They had also installed the heating in St. Pancras Station, where they were appointed without a competition.[129]

Hunt disagreed. He argued that since the plans were Street's and not Haden's (a technically correct but unrealistic description of the situation), "any first rate Mechanical Engineer" should be able to carry them out.[130] Although he was not prepared to say that the estimate submitted by Haden was excessive, he still could not advise the first commissioner to accept it "without the test of a competition." Adam adopted this advice and ordered a competition on May 10.[131]

Mitford then renewed his request to Street for a list of capable contractors, and for the next month a strongly felt exchange of letters went on between the Office of Works and the architect. Street again advised Mitford that he was unable to name other firms which commanded his confidence. "My experience," he wrote, "is that a great many men undertake to warm and ventilate buildings and that very few of them succeed."[132] He pledged to cooperate with whoever was hired, but he refused to accept the responsibility unless the Hadens were employed to execute the design that was virtually if not legally their own. Hunt drafted an annoyed memo in response, asserting that it was Street's duty "to prepare and be responsible for all the details, structural or otherwise which may be necessary in order to make the Building complete in all its parts and hand it over to the Department in a fit state for occupation."[133] If the architect refused to be liable for the heating system, Hunt suggested, as he had in 1871, that he might "hand it over to some other competent person able and willing to take the burden upon himself." A warning was sent to Street.[134]

In reply, the architect reluctantly sent a list of nine contractors, of whom he warned, "as I have not employed many of them I am quite unable to say that they possess my confidence."[135] He was also still unwilling to accept any responsibility. "I am not an Engineer," he wrote. "I have never warmed a public building, and I never before heard that an architect was required to undertake such duties." This further upset Hunt, who again recommended that either Street should be required to assume full responsibility for the work or that he should be replaced. He concluded, "I should be very sorry to be driven to such an alternative as this, but in the face of this Letter, in which Mr. Street practically tells us he not only knows nothing but is not expected to know anything of the subject I cannot possibly advise the First Commissioner to allow him to proceed with the work."[136] Another warning was passed on to Street, threatening that the Office of Works might be compelled to "seek some competent person to undertake the work and to assign to him the architect's commission in respect thereof."[137]

From Street this occasioned a further protest that he had willingly accepted the traditional responsibility for "those works in connection with warming and ventilating which are usually and can be conveniently included in a *Builders* contract, and which it is customary for an architect to make plans for."[138] He again counseled,

> If, contrary to my advice, you employ some one who has not had constant experience of such large works, who is not responsible for the scheme in any sense whatever, and who cannot therefore be asked to guarantee any certain results, it is my plain duty to tell you that in my judgement there will be the gravest risk of a comparative failure, or at least of troublesome and probably expensive alterations in the scheme after the tenders have been sent in.

Hunt, who had championed the claims of Street on other occasions, now lost sympathy with him. He first wrote to Mitford that the fact that Street's commission was based on the entire cost of the building, including the complete heating system, proved his responsibility.[139] A few days later his views had hardened even more, and he advised Mitford,

> Mr. Street would not hesitate to be responsible for the success of his own scheme if only he could employ Messrs. Haden to do the work at their own price. This is practically admitting that the scheme is Haden's and not Mr. Street's and if we were to employ Haden to do the work as Mr. Street desires we had better hold Haden liable and dispense with Mr. Street's services altogether and save 5 percent on the outlay. This of course cannot be done and therefore unless Mr. Street will admit unreservedly that he is to be held responsible for the efficiency and success of his scheme, I am decidedly of the opinion that it would not be prudent to allow the works to proceed under his direction.[140]

Based on this memorandum, an ultimatum was sent to the architect on June 7: "Unless you wish to resign the superintendence of the Work together with the commission as architect thereon, the Board must hold you responsible for the execution and efficiency of a scheme which was so manifestly included in your agreement."[141]

Street must have noticed that his employers were growing weary of his intransigence, but only now did he seem to realize that they seriously contemplated his removal from part of the design. He replied: "I do not believe any architect has ever done more to assist a client in such matter than I have done in this case, and I have never asked, nor do I intend to ask after [a] great part of the work has been done, to be relieved from the work."[142] He at last consented to put the specifications in shape for the use of bidders, and he reported that these were ready on August 6.[143] The Office of Works then set about preparing the terms of the contract and the invitations to tender, and by the end of August everything appeared to be in order.[144]

However, the tenders were never invited. Almost immediately after resuming office as first commissioner, William Adam had appealed to Gladstone to be appointed governor of Madras.[145] He was apparently fond of India, where he had served as private secretary to the governor of Bombay in the 1850s, and that autumn the transfer was approved. On November 11, 1880, George John Shaw-Lefevre (1831–1928) was named to succeed him at the Office of Works. Shaw-Lefevre's sister had married the son to the fourth earl of Aberdeen, who had employed Street to design the chapel at Haddo House in 1879, and Shaw-Lefevre later professed that he was himself a long term friend of the architect.[146] This association may have disposed the new first commissioner to be indulgent toward Street, and in a meeting with the architect on January 18, 1881, he agreed that too much time had already been lost for him to allow any further delay for a competition. He authorized the signing of a contract with Haden.[147] Hunt was upset by this immediate capitulation, but the first commissioner was not to be dissuaded. "I have mentioned the subject to the Secretary of the Treasury and told him I will take the responsibility upon this Department," he wrote, suggesting that, as A. B. Mitford later recalled, Shaw-Lefevre did have a knack for getting his way with the chancellor of the Exchequer.[148] In March, a contract was signed for £36,225, rather less than the sum named in the estimate of December 1879.

After much uncertainty, Street was thus spared the uncongenial task of supervising the installation by one contractor of a heating system designed by another. Nor was he compelled to commit himself fully in an area where he had little technical expertise. Because G. N. Haden and Son were competent and honorable tradesmen, the law courts also received an effective apparatus without the terrible difficulties that beset the Houses of Parliament. But Street never won the argument over the responsibility of the architect for heating and ventilation, although the Office of Works no longer pursued the matter very vigorously. When his son submitted a request in 1884 for an additional commission for the heating contract, arguing that it had not been a part of the original responsibility of the architect, Sir Henry Hunt memoed stiffly, "Mr. Street was over and over again informed that the Warming and Ventilating of this Building were included in his Agreement of 23rd September 1870 and therefore I cannot recommend the Board recognise the claim now made."[149]

Builders

IN ADDITION to the difficulties encountered by the Office of Works in dealing with the architect, it faced further disputes in working with the construction contractors at the law courts. With them, too, patterns of practice were in transition, complicating the ordinary problems of broken deadlines, strikes, and bankruptcy which beset the construction of the new building.

Street was eager to get his design into the hands of the builders as soon as possible. On August 4, 1870, when his simplified floor plan was approved by the Royal Commission, he wrote to Douglas Galton at the Office of Works to ask that trial borings be made at the site and that the foundation contract be prepared. Since detailed plans had not yet been readied, Street proposed that contractors might be invited to submit bids based on the price per cubic yard of foundation work, rather than for the gross amount.[150] Henry Hunt objected to this unorthodox and old-fashioned manner of proceeding, demanding that tenders be submitted in the usual form. This required the completion of a full set of plans and specifications first. He was also unhappy with the separation of the foundation from the main construction contract, but he was willing to allow this in the "exceptional case" of the law courts.[151] Galton concurred in this opinion, and in early October, Acton Ayrton, who was also anxious for work to begin, approved Hunt's plan.[152]

In November, Street set to work making the necessary plans and specifications for the foundations, and he submitted a list of suggested builders.[153] This does not survive, but it seems to have formed the basis for the roster of twenty-one contractors invited by the Office of Works to tender on December 21.[154] Included were most of the giant general contractors of the day, firms like Lucas Brothers, Holland and Hannen, Dove Brothers, William Cubitt and Company, Henry Lee and Sons, George Myers and Sons, George Trollope and Sons, and William Brass. Except for Holm and Nicol of Liverpool, all were based in London. They were asked to submit their tenders before 1 P.M. on December 28, 1870.

The builders met together on December 15 and agreed to employ two firms of surveyors jointly, commissioning them to prepare the bill of quantities on which bids would be calculated. But they also agreed that the deadline was too soon and that they would have to see the conditions of the proposed contract, not yet drafted by the Office of Works, by December 19.[155] These requests were forwarded to Street, who sent them on to the office with his endorsement. He observed, "Christmastide is, I suppose, not the most convenient time for getting work done," and he recommended an extension of the deadline until January 14, 1871.[156] The builders' requests were granted.[157]

However, difficulties quickly arose after the contractors had studied the harsh provisions of the contract. These included penalties even in the event of unforeseeable delays, a clause permitting the government to add features not shown on the contract plans, and a prohibition against protesting the certificates issued by the architect. As it happened, the building trades were just then very sensitive to the dangers of such one-sided contracts, having been alerted to them by the decision in the case of *Jones v. St. John's College*, issued the previous November. In that ruling, substantial penalties for exceeding a deadline had been levied against a builder, even though the client's request for additional work caused the delay. The contract, however, had stipulated that all construction, including extras, was to be completed by a given date.[158] Thus warned and rallied to something like professional solidarity, the bidders for the foundations of the law courts refused to accept the terms proposed by the government. Rather than submit their tenders, they sent a deputation to Ayrton on January 7. The first commissioner evidently found the arguments of a group of influential businessmen more convincing than the unsupported protests which he often heard from the artists in his employ, and the contract was promptly rewritten. Concessions were made to the builders on every disputed point, and the time allowed for completion of the work was increased from seven to twelve months.[159]

Ayrton took advantage of the delay caused by this dispute to revise the specifications slightly. Street had just submitted the drawings which showed the great, freestanding clock tower at the southeast, a proposal immediately rejected by the Office of Works. Thus, when Ayrton advised the builders on January 13 of the modified contract terms, he also asked them to record the cost of the foundations for the tower as a separate item in their bids. The new deadline for tendering was 1 P.M. on January 20, 1871.[160]

Nineteen tenders were duly received. One contractor had withdrawn during the first stage of the bidding, another failed to submit a final tender, and a third delivered his bid too late. These three were partially offset by the firm of G. B. Gammon and Sons, which submitted a tender without an invitation. Gammon's was the highest bid, at £68,734, separated by nearly £32,000 from the low tender of £36,775 put in by Dove Brothers.[161] This enormous range was noted with "astonishment" by the *Builder*, while the *Building News* observed that it appeared that tendering had become a "game of chance."[162] A correspondent in the latter journal suggested that many contractors agreed to tender for such contracts merely to get their names into the papers and that they did not take the time to prepare careful estimates.[163]

G. E. Street was immediately consulted by the Office of Works, and he advised the acceptance of Dove's tender, which fell below his own estimate of £37,000–40,000.[164] Ayrton accepted Street's advice, and after the approval of the Treasury had been obtained, a contract for £35,060 was signed at the Office of Works on February 2 at 3 P.M.[165] The contract amount had been reduced by omitting the foundations for the clock tower, but Street at least had the reassurance of seeing some progress being made toward the execution of his design, albeit in altered form.

Dove Brothers, although the low bidders, was not an insubstantial firm, risking all to win a large contract. They were probably to be counted among the top three London general contractors of the 1860s, a position they earned chiefly through the construction of churches.[166] Originally four brothers were involved in the company, but in 1862 only three joined in signing a formal partnership agreement. The senior partner was Benjamin Dixon Dove, who lived unostentatiously at their building yard at 15 Studd Street, Islington. This was a convenient location for the use of Regent's Canal to transport heavy materials cheaply. The lists of tenders and the reports of contruction progress published in the *Building News* show that the Doves were the low and usually successful bidder for more than a dozen contracts between 1868 and 1870. None of these exceeded £10,000, however, underscoring the great scale of the contract for the law courts. But at least one of their churches from this period, St.

Mary Abbotts, Kensington, by G. G. Scott, was a work of national importance, and in 1869–70, they built the tower of Street's St. Peter, Bournemouth, for £2995.[167]

The terms of the law courts contract required completion of the foundations by February 1, 1872, but work was not finished until May 18. In principle, Dove Brothers was liable for a penalty of £100 per week for this delay, but in March Street appealed to the Office of Works against the strict enforcement of this clause. The slower, more careful rate of construction had been "an advantage to the work," he argued, and he went on, "I should be very sorry that Messrs Dove should be fined if they go on as they have hitherto. They appear to me to have done their work well and carefully, but perhaps have not quite realized from the first how much time this work would take."[168] Although Street later refused to accept any personal responsibility for the delay, blaming it on Dove Brothers' failure to employ "a sufficiently large force of men," he continued to argue that no penalty was called for. The work had benefited, he said, and, since the main contract was not even ready for tendering, no harm had been done to the schedule. Ultimately the Office of Works accepted this point of view.[169]

Indeed, there was little to complain about with respect to the Dove contract. In the course of construction Street had been able to pare a further £3541 from the total amount, as he worked out the final design more exactly.[170] Moreover, the excavations revealed a freshwater spring which, it was predicted, would be able to supply half the needs of the building. Of its waters Street reported enthusiastically: "It has been drunk by the workmen, and comes to our drains through gravel and sand, and looks extremely good."[171] Finally, the Doves' workmanship was sound. However, they later seemed to regret their low bid, unsuccessfully petitioning for an additional £2250 to compensate them for the unexpected expenses that they had incurred when they encountered clay where the test borings had shown gravel.[172]

The main building contract did not proceed as smoothly. Tendering was delayed for years by the controversy surrounding the final plan and for many additional months while the very complex quantities were calculated. Once the bids were received, further delay occurred while the Office of Works sought to reduce the expense of Street's plan, and there was even more waiting when the successful contractor disputed the terms of the contract. When work finally began, the builder was out-matched by the enormity of the undertaking and by the worsening state of the economy.

Preparations for the main contract began poorly because of the long debate over site, cost, and plan, but even when these issues were resolved, a huge amount of time was lost waiting for Street to prepare the extraordinarily complete book of specifications and the 248 contract drawings. These, in turn, demanded a spectacular exertion from the surveyors, working in consultation with the architect, in order to draft the bill of quantities on which the tenders could be based. Although the surveyors employed by the architect began their work in May 1871, even before the Treasury overrode Ayrton and while Street was still making contract drawings, it was not until late in 1872 that preparations could be made to invite bids. In January 1872, in the midst of this long preliminary effort, Street explained his own role: "I am engaged day after day in answering questions, and making explanatory drawings [in additon to the contract drawings] for the Surveyors, and all these answers and explanations are incorporated from time to time in a specification book from which finally I propose to form the complete specification for the work."[173]

At last, on December 2, 1872, Street reported that the plans and specifications were ready.[174] Following instructions from Ayrton, he had organized the materials to allow the construction work to be divided into separate contracts for the main block and the east wing, perhaps to be awarded to different builders. The architect suggested that the list of those invited to bid for the foundations should form the basis of the list for these contracts. Hunt, however, thought that additional invitations should be issued to provincial firms, and Galton agreed.[175] Thus, when preliminary letters of inquiry were dispatched to twenty-four contractors on December 11, the large London builders, with Dove among them, again dominated the roster of invitees, but four additional firms from Birmingham and Manchester had joined Holm and Nicol of Liverpool to represent provincial interests more forcefully.[176] This gesture was apparently felt to be necessary in constructing a national building, but the reasoning that lay behind it was never clearly articulated.

It was not until mid-January 1873 that the results of the first letters were forwarded to Street.[177] Most of the non-Londoners had declined to compete, although a total of eighteen signified that they were interested. At the last minute four more names were added to the list, before the formal invitations to tender were sent out on February 27.[178] The deadline was originally set for March 15, but five days before the bids were due it was extended to the 25th. On the latter date nineteen contractors submitted tenders for one or more of the three contracts that were offered: for the entire building, for the main block of great hall and courtrooms, and for the eastern block of offices. The lowest bids for all contracts were discovered to be those of Joseph Bull and Sons of Southampton, one of the firms added to the list after replies had been received from the initial inquiries.[179]

This time the range of tenders was less spectacular. To erect the entire building in the preferred material, Portland stone, they varied from the Bulls' low of £744,344 to the high of £994,700 bid by Peto Brothers of Pimlico. Bull and Sons, however, were substantially below the next-to-lowest tender of George Baker and Son of Lambeth, who had come in with £816,675. Dove Brothers, chastened by their small profit (or perhaps a loss) on the foundations, was tenth with £924,100.

Street recommended that Bull and Sons be employed, but a quarrel ensued because their tender exceeded the statutory limit of £710,000, a sum which was also to pay the separate contracts for heating and lighting equipment. The Office of Works demanded that the design be modified to reduce costs, as already discussed, and during the dispute both Ayrton and Street negotiated privately with the Bulls. This led to substantial confusion, and it was not until July 2, when Street and Bull were advised by the Office of Works that the Treasury had sided with Street, that the position of the contractor became clear.[180]

The selection of Bull and Sons must have surprised most observers. Their Belvidere Works lay beside the River Itchen in Southampton, and they had established a successful but not enormous practice in the south of England. They did a substantial amount of railway work, chiefly for the London and Southwestern Railway, but their architectural output was limited, and a survey of the tender and construction news columns of the *Building News* from 1868 to 1872 reveals only ten apparent or confirmed contracts. These did include several important structures, including John Gibson's National Provincial Bank in Southampton and the Godwinesque Winchester Guildhall by Jeffrey and Skiller.[181] However, nothing about their previous accomplishments suggested that they were likely to win the right to build the largest public building of that generation. The success of Bull and Sons was clearly the result of offering the lowest bid to an economy-minded Government, and the case of their employment was to demonstrate the folly of making such decisions on the basis of price alone.

The head of the firm was Joseph Bull, born in Southampton in 1803. He and his wife Sarah lived in Orchard Lane and later in Paget Street in that city, and he had established himself as a builder at least by the 1830s. Three of his sons entered the business: Edward Charles, baptized in 1840, and Henry William and Frederick W., both evidently born after 1846.[182] Another son seems to have become an architect, going into partnership with C. A. Monday, with whom he designed the Norman church of St. Matthew, Southampton, constructed by the family firm and consecrated in 1870.[183] Monday was later placed in charge of all the architectural drawings for the law courts by the Bulls. The story of the company was one of comfortable prosperity and of local importance, all of which was sacrificed in the pursuit of a contract which was probably too large and far away for the resources of the firm, and which was undertaken on the eve of deteriorating financial conditions in the country at large.

The Bulls' shortcomings were almost immediately demonstrated, bringing Street into an unaccustomed alliance with the Office of Works, a relationship that became more natural when W. P. Adam succeeded Ayrton as first commissioner in August 1873. The first indication that their builder would prove uncooperative came a few weeks after the design controversy had been resolved and the way seemed to be clear at last for rapid progress. In a letter to the secretary of works on July 18, the Bulls raised two points of dispute whose lengthy debate was to delay the signing of the contract until the next year. First, basing their case on the precise wording of the invitation to tender, which had requested a bid for the fitting of only a single, sample court, they refused to undertake the construction of all of the courtrooms at their bid price of £804. Second, they reasoned that they were due "some consideration for the delay of nearly four months and the inconvenience and loss we have entertained since the delivery of our tender which it is obvious in the present state of the labor market has been much to our disadvantage."[184] On neither issue were Street or the Office of Works at first willing to give much ground, but in each case some accommodation had to be reached before work could begin.

The first reply to Bull and Sons was based on a memo by Henry Hunt, who suggested that they could be released from their bid of £804 only if the final plans for the other seventeen courtrooms differed from the single sample design on which their tender was based. On the other question, he argued, reasonably, that delays were common at the outset of "a great work of this kind" and that all of the bidders had known the state of the construction market, where prices had been rising steadily for several years.[185] Shortly after this message was conveyed to the contractors, Street met with them to attempt to persuade them that they were being unrealistic, but he was unsuccessful. Already they seemed to recognize that they were in over their heads, and they grasped at every opportunity to reduce their responsibilities and increase their income.

On September 1, several of the Bulls met with Hunt, Galton, and Charles Poland, who represented Street. They explained that their sample courtroom tender had included a clerical error which resulted in a bid £300 lower than intended. The Bulls were understandably anxious that this mistake for one court should not be multiplied by eighteen. The hardships caused by the delay were also discussed, but most importantly, the builders introduced a number of additional requests which revealed even more tellingly the weaknesses of their organization and finances. In lieu of the heavily framed timber scaffolding which Street had included in the specifications, they asked to substitute lighter, cheaper pole scaffolding where sufficient. They further requested that they be released from the clause requiring them to work all stone on the site, preferring to do some of that labor at their yard in Southampton. They also asked to be granted an advance toward the purchase of machinery.[186] All of these proposals indicated that the firm was short of capital and geographically overextended.

Street, Galton, and Hunt were adamantly opposed to any concession to these new demands, and in mid-September, Hunt prepared a briefing memorandum on the situation for Adam, the new first commissioner, who was only then becoming active in the business of the office.[187] Hunt was, however, now more flexible with respect to the original claims. He allowed that the Bulls had made a "bona fide error" in their courtroom tender, and he urged that £5100 be added to the contract on account of this. Moreover, he was willing to see some "fair and reasonable" compensation offered on account of the delay, a difficulty which would not have arisen, he suggested, if Ayrton had not so stubbornly resisted Hunt's counsel of moderation in reshaping the design. "But," he went on, "the First Commissioner was pleased to take a different view of the subject and of course I do not presume to doubt the correctness of his decision." Evidently, with Ayrton gone, Hunt now found it possible to suggest more generous terms, and he also saw that it was desirable to separate himself as much as possible from the policies of his late, unpopular chief.

W. P. Adam was by nature disposed to adopt this conciliatory line, and in early October, he directed that Bull and Sons should be offered an additional £5100 for the courtroom fittings and that the cash reserve, which was to be withheld until their work was completed, should be reduced from £23,000 to £15,000 in compensation for the delay.[188] The builders, however, were still uneasy, for they estimated that they had already lost £10,000. Further, they replied that any arrangement with respect to the courtrooms must remain tentative until detail drawings for all of the rooms were available. And they added yet another request indicative of their weaknesses, asking that joinery work, which they intended to fabricate and store in Southampton, should be paid for before it was brought up to London.[189] Street, Galton, and Hunt again agreed not to give in to this type of demand, and on October 28, the Bulls were advised that no further concessions would be made.[190] A week later, when no reply had been received, they were requested to answer "without further delay."[191] The Office of Works once more resorted to the familiar practice of issuing an ultimatum, but this time Street was comfortably on their side.

This tested technique had negative effects on the prospects for amicable cooperation. The Bulls immediately replied in fury,

> *We were ready in March last* to execute a Contract in accordance with our Tender. We must recall your attention to the fact that it *was the Board* and not we who disturbed the foundation of the Contract by proposing on the 31st May last (more than two months after the delivery of the tenders) *first to include the fittings of 18 Courts* in the Contract, we having tendered on the Board's own request for the fittings of *one* only, and *then* to reduce the amount of the tender *by £100,000.*[192]

Rather than accept the terms offered by the Government with respect to the seventeen disputed courtrooms, they now proposed that all courtroom fittings be omitted and made the subject of a later, supplemental contract. This proposal was accepted by the Office of Works as the only route out of the impasse, and so a working agreement was reached, the Bulls reserving only the right to refer their claim for delay compensation to arbitration in the future.[193]

The priced bill of quantities, which Bull and Sons were to provide for inclusion in the contract, took rather longer to prepare than anticipated. All was not in readiness for signing until the last week of January 1874. The further delay caught Street unawares, for he had already had the signature blocks on all of the contract drawings provisionally dated "December 1873," and the contractors themselves had told the press that work would begin on January 5.[194] Even when the documents were prepared, the Bulls were unable to come to London for a week, and Street was unavailable until Saturday, February 7.[195] On that date, at noon, Street met with the builders to sign the drawings and the contract. There were so many drawings that this mechanical task required five hours.[196] In its final form the contract set deadlines of August 8, 1877, for the eastern block and June 1, 1880, for the main block. The contract amount was £693,429, having been reduced by the sum approved by the Treasury and also by the removal of all courtroom fittings. A further amount was subtracted because it had been agreed to make all decorative stone-carving the subject of a separate contract.[197]

Construction finally commenced on May 1, by which time the Conservatives had returned to office. There was no official desire to publicize the much-delayed event, and, just as the first stone of the Houses of Parliament was laid without fanfare by Barry's wife, the law courts got underway with a quiet family ceremony. Only about a dozen guests were present, and most of them were Bulls. The first brick was laid by Henry W. Bull, followed by one laid by his wife, another by his son, and one each by all of those present. This went on unobtrusively at the northeast corner of the building.[198] The subdued poignancy of the event contrasted sharply with the acrimonious disputes over the design and the terms of the contract that had preceded it, and also with the years of difficulty that lay ahead.

As foreshadowed by their efforts to amend the contract, Bull and Sons sank quickly into trouble. By February 1874 Street was compelled to write to them, complaining of their slow progress. He was particularly alarmed by their neglect of work on the main block, and he kept up the pressure with a continuous stream of letters throughout the spring and summer of 1875. Finally, on September 14, he directed his clerk to advise the builders that

> Mr. Street . . . is extremely surprised at your almost entire neglect of the works on the more important portion of your Contract, in spite of his often

repeated directions to you to go on with them. For the last nine months very little indeed has been done to this portion of the work and Mr. Street is confident that you will never recover the lost time, and that it will hardly be possible for you to complete the works within the period settled by the Contract.

A month later he provided the Office of Works with a gloomy progress report.[199] Part of the blame for the setbacks lay with the severe winter weather, which halted work for a month and a half in 1874–75. But the chief difficulty, Street explained, was that the Bulls, like the Doves, did not employ enough men and machinery. A year earlier 350 workers had been on the job, and this had slowly risen to 540 by August 1875. The contractors were adding "considerably" to their machinery, and with more masons and laborers Street felt that it was still "within the bounds of possibility" that the contracts would be completed on schedule. Still, he was not sanguine about the prospect for such improvements. Contemporary accounts did report a large increase in the numbers of men and machines, bringing the force to more than one thousand and tripling the number of steam-powered masonry saws, but relations with the contractor remained strained.[200]

The plight of Bull and Sons was principally financial in nature. Having been denied an advance payment with which to purchase equipment, they were slow in bringing together the necessary resources for the construction of a great building. Their acute money problems also led them to question the details of the certificates for completed work which Street prepared as the basis for their remuneration. To protect himself, Street was compelled to hire James Gandy to survey the work regularly and provide corroborating figures. As discussed, Gandy's pay itself became a point of dispute between the architect and the Office of Works, but Street was able to convince them that the surveyor's frequent measurements of the construction were necessary by maintaining,

> Because with the sort of Contractors we have we should quite certainly have a demand for an Arbitration once a year as provided by the Contract unless I could meet them with this array of carefully prepared figures agreed to on their behalf by their Surveyors [who met with Gandy]. For my own purposes they are not necessary. I could now undertake to certify with a very close approach to accuracy without any such elaborate measurements.[201]

The Bulls' financial distress necessitated this considerable extra expenditure and enormous additional labor on the part of those who employed and supervised their services.

But although it complained, the government had a vested interest in keeping its builder solvent. If Bull and Sons collapsed before the completion of the building, prodigious delays would inevitably ensue, and so, while lamenting their dilatoriness, special arrangements were made to ease their severe cash flow problems. Toward the end, certificates for payment to the contractors were issued weekly, and this rapid funneling of cash led, not altogether inadvertently, to sizable overpayments. These were treated as advances. As Arthur Edmund Street explained after the death of his father:

The history of the overpayment of the contractors was their continued financial weakness which made it everyone's interest to keep them going by ad-
vancing at times rather more than they were entitled to. In 1878 it was discovered that the Contractors were overpaid nearly £2600, but in the face of
this £6000 extra was certified for (Certificate Number 47) at the request or
with the consent of [the Office of Works] for the purpose of bolstering up
Messrs. Bull. Six months later Messrs. Bull were found to have had £13,000
too much, but £5000 was advanced (Certificate Number 55) on the same
grounds and under the same authority.[202]

Despite this generosity the Bulls were always on the brink of disaster. First and
second mortgages were obtained on their equipment during the progress of the
construction, and they were consistently slow in honoring the financial claims made
against them. In January 1878, Street brought it to the attention of the Office of
Works that the Bulls had paid nothing to the subcontracting stonecarvers since the
previous September. Arrangements were then made to pay the carvers directly.[203]
Similarly, in February 1879, Street reported that the Bulls had failed to pay their
own surveyors for about a year, and that the surveyors had consequently refused to
meet with Gandy to discuss the certificates. Again he asked that direct payments be
arranged, but this time Henry Hunt objected that the practice would set a dangerous
precedent.[204]

Further evidence of the serious problems of Bull and Sons can be gleaned from
a variety of sources. For instance, in 1882, when electric lighting was being installed
in the new building, the engineering contractor declared that the Bulls' steam boilers
were too dangerous to use even temporarily for powering the generators. They had
suffered from want of proper maintenance, and the builders now refused to repair
them.[205]

Ultimately, no combination of complaint and generosity could save the contractors. The main block of the building was completed and the law courts were
officially opened in December 1882, 121 weeks behind schedule, and the next
month receivers were named for Joseph Bull and Sons, now headed by William
Henry Bull. Their debts were estimated at first at £190,000, although an amount
about half that figure was later quoted.[206] In their defense, the builders claimed that
the government owed them an additional £89,752, of which about £60,000 was said
to be penalties for contract violations and the rest for added work. To counter this,
the Office of Works was prepared to assert its claim for lateness fines, and so the case
was referred to arbitration. Representatives and surveyors (with Gandy again serving
on the government side) were appointed by both parties in 1883, and Lord Halsbury
was named as umpire in 1886, but the Bull family never assembled their case.
Repeated postponements were granted at their request, but none was allowed after
September 1894, at which date they had still failed to come forward with their
evidence.

The government was pleased at this final victory by default, but it was a sad
and antiheroic end for so great an enterprise. Almost ten years earlier Sir Henry
Hunt had urged the speedy settlement of the case, observing: "As I happen to be
the only person in the Department who is thoroughly acquainted with all that has
been done and said from first to last in regard to this Contract there is the contin-

gency of a Man of my Age surviving or holding office for a Year or more."[207] Hunt, in fact, retired in 1886 at the age of seventy-six, thus breaking the last link with the early stages of the project. He died three years later. Street had died in 1881, and Ayrton and Layard, long out of office, died in 1886 and 1894, respectively. Thus, by the time the last legal hurdles were cleared, the Royal Courts of Justice were already the work of a dead generation.

Building Workers

THE BULLS' demise had been speeded by the expenses incurred in defeating a seven-month strike of the Society of Operative Stonemasons in 1877–78. This episode was of great importance to the trade union movement, marking the end of a decade of substantial gains and ushering in a new type of more moderate labor leadership. The outcome of the strike, like the fate of Bull and Sons, was heavily influenced by the state of the national economy, which, by the mid-seventies, was entering the period of decline that followed the mid-Victorian boom. By that date, Britain was being challenged for the first time by the industrial power of Germany and the agricultural might of North America.[208]

The stonemasons' strike was in support of the so-called "Nine-Hours Movement," and the history of that struggle to shorten the working day from ten hours (as established by legislation in 1847) was to a large extent the history of the stonemasons' union itself. They had first asked for nine hours in 1853, and had quickly established themselves in the vanguard of labor militancy. In particular, the London chapter of the Operative Stonemasons (O.S.M.) was famous for its independence and radicalism, persisting in the old brand of direct action, strike-oriented strategy that began to go out of style during the prosperous decades after 1850. The new moderate attitude among unionists, which favored arbitration for the resolution of differences, spawned the Trades Union Congress (T.U.C.), founded in 1868. The story of the masons shows them struggling with these new values and, in the end, succumbing.

Three major episodes of working hours agitation prepared the ground for the climactic strike of 1877–78. In November 1858, the masons joined with the other London building trades in petitioning and ultimately striking for a nine-hour day, even though their national executive had failed to support their action. The employers, who had just banded together to form the National Association of Master Builders, responded with a lockout and then offered to rehire any of the twenty-five thousand unemployed workers who signed an anti-union "document." However, the strikers held out against this attempted union breaking, and the last contractor finally rehired his men in February 1860.

Although they had not won shorter hours, the building trades were united by this effort, and another set of nine-hour demands was drafted in March 1861. Their unity was shortlived, however, and only the bricklayers briefly joined the masons in a supporting strike. The ever independent stonemasons persisted alone with what one historian has called "astonishing and almost suicidal determination," but they were once more cut off by their national organization in June 1862, and the long strike then failed.[209] The owners had again responded to this offensive with their own demands, and after their victory these were enacted. Hourly rates now replaced fixed daily pay scales, without which, the employers reasoned, no worker would ask for shorter hours.

In the third battle, which came nearly ten years later, the new mood of moderation seemed to have reached even the stonemasons. The T.U.C. had been founded in the meantime, and the Trade Union Act of 1871 had given unions new legal rights and increased respectability. In this climate the London masons began to agitate in January 1871 for what was called "nine and nine"—nine hours of work per day (fifty-one hours of work per week, with a short Saturday) at nine pence per hour. The concomitant demand for a higher hourly rate was intended to offset the reduction in working time. The carpenters and joiners enlisted as allies, and the owners were given until July 1 to reply to their demands. However, the carpenters overeagerly struck against two firms on June 1, and this was answered by the contractors with a general lockout.

The masons responded to this challenge in an unexpected way. The new national secretary of the O.S.M., a nonmilitant, again denied the Londoners the support of the national treasury, but the London chapter itself was now headed by a man of the new breed, Henry Broadhurst, who was later the general secretary of the T.U.C. and a member of Parliament. Broadhurst argued that the masons were entitled to make whatever terms they could, and in separate meetings with the masters they hammered out a compromise. The settlement of 8½ pence per hour, with fifty-two hours of work per week for most of the year and forty-seven hours during the twelve weeks of mid-winter, infuriated other London trade unionists. More old-style militancy was expected from the masons.

Six years later, the London masons seemed determined to redeem their reputation, and the law courts became a hostage to their action. On the first day of 1877, they served general notice that after July 30 they would expect to see the prevailing wage of nine pence raised by a penny and to work a shorter day. However, as the long spring wore on, the economy began to slide into a depression which ultimately reached even the relatively sheltered building industry. The employers met only once with representatives of the masons, and, pointing to the financial situation, they rejected their claim. As a result 1700 men came out on strike that summer. At first the strikers seemed to be making headway, as approximately one hundred smaller contractors acceded to their demands. But they failed to gain support from other unions, who were now content to let the masons go their own way, and they were generally criticized by moderate labor leaders for launching an offensive at an inopportune time. The weekly *Industrial Review*, the mild succcessor of the militant *Beehive*, supported the settlement of disputes through arbitration, and editorialized against what they called a "mere trial of strength."[210] The London Trades Council also passed a resolution in October regretting that the stonemasons had struck without consulting their brethren in other fields.[211] The thinking of laborites was still shaped by classical economics, and few questioned that a period of recession was an impossible time in which to seek higher wages.

Moreover, despite the willingness of many of the smaller firms to give ten pence per hour to their men, a dozen of the major general contractors refused to give an inch. This kept six hundred or more masons out of work, and these had to be supported by funds drawn from the national headquarters—which backed the strik-

ers—or from special levies among those who had returned to work. The struggle soon focused on the two largest projects where the contractors had refused to come to terms: the Temple Gardens Building, a block of chambers designed by E. M. Barry for the Inner and Middle Temples, where the builder was G. W. Booth, and the law courts.

In September, the contest entered a much more serious phase when the Master Builders Association began to import foreign masons as strikebreakers. Seven Germans arrived first, and agents of the builders soon fanned out to Italy, Canada, and the United States, where they offered guaranteed employment for six months without mentioning the strike. The trickle of foreigners grew into a flood, with 571 masons coming to London before the strike ended. One hundred sixty-nine came from North America and fifty-two from Holland; the remainder were largely German and Italian. In addition to these forces, approximately six hundred less scrupulous British provincial stonemasons, many from Scotland, came to take advantage of the situation.[212] The Bulls, who had employed 550 masons before the strike, had 40 foreigners at work by October and approximately 300 were on the site by November. Their force was about half German and half Italian, and they also succceeded in luring some forty Englishmen back to work at nine pence.[213] Henry William Bull himself visited the quarries of Belgium, Austria, and Germany to recruit workers late in November, and he returned with 129 masons. He also hired a German architectural student named Rees, from Ludwigsburg, to serve as their foreman, and another student to be his assistant.[214]

Naturally, the introduction of foreign blacklegs raised an enormous storm of protest, even from those who had not supported the strike at first. Referring specifically to the law courts, the *Industrial Review* queried,

> Was it ever heard of that, in a country so boastful of its freedom and justice as ours, great public works, for which every man, gentle or simple, pays his share, should be carried out by the importation of foreign craftsmen, to the exclusion of native artisans, and especially that a great national edifice should be bungled by the scum of European artificership, while the first masons in the world are turned off, to walk the streets of their own capital, with empty stomachs, and to bury their compulsory idle hands in the void depths of their trouser pockets.[215]

As resentment grew, scattered incidents of violence occurred, and after one encounter between a group of German masons and the son of an English plasterer, Henry Bull appeared in court to testify on behalf of his new men. They were released on their own recognizance after he paid their fine and a surety of twenty pounds.[216]

To safeguard their foreign workers, the Bulls housed and fed them on the site. Some slept in the shop over the architect's office, and a dining hall and kitchen were set up in the crypt of the eastern block, now nearing completion (Fig. 128). Separate messes were provided for the Germans and the Italians, and the latter were duly served "their beloved macaroni."[217] Three generous meals and lodging could be had for only three shillings per day, and dinner, for example, consisted of a pint of beer and an unlimited quantity of soup, meat, and potatoes. Life was arduous for the foreigners, however. They worked a week of six twelve-hour days for nine pence

128 The dining room for foreign masons in the basement of the eastern wing. 1877. (Illustrated London News, 3 November 1877.)

per hour, and, of course, they were held as voluntary prisoners behind the hoardings of the site.[218] The Society of Operative Stonemasons drafted a memorial, protesting the use of a government building as a "common lodging-house," which was presented to G. J. Noel, the first commissioner of works.[219] But they were told in reply that the Bulls' action was legal, and, indeed, Noel later wrote to the Treasury, commending "the very active and successful measures which [the builders] took in combatting the masons' strike."[220]

The arrival of the foreigners also imposed a further financial burden on the striking union. Such was international labor solidarity that many and perhaps most of the workers from abroad refused to go to work when they discovered that a strike was in progress. The stonemasons decided to send these men home at the expense of the strike fund, and so these costs were added to the support payments which were already being made to the strikers. Strike pay was maintained at or near eighteen shillings per week for single men, with an additional shilling for married workers and one more for each child. These costs were borne both by London masons lucky enough to return to work and by a small tax on provincial masons.

The union continued to claim that more and more builders were conceding the ten pence hourly rate, and perhaps a total of 120 firms did capitulate. But the larger firms, like Cubitt, Trollope, Dove, and Bull, had discovered that they could beat the strikers. Sufficient blacklegs had been recruited to get them through the winter season, at which time there was less work to do anyway. When the strikers asked to discuss their demands with the employers in November, the master builders voted not even to consider the proposition. The Bulls were present at the meeting when they chose instead to listen to a report on the masonry work being done at the law courts; the speaker concluded that no better workmanship had been seen in years.[221] Early in 1878 the builders declined the offer of arbitration made by George Godwin, the editor of the *Builder*, saying that they already had sufficient men at work.[222]

Finally, late in 1877, even some of those contractors who had originally granted ten pence per hour began to give notice that they would cut back to nine.[223] A number of the provincial unions also began to call for an end to the strike in the capital, for which they had paid heavily. Although continuation of the action was approved by a vote of all the lodges in the country, the end was now not far away.[224] The London Trades Council voted in February against sponsoring demonstrations in support of the masons, the *Industrial Review* began to question the statistics which had seemed to show that the strike was succeeding, and early in March the union voted to allow its members to return to work at 9½ pence per hour.[225] Then on March 14, the workers gave way entirely, agreeing to accept the old rate of nine pence. The Operative Stonemasons had spent a total of £24,605, of which £15,775 had been drawn from national funds, and continued expenditure on that scale could not be sustained.[226]

The failure of the strike was not interpreted only as a sign that the economy was weakening. It was also seen as proof that traditional labor militancy was now obsolete. The new strategy of moderate demands and settlement through arbitration appeared to have been vindicated, and the *Industrial Review* counseled: "The rank and file of the union must learn in the future to be guided, more than they have in the past, by some of their trusted leaders."[227] A new era in labor relations was dawning.

For old-style unions, like the Society of Operative Stonemasons, the strike was the high-water mark of power. Their crude, rough-and-tumble strategy had been sometimes effective during the early years of the mid-Victorian boom, but the subtle and intractable economic problems of the last quarter of the nineteenth century were better solved by conciliatory techniques. In the course of the strike, the membership of the masons' union reached an all time peak of 27,110, but by 1880 the roster had dwindled to 14,299 and the union was burdened with £2358 in debts.[228] Many of the men who returned to work for Bull after the strike were nonmembers.

Perhaps the most galling symbol of the defeat of 1878 was that approximately 140 foreign masons, most of them Germans, were allowed to continue to work at the law courts, and 70, with their German foreman, remained as late as 1879. This fulfilled the pledge made by the master builders to look after the interests of those who had enabled them to defeat the O.S.M., but it was necessary to arrange for the foreigners to work in a separate shop, divided from that of their British coworkers by the boiler room.[229]

Chapter 7

Under Construction

"That Simile of the Beehive."
—*Times*, August 25, 1874

AFTER the design for the law courts was established, a decade of work still lay ahead. There was a huge construction project to organize, and, as the building took shape, a number of substantial changes were introduced into the plans. Toward the end of the decade, fittings and decorations had to be designed and mechanical services installed. Even the fate of Sir Christopher Wren's crumbling Temple Bar remained to be decided.

Construction

BY THE 1870s erecting a great building was no longer an extraordinary undertaking. Decades of railway development had established reliable construction techniques and efficient equipment, making the process swift and the results predictable. Thus the building of the law courts was a far less glamorous activity than building the Houses of Parliament had been a generation earlier, at the dawn of the Railway Age. But the construction history of the courts remains a story of enormous technical competence and great organizational ability, accomplished despite the many difficulties that beset the major contractor, Bull and Sons. Indeed, the *Builder* reported that there had never been a more scientific *chantier* than that set up for the law courts, even in Paris during the height of the construction boom of the Second Empire.[1]

Of course, with Dove Brothers, the well-established winners of the foundation contract, efficiency and competence were fully expected. The work was not unusual and the contractor was properly prepared, and so construction of the new building began without incident in the spring of 1871.[2] The houses which had occupied the site had been razed much earlier—the obvious readiness of the site had long provided an embarrassing contrast with the unreadiness of the building plans—and the Doves were able to begin work immediately after signing their contract.

First, approximately 170,000 cubic yards of material had to be excavated. This naturally was a more taxing undertaking in the heart of London than it might have been in the country, owing to the difficulty of disposing of the unwanted earth. At times other contractors paid a high premium for such construction fill, but that type of demand was slack at the moment. As a result, the Doves had to pay "pretty smartly" just to have the waste taken away. Ultimately, much of the debris from the law courts site was used in railway work. No power equipment seems to have been employed in the excavation, the bulk of which was accomplished by three hundred workmen using shovels and hand barrows (Fig. 129). Wooden walkways were laid to ease maneuvering of the barrows, and the excavated material was transferred to horsecarts and then conveyed down to the river, where it was loaded onto barges and taken away.

A great variety of materials were discovered in the course of this work. The ordinary earth had to be disposed of, but large deposits of sand and gravel and great quantities of brick were carefully sorted and set aside. These were later used in making concrete.

The kind of concrete foundation mat which Dove laid for the law courts had become a fairly common feature. Robert Smirke had pioneered the system at the British Museum and the Millbank Penitentiary, and Charles Barry had used it at the Houses of Parliament more than thirty years earlier.[3] But for the law courts a power mixer was introduced in preparing the concrete, consisting of a portable steam engine attached to "a hollow cast iron cylinder, in the interior of which revolves a shaft containing six strong arms." The concrete mixed in this apparatus was composed of one part Barrow lime and six parts gravel and broken brick. The dry ingredients were poured into the hopper of the mixer, where they passed under a jet of water and then dropped through the rotating blades. The ready concrete exited from the bottom of the mixing cylinder and was shoveled into wheel barrows. These were then run out along the catwalks to the parts of the foundation then being filled, and the concrete was dumped into place from a height of fifteen feet. This rather primitive method of laying concrete—the same employed at the Houses of Parliament—had been criticized in the intervening period.[4] Critics objected to the system again at the law courts, arguing that dropping the concrete from a height

129 Foundation excavations, looking toward St. Clement Danes. 1871. (Graphic, 26 August 1871.)

allowed the components of different densities to separate.[5] But neither the Houses of Parliament nor the law courts seemed to suffer any foundation failures.

The foundation mat at the law courts generally ranged from five to ten feet in thickness, depending on the weight of the superstructure, but under the southeast tower the foundations were extended to a depth of seventeen feet. In most places they were footed on clay. In order to allow for different rates of settling, the very heavy central hall was built on a section of the mat that was not connected to the foundations for the rest of the building (see Fig. 94).

Despite Street's complaint that insufficient men were employed, and even though the contract was completed behind schedule, Dove Brothers were unquestionably competent. Street demonstrated his belief in their ability when he opposed charging them with deadline penalties. Their talent for running a work place that was at once well-managed and happy was symbolized by the great Thanksgiving dinner with which they rewarded their workmen in February 1872. A paid holiday was declared, and the men feasted on boiled and roasted joints of meat, vegetables, beer, and plum pudding.[6] It is difficult not to contrast this celebratory meal with the dining provisions that Bull and Sons had to make on the site for their foreign masons during their far less happy period of work at the law courts.

However, despite their shortcomings, the Bulls did manage to put on a fairly complete demonstration of up-to-date building methods when they took over the site in 1874. Their efforts were sympathetically noted by the press, who were undoubtedly glad to see some substantial progress being made on the building after so many years of delay. After signing the contract on February 7, the builders were on the property on Wednesday, February 18, making plans for erecting the necessary workshops and storage facilities.[7] The first brick having been laid on May 1, preparatory work was in full swing by June at the Bulls' yard in Southampton, and the first Portland stone was delivered to the site on July 16.[8] By late August the activity behind the hoardings of the Carey Street site could be described by the *Times* as "a scene which may well recall that simile of the beehive to which Virgil likened the labours of the builders of Carthage."[9]

The site was carefully organized to speed the progress of the work. Toward its eastern side, within the area of the intended courtyard, Dove Brothers had erected a building for the architect's office and the modeling loft. On the western side, where there was to be a substantial tract of unused land, the workshops were built and large yards for storage were laid out. Much of this preliminary construction was of brick, for it was realized that these were not really temporary structures, and, before the end, they would shelter the workers through eight winters.

This layout facilitated a steady flow of work across the site. The large or full-scale drawings were produced in the architect's office as the work advanced, and, supplemented when necessary with clay models from the adjacent modeling shed, they were sent over to the template "lodge," located over the engine house on the western side of the yard. There, under the direction of Frederick Clarke, the masons' foreman, and C. A. Monday, the Bulls' architectural adviser, full-scale drawings of each block were prepared and numbered to show their proper placement. The drawings were then transferred to a planed and whitened wall of boards rather than to the more usual lofting floor, and from them zinc templates were cut to be used in the workshops downstairs.[10]

While this work was being done, the stone was arriving at the courts. As in the case of the Houses of Parliament, the stone blocks, each weighing six to ten tons, were probably brought to London by canal barges which could be unloaded at the Embankment quite close to the new building. The material was stacked in a storage depot at the western side of the site with the aid of a forty-ton capacity "traveler," a gantry crane that ran on elevated tracks. At first one such derrick was used, but two more, each with its own steam engine, were later put into service.[11] As stipulated by the contract, the stone arrived on the site unworked, and, as needed, blocks were moved by the travelers from the depot into the workshops, where they could be cut under the supervision of the assistants of the architect.

Lit by gas, the masons' shops were arranged on either side of the engine house, with a subforeman in charge of each workroom. Most of the heavy, repetitive work was accomplished with the assistance of power tools, all of which were driven by two of Annan's patent boilers, thirty feet long and eight feet in diameter, attached to two sixty-horsepower horizontal engines built by Wheatley, Kirk, and Price of Manchester. At first, the masons employed twelve stonecutting saws and three revolving rubbing tables, on which blocks were placed while their surfaces were being smoothed. By 1875, urged by Street to increase their machinery, the Bulls had installed a total of forty saw frames and twelve rubbing tables. Blocks were moved from machine to machine on tramways laid throughout the shops, and they were hoisted into working position by small hand cranes located at each work place. None of this was innovative, although the scale of the undertaking was certainly impressive. However, the use of Hunter's patent molding cutting machines, introduced at the law courts by 1875, was a new departure in masonry technique. As described to a visiting party of the Society of Engineers in 1878, these devices saved a great deal of manual labor: "The most intricate mouldings are cut upon the straight by bringing the arrise of the block of stone against a revolving shaft, upon which are fixed movable arms, bearing specially designed nails; these press head-foremost upon the stone, and cause the desired indentations, which have, however, afterwards to be touched up by hand."[12] Only curved moldings had to be executed entirely by hand.

Street reacted ambiguously to this mechanization. Given the attention he lavished on molded detail, he hinted to a visiting group from the Architectural Association that he really preferred hand-produced to machine-cut masonry.[13] But although Street ordered that the visible surfaces of all blocks be given a final hand rubbing, his medievalism had long ago outgrown the impulse to demand a complete revival of ancient crafts and craftsmanship. He had only briefly espoused the socially motivated medievalism, with its emphasis on this revival, that was endorsed by Pugin and Ruskin and which was later taken up by the art worker socialists who followed William Morris. Street was sufficiently pragmatic to accept the role played by machinery in speeding and cheapening the construction of the law courts, so long as it did not seriously interfere with his artistic objectives.[14]

Once worked, the stone was shifted out to the building where the "fitters" or "fixers" took it in hand. With the aid of several steam-driven winches, the blocks were hoisted, and then moved into position by the more than sixty hand-operated travelers which rolled along tramways laid at various heights throughout the rising structure. Where needed, portable engines were set up to power the mortar mills

and blacksmith forges which produced the materials to set and clamp the masonry in place. In order to provide a framework to support all of this mechanized activity, the scaffolding was entirely "framed," being constructed of sawed timbers secured by iron fasteners, rather than the cheaper "pole" scaffolding which was usually lashed together and which the Bulls had unsuccessfully sought to substitute in the contract. Framed scaffolding was not a new system—it had been employed at the Houses of Parliament—but it was still an unusual technique, and the complex work of designing the wood framing had to be undertaken by the contractor's chief foreman, Thomas Epps.[15] Unlike the Houses of Parliament, where a complex movable scaffolding was devised for the Victoria Tower and where the clock tower was built using an ingenious system of internal scaffolding, the law courts required no special provisions for its more modest towers. As shown in a contemporary engraving, the southeast tower was erected within the same type of braced wooden scaffolding that was used for the rest of the building (Fig. 130).

With the aid of machinery, work continued at a reasonable rate for much of the year. Severe winter weather, however, was an intractable foe, and during two freezing periods work was stopped for a considerable time. In 1874–75, no outside work was possible between December 15 and January 23, and in 1878–79, just as work was regaining momentum after the strike, a harsh winter halted construction from December 10 until March 28. When frost set in before mortar had cured sufficiently, it was sometimes necessary to dismantle enormous sections of wall and reassemble them.[16] Of course, activity was still possible in the workshops during freezing weather, and during the 1878–79 winter the masons were able to prepare all of the stone required to finish out the great hall the following summer.[17] To a certain extent, too, the occasional stoppage of outside work was an advantage, for the masons were otherwise hard pressed to keep ahead of the fitters, even though the stonecutting machinery usually ran until nine in the evening.

As noted, Street was initially dissatisfied with the number of workers that the Bulls put on the job. Various reports indicate that fewer than 400 men were at work during the first summer of construction in 1874, but a year later approximately 1000 were laboring on the site, of whom 300 were masons, 300 were fitters, and the remainder laborers. At the time of the strike in 1877, 550 masons alone were employed, and in 1878 it was reported that there were 1500 men at work, of whom 400 or 500 were masons. The number of masons fell because the amount of stonework declined as the building neared completion.[18]

Indeed, except for the first year and the period of the strike, it seems that more than one thousand men were usually on the site during fair weather. By contrast, that number was never exceeded at the Houses of Parliament, where construction was much slower.[19] Foundation work at Westminster had begun in 1838, and interior fittings were still being completed when E. M. Barry was dismissed from his supervisory position in 1870. At the law courts, the foundations were begun in the spring of 1871, but although two years elapsed between their completion and the commencement of the main contract in the spring of 1874, the building was ready for full occupancy by the end of 1882. This was, of course, behind schedule, but the Bulls' performance was still acceptable. As to their workmanship—at least with masonry—Street admitted that he had "no complaint to make on this score."[20]

130 *The clock tower in scaffolding and Temple Bar. November 1877. (Illustrated London News, 22 December 1877.)*

Perhaps, in fact, the builders pressed their men to work rather too rapidly. Although comparative statistics are unavailable, it seems that there were an unusual number of accidents at the law courts, at least two of which are known to have been fatal. On April 26, 1875, a block weighing only three hundred pounds was being lifted into place at the southwest corner of the building by a jib crane with a three-ton capacity. It slipped from its chains and fell fifteen feet, killing William Roberts of Somers Town.[21] A little more than a year later, Thomas Walker of Wiltshire died in agony at King's College Hospital after falling more than fifty feet from the scaffolding and landing on his head.[22] In the period between these two accidents, four other men were hospitalized by injuries sustained at the law courts.[23] Finally, Frederick Clarke, the masons' foreman, barely escaped death on December 27, 1877, after the snapping of a chain with which a two-ton block was being hoisted in the south stairway of the eastern wing. Clarke had been standing beneath the stone, but he was able to step into a corner as it hurtled past.[24]

More care seems to have been taken with the selection than with the safe handling of materials. Although the invitations to tender had required estimates for several types of building stone, in the end, the major part of the fabric of the law courts was built of Portland stone, the durable and sparkling white limestone from the Isle of Portland in Dorset which had been the favored building material in London since about 1600.[25] Recently the Foreign Office and Holborn Viaduct had utilized Portland stone, and architects had generally rejected substitutes. In particular, the huge experiment with northern magnesian limestone at the Houses of Parliament was now judged to have been a failure.[26] For exterior work at the law courts, Portland stone from the hard, central stratum called the "Whitbed" was specified. This was difficult to saw and therefore expensive to work, but it was also resistant to the acidic atmosphere of the metropolis. Portland stone in general possesses a remarkable self-cleansing ability, and the rain-washed surfaces of the law courts were still surprisingly white when the entire building was scrubbed clean a few years ago. For interior work Street specified the finer but less durable "base" or "best" bed of Portland stone.

A small number of other building stones were employed in limited quantities to achieve the subdued effects of polychromy that Street sought. From 1860 onward, constructional color had played an ever decreasing role in his work, but he did specify red granite shafting for some of the upper windows of the Strand façade and for the arcade screening the eastern wing. Almost surely for economic reasons, tinted concrete was later substituted for granite (see Fig. 110). Within the great central hall, a rather more colorful and varied combination of materials was used, noticeably warming the atmosphere and alluding unmistakably to English medieval precedent (see Figs. 113, 115). The dark gray Purbeck "marble" shafts of the blind arcade over the benches and the window enframements particularly recall the use of that material at Westminster Abbey, Lincoln, and Salisbury. For some shafting of the main piers Street employed polished Aberdeen red granite in a more thoroughly Victorian spirit, and for the walling within the blind arcade of the lower wall he alternated yellow and cream bands of polished Jura marble and Corsham stone. Some of the small detached columns which flanked the doorways leading to the witness stairs were of light gray Derbyshire fossil granite. For the north and south balconies of the hall, Street specified handrails and supporting columns of creamy

Hopton Wood limestone, polished to strengthen its subtle color contrast with the surrounding Portland stone (see Fig. 114). The vaulting webs were of light Corsham stone, again contrasting only slightly with the Portland.

Most of the eastern block of the building was clad in brick, and the use of that material increased at the northeast corner during the process of construction (see Fig. 119). The structural bricks were of ordinary manufacture, equivalent to the best Cowley or Sittingbourne stock bricks. But for the facings, Street ordered the molding of special red bricks of unusual dimensions, longer and wider, but also flatter than was standard. These purpose-made bricks were 10 by 5 inches (compared to the usual 8 by 3½), and they were only 2⅛ inches thick (in contrast to the ordinary thickness of 2¾). This permitted five courses per foot instead of four, giving a measure of structural reality to the longer, continuous horizontals which Street had espoused in theory. He had written much earlier that "all construction is necessarily horizontal."[27]

All masonry, stone and brick, was laid in mortar prepared to the directions of the Patent Selenitic Mortar Company. An exact recipe was provided for its mixing in a steam-powered mill:

> The mortar is to be mixed as follows viz. throw into the pan of the edge runner two or three pails of water to the first of which 4 lbs of plaster of Paris has been added and gradually introduce a bushel of fresh grey stone ground lime and continue to grind the whole for three or four minutes until the same becomes a creamy paste and then put [in] five or six bushels of clean sharp sand and then grind the whole for nine or ten minutes longer. The mortar is to be used fresh.

Interior plastering was done with the Portland cement of the Patent Selenitic Cement Company. Its manager wrote to the *Building News* in 1879, elated that a writer had mistaken its product for Keene's cement, a more costly material.[28]

Street demonstrated his respect for modern methods by approving the use of a number of structural innovations and the extensive use of iron. He did not believe, however, that iron construction possessed any artistic value, and in 1852 he had dismissed its applications as "simply engineering." He also told the students at the Royal Academy in 1881 that he believed the potential uses of iron as a hidden strengthener were "rather temptations than anything else."[29] But a building the size of the law courts could scarcely have been built without ferrous materials, and their use in Britain by that time was taken for granted. To be sure, to satisfy Street's scruples, pains were taken to leave a large proportion of the ironwork honestly visible. There was also much less iron employed than at the Houses of Parliament, for example, where the fear of another destructive fire had dictated its widespread introduction. At the law courts the roofs were of ordinary timber construction, covered with green Bangor slates, whereas at Parliament the roofing had been of cast-iron plates, supported by a system of wrought-iron frames. Of course, in the years that passed between the design of the two buildings, much had been learned about the vulnerability of iron to fire damage, and it was no longer seen as a prerequisite of fireproof construction.

Most of the structural iron was used in floor girders, which were borne for the most part by masonry walls. Iron columns were rare. The girders were largely of an

"I" section, constructed by bolting or riveting together a specified number of flanged iron members. Some elements were triply reinforced, and spans of more than thirty feet and iron weights of more than one hundred pounds per linear foot were not uncommon. The mightiest girder of all was a box section, 24 by 12 inches, with a weight of 364 pounds per foot. It spanned the record and writ office in the eastern block. All ironwork was tested hydraulically by an inspector who was appointed by Street. In the main building all exposed beams were required to have an iron or zinc trefoil molding attached to the soffit, but in the east wing much unadorned ironwork was permitted. In the corridors of that part of the building, and especially beneath the central skylight, there was more ferrous structural material visible than Street allowed in any other building (Fig. 131).

The photograph of the hallway in the east wing also shows another important structural system that was used in conjunction with the iron girders. The shallow vaults of the ceiling, whose overall effect is a gentle scalloped or wave pattern, are Dennett's fireproof arches. These were used throughout the building, and, unconcealed, they comprised the ceilings of most of the corridors and ordinary offices. The system consisted of concrete arches, as thin as 2½ inches at the crown, with spans of up to twelve feet. They rested on the flanges of the iron girders and were built over wooden centering which was removed when the concrete cured. Almost any variety of arch, vault, or dome could be formed. A. and R. Dennett and Company of 3 Craven Street, Strand, and Station Street, Nottingham, were the patentees, and their invention had been in use since 1856. G. G. Scott had employed the system at the Foreign Office, and his testimonial was quoted in the company's advertisements: "I can bear witness to its strength and extreme convenience of application."[30] At the law courts, Street specified the use of the Dennett patent, and the arches were built by the Dennetts' own workmen.

Another even more recent, but nonstructural, innovation adopted at the law courts was Bullivant's Patent Air-Proof and Noiseless Window Sash. Patented in 1867 by T. Bullivant, this device was really no more than an intelligent modernization of the common guillotine window.[31] Bearing surfaces were made of metal, and the ordinary wooden beading which guided the sash up and down was replaced by metal bars which engaged grooves on each side of the sash. These bars were spring loaded to prevent rattling and drafts. The sash cord pulleys were of an easily replaced design, and, for smaller windows, sash cords could be eliminated entirely and replaced by thumbscrew brakes. Provision was made to incorporate a roller shade in the head of the window, and the sash could be removed for cleaning or repair by removing a single screw. The design had been adopted recently by the architect Henry Currey at St. Thomas's Hospital, which faced the Houses of Parliament from across the Thames. Street's eagerness to utilize a new window system at the law courts can probably be attributed to the fact that the foes of Gothic architecture were especially critical of Gothic windows. A modern medievalist had to defend his work repeatedly against charges of gloom and drafts, and the use of any sort of sash window instead of the more historically correct casement type can be seen as a response to this complaint. The adoption of the most up-to-date type of sash window, of the kind just chosen for an enormous classical hospital, might have been an attempt to refute all such criticism conclusively.

131 *Skylight over central corridor in east wing.*

Modification of the Design

ALTHOUGH the specifications attached to the contract had been complete, as the construction progressed several modifications were required by the Office of Works, requested by Street in an effort to improve his design, or made by the architect on his own authority. The three most important alterations were the provision of additional courtrooms, the placement of a flèche on the ridge of the roof of the great hall, and the introduction of substantially more brickwork at the northeast corner of the building than was shown in the contract drawings.

The need for additional courtrooms became apparent soon after construction began. In 1873, the Judicature Act was passed, fusing equity and common law and creating a single Court of Appeal, for which Street had made no provision in the approved design. In July 1874 Lord Chancellor Cairns sent a memo to the Office of Works, explaining the needs of the new appeals procedure, and Douglas Galton quickly took the matter in hand, intending to see that the plans were altered to include three more courts before construction was far advanced.[32] Bull and Sons had only been on the site for a few months.

Galton had assumed that the additional courtrooms would be accommodated in an annex to the building, placed either north of Carey Street or on the northwest corner of the acquired site, to be extended slightly by purchasing a few of the wretched houses adjacent to King's College Hospital. Street preferred the second location, which offered a better chance to create a coherent relationship between the annex and the main building, and Henry Hunt reckoned that it was also the cheaper alternative.[33]

Street's calculation for the cost of the appeals court building was £125,000, and in August he prepared two floor plans.[34] These showed a rather complicated compression of the major features of the main building, preserving a central hall—for the bar, not the public—and separate accesses and corridors for the different types of visitors to the courts. One large court and two smaller, auxiliary courtrooms were provided, in addition to all of the necessary offices and consultation rooms. The elevations would have been highly irregular, but this would have complemented the asymmetrical placement of the building. A bridge was intended to link the appeals court to the main block.

However, no action was ever taken on the basis of this design, for in November, Sir Henry Lennox issued a curt memorandum: "This land will not be required to be purchased."[35] Even the Conservative administration was unwilling to inflate the price of the law courts when construction of the superstructure was just beginning. In addition, the Tories had serious objections to the appeals system created by the Judicature Act, and it is possible that they did not wish to grant it their *de facto* approval by including provision for it in the building program.

Of course, this left for the future the creation of the needed additional courts. On April 21, 1877, Cairns summoned Mitford, Hunt, Street, and a Treasury secretary to a meeting at the House of Lords, where he outlined a more modest plan for the required accommodation.[36] He asked that the two large arbitration rooms at the front of the building on the ground floor, directly beneath courts ten and eleven, be converted into courtrooms (see Fig. 103). These would suffice for the time being, Cairns believed, but he also asked that the bar corridor be extended westward through the large courtroom at the northwest corner of the hall, one of the two outsize courtrooms provided in the building. (This court is labeled "B. Lord Justices" in Fig. 93.) The extension would permit connection to an annex if one like that considered in 1874 were eventually built. Approval was quickly given to this scheme.

The conversion of the arbitration rooms was an easy matter, requiring only a small alteration to connect them to the judges' corridor. Street prepared the necessary instructions for this work in July 1877.

At the same time he designed rather more drastic alterations to allow communication with a future western annex.[37] A corridor was cut through the largest of the western courtrooms, as Cairns had suggested, sharply reducing its size (court seventeen in Fig. 104). Street had estimated that this work would cost £2500, but the expenditure rose to £3282 because most of the materials for the original design had already been prepared.[38] Anticipating the needs of the future annex, Street strongly urged the immediate purchase of the "dilapidated" houses next to King's College Hospital. The Office of Works endorsed this recommendation, but it was rejected by the Treasury.[39]

Soon it was discovered that the two additional courtrooms created by this improvisation would be insufficient for the anticipated volume of legal business, and in 1881 a further makeshift arrangement was contrived. The northern bar room was converted into the twenty-first court in the building, and this large and airy chamber, with windows looking directly onto Carey Street, was specifically designated as the new Court of Appeal.[40] The mass of masonry rising behind the Bench was the chimney breast of what had been intended for use as a common room for lawyers (Fig. 132).

Only in 1908 was the long-postponed western extension approved. The plans incorporated four courtrooms, with the Court of Appeal remaining in the old building (visible in pages 2–3). The designer was Sir Henry Tanner (1849–1938),

132 North bar room refitted as courtroom one, the Court of Appeal. (Pictorial London. London: Cassell and Company, 1906.)

who was then chief architect of the Office of Works, where he had begun his career in 1871 as an assistant. He copied mechanically much of his detail from the original design, his prominent stair tower being an elongated version of the public stairs of Street's main façade.

Street accomplished more with the second major revision of the building, the introduction of a wood and lead flèche in place of the stone turret that had been struck from his plans for the central hall in order to reduce costs. Even the *Builder* had protested against its removal in 1874.[41] Street began his own campaign for the flèche in 1876, when he described his plans for one to a visiting group from the Architectural Association.[42] Disraeli was now prime minister, and Street and several other publicly employed architects chose this opportunity to appeal for a reversal of the tightfisted policy of the Liberals toward architecture. In that same year, Waterhouse also began to lobby for the reintroduction of the monumental entrance towers that had been excised from the Natural History Museum by Ayrton, and he succeeded in winning Treasury approval in January 1878.[43] G. G. Scott, too, had similarly but less successfully approached the Conservatives in 1874, immediately after they took office, seeking to restore the towers that Ayrton had ordered cut from the Whitehall façade of his government offices.[44]

Having announced his intentions in 1876, Street waited until January 9, 1879, before proposing the flèche to the Office of Works.[45] He seems to have been waiting to see whether savings could be made elsewhere in the building that might be redirected. At last this windfall was discovered in the general contract for the east wing, then nearing completion, and so Street could ask with some confidence to be allowed to obtain estimates for his substitute turret, "without [which] the whole design of my building will be most grievously maimed."

Authorized to proceed, Street prepared a design and submitted an estimate of £3500 on February 22.[46] Not unfairly, he argued,

> I hope the First Commissioner will feel that up to this time I have shewn the strictest moderation in asking for any additional allowances for the sake of adding Architectural features to my design. I think that in point of fact this is the first addition to the building which I have asked for on this ground, and . . . I can say with confidence that it is also the last alteration or addition of an artistic kind which I shall have to ask for.

His proposal was enthusiastically received. Mitford called the flèche "a fine feature," and Hunt, agreeing, showed accustomed eagerness to separate himself from the policies of his parsimonious former chief. He wrote: "I did all I could to prevent the Turret as originally designed from being omitted but Mr. Ayrton to save expense decided otherwise."[47]

In December, Street submitted a final design for the flèche, which differed in some ways from the original design.[48] Subsequently, he also moved the spire toward the Strand façade. While the original stone turret had been located at the center of the roof, annotations on a contract drawing show that the flèche was first intended to be placed further south, over the second buttress of the hall. Finally, in June 1880 it was advanced further still, to the first buttress, where it was constructed (see Fig. 99). This substantially increased its visibility from the Strand and its contribution to the composition of the main façade (Fig. 133).

133 The flèche and the south gable of the hall. 1879–80. (NMR)

Street was soon compelled to report the unhappy news that rather than £3500, the flèche was likely to cost between £5200 and £5300. He had, however, been able to substitute brick for ashlar in the parapets of the central hall, where he had determined that it would be invisible from the ground, and this had produced an offsetting saving of £2402 (substitution visible in Fig. 99). He proposed that the contract for the flèche be awarded to Messrs. Beard, Dent, and Hellyer, rather than to the Bulls, whose tender for leadwork he considered to be high. This proposal was adopted, resulting in further economy.

Street seems to have ordered the third major alteration of the design without seeking official approval. This was possible because his revisions, which were confined to the brickwork at the northeast corner of the building, demanded no increased expenditure and did not seriously alter the overall massing or the plan. But in artistic terms, the changes were enormously significant, creating the most visually exciting part of the design.

Street's original intentions at the northeast corner of the law courts were shown in the small-scale elevation he prepared in 1870, and these were little altered in the contract drawings for the final design (see Figs. 96, 116, 117). At the corner, he had to engineer the gradual transition from brick, the predominant material of the eastern office wing, to ashlar, the material of the main block. He proposed to do this at first by making the Carey Street tower, the smaller brother of the Strand clock tower, half brick and half Portland stone, with the latter material employed above the midpoint. Thereafter, as the building marched westward down Carey Street toward the ashlar main block, brick was to appear again only briefly in the pavilion which stood beside the gateway into the quadrangle. The tower was to be marked by a great winged figure of Justice, standing under the relieving arch that embraced the two largest windows of its north face. The treatment was intelligible but rather splotchy, as the amount of brick decreased and the building was progres-

134 Altered northeast tower. New elevations, November 1875. (PRO Works 30/2039.)

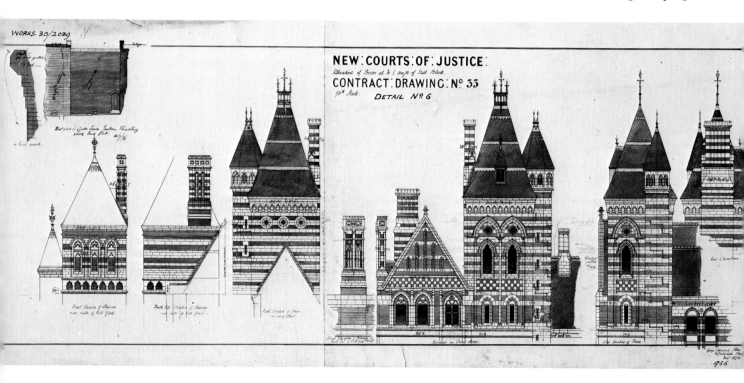

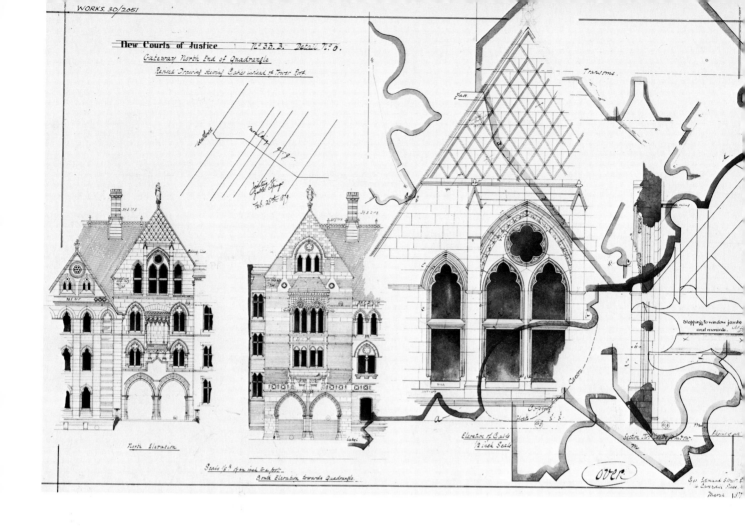

New Courts of Justice — No 33.3. Detail No 3.
Gateway North End of Quadrangle
Revised Drawing showing Gable instead of Tower Roof

North Elevation

South Elevation towards Quadrangle

Elevation of Gable
12 inch Scale

135 Altered linking wing be-
tween northeast tower and
main block. Elevations and
molding profiles, March 1877.
(PRO Works 30/2051.)

sively lithified as it made the transition. The high roof and the crocketted gable placed over the gateway into the courtyard were also somewhat unsatisfactory. Their spikey angularity contrasted unpleasantly with the massive sobriety of most of the rest of the design.

These weaknesses may be attributable to the fact that the north façade had escaped Ayrton's criticism and had never been revised. But soon enough Street noticed the deficiencies on his own, and he was tinkering with some of the details of the Carey Street elevation as early as July 1874, before the Bulls had been very long on the site.[49] The following May, he moved firmly to revise the appearance of the northeast tower, and a beautiful finished drawing of the revisions was prepared in November (Fig. 134). Much more brick was introduced above the midpoint, and it became the predominant material of the whole. This established the tower as a part of the brick-faced eastern wing, rather than a mongrel feature interposed be-tween it and the ashlar main block. The transition was made decisive rather than gradual, and the tower was given a powerful unity—both alterations which comple-mented the strength and clear-cut massing of the overall design. Moreover, the great allegorical figure, an unusual component in a building by Street, was eliminated, and the single large relieving arch was replaced by two smaller arches.

Evidently satisfied by the effect of these changes, Street soon introduced further revisions of a complementary nature. By March 1877 he had done away with the fussy French roof and dormer over the northern entrance to the quadrangle. In their place he designed a handsome, diapered gable whose simpler form was a better neighbor for the new, forceful tower (Fig. 135; compare with Fig. 116). The same

136 *The Carey Street façade.*

137 *The northeast tower.*

spirit motivated a final revision which Street made in the northern façade a month later, when he removed the swept-back roofs with which he had originally crowned the corner pavilions of the main block. He substituted two triple gables of bolder outline and more easily read detail (Fig. 136; compare with Fig. 117).[50]

The result of these changes was a triumph (Fig. 137). Street was able to employ color to unify the strong individual elements of this part of the design far more successfully than elsewhere. Indeed, the differences between the northeast tower and the rest of the building are so striking that Sir Nikolaus Pevsner was prompted

to suggest that it was the work of Philip Webb, whom he mistakenly identified as Street's assistant at this time.[51] It is true that in the insistent use of orange red brick—increased in the revised design—and in its brilliant contrast with the white of the Portland stone, the effect is not unlike that achieved by the younger, Queen Anne architects with their cheerful juxtaposition of brickwork and white sashes. The picturesque concatenation of gables, again an effect increased in revision, also linked the work with that of the younger men. Indeed, while Webb was not the designer, his work does provide specific analogies for the kind of vigorous brick and Portland architecture which Street adopted. Webb had built a small office building nearby at 19 Lincoln's Inn Fields in 1868–70, which may even have exerted a direct influence on the design of the Bell Yard façade (Figs. 138, 139). Certainly there is a strong coloristic and compositional resemblance between the office building and Street's gabled pavilions, with their similar stacks of two-window bays, framed by strap buttresses. The relationship between the master and his former assistants, Webb and Shaw, was a lively one.

Fittings, Furniture, and Decoration

AS THE LAW COURTS gradually rose from behind the hoardings along the Strand, Street's concerns shifted to equipping and decorating the great building. In this area, although restricted by the austerity which Ayrton had imposed on the project, he exercised a relatively free hand. The ensemble of sculpture, furniture, metalwork, stained glass, and pavings which he created for the law courts is worthy of serious study, even if the final effect is much less sumptuous than that achieved at the Houses of Parliament.

The decorative stonecarving for the law courts was a subject in which Street showed particular interest. To be sure, his design, which relied for effect on the composition of large masses, did not require extensive sculptural enrichment, and so the architect had been willing to reduce the amount set aside for carving from £35,000 to £20,000 in order to win approval for his plans. But Street had seen to it that what decorative stonecarving remained was eliminated from the Bulls' contract and that a clause was introduced to permit him to select and supervise the carvers himself. When the time came for the ornamental work to begin, in the spring of 1876, Street was free to give the work to whomever he pleased.

Not surprisingly, his choice was Thomas Earp, the gifted sculptor who had carved the pulpits, reredoses, or other decorative work for more than a score of Street's churches. The architect wrote directly to Earp, whose works were at 49 Kennington Road, Lambeth, asking him under what terms he would undertake the decoration of the law courts. In late March, the sculptor replied, giving an interesting schedule of the wage rates which then prevailed, but declining to make a lump sum estimate.[52] Ordinary carvers, Earp reported, were paid at least 1s. per hour (2d. more than the strike demand made by the masons a year later), while the foliage and animal carvers might receive 1s. 6d. Figure carvers and sculptors, the aristocrats of the trade, could earn between 1s. 6d. and 2s., or even more. Earp proposed to assemble a crew with wages ranging from 1s. 1d. to 1s. 6d., with an average rate of 1s. 3d. It would be necessary, he advised Street, to retain the full-time services of a smith or at least a boy to sharpen tools.

Street forwarded this information to the Office of Works, asking for permission

138 Two gables of the eastern façade.

139 Philip Webb. 19 Lincoln's Inn Fields, London. 1868–70.

to employ Earp without a contract specifying a fixed sum. An inflexible agreement for the carving, he argued, would make it "impossible to get it done in the best way."[53] Henry Hunt, surprisingly, offered no objection, and so Lord Henry Lennox, the Tory first commissioner, approved this unusually open-ended arrangement.[54] It was still understood that only £20,000 was to be spent, with an extra £533 allowed for scaffolding, but Street had succeeded in giving the work to the subcontractor of his choice on very favorable terms.

Thomas Earp employed approximately twenty carvers at the law courts, who worked under his foreman, H. T. Margetson of Chelsea. Earp himself may have lent a hand in the work, as did Margetson. Everything was done under Street's supervision, and in Earp's statement of terms he had acknowledged that all "designing, modelling, and ordering" was to be done by the architect. To this end, unusually detailed drawings and even clay models were prepared to guide the sculptors.

Street also designed the iconographic program for the sculpture. At the law courts this was a rather simple business, for interest in architectural symbolism had declined since the heyday of Pugin and the Ecclesiologists in the 1840s. The removal of the personification of justice from the northeast tower was in keeping with this shift away from didacticism. In its absence, only about forty armorial shields, four freestanding gable figures, and a few smaller personifications remained to suggest the purpose of the building. The statues were the most significant elements of this program. Moses, carrying the tablets of the law, was portrayed over the central door of the north façade (see Fig. 136). His isolation from the other three figures who adorned the southern entrance was probably intentional, for he represented the old fixity of the Hebraic code. The southern figures, representing more liberal forces, were dominated by the figure of Christ, who released Christians from Jewish law, standing on the gable of the great hall (see Fig. 133). Mounted on smaller, flanking gables were two other, temporal rulers. To the east stood King Alfred the Great, the author of the Book of Laws which provided the starting point for the adaptable system of English common law. To the west was mounted a representation of Solomon, the sagacious interpreter of seemingly harsh statutes. The iconography thus emphasized the essentially flexible, Christian, and English qualities of British jurisprudence—appropriate themes for the great era of Victorian law reform.

Most of the many shields, placed between the windows of the topmost story, were carved with the coats of arms of eminent living jurists. Street, probably with the assistance of his brother, compiled a list of those worthy of this distinction, and he wrote to each to ask permission for the use of their arms.[55] In the central gable of the north façade the royal arms were displayed, together with those of the lord chancellor and lord chief justice in 1880 (Lords Selborne and Coleridge) and of the Inns of Court.[56] The northern elevation also bore representations of the legal virtues, mounted on shields. Concordia, Prudentia, Rhetorica, and Lex were accommodated between the upper windows of the central block, while Fides, Spes, and Iustitia stood watch over the passage into the internal courtyard. There was little incidental sculpture, but it was possible to include likenesses of Street and Henry Bull on the corbels supporting the oriel on the north side of the courtyard. Modeled by Margetson, these figures stirred some controversy. Street reportedly failed to recognize his own portrait, while a hostile question was asked in Parliament about the appropriateness of honoring an "obscure contractor."[57] On either side of the northern judges' entrances, the molding stops were decorated with the figures of cats and dogs, a lighthearted allusion to litigious squabbling.

The remainder of the carving was predominantly floral, in the stiff leaf style of the early thirteenth century. It does not at first seem plentiful or particularly rich in effect, but it is skillfully concentrated to wring the most out of a small budget. The main entrance was elaborately carved, and the Strand façade was bound together by

140 *Public stair tower and the flèche.*

the great frieze of emblematic British plants running between the ground and first floors (see Figs. 110, 111). The public stair towers were also loci of intensive carving, in part utilizing the same motifs (Fig. 140). Some of the exterior spandrels and, most notably, the tympana over some of the doors leading from the central hall were richly diapered, giving an almost festive and quintessentially English feeling of decorative enthusiasm (see Fig. 115).

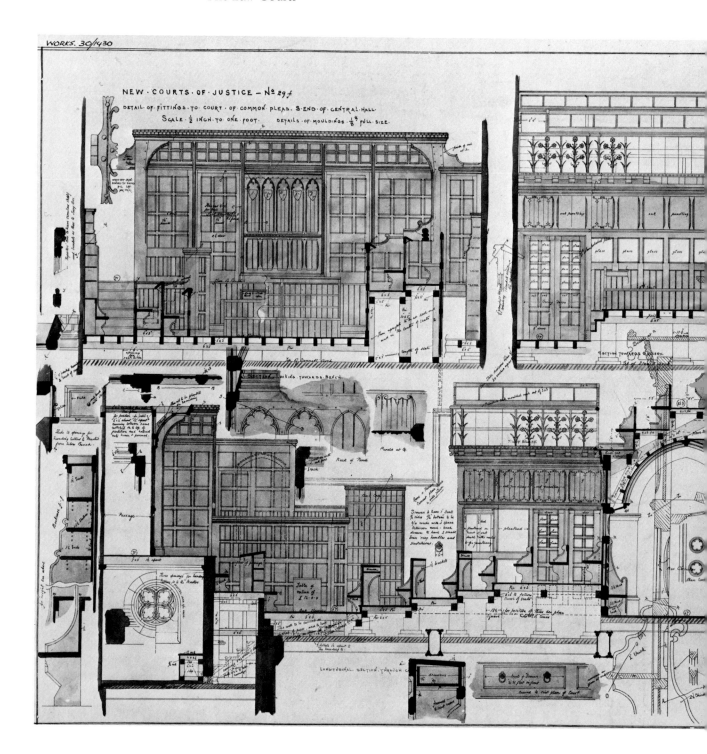

141 Sample design for the fittings in courtroom ten. Contract drawing, c. 1871–72. Execution differs. (PRO Works 30/1430.)

The majority of the sculpture was carved in place, utilizing the scaffolding erected by the builders. This saved some expense, but because the carving work was done without a fixed estimate, it was difficult to calculate costs in advance. Sometimes, there were pleasant surprises, as when a saving of nearly £400 was realized on the carving for the eastern wing, for which £6749 had been allocated.[58] But for the decorative carving on the main block, a substantial cost overrun devoured this surplus and drove the total expense £4527 above the ceiling. In July 1881, as the

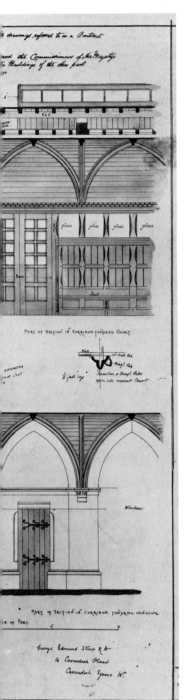

carvers rapidly neared the declared budget limit, Street was compelled to ask for permission to spend more.[59] He apologized later: "I am extremely vexed that there should be a large deficiency," and he admitted that his estimate had been no more than "a guess at the amount the work might cost."[60] The rather lenient first commissioner G. J. Shaw-Lefevre allowed the excess. No doubt the savings recorded elsewhere made this liberality easier.

With furniture and woodwork, Street had more difficulty in obtaining his wishes, although ultimately most of the building was furnished according to his designs. He was least successful in outfitting the eastern wing, the first part of the law courts to be completed, but that initial setback seems to have stirred him to fight more vigorously for his ideas in the rest of the building.

The eastern block, for which a separate contract was signed with Bull and Sons, was due to be completed in August 1877. Although this deadline was missed, the eastern offices were still the first part of the building to be occupied, and it was there that the issues of furnishing and outfitting were faced for the first time. In July 1877 Noel, the first commissioner, asked the Treasury to approve the designing of special furniture by the architect which would be worthy of "a Building of so important a character."[61] This request was evidently made at the urging of Street.

The Treasury was unsympathetic, replying, "The uses to which most of the furniture is put are of the roughest possible character and it would in their Lordships view be right that existing furniture in existing offices be used as far as it will go."[62] Street therefore delegated Augustus Tanner to study the available stocks of furniture. When at last the east wing was opened after the Easter holiday in 1879, new fittings were provided only for the chancery pay department, and these were of stock manufactured designs.[63]

For the main building, Street was determined to arrange matters differently. Because the built-in wooden fittings and the roofing of the courtrooms had been left out of the principal contract, after the Bulls refused to accept the terms proposed by the Office of Works, in the late seventies this work was put out for separate tendering. Street took this opportunity to abandon his original plan to complete almost all the courtrooms according to two basic designs, one for use on the east side of the hall and the other on the west (Fig. 141). This layout had been intended to give a sharp sense of territoriality to the two sides of the building, in keeping with its division between common law and equity. In the same way, the witness stairs on either side of the great hall were of slightly different designs: semicircular in plan on the east and polygonal on the west.

The creation of a unified court system by the Judicature Act had made this division meaningless, and in July 1878 Street proposed instead "varied designs for the whole eighteen [courtrooms], so that no two shall be alike."[64] He promised that this would lead to no increase in cost and forwarded thirty-one detail drawings to the Office of Works.[65] His proposition was approved.

Only one example of each of the original designs was executed: court six to the east and court sixteen to the west (Fig. 142, located on Fig. 104). Room sixteen was covered by a flat ceiling supported on webs of wooden vaulting, pierced by a semicylindrical skylight. For room six, Street specified a trefoil wooden barrel vault, glazed in its central lobe.

142 *Courtroom sixteen, ceiling. (Archives Department, Westminster City Libraries. M. D. Trace photograph.)*

The remaining courts on the first floor furnished further entries in the encyclopedia of wooden roofing forms which Street compiled at the law courts, having discovered that he could thus vastly increase the variety of his design without altering the long-established masonry contract. Courts ten and eleven, located in the front of the building, were built to virtually the same sumptuous design, entirely covered by wooden vaulting (Fig. 143). This compensated for the fact that they were slightly smaller than the other rooms. The roughly corresponding courts at the north end of the building, numbers two and nineteen, were also built to very similar plans. They were both covered by flat, paneled ceilings, raised in the center in a kind of unglazed monitor. All of the remaining courtrooms, like those of the original specimen designs, were provided with skylights. Court four, the largest courtroom and designated for the use of the lord chief justice, was given a flat ceiling supported on knees (Figs. 144, 145). At the center rose an exceedingly tall and narrow monitor, with windows on four sides. Courtroom three was lit by a skylight set into a raised ceiling which was borne by coved cornices at the front and back of the room (Figs. 146–148). Further combinations of ceilings, vaults, skylights, and monitors were worked out for the other courts.

143 Courtroom eleven, looking toward gallery. (Illustrated London News, 30 December 1882.)

144 *Courtroom four, the Lord Chief Justice's Court, looking toward the bench. (NMR)*

145 *Courtroom four, the Lord Chief Justice's Court, ceiling. (Archives Department, Westminster City Libraries. M. D. Trace photograph.)*

All courtrooms were similarly arranged, with inclined seating on the main floor, facing the clerks' tables and the bench. The public gallery stretched across the rear of the room, and a balcony was let into the masonry at the side to provide an exceptional vantage for the jury. The great height of the rooms, emphasized by the skylights and lofty clerestory windows and by the placement of the jurors and spectators above the principal floor, contrasted markedly with their quite limited and crowded horizontal space. It was thus that Street insured good visibility and hearing without sacrificing light and air.

146 Courtroom three, looking
toward the bench. (Archives Department, Westminster City Libraries. M. D. Trace photograph.)

147 Courtroom three, ceiling. (Archives Department, Westminster City Libraries. M. D. Trace photograph.)

148 Courtroom three, looking toward gallery. (Archives Department, Westminster City Libraries. M. D. Trace photograph.)

Although these designs were approved in 1878, the very slow progress of Bull and Sons with the main contract delayed the start of work on the courtrooms for several years. In April 1880 Street at last submitted his final set of drawings.[66] Four months later he also submitted four lists of four firms which might be invited to tender for the four parts into which the contract was to be divided, and these were approved by the Liberal Government which had taken office in the meantime.[67] The process of calculating quantities for the varied designs was then begun, but, as Street explained in August, the work proved to be "long and troublesome."[68] Not until November 23 were invitations for the eastern side finally issued to builders, and the invitations for the western rooms, where the work of the Bulls was even less far advanced, were not sent out until March 14, 1881.[69]

In all, tenders were invited from seventeen contractors, thirteen of whom submitted bids. Because of the mixed nature of the work, an unusual variety of firms was invited, ranging from huge general contractors like George Trollope and Sons, William Cubitt, Holland and Hannen, and Dove Brothers, to furniture makers like Holland and Sons, Gillow and Company, and Collinson and Lock. There was a relatively high percentage of provincial invitees, comprising five in all, and ultimately three of the four contracts were awarded to non-Londoners. Henry Lovatt of Darlington Street, Wolverhampton, was the low bidder at £6296 for courtrooms sixteen to nineteen (the northwestern courts) and for numbers two to five (the northeastern rooms) at £7887. Jackson and Graham, the Oxford Street furniture makers, tendered a low £9247 for rooms six to ten (at the southeast), and Bull and Sons of Southampton won the contract for the southwestern courts, numbers eleven to fifteen, with a bid of £8700. Street, who had nominated most of the invited bidders, approved these awards, but with respect to Bull he did so "with some hesitation owing to the dilatory character of their proceedings."[70] The Bulls also received the commission for refitting the northern bar room as court one. The contracts for the eastern courts were signed on March 15, 1881, after sufficient further delay to cause Henry Lovatt to register a complaint, and the western contracts were signed on May 27.[71]

The fitting up of the courtrooms was accomplished with Street's usual close supervision. A total of seventy-nine drawings were appended to the four contracts, and provision was made for the architect's continuous direction.[72] Like the stone-carvers, the woodcarvers were to be men "of thorough ability approved by the Architect," and it was specified that "models [are] to be made of clay and submitted to the Architect from time to time for examination and alteration."

The woodwork of the ceilings and fittings was of oak, although deal had been used in the eastern block and in the lesser offices of the main building. Its selection and preparation were carefully detailed: "The Wainscot is to be the very best Riga clean well seasoned and carefully selected, free from sap and in all respects equal to a sample to be sent to the Architect's Office at the time the tenders are made. . . . The Wainscot to be stained with Ammonia in a close room to such a degree of darkness as the Architect may require and is not to be oiled or finished in any other way." All of the builders seem to have done much of the preparatory fabrication in their yards, where they also dried the woodwork before bringing it to the law courts for installation. For Bull and Lovatt this meant that the materials had to be transported the considerable distances from Southampton and Wolverhampton, respectively. In the interest of fire prevention, work in the courtrooms was to be done without the use of candles, although gas lighting was permitted. This may have saved the whole project from such a disaster as befell the unlucky Bulls, much of whose already completed woodwork was destroyed by a fire at their Southampton works.[73]

This fire, together with a great number of small alterations which were ordered by the court officers while the work was in progress, substantially delayed the completion of the contracts. The deadlines had been January 30, 1882, for the eastern courts and February 25 for the western rooms, but Bull and Sons, apparently the last to finish, only concluded their work on September 19, 1883. Nevertheless, the building was officially opened on December 4, 1882, and it was in nearly full use early the next year.

Quality control was also a problem, at least with the Bulls' work. Although no long-term difference in the durability of the workmanship of the three builders has been observed, Street was profoundly dissatisfied with the work that was sent up from Southampton. Of Bull and Sons he lamented: "The truth is that it is almost hopeless to get first rate work—especially joinery—from our contractors—and as all their work comes to the building unseasoned it is an advantage to have it there exposed to the weather some time so that the defects may show themselves and may be remedied."[74] Street must have been thankful that all of the courtrooms were not executed by the main contractor, as had been originally intended.

No movable furniture was provided for the main building by these contracts, but Street was encouraged by the willingness of the Government to accept his varied designs for the courtrooms to campaign for the right to design such furniture as well. He hoped to avoid an extension of the policy of re-use adopted in the eastern office block, as he explained in January 1879:

> I need hardly say that I have been much disappointed to find that the whole of the East wing is to be furnished with old furniture or with furniture over the design of which I appear to have no control. I trust that in the many important parts of the main building for which such a course as the use of old furniture from the Government stores can hardly be contemplated I may be allowed to make the necessary drawings and designs; and in order that the work may be executed in good time I should like to have the authority to do so ere long.[75]

The Office of Works deferred its decision but warned that, in any event, Street should expect no additional commission for designing furniture. Accustomed by now to official attitudes, he accepted these terms without comment.[76]

Within the year, furniture became a subject that could no longer be postponed. In December 1879, the judges had begun to look forward to moving into the main block of the new building, and the Office of Works was asked to secure furniture for the bar room and the judges' chamber hall, a common room and waiting room located adjacent to the bar room in the southeastern part of the building. Perhaps prompted by the architect, the judges specifically asked that designs be made by Street.[77] The Office of Works and the Treasury, still under Conservative control, were quick to sanction this proposal when it came from the future tenants of the law courts, and on December 30, the good news was relayed to Cavendish Place.[78]

149 *The bar room. Writing table, probably executed by Collinson and Lock.*

Within two weeks Street's furniture plans were nearly complete, and he was on his way toward winning the right to design much of the furniture in the more important rooms of the building.[79]

Furniture design was for Street an important part of the work of the architect, and it was a part of his life as well, for through his second wife, Jessie Mary Anne Holland, he was related to the prominent London furniture makers, Holland and Sons.[80] Jessie, who had been a close friend of his first wife, Mariquita, herself died only shortly after returning from their wedding trip in 1876, but strong ties to her family remained intact. Holland and Sons were among those recommended by Street to tender for the furniture of the bar room and the judges' hall.

The other companies he listed included the leading, progressive manufacturers of the day. In addition to Holland, he recommended Gillow and Company, Jackson and Graham, Collinson and Lock, and the less fashionable George Trollope and Sons, all of whom were later invited to tender for the courtroom fittings as well. When the tenders for the furniture contract were opened on February 11, 1880, the lowest was found to come from Collinson and Lock. Their bid was so low—a mere £438, compared to the £693 tendered by Trollope, the next lowest—that Street was compelled to advise that it be accepted, even though the sample of wood that they had submitted was inferior to those provided by the other bidders.[81] A contract with Collinson and Lock was signed on February 21.[82]

Theirs was a relatively young firm, founded by Frank Collinson and George Lock in 1870, which had risen rapidly to the top of the field by capitalizing on the new taste in decorative arts which accompanied the fad for Queen Anne architecture.[83] Their designers included the architects T. E. Collcutt, who gave their premises at 109 Fleet Street an up-to-date façade, and E. W. Godwin. Collinson and Lock were probably the manufacturers of the benches and writing tables presently in the bar room and judges' hall, for although there are no makers' marks, the furniture resembles that shown in contemporary views of the rooms (Figs. 149, 150).

150 *The bar room, looking west.* (Illustrated London News, 6 January 1883.)

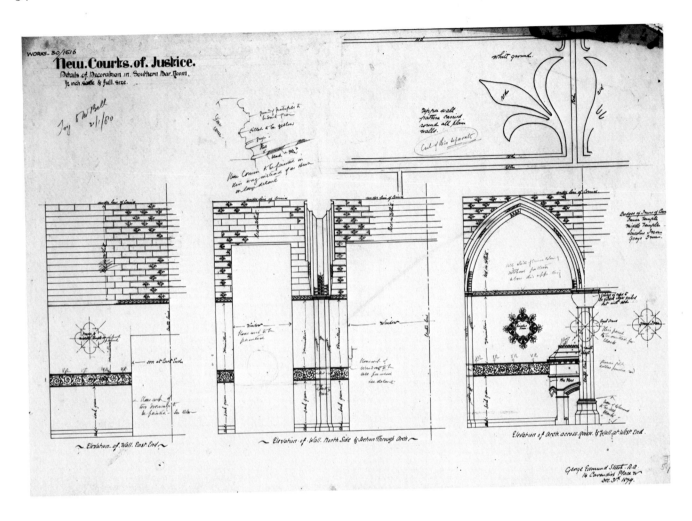

New. Courts. of. Justice.
Details of Decoration in Southern Bar Room,
½ inch scale & full. size.

151 *The bar room. Painting details, 31 December 1879. "VR" monogram inserted later. (PRO Works 30/1516.)*

To complement his furniture, Street also designed a sumptuous scheme of painted and carved decoration for the bar room (Figs. 151, 152). Unlike much of the ornamental work in the building, this was completed before his death in 1881, and it suggests what he might have wrought elsewhere as well. The recently restored wall painting is particularly vivid, making the rising walls in turn dark green, vermilion, and cream with red fleur-de-lis. A girdle of floral pattern, with the royal monogram worked in, encircles the room at eye level, and above it are painted the arms of the Inns of Court. The soffits of the arches are painted with a dogtooth pattern, and some parts of the richly carved fireplace are colored—a practice commoner in the work of Burges than of Street. There is a profusion of gilding, and an oriental carpet originally covered the floor.

The judges' hall was more austere in its decoration, in keeping with its more utilitarian function as a waiting room for those visiting the offices of the judges and the legal departments (Fig. 153). There was no wall painting, and the fireplace was of a much simpler design. Masonry detail in this room was blunter, and nearly as massive as exterior work. Extremely bold, uncomplicated corbels supported the open timber roof, and at the northwest corner the bulbous base of a stair tower was allowed to project unceremoniously into the room. The columns of the two-story arcade, which opened onto two floors of offices in the eastern wing, were of unusually short proportions.

152 *The bar room fireplace. The grate is not original.*

153 *The judges' hall, looking southeast.*

Street's success in obtaining the authority to design the furniture for these two rooms emboldened him to ask again to be allowed to design the furniture for the other important rooms of the main block. In May 1881 he wrote to Algernon Mitford, expressing his "hope that the other rooms are not to be fitted up in the same fashion as in the East Wing."[84] This question could no longer be avoided, for at Easter several office staffs had been able to move into the upper two floors of the main building, and a number of judges were anxious to move into their new quarters as well. Street was therefore asked to prepare specifications and an estimate for the furniture required in the courtrooms and the judges' offices.[85]

In mid-August Street's plans were nearly ready, and he also made his now usual request that the contract be awarded to the firm of his choice.[86] He argued that the impatience of the judges left no time for competitive bidding. To execute his designs Street first considered Collinson and Lock, who had already built furniture for the bar room and judges' hall. But he had found that their work "though good is I think not quite the very best that could be made," and so he asked that the new, much larger contract for the main block be given to Holland and Sons, the firm owned by the family of his late wife. He had already put some business in their hands by engaging them to move furniture into the law courts during 1880 and early 1881.[87] There was perhaps some favoritism in this, although the Hollands were also a highly reliable company.

However, the Liberals had returned to office, and they rejected Street's arguments and ignored the growing clamor of court officials who were anxious to move into the new building.[88] The need for a swift, noncompetitive contract award thus evaporated, and on the last day of August G. J. Shaw-Lefevre ordered that the furniture be put out for bidding. Street was now increasingly incapacitated by his final illness, and he was slow in completing the designs. Tenders were not invited until January 1882, a month after his death.

The same five firms which had bid for the bar room and judges' hall furniture were once more asked to compete. The tenders, based on twenty-four drawings, were received on February 14. This time Gillow and Company were the lowest at £9064, followed by Collinson and Lock, Holland and Sons, and Jackson and Graham.[89] But Gillow did not receive the entire contract. Instead, seized by a renewed sense of urgency, the Office of Works decided to divide the furniture among the three lowest bidders in order to speed construction. Gillow thus had to share the commission with Collinson and Lock, and Holland and Sons. The expenditure necessary to perform the work in this manner was calculated at £9512.

Before contracts were signed with these three firms, Street's successors at the law courts, his son Arthur Edmund Street and Arthur Blomfield, obtained substantial increases in the quantity of furniture to be produced. In July, the first commissioner approved the construction of architect-designed furniture for about 150 additional rooms on the courtroom floor as well as for the witness, jury, robing, and arbitration rooms on the ground floor, and a detailed schedule of all the furniture requirements was drafted by James Gandy, the surveyor.[90] Each of the twenty-nine judges' offices was to be provided with six chairs, two armchairs, a table with drawers, an occasional table, a wardrobe, a looking glass, a hat stand, an umbrella stand, one firescreen, a fender, a set of fire irons, a washstand, a desk slope, a Persian carpet, and a rug. More than one thousand side chairs were ordered for use in various rooms. Only a few of these additional pieces of furniture were noted as requiring fresh designs, and so the great majority were presumably manufactured following the patterns that Street had made in the summer before his death. The enlarged furniture order was officially approved in early August, and it appears that the additional work was added to that already apportioned among the three low bidders, who signed new contracts.[91]

The three firms that manufactured this great quantity of furniture were all substantial, London-based builders with West End addresses. Collinson and Lock, who had won the first contract for movable furniture in the law courts, were now also engaged in providing furnishings for the Savoy Theatre. Given the dissatisfaction expressed by Street with the quality of their work, their second contract was limited for the most part to the repetition of designs they had already produced. Chairs predominated in this, and it may be assumed that Collinson and Lock provided a majority of the surviving portable seating.

Holland and Sons were a larger and older firm, dating back to about 1815, and they had provided much of the furniture for the new Houses of Parliament.[92] But, like Collinson and Lock, they were also to be counted among the more progressive furniture makers of the period. At mid-century they had executed the designs of both Henry Cole and Gottfried Semper, and in the seventies they were the first to employ the designer Bruce Talbert, whose popular work lay somewhere between that of Burges and Godwin. When Holland and Sons contracted for the law courts, their principal offices were at 23 Mount Street, Grosvenor Square, and the firm was headed by three partners: William James Holland, Jessie Street's brother; George Edmund Holland, her significantly named cousin; and an outsider named George Illingworth.[93]

The third firm, and the low bidder for the original, undivided furniture contract, was Gillow and Company, whose shop was at 176 Oxford Street. The longest established of the three, this firm had shared a large part of the work at the Houses of Parliament with the Hollands.[94] Gillow's records show that between October 11, 1882, and March 8, 1883, twenty-two designs for furniture were executed for the law courts.[95] These included tables, washstands, wardrobes, mirrors, benches, mail boxes, folding screens, book wagons, and chairs.

Street also designed the ornamental ironwork for the building, and he contrived to have the £2204 allotted for it taken out of the Bulls' contract, so that he could give the work to a specialist. In June 1881 he privately invited bids from three smaller firms. The lowest tender, for £1746, came from Thomas Potter and Sons of 44 South Molton Street, which had already installed much of the piping and other equipment for the gas lighting system.[96] The saving which this represented from the allocated amount permitted the addition to the contract of iron maintenance catwalks outside the windows of the hall, and the Office of Works, which shared Street's frustration with Bull and Sons, was quick to approve the assignment of this work to a builder who was both cheaper and better.[97]

At the same time Street was making preparations for the glazing of the hall windows. These he proposed to decorate with the coats of arms of the lord chancellors of England, and again he found an outside craftsman who was willing to complete the work within the price agreed to by the Bulls, James Bell of 98 Great Russell Street. When Bell went to the College of Heralds to research the stipulated program, he found that 140 shields of past chancellors were known, whereas the design made by Street on which Bull and Sons had founded their estimate included only 72 shields. No equitable means of denying representation to some of the 140 could be devised, and so application was made to the Office of Works for a slight increase in spending. A total outlay of £340 was approved.[98]

The scheme which Street designed was intended to admit as much light as possible, and the result was quite the opposite of the gloomy hall that James Fergusson had almost hysterically predicted a decade earlier. Most of the glass was clear, punctuated only by the small, regularly placed coats of arms. As Street had explained when requesting the increase in expenditure, he did "not wish ever to see richly colored glass introduced," and he shared a distaste for dark glass with most architects of his generation. In 1852 he had admonished an assembly of the Ecclesiological Society: "The object of a window being to let in light, that glass is the worst which again artificially shuts out light."[99] He went on to tell his audience that stained glass ought to be considered an architectural embellishment, not a medium for moral instruction.

The decoration of the central hall was completed by the laying of a floor of stone mosaic. This was the last detail which Street designed before being incapacitated by his final illness, and approval for his plans came only on December 12, 1881, when he was less than a week from death. Augustus Tanner touchingly urged the acceptance of this last work, which was somewhat more costly than the floor specified at first, out of "duty on behalf of Mr. Street."[100] Once more, this part of the decoration had been excised from the Bulls' contract, and Street had found a more qualified firm to take over. The competence of Burke and Company, whose manufactory was in Paris but who maintained an office at 17 Newman Street, Oxford Street, inspired Street to make a new, more elaborate design, costing thirty-eight shillings per square yard rather than the specified twenty-two shillings. Fortunately, a substantial savings had turned up in the heating contract, allowing a total of £2112 to be spent on the floor of the great hall. However, Street's further recommendation that the upper walls of the hall be incrusted with mosaics was never adopted.

Heat and Light

IN ADDITION to designing the decoration and furnishings, Street contributed to the arrangements for heating and lighting of the law courts. Although he successfully resisted accepting full responsibility for the heating system, his ideas did influence its final form. He played a lesser role in providing the building with one of the first systems of electric lighting in Britain.

Like the plan of the building itself, the design of the heating and ventilating system had to be revised several times. In his competition entry Street had given only sketchy details of an intended low pressure hot water heating scheme, and this had failed to satisfy Dr. John Percy, the technical adviser of the Royal Commission. Percy preferred hot air heat, because it did not rely on potentially dangerous piping, and he had warned: "I should advise the Commissioners to hesitate long before they accept this proposal."[101] Street earnestly sought to learn from his mistakes in the competition, and, accordingly, he revised the heating plan in preparing the contract drawings in 1872. He now introduced hot air warming in the courtrooms themselves, while retaining hot water heat in the rest of the building. The great ventilation stacks which flanked the central hall in this design were an integral part of his system, for it was through them that foul air was to be removed after being extracted from the upper parts of the courts (see Fig. 99). Steam-heating coils were to be installed in the stacks to promote the flow of air, drawing clean air, warmed to the proper temperature, into the courtrooms at floor level. A single power plant served all the courts.

When the tall extractor towers were given up for the sake of economy, such a plan had to be abandoned, and before a new scheme could be designed a contract had been signed with Bull and Sons that made no mention of heating. In the summer of 1874, Street prepared a new proposal that divided the courtrooms among several, smaller heating systems, each with its own more modest ventilating stack.[102] This was set aside, however, until the building was more nearly complete.

The first part of the law courts to require a heating plant was the eastern wing, and there a very simple and entirely separate apparatus was installed in 1877. The system, manufactured and partly designed by G. N. Haden and Son, used low pressure water as the warming medium.[103] A boiler was placed in the central part of the cellar to provide for most of the wing, and a second, adjacent boiler was installed to heat eight rooms located on upper floors by means of a separate network of piping. An average temperature of only fifty-six degrees was maintained.

Not all heat came from central boilers, however. Most ordinary offices were provided with coal-burning fireplaces in which were installed patent ventilating stoves of the design developed by Douglas Galton, Ayrton's director of works. The principle of these stoves was to use the convection currents created by the fire to draw fresh air into the room. They apparently worked well enough for Street to adopt them despite his poor relations with Galton, and the same apparatus was also used in many rooms in the main building. However, the architect did reserve the right to design his own cast-iron face pieces for the Galton stoves.[104]

Despite the use of the Galton patent, the heating system adopted in the east wing was fundamentally conservative. This was undoubtedly a reaction against the overly intricate provisions which had caused such dissatisfaction at the Houses of Parliament.

The same conservatism underlay the ultimate design for the heating system of the main building—the "somewhat ruder and simpler" system that Street and Frederick Blake designed to replace the mammoth and costly plans drafted by Charles Hood in 1879. The Street–Blake design returned to the principles of the proposal shelved in 1874 and divided the courtrooms into four groups, each heated by a separate hot air system of moderate size.[105] The design of these plants was based on successful systems already installed in smaller buildings, insuring that the law courts, unlike the Houses of Parliament, were never made an experimental laboratory for ventilation engineers. The other rooms which required warming were connected into a system of low pressure hot water, like that used in the east wing.

Heat was provided by six fifty-horsepower tubular boilers located in the vast crypt beneath the central hall. A pair at each end of the crypt generated hot water, while two additional boilers placed at the north end created steam. The hot water was channeled off into four systems of heating pipes which ran through the corridors and beneath the warming chambers of the hot air system, located below each courtroom, through which air passed before ascending into the courts. The circulation of air in the courtrooms was promoted by thermal convection which was generated by coils installed in the small ventilation stacks between each pair of courts. These coils were heated with steam from the two extra boilers in the north crypt. Fans powered by the same boilers were also provided because convection alone had not insured sufficient ventilation at the Houses of Parliament. The system was designed to draw in fresh air from the light areas and to move six thousand cubic feet each minute, enough to renew the atmosphere in the courtrooms six times every hour.

In addition to heating, provision was made for cooling the courts. Beside each warming chamber was located a cooling chamber, and by means of baffles the air flow could be divided between the two rooms in any proportion, producing a final mixture of air at the desired temperature, regardless of the season. Although it was originally intended to cool the air by passing it through a cleansing spray of water which had been chilled by an ice-making machine, ether was later adopted as the cooling agent. By this means it was hoped that the courtrooms could be maintained, summer and winter, between fifty-eight and sixty degrees, but a group of visiting architects was told in 1886 that a range of sixty-four to sixty-eight degrees was the operational norm.

In contrast with the conservative heating system, the provisions made for lighting the new building were innovative and even adventuresome. The law courts were the first government building in Britain to be permanently lit by electricity, and the development of a satisfactory system took several years of more or less experimental work. Although Street had died before the final lighting plans were approved, he had seen to it during his lifetime that nothing was done to impede the adoption of the new invention.

When the east wing was nearing completion, electricity was not yet a practical alternative to gas, and so in 1876 plans were made for conventional lighting in that part of the building. Tenders were invited in April 1877, and Thomas Potter and Sons, who later contracted for the ornamental ironwork, were the low and successful bidders at £3994.[106]

By 1879, when lighting for the main building came to be considered, the situation had changed dramatically. A wide variety of functioning incandescent lamps had been produced in Europe and America, and Joseph Wilson Swan, in Newcastle, and Thomas Alva Edison, in New Jersey, were racing to perfect a cheap, long-lasting filament. Swan, who had experimented with filaments of cotton (the eventually favored material) as early as 1848, had more recently devoted his attention to photography. But in 1877 he recommenced his electrical research, and in 1879 he perfected the all-glass bulb, whose perfect vacuum greatly lengthened filament life. Edison's work along similar lines was made to seem more significant because of his keen sense of showmanship. In September 1878, he had publicly announced his determination to find a better filament, and this attracted a number of wealthy backers. His experiments continued for fourteen months, amid a barrage of contrived publicity, and the telegrams from America that regularly reported impending breakthroughs created chaos in the trade of gas shares in London. Finally, on October 12, 1879, Edison demonstrated to the press his successful filament, a piece of carbonized cotton thread. It is thus not surprising that when Street wrote to the Office of Works sixteen days later, asking for instructions for the lighting of the main building, Mitford noted that strong pressure for the use of electricity was to be expected. Hunt predicted, "It is not impossible that the Electric Light may be introduced in the Courts of Justice or some parts of them."[107]

Despite this prospect, it did not seem prudent to commit the Government to an untested system, and so the Office of Works directed Street to have Potter lay gas mains in the main building (at prices based on his previous tender) but to defer the installation of the actual lighting fixtures.[108] In this way, the pipes, which would be very costly to lay once the building was completed, would be available in case electrical lighting proved unworkable. Street showed more confidence in the new technology, and in December he suggested that it was needless to provide for gaslight throughout the building: "It has occurred to me that it might be well at present to make provision for lighting *rooms and corridors only* with gas, upon the assumption that Electric light might with great advantage be applied to the lighting of the central Hall and all of the Courts."[109] But the cautious Office of Works insisted on installing gas lines everywhere, just in case.[110]

Thereafter, nothing was done about lighting until after Street's death in December 1881. But the architect did make a final, cautiously optimistic public statement about electric light on April 25, 1881, during a demonstration of lamps at the R.I.B.A. Street announced that he was only waiting for an inventor to develop lamps capable of producing a steady light before introducing them at the law courts. Significantly, the speaker that evening, John Slater, had especially praised the lamps produced from a new design by Swan. They were, Slater said, cheap, simple, and very steady.[111] With them, Swan had successfully duplicated Edison's use of carbonized cotton, and he had improved the process by toughening the filament with sulfuric acid. This brought the new technology to England and paved the way for its wider application there. Indeed, two years later, Swan successfully prosecuted a patent infringement case against Edison, based on his own, earlier work with cotton filament. In the end, a joint Swan–Edison company was formed to make electric lamps outside America.

Encouraged by these developments, two months after the death of Street his successors pressed the Office of Works for the adoption of electricity in the strongest possible terms. They reported, "We have no doubt ourselves that before the building is completed the Electric light in some form or other will have been so far perfected as to render it available for every department, and that it will be found in every respect preferable to gas."[112] An exhibition of lighting equipment was scheduled for that spring at the Crystal Palace, and they suggested that a decision be made after inspecting the competing designs there.

Apparently on the strength of their display at the Crystal Palace, in May an estimate for an experimental system of lighting was sought from R. E. Crompton and Company, Mansion House Buildings, London, who were licensees of the Swan design. No order was placed immediately, and over the summer, with the opening of the building looming at the end of the year, interest gradually shifted away from an experiment and toward a permanent, complete system, servicing all rooms in the main block.[113] Early in September Arthur Blomfield submitted Crompton's tender of £9000 for such an installation, noting that when added to the £3000 that had already been spent laying obsolete gas mains, this would result in an excess of £6000 over the £6000 set aside for lighting the main building. But Blomfield argued that "no one would now be satisfied with gas and I think it would be very false and shortsighted economy to adopt it to the exclusion of the electric light."[114] This reasoning carried the day, and a few days later Crompton and Company were authorized to proceed with the installation of fifteen hundred Swan incandescent lamps. These were of Swan's new Edison-like design, which had been given their first extensive trial at Cragside, the spectacular house which Norman Shaw designed for Sir William Armstrong, the armaments manufacturer.[115] They had also been installed recently at the Savoy Theatre.

In October, with the opening of the building only two months away, rapid preparations were begun to provide some electric light for that occasion. The deadline did not pose a great problem for the installation of the lights themselves, for although it was not possible to fit all the permanent fixtures that Blomfield had designed, temporary light standards were easily substituted. But a more serious problem had to be overcome with respect to the power system. This was a critical matter, for in the days before electrical grids and central generating plants, each building had to make its own electricity. Street had intelligently foreseen this necessity, and he had specified extra large heating boilers which could also be used to power dynamos, should electric light be adopted. There was some unused horsepower in one of the engines that drove the ventilating equipment as well. However, it was soon discovered that this engine did not drive off its flywheel, as was necessary, and orders had to be given for mounting a new machine next to it in the crypt. Since this could not be accomplished in time for the opening, then scheduled for late November, a frantic search was launched for a temporary power source. It was at this time that the Bulls' two engines and boilers, with their combined capacity of 160 horsepower, were inspected and found to be unsafe for even two or three months of use. As a final resort, Crompton and Company hired a portable steam engine and boiler which were set up in an iron shed to the west of the building, and these provided the power for the inauguration of the law courts. For state reasons this ceremony was postponed until early December.[116] In February 1883, the contractors reported that the installation of the permanent lights in the eastern courtrooms was completed, and in June they reported the same for the west.[117]

Generating power remained insufficient, however, throughout the first years of operation.[118] First the power of the dynamos was boosted, without noticeable effect, and finally, in the summer of 1884, £1500 was spent on new engines. Although these were not ready for the start of the fall term and oil lamps had to be used for a short period, when they were set to work the lighting was increased to acceptable levels.

As finally constituted, the lighting plant was powered by two Galloway boilers which fired two single cyclinder horizontal engines, each developing 105 horsepower.[119] Either of these engines alone was capable of driving all the dynamos, to which they were connected by a complex system of gears. Six Crompton-Burgin dynamos were coupled in parallel to light the twenty-candle-power Swan lamps which were placed in most rooms and corridors. The great hall was lit by six four thousand-candle-power Crompton Crabb arc lamps, divided into two series, each of which was powered by its own Burgin dynamo. In addition, a small Williams twenty-five-horsepower engine was used to turn the single dynamo which powered the forty-five lamps required even in bright weather. This rather complex system, perfected only after two years of testing, contrasted markedly with the simple and conservative provisions made for heating.

Temple Bar

AS THE WORK proceeded in contracting, fitting out, and equipping the new law courts, Street also strove to improve the setting of the great edifice. He had attempted unsuccessfully to secure the demolition of St. Clement Danes, the work of Christopher Wren and James Gibbs, and when Wren's Temple Bar later came under his authority he succeeded in having it removed. Although he published a pamphlet in 1871 urging the respectful treatment of St. Paul's Cathedral, it cannot be said that he had become a warm admirer of the English Baroque.[120]

Temple Bar had been built in 1672 to mark the site of one of the medieval gates of the City of London. It had become a serious impediment to traffic on the Strand by the middle of the nineteenth century, and the competition designs for the law courts, including Street's, had foreseen its replacement by a wide-span bridge, connecting the law courts with the Temples. This costly feature was eliminated from the adopted plan, leaving Temple Bar to remain an obstructive and incongruous neighbor for the rising building (see Fig. 130).

Street did not take direct action to secure the removal of Temple Bar, but the weakened physical condition of the ancient, traffic-buffeted structure soon made its demolition an unavoidable issue. The adjacent construction work may have accelerated the decay of the archway, and it stood unbuttressed after the abutting houses were removed. On July 31, 1874, passersby reported that the southern half of the central arch had shifted and that a fissure had opened near the keystone on the west side.[121] Traffic was temporarily stopped and orders were given to shore up the sagging keystone. Vehicles passing through the gateway were hereafter limited to a walking pace (Fig. 154). Street, alarmed that he might be charged with negligent damage to the venerable monument, made his own survey, and he concluded that bracing timbers had properly compensated for the removal of the abutting buildings.[122] The cracks, he suggested, were old ones which had simply lost their filling, and his hypothesis was confirmed a few days later when a policeman testified that he had seen city workmen chipping out mortar.[123]

In any case, Temple Bar now became the subject of public and official discussion. The Court of Common Council of the City of London Corporation debated its removal in December 1874, and the commissioners of sewers considered the problem in March 1875. Staunch defenders of the structure then rallied, as they had for St. Clement's, and both bodies deferred their decisions.[124] However, the subject was ineluctable, and the Court of Common Council voted in September 1876 to recommend demolition.[125]

During 1877 plans were brought forward for the replacement of Temple Bar with a small marker on a pedestrian island in the center of the Strand.[126] The City of London prepared plans for this which were accepted by Street and approved by the Office of Works and the appropriate municipal authorities.[127] Demolition of Temple Bar began on January 2, 1878, and within two weeks only the side piers remained. These were left in place until construction work on both sides of the Strand was completed. The whole of Wren's gate was ultimately re-erected at Theobald's Park, Hertfordshire.[128]

154 Christopher Wren. Temple Bar. 1672. East façade in 1877, after the insertion of bracing timbers. (Fine Arts Library, Harvard University.)

In 1880 the City decided to build something more than a simple marker on the site of Temple Bar, and in April Horace Jones, the City architect, prepared drawings for a tall, classical monument to be decorated with sculpture. A plan but no elevation was shown to Street, who was thus kept from making an artistic evaluation of the work, even though it would always be seen in conjunction with his own great building. He did, however, attack the wisdom of replacing one traffic obstruction with another. To the Office of Works, Street protested: "As Temple Bar is removed I cannot but feel that it is most undesirable that your Board should assist in any way in the erection of the proposed memorial in its place. The effect is simply to take several feet off a pavement which will always be crowded, and to make this great sacrifice for the sake of a really useless erection in a most inconvenient position."[129] Although Street and City officials worked out a compromise on the placement of curb lines, the architect remained largely unsatisfied, and he made his views public in several letters to the *Times* that fall.[130]

By then, however, it was too late. The first stone of the monument had been laid on August 10, and on November 10 the completed work was unveiled by Prince Leopold.[131] The building contractor was John Mowlem, Burt, and Freeman of Millbank, and the sculpture was executed by several artists. The large iconographic

155 *Horace Jones. Temple Bar monument, beneath the clock of the law courts. 1880. Griffin by Charles B. Birch.*

program, which had been approved by the Queen and the Prince of Wales, celebrated its connections with the City of London. Each was portrayed in a full-length statue, and relief panels depicted Her Majesty's first entrance into the City as Queen in 1837 and the procession to St. Paul's in 1872 for a service of thanksgiving after the Prince's recovery from a nearly fatal illness. A spiky griffin by Charles B. Birch surmounted the whole (Fig. 155).

The florid design, which contrasted unfavorably with the massive sobriety of the law courts, had few defenders. The *Architect* criticized the hastily conceived project and lamented the failure to study the design with a large model before beginning construction.[132] The *Building News* hoped that when the Queen opened the new building she would be shown the griffin and order its immediate removal.[133]

Courts of Justice

WORKS. 30/1987

N.º 37 T.

Design for clock dial and case.

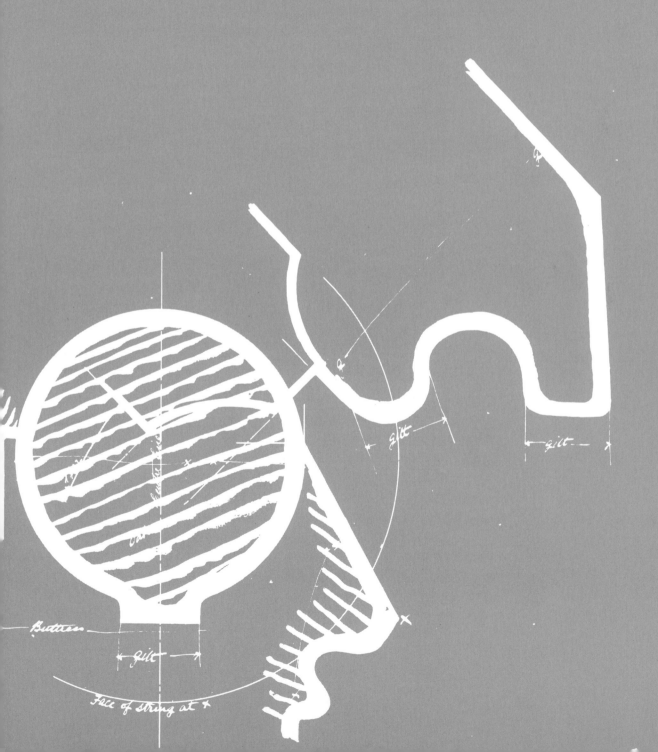

Chapter 8

Epilogue

"Within Sight of the Port."
—Westminster *Guardian*, December 21, 1881

IN 1881, before all the scaffolding was removed from the law courts, George Edmund Street died. He was only fifty-seven, but in the last year of life all the high honors of his profession had come to him; at his death he was the president of the R.I.B.A., professor of architecture, and the treasurer of the Royal Academy. New tastes were now in favor, but in a special sense his friend Arthur Blomfield was correct when he asserted that Street was "universally admitted to be the first architect of the day."[1] His final year was also touched with personal happiness, for his much beloved son was engaged to be married, and this promised to revivify the household which still mourned the deaths of Street's two wives.

Throughout that last year Street had grown increasingly tired. However, the pace of his private practice, slowed by long years of commitment to the law courts, started to accelerate again, with new churches for the American congregations in Paris and Rome as symbols of his international reputation. In June he felt the first effects of serious illness, and he invited his son to join him on a Continental holiday.[2] They visited a score of German cities in a few weeks, but Street began to complain of the gout, and so they cut short their tour and returned home to Holmdale. During the summer he began to suffer from chronic headaches, and on August 6 this was diagnosed as a symptom of overwork and he was again ordered abroad, this time to take the waters. Fortunately, he was able to arrange to travel with the architect John L. Pearson, and, setting off in late August, the two spent about a month at the French Alpine spas of St. Gervais, Chamonix, and Aix-les-Bains. They were joined briefly by another architect friend, Ewan Christian, and Street was able to arrange a side trip to inspect his own churches at Vevey and Lausanne in Switzerland. But the headaches persisted.

Back in England, Street seemed to improve, and by October the headaches had disappeared. In the first week of November he went on a sketching trip with his son Arthur in Suffolk, and on the seventh he opened the winter session of the R.I.B.A. with the traditional presidential address. He was in York on the ninth, and the seventeenth found him at the law courts for what was to be the last time. The next day he was again joined by his son in surveying an old building in Salisbury. On November 19 they set off early in the day to return to Holmbury St. Mary. Street drowsed on the train, and while making the three-mile walk from the station to the house his steps faltered, and he began to speak to Arthur of his mother, Mariquita, as though she were still alive. He had suffered a stroke.

Two days later Street was brought up to London where once more he seemed to recuperate. He did no work, and plans began to be made for a long trip to Egypt in the company of his friend Frank Walton, the painter. December 16 was set as the departure date. But on the fifteenth, while having dinner with Walton, he had a second stroke, this time with paralytic effects.[3] Street was carried to bed, and the next morning he spoke his undramatic last words to Arthur: "I am glad to hear your voice." Unconscious, he died quietly at 10:15 P.M. on Sunday, December 18. Never seen by him, the great hall of the law courts had been cleared of scaffolding only ten days earlier. As the Westminster *Guardian* observed, "It is as when the ship founders within sight of the port—as when the racer drops within reach of the goal."[4]

The churchyard at Holmbury St. Mary was the obvious place for interment, and a funeral was arranged for December 23. But the nation wished nobler treatment for the architect of the greatest public building of his generation, and, at the request of the R.I.B.A. Council and Sir Frederick Leighton, president of the Royal Academy, burial in Westminster Abbey was approved. The funeral on December 29 began with a cortege at two o'clock to bring the body from 14 Cavendish Place to Westminster, passing Big Ben as the towering clock struck three.[5] The plain oak coffin, bearing a brass Gothic name plate made by Holland and Sons, was followed by seven coaches of family and private friends, four coaches for the Council of the Royal Academy, nine coaches for the past and present officers of the R.I.B.A., a single carriage for the officers of the Architectural Association, and many private vehicles.[6] Among the private carriages was that of the Prince of Wales.

In the abbey, Street was borne to the crossing, where the first part of the service was read by Canon Duckworth. His pallbearers, who reflected the varied achievements of his career, were A. J. Beresford-Hope, M.P. (past president of the R.I.B.A. and representative of the Architectural Museum), Sir Frederick Leighton (president of the Royal Academy), G. J. Shaw-Lefevre (first commissioner), Edwin Freshfield (representing the Society of Antiquaries), Professor T. Hayter Lewis (acting president of the R.I.B.A.), the bishop of Winchester (Dr. Harold Browne), Mr. Justice Kay (representing the lord chancellor), and W. H. Gladstone, M.P. (representing his father, the prime minister). The presence of the last was a reminder of the continued cordial relations between Street and the great Liberal politician. He had taken breakfast with Gladstone as recently as 1879, and later that year he returned the hospitality, entertaining him at Holmbury St. Mary shortly after the dedication of his new church.[7] Fittingly, Gladstone was again premier now that the law courts were nearing completion and as their architect had reached his final rest.

The congregation at the abbey was a large one, filling the crossing and transepts and overflowing into the rest of the church. The *Architect* observed that a larger and more varied group of artists had never assembled in memory of one of their fellows. Among those in attendance were a number of former assistants and several men from the present office, including Augustus Tanner and James Gandy. The foremen from the law courts were also present.

After the first part of the service the choir sang "How Blessed Are the Departed," and the body was moved to the grave. Street was to lie in the nave of the abbey, just to the east of Sir George Gilbert Scott, whom, with visible emotion, he had served as a pallbearer three and a half years before. Sir Charles Barry lay just beyond Scott, and so the creators of the great national monuments of the Victorian age—the Houses of Parliament, the Albert Memorial, and the Royal Courts of Justice—were brought together in death. It was widely assumed that Street would have joined his neighbors in receiving the distinction of knighthood had he lived to see the completion of his largest work.

Dr. Bradley, the dean of Westminster, read the final part of the service, the choir sang "His Body is Buried in Peace," and, as the friends of George Edmund Street pressed forward for a final glimpse of the coffin, now nearly covered with flowers, the organ of the abbey thundered the "Dead March" from Handel's *Saul*. George Frederick Bodley, a friend of Street since their days together in Scott's office, later designed a brass monument to cover the grave.

Arthur Edmund Street (1855–1938) was his father's sole heir. In that role he inherited not only an estate valued at £55,136, making him a millionaire in modern terms, but also the responsibility for completing the unfinished architectural commissions.[8] His association with some of his father's buildings continued until the end of the century, and at the law courts the final work lasted for a few years after the new building was opened on December 4, 1882.

Arthur Street took up the duty of finishing his father's work with passionate intensity. On the day after the death he wrote to the first commissioner to claim the right to carry on in his place:

> It is my sad duty to inform you of the death of my father. . . . In his untimely death I have the consolation of knowing that he was happy in having virtually completed the Courts of Justice which will stand as the great work of his life. During the last three weeks, when he had to rest quietly in his room, he alluded several times with great satisfaction that every essential drawing had already been prepared by himself and that over 3000 had been made with his own hand. There remains now really only the carrying out what he had designed and fully explained to myself and his trusted assistants.
>
> And I beg very respectfully to assure you that every sentiment will impel me to see that the great work is finished as my father had intended. With regard to the many works that are not completed in design as are the Law Courts I may at a time like this perhaps be permitted to say that my father in view of a prolonged absence from England [the planned trip to Egypt] had considered how he was to be aided by an architect somewhat younger than himself, but of acknowledged reputation and ability. I have now of course to take that step, seeing that my father's absence is indeed for ever.[9]

Arthur was only twenty-six, and despite several years of experience in his father's office, he was largely the product of an education of Eton and Oxford and little prepared for the harsher realities of architectural practice. His letter alludes to the fact that his father had counseled him, in the event of his death, to obtain the assistance of Arthur W. Blomfield (1829–99), a family friend and a careful, conservative architect. On December 23, Arthur Street asked the Office of Works that he and Blomfield receive a joint commission to complete the law courts.[10] This was granted.

The bulk of the responsibility assumed by Street's successors was for the execution of works that were already designed and contracted for. Only with respect to furnishing and lighting did they possess any substantial artistic freedom. Blomfield was apparently the designer of the additional furniture, the courtroom clocks, and the lighting fixtures which had to be ordered in the course of 1882. Arthur Street was given the job of designing a large number of additional doors which were ordered

156 *The Strand façade from the roof of St. Clement Danes, showing the western railing under construction. c. 1884. (Fine Arts Library, University of Pennsylvania.)*

in 1883, after experience with the working of the building indicated the desirability of partitioning some of the stairways and corridors.[11] He also planned the great stone and iron railing that enclosed the open land west of the building, for which his father had left no drawings (Fig. 156).[12]

Blomfield and A. E. Street also made the first provisions to circumvent the careful separation of circulation patterns which had played so large a role in the architect's instructions. The first evidence of a more pragmatic approach to the use of the building came in 1885 when they inserted a small stair at the north end of the great hall to facilitate direct north–south circulation between the front and back doors, which were separated by a floor level. Street had originally been instructed to frustrate such circulation lest the hall become a thoroughfare.[13]

In later years, the exclusion of the public from the central hall came to seem less and less appropriate. As early as 1883 a questioner in the House of Commons complained of its inaccessibility and recounted that even the prime minister had had difficulty getting past the guards.[14] In 1893 *Punch* ridiculed the vast space in which only a solitary figure could be seen:

> That thing of beauty was meant to be
> For ever a joy,
> Just built to accommodate, as we see,
> One messenger boy.[15]

In this century the hall has been opened to the public. Indeed, present-day security provisions have required the closing off of all the stairs, corridors, and galleries which were designed as separate accommodation for spectators. Many of the other features of the separate circulation systems have also been abandoned, although the judges' corridor remains a private preserve.

Street and Blomfield were responsible for finally settling the several disputes which were still unresolved at the time of the architect's death. Street's pay continued to be an issue of contention with the Office of Works, and it was only in 1884 that Arthur was forced to give up the claim for an additional commission for the design of the heating system. He protested at last: "I am too weak to put myself in opposition to your office and must accordingly yield the point."[16] They also had to reply to the charges made by Bull and Sons in defending themselves against their creditors. In this, ignorant of the complexities of the case, they were at a disadvantage, and Arthur admitted that he was sure that the contractor would not have made his allegations at all if his father had lived.[17] Henry Hunt took a characteristically more bitter view of the situation, observing, "Mr. Arthur Street is young and inexperienced. Mr. Arthur Blomfield, though a most able, judicious and upright Man, has only been connected with the work since Mr. Street's death."[18] But in the end the Bulls' case was shown to be the weaker one.

By 1885 most of the construction was complete, the last annual appropriation had been made, and, indeed, the building had been in use for two years. In a later statistical summary, the Office of Works used 1885 as the cutoff date when calculating overall construction costs.[19] That study reported a total expenditure of £1,973,221, an increase of only 32 percent over the ceiling of £1.5 million which was first proposed 25 years before. Of that sum, £934,818 had been spent on the site and miscellaneous preliminary expenses, and £5005 had been paid to reimburse Lincoln's Inn for the removal of the Court of Chancery. A further £29,510 had been expended for rates, taxes, and caretaking, and £2023 was spent for the opening ceremony. A total of £1,003,888 was thus devoted to design and construction, including £39,464 paid in architect's and surveyors' fees. Street and his successors received a commission of slightly more than £35,000.

The Royal Courts of Justice were officially opened on December 4, 1882, amid pageantry that shamed the humble foundation-laying ceremony. Even the weather cooperated, providing "one of the brightest and fairest of December days that can shine in England."[20] It was a happy occasion of public pomp and display, even though the ceremony took place less than seven months after the horrific murder of Lord Frederick Cavendish in Ireland and was conducted under the threat of further Fenian terrorism. Secretary of Works Algernon Mitford kept in constant communication with the chief commissioner of police while planning the event, and very tight security was provided for the Queen's visit to the new building.[21] On the eve of the ceremony, Mitford and a detachment of police searched the building and

157 Queen Victoria arriving at the main entrance for the opening ceremony, 4 December 1882. (Graphic, 9 December 1882.)

158 *Queen Victoria departing from the quadrangle after the ceremony, 4 December 1882. (Illustrated London News, 9 December 1882.)*

discovered a mysterious box in the crypt, beneath the place where Her Majesty was to stand, but it was found to contain only some broken pieces of tile. More ominously, it was learned after the Queen's visit that a known Fenian, using impeccable letters of reference, had been able to enlist in the regiment of volunteers who provided the honor guard at the entrance to the courts. This man had, in fact, stood with the honor guard, but for some unknown reason he failed to act against the Queen.

Nothing of this was apparent to the public, however. Victoria arrived from Windsor aboard a special train, then passed in her carriage through crowds gathered for the occasion from Paddington Station by way of Pall Mall and the Strand to the law courts. Near the courts the streets were lined with banner-draped masts, and a grandstand was erected around St. Clement Danes (Fig. 157). Her Majesty arrived at the southern door at noon, preceded an hour earlier by the judges, who had paraded to their new home from Westminster Hall. Before her arrival the prime minister, the Cabinet, and other royalty had also come to take their places, and the Lord Mayor, aldermen, and Common Council of the City of London had arrived in a procession heralded by trumpeters and led by mounted police. At the entrance she was met by G. J. Shaw-Lefevre, the first commissioner, who conducted her to the dais at the north end of the hall. He then presented the key of the building on a velvet cushion. She touched it, signifying her acceptance, and it was passed by the home secretary to Lord Selborne, the lord chancellor. Selborne, the author of the Judicature Act, had been made an earl on the occasion of the opening, and after receiving the key he addressed the Queen: "These Royal Courts of Justice, stately enough to satisfy even those who are most accustomed to Westminster Hall, will not, like Westminster Hall, recall the memories of Norman or Plantagenet, of Tudor or Stuart Kings; but they will be for ever associated with the name of your Majesty." An enduring symbol of Victorian law and art, the law courts have fulfilled his prediction.

The Royal Courts of Justice were declared open forever, a fanfare was sounded from the north balcony of the hall, and the royal procession departed into the courtyard (Fig. 158). There Henry W. Bull and Edward C. Bull were presented, and Arthur Street was also introduced. But Blomfield, mourning the recent death of his wife, was absent. The Queen left by carriage, and many of the other guests proceeded to luncheons at Gray's Inn, Lincoln's Inn, the Middle Temple, and the Inner Temple. Each of the Inns of Court was host to at least one royal prince. Before Her Majesty regained her coach, an address from the workmen, signed by their foremen, was read. It concluded, "Our one regret is that the great master whose designs we have carried out should not have been spared to see this day." Queen Victoria responded, "I join with you in the expression of sincere regret that the designer of this noble edifice should not have lived to see the completion of his work."

The great building was itself all the monument that Street required, but his friends and admirers saw to it that his memory was honored more specifically. The meeting of the R.I.B.A. on December 19, 1881, was given over to a eulogy, and the same occurred at the Architectural Association on January 1.[22] On the day of the funeral the dean of York eulogized the architect in opening the Deanery library, which Street had restored.[23] Street was also the subject of an afternoon sermon at Westminster Abbey on New Year's Day.[24]

His friends arranged for two tangible memorials which linked Street's memory directly to the law courts. The first was a monument placed in the second bay of the great hall (Fig. 159). A group of those close to him gathered at the R.I.B.A. on February 3, 1882, to plan for such a memorial, and they adopted a long list of members, the most active of whom were A. J. Beresford-Hope, Arthur Blomfield, and Alfred Waterhouse, but also including the Prince of Wales, the lord chancellor,

159 Henry Hugh Armstead, sculptor, and Arthur W. Blomfield, architect. The Street memorial in the central hall. 1882–86. (NMR)

past and present first commissioners, and several bishops and lawyers.[25] On April 4 they met again in the hall of the law courts and unanimously chose Henry Hugh Armstead to be the sculptor of the monument.[26] A personal friend of Street, he had studied Gothic art more thoroughly than most other academic sculptors. It was also agreed that Blomfield should design the architectural setting for the work, and the meeting concluded with a tour of the building for the Prince of Wales.

The ambitious plans of the memorial committee, which hoped to erect a full-length statue, were delayed at first by shortness of funds. By June only £1600 had been subscribed, and in July the Treasury rejected Shaw-Lefevre's request of £420 for the architectural part of the monument.[27] Only in December 1884 could the work begin, the deficit having been made up by Arthur Street.[28]

On March 24, 1886, the monument was unveiled by Lord Herschell, the new lord chancellor.[29] G. E. Street was shown seated within a niche, with dividers in hand and a plan spread out across his knees. Wrapping the pedestal on three sides was a marble frieze which portrayed the various arts and trades of architectural construction, and in it Street himself was represented several times as a supervisor. A small death mask was also incorporated in the front panel. A separate portrait bust carved by Armstead at the same time was acquired by the R.I.B.A.

The second monument to Street at the law courts, the great clock in the southeast tower, was a less formal but more poignant reminder of his achievement. It was set in motion on December 18, 1883, the second anniversary of his death. Street himself had designed the clock case in 1877, which was built by Thomas Potter and Sons, the plumbing and ironwork contractors (Fig. 160).[30] However, the construction of the clockworks was postponed that time and again in 1881.[31] Not until 1882, after Street's death, did the Office of Works obtain permission from the Treasury to complete the mechanism. Following the advice of the astronomer royal, W.H.M. Christie, the job went to Gillett and Bland of Croydon without full specifications. A contract was signed for approximately £1700.[32]

The clockworks designed by Gillett and Bland were of a new type, like those which they had installed in the Manchester Town Hall four years earlier. The hands

160 Clock case. Plan, elevations, and molding profiles, July 1877. (PRO Works 30/1987.)

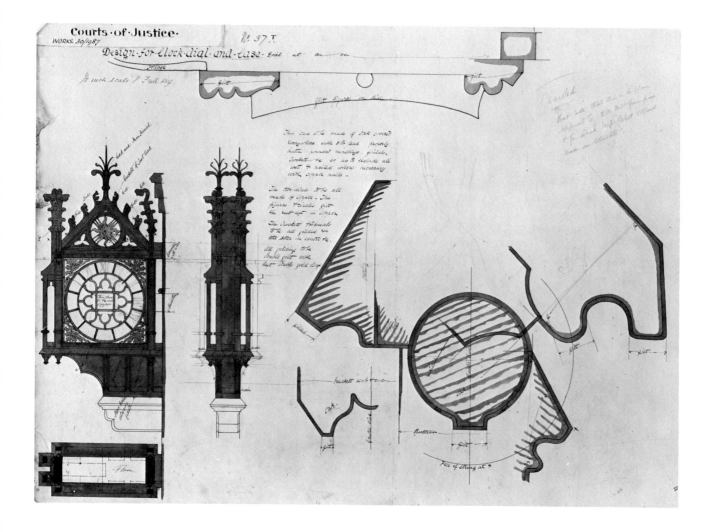

advanced by leaps every thirty seconds rather than moving continuously, recording the passage of time very legibly. However, the system required special clock faces with clearly readable thirty-second markings, and it was necessary to replace the elaborate and already deteriorating dials that Street had designed in 1877 with a baldly functional design made by Charles Bland.[33] The clock was lit from within by gas, for nighttime visibility, and it announced the time by night and day with six bells, sounding the St. Mary of Cambridge chimes. The hour bell weighed 6800 pounds. Accuracy within one second per week was guaranteed.[34]

The idea of starting the clock on the anniversary of Street's death may have developed only after Gillett and Bland reported that the clock might be put into service any time after December 8, 1883.[35] A lack of premeditation seems to be reflected in the fact that both Blomfield and Arthur Street were unavoidably absent from the ceremony, and the ritual of cutting the cord to release the pendulum had to be performed by James Gandy, the surveyor. Nevertheless, the clock was a most effective memorial, its mechanical heartbeat taking up the cadence at the place where Street's own vitality had been slowly drained away.

Those who memorialized George Edmund Street were honoring a man who stood at the head of his profession. He held its highest offices, and he had spent the last fifteen years of his life designing and overseeing the construction of the greatest public building of the second half of the nineteenth century. But Street's eminence at the time of his death was peculiarly tenuous. His art was quite remote from the interests of most younger architects, and the law courts were not widely admired. For some time Street had forcibly detached himself from the day-to-day activities of the architectural profession, and his acceptance of important official positions in his last year did not entirely return him to the fold.

Street's separate and independent position was apparent in his attitude toward competitions during his last years. He entered only two contests after winning the commission for the law courts, and he was pleased with the results of neither. The first was the competition for the new Examination Schools at Oxford, which Street entered in 1868.[36] The entry of Thomas N. Deane was preferred, but university authorities overturned the award and called for a new competition. Street refused to compete again, arguing that the job properly belonged to Deane, and the results of the second contest were thrown out in turn themselves. The problem was only resolved when Thomas Graham Jackson won a third competition in 1875–76.

Anticipating a more honorable contest, Street also submitted a design for Edinburgh cathedral in 1872. In this G. G. Scott was victorious, and although Street felt no personal hostility for his old employer, he was incensed again at the manner in which the affair was conducted.[37] Of the six competitors, only Street and William Burges had observed the stated budget ceiling, and Ewan Christian, the professional assessor, wrote a report which favored Street's entry. However, the cathedral building fund trustees awarded the palm to Scott.[38] Street protested bitterly, "If I had supposed that the trustees . . . were to be the judges, as I am not a madman, I should not have thought twice before refusing to compete," and he vowed, "I have been tempted for the last time."[39] G. E. Street, who had won his own greatest commission in a controversial competition, never did compete again.[40]

Street's independence also shaped his relationship with the Royal Academy and the R.I.B.A. An artist and a Goth, he felt ill at ease with the changing taste and temperament of his colleagues in those organizations, among whom professionalism and classicism were on the rise. Nevertheless, he was elected to the highest offices in both organizations by the time of his death.

Street was voted an associate of the Royal Academy in 1866, but because the tide had turned very quickly against medievalists, he made slow progress up the Academy's *cursus honorum.* At almost every turning his advance was blocked by his young nemesis, E. M. Barry, whose classical preferences accorded better with the tastes of the dominant figural artists of the academy. Barry had already been elected an associate in 1861, at the astonishingly young age of thirty-one. When both were nominated for full membership in 1869, a symbolic rematch of the law courts competition was staged, and Barry emerged the victor by a margin of three votes.[41] Street was again defeated in December 1870, and it was only in the spring of 1871 that he became a full academician.[42]

In the year of his election, Street and Barry both substituted for the ailing G. G. Scott and gave the Royal Academy architecture lectures.[43] Then, when Scott formally retired, Barry bested Street once more by winning the permanent position of professor in 1873. The classical eclecticism which he espoused in half a dozen years of dull lectures may have suited the tastes of the Queen Anne decade, but they inspired little enthusiasm.[44] The *Architect* attributed the selection of Barry to his seniority as an academician, observing that Street could have composed lectures with "a certain authority which may be wanting in those that are now being delivered."[45]

However, Street was yet again defeated by Barry, by a vote of fourteen to eight, in the 1879 election for the professorship, and it was only in 1880, after Barry's death, that he at last attained that office.[46] Street lived to give only one course of lectures, in February and March 1881, and he made them an unswerving reaffirmation of the ideals which he had possessed since the earliest days of his career. Almost proudly aloof from contemporary issues, he made few concessions to the changing interests of younger architects, even though his own work had reflected a sometimes sympathetic interest in their activities. Where his own opinions had altered over the years, as on the issues of foreign precedent and the picturesque, he minimized the differences between his early and recent statements and took a middle approach. In an age of contradiction and change, Street sought to identify permanent guideposts.[47]

Street's relationship with the R.I.B.A. tells a similar story of individualism. As early as 1860 he had "had some fun" with the classicists who then governed that body by joining with other Goths in attempting to upset the official slate of candidates.[48] Their attempt failed, but over the next few years their strength grew, and in 1865 Beresford-Hope, a Goth, won the presidency. By then Street was himself a vice president, and his rapprochement with the establishment was signaled by his willingness to accept the institute gold medal in 1874, after John Ruskin turned it down. Ruskin had rejected the honor in order to scold the architectural profession for their restoration work, and Street, as his son recalled, "loyally" picked up the medal "with its gilt rubbed off."[49]

However, Street's relationship with the R.I.B.A. soon deteriorated, and a Barry again participated in the story. This time it was Charles, the older brother of E. M. Barry, who was president of the institute from 1876 to 1879 and the first representative of the younger generation to hold that post. In his first year of office he inaugurated a reform of the bylaws which established a nearly automatic line of succession: council members would rise inexorably to be vice-presidents and vice-presidents would climb in seniority until reaching the presidency itself. The professionalists, who sought a more rigidly organized profession, complete with formal education requirements and qualifying examinations, saw this as a positive reform. However, like most artist architects, Street disliked the new procedure even though his own position as second vice-president was advantageous.[50] He made a dramatic protest in 1879, when Barry retired and was automatically succeeded by John Whichcord. According to the new bylaws, Street was now in line to be senior vice-president himself, and thus sure to be elected president in 1881, following Whichcord's expected two-year term. But he resigned rather than accept this automatic promotion, citing his large responsibilities as a member of the Council of the Royal Academy, but also recommending that "any chance of getting new blood . . . ought to be seized." The *Architect* reported that many felt that Street and not Whichcord should be the new president anyway and approved this gesture. It argued that the head of the institute should be "the best man for the moment who can be got."[51]

This set the stage for even more drama at the next election in the spring of 1881. Street's resignation had left Professor T. Hayter Lewis in line for the presidency, but Lewis retired in favor of Horace Jones, the City architect and the designer of the ungainly Temple Bar monument which stood beside the law courts. What was quickly identified as a contest between the council nominee, Jones, and the favorite of the nonprofessionalists, Street, was thus also spiced with personal rivalry. The *Architect* launched Street's campaign with an editorial on March 12 which was very personal in tone, condemning the system whereby "the presidential chair is to be usurped by haphazard nobodies in succession for ever and ever."[52] Referring specifically to Street, the article concluded, "What we affirm is that an important artistic society ought to have at its head, not merely the casual representative of nothing in particular, but some one if possible who can stand upright before a censorious world as a recognised leader of his generation."

What ensued was the first contested presidential election in twenty years, and many were tempted to liken it to the "Battle of the Styles" of that earlier time. But while Street's supporters included many Goths, there were classicists among them as well, united in the battle of art against professionalism. For example, a circular letter on behalf of his candidacy was published by Robert W. Edis, the well-known Queen Anne specialist, and Richard Phené Spiers, the fervent admirer of French academic classicism.[53] This joined many supportive statements from medievalists. William Burges wrote less than a month before his death to call for a return to the "old mode of election," and Street's friend Arthur Blomfield warned, "I think that the Institute would make a very grave mistake were it any longer to pass over Mr. Street, who is universally admitted to be the first architect of the day."[54] William White, a colleague from the years in Scott's office, wrote to say that Street had "influenced for good the development of all art in the present generation, far more than . . . any other individual member of the Institute."[55] Street's formal nomination papers were filed by James Brooks.

Opposition to his election from the professionalists was strong. Two former members of the R.I.B.A. Council predictably wrote to the journals to protest any deviation from the rules.[56] The *Builder* remained very cool toward Street supporters, in contrast with the receptive neutrality of the *Building News* and the open endorsement of the *Architect*.[57] T. Roger Smith raised the loudest single voice in opposition, correctly complaining that Street was unlikely to support architectural registration examinations of the type that the professionalists favored.[58] In a long memo published before the election, he recited the legal bases for the selection of Jones and argued that Street had taken himself out of the running by resigning in 1879.[59]

It was apparent that Street stood a good chance of being elected, and fears that this would create a rift in the institute led Horace Jones himself and Charles F. Hayward, F.R.I.B.A., to propose compromises which would insure Street the presidency at a later date. Street rejected these, explaining in his reply to Hayward that he could not leave his friends "in the lurch."[60]

The dispute climaxed at the tense and heavily attended annual meeting of the R.I.B.A. on May 9, when the presidential election was held.[61] While the vote was being counted, what the *Building News* called "a smart passage of arms" erupted, but this was halted by the announcement that Jones had been defeated by a margin of eighty-three to eighty-seven. The *Architect* jubilantly celebrated the demise of the policy of "inelastic *succession* instead of special *selection.*" It also correctly interpreted this as a defeat for professionalism in the "battle of Art with No-Art," rather than the victory of Gothic over classical. This new line of battle would be drawn more clearly a decade later when the "Profession or Art" controversy reached its stormiest moments.[62]

In victory, Street sought to be conciliatory. He studiously avoided controversy in his inaugural address, delivered on November 7 when he was less than six weeks from death, by devoting most of his discussion to what he called contemporary "vernacular architecture"—the work of ordinary builders. Street stressed the need to improve the quality of construction, and he even argued that "the best artist is the most practical man."[63] But many were deaf to his effort to reunite artists and professionalists, hearing only what they expected to hear. For example, the *Building News* reported that "for the first time during a long series of presidential addresses, we have heard art placed first and spoken of as the real object of the Royal Institute of British Architects."[64] That was what Street stood for, but it was not the gist of what he said on that occasion.

Street's final election to high office was not accompanied by the wide acceptance of his Gothic architecture, and that is evident from the criticism which the law courts received as they neared completion. As they had from the start, the bold and picturesque aspects of the design disappointed observers whose tastes were classical, and the numbers of such observers continued to grow. The harsh reality was that the law courts were the "grave of the [Gothic] Revival," as Goodhart-Rendel remembered that they had been called.[65]

As the building rose amid its scaffolding, those who had made a career of criticizing Street redoubled their efforts. George Cavendish Bentinck, M.P., complained in 1877 that the architect "threw away his opportunity, and from sheer ignorance of the principles of his art has broken this great space into at least fourteen

161 *The law courts from the roof of St. Clement Danes, c. 1890. (Guildhall Library, City of London.)*

compartments, pierced them with irregular and deformed windows, and intends to add a lopsided tower which . . . will not be worth the cost of its foundations."[66] But in addition to this expected opposition, even heretofore friendly voices turned critical as the shape of the law courts became visible. The negative tone of this criticism was intensified by the fact that it was the east wing, with its polychromy and multiple towers, which was first unveiled. The *Building News,* although initially Street's ally, became increasingly skeptical about his work. Upon seeing the eastern block in 1876, the editors lamented, "While we admire the details *per se,* the composition would have been vastly more impressive and significant as the seat of English justice if more continuity and balance had been preserved in them and less of the picturesque elements introduced."[67] Even John P. Seddon, whose competiton design was like Street's in its picturesque muscularity, admitted at the memorial meeting of the Architectural Association that Street's secular designs were "too monastic" and broken up.[68]

There was very little appreciation in the last quarter of the nineteenth century for a large public building that was adapted to a crowded, urban environment, in which only a rooftop vantage afforded a view of the entire design (Fig. 161). None admired how the scale of the law courts complemented the domestic character of the surrounding Inns of Court, or how its short lengths of self-contained façade were adjusted to actual points of view. Amid the bathos of late Victorian imperial classicism, the strengths of Street's design were perceived as weaknesses. Its bold gestures were seen as licentiousness, while its flexibility was interpreted as disunity.

Only a waggish writer of the next generation, P. G. Wodehouse, could properly evaluate the manner in which the building came to grips with its extraordinarily difficult site. In 1925 he recounted the advice that his hero Bertie Wooster had received from his Uncle Henry:

> Never forget, my boy, . . . that if you stand outside Romano's in the Strand, you can see the clock on the wall of the Law Courts down in Fleet Street. Most people who don't know don't believe it's possible, because there are a couple of churches in the middle of the road, and you would think they would be in the way. But you can, and it's worth knowing. You can win a lot of money, betting on it with fellows who haven't found it out (Fig. 162).[69]

Uncle Henry's great wisdom was lost to most of Street's contemporaries, and the architect's final honors were due more to admiration for his character than to respect for his art. This was a reflection of the new temper of the times, in which it was not only unfashionable to emulate Gothic architecture, but impossible to argue with conviction about the supremacy of any historical style. In the void of the resulting artistic pluralism, personal values became the only standard for evaluation. Fortunately, Street's character withstood easily the most searching examination, and personal admiration abounded in the reminiscences of him. The admiring obituary notice in the *Architect* employed the jingoistic vocabulary of the late Victorian Empire:

162 The clock of the law courts, visible beyond the spires of St. Mary-le-Strand and St. Clement Danes.

> Street was, every inch of him, a downright Englishman; and this work of his had been done in that thoroughly robust English spirit which all over the world confronts difficulties and dangers as incentives only to greater effort,

greater self-confidence, and greater endurance. A more courageous man in his way never lived in England or out of it. If we provoke a smile, no matter: but every line of his pencil was a blow. His work was fighting work from his boyhood till his death. He was the perfect embodiment of the Romanticism militant of his generation. In a Gothic age he was wholly Gothic, the most Gothic of all Goths.[70]

A. J. Beresford-Hope was of Street's own High Victorian generation, but he, too, emphasized the personal: "I feel there is very little for me to add as to his honesty, his boldness, the way he conquered people by the conviction that about him there was no trickery, no diplomacy in a bad sense, his fearless, earnest advocacy of what was right, and true, and beautiful—beautiful in the moral and in the material world."[71] Personal traits do explain how George Edmund Street molded both men and things—without guile or pretense. They explain why the letter files of the Office of Works are filled with heated correspondence, and also why the design of the Royal Courts of Justice is infused with confidence and strength.

Notes

Notes to the Preface

1. John Summerson, *Victorian Architecture: Four Studies in Evaluation* (New York: Columbia University Press, 1970), p. 115.
2. Nikolaus Pevsner, *London I: The Cities of London and Westminster*, 3d ed. rev. (Harmondsworth, England: Penguin Books, 1973), p. 321.

Notes to Chapter 1

1. Lincolniensis [letter], "The New Law Courts," *Times*, 18 November 1867, p. 11.
2. Webb was employed by GES from May 1854 until May 1858, latterly as his chief assistant. Shaw headed the office from 1859 until 1862. Morris was a pupil, signing articles on 21 January 1856, but he left before the end of the year. See: William R. Lethaby, *Philip Webb and His Work* (1935; reprint ed., London: Raven Oak, 1979), pp. 13–26, 235; Andrew Saint, *Richard Norman Shaw* (New Haven and London: Yale University Press, 1976), pp. 15–18; and John William Mackail, *The Life of William Morris* (London: Longmans, Green, and Company, 1899) 1:85–112.
3. Robert Kerr, "English Architecture Thirty Years Hence," *Builder*, 17 May 1884, p. 729.
4. The standard biographical study of GES is by Street's son, Arthur Edmund Street, *Memoir of George Edmund Street, R.A., 1824–1881* (1888; reprint ed., New York: Benjamin Blom, 1972). See also the article in the *Dictionary of National Biography* by Paul Waterhouse and the introductory essay in Georgina G. King, ed., *George Edmund Street: Unpublished Notes and Reprinted Papers* (New York: Hispanic Society of America, 1916). The obituaries include: "The Late Mr. G. E. Street, R.A.," *Architect*, 24 December 1881, pp. 413–14; "Fine Arts: Mr. George Edmund Street, R.A.," *Athenaeum*, 24 December 1881, pp. 857–58; "The Late G. E. Street, R.A.," *Builder*, 24 December 1881, pp. 777–79; "George Edmund Street, R.A.," *Building News*, 23 December 1881, pp. 813–15; "Mr. George Edmund Street, R.A.," *The Guardian* [Westminster], 21 December 1881, pp. 1821–22; and "Obituary," *Times*, 19 December 1881, p. 9. Consult the bibliography for recent studies of individual buildings.
5. GES [letter], "The Use of Lychnoscopes Suggested by the Paintings in Eton College Chapel," *Ecclesiologist* 8 (1847–48): 288–90.
6. "The Royal Palace of Justice," *Architect*, 9 December 1882, p. 355.
7. GES [letter], "On the Proper Characteristics of a Town Church," *Ecclesiologist* 11 (1850): 227–33; GES, "The True Principles of Architecture, and the Possibility of Developement," *Ecclesiologist* 13 (1852): 247–62; GES, "On the Revival of the Ancient Style of Domestic Architecture," *Ecclesiologist* 14 (1853): 70–80; and GES, *An Urgent Plea for the Revival of True Principles of Architecture in the Public Buildings of the University of Oxford* (Oxford and London: John Henry Parker, 1853).
8. GES [letter], "Naumburg Cathedral," *Ecclesiologist* 15 (1854): 381–86; GES, "The Churches of Lübeck," *Ecclesiologist* 16 (1855): 21–36; GES [letter dated 8 March 1855], "Erfurt and Marburg," *Ecclesiologist* 16 (1855): 73–82; GES [letter], "An Architect's Tour to Munster and Soest," *Ecclesiologist* 16 (1855): 361–72; GES, "Mr. Street on German Pointed Architecture," *Ecclesiologist* 18 (1857): 162–72; GES, *Brick and Marble in the Middle Ages: Notes on Tours in the North of Italy*

(London: John Murray, 1855 [second edition, 1874]); GES, "Architectural Notes in France," *Ecclesiologist* 19 (1858): 362–72, and 20 (1859): 18–26, 91–100, 178–84, 332–40; GES, "On Italian Pointed Architecture," *Ecclesiologist* 22 (1861): 353–67, and 23 (1862): 1–16; GES, "On the Churches of Le Puy en Velay in Auvergne," *Papers Read at the Royal Institute of British Architects* 1860–61: 97–120; GES, "Brickwork in the Middle Ages," *The Church Builder* no. 5 (January 1863): 9–18, no. 6 (April 1863): 53–64, no. 7 (July 1863): 94–107, no. 9 (January 1864): 5–17, no. 12 (October 1864): 154–65, no. 17 (January 1866): 20–33; GES, *Some Account of Gothic Architecture in Spain* (London: John Murray, 1865 [second edition, 1869]).

9. GES, "A Lecture Delivered at the Royal Academy Last Session," *Architect*, 16 December 1871, pp. 299–301, 23 December 1871, pp. 310–12, 30 December 1871, pp. 323–25; GES, "A Second Lecture Delivered at the Royal Academy Last Session," *Architect*, 17 February 1876, pp. 78–80, 24 February 1872, pp. 88–90, 2 March 1872, pp. 103–4; the Royal Academy lectures of 1881 were reprinted as an appendix in AES, *Memoir*, and they were also published in the *Architect*, *Builder*, and *Building News*.

10. From the point of view of architectural theory, GES's other important publications are: "The Study of Foreign Gothic Architecture, and Its Influence on English Art," in *The Church and the World*, ed. Orby Shipley (London: Longmans, Green, Reader, and Dyer, 1866) 1:397–411; "Architecture in the Thirteenth Century," in *The Afternoon Lectures on Literature and Art*, eds. Robert H. Martley and R. Denny Urbin, 4th series (London: Bell and Daldy; Dublin: Hodges and Smith and McGee, 1867), pp. 1–45; "On Some of the Differences of Style in Old Buildings," *Papers Read at the Royal Institute of British Architects* 1869–70: 25–46; "Architecture, Thirteenth Century," *St. Paul's Ecclesiological Society Transactions* 1 (1881–1885): 71–76; "The Opening Address, 1881–1882," *Royal Institute of British Architects Proceedings* 1881–82: 55–68.

11. AES, *Memoir*, p. 282.

12. John Ruskin, rough draft for *The Stones of Venice*, volume 3; quoted in E. T. Cook and Alexander Wedderburn, eds., *The Works of John Ruskin*, Library edition, volume 11 (London: George Allen; New York: Longmans, Green and Company, 1904), p. xvii.

13. A. W. N. Pugin, *True Principles of Pointed or Christian Architecture* (London: John Weale, 1841), p. 1.

14. James Fergusson, *An Historical Inquiry into the Principles of Beauty in Art, more especially with Reference to Architecture* (London: Longman, Brown, Green and Longmans, 1849), p. 155.

15. GES, "True Principles of Architecture," p. 250.

16. AES, *Memoir*, p. 327.

17. GES, "On the Future of Art in England," *Ecclesiologist* 19 (1858): 240.

18. GES, "True Principles of Architecture," pp. 249–50.

19. AES, *Memoir*, p. 342.

20. GES, "True Principles of Architecture," p. 249. He reaffirmed this belief twenty-nine years later: AES, *Memoir*, p. 337.

21. AES, *Memoir*, p. 337.

22. GES, "True Principles of Architecture," p. 247.

23. *Ibid.*, p. 262.

24. GES, *Gothic Architecture in Spain*, p. 464.

25. Quoted in AES, *Memoir*, p. 117.

26. GES, "Proper Characteristics of a Town Church," p. 227.

27. GES, "Architectural Notes in France—No. I," p. 363.

28. AES, *Memoir*, p. 106.

29. GES, "Proper Characteristics of a Town Church," p. 228; and GES, "Revival of the Ancient Style of Domestic Architecture," p. 80.

30. GES, *Gothic Architecture in Spain*, pp. 428–29.

31. GES, *Brick and Marble in the Middle Ages*, p. 267.

32. GES, letter quoted in "The New Church in the Parish of S. Giles, Oxford," *Ecclesiologist* 20 (1859): 391.

33. For the use of these terms see: GES, *Brick and Marble in the Middle Ages*, p. 263; AES, *Memoir*, pp. 77, 350; GES, "Proper Characteristics of a Town Church," p. 230; GES, "True Principles of Architecture," pp. 253–54.

34. GES, "True Principles of Architecture," p. 253.

35. E.g., ibid., pp. 247–61.

36. GES, "German Pointed Architecture," p. 163.

37. Royal Academy lectures, 1881; AES, Memoir, p. 374.

38. GES, "On the Probability of Certain Churches in Kent and Surrey Being by the Same Architect, with a Suggestion for a Guild of Architects," Ecclesiologist 11 (1850): 40; and GES, "Future of Art in England," p. 240.

39. Royal Academy lectures, 1881; AES, Memoir, p. 375.

40. GES, "Architectural Notes in France—No. IV," p. 180.

41. GES, "Churches of Le Puy en Velay in Auvergne," p. 97.

42. GES, "German Pointed Architecture," p. 163.

43. GES, Gothic Architecture in Spain, p. 441.

44. Ibid., pp. 422, 445–46.

45. GES, Brick and Marble in the Middle Ages, p. 256.

46. Ibid., p. 268.

47. John Ruskin, The Stones of Venice, volume 1 [1851], in Cook and Wedderburn, eds., Works of John Ruskin, 9:38.

48. GES, "True Principles of Architecture," pp. 247–61; and Pugin, True Principles of Pointed or Christian Architecture.

49. G. G. Scott, "On the Question of the Selection of a Single Variety of Pointed Architecture for Modern Use, and of Which Variety Has the Strongest Claims for Such Selection," in A Plea for the Faithful Restoration of Our Ancient Churches (London: John Henry Parker, 1850), pp. 113–16.

50. Ibid., p. 139.

51. G. G. Scott, Remarks on Secular and Domestic Architecture, Present and Future (London: John Murray, 1857 [second edition, 1858]).

52. Ibid., p. 192.

53. Of course, Pugin's categorical pronouncements were also the shared heritage of the High Victorians, including John Ruskin himself.

54. GES's report is partially quoted in "The New Government Offices: Mr. Street's Prize Design for the Foreign Department," Illustrated London News, 24 October 1857, pp. 411–12.

55. GES, "Architectural Notes in France—No. IV," p. 179.

56. But the commission went to a Frenchman.

57. Stefan Muthesius interprets High Victorian architecture as a whole in terms of the qualities here identified as Early French. See: The High Victorian Movement in Architecture, 1850–1870 (London and Boston: Routledge and Kegan Paul, 1972). So does George Hersey, who, in the effort to impose a semiotic interpretation on the period, invests them with specific sexual meaning. See: High Victorian Gothic: A Study in Associationism (Baltimore and London: Johns Hopkins Press, 1972). See also: Mark Girouard, The Victorian Country House, 2d ed. (New Haven and London: Yale University Press, 1979), pp. 54–57.

58. So described by Kingsley in his sermon "David"; quoted in Fanny E. Kingsley, ed., Charles Kingsley: His Letters and Memories of His Life, 7th ed. (London: Henry S. King and Company, 1877) 2: 211–14.

59. George R. Parkin, Edward Thring, Headmaster of Uppingham School: Life, Diary, and Letters (London and New York: Macmillan and Company, 1898) 1:79.

60. Ibid., p. 106. The school room was built in 1862–63. The chapel was built in 1863–65, with a porch and turret of 1871–73.

61. Ibid., p. 91.

Notes to Chapter 2

1. Bentham Papers, University College Collection, box 27, p. 172. Quoted in Mary P. Mack, Jeremy Bentham: An Odyssey of Ideas, 1748–1792 (London, Melbourne, and Toronto: Heinemann, 1962), pp. 66–67. See also: George W. Keeton and Georg Schwartzenberger, eds., Bentham and the Law: A Symposium (London: Stevens and

Sons, 1948); and John Forrest Dillon, "Benthamite Influence in the Reforms of the Nineteenth Century," in *Select Essays in Anglo-American Legal History*, volume 1, Ernst Freund, William E. Mikell, and John H. Wigmore, eds. (Boston: Little, Brown and Company, 1907).

2. The history of legal reform may be studied in part in Brian Abel-Smith, *Lawyers and the Courts: A Sociological Study of the English Legal System, 1750–1965* (London: Heinemann, 1967); Freund, Mikell, and Wigmore, eds., *Anglo-American Legal History*; William Searle Holdsworth, *A History of English Law*, 3d ed., volume 1 (London: Methuen and Company, 1922); Richard Meredith Jackson, *The Machinery of Justice in England*, 4th ed. (Cambridge: Cambridge University Press, 1964). A definitive history of this movement has not yet appeared.

3. Usefully discussed in William Searle Holdsworth, *Charles Dickens as a Legal Historian* (New Haven: Yale University Press, 1928).

4. *Bleak House*, chapter 24.

5. Holdsworth, *Dickens*, pp. 121–22.

6. *Ibid.*, pp. 85–87.

7. Charles Synge Christopher, Baron Bowen, "Progress in the Administration of Justice during the Victorian Period," in *Anglo-American Legal History*, eds. Freund, Mikell, and Wigmore, 1:521.

8. Holdsworth, *Dickens*, pp. 90ff.

9. Christopher, "Administration of Justice," 1:520–21.

10. Abel-Smith, *Lawyers and the Courts*, p. 41.

11. Christopher, "Administration of Justice," 1:523–29.

12. "American Justice: ABC's of How It Really Works," *U.S. News and World Report*, 1 November 1982, p. 52.

13. James Beresford Atlay, *The Victorian Chancellors* (London: Smith, Elder and Company, 1906) 1:284–85.

14. *Ibid.*, p. 309.

15. *Ibid.*, p. 295.

16. *Ibid.*, p. 297.

17. Quoted in *ibid.*, p. 320.

18. *Ibid.*, p. 326.

19. *Ibid.*, p. 314.

20. In our context, the natural comparison is with architecture, where the R.I.B.A. was founded in 1834 and the Architectural Association in 1847.

21. Michael Birks, *Gentlemen of the Law* (London: Stevenson and Sons, Limited, 1960), chapters 10 and 11; Harry Kirk, *Portrait of a Profession: A History of the Solicitors Profession, 1100 to the Present Day* (London: Oyez Publishing, 1976), chapter 11.

22. Abel-Smith, *Lawyers and the Courts*, p. 34, n. 6.

23. "Professional Prospects," *Law Times*, 12 June 1852, p. 82.

24. "Proceedings of Law Societies: Society for Promoting the Amendment of the Law," *Law Times*, 28 June 1851, p. 119. The examples of Scotland and certain states in the United States, where no common law and equity distinctions were made, were often cited. David Dudley Field, a member of the New York commission that had overseen law reform there, was a frequent witness before the Society for Promoting the Amendment of the Law in 1850 and 1851: "Proceedings of Law Societies: Society for Promoting the Amendment of the Law, Eighth Annual Address of the Council," *Law Times*, 1 November 1851, pp. 65–66; "Fusion," *Law Times*, 3 January 1852, p. 137; "Proceedings of Law Societies: Society for Promoting the Amendment of the Law," *Law Times*, 3 January 1852, p. 142. The *Law Times* ran a series called "A Sketch of the Scotch Law Courts": *Law Times*, 6 December 1851, pp. 106–7; 20 December 1851, pp. 123–24; 10 January 1852, pp. 146–47; 24 January 1852, pp. 162–63; 7 February 1852, pp. 182–84; 27 March 1852, pp. 2–3; 24 April 1852, pp. 30–31; 15 May 1852, pp. 50–51; 6 November 1852, pp. 75–76; 25 November 1852, pp. 141–42.

25. "Law and Equity," *Law Times*, 2 August 1851, p. 165.

26. "Common Law Procedure Bill," *Law Times*, 12 June 1852, p. 82.

27. "The New Era," *Law Times*, 19 June 1852, pp. 89–90.

28. "The Law and the Lawyers," *Law Times*, 29 January 1859, p. 217.

29. Nikolaus Pevsner, *London I: The Cities of London and Westminster*, 3d ed. rev.

(Harmondsworth, England: Penguin Books, 1973), pp. 521, 530. Except where noted, the discussion of Soane's courts relies upon J. Mordaunt Crook and M. H. Port, *The History of the King's Works, Volume VI, 1782–1851* (London: Her Majesty's Stationery Office, 1973), pp. 504–12.

30. *Hansard*, ns 10 (1 March 1824): pp. 632–33.

31. The interiors are well illustrated in Dorothy Stroud, *The Architecture of Sir John Soane* (London: Studio Books, 1961).

32. "The Law and the Lawyers," *Law Times*, 18 June 1864, p. 367.

33. "The Bench and the Bar: Ventilation of the London Law Courts," *Law Times*, 24 March 1866, p. 338.

34. As explained in the testimony in "Report from the Select Committee on Courts of Law and Equity," *BPP*, volume 10 in 1842.

35. *Ibid.*, p. 85.

36. "Report of the Commissioners Appointed to Inquire into the Expediency of Bringing together into One Place or Neighbourhood All the Superior Courts of Law and Equity, the Probate and Divorce Courts, and the High Court of Admiralty, and the Various Offices Belonging to the Same; and into the Means which Exist or May Be Supplied for Providing a Site or Sites, and for Erecting Suitable Buildings, for Carrying out this Object," *BPP*, volume 31 in 1860, p. vii.

37. "Report of the Commissioners," p. 96.

38. A Subscriber, "Correspondence," *Law Times*, 16 November 1844, p. 125. Although the chancery courts did not move all of their sittings to Lincoln's Inn until somewhat later, the practice of sitting there for part of the year was well established by this date.

39. "The Law and the Lawyers," *Law Times*, 8 July 1863, p. 508.

40. "Select Committee on Courts of Law and Equity," p. 30.

41. *Ibid.*, pp. 83–84.

42. "Report of the Commissioners," pp. 68–70.

43. "The Lawyer: Removal of the Courts from Westminster," *Law Times*, 24 April 1852, p. 35.

44. *Hansard*, ns 25 (7 July 1830): 1072–73.

45. *Hansard*, 3s 14 (1 August 1832): 991. *Hansard*, 3s 31 (9 February 1836): 236.

46. PRO Works 12/32/4 f.14, printed copy of Law Society resolution.

47. Atlay, *Victorian Chancellors*, 2:441.

48. *Hansard*, 3s 57 (27 April 1841): 1162–65.

49. The pamphlet, which appeared in two editions, is unsigned, but it may be quite securely attributed to Harvey Gem, a solicitor, who was a strong proponent of the Law Society plan. Its two editions are: *Westminster Hall Courts: Facts for the Consideration of Parliament before the Final Adoption of a Plan Perpetuating the Courts of Law on a Site Injurious and Costly to the Suitor* (London: J. Hatchard and Son, 1840); and *Arguments for the Removal of the Courts of Law and Equity from Westminster to Lincoln's Inn Fields* (London: J. Hatchard and Son, 1841).

50. Testimony on 25 May 1841, "Select Committee on Courts of Law and Equity," p. 86.

51. *Ibid.*, pp. 99–105.

52. "The Law and the Lawyers," *Law Times*, 30 January 1864, p. 146.

53. Barry could have seen these designs in A.-P. Prieur and P.-L. Van Cléemputte, *Collection des prix que la ci-devant Académie d'Architecture proposait et couronnait tous les ans* (Paris: Van Cléemputte, 1787–96); and L.-P. Baltard and A.-L.-T. Vaudoyer, *Grands Prix d'architecture couronnés par l'Académie Royale des Beaux-Arts de France* (Paris: The authors, 1834).

54. David van Zanten, "Architectural Composition at the Ecole des Beaux-Arts from Charles Percier to Charles Garnier," in *The Architecture of the Ecole des Beaux-Arts*, ed. Arthur Drexler (New York: Museum of Modern Art, 1977), pp. 162ff.

55. Testimony on 18 May 1841, "Committee on Courts of Law and Equity," pp. 73–74.

56. Testimony of Charles D. Singer on 8 June 1841, *ibid.*, pp. 88–90.

57. Testimony on 18 May 1841, *ibid.*, p.67.

58. Testimony on 8 June 1841, *ibid.*, p. 97.

59. Testimony of William Cadogan on 8 June 1841, *ibid.*, p. 91.

60. Testimony on 11 May 1841, *ibid.*, p. 10.

61. Cadogan testimony on 25 May 1841, *ibid.*, pp. 85–87; Barry testimony on 8 June 1841, *ibid.*, p. 101.

62. *E.g.*, *ibid.*, pp. 15, 87, 99.

63. *E.g.*, *ibid.*, p. 38.

64. Testimony on 13 May 1841, *ibid.*, p. 33.

65. Testimony on 14 May 1841, *ibid.*, p. 38.

66. *Hansard*, 3s 67 (16 March 1843): 1073–74; see also a second, brief Lords debate in *Hansard*, 3s 68 (28 April 1843): 1013–14.

67. Barry testimony, "Report from the Select Committee on Courts of Law and Equity; together with the Minutes of Evidence, and Index," *BPP*, volume 12 in 1845, pp. 5–8.

68. *Ibid.*, p. 18.

69. *Ibid.*, pp. 11–12.

70. *Ibid.*, pp. 12–13.

71. The controversy was renewed by a pamphlet in support of the Lincoln's Inn Fields site: Robert Alfred Routh and Charles Wetherell Brown, *An Address to The Legal World on the Centralisation of the Courts of Law and Equity* (London: S. Taylor, 1851). The Law Society countered with petitions in April 1852 and January 1853, and in 1853 its success was reflected in Harvey Gem's momentary abandonment of his strong support for the fields: An Old Law Reformer [Harvey Gem], *The New Houses of Parliament and the Law Courts: Are the Law Courts to Remain at Westminster?* (Brighton: Curtis and Company, 1853).

72. "Proceedings of the Law Societies: Incorporated Law Society, Removal of the Courts of Law," *Law Times*, 21 January 1854, pp. 170–71.

73. PRO Works 12/32/3 f.2 (26 January 1854), minute on the meeting.

74. Various meetings of the trustees and of the freeholders and leaseholders of the fields are reported in "Legal Intelligence: The Proposed New Law Courts," *Law Times*, 18 February 1854, p. 210; PRO Works 12/32/3 f.7 (8 February 1854), printed announcement of meeting on February 16 for freeholders and leaseholders;

Works 12/32/3 f.8 (16 February 1854), resolutions passed at that meeting; Works 12/32/3 f.10, record of voting at that meeting.

75. An Old Law Reformer [Harvey Gem], *Where Shall the New Law Courts Be Built?* (London: T. F. A. Day, 1854).

76. The society published an open letter in May 1856: "Courts of Justice for the Metropolis: Suggestions for Providing the Funds Required for the Erection of Courts and Offices for the Administration of Justice in the Metropolis," copy at PRO Works 12/32/4 f.5. In December the officers called on the first commissioner: Works 12/32/4 f.6 (8 December 1856), Alfred Austin (secretary of works) to Edward White (president of the Law Society).

77. *Hansard*, 3s 137 (30 March 1855): 1402–3.

78. PRO Works 12/32/4 f.10 (23 November 1858), Manners to Young.

79. Text of the bill: *BPP*, 1s, volume 2 in 1859.

80. "Plans for the New Courts," *Law Times*, 4 June 1859, p. 139. Designed by Philip Hardwick.

81. Incorporated Law Society, *Observations on the Proposed Concentration of the Courts of Justice and All the Requisite Offices in the Vicinity of the Inns of Court and on the Means of Defraying the Expense* (London: Spottiswoode and Company, January 1, 1859), p. 6.

82. "Plans for the New Courts," *Law Times*, 4 June 1859, p. 139.

83. "Report of the Commissioners."

84. *Victorian Chancellors*, 2:223; "Report of the Commissioners," p. 34.

85. Thomas Sadler, *Edwin Wilkins Field: A Memorial Sketch* (London: Macmillan and Company, 1872).

86. "Report of the Commissioners," pp. 21, 33.

87. *Ibid.*, p. 35.

88. *Ibid.*, pp. 24, 34.

89. He complained that the hearings were rigged and wrote another pamphlet: Harvey Gem, *Strictures on the Report of Her Majesty's Commissioners for the Concentration of the Law Courts, and on Their Recommendations as Regard Site* (London: W. Heath, 1861).

90. "Report of the Commissioners," p. xxxii.

91. *Ibid.*

92. *Ibid.*, pp. 90–96.

93. *Ibid.*, pp. 70–75, 84–89.

94. Abraham defended himself spiritedly: "Minutes of Evidence Taken Before the Select Committee on the Courts of Justice Building Act (Money) Bill," *BPP*, volume 14 in 1861, p. 5.

95. *Ibid.*

96. "The Courts of Justice Competition," *Civil Engineer and Architect's Journal*, 1 March 1867, p. 66.

97. "Select Committee on the Courts of Justice Building Act (Money) Bill," p. 2.

98. PRO Works 12/1 f.7.

99. Quoted in Thomas Arthur Nash, *The Life of Richard Lord Westbury* (London: Richard Bentley and Son, 1888) 2:2.

100. PRO Works 12/1 f.27, Lincoln's Inn petition. Frederick Lygon and Charles Selwyn were the complainers; *Hansard*, 3s 163 (27 June 1861): 1682–84.

101. *Hansard*, 3s 163 (27 June 1861): 1684.

102. PRO Works 12/1 f.22 (8 April 1861), Henry Hunt memo.

103. *Hansard*, 3s 161 (15 February 1861): 463–68.

104. *Hansard*, 3s 163 (27 June 1861): 1683.

105. "Select Committee on the Courts of Justice Building Act (Money) Bill," pp. 23–30.

106. BL Add. MS. 44636 ff. 55–58.

107. *BPP*, volume 51 in 1861.

108. *Hansard*, 3s 164 (19 July 1861): 1188–89.

109. PRO Works 12/1 f.59 (17 June 1862), Lincoln's Inn petition. Wason's many letters to the Office of Works are in Works 12/32/5. Finally, on January 2, 1863, Alfred Austin, the secretary of works, advised the first commissioner against answering Wason's latest missive: "It contains insulting and groundless charges which you have already called upon him in vain to retract" (f.21). Wason's response was a forty-page pamphlet, reprinting his entire correspondence with the office. And when the law courts site was an issue again in 1869, he once more put forward his Westminster scheme in a printed letter addressed to the Commons: Works 12/32/2 f.162 (31 July 1869).

110. Reported in PRO Works 12/32/3 f.13 (3 July 1862), William Mannin (secretary of the trustees) to Cowper.

111. *Hansard*, 3s 165 (14 March 1862): 1563–64.

112. *Hansard*, 3s 166 (10 April 1862): 798–800.

113. *Ibid.*, pp. 803–10.

114. *Ibid.*, p. 813.

115. *Ibid.*, p. 817.

116. *Ibid.*, p. 814.

117. See Henry Roseveare, *The Treasury: The Evolution of a British Institution* (London: Allen Lane, the Penguin Press, 1969), chapter 7.

118. Nash, *Westbury*, 2:45.

119. These personal factors are discussed in "The Law and the Lawyers," *Law Times*, 26 April 1862, p. 325; and "The Law and the Lawyers," *Law Times*, 8 July 1863, p. 508.

120. *Hansard*, 3s 170 (27 March 1863): 25; *Hansard*, 3s 170 (18 May 1863): 1838–39; *Hansard*, 3s 171 (5 June 1863): 405.

121. PRO Works 12/1 f.67 (15 October 1863), Cheffins to Austin, with Hunt memo (20 October 1863).

122. *Hansard*, 3s 173 (12 February 1864): 496; *Hansard*, 3s 173 (10 March 1864): 1756; *Hansard*, 3s 174 (15 April 1864): 1142; *Hansard*, 3s 174 (21 April 1864): 1420–21; *Hansard*, 3s 174 (3 May 1864): 2052.

123. "Law Societies: Incorporated Law Society of the United Kingdom, Annual Report of the Council to the General Meeting of the Members, July 8, 1864," *Law Times*, 10 September 1864, pp. 495–96.

124. *BPP*, volume 29 in 1864.

125. PRO Works 12/1 f.77 (18 June 1864), draft of minute.

126. *Hansard*, 3s 176 (27 June 1864): 368–70.

127. "The Ways and Means for the New Law Courts," *Law Times*, 26 March 1864, p. 239.

128. Quoted in Nash, *Westbury*, 2:100. Gladstone was not alone in proposing an increase in fees to pay for the courts: Robert Alfred Routh and Charles Wetherell Brown, *Centralisation of the Courts of Law and Equity*, p. 7. A Law Society deputation also recommended that he adopt such an

expedient in May 1862: "The Bench and the Bar: Concentration of the Law Courts, Deputation to the Chancellor of the Exchequer," *Law Times*, 10 May 1862, pp. 354–55. Gladstone asked for a memo on their proposal: BL Add. MS. 44636 ff. 55–58, notes on the 1861 Treasury minute.

129. Reported in *Hansard*, 3s 177 (16 February 1865): 297.

130. Letter to C. G. Loring quoted in Sadler, *Field*, p. 39.

131. PRO Works 12/1 f. 94 (27 July 1864), Hamilton (Treasury secretary) to Cowper.

132. PRO Works 12/1 ff. 119–20 (3 February 1865), Pennethorne to Cowper.

133. PRO Works 12/31/2 f. 7 (3 December 1864), Office of Works to Pennethorne.

134. PRO Works 12/1 f. 132 (18 February 1865), Pennethorne to Cowper.

135. PRO Works 12/1 ff. 143–45 (24 February 1865), Pennethorne to Cowper; "Minutes of Evidence Taken before the Select Committee on the Courts of Justice Concentration (Site) Bill; with the Proceedings of the Committee," *BPP*, volume 12 in 1865, pp. 1–7.

136. PRO Works 12/1 f. 179 (28 June 1865), Cowper to Pennethorne.

137. PRO Works 12/1 ff. 143–45 (24 February 1865), Pennethorne to Cowper.

138. *Hansard*, 3s 178 (23 March 1865): 179–80. Pennethorne's appointment *had* been considered in the wake of the unsatisfactory competition for the government offices in 1857. This may have aroused Selwyn's suspicions in 1865.

139. PRO Works 12/1 f. 147 (25 February 1867), Pennethorne to Cowper.

140. *Hansard*, 3s 177 (10 February 1865): 166–67.

141. *Hansard*, 3s 178 (28 April 1865): 1182.

142. *Ibid.*, 1173.

143. *Hansard*, 3s 176 (27 June 1864): 372.

144. Stanhope in *Hansard*, 3s 177 (20 March 1865): 1911; Lygon in *Hansard*, 3s 178 (30 March 1865): 490.

145. PRO Works 12/1 ff. 169–70 (10 April 1865), Pennethorne to Cowper.

146. "Select Committee on the Courts of Justice Concentration (Site) Bill," pp. 7–8.

147. PRO Works 12/1 f. 142, Abraham's estimate of working-class displacement.

148. "Select Committee on the Courts of Justice Concentration (Site) Bill," pp. 8–9.

149. *Hansard*, 3s 177 (28 February 1865): 929.

150. *Ibid.*, 934.

151. Atlay, *Victorian Chancellors*, 2:268–74.

152. *Hansard*, 3s 177 (23 February 1865): 606.

153. All of the following discussion of the Royal Commission is based on "Report of the Commissioners Appointed to Advise and Report as to the Buildings Proper to Be Erected, and the Plans upon which such Buildings Shall Be Erected for the New Courts of Justice," *BPP*, volume 20 in 1871.

154. *Ibid.*, p. 9

155. For Burnet, see Crook and Port, *King's Works*, p. 221.

156. "Report of the Commissioners . . . as to the Buildings Proper to Be Erected," pp. 140–41.

157. *Ibid.*, p. 26.

158. *Ibid.*, p. 140.

159. Webster's talk was entitled "The Palace of Justice—The Site, Approaches, and Arrangements of the Courts and Offices of Judicature." It was reported in "Proceedings of Law Societies: Law Amendment Society," *Law Times*, 6 January 1866, pp. 140–42.

160. AES, *Memoir*, pp. 41, 258–59.

161. For a discussion of Conservative attitudes toward Reform see Robert Blake, *Disraeli* (London: Eyre and Spottiswoode, 1966).

162. The term is applied to architecture in A. J. Beresford-Hope, *The Common Sense of Art* (London: John Murray, 1858), p. 13.

163. GES, "On Italian Pointed Architecture," *Ecclesiologist* 22 (1861): 363.

164. Rough draft of the *The Stones of Venice*, volume 3, chapter 4. Quoted in E. T. Cook and Alexander Wedderburn, eds., *The Works of John Ruskin*, Library edition, volume 11 (London: George Allen; New York: Longmans, Green and Company, 1904), p. xvii.

Notes to Chapter 3

1. For previous discussion of the competition see: Joseph Kinnard, "G. E. Street, the Law Courts and the 'Seventies," in *Victorian Architecture,* ed. Peter Ferriday (London: Jonathan Cape, 1963,) pp. 221–34; M. H. Port, "The New Law Courts Competition, 1866–67," *Architectural History* 11 (1968): 75–93; John Summerson, "The Law Courts Competition of 1866-67," *R.I.B.A. Journal* 77 (1970): 11–18; and John Summerson, "A Victorian Competition: the Royal Courts of Justice," *Victorian Architecture: Four Studies in Evaluation* (New York: Columbia University Press, 1970), chapter 4.

2. This era has been studied recently by two authors, to whom much of the following discussion is indebted. See: Maurice Cowling, *1867: Disraeli, Gladstone and Revolution; The Passing of the Second Reform Bill* (Cambridge: Cambridge University Press, 1967); and F. B. Smith, *The Making of the Second Reform Bill* (Cambridge: Cambridge University Press, 1966).

3. W. F. Monypenny and G. E. Buckle, *The Life of Benjamin Disraeli, 1st Earl of Beaconsfield* (London: John Murray, 1912) 2:262.

4. Thomas Carlyle, "Shooting Niagara: and after?" *Macmillan's Magazine,* August 1867, pp. 319–36.

5. J. Mordaunt Crook and M. H. Port, *The History of the King's Works, Volume VI, 1782-1851* (London: Her Majesty's Stationery Office, 1973), pp. 430–37.

6. David Watkin, *The Life and Work of C. R. Cockerell* (London: A. Zwemmer, 1974), pp. 207–13.

7. "Report of the Commissioners Appointed to Advise and Report as to the Buildings Proper to Be Erected, and the Plans upon which Such Buildings Shall Be Erected for the New Courts of Justice . . . ," *BPP,* volume 20 in 1871, pp. 12, 14.

8. G. G. Scott, *Personal and Professional Recollections* (London: Sampson Low, Marston, Searle, and Rivington, 1879), p. 273. "The New Law Courts' Competition," *Building News,* 11 January 1867, p. 18.

9. Lincolniensis [letter], "The New Law Courts," *Times,* 18 November 1867, p. 11.

10. "Report of the Commissioners," pp. 13–14.

11. *Ibid.,* pp. 22, 24.

12. Scott, *Recollections,* p. 193.

13. F. H. W. Sheppard, ed., *Survey of London, Volume 38, The Museums Area of South Kensington and Westminster* (London: University of London, 1975), p. 206. M. H. Port, ed., *The Houses of Parliament* (New Haven and London: Yale University Press, 1976), pp. 177–78.

14. Palmer's relationship with Waterhouse is discussed by Mark Girouard in "Blackmoor House, Hampshire: The Property of the Earl of Selborne," *Country Life,* 29 August 1974, pp. 554–57; 5 September 1974, pp. 614–17. The documentation is contained in the BAL, Waterhouse Letterbook 1864–67, volume 2, especially: p. 11 (23 November 1866), Waterhouse to Palmer, enclosing plans; pp. 227–28 (12 December 1866), Waterhouse to Palmer, enclosing bill for £154.5.4; pp. 731–32 (25 February 1867), Waterhouse to Laura Palmer, arranging consultation; pp. 876–77 (12 March 1867), Waterhouse to Palmer, concerning estate buildings and church; p. 973 (19 March 1867), J. Willey [for Waterhouse] to Laura Palmer, concerning invitations to Waterhouse, who was ill.

15. BL Add. MS. 44536 f.19v (7 February 1866), Gladstone to Stirling-Maxwell, asking him to serve. Add. MS. 44409 f.191 (8 February 1866), Stirling-Maxwell to Gladstone, accepting.

16. Scott, *Recollections,* p. 184.

17. John Morley, *The Life of William Ewart Gladstone* (New York: Macmillan Company, 1903) 2:217–18.

18. The diaries are preserved at the Lambeth Palace Library. The relevant volumes have been published: H. C. G. Matthew, ed., *The Gladstone Diaries, V: 1855–1860, and VI: 1861–1868* (Oxford: Oxford University Press, 1978).

19. BL Add. MS. 44782 ff.94 and 139 (20 May 1858 and 2 May 1860), breakfast lists. Diaries as noted in n. 18.

20. BL Add. MS. 44782 f.37 (4 May 1854), breakfast list.

21. Diaries, 19 August 1859.

22. Diaries, 28 March 1858 and 23 July 1858.

23. BL Add. MS. 44530 ff.67v–68r (30 August 1859), Gladstone to Scott, in which he says: "The widespread reputation you have acquired is to you too great a trea-

sure to be hazarded for the sake of any particular employment."

24. Diaries, 14 October 1864. "The Designs for the Law Courts," *Building News*, 1 March 1867, p. 163.

25. AES, *Memoir*, p. 41.

26. Recorded in Diaries; not extant.

27. AES, *Memoir*, p. 41.

28. Diaries, 8 June 1857 and 9 June 1857.

29. Diaries, 22 February 1863 and 12 April 1863.

30. BL Add. MS. 44404 f.172 (10 December 1964), GES to Gladstone, Add. MS. 44534 f.169r (13 December 1864), Gladstone to GES.

31. BL Add. MS. 44405 f.190 (27 February 1865), GES to Gladstone.

32. Diaries, 28 February 1865, 1 March 1865, 13 March 1865.

33. *Hansard*, 3s 182 (22 March 1866): 775.

34. *Ibid.*, p. 777.

35. Gladstone diaries.

36. *Hansard*, 3s 181 (20 February 1866): 813–14.

37. AES, *Memoir*, p. 51.

38. See the biographical memoir by Alfred Barry in Edward M. Barry, *Lectures on Architecture Delivered at the Royal Academy* (London: John Murray, 1881).

39. "The Designs for the Law Courts," *Building News*, 1 March 1867, p. 163.

40. Hermione Hobhouse, "Philip and Philip Charles Hardwick, an Architectural Dynasty," in *Seven Victorian Architects*, ed. Jane Fawcett (University Park, Pennsylvania: Pennsylvania State University Press, 1977), pp. 32–49.

41. Stuart Allen Smith, "Alfred Waterhouse, Civic Grandeur," in *ibid.*, pp. 92–121.

42. "The New Courts of Law," *Times*, 11 February 1867, p. 12.

43. "Report of the Commissioners," p. 6.

44. As noted above, Waterhouse's designs for Roundell Palmer postdate the competition.

45. "Report of the Commissioners," p. 22.

46. These events are recorded in the letters of G. E. Street and E. M. Barry to Lord Derby, the prime minister, both dated 20 January 1868: PRO T1/6835B/19182 ff.1696 and 1697. Reprinted in "New Courts of Justice: Copy 'of Correspondence with the Two Architects Recommended by the Judges of Designs for the New Courts of Justice,'" *BPP*, volume 47 in 1868–69, pp. 1–3. See also: "Report of the Commissioners," p. 24.

47. "Report of the Commissioners," p. 24. Their resignations were reported in Parliament on March 12. *Hansard*, 3s 182 (12 March 1866): 17.

48. "Report of the Commissioners," p. 24.

49. *Ibid.*

50. "The Law and the Lawyers," *Law Times*, 10 March 1866, p. 293.

51. *Hansard*, 3s 182 (22 March 1866): 777. The full debate, from which all subsequent quotations are taken, includes columns 775–96.

52. "Report of the Commissioners," p. 35.

53. *Ibid.*

54. Diaries, 3 April 1866.

55. *Hansard*, 3s 183 (30 April 1866): 180–84.

56. *Hansard*, 3s 183 (18 May 1866): 1178. Tite and Beresford-Hope did not support this further enlargement, and Gladstone also spoke against it.

57. "Report of the Commissioners," p. 46.

58. PRO Works 12/33/1 f.20 (21 August 1866), Godwin to Manners. Works 12/33/1 f.21 (27 August 1866), Office of Works to Godwin.

59. "Report of the Commissioners," p. 22 and PRO Works 12/33/1 ff.1–2 (23 February 1865), Lockwood and Mawson to Cowper. Works 12/33/1 ff.4–6 (24 March 1866), Goodchild to Cowper. Works 12/33/1 ff.12–13 (23 March 1866), J. and H. Francis to Cowper. Works 12/33/1 f.15 (26 March 1866), Beeston and Brereton to Cowper. Works 12/33/1 ff.17–18 (12 April 1866), Dales to Cowper.

60. Illustrated in the *Builder*, 13 August 1864, pp. 600–601.

61. Scott, *Recollections*, p. 274.

62. "The Designs for the Law Courts," *Times*, 2 July 1868, p. 10.

63. BAL, Waterhouse Letterbook 1864–67, volume 2, p. 21 (24 November

1866), Waterhouse to John T. Hibberd; pp. 300–301 (22 December 1866), Waterhouse to J. D. Burton.

64. "Report of the Commissioners," p. 25.

65. Ibid., pp. 42–43.

66. Ibid., pp. 38–39. The instructions also referred approvingly to the existing courts of the master of the rolls and the court of Exchequer in London, the crown courts at Cambridge, and the new courts at Brecon, Wales. Ibid., p. 137.

67. Ibid., p. 26.

68. Ibid., pp. 40–41. The various maps referred to here and subsequently have not survived, but a good idea of the greatest extent of the demands is provided by a plan prepared in 1868, Fig. 78.

69. Ibid., p. 47.

70. Ibid.

71. Ibid., pp. 51–53.

72. Ibid., pp. 41–42. Proposed by Scott on June 16. Approved on July 9.

73. PRO Works 12/34/2 ff. 1–3 (2 November 1866), Hunt to Cowper.

74. "Report of the Commissioners," pp. 48–53.

75. Ibid., pp. 45, 48, 50–51, 53. Related papers are located in PRO Works 12/35/2.

76. "Report of the Commissioners," p. 57.

77. After the competition, the drawings were returned to the architects. Two Burges interiors are preserved at the Victoria and Albert Museum; three Scott exterior perspectives and one elevation are preserved at the Royal Courts of Justice, and one exterior and three interior views of his design are owned by the BAL Drawings Collection; Street's bird's-eye view is held by the Architectural Association; and two exterior perspectives by Waterhouse are at the BAL. However, some record of all the other designs was published. Floor plans and sections of each entry were lithographed by the commission for the use of the judges. These were bound in folio volumes with the title New Courts of Justice: Design Submitted by . . . by Day and Son of London, the lithographers, with the date 1867. The Builder and Building News, between them, published perspectives of every design except for that of Abraham, and some details; and the Builder printed block plans of many of the entries as well. The most useful of the printed sources are the volumes that at least seven of the competitors published at their own expense, comprised of photographs of their rendered drawings: William Burges, Law Courts Commission: Report to the Courts of Justice Commission (London: George Edward Eyre and William Spottiswoode, 1867); Henry B. Garling, New Courts of Justice: Design Submitted by Mr. Henry B. Garling (London: Day and Son, 1867); Henry F. Lockwood, Design for the Concentration of the Law Courts (n.p., [1867]); George Gilbert Scott, Design for the New Law Courts (London, 1867); John P. Seddon, New Law Courts: Description of Design (London: George Edward Eyre and William Spottiswoode, 1867) [Seddon's major perspective, not included in this volume, is recorded in a photograph at the BAL Drawings Collection]; George Edmund Street, Explanation and Illustrations of His Design for the Proposed New Courts of Justice (London: J. E. Taylor and Company, 1867); Alfred Waterhouse, Courts of Justice Competition. General Description of Design (London: George Edward Eyre and William Spottiswoode, 1867). In addition, photographs of several of Brandon's drawings are preserved at the BAL Drawings Collection. The most complete collections of these volumes are held by the BAL and the library of the Property Services Agency, Department of the Environment, Croydon. It should be noted that no record of Abraham's elevations has been unearthed.

78. [leading article], Times, 19 November 1867, p. 6.

79. "The New Courts of Law," Saturday Review, 9 February 1867, p. 172.

80. "The New Law Courts," Ecclesiologist 28 (1867): 113.

81. "The New Courts of Law," Saturday Review, 9 February 1867, p. 172. "Art: the New Law Courts' Designs," Spectator, 23 March 1867, p. 212. "The New Courts of Law," Times, 11 February 1867, p. 12.

82. "Designs for the Proposed Law Courts," Builder, 16 February 1867, p. 109.

83. James Fergusson, "The Law Courts Designs," Builder, 16 April 1867, pp. 238–39.

84. [Philip Smith and J. T. Emmett],

"The New Courts of Law: Courts of Justice Commission, Instructions for the Competing Architects," *Quarterly Review*, 123 (July 1867): 107–8. [Attribution from *Wellesley Index to Victorian Periodicals*.]

85. *Hansard*, 3s 185 (22 February 1867): 817, 820.

86. Robert Kerr, "English Architecture Thirty Years Hence," *Builder*, 17 May 1884, p. 729.

87. See chapter 1. John Ruskin, *The Stones of Venice*, volume 1, in E. T. Cook and Alexander Wedderburn, eds., *The Works of John Ruskin*, Library edition, volume 9 (London: George Allen; New York: Longmans, Green and Company, 1903), p. 38. GES, "The True Principles of Architecture, and the Possibility of Developement," *Ecclesiologist* 13 (1852): 253.

88. Journals with evaluative reviews (those with stars favored Burges): *Athenaeum, Belgravia, Builder, Building News* (*), *Chronicle* (*), *Civil Engineer and Architect's Journal* (*), *Ecclesiologist* (*), *Engineer, Illustrated London News, Law Times* (*), *Quarterly Review, Saturday Review* (*), *Solicitors' Journal, Spectator, Standard* (*), *Times*. No attempt has been made to study the views of provincial newspapers. Only one foreign review has been found (see n. 141).

89. Burges, *Law Courts Commission*, p. 16.

90. *Ibid.*

91. "The New Law Courts," *Ecclesiologist* 28 (1867): 117–18.

92. "The Competition for the Law Courts," *Saturday Review*, 4 May 1863, p. 563.

93. "The Courts of Justice Competition: Article X," *Building News*, 22 March 1867, pp. 202–3.

94. "The Courts of Justice Competition," *Civil Engineer and Architect's Journal*, 1 April 1867, p. 98.

95. [leading article], *Standard*, 15 March 1867, p. 4.

96. "The Courts of Justice Competition: Article X," *Building News*, 22 March 1867, pp. 202–3.

97. "The Law and the Lawyers: The New Courts of Justice," *Law Times*, 27 July 1867, p. 190.

98. Burges, *Law Courts Commission*, p.16.

99. The courtroom and judges' hall interiors, both photographically reproduced in the illustrated edition of the report, are by Haig. The former is now at the Victoria and Albert Museum. The bird's-eye view and the view of Temple Bar (*Building News*, 3 May 1867) are probably his work.

100. Dudley Harbron, *The Conscious Stone. The Life of Edward William Godwin* (London: Latimer House, 1949), p. 57. J. Mordaunt Crook, *William Burges and the High Victorian Dream* (Chicago: University of Chicago Press, 1981), p. 247.

101. "The New Law Courts," *Ecclesiologist* 28 (1867): 119.

102. "Fine Arts: The Courts of Justice," *Athenaeum*, 16 February 1867, p. 227.

103. "Art: The New Law Courts' Designs," *Spectator*, 23 February 1867, p. 213. [Philip Smith and J. T. Emmett], "The New Courts of Law. Courts of Justice Commission: Instructions for the Competing Architects," *Quarterly Review* 123 (July 1867): 111. "New Courts-of-Justice Designs," *Belgravia*, March 1867, p. 42. "The New Courts of Law," *Times*, 11 February 1867, p. 12.

104. "The New Courts of Law," *Times*, 11 February 1867, p. 12. "The Courts of Justice Competition," *Civil Engineer and Architect's Journal*, 1 March 1867, p. 70. The plan was also praised in "The New Law Courts," *Solicitors' Journal*, 16 February 1867, pp. 353–54. The design was ranked as one of three most likely winners (together with those of Scott and Lockwood) in "The Designs for the New Law Courts," *Engineer*, 15 February 1867, p. 140.

105. "The Courts of Justice Competition: Article IV," *Building News*, 8 February 1867, p. 95.

106. "Report of the Commissioners," p. 140.

107. Waterhouse, *Courts of Justice Competition*, p. 20.

108. "Art: The New Law Courts' Designs," *Spectator*, 23 February 1867, p. 213. The exterior appearance was also favorably reviewed in "New Courts-of-Justice Designs," *Belgravia*, March 1867, p. 40; and "The Competition for the Law Courts," *Saturday Review*, 4 June 1867, p. 562.

109. "The Courts of Justice Competition: Article IV," *Building News*, 8 February 1867, p. 95.

110. "Fine Arts: The Courts of Justice," *Athenaeum*, 9 March 1867, p. 327.

111. "The Designs for the New Law Courts," *Engineer*, 15 February 1867, p. 140; and "The Courts of Justice Competition," *Civil Engineer and Architect's Journal*, 1 March 1867, p. 70.

112. "The New Law Courts," *Ecclesiologist* 28 (1867): 131; "The Designs for the New Law Courts," *Chronicle*, 11 May 1867, p. 162; "The Competition for the Law Courts," *Saturday Review*, 4 May 1867, p. 562; and "New Courts-of-Justice Designs," *Belgravia*, March 1867, p. 40.

113. "The Courts of Justice Competition: Article IV," *Building News*, 8 February 1867, p. 96.

114. Seddon, *New Law Courts*, p. 4. The French character of his design was identified in "New Courts-of-Justice Designs," *Belgravia*, March 1867, p. 42; and "The Courts of Justice Competition: Article VI," *Building News*, 22 February 1867, p. 137.

115. One of these photographs was published in his *Description*. Four others are at the BAL Drawings Collection. He also submitted two smaller models of an equity court and a principal staircase.

116. "Fine Arts: The Courts of Justice," *Athenaeum*, 23 March 1867, p. 391.

117. "The Courts of Justice Competition: Article VI," *Building News*, 22 February 1867, p. 137.

118. "The New Courts of Law," *Times*, 11 February 1867, p. 12. "Art: The New Law Courts' Designs," *Spectator*, 23 February 1867, p. 212.

119. "Designs for the Proposed Law Courts," *Builder*, 16 February 1867, p. 109.

120. "The New Law Courts," *Solicitors' Journal*, 23 February 1867, p. 373.

121. Seddon, *New Law Courts*, p. 6.

122. "The Designs for the New Law Courts," *Engineer*, 15 February 1867, p. 140.

123. [Philip Smith and J. T. Emmett], "The New Courts of Law: Courts of Justice Commission, Instructions for the Competing Architects," *Quarterly Review* 123 (July 1867): 111.

124. "The Competition for the Law Courts," *Saturday Review*, 4 May 1867, p. 562.

125. "The Designs for the New Law Courts," *Chronicle*, 11 May 1867, p. 161. Other reviews which found the design too churchlike included: "New Courts-of-Justice Designs," *Belgravia*, March 1867, p. 40; "Fine Arts: The Courts of Justice," *Athenaeum*, 16 February 1867, p. 227; "The Courts of Justice Competition," *Civil Engineer and Architect's Journal*, 1 April 1867, p. 101; "The Courts of Justice Competition: Article XI," *Building News*, 29 March 1867, p. 219; "Designs for the Proposed Law Courts," *Builder*, 9 February 1867, p. 89.

126. Quoted in "Designs for the Proposed Law Courts," *Builder*, 9 February 1867, p. 89.

127. John Summerson, *Victorian Architecture: Four Studies in Evaluation* (New York: Columbia University Press, 1970), pp. 108–9.

128. "The Competition for the Law Courts," *Saturday Review*, 4 May 1867, p. 561.

129. "The Courts of Justice Competition: Article IX," *Building News*, 15 March 1867, pp. 186–87. Other critics of the disconnected façade were: "Designs for the Proposed Law Courts," *Builder*, 16 February 1867, p. 108; "The Designs for the New Law Courts," *Engineer*, 15 February 1867, p. 140; "Art: The New Law Courts' Designs," *Spectator*, 23 February 1867, p. 213; "The Designs for the New Law Courts," *Chronicle*, 11 May 1867, p. 161.

130. "New Courts-of-Justice Designs," *Belgravia*, March 1867, p. 43.

131. *Ibid.*, p. 38.

132. Quoted in "The Courts of Justice Competition," *Civil Engineer and Architect's Journal*, 1 April 1867, p. 103.

133. *Ibid.*, p. 104. "The Competition for the Law Courts," *Saturday Review*, 4 May 1867, p. 561.

134. On Lockwood's popularity see: "The Courts of Justice Competition Article VII," *Building News*, 1 March 1867, pp. 153–54; and "The Competition for the Law Courts," *Saturday Review*, 4 May 1867, p. 561.

135. "The Designs for the New Law Courts," *Engineer*, 15 February 1867,

p. 140. Favored equally were Waterhouse and Scott.

136. "The Designs for the Law Courts," *Builder*, 23 March 1867, p. 208.

137. "The Courts of Justice Competition," *Civil Engineer and Architect's Journal*, 1 March 1867, p. 72.

138. "The Competition for the Law Courts," *Saturday Review*, 4 May 1867, p. 561. Similar views were expressed in: "The Courts of Justice Competition: Article VII," *Building News*, 1 March 1867, pp. 153–54; [Philip Smith and J. T. Emmett], "The New Courts of Law: Courts of Justice Commission, Instructions for the Competing Architects," *Quarterly Review*, 123 (July 1867): 111–12; "New Courts-of-Justice Designs," *Belgravia*, March 1867, p. 44; "Art: The New Law Courts' Designs," *Spectator*, 23 February 1867, p. 212.

139. "The Courts of Justice Competition: Article VIII," *Building News*, 8 March 1867, p. 169.

140. "New Courts-of-Justice Designs," *Belgravia*, March 1867, p. 46.

141. "The New Law Courts Designs," *Illustrated London News*, 23 February 1867, p. 194. In the only review that has been found in a journal from the Continent, Alfred Strong complimented Garling's entry: "Statt einer Gruppe unabhängiger Häuser haben wir hier eine imposante ruhige Masse." "Der Neue Justizpalast in London," *Allgemeine Bauzeitung* 32 (1867): 205.

142. Garling, *New Courts of Justice*, diagram opposite p. 4.

143. Quoted in "The Courts of Justice Competition," *Civil Engineer and Architect's Journal*, 1 April 1867, p. 99.

144. Edward M. Barry, *Lectures on Architecture Delivered at the Royal Academy* (London: John Murray, 1881), pp. 351–52.

145. "The National Gallery Competition," *Building News*, 11 January 1867, p. 16.

146. "The Courts of Justice Competition," *Building News*, 25 January 1867, p. 58.

147. "The Courts of Justice Competition," *Civil Engineer and Architect's Journal*, 1 April 1867, p. 102.

148. "The New Courts of Law," *Times*, 11 February 1867, p. 12. Other un-

favorable reviews included: "The New Law Courts," *Ecclesiologist* 28 (1867): 116; "The Designs for the New Law Courts," *Engineer*, 15 February 1867, p. 140; "The Competition for the Law Courts," *Saturday Review*, 4 May 1867, p. 562; "The Designs for the New Law Courts," *Chronicle*, 11 May 1867, p. 162.

149. "Designs for the Proposed Law Courts," *Builder*, 9 February 1867, p. 89.

150. "The Law Courts Competition," *Builder*, 22 June 1867, p. 444.

151. Scott discussed the Gothic dome in his 1873 Royal Academy lectures (written in 1872). He told his audience, "That [Gothic] revival needs but such a welcoming of all that is good and noble to render it *complete*, and no feature possesses these qualities in a higher degree than the cupola. Let us, therefore, make it our own." G.G. Scott, *Lectures on the Rise and Development of Mediaeval Architecture* (London: John Murray, 1879), 2:289.

152. "Fine Arts: The Courts of Justice," *Athenaeum*, 23 February 1867, p. 259.

153. "The Courts of Justice Competition," *Civil Engineer and Architect's Journal*, 1 March 1867, p. 68. "The Courts of Justice Competition: Article III," *Building News*, 1 February 1867, pp. 79–80. Other fundamentally negative reviews of his elevations included: "The New Law Courts," *Ecclesiologist* 28 (1867): 120; "Art: The New Law Courts' Designs," *Spectator*, 23 February 1867, p. 213; "The Designs for the New Law Courts," *Chronicle*, 11 May 1867, p. 162; [Philip Smith and J. T. Emmett], "The New Courts of Law: Courts of Justice Commission, Instructions for the Competing Architects," *Quarterly Review* 123 (July 1867): 110.

154. "The New Courts-of-Justice Designs," *Belgravia*, March 1867, p. 37. Of course, Scott's enormous reputation salvaged some compliments for him. He was identified as one of the favorites, along with Waterhouse and Lockwood, in "The Designs for the New Law Courts," *Engineer*, 15 February 1867, p. 140. It criticized his design for "want of solemnity," however. The *Standard* also initially favored Scott: "Designs for the New Courts of Justice," *Stan-*

dard, 9 February 1867, p. 6. Later, it switched allegiance to Burges.

155. Quoted in "The Courts of Justice Competition: Article III," *Building News*, 1 February 1867, p. 80.

156. "Fine Arts: The Courts of Justice," *Athenaeum*, 23 February 1867, p. 259.

157. GES, *Proposed New Courts of Justice*, p. 32.

158. See chapter 1.

159. GES, *Proposed New Courts of Justice*, p. 16.

160. *Ibid.*, p. 31. An allusion to the *salle des pas perdus* in the Palais de Justice, Paris, may also have been intended. There the medieval plan, with a row of central columns, was preserved by a Renaissance rebuilding.

161. Scott, *Recollections*, p. 213 (from the portion written in 1864). Stefan Muthesius, *The High Victorian Movement in Architecture, 1850–1870* (London and Boston: Routledge and Kegan Paul, 1972), pp. 138–40.

162. Paul Joyce has discussed the early examples of Street's return to English precedent with the author.

163. "The Study of Foreign Gothic Architecture, and Its Influence on English Art," *The Church and the World: Essays on Questions of the Day*, ed. Orby Shipley. (London: Longmans, Green, Reader, and Dyer, 1866), pp. 397–411. "Architecture in the Thirteenth Century," *The Afternoon Lectures on Literature and Art*, eds. Robert H. Martley and R. Denny Urbin 4s (London: Bell and Daldy, and Dublin, Hodges and Smith, and W. McGee, 1867), pp. 1–45. Both by GES.

164. "The Study of Foreign Gothic Architecture," p. 400.

165. *Ibid.*, pp. 398, 400.

166. "Architecture in the Thirteenth Century," p. 16.

167. GES, "A Lecture Delivered at the Royal Academy Last Session," *Architect*, 23 December 1871, p. 311. Read on 9 March 1871.

168. GES, "Architecture, Thirteenth Century," *St. Paul's Ecclesiological Society Transactions* 1 (1881–85): 71. Read 21 May 1879.

169. "Fine Arts: The Courts of Justice," *Athenaeum*, 23 March 1867, p. 391.

170. [Philip Smith and J. T. Emmett], "The New Courts of Law: Courts of Justice Commission, Instructions for the Competing Architects," *Quarterly Review* 123 (July 1867): 112.

171. "The Designs for the Law Courts," *Builder*, 2 March 1867, p. 144.

172. "The Courts of Justice Competition: Article V," *Building News*, 15 February 1867, p. 117.

173. "The Designs for the New Law Courts," *Chronicle*, 11 May 1867, p. 162.

174. "The New Law Courts," *Ecclesiologist* 28 (1867): 117.

175. "The Competition for the Law Courts," *Saturday Review*, 4 May 1867, p. 562. "The Courts of Justice Competition," *Civil Engineer and Architect's Journal*, 1 April 1867, p. 99. "The Courts-of-Justice Designs," *Belgravia*, March 1867, p. 41.

176. GES, *Proposed New Courts of Justice*, pp. 6–7.

177. "Designs for the Proposed Law Courts," *Builder*, 16 February 1867, p. 108.

178. GES, *Proposed New Courts of Justice*, p. 10.

179. "Designs for the Proposed Law Courts," *Builder*, 16 February 1867, p. 108.

180. "Report of the Commissioners," p. 58.

181. AES, *Memoir*, p. 52.

182. GES, *Some Remarks in Explanation of his Designs for (1) Rebuilding and (2) Enlarging the National Gallery* (London: J. E. Taylor and Company, 1867), p. 24.

183. "The National Gallery Competition," *Building News*, 11 January 1867, p. 16.

184. GES, *Proposed New Courts of Justice*, p. 26.

185. Gladstone Diaries.

186. *Hansard*, 3s 182 (22 March 1866): 776.

187. "Report of the Commissioners," p. 6. For representative correspondence see: BAL, Waterhouse Letterbook 1864–67, volume 2, p. 266 (18 December 1866), Waterhouse to Field; pp. 475–76 (14 January 1867), Waterhouse to Field; pp. 565–66 (29 January 1867), Waterhouse to Field.

188. One on the Spot [letter], "Fair

Play for the New Law Courts," *Builder*, 23 February 1867, p. 135.

189. "Fair Play for the Law Courts Designs," *Builder*, 16 March 1867, p. 193. Further discussion of Field's conduct: A Member of the Solicitors' Committee [letter, author thus identified by publishing error], "Fair Play for the Law Courts Competition," *Builder*, 2 March 1867, p. 154; Alfred Bell and Member of the Solicitors' Committee [letters], "Fair Play for the Law Courts," *Builder*, 9 March 1867, p. 175. Waterhouse was not specifically named as the beneficiary of Field's favoritism, but the letter printed on March 2 links the secretary's efforts to other endeavors on behalf of Waterhouse.

190. *Hansard*, 3s 185 (22 February 1867): 824. BAL, Waterhouse Letterbook 1864–67, volume 2, p. 711 (23 February 1867), Waterhouse to Field; p. 784 (28 February 1867), Waterhouse to Field; p. 790 [A] (1 March 1867), Waterhouse to Powell; p. 790 [B] (1 March 1867), Waterhouse to Field.

191. A Member of the Solicitors' Committee [letter, author thus identified by publishing error], "Fair Play for the Law Courts Competition," *Builder*, 2 March 1867, p. 154.

192. BAL, Waterhouse Letterbook 1864–67, volume 1, pp. 556–57 (18 February 1865), Waterhouse to Henry Paull; p. 558 (18 February 1865), Waterhouse to Thomas Bazley; p. 633 (3 March 1865), Waterhouse to Charles Bursiton.

193. A Member of the Solicitors' Committee [letter, author thus identified by publishing error], "Fair Play for the Law Courts Competition," *Builder*, 2 March 1867, p. 154.

194. BAL, Waterhouse Letterbook 1864–67, volume 2, p. 54 (28? November 1866), Waterhouse to J. D. Burton (photographer). Many more letters follow on this subject.

195. BAL, Waterhouse Letterbook 1864–67, volume 2, pp. 643–44 (11 February 1867), Waterhouse to Field; p. 649 (12 February 1867), Waterhouse to Field; pp. 662–63 (13 February 1867), Waterhouse to Field. He expressed similar feelings to Henry A. Hunt of the Office of Works on

26 April 1867. This letter is preserved in the copy at the Library of the Property Services Agency, Department of the Environment, Croydon, of Waterhouse's *Courts of Justice Competition*.

196. "Report of the Commissioners," p. 66.

197. E. W. Pugin [letter], "The New Law Courts," *Times*, 13 September 1871, p. 10, dated 9 September 1871.

198. E. W. Pugin [letter], "English Architecture," *Standard*, 18 March 1867, p. 3, dated 16 March 1867. In addition, see: E. W. Pugin [letter], "Modern Architecture," *Standard*, 5 April 1867, p. 7; and E. W. Pugin [letter], "Correspondence: The New Law Courts," *Building News*, 28 June 1867, pp. 448–49, dated June 1867.

199. *Westminster Gazette*, March 1867, reprinted in "The Designs for the New Palace of Justice," *Building News*, 15 March 1867, pp. 197–98. The anonymous author of this essay also wrote three letters pointedly attacking Burges: "Modern Architecture," *Standard*, 5 April 1867, p. 7; "Modern Architecture," *Standard*, 17 April 1867, p. 5, dated 9 April 1867; and "Modern Architecture," *Standard*, 25 April 1867, p. 5. These prompted a defense of Burges by the correspondent "Philocalus": "English Architecture," *Standard*, 21 March 1867, p. 3, dated 19 March 1867; "Modern Architecture," *Standard*, 9 April 1867, p. 5; and "Modern Architecture," *Standard*, 20 April 1867, p. 2.

200. "The Law Courts: Mr. Street and the 'Times,'" *Architect*, 2 September 1871, p. 113.

201. "Report of the Commissioners," p. 56.

202. *Ibid.*, p. 60.

203. *Ibid.*, pp. 67–70. Some tied first place points were awarded.

204. *Hansard*, 3s 182 (22 March 1866): 780.

205. "Report of the Commissioners," p. 61.

206. *Ibid.*

207. *Hansard*, 3s 185 (22 February 1867): 814–20. *Hansard*, 3s 186 (3 May 1867): 2018–20.

208. "Report of the Commissioners," pp. 62–66.

209. *Ibid.*, pp. 73–79.

210. *Ibid.*, p. 70.

211. Port, ed., *Houses of Parliament,* p. 227.

212. "Report of the Commissioners," p. 72.

213. Scott's letter of 9 January 1867 and Garling's of 16 January 1867 appear in *ibid.*, p. 57. Scott also circulated a printed version of his letter, dated 14 February 1867, a copy of which is among Gladstone's papers: BL Add. MS. 44607 ff.61–62.

214. "Report of the Commissioners," pp. 100, 101, 103. PRO Works 12/33/1 ff.74–75 (1 July 1867), Abraham to the commission, printed.

215. Published in "New Courts of Justice: Copy of Treasury Minute of the 23rd Day of December 1865, of the Award of the Judges, and, Further Correspondence Relative thereto," *BPP,* volume 55 in 1867–68, p. 2.

216. "The Law Courts Competition," *Builder,* 10 August 1867, p. 593.

217. *Hansard,* 3s 190 (29 June 1868): 330.

218. *Ibid.,* 333.

219. *Hansard,* 3s 190 (15 May 1868): 367.

220. *Hansard,* 3s 190 (29 June 1868): 337.

221. "The Law Courts: Mr. Street and the 'Times,' " *Architect,* 2 September 1871, p. 113.

222. As noted below, in 1868 Street sought Gladstone's assistance in defeating an effort to overturn his appointment. Street appealed again to Gladstone in 1871 and 1873 when the Office of Works was reluctant to approve his plans. (See chapter 5.) Further circumstantial evidence suggests that Gladstone's architectural taste at the time of the competition may have been inclined in favor of Street. His diaries (19–22 December 1866) show that he had been reading Viollet-le-Duc's *Essay on Military Architecture* (1860), and its illustrations of strong, simple, fortification architecture may have turned his attention toward what elements of early French muscularity remained in Street's work. Gladstone is also known to have been familiar with the reviews of the designs printed in the *Quarterly Review* and

the *Spectator.* The former, which preferred Street while condemning the whole of the competition on general grounds, is cited in the diaries on 18 July 1867. The latter, which preferred Waterhouse but also commended Street, Burges, and Brandon, is preserved among Gladstone's papers: BL Add. MS. 44607 ff.66–67.

223. It should be noted that the private papers of the judges, so far as they are known, have been consulted. Nothing in the letters and diaries of Cockburn, Gladstone, or Palmer casts any further light on the decision.

224. "New Courts of Justice," pp. 2–3.

225. The Treasury had asked the Office of Works to suggest a surveyor on 18 March 1867, and on 29 March 1867 Gardiner was recommended. He was paid £525. PRO Works 12/33/1 ff.22–29. "Report of the Commissioners," p. 104.

226. The percentage increases and Gardiner's estimates for the other architects are: Abraham (16%, £1,428,542), Brandon (45%, £2,052,968), Burges (9%, £1,733,257), Deane (32%, £1,419,916), Lockwood (45%, £1,789,934), Scott (35%, £1,726,494), Seddon (30%, £2,665,953).

227. *Hansard,* 3s 189 (9 August 1867): 1221.

228. Gladstone's letters are recorded in his diary. They are not extant.

229. BL Add. MS. 44413 f.180 (4 October 1867), Cockburn to Gladstone.

230. "New Courts of Justice," p. 3.

231. PRO Works 12/33/1 ff.78–79, printed copy. Brandon also seems to have published a brochure, referred to by Street in "Report of the Commissioners," p. 105.

232. "Report of the Commissioners," p. 105.

233. Scott, *Recollections,* p. 275.

234. G. G. Scott [letter], "The Law Courts Competition," *Builder,* 24 August 1867, p. 630.

235. Scott, *Recollections,* p. 275.

236. "Report of the Commissioners," p. 106.

237. *Ibid.*

238. PRO T1/6776A/4420 f.1469 (20 November 1868), Deane to Treasury.

239. GES, *The New Courts of Justice:*

Notes in Reply to Some Criticisms, 2d ed. (London: Oxford, and Cambridge, Rivingtons, 1872), p. 23. Barry also spoke of their consultation in E. M. Barry [letter], "Fine Arts. The Law Courts," *Athenaeum*, 21 February 1872, pp. 247–48.

240. "Report of the Commissioners," pp. 105–6.

241. *Ibid.*, p. 105.

242. PRO T1/6835B/19182 f.1696 (20 January 1868), Barry to Derby. Published in "Copy of Correspondence with the Two Architects Recommended by the Judges of Designs for the New Courts of Justice," *BPP*, volume 47 in 1868–69, p. 2.

243. PRO T1/6835B/19182 f.1697 (20 January 1868), GES to Derby. Published in "Copy of Correspondence with the Two Architects," p. 3.

244. Scott, *Recollections*, p. 191.

245. [leading article], *Times*, 19 November 1867, p. 7.

246. "The New Law Courts," *Ecclesiologist* 28 (1867): 292.

247. "The Designs for the New Law Courts," *Building News*, 6 December 1867, p. 841. The endorsement of Burges in this article is strongly implied but not stated explicitly.

248. "The Courts of Law Competition," *Builder*, 28 December 1867, p. 936.

249. William Watkiss Lloyd, "The New Law Courts," *Builder*, 7 December 1867, pp. 884–85.

250. E. W. Pugin [letter], "The New Law Courts," *Times*, 15 August 1867, p. 9.

251. W. E. G. [letter], "The New Law Courts," *Times*, 20 August 1867, p. 10, dated 17 August 1867. This cannot be Gladstone.

252. GES [letter], "The New Law Courts," *Times*, 4 September 1867, p. 7.

253. E. W. Godwin [letter], "The New Law Courts," *Times*, 20 August 1867, p. 10.

254. M. D. Wyatt [letter], "The New Law Courts," *Times*, 20 November 1867, p. 12, dated 19 November 1867.

255. *Hansard*, 3s 190 (29 November 1867): 417–18. *Hansard*, 3s 190 (14 February 1868): 732–33.

256. *Hansard*, 3s 192 (12 May 1868): 105–7.

257. *Hansard*, 3s 192 (14 May 1868): 290.

258. *Hansard*, 3s 192 (15 May 1868): 362–71.

259. *Hansard*, 3s 192 (29 May 1868): 1045.

260. *Ibid.*, p. 1051.

261. "Report of the Commissioners," pp. 105–6.

262. *Ibid.*, p. 108.

263. It is referred to in a memorandum written on PRO T1/6776A/4420 f.3679.

264. PRO T1/6776A/4420 f.3679 (26 February 1868), Barry to G. W. Hunt. Printed in "Copy of Correspondence with the Two Architects," pp. 4–5.

265. "Report of the Commissioners," p. 108.

266. *Ibid.*

267. *Ibid.*

268. PRO T1/6835B/19182 f.8056.

269. "Report of the Commissioners," pp. 106–7.

270. A copy of the letter to Street is PRO Works 12/33/1 f.80 (9 June 1868), G. Sclater Booth (Treasury secretary) to GES.

271. GES [letter], "Correspondence: Mr. E. M. Barry and Mr. Street," *Building News*, 23 February 1872, p. 161, dated 19 February 1867. The *Builder*'s report is "The New Law Courts," *Builder*, 6 June 1868, p. 406.

272. GES [letter], "Correspondence: Mr. E. M. Barry and Mr. Street," *Building News*, 23 February 1872, p. 161, dated 19 February 1867.

273. GES [letter], "Fine Arts: The Law Courts," *Athenaeum*, 2 March 1872, p. 278.

274. Quoted in BL Add. MS. 44415 ff.237–40 (29 June 1868), GES to Gladstone.

275. E. M. Barry [letter], "Fine Arts: The Law Courts," *Athenaeum*, 21 February 1872, p. 247. E. M. Barry, *The New Law Courts and the National Gallery: Facts Relating to the Late Competitions, With a Reply to Portions of Mr. Street's Recent Pamphlet* (London: Macmillan and Company, 1872), p. 13.

276. GES, *The New Courts of Justice: Notes in Reply to Some Criticisms*, pp. 22–23.

277. PRO T1/6835B/19182 f.8870 (10 June 1868), GES to Treasury.

278. Quoted in BL Add. MS. 44415 ff.237–40 (29 June 1868), GES to Gladstone.

279. Printed in "New Courts of Justice," p. 7. The original is not extant.

280. Copy of the original: PRO Works 12/33/1 ff. 83–90 (8 June 1868), Barry to G. Sclater Booth (Treasury secretary). E. M. Barry [letter], "The New Law Courts," Times, 15 June 1868, p. 5. The letter was also printed as "General Correspondence: The New Law Courts," Solicitors' Journal, 20 June 1868, pp. 701–2. It was quoted in "The Proposed Law Courts," Builder, 13 June 1868, p. 421; and "The Law and the Lawyers: The Architect of the New Law Courts," Law Times, 20 June 1868, p. 140.

281. PRO T1/6835B/19182 f.9532 (13 June 1868), Barry to G. Sclater Booth (Treasury secretary).

282. Hansard, 3s 192 (19 June 1868): 1837–38.

283. Ibid., 1844.

284. Ibid., 1838–42.

285. Printed in "New Courts of Justice," pp. 12–14. The original is not extant.

286. BL Add. MS. 38995 ff.233–34 (24 June 1868), GES to Layard.

287. Thomas H. Street [letter], "General Correspondence: The New Law Courts," Solicitors' Journal, 4 July 1868, pp. 749–50.

288. BL Add. MS. 44415 ff.237–40 (29 June 1868), GES to Gladstone.

289. Hansard, 3s 193 (29 June 1868): 329.

290. Ibid., 330.

291. Ibid., 333–34.

292. Ibid., 341–42.

293. Reported in "Our Office Table," Building News, 3 July 1868, p. 459. Hansard, 3s 193 (29 June 1868): 343.

294. PRO T1/6835B/19182 f.10299 (29 June 1868), Barry to G. Sclater Booth (Treasury secretary). Printed in "Copy of Correspondence with the Two Architects," p. 5. The 20 January 1868 letters were not published until 1869.

295. E. M. Barry [letter], "New Law Courts," Builder, 18 July 1868, p. 534. E. M. Barry [letter], "Solicitors' Journal:

The New Law Courts," Law Times, 18 July 1868, p. 224. E. M. Barry [letter], "General Correspondence: New Law Courts," Solicitors' Journal, 18 July 1868, p. 788.

296. E. M. Barry [letter], "The New Law Courts," Times, 3 July 1868, p. 11.

297. PRO T1/6835B/19182 f.11418 (21 July 1868), Barry to G. Sclater Booth (Treasury secretary). Printed in "Copy of Correspondence with the Two Architects," pp. 5–8.

298. E. M. Barry [letter], "Solicitors' Journal: The Architect of the New Law Courts," Law Times, 1 August 1868, pp. 264–65. E. M. Barry [letter], "The New Law Courts," Times, 1 August 1868, p. 4, dated 31 July 1868. "General Correspondence: The New Law Courts," Solicitors' Journal, 1 August 1868, p. 824.

299. PRO T1/6835B/19182 f.11418, Clerke memo dated 23 July 1868.

300. BL Add. MS. 44536 f.79v (19 December 1868), Gladstone to Barry. Barry's letter of 30 November 1868 is not extant.

301. PRO T1/6835B/19182 f.19182 (21 December 1868), Barry to Treasury secretary. Printed in "Copy of Correspondence with the Two Architects," pp. 8–10.

302. PRO T1/6835B/19182 f.19182, Clerke memo dated 26 December 1868.

303. "The Proposed Law Courts," Builder, 13 June 1868, p. 421.

304. "The Proposed Law Courts," Builder, 1 August 1868, p. 577.

305. "The Royal Institute of British Architects: Opening Night," Builder, 7 November 1868, pp. 814–15.

306. "The Law and the Lawyers: The Architect of the New Law Courts," Law Times, 20 June 1868, p. 140.

307. "The Law and the Lawyers," Law Times, 27 June 1868, p. 156. "The Law and the Lawyers: A Palace of Law," Law Times, 25 July 1868, p. 237.

308. "General Correspondence: New Law Courts," Solicitors' Journal, 18 July 1868, p. 788, editor's note after Barry's 29 June 1868 letter.

309. [leading article], Times, 30 June 1868, p. 11.

310. "The New Law Courts and the National Gallery," Building News, 12 June

1868, p. 401. "The New Law Courts," *Building News*, 26 June 1868, p. 432.

311. "Our Office Table," *Building News*, 3 July 1868, p. 459.

312. G. G. Scott [letter], "The Designs for the Law Courts," *Times*, 2 July 1868, p. 10, dated 1 July 1868.

313. E. W. Pugin [letter], "The New Law Courts," *Times*, 23 June 1868, p. 11, dated 20 June 1868.

314. E. M. Barry [letter], "Fine Arts: The Law Courts," *Athenaeum*, 21 February 1872, p. 248.

315. Scott, *Recollections*, pp. 276–77.

Notes to Chapter 4

1. BL Add. MS. 38995 ff.233–34 (24 June 1868), GES to Layard.

2. PRO T1/6835B/19182 f.8870 (10 June 1868), GES to G. Sclater Booth (Treasury secretary).

3. "Report of the Commissioners Appointed to Advise and Report as to the Buildings Proper to Be Erected and the Plans upon which Such Buildings Shall Be Erected, for the New Courts of Justice . . . ," *BPP*, volume 20 in 1871, p. 109.

4. *Ibid.*

5. PRO Works 12/33/1 f.98 (23 June 1868), GES to Alfred Austin (secretary of works); Works 12/33/1 f.99 (26 June 1868), GES to Austin; Works 12/33/1 f.100 (26 June 1868), Austin to Treasury lords; Works 12/33/1 ff.101–2 (3 July 1868), G. Sclater Booth (Treasury secretary) to Manners; Works 12/33/1 f.103 (6 July 1868), Austin to GES; Works 12/33/1 f.109 (9 October 1868), Office of Works memo on coal and gas; Works 12/33/1 f.110 (12 October 1868), Austin to GES; T1/6835B/19182 f.9925 (23 June 1868), Field to G. Sclater Booth.

6. "Report of the Commissioners," pp. 109–10.

7. *Ibid.*, p. 110.

8. *Ibid.*, p. 121.

9. So called by Robert Lowe on July 9, 1869. Street adopted the term. "Report from the Select Committee on the New Law Courts; together with the Proceedings of the Committee, Minutes of Evidence, and Appendix," *BPP*, volume 10 in 1868–69, p. 34.

10. "Report of the Commissioners," pp. 110–12.

11. GES, *New Law Courts: Block Plans and Sections Prepared by George Edmund Street, A.R.A., the Architect to the New Courts, and Approved by the Courts of Justice Commission, 23rd July 1868; Details Added, October 1868* (London: Kell Brothers, 1868).

12. PRO Works 30/2235. This detail drawing of a typical courtroom, in plan and section, was prepared after the approval by the commission of the general plans in July. "Report of the Commissioners," p. 120.

13. PRO Works 12/34/4 ff.62–68, undated report by GES, c.1871.

14. "Report from the Select Committee," p. 52.

15. "Report of the Commissioners," p. 121.

16. "The New Law Courts," *Building News*, 19 May 1876, p. 489.

17. "Manchester Townhall Designs," *Building News*, 13 March 1868, pp. 176–77.

18. Society for the Encouragement of Arts, Manufactures, and Commerce, *Proceedings of a Committee Appointed by the Council of the Society of Arts, to Report upon the Best Way of Dealing with the Thames Embankment* (London, 1869), p. 34. The drawing is lost.

19. "The Architectural Conference: English Architecture Thirty Years Hence," *Builder*, 17 May 1884, p. 714.

20. Andor Gomme, Michael Jenner, and Bryan Little, *Bristol: An Architectural History* (London: Lund Humphries, 1979), pp. 316–17, 429.

21. In the revised plan the probate department had asked for twin towers instead of one. One was for original wills, the other for copies.

22. "Report of the Commissioners," p. 120.

23. *Ibid.*, pp. 121–23.

24. *Ibid.*, pp. 123–24.

25. *Ibid.*, p. 124; copy at PRO Works

12/33/1 ff.158–60 (25 January 1869), George Hamilton (Treasury secretary) to Field.

26. "Report of the Commissioners," p. 124.

27. PRO Works 12/33/1 f.161 (5 February 1869), George Russell (assistant secretary of works) to Treasury lords.

28. As reported by George Pownall to William Cowper, the former first comissioner, on 22 May 1869. Letter printed in "Copy of the Report from the Surveyor of Her Majesty's Works and Public Buildings to the First Commissioner on the Sites Prospect for the Courts and Offices of Law," *BPP*, volume 47 in 1868–69, p. 6. Copy also in Layard Papers: BL Add. MS. 38996 f.212.

29. By Robert Lowe: *Hansard*, 3s 195 (20 April 1869): 1254; and *Hansard*, 3s 196 (10 May 1869): 558.

30. "Report of the Commissioners," pp. 112–13. Pownall's estimate was actually for £667,120, but it was rounded upward by the commission. His original estimate is PRO Works 12/36/2 ff.3–4 (18 July 1868), Pownall to Austin. It is reprinted in appendix 4 of "Report from the Select Committee," p. 180.

31. PRO Works 12/36/2 f.23 (August 1868), Treasury to Manners.

32. PRO Works 12/36/2 ff.24–25 (18 August 1868), Cheffins to Austin.

33. PRO Works 12/36/2 f.92 (December 1868), Cheffins to Austin.

34. "Report of the Commissioners," pp. 111–13.

35. They assumed that Street had not so reduced accommodation in the great plan as to warrant a lower estimate.

36. Letter of M. H. Foster to Hunt (23 October 1868), reprinted as appendix 5 of "Report from the Select Committee," pp. 181–82.

37. "The Law and the Lawyers: A Palace of Law," *Law Times*, 25 July 1868, p. 237.

38. [leading article], *Times*, 22 July 1868, p. 9.

39. Reported in "The Royal Institute of British Architects: Opening Night," *Builder*, 7 November 1868, pp. 814–15.

40. *Ibid.*

41. For Layard see: William N. Bruce, ed., *Sir Henry Layard, G.C.B., D.C.L.: Autobiography and Letters*, 2 vols. (London: John Murray, 1903); and Gordon Waterfield, *Layard of Nineveh* (London: John Murray, 1963).

42. Layard recorded his excavations in: *Nineveh and Its Remains* (London: John Murray, 1849); and *Nineveh and Babylon* (London: John Murray, 1853).

43. For Lowe see: Arthur Patchett Martin, *The Life and Letters of the Right Honourable Robert Lowe, Viscount Sherbrooke*, 2 vols. (London and New York: Longmans, Green and Company, 1893); and James Winter, *Robert Lowe* (Toronto and Buffalo: University of Toronto Press, 1976).

44. [Robert Lowe], "Mr. Gladstone's Financial Statements," *Home and Foreign Review* 4 (1864): 18.

45. F. H. W. Sheppard, ed., *Survey of London, Volume 38, The Museums Area of South Kensington and Westminster* (London: University of London, 1975), p. 207.

46. Layard may also have discussed the matter with him privately at an earlier date. See BL Add. MS. 38996 ff.40–41 (20 January 1869), GES to Layard.

47. PRO Works 12/1 ff.280–81 (14 December 1868), GES to Layard.

48. BL. Add. MS. 38996 ff.1–2 (5 January 1869), Layard to Lowe. The directions to GES are quoted in Add. MS. 38996 ff.42–43 (21 January 1869), GES to Edmund Oldfield (Layard's private secretary).

49. BL Add. MS. 38996 ff.5–6 (5 January 1869), GES to Oldfield.

50. BL Add. MS. 38996 f.15 (6 January 1869), Layard to Lowe.

51. Reported in BL Add. MS. 38996 ff.42–43 (21 January 1869), GES to Oldfield.

52. BL Add. MS. 38996 f.32 (14 January 1869), Layard to Lowe.

53. BL Add. MS. 38996 f.38 (20 January 1869), Oldfield to GES. Add. MS. 38996 ff.40–41 (20 January 1869), GES to Layard.

54. Inner Temple [letter], "Correspondence: The Site of the New Law Courts," *Law Journal*, 1 January 1869, pp. 11–12. The site controversy is discussed in M.H.

Port, "From Carey Street to the Embankment—and back again!" *London Topographical Record* 24 (1980): 167–90.

55. BL Add. MS. 38996 f.50 (20 January 1869), Trevelyan to Layard.

56. C. E. Trevelyan [letter], "The New Law Courts," *Times*, 5 January 1869, p. 11, dated 1 January 1869.

57. [leading article], *Times*, 6 January 1869, p. 6.

58. Letters from Trevelyan: "The New Law Courts," *Times*, 20 January 1869, p. 10, dated 19 January 1869; "The New Law Courts," *Times*, 28 January 1869, p. 7, dated 27 January 1869; "The New Law Courts," *Times*, 1 February 1869, p. 12, dated 30 January 1869; "The New Law Courts," *Times*, 6 February 1869, p. 9, dated 5 February 1869; "The New Law Courts," *Times*, 25 February 1869, p. 6, dated 22 February 1869.

59. For example: A Surveyor [letter], "Site of New Law Courts," *Times*, 3 February 1869, p. 10, dated 2 February 1869.

60. G. E. Street [letter], "The New Law Courts," *Times*, 29 January 1869, p. 5, dated 28 January 1869. *Correspondence Relating to the Site of the New Courts and Offices of Law* (London: F. B. Day, 1869). The pamphlet is extremely rare, and no copy of it at all may survive. A copy held by the British Library was destroyed in the Second World War.

61. "Fine Arts: Fine Art Gossip," *Athenaeum*, 6 June 1868, p. 802. "Our Weekly Gossip," *Athenaeum*, 23 January 1869, p. 133. But the editors changed colors again after the Embankment site was rejected, calling it "the worst conceivable site" in "Fine Arts: The Courts of Justice," *Athenaeum*, 19 February 1870, p. 266.

62. "The Site of the Law Courts," *Saturday Review*, 23 January 1869, p. 111; "The Law Courts and the Thames Quay," *Saturday Review*, 13 February 1869, pp. 213–14; "Carey Street for the Law Courts," *Saturday Review*, 7 August 1869, pp. 182–84.

63. "The New Law Courts," *Law Journal*, 8 January 1869, p. 20; "The Site of the New Law Courts," *Law Journal*, 12 February 1869, pp. 96–97; "The Battle of the Sites," *Law Journal*, 26 March 1869, p. 179; "The Sites Controversy," *Law Journal*, 23 April

1869, pp. 227–28; "The Battle of the Sites," *Law Journal*, 30 April 1869, pp. 236–37; "The Battle of the Sites," *Law Journal*, 14 May 1869, pp. 265–66; "The Battle of the Sites," *Law Journal*, 25 June 1869, pp. 349–51.

64. [leading articles], *Solicitors' Journal*, 30 January 1869, p. 239; 6 February 1869, p. 257; 1 May 1869, p. 515; 22 May 1869, p. 585; 29 May 1869, p. 605; 26 June 1869, p. 694; 7 August 1869, p. 828. "The Incorporated Law Society and the New Law Courts," *Law Times*, 13 February 1869, pp. 281–82. Compare their earlier support for the Embankment: "The New Law Courts," *Law Times*, 9 January 1869, p. 183; and "The Law Courts," *Law Times*, 30 January 1869, pp. 241–42.

65. "The New Law Courts and the Offices," *Builder*, 13 February 1869, pp. 117–18.

66. "The New Law Courts," *Building News*, 22 January 1869, p. 62. See also: "The Incorporated Law Society on the Site for the New Law Courts," *Building News*, 12 February 1869, p. 133; "The Law Courts," *Building News*, 23 April 1869, p. 358; "The New Law Courts," *Building News*, 30 April 1869, p. 380; "The Proposed New Law Courts," *Building News*, 4 June 1869, p. 511; "The Proposed Law Courts," *Building News*, 11 June 1869, p. 523. But two signed articles favorable to the Embankment were printed: C. Bruce Allen, "A Thought about the Law Courts," *Building News*, 5 February 1869, p. 107; and R. Y., "Thames Embankment Projects," *Building News*, 19 March 1869, pp. 245–47.

67. "The Carey Street Site for a Palace of Industry," *Architect*, 23 January 1869, pp. 45–46; "The Site of the New Law Courts," *Architect*, 30 January 1869, pp. 61–62; "The New Law Courts," *Architect*, 13 February 1869, pp. 85–86; "Is the Embankment Site too Small or not?" *Architect*, 13 February 1869, p. 86; "The Thames Embankment and Its Approaches," *Architect*, 27 February 1869, p. 113; "Match Extraordinary: Lincoln's Inn against All England," *Architect*, 27 February 1869, p. 114; "Mr. Shields' Report on the New Law Courts Site," *Architect*, 27 March 1869, p. 166; "The Embankment Site for the Law Courts," *Architect*, 24 April 1869, pp. 213–14; "The New Site of

the Law Courts," *Architect*, 1 May 1869, p. 230; "Items of News from Our Special Correspondents and Others: Mr. Street's New Designs for the Law Courts," *Architect*, 29 May 1869, p. 288; "The Law Courts as They Are to Be," *Architect*, 5 June 1869, pp. 290–91; "The Architect: The Parliamentary Session," *Architect*, 14 August 1869, pp. 73–74.

68. Society for the Encouragement of Arts, Manufactures, and Commerce, *Proceedings*.

69. *Ibid.*, pp. 17–18.

70. BL Add. MS. 38996 f.61 (5 February 1869), Trevelyan to Layard.

71. "Match Extraordinary: Lincoln's Inn against All England," *Architect*, 27 February 1869, p. 114.

72. Society for the Encouragement of Arts, Manufactures, and Commerce, *Proceedings*, pp. 54–55.

73. *Ibid.*, p. 14.

74. *Ibid.*, pp. 39–40.

75. Incorporated Law Society, *The New Law Courts: Statement by the Council of the Incorporated Law Society on the Suggested Change of Site* (London, 1869), pp. 9, 12–13.

76. Reported in "Solicitors' Journal," *Law Times*, 6 March 1869, p. 351.

77. PRO Works 12/32/2 f.17 (17 February 1869), resolutions of the Articled Clerks Society.

78. Philip Rickman (secretary, Metropolitan and Provincial Law Association), *The So-called "Embellishment" of London at the Expense of the Suitors* (London: n.p., 1869), dated 17 March 1869.

79. In the interim, Gregory served as best man at the wedding of Layard and Enid Guest on March 9. Waterfield, *Layard*, p. 310.

80. See "Mr. Shields' Report on the New Law Courts Site," *Architect*, 27 March 1869, p. 166.

81. "Copy of the Report Made by Mr. F. W. Shields, C.E., on the Subject of the Site for the New Courts of Justice and Their Approaches," *BPP*, volume 47 in 1868–69, pp. 1, 2.

82. *Ibid.*, p. 2.

83. *Ibid.*, p. 3.

84. PRO Works, 12/32/2 f.8 (February 1869), Hunt memo.

85. *Hansard*, 3s 196 (10 May 1869): 543.

86. BL Add. MS. 38996 f.50 (20 January 1869), Trevelyan to Layard, *re* petition drive. Add. MS. 38996 ff.104–5 (25 February 1869), Trevelyan to Layard, reporting resolution of Middle Temple in support. Add. MS. 38996 f.160 (13 April 1869), Trevelyan to Layard, reporting similar resolution of Inner Temple.

87. BL Add. MS. 38996 ff.162–63 (19 April 1869), Fitzroy Kelly to Layard.

88. BL Add. MS. 44536 f.125v (9 March 1869), Gladstone memo.

89. *Hansard*, 3s 195 (20 April 1869): 1216.

90. *Ibid.*, 1217.

91. *Ibid.*, 1220.

92. *Ibid.*, 1258.

93. *Ibid.*, 1259.

94. *Ibid.*, 1264.

95. *Ibid.*

96. *Ibid.*

97. *Ibid.*, 1262–63.

98. [leading article], *Times*, 22 April 1869, p. 9.

99. [leading article], *Times*, 20 April 1869, p. 9; [leading article], *Times*, 21 April 1869, p. 9.

100. *Hansard*, 3s 195 (20 April 1869): 1270.

101. No record survives of his first instructions. The request was probably made in person.

102. At the last meeting of the Society of Arts committee.

103. Gladstone and Lowe had considered such an option in March: BL Add. MS. 44536 f.125v (9 March 1869), Gladstone memo; PRO Works 12/1 f.299 (9 March 1869), Lowe to Layard. Henry Hunt proposed that Street prepare an alternative design: PRO Works 12/32/2 f.52 (13 May 1869), Hunt memo; Works 12/32/2 f.56 (13 May 1869), Layard to Treasury lords; Works 12/32/2 f. 57 (13 May 1869), Russell to GES; and Works 12/32/2 f.58 (22 May 1869), George Hamilton (Treasury secretary) to Layard.

104. BL Add. MS. 38996 ff.166–68 (28 April 1869), GES to Layard.

105. BL Add. MS. 38996 ff.202–3 (19 May 1869), GES to Layard. "Copy of Plans for the New Law Courts on the Embank-

ment Site, with a Letter from the Architect," *BPP*, volume 47 in 1868–69. The only original drawing to survive is the Howard Street site plan. PRO Works 30/1277.

106. BL Add. MS. 38996 ff. 3–4 (5 January 1869), Lowe to Layard.

107. *Hansard*, 3s 195 (20 April 1869): 1265.

108. "The Law Courts," *Building News*, 23 April 1869, p. 358.

109. "The Royal Institute of British Architects: Opening Night," *Builder*, 7 November 1868, pp. 814–15.

110. See: BL Add. MS. 38996 f. 15 (6 January 1869), Layard to Lowe. *Hansard*, 3s 196 (10 May 1869): 549.

111. "The Office of Works," *Builder*, 31 July 1869, p. 601.

112. "The New Law Courts," *Building News*, 22 January 1869, pp. 62–63.

113. The perspective was shown at the Royal Academy in 1870, number 789. Published twice by the *Building News*, on 23 April 1871 and 25 August 1882, but now lost.

114. Professor Irene Winter of the University of Pennsylvania brought Layard's reconstruction of Nimrud to the author's attention.

115. Society for the Encouragement of Arts, Manufactures, and Commerce, *Proceedings*, pp. 36–37.

116. *Hansard*, 3s 196 (10 May 1869): 549.

117. "Copy of Plans for the New Law Courts," pp. 6–7. Note that the plans, prepared before the perspective, show both ventilating towers at the east end of the hall, rather than one at each end. Many other, smaller inconsistencies can also be detected.

118. "Report from the Select Committee," p. 55.

119. *Hansard*, 3s 196 (10 May 1869): 544.

120. "Copy of Plans for the New Law Courts," p. 11.

121. "Report from the Select Committee," pp. 41–42.

122. *Ibid.*, p. 55.

123. BL Add. MS. 38996 ff. 202–3 (19 May 1869), GES to Layard.

124. [leading article], *Times*, 12 May 1869, p. 9.

125. "The Site for the Law Courts," *Builder*, 15 May 1869, p. 381.

126. Roundell Palmer, *Memorials, Part II: Personal and Political, 1865–1895*, ed. Sophia M. Parker (London: Macmillan and Company, 1898), 2:25.

127. BL Add. MS. 38996 ff. 192–93 (12 May 1869), lithographed letter from J. H. Bolton (president, Law Society); Add. MS. 38996 ff. 222–23 (26 May 1869), lithographed letter from J. H. Bolton. Copies of the form letters, circulated in May and June, are BL Add. MS. 38996 ff. 194 and 210–11. Trevelyan complained of this practice to Layard in Add. MS. 38996 ff. 281–82 (12 June 1869).

128. The meeting is reported in [general columns], *Solicitors' Journal*, 29 May 1869, p. 605. A resolution passed in Liverpool on May 14 is noted in "The New Law Courts: Observations of the Incorporated Law Society of Liverpool," *Solicitors' Journal*, 29 May 1869, pp. 610–11. The Society of the Attorneys and Solicitors of Ireland also circulated a printed letter: BL Add. MS. 38996 f. 290 (16 June 1869).

129. GES referred to the map in his report of 21 May 1869. No copy has been located. Pownall's estimate was printed in "Report of the Commissioners," pp. 124–25.

130. "Report from the Select Committee," pp. 32, 11.

131. *Ibid.*, p. 34. GES replied that he had merely locked the back door into his private office to guard against needless interruption. Burnet was still welcome to visit via the front door, which was attended by one of Street's clerks. *Ibid.*, p. 47.

132. "Report of the Commissioners," pp. 124–25.

133. "Copy of the Report of the Committee Appointed by the Courts of Justice Commission to Examine All the Plans Submitted to the Commission with a View to Ascertain the Dimensions and Measurements," *BPP*, volume 47 in 1868–69. "Report of the Commissioners," p. 129.

134. BL Add. MS. 38996 ff. 226–27 (27 May 1869), GES to Layard.

135. "Report from the Select Committee," p. 33.

136. PRO Works 12/32/2 f. 79 (18 June 1869), Russell to GES.

137. PRO Works 12/32/2 ff.82–93 (21 June 1869), GES to Layard; a lithographed copy: BL Add. MS. 38996 ff.297–98.

138. "Copy of the Report from the Surveyor of Her Majesty's Works and Public Buildings to the First Commissioner on the Sites Proposed for the Courts and Offices of Law," *BPP*, volume 47 in 1868–69, pp. 7, 4.

139. BL Add. MS. 38996 f.204 (20 May 1869), Trevelyan to Layard.

140. See the following letters from Trevelyan to Layard in this respect: BL Add. MS. 38996 ff.176–77 (5 May 1869); Add. MS. 38996 f.218 (26 May 1869); Add. MS. 38996 ff.245–46 (31 May 1869); Add. MS 38996 ff.251–52 (1 June 1869); Add. MS. 38996 ff.270–71 (5 June 1869); Add. MS. 38996 ff.278–79 (11 June 1869); Add. MS. 38996 ff.281–82 (12 June 1869).

141. "The Site for the New Law Courts," *Solicitors' Journal*, 26 June 1869, pp. 706–7.

142. First inquiry is PRO Works 12/32/ 2 f.62 (31 May 1869), Russell to Henry Cole. The model does not seem to have survived. A long controversy over payment for the model involved Layard's successor, A. S. Ayrton.

143. BL Add. MS. 44536 f.170v (5 June 1869), Gladstone to Layard; Add. MS. 38996 ff.276–77 (9 June 1869), Earl de Grey (secretary to the Queen) to Layard.

144. E. M. Barry [letter], "The New Law Courts," *Times*, 14 June 1869, p. 5, dated 12 June 1869.

145. "Copy of Correspondence with the Two Architects Recommended by the Judges of Designs for the New Courts of Justice," *BPP*, volume 47 in 1868–69.

146. "The Courts of Justice Site," *Law Journal*, 11 June 1869, p. 319.

147. *Hansard*, 3s 197 (22 June 1869): 458–63.

148. BL Add. MS. 38996 ff.301–2 (25 June 1869), Trevelyan to Layard. Other letters of Trevelyan to Layard: Add. MS. 38996 f.305 (28 June 1869); Add. MS. 38996 ff.311–12 (30 June 1869); Add. MS. 38996 ff.313–14 (1 July 1869); Add. MS. 38996 ff.315–16 (3 July 1869).

149. "Report from the Select Committee," pp. 69, 173–76.

150. *Ibid.*, p. 123.

151. *Ibid.*, pp. 166–70.

152. BL Add. MS. 44783 f.211 (22 July 1869), guest list.

153. "Report from the Select Committee," p. xiv.

154. *Ibid.*, pp. iv–v.

155. *Hansard*, 3s 198 (10 August 1869): 1529.

156. Suggested in BL Add. MS. 38997 f.18 (15 October 1869), GES to Layard.

157. PRO Works 12/32/3 ff.110–12 (11 August 1869), Robertson to Layard.

158. BL Add. MS. 38996 ff.200–201 (18 May 1869), Lowe to Layard.

159. BL Add. MS. 38996 f.359 (9 August 1869), Granville to Layard.

160. BL Add. MS. 38997 ff.6–7 (4 October 1869), Lord Clarendon (foreign secretary) to Layard; Add. MS. 38997 ff.10–14 (11 October 1869), Layard to Lord Clarendon.

161. BL Add. MS. 38997 ff.15–17 (12 October 1869), Layard to Gladstone.

162. Waterfield, *Layard*, p. 312.

163. Winter, *Lowe*, p. 249.

164. BL Add. MS. 38997 ff.43–44 (25 October 1869), GES to Layard.

165. BL Add. MS. 38997 ff.71–76 (29 October 1869), Elcho to Layard.

Notes to Chapter 5

1. BL Add. MS. 44422 ff.168–70 (13 October 1869), Gladstone to Ayrton.

2. BL Add. MS. 44422 ff.187–90 (15 October 1869), Ayrton to Gladstone.

3. Reported with dismay in "The Functions of the Minister of Public Works," *Building News*, 12 November 1869, p. 362; and "Mr. Ayrton," *Architect*, 13 November

1869, p. 235. See also: William N. Bruce, ed., *Sir A. Henry Layard, G.C.B., D.C.L.: Autobiography and Letters from His Childhood until His Appointment as H.M. Ambassador at Madrid* (London: John Murray, 1903) 2:258.

4. "Mr. Layard on the Functions of the Minister of Public Works," *Building News*,

12 November 1869, p. 366; and "Mr. La-yard on Pompeii and Public Work," *Architect*, 13 November 1869, p. 237–38.

5. "Alliteration with Ayrton," *Punch*, 27 November 1869, p. 218.

6. Much of the following information on the Office of Works comes from "Her Majesty's Office of Works and Public Buildings," *Builder*, 8 September 1877, pp. 897–99.

7. BL Add. MS. 44538 f.58r (22 January 1870), Gladstone to Lowe; Add. MS. 44301 ff.118–19 (22 January 1870), Lowe to Gladstone; Add. MS. 44538 ff.58r–58v (22 January 1870), Gladstone to Ayrton, apologizing. Lowe traveled with Galton in North America in 1856: A. Patchett Martin, *The Life and Letters of the Right Honourable Robert Lowe, Viscount Sherbrooke, G.C.B., D.C.L.* (London and New York: Longmans, Green and Company, 1893), 2:127ff.

8. Described in great detail and illustrated in "Report to the Right Hon. the Earl de Grey and Ripon, Secretary of State for War, Descriptive of the Herbert Hospital at Woolwich," *BPP*, volume 26 in 1865.

9. By Galton: *An Address on the General Principles Which Should Be Observed in the Construction of Hospitals, Delivered to the British Medical Association of Leeds, July 29, 1869* (London: Macmillan and Company, 1869); *Observations on the Construction of Healthy Dwellings; Namely Homes, Hospitals, Barracks, Asylums, Etc.* (Oxford: Clarendon Press, 1880); *Healthy Hospitals: Observations on Some Points Connected With Hospital Construction* (Oxford: Froude, 1893).

10. "Her Majesty's Office of Works and Public Buildings," *Builder*, 8 September 1877, p. 898.

11. BL Add. MS. 44301 f.43 (24 March 1869), Lowe to Galton.

12. "Mr. Ayrton on Architecture," *Architect*, 24 December 1870, p. 363.

13. G. G. Scott, *Personal and Professional Recollections* (London: Sampson Low, Marston, Searle, and Rivington, 1879), p. 273.

14. F. H. W. Sheppard, ed., *Survey of London, Volume 38, The Museums Area of South Kensington and Westminster* (London: University of London, 1975), pp. 209–10.

15. M. H. Port, ed., *The Houses of Parliament* (New Haven and London: Yale University Press, 1976), pp. 187–88. The quotation is from W. Lawrence: *Hansard*, 3s 201 (13 May 1870): 717.

16. BL Add. MS. 44538 f.67v (1 February 1870), Gladstone to Lowe; Barry had just met with Gladstone.

17. Barry's letter is lost. BL Add. MS. 44538 f.140r (4 May 1870), Gladstone to Barry. Reported in Add. MS. 44538 ff.139v–40r (4 May 1870), Gladstone to Ayrton.

18. Two letters from Palmer to Ayrton (18 November 1869 and 20 November 1869) are recorded in the notes of R. J. Lambert. Present location unknown. (Courtesy of Paul Joyce.)

19. PRO Works 12/33/2 ff.13–14 (1 January 1870), GES to Ayrton.

20. *Hansard*, 3s 199 (11 February 1870): 168.

21. PRO Works 12/33/1 f.175 (22 February 1870), Ayrton memo.

22. PRO Works 12/33/1 ff.178–92 (25 March 1870), GES to Ayrton.

23. PRO Works 12/33/1 f.194 (28 March 1870), Ayrton to Galton.

24. PRO Works 12/33/1 ff.198–99 (19 April 1870), GES to Galton.

25. PRO Works 12/34/1 ff.17–23 (27 June 1870), report of Galton and Hunt.

26. PRO Works 12/34/1 ff.1–6 (17 June 1870), GES to Ayrton.

27. *Ibid.*

28. PRO Works 12/34/1 ff.17–23 (27 June 1870), report of Galton and Hunt.

29. PRO Works 12/34/1 ff.24–27 (2 July 1870), Ayrton to Treasury lords.

30. *Ibid.*

31. PRO T1/7004B/19487 f.12726 (7 July 1870), Lowe's draft of minute. Works 12/34/1 f.28 (8 July 1870), James Stansfield (Treasury secretary) to Ayrton enclosing Works 12/34/1 ff.30–33 (7 July 1870), Treasury minute.

32. James Winter, *Robert Lowe* (Toronto and Buffalo: University of Toronto Press, 1976), p. 248.

33. PRO Works 12/34/1 ff.30–33 (7 July 1870), Treasury minute.

34. PRO Works 12/34/1 f.29 (11 July 1870), Russell to Field; and Works 12/34/1 f.36 (16 July 1870), Russell to Field.

35. PRO Works 12/34/1 ff.37–51 (14 July 1870), GES memo on 7 July 1870 Treasury minute.

36. "Report of the Commissioners Appointed to Advise and to Report as to the Buildings Proper to Be Erected, and Plans upon which Such Buildings Shall Be Erected for the New Courts of Justice," *BPP*, volume 20 in 1871, p. 130.

37. PRO Works 12/34/1 f.51 (20 July 1870), GES to James Stansfield (Treasury secretary).

38. PRO Works 12/34/1 ff.37–51 (14 July 1870), GES report on his design and memo on 7 July 1870 Treasury minute.

39. "Report of the Commissioners," pp. 130–31.

40. *Ibid.*, p. 131.

41. *Ibid.*, and PRO Works 12/40/2 f.3 (13 August 1870), R. W. Lingen (Treasury secretary) to Ayrton.

42. Reported in PRO Works 12/34/4 ff.100–101 (5 May 1871), GES to Galton.

43. PRO Works 12/34/4 ff.111–12 (26 May 1871), GES to Callander (assistant secretary of works).

44. "The Proposed New Law Courts," *Building News*, 4 June 1869, p. 511. "Architecture at the Royal Academy," *Building News*, 20 May 1870, p. 370.

45. "Architecture at the Royal Academy," *Builder*, 7 May 1870, p. 358.

46. *Hansard*, 3s 204 (10 February 1871): 121.

47. PRO Works 12/34/4 ff.60–61 (2 January 1871), GES to Ayrton.

48. Winter, *Lowe*, p. 251.

49. This controversy is discussed in the next chapter.

50. PRO Works 12/34/4 ff.60–61 (n.d.), Hunt and Galton to Ayrton.

51. PRO Works 12/34/4 ff.70–71 (14 January 1871), Office of Works to GES.

52. PRO Works 12/34/4 ff.74–75 (13 February 1871), Ayrton to Treasury lords.

53. PRO Works 12/34/4 ff.76–77 (16 March 1871), R. W. Lingen (Treasury secretary) to Ayrton.

54. PRO Works 12/34/4 ff.80–86 (30 March 1871), Ayrton to Treasury lords, enclosing Galton's report of 28 March 1871.

55. PRO Works 12/34/4 ff.87–89 (6 April 1871), William Law (Treasury secretary) to Ayrton.

56. PRO Works 12/34/4 ff.91–93 (22 April 1871), GES to Russell, enclosing list of drawings.

57. PRO Works 12/34/4 f.96 (2 May 1871), GES to Ayrton.

58. PRO Works 12/34/4 ff.97–98 (5 May 1871), Ayrton to Treasury lords; and T1/7140/19533 f.7777 (5 May 1871), Ayrton to Treasury lords.

59. PRO T1/7140/19533 f.7777, draft of letter to Ayrton, realized as Works 12/34/4 ff.106–8 (26 May 1871), R. W. Lingen (Treasury secretary) to Ayrton.

60. PRO Works 12/34/4 ff.111–12 (26 May 1871), GES to Callander.

61. PRO Works 12/34/4 f.115 (5 June 1871), Ayrton to Treasury lords.

62. PRO Works 12/34/4 ff.136–37 (16 December 1871), GES to Galton.

63. PRO Works 12/34/4 f.120–21 (4 August 1871), William Law (Treasury secretary) to Ayrton.

64. PRO Works 12/34/4 f.122 (5 August 1871), Ayrton to Treasury lords.

65. PRO T1/7140/19533 f.12677 (7 August 1871), Ayrton to Treasury lords, with margin notes by Treasury official.

66. Stevens also appealed to Gladstone, as did Street (see below). See: "The Wellington Monument in S. Paul's Cathedral," *Building News*, 12 August 1870, pp. 109–10; Martin, *Lowe*, 2:380–81; John Physick, *The Wellington Monument* (London: Her Majesty's Stationery Office, 1970), pp. 83–94.

67. On Dublin see: BL Add. MS. 44429 f.8 (2 January 1871), GES to Gladstone; Add. MS. 44539 f.126v (6 January 1871), Gladstone to GES. Gladstone feared that his gift might be refused owing to his support for the disestablishment of the Anglican Church in Ireland.

68. BL Add. MS. 44431 f.121 (11 July 1871), GES to Gladstone; and Add. MS. 44784 f.45 (13 July 1871), guest list.

69. AES, *Memoir*, pp. 207–8.

70. "The New Law Courts," *Building News*, 13 October 1871, p. 261. The earliest representation of the new design is the version of drawing number 25H published in the *Building News* on 1 December 1871. It is dated November 1871. The nearly identical contract drawing numbered 25H is dated November 1872, however. Copies of the lat-

ter are PRO Works 30/1418 and Works 30/2272.

71. "The New Law Courts—IV," *Building News*, 3 November 1871, p. 321.

72. Publication of the design: *Building News* (17 November 1871), west half of Strand elevation; *Architect* (25 November 1871), both halves of Strand elevation; *Building News* (1 December 1871), elevation, section and plan of public stairs; *Builder* (2 February 1871), west half of Strand elevation; *Building News* (8 December 1871), east part of Strand elevation; *Architect* (9 December 1871), longitudinal section of central hall; *Architect* (16 December 1871), central hall details.

73. He seems to sanction its publication in *The New Courts of Justice: Notes in Reply to Some Criticisms*, 2d ed. (London, Oxford, and Cambridge: Rivingtons, 1872), p. 17. The view may have been based on a reworking of the perspective that he submitted to the Treasury.

74. Brewer's perspective was published: *Building News*, 1 December 1882.

75. PRO Works 12/34/4 ff. 127–28 (30 November 1871), GES to Galton.

76. PRO Works 12/34/4 ff. 131–35 (15 December 1871), Russell to GES. Works 12/34/2 ff. 13–17 (15 January 1872), GES to Russell, enclosing a list of drawings. Works 12/34/2 ff. 35–36 (16 January 1872), GES to Galton.

77. PRO Works 12/40/3 ff. 2–3 (27 January 1872), Ayrton to Treasury lords; and T1/7227A/16134 f. 1839 (27 January 1872), Ayrton to Treasury lords (the same).

78. PRO Works 12/40/3 f. 4 (5 February 1872), William Law (Treasury secretary) to Ayrton. GES was advised the next day: Works 12/40/3 f. 8 (6 February 1872), Russell to GES.

79. "Chips," *Building News*, 11 August 1871, p. 110.

80. "The Law Courts," *Builder*, 4 November 1871, p. 872. "St. Clement Danes," *Architect*, 25 November 1871, p. 264.

81. For example, see Edmund Sharpe [letter], "The New Law Courts," *Times*, 15 January 1872, p. 4, dated 9 January 1872.

82. Notably raised by G. B. Gregory. *Hansard*, 3s 203 (28 July 1870): 1111–13;

and *Hansard*, 3s 204 (10 February 1871): 120.

83. *Hansard*, 3s 208 (20 July 1871): 53.

84. James Fergusson, "The New Law Courts," *Builder*, 1 July 1871, p. 503.

85. "The Proposed New Courts of Justice," *Builder*, 2 December 1871, p. 949.

86. "Epilogue," *Builder*, 30 December 1871, pp. 1017–18; and "The Designs for the Law Courts," *Builder*, 30 March 1872, p. 237.

87. The Times, *The History of the Times [Volume 2]: The Tradition Established, 1841–1884* (London: The Times, 1939), pp. 439–40. "The New Courts of Justice," *Times*, 19 August 1871, p. 11.

88. [leading article], *Times*, 11 September 1871, p. 9.

89. "The New Law Courts," *Times*, 6 December 1871, p. 3.

90. "The New Law Courts," *Illustrated London News*, 23 September 1871, p. 287.

91. "Flemish Town Halls and the New Law Courts," *Graphic*, 28 October 1871, p. 418.

92. E. B. Denison [letter], "Modern Architecture," *Times*, 1 September 1871, p. 6. E. B. Denison [letter], "The Law Courts," *Times*, 21 October 1871, p. 9, dated 19 October 1871. See also his letters: "Architecture of the Law Courts," *Times*, 7 September 1871, p. 8, dated 5 September 1871; "The New Law Courts," *Times*, 1 December 1871, p. 6, dated 30 November 1871; and "Modern Architecture," *Times*, 29 December 1871, p. 8, dated 28 December 1871.

93. E. W. Pugin [letter], "The New Law Courts," *Times*, 22 January 1872, p. 10. Other Pugin letters: "The New Law Courts," *Times*, 13 September 1871, p. 10, dated 9 September 1871; "The New Courts of Justice," *Times*, 30 November 1871, p. 5, dated 29 November 1871; "The Threatened Courts of Justice," *Times*, 2 December 1871, p. 5; "Modern Architecture," *Times*, 19 December 1871, p. 4, dated 16 December 1871.

94. Anti-Gothic letters: "The Proposed Courts of Justice," *Times*, 5 September 1871, p. 7, dated 1 September 1871; "The New Courts of Law," *Times*, 9 Sep-

tember 1871, p. 4, dated 8 September 1871; "New Law Courts," *Times*, 16 September 1871, p. 4, dated 15 September 1871. Sydney Smirke [letter], "The New Law Courts," *Times*, 19 October 1871, p. 11, dated 16 October 1871.

95. F.R.I.B.A. letters: "The New Law Courts," *Times*, 27 November 1871, p. 5, dated 23 November 1871; "The New Law Courts," *Times*, 5 December 1871, p. 12, dated 4 December 1871; "The New Law Courts," *Times*, 5 January 1872, p. 3, dated 3 January 1872; "The New Law Courts," *Times*, 19 January 1872, p. 11, dated 17 January 1872; "New Law Courts," *Times*, 1 April 1872, p. 9, dated 29 March 1872.

96. L. A. Marchand, *The Athenaeum: A Mirror of Victorian Culture* (Chapel Hill, North Carolina: University of North Carolina Press, 1941), p. 226.

97. "Fine Arts: New Courts of Justice," *Athenaeum*, 29 July 1871, p. 151.

98. "Fine Arts: The Courts of Justice," *Athenaeum*, 6 January 1872, pp. 21–22. "Fine Arts: Mr. Street and His Critics," *Athenaeum*, 13 January 1872, pp. 54–55.

99. "The Law Courts and Their Critics," *Saturday Review*, 23 December 1871, p. 804. See also "Mr. Fergusson, Mr. Street, and the Law Courts," *Saturday Review*, 13 January 1872, pp. 42–45.

100. "The New Law Courts," *Building News*, 14 July 1871, p. 28.

101. E. W. Godwin, "The New Law Courts," *Building News*, 28 July 1871, p. 73.

102. It republished the first critical review from the *Times:* "The New Courts of Justice," *Building News*, 25 August, 1871, p. 150. It also reprinted a hostile article entitled "Modern Architecture" from the *Pall Mall Gazette* as "Non-professional Opinion on the New Law Courts," *Building News*, 22 September 1871, pp. 211–12. "The New Law Courts," *Building News*, 13 October 1871, pp. 261–62; 20 October 1871, pp. 284–86; 27 October 1871, pp. 298–99; 3 November 1871, pp. 320–21. E. W. Pugin attributed the favorable articles to Charles Boutell, the eminent medievalist: E. W. Pugin [letter], "The New Courts of Justice," *Times*, 30 November 1871, p. 5, dated 29 November 1871; and E. W. Pugin [letter], "The Threatened Courts of Justice," *Times*,

2 December 1871, p. 5. Boutell did send two pro-Street letters to the *Building News* at this time: "Correspondence: Architectural Heraldry," *Building News*, 17 November 1871, pp. 375–76; and "Correspondence: The New Law Courts," *Building News*, 5 January 1872, p. 22, dated 3 January 1872.

103. *E.g.*, the second *Times* review was reprinted as "The New Law Courts," *Building News*, 8 December 1871, pp. 426–27. Fergusson's critique from *Macmillan's* [see n. 122] was reprinted as "Modern Architecture and the New Law Courts," *Building News*, 29 December 1871, pp. 500–501. A hostile notice from the *Lambeth Review* was reprinted as "A Plea for Gothic," *Building News*, 29 March 1872, pp. 252–55. The unfavorable article from the *Quarterly Review* of April 1872 [see n. 129] was printed as "Modern Architecture," *Building News*, 26 April 1872, pp. 333–35. Two critical, signed articles were also published: C. B. Allen, "Modern Gothic as Practised and the Law Courts," *Building News*, 8 December 1871, pp. 437–38; and G. H. G., "Architecture or Archaeology?" *Building News*, 19 January 1872, p. 57.

104. "The New Law Courts—II," *Building News*, 20 October 1872, p. 285.

105. "The New Law Courts," *Building News*, 8 December 1871, p. 428. "Damnatory Art Criticism," *Building News*, 5 January 1872, pp. 1–2.

106. "Mr. Fergusson on the Law Courts," *Architect*, 15 July 1871, p. 26.

107. "The Law Courts: Mr. Street and the 'Times,' " *Architect*, 2 September 1871, p. 113. "The Law Courts: Mr. Street's Design," *Architect*, 9 September 1871, p. 127.

108. "The 'Times' and the New Law Courts," *Architect*, 30 September 1871, pp. 164–66.

109. " 'The Times' v. Architects," *Architect*, 16 December 1871, p. 297. " 'Modern Architecture!' " *Architect*, 30 December 1871, p. 321.

110. "Architecture in 1871: The Law Courts," *Architect*. 6 January 1872, p. 4. "Fergussonic Architecture; or, the Coming Style," *Architect*, 3 February 1872, pp. 53–54.

111. The reprint is "The New Courts

of Justice," *Law Journal*, 25 August 1871, pp. 585–86. [The *Law Times* also reprinted the review as well as a number of hostile letters from the *Times*, but took no further interest in the matter. "The Bench and the Bar," *Law Times*, 26 August 1871, pp. 312–13; and "The Bench and the Bar," *Law Times*, 16 September 1871, pp. 362–63.] "The Law Courts," *Law Journal*, 25 August 1871, p. 576.

112. "The New Law Courts," *Law Journal*, 15 September 1871, p. 623.

113. "The New Law Courts," *Law Journal*, 6 October 1871, pp. 669–70.

114. See "The New Law Courts," *Law Journal*, 1 December 1871, pp. 809–10; and "The New Law Courts," *Law Journal*, 29 December 1871, p. 879.

115. "The New Law Courts," *Law Journal*, 29 March 1872, p. 209.

116. "The Drawings for the New Courts of Justice," *Builder*, 16 December 1871, p. 989; "Miscellanea: The New Law Courts," *Builder*, 23 December 1871, p. 1012.

117. Edward J. Tarver [letter], "Correspondence: The New Law Courts," *Architect*, 30 December 1871, p. 330.

118. John P. Seddon [letter], "Modern Architecture," *Times*, 28 December 1871, p. 5.

119. Edmund Sharpe [letter], "The New Law Courts," *Times*, 15 January 1872, p. 4. Sharpe's remarks were widely reprinted: "Correspondence: New Law Courts," *Architect*, 20 January 1872, pp. 38–39; "Correspondence: New Law Courts," *Building News*, 19 January 1872, p. 58.

120. Thomas H. Wyatt, "Opening Address for the Session 1871–72," *Papers Read at the Royal Institute of British Architects 1871–72*: 10.

121. Thomas H. Wyatt [letter], "The New Law Courts," *Times*, 28 November 1871, p. 5.

122. James Fergusson, "The New Law Courts," *Macmillan's Magazine*, January 1872, p. 254.

123. *Ibid.*, p. 253. Fergusson's essay was reprinted as "The New Law Courts," *Times*, 27 December 1871, p. 8; and "Modern Architecture and the New Law Courts,"

Building News, 29 December 1871, pp. 500–501. He also wrote two subsequent letters to the *Times*: "Modern Architecture," *Times*, 29 December 1871, p. 8, dated 28 December 1871; and "Modern Architecture," *Times*, 30 December 1871, p. 3, dated 29 December 1871.

124. GES, *The New Courts of Justice: Notes in Reply to Some Criticisms*, 2d ed. (London, Oxford, and Cambridge: Rivingtons, 1872), p. 21.

125. *Ibid.*, p. 10.

126. *Ibid.*, p. 20.

127. *Ibid.*, pp. 9, 16.

128. James Fergusson [letter], "Fine Arts: The New Law Courts," *Athenaeum*, 20 January 1872, p. 85, dated 16 January 1872.

129. [John T. Emmett], "The State of English Architecture," *Quarterly Review* 132 (April 1872): 295–335. [Attribution from the *Wellesley Index of Victorian Periodicals*.]

130. PRO T1/7140/19533 f.14840 (21 September 1871), Barry to Lowe.

131. E. M. Barry [letter], "The New Law Courts," *Times*, 9 December 1871, p. 9, dated 8 December 1871.

132. E. M. Barry, *The New Law Courts and the National Gallery: Facts Relating to the Late Competitions, with a Reply to Portions of Mr. Street's Recent Pamphlet* (London: Macmillan and Company, 1872).

133. "Fine Arts: Mr. E. Barry and Mr. Street," *Athenaeum*, 3 February 1872, p. 151. The second edition of Street's pamphlet is cited in n. 124.

134. These events are reconstructed in chapter 4. See: E. M. Barry [letter], "Correspondence: Mr. E. M. Barry's Designs for the New Law Courts," *Building News*, 16 February 1872, p. 140, dated 13 February 1872; E. M. Barry [letter], "Fine Arts: The Law Courts," *Athenaeum*, 21 February 1872, pp. 247–48, dated 21 February 1872; GES [letter], "Correspondence: Mr. E. M. Barry and Mr. Street," *Building News*, 23 February 1872, pp. 161–62, dated 19 February 1872; GES [letter], "Fine Arts: The Law Courts," *Athenaeum*, 2 March 1872, pp. 278–79, dated 26 February 1872. Also: E. M. Barry [letter], "The Law Courts Competition," *Builder*, 17 February 1872, pp. 123–24.

135. G. Cavendish Bentinck [letter], "The New Law Courts," *Times*, 11 Septem-

ber 1871, p. 5, dated 8 September 1871. *Hansard*, 3s 210 (22 March 1872): 581.

136. *Hansard*, 3s 210 (22 March 1872): 584.

137. *Ibid.*, 586.

138. *Hansard*, 3s 212 (5 July 1872): 699.

139. *Hansard*, 3s 213 (3 August 1872): 415–16.

140. The builders and the process of tendering are discussed in the next chapter.

141. Plain-speaking [letter], "Mr. Street and the New Law Courts," *Builder*, 10 February 1872, p. 109.

142. The firm of Bull and Sons is discussed in the next chapter. PRO Works 12/40/3 ff.27–28 (26 March 1873), Russell to GES.

143. PRO Works 12/40/3 ff.31–34 (27 March 1873), GES to Russell; and Works 12/40/3 f.35 (27 March 1873), GES to Russell. K. Maiwald, "An Index of Building Costs in The United Kingdom, 1845–1938," *Economic History Review* 2s 7 (1954–55): 192.

144. PRO Works 12/40/3 ff.36–40 (29 March 1873), Hunt memo.

145. "The Wardour (Chilmark) and Tisbury Stone Company," *Building News*, 16 April 1869, p. 335.

146. PRO Works 12/40/3 ff.41–48 (3 April 1873), Ayrton to Treasury lords; and T1/7329A/20026 f.5417 (3 April 1873), Ayrton to Treasury lords (the same).

147. PRO Works 12/40/3 f.49 (18 April 1873), William Law (Treasury secretary) to Ayrton; and T1/7329A/20026 f.5417, draft of the same.

148. PRO Works 12/40/3 ff.50–59 (1 May 1873), GES to Ayrton, enclosing schedule of reductions.

149. PRO Works 12/40/3 ff.60–70 (9 May 1873), Russell to GES, based on Galton's hostile evaluation: Works 12/40/3 f.59['] (7 May 1873), Galton to Ayrton.

150. PRO Works 12/40/3 ff.76–86 (15 May 1873), GES to Russell.

151. PRO Works 12/40/3 ff.88–89 (17 May 1873), Russell to GES.

152. PRO Works 12/40/3 ff.102, 104 (22 May 1873), GES to Ayrton.

153. PRO Works 12/40/3 f.90 (20 May 1873), Charles Strenge (Treasury secretary)

to Ayrton; and T1/7329A/20026 f.7524 (19 May 1873), draft of the same.

154. PRO Works 12/40/3 ff.105–9 (26 May 1873), Russell to GES.

155. BL Add. MS. 44438 f.325 (27 May 1873), GES to Gladstone. This letter retracts the appeal written that morning (which is not preserved) and reports his satisfactory meeting with Lowe.

156. PRO Works 12/40/3 f.122 (6 June 1873), GES to Russell.

157. PRO Works 12/40/3 f.124 (9 June 1873), Russell to GES.

158. PRO Works 12/40/3 f.125 (14 June 1873), Russell to GES.

159. PRO T1/7329A/20026 f.9072 (11 June 1873), GES to Treasury lords.

160. *Ibid.* PRO Works 12/40/3 ff.126–33 (June 1873, received 16 June 1873), William Law (Treasury secretary) to Ayrton.

161. PRO Works 12/40/3 ff.134–38 (16 June 1873), GES to Russell.

162. PRO Works 12/40/3 ff.139–43 (19 June 1873), Ayrton to Treasury lords; and T1/7329A/20026 f.9384 (19 June 1873), Ayrton to Treasury lords (the same).

163. BL Add. MS. 44439 f.52 (17 June 1873), GES to Gladstone.

164. BL Add. MS. 44784 f.146 (19 June 1873), guest list; and Add. MS. 44784 f.148 (26 February 1873), guest list.

165. BL Add. MS. 44641 ff.135–36, Gladstone Cabinet diary for 21 June 1873. Add. MS. 44542 ff.128v–29r (21 June 1873), Gladstone to Ayrton, asking him to attend.

166. PRO T1/7329A/20026 f.9384, George Hamilton's notes for Lowe; and BL Add. MS. 44641 ff.140–43, Gladstone's notes.

167. Gladstone's draft is BL Add. MS. 44641 f.140. Full text is Add. MS. 44452 ff.131r–31v (28 June 1873), Gladstone to Ayrton.

168. PRO Works 12/40/3 ff.154 (1 July 1873), R. W. Lingen (Treasury secretary) to Ayrton.

169. PRO Works 12/40/3 ff.155–56 (2 July 1873), Callander to GES.

170. Recorded in the notes of R. J. Lambert now in the possession of Paul Joyce. Whereabouts of original unknown.

171. Discussed in BL Add. MS 44641

ff. 158–61, Gladstone's notes for Cabinet meeting of 12 July 1873.

172. *Ibid.*

173. BL Add. MS. 44542 f. 139r (19 July 1873), Gladstone to Ayrton.

174. *Hansard*, 3s 214 (10 February 1873): 196–97; *Hansard*, 3s 215 (21 April 1873): 791–93; *Hansard*, 3s 216 (23 May 1873): 396–408; *Hansard*, 3s 217 (15 July 1873): 398–99; *Hansard*, 3s 217 (28 July 1873): 1098–1100.

175. Anthony Trollope, *The Prime Minister* (Oxford: Oxford University Press, 1938) 1: 413.

176. Winter, *Lowe*, pp. 289–91.

177. When he was removed from the Office of Works to the post of judge advocate general, Gladstone instructed him, at the request of the Queen, to conduct all business with her in writing. BL Add. MS. 44439 f. 268 (5 August 1873), Gladstone to Ayrton.

178. F. Tomline and Gilbert A' Beckett [W. S. Gilbert], *The Happy Land: A Burlesque Version of "The Wicked World"* (London: J. W. Last and Company, 1873), p. 21.

179. BL Add. MS. 44302 ff. 137–38 [received 4 August 1873], Lowe to Gladstone.

180. BL Add. MS. 44641 f. 191, Gladstone's notes for Cabinet meeting of 6 August 1873.

181. BL Add. MS. 44439 f. 268 (6 August 1873), Gladstone to Ayrton.

182. BL Add. MS. 44439 ff. 281–84 (8 August 1873), Ayrton to Gladstone. He again asked for consideration for Galton in Add. Ms. 44440 ff. 141–43 (3 October 1873), Ayrton to Gladstone. Galton was finally knighted in 1887.

183. This episode is discussed further in the next chapter.

184. "Some Recent Examples of Church Architecture," *Building News*, 13 August 1869, pp. 121–22.

185. "Crude Architecture," *Architect*, 1 July 1871, pp. 1–3.

186. John T. Emmett, ["The State of English Architecture,"] *Quarterly Review* 132 (April 1872): 302.

187. James Fergusson [letter], "Fine Arts: The New Law Courts," *Athenaeum*, 20 January 1872, p. 85, dated 16 January 1872.

188. GES, "On Some of the Differences in Style in Old Buildings," *Papers Read at the Royal Institute of British Architects* 1868–69: 25–46.

189. GES, *Remarks and Suggestions on the Scheme for the Completion of St. Paul's Cathedral* (London, 1871).

190. Paul Joyce described this feature of Holmdale to the author.

Notes to Chapter 6

1. Quoted in AES, *Memoir*, p. 284.

2. Details of GES's routine are derived largely from AES, *Memoir*, chapter 13.

3. The drawing labeled "Courts of Justice No. 5" among the Dove drawings at the BAL shows this building. The new entrance is indicated in the letterhead of PRO Works 12/40/3 f. 256 (12 March 1877).

4. Tanner's position in GES's office was described by Hunt in PRO Works 12/45/3 ff. 17–20 (1 March 1883); "Obituary: Augustus W. Tanner," *R.I.B.A. Journal* 30 (1922–23): 626–27; his election as an A.R.I.B.A. is noted in "Royal Institute of British Architects," *Architect*, 5 February 1870, p. 68. Tanner served for about thirty-eight years as a district surveyor, beginning in 1883.

5. Information from Paul Joyce.

6. Holland was perhaps related to the furniture makers, William Holland and Sons. Street's second wife, Jessie Marie Anne Holland, was William Holland's granddaughter and had been a friend of the Streets for many years before their marriage. (AES, *Memoir*, p. 230.) Holland signed the contract drawings for St. John the Divine, Kennington (at the BAL Drawings Collection), St. Andrew, East Heslerton (BAL), Wellington Barracks Chapel (BAL), All Saints, Middlesborough (BAL), St. Paul's, Rome (BAL), Holmbury St. Mary (Victoria and Albert Museum), and St. George, Clun (Victoria and Albert Museum).

7. "Miscellanea: The Late Mr. William Young," *Builder*, 20 January 1877, p. 72.

8. "The New Law Courts," *Building News*, 16 August 1878, p. 156.

9. Augustus W. Tanner, "Some Recollections of the Late Mr. Street and the Building of the Law Courts," *British Architect*, 1 December 1882, p. 568. PRO Works 12/40/2 f.1 (4 August 1870), GES to Galton.

10. PRO Works 12/40/2 f.2 (7 August 1870), Hunt memo; Works 12/34/4 ff.1–2 (26 November 1870), GES to Galton.

11. PRO T1/7140/19533 f.19533 (20 December 1871), Ayrton to Treasury lords.

12. PRO Works 12/34/2 ff.55–56 (19 June 1878), GES to Mitford (secretary of works).

13. "Progress at the New Law Courts," *Builder*, 4 October 1879, p. 1104. "The Royal Courts of Justice," *Illustrated London News*, 9 December 1882, pp. 601–2.

14. For surveying practice see: Frank Jenkins, *Architect and Patron* (London, New York, and Toronto: Oxford University Press, 1961), pp. 203–4.

15. "In gross" contracts were a recent development, used in part for the Houses of Parliament and for the entire Royal Exchange. Francis Michael Longstreth Thompson, *Chartered Surveyors: The Growth of a Profession* (London: Routledge, 1968), p. 88.

16. Robert Kerr, "English Architecture Thirty Years Hence," *Builder*, 17 May 1854, p. 729.

17. J. P. Seddon, "George Edmund Street, R.A.," *Architect*, 24 December 1881, p. 406.

18. AES, *Memoir*, pp. 281–82.

19. Andrew Saint, *Richard Norman Shaw* (New Haven and London: Yale University Press, 1976), pp. 15–16.

20. Quoted in AES, *Memoir*, p. 283.

21. Basil H. Jackson, ed., *Recollections of Thomas Graham Jackson, 1835–1924* (Oxford: Oxford University Press, 1950), pp. 58–61.

22. This technique is illustrated in the case of H. H. Richardson in Mariana Griswold Van Rensselaer, *Henry Hobson Richardson and His Works* (Boston: Houghton, Mifflin and Company, 1888), pp. 128–29.

23. Quoted in AES, *Memoir*, pp. 283–84.

24. Tanner, "Recollections of the Late Mr. Street," p. 567.

25. "The Late G. E. Street, R.A.," *Builder*, 24 December 1881, p. 779.

26. AES, *Memoir*, pp. 280–81.

27. Tanner, "Recollections of the Late Mr. Street," p. 567.

28. Quoted in AES, *Memoir*, p. 323. There are two sketchbooks at the Royal Academy and four at the BAL Drawings Collection.

29. *E.g.*, M [letter], "Correspondence: Convent of St. Margaret, East Grinstead," *Building News*, 25 December 1868, p. 882.

30. The only known colored renderings are a watercolor perspective of Bristol Cathedral at the Bristol City Art Gallery, a watercolor of St. Paul's, Rome, owned by the church, and Brewer's bird's-eye view of the law courts, tinted with sepia.

31. One of his landscape watercolors is reproduced as the frontispiece in Georgina G. King, ed., *George Edmund Street: Unpublished Notes and Reprinted Papers* (New York: Hispanic Society of America, 1916).

32. For GES's dissatisfaction with his use of color, see AES, *Memoir*, p. 286.

33. One such sketch, dated 1 September 1876, was published in the *Building News*, 23 October 1885. As these were given directly to the workmen they were not preserved among the working drawings now at the Public Record Office.

34. Quoted in AES, *Memoir*, p. 329.

35. Tanner, "Recollections of the Late Mr. Street," p. 568; see also AES, *Memoir*, p. 136.

36. An unidentified school at Wantage, the restored church at Sheviock, Cornwall, and All Saints, Boyne Hill. Noted in AES, *Memoir*, p. 13.

37. G. G. Scott, *Personal and Professional Recollections* (London: Sampson Low, Marston, Searle and Rivington, 1879), pp. 215–16.

38. Quoted in AES, *Memoir*, p. 284.

39. Victoria and Albert Museum.

40. PRO Works 12/34/2 ff.13–16 (15 January 1872), GES to Russell (secretary of works). Works 12/40/3 f.35 (27 March 1873), GES to Russell.

41. Multiple copies of most of the drawings exist in the PRO Works 30 class. The signed set of contract drawings is Works 30/2245–2492. GES's private papers were destroyed in the Second World War.

42. AES, *Memoir*, p. 277.

43. The copy of the contract signed by GES is Works 12/33/1 f.204 (23 September 1870). An altered draft is Works 12/33/1 f.203.

44. For the R.I.B.A. code see: Jenkins, *Architect and Patron*, p. 214.

45. Thompson, *Chartered Surveyors*, p. 90.

46. The decision of the law officers was reported to Ayrton in a 23 September letter; see "Upshot of Mr. Barry's Case," *Building News*, 30 September 1870, p. 236. For *Ebdy v. McGowan* see: "Architects and the Law," *Building News*, 25 November 1870, pp. 381–82. For the parallel American situation see: James F. O'Gorman, *H. H. Richardson and His Office* (Cambridge, Massachusetts: Harvard College Library, 1974), pp. 13–16.

47. "The New Conditions of the Office of Works for Architects," *Architect*, 5 November 1870, p. 254.

48. GES [letter], "Correspondence: The New Conditions of the Office of Works," *Architect*, 12 November 1870, p. 282, dated 7 November 1870.

49. PRO Works 12/33/2 ff.1–3 (18 November 1869), GES to James Stansfield (Treasury secretary).

50. PRO Works 12/33/2 ff.23–26 (18 March 1870), William Law (Treasury secretary) to Ayrton. Works 12/34/4 f.91 (22 April 1871), GES to Russell.

51. PRO Works 12/33/2 ff. 38–39 (15 January 1872), GES to Russell.

52. PRO Works 12/33/2 f.40 (22 January 1872), Hunt memo. Works 12/40/3 f.168 (30 July 1873), GES to Ayrton. Payment authorized in November 1873: Works 12/33/2 f.56 (19 November 1873), Adam to Treasury lords; Works 12/33/2 f.57 (29 November 1873), William Law (Treasury secretary) to Adam; Works 12/33/2 f.58 (4 December 1873), GES to Russell.

53. The meeting was reported in a letter and memorandum which GES submitted to Ayrton the next day: PRO Works 12/33/2 ff.4–12 (13 December 1869), GES to Ayrton.

54. PRO Works 12/33/2 ff.23–26 (18 March 1870), William Law (Treasury secretary) to Ayrton.

55. In PRO Works 12/33/2 ff.4–12 (13 December 1869), GES to Ayrton, this is cited as £2000, apparently by error.

56. Second meeting reported in PRO Works 12/33/2 ff. 13–14 (1 January 1870), GES to Ayrton. Works 12/33/2 ff. 16–22 (17 January 1870), Ayrton to Treasury lords.

57. PRO Works 12/33/2 ff.23–26 (18 March 1870), William Law (Treasury secretary) to Ayrton.

58. Copy is PRO Works 12/34/4 ff.6–9 (25 November 1870), GES to James Stansfield (Treasury secretary).

59. PRO Works 12/34/4 ff.12–14 (13 December 1870), Ayrton to Treasury lords.

60. PRO Works 12/34/4 f.16 (29 December 1870), Charles Strenge (Treasury secretary) to Ayrton. Meeting reported in PRO Works 12/34/4 f.117 (7 June 1871), GES to Russell; Works 12/33/2 ff.47–48 (13 August 1873), GES to Russell; and Works 12/33/2 ff.120–29 (16 November 1875), GES memo on claims.

61. PRO Works 12/33/2 ff.31–32 (23 March 1871), Hunt report; Works 12/33/2 ff.33–37 (24 March 1871), Galton report.

62. PRO Works 12/34/4 f.79 (27 March 1871), Ayrton to Treasury lords. Works 12/34/4 ff.94–95 (1 May 1871), Ayrton to Treasury lords.

63. PRO Works 12/34/4 ff.104–5 (16 May 1871), William Law (Treasury secretary) to Ayrton; Works 12/34/4 ff.113–14 (30 May 1871), William Law to Ayrton; Works 12/34/4 f.116 (6 June 1871), Russell to GES.

64. PRO Works 12/34/4 f.117 (7 June 1871), GES to Russell.

65. PRO Works 12/34/4 f.119 (9 June 1871), Russell to GES; Ayrton's draft of this letter is on the back of f.117.

66. PRO Works 12/33/2 ff.43–44 (20 November 1872), GES to Russell.

67. PRO Works 12/40/3 f.168 (30 July 1873), GES to Ayrton.

68. *Ibid.* (4 August 1873), Hunt memo; (9 August 1873), Galton memo.

69. PRO Works 12/40/3 f.172 (11 August 1873), Russell to GES.

70. Lord Redesdale (A. B. Mitford), *Memories* (New York: E. P. Dutton and Company, [1915]) 2:687.

71. PRO Works 12/33/2 f.49 (25 September 1873), GES to Russell. Works

12/33/2 ff.50–53 (26 September 1873), GES to Russell, requesting arbitration.

72. Street reminded the Office of Works of his claims in the interim: PRO Works 12/33/2 ff.60–61 (10 November 1873), GES to Russell; Works 12/33/2 f.63 (28 January 1874), GES to Russell.

73. PRO Works 12/33/2 f.54 (30 September 1873), Adam memo.

74. PRO Works 12/33/2 ff.64–66 (4 November 1873), Hunt and Galton report.

75. PRO Works 12/33/2 f.62 (10 February 1874), Adam to GES.

76. PRO Works 12/33/2 ff.67–68 (14 February 1874), GES to Adam.

77. PRO Works 12/33/2 f.69 (21 February 1874), Adam memo.

78. Hughenden papers.

79. Lord Redesdale, *Memories*, 2:683.

80. Hughenden papers, B/XX/Lx/488b, Disraeli's report of the Cabinet decision; B/XX/Lx/488c (15 July 1876), Disraeli to Lennox, requesting his resignation.

81. Lennox refers to Galton's eight week absence in Hughenden papers, B/XX/Lx/414 (16 April 1874), Lennox to Disraeli. On 27 October 1875 Galton is referred to as the "late Director of Works" in an interoffice memo: PRO Works 12/41/2 f.3 (27 October 1875). He received a £1000 pension although only fifty-three according to "Her Majesty's Office of Works and Public Buildings," *Builder*, 8 September 1877, p. 898.

82. Lord Redesdale, *Memories*, 2:703. For his appointment see: Hughenden papers, B/XX/Lx/413 (14 April 1874), Lennox to Disraeli; and B/XX/Lx/417 (27 April 1874), Lennox to Montagu Corry (Disraeli's private secretary). Lennox wished to promote Robert J. Callander, the assistant secretary, but Disraeli insisted on Mitford.

83. A. B. Mitford, *Tales of Old Japan* (London: Macmillan and Company, 1871). A. B. Mitford, *The Attaché at Peking* (London and New York: Macmillan and Company, 1900). Mitford was the grandfather of the celebrated Mitford sisters of the twentieth century.

84. Referred to in PRO Works 12/33/2 ff.72–73 (13 August 1874), Lingen (Treasury secretary) to Lennox.

85. *Ibid.*

86. The meetings are reported in PRO Works 12/33/2 ff.74–75 (19 January 1875), GES to Hunt (?); and Works 12/33/2 ff.120–29 (16 November 1875), GES memo on his pay claims.

87. PRO Works 12/33/2 f.77 (27 January 1875), Mitford to GES. Works 12/33/2 ff.78–81 (28 January 1875), GES to Mitford.

88. Memo to P. H. Lawrence on PRO Works 12/33/2 ff. 78–81. Reply to GES is Works 12/33/2 f.82 (6 February 1875), Mitford to GES.

89. PRO Works 12/33/2 ff.94–96 (8 February 1875), GES to Mitford.

90. PRO Works 12/33/2 ff.83–93 (13 March 1875), Hunt memo.

91. *Ibid.* Galton's memo is dated 17 March 1875. Lawrence's is 18 March 1875.

92. PRO Works 12/33/2 f.104 (1 June 1875), Mitford to GES.

93. PRO Works 12/33/2 ff.97–98 (13 May 1875), GES to Mitford. Works 12/33/2 f.100 (1 June 1875), Mitford to Lennox.

94. PRO Works 12/33/2 ff.102–3 (3 June 1875), GES to Mitford; Works 12/33/2 f.104 (1 June 1875), Mitford to GES; Works 12/33/2 f.105 (17 June 1875), Hunt memo, (21 June 1875), Galton memo, (10 August 1875), Lennox memo; Works 12/33/2 f.106 (12 August 1875), Mitford to GES. Works 12/33/2 ff.107–8 (6 October 1875), GES to Mitford.

95. *Ibid.* (18 October 1875), memos proposing meeting with GES; Works 12/33/2 ff.120–29 (16 November 1875), GES memo on claims; Works 12/33/2 ff.130–31 (13 December 1875), Hunt memo on meetings with GES.

96. PRO Works 12/33/2 ff.132–33 (17 December 1875), Mitford to GES.

97. PRO Works 12/33/2 ff.134–35 (20 December 1875), GES to Mitford.

98. PRO Works 12/35/1 ff.1–3 (6 November 1878), Hunt to Noel (first commissioner).

99. PRO Works 12/35/1 ff.4–5 (10 December 1878), Hunt to Mitford.

100. PRO Works 12/45/3 ff.53–59 (8 March 1884), Blomfield and AES to Mitford; Works 12/33/2 f.172 (23 December 1884), Hunt memo. Gandy had asked for £3663, however.

101. The first letters exchanged by GES and Ayrton, dated 13 December 1869 and 14 December 1869, have not been found. They are referred to in PRO Works 12/34/4 ff.138–39 (19 December 1871), GES to Russell.

102. The contractor was G. N. Haden and Son. Jack Simmons, *St. Pancras Station* (London: George Allen and Unwin, 1968), p. 55.

103. For an account of the heating of the Houses of Parliament see: Denis Smith, "The Building Services," chapter 11 in *The Houses of Parliament,* ed. M. H. Port (New Haven and London: Yale University Press, 1976).

104. PRO Works 12/34/4 ff.141–42 (23 December 1871), Hunt memo.

105. PRO Works 12/34/4 ff.143–44 (23 December 1871), Russell to GES.

106. PRO Works 12/41/2 f.1 (8 August 1874), GES to Galton; Works 12/41/2 ff.5–27 (n.d.), GES's heating plan. The technical details of this are discussed in chapter 7.

107. PRO Works 12/41/2 f.31 (12 April 1877), GES to Mitford; Works 12/41/2 f.75 (1877), GES's specifications for the heating of the east wing.

108. PRO Works 12/41/2 f.31 (16 April 1877), Hunt memo.

109. PRO Works 12/41/2 f.34 (30 April 1877), Haden's tender. Works 12/41/2 f.51 (27 July 1877), A. K. Stephenson (solicitor) memo, reporting signing of contract.

110. PRO Works 12/41/2 f.36 (3 May 1877), GES to Mitford. Haden contracted for the heating of GES's St. Michael, Frosterley, Durham, consecrated on 27 May 1869. "Building Intelligence: Churches and Chapels," *Building News,* 4 June 1869, p. 512.

111. PRO Works 12/41/1 f.6 (29 July 1878), GES to Mitford. Works 12/41/1 f.7 (31 July 1878), Mitford to GES.

112. PRO Works 12/41/1 f.8 (5 November 1878), GES to Mitford; Works 12/41/1 f.9 (8 November 1878), Percy to Mitford; Works 12/41/1 f.10 (11 November 1878), Percy to Mitford; Works 12/41/1 f.11 (15 November 1878), Percy to Mitford. The technicalities of the heating plan are discussed in chapter 7.

113. PRO Works 12/41/1 f.13 (6 December 1878), Hood to Mitford; Works 12/41/1 f.19 (24 January 1878), Mitford to Hood. Hood's letterhead listed "Iron Merchants, Engineers, Manufacturers of Hot Water, Steam, Hot Air, Gas and Cooking Apparatus, Hydraulic Machinery, Water Works, Gas Works, General Castings and Builders Iron Work."

114. PRO Works 12/41/1 f.21 (1 April 1879), Hood to Mitford. The report itself has not been found.

115. PRO Works 12/41/1 f.22 (22 April 1879), Percy memo.

116. PRO Works 12/41/1 ff.25–29 (26 April 1879), GES to Mitford.

117. PRO Works 12/41/1 f.30 (29 April 1879), Mitford to Hunt.

118. PRO Works 12/41/1 ff.32–33 (2 May 1879), Hunt to Mitford.

119. Meeting reported in PRO Works 12/41/1 ff.60–63 (8 May 1880), GES to Mitford. Works 12/41/1 ff.32–33 (12 May 1879), Noel memo; Works 12/41/1 f.31 (15 May 1879), Mitford to GES.

120. PRO Works 12/41/1 ff.34–36 (16 July 1879), GES to Mitford.

121. *Ibid.* (24 July 1879), Hunt memo.

122. PRO Works 12/41/1 ff.38–40 (26 July 1879), Noel to Treasury lords; Works 12/41/1 ff.41–42 (5 August 1879), Lingen (Treasury secretary) to Noel.

123. PRO Works 12/41/1 ff.43–44 (8 December 1879), GES to Mitford.

124. *Ibid.* (10 December 1879), Hunt memo.

125. GES proposed this arrangement on 23 January 1880, and they accepted. PRO Works 12/41/1 f.54 (7 February 1880), Haden and Son to GES.

126. PRO Works 12/41/1 f.58 (30 March 1880), Tanner to Mitford, submitting specifications, which have not themselves been found.

127. PRO Works 12/41/1 f.57 (3 May 1880), Hunt to Mitford; Works 12/41/1 f.59 (6 May 1880), Mitford to GES. Adam had spent the intervening years as Liberal whip.

128. PRO Works 12/41/1 ff.60–63 (8 May 1880), GES to Mitford.

129. Simmons, *St. Pancras Station,* p. 55.

130. PRO Works 12/41/1 ff.64–65 (10 May 1880), Hunt memo.

131. *Ibid.*

132. PRO Works 12/41/1 f.67 (13 May 1880), GES to Mitford.

133. PRO Works 12/41/1 ff.68–69 (17 May 1880), Hunt memo.

134. PRO Works 12/41/1 f.71 (19 May 1880), Mitford to GES.

135. PRO Works 12/41/1 f.73 (19 May 1880), GES to Mitford.

136. PRO Works 12/41/1 f.72 (24 May 1880), Hunt memo.

137. PRO Works 12/41/1 f.74 (25 May 1880), Mitford to GES.

138. PRO Works 12/41/1 ff.76–78 (26 May 1880), GES to Mitford.

139. PRO Works 12/41/1 ff.79–80 (31 May 1880), Hunt to Mitford.

140. PRO Works 12/41/1 ff.82–83 (4 June 1880), Hunt to Mitford.

141. PRO Works 12/41/1 f.84 (7 June 1880), Mitford to GES.

142. PRO Works 12/41/1 f.85 (8 June 1880), GES to Mitford.

143. PRO Works 12/41/1 f.96 (6 August 1880), GES to Mitford.

144. PRO Works 12/41/1 ff.97–108, various correspondence pertaining to the preparation for bidding (10 August–18 October 1880).

145. BL Add. MS. 44095 ff.112–13 (12 June 1880), Adam to Gladstone.

146. Christopher Hussey, "Haddo House, Aberdeenshire," *Country Life,* 18 August 1966, pp. 378–81; 25 August 1966, pp. 448–52. "The Memorial to the Late Mr. G. E. Street," *Building News,* 7 April 1882, p. 417.

147. The meeting is reported in PRO Works 12/41/1 f.109 (24 January 1881), GES to Mitford.

148. PRO Works 12/41/1 f.110 (1 February 1881), Hunt to Mitford; and (10[?] February 1881), Shaw-Lefevre to Mitford. Lord Redesdale, *Memories,* 2:688.

149. PRO Works 12/33/2 f.167 (21 July 1884), Hunt to Mitford. In 1880, GES had made a similar claim himself, which was rejected. He had then complained: "If the First Commissioner is really of [the] opinion that I am to do the works you enumerate without payment I submit—of course under protest." Works 12/33/2 ff.154–55 (11 June 1880), GES to Mitford.

150. PRO Works 12/40/2 f.1 (4 August 1870), GES to Galton.

151. PRO Works 12/40/2 f.2 (7 August 1870), Hunt memo.

152. PRO Works 12/40/2 f.1 (8 August 1870), Galton memo, (5 October 1870), Ayrton memo.

153. PRO Works 12/40/2 f.7 (18 November 1870), GES to Galton. The foundation plans are now at the BAL Drawings Collection.

154. PRO Works 12/40/2 ff.9–10 (12 December 1870), Russell to GES.

155. PRO Works 12/40/2 f.13 (15 December 1870), builders' resolutions. The surveyors were Hunt and Steward, and Widnell and Trollope.

156. PRO Works 12/40/2 f.12 (15 December 1870), GES to Ayrton.

157. PRO Works 12/40/2 f.14 (19 December 1870), Callander to GES, announcing approval.

158. The 18 November 1870 trial is reported in "Law Report: Court of Queen's Bench . . . Jones v. St. John's College, Oxford," *Times,* (19 November 1870), p. 11.

159. The builders' complaint and the meeting are reported in: "The London Builders and the Law Courts," *Builder,* 14 January 1871, p. 34; "The London Builders and the Law Courts," *Builder,* 21 January 1871, p. 44; "Our Office Table: The New Courts of Justice," *Building News,* 6 January 1871, p. 22; "Our Office Table: The New Law Courts," *Building News,* 13 January 1871, p. 39; "The New Courts of Justice," *Architect,* 7 January 1871, p. 14; "The New Courts of Justice," *Times,* 5 January 1871, p. 3; "The New Courts of Justice," *Law Journal,* 6 January 1871, p. 31; "The New Law Courts," *Law Journal,* 13 January 1871, p. 48.

160. PRO Works 12/40/2 f.19 (13 January 1871), printed invitation to tender; Works 12/40/2 f.20 (13 January 1871), Russell to Henry Lee (chairman of builders committee); Works 12/40/2 f.21 (13 January 1871), Russell to GES.

161. PRO Works 12/40/2 ff.23–24, table of tenders and the Doves' tender.

162. "Tenders for the New Law Courts: Foundations," *Builder,* 28 January 1871, p. 71; "The Foundations for the New Law

Courts," *Building News*, 27 January 1871, p. 73.

163. F. [letter], "Correspondence: New Law Courts," *Building News*, 17 February 1871, p. 136. See also: J. M. L. [letter], "Correspondence: New Law Courts," *Building News*, 10 February 1871, p. 118.

164. PRO Works 12/40/2 f.25 (20 January 1871), Russell to GES. Works 12/40/2 f.26 (21 January 1871), GES to Russell.

165. PRO Works 12/40/2 f.30 (23 January 1871), Ayrton to Treasury lords; Works 12/40/2 f.31 (1 February 1871), Charles Strenge (Treasury secretary) to Ayrton; Works 12/40/2 f.33 (3 February 1871), P. H. Lawrence (solicitor of works) to Ayrton.

166. Much of what follows about Dove Brothers comes from John Summerson, *The London Building World of the Eighteen-sixties* (London: Thames and Hudson, 1973), pp. 10–15.

167. "S. Mary Abbotts Church, Kensington," *Building News*, 3 June 1870, p. 413; Ian McQueen, *Bournemouth St. Peter's* (Milbourne Port, Sherborne, Dorset: Dorset Publishing Company, 1971), pp. 69–70.

168. PRO Works 12/40/2 f.45 (16 March 1872), GES to Russell.

169. PRO Works 12/40/2 f.57 (6 June 1872), GES to Russell; Works 12/40/2 f.67 (14 December 1872), GES to Russell; Works 12/40/2 ff.70–71 (4 January 1873), Russell to GES.

170. PRO Works 12/40/2 f.67 (14 December 1872), GES to Russell.

171. PRO Works 12/40/2 f.53 (30 May 1872), GES to Russell.

172. PRO Works 12/40/2 f.66 (13 December 1872), Dove to GES (copy). The technical issues involved in laying the foundations are discussed in chapter 7.

173. PRO Works 12/34/2 ff.13–16 (15 January 1872), GES to Russell.

174. PRO Works 12/40/3 f.10 (2 December 1872), GES to Ayrton.

175. PRO Works 12/40/2 ff.64–65 (6 December 1872), Hunt memo. Works 12/40/3 f.10 (6 December 1872), Galton to Ayrton. Works 12/40/3 ff.11–13 (9 December 1872), Russell to GES.

176. PRO Works 12/40/3 f.15 (11 December 1872), draft of letter to builders, with list of invitees.

177. PRO Works 12/40/3 ff.18–19 (14 January 1873), Russell to GES.

178. PRO Works 12/40/3 f.19 was amended, apparently by Galton, to include 4 firms; Works 12/40/3 f.25 (27 February 1873), printed invitation.

179. PRO Works 12/40/3 f.29 (25 March 1873), Galton's compilation of tenders. Works 12/40/3 f.114 (25 March 1873), Bulls' tender for main block. Works 12/40/3 f.115 (25 March 1873), Bulls' tender for eastern block. Works 12/40/3 f.116 (25 March 1873), Bulls' tender for the entire building. Works 12/40/3 f.117, table of tenders for entire building in Galton's hand. Works 12/40/3 f.118, table of tenders for main block in Galton's hand. Works 12/40/3 f.119, table of tenders for eastern block in Galton's hand.

180. PRO Works 12/40/3 ff.157–58 (2 July 1873), Callander to Bull.

181. "Trade News: Tenders," *Building News*, 2 June 1871, p. 441.

182. The author is grateful to S. D. Thomson, city archivist of Southampton, who found most of this information in the parish registers of the Above Bar Congregational Church and the Church of St. Mary.

183. "Building Intelligence: Churches and Chapels," *Building News*, 17 June 1870, p. 458. Monday was reported to be in charge of the Bulls' technical documents in "Our Office Table," *Building News*, 14 January 1876, p. 54; and "Retrospective," *Builder*, 30 December 1876, p. 1255. The spelling of his name is given variously as Monday, Munday, and Mondey.

184. PRO Works 12/40/3 f.163 (18 July 1874), Bull to Russell.

185. PRO Works 12/40/3 f.164 (21 July 1873), Hunt memo; Works 12/40/3 f.165 (24 July 1873), Callander to Bull.

186. PRO Works 12/40/3 ff.204–5 (2 September 1873), Bull memorandum on 1 September 1873 meeting.

187. PRO Works 12/40/3 f.190 (5 September 1873), GES to Galton. Works 12/40/3 ff.188–89 (6 September 1873), GES to Russell. Works 12/40/3 ff.190–201 (15 September 1873), Hunt to Adam. Works 12/40/3 f.202 (23 September 1873), Galton to Adam.

188. PRO Works 12/40/3 f.203 (2 October 1873), Adam memo; Works 12/40/3 ff.206–9 (9 October 1873), Callander to Bull.

189. PRO Works 12/40/3 ff.211–12 (18 October 1873), Bull to Russell.

190. PRO Works 12/40/3 f.214 (23 October 1873), GES to Russell, with (23 October 1873), Galton memo, and (23 October 1873), Hunt memo.

191. PRO Works 12/40/3 f.216 (6 November 1873), Callander to Bull.

192. PRO Works 12/40/3 f.218 (7 November 1873), Bull to Russell.

193. PRO Works 12/40/3 f.222 (18 November 1873), Bull to Russell.

194. "The Law Courts," *Builder*, 13 November 1873, p. 982; and "The Law Courts," *Builder*, 10 January 1874, p. 35.

195. PRO Works 12/40/3 ff.235–36 (28 January 1874), GES to Office of Works, enclosing (27 January 1874), Bull to GES.

196. "General," *Architect*, 14 February 1874, p. 94.

197. The contracts for the east block and the main building, together with the priced bills of quantities, are preserved at the Library of the Property Services Agency, Department of the Environment, Croydon. The signed contract drawings are PRO Works 30/2245–2492.

198. See the accounts in: "Miscellanea: The New Law Courts," *Builder*, 9 May 1874, p. 405; [E. D.], *The Royal Courts of Justice: Illustrated Handbook* ([London?]: printed for the author, 1883); and Tanner, "Recollections of the Late Mr. Street," p. 567. For Parliament see: Port, ed., *The Houses of Parliament*, p. 101.

199. PRO Works 12/45/2 ff.16–19 (12 October 1875), GES to Mitford. This letter quotes his complaint to Bull of 14 September 1875 and ten previous letters to the contractor that year.

200. "The New Law Courts," *Times*, 1 September 1875, p. 9. The figures contradict those quoted by GES.

201. PRO Works 12/35/1 ff.1–3 (6 November 1878), GES to Noel.

202. PRO Works 12/33/2 ff.170–71 (3 August 1884), AES to Mitford. See also: Works 12/45/3 ff.17–20 (1 March 1883), Hunt to Mitford.

203. The correspondence relating to this is PRO Works 12/42/5 ff.7–14 (25 January–12 February 1878).

204. The relevant correspondence is PRO Works 12/35/1 ff.11–14 (19–20 February 1879).

205. PRO Works 12/41/3 ff.32–33 (17 October 1882), Crompton (electrical engineer) to Mitford; Works 12/41/3 f.35 (9 November 1882), Crompton to Mitford.

206. For statistics on the deadline see: PRO Works 12/45/3 ff.23–26 (10 May 1883), Hunt to Mitford. The chancery order for the Bulls' liquidation is Works 12/45/3 ff.6–8 (26 January 1883). Information on the liquidation is drawn from correspondence in Works 12/45/3, *passim*, especially ff.100–113, a summary of the case, apparently prepared in 1895. See also: "Miscellanea: The Contractors for the New Law Courts," *Builder*, 13 January 1883, p. 62; and "The Royal Courts of Justice: The Contractors' Claims for 'Extras,'" *Builder*, 10 February 1883, p. 187. The liquidation was by "settlement" rather than by bankruptcy.

207. PRO Works 12/45/3 f.80 (24 March 1885), Hunt to Mitford.

208. The account that follows is drawn from a number of sources. The best general histories of British trade unionism in this period are Henry Pelling, *A History of British Trade Unionism*, 3d ed. (Harmondsworth, England: Penguin Books, 1976); and Sidney Webb and Beatrice Webb, *The History of Trade Unionism* (London, New York, and Toronto: Longmans, Green, and Company, 1920). There are two histories of building workers, both strongly pro-labor: William S. Hilton, *Foes to Tyranny: A History of the Amalgamated Union of Building Trade Workers* (London: The Amalgamated Union of Building Trade Workers, 1963); and Raymond W. Postgate, *The Builders' History* (London: Labour Publishing Company, [1923]). For detailed information about the 1877–78 strike, the best source is the weekly workingmen's newspaper, the *Industrial Review*. Edited by George Potter, this was the successor to his earlier, more radical *Beehive*. Because of the manner in which articles were written, it is sometimes difficult to assign precise dates to the events dis-

cussed in the *Review,* but its account is far more complete than that in the architectural journals.

209. Hilton, *Foes to Tyranny,* p. 144.

210. "The London Stone Masons," *Industrial Review,* 25 August 1877, p. 8.

211. Reported in "The London Trades Council and the London Stone Masons," *Industrial Review,* 27 October 1877, pp. 4–5.

212. These figures were reported by Henry Broadhurst after the strike. See: "The Masons of London and the Strike," *Industrial Review,* 6 April 1878, p. 4.

213. "The London Stone Masons' Strike," *Industrial Review,* 27 October 1877, p. 4; "The London Stone Masons' Strike," *Industrial Review,* 10 November 1877, p. 3; "The London Stone Masons' Strike," *Industrial Review,* 24 November 1877, p. 3. The last article maintained that only 60 foreigners were at work at the courts. The figures were much disputed.

214. "The London Stone Masons' Strike," *Industrial Review,* 1 December 1877, p. 4; Tanner, "Recollections of the Late Mr. Street," p. 568.

215. "The London Stone Masons," *Industrial Review,* 15 December 1877, p. 9.

216. "German Violence Protected by Law," *Industrial Review,* 19 January 1878, p. 1.

217. Quoted from the *Daily News* (5 November 1877) in "A Foreign Colony in London," *Industrial Review,* 10 November 1877, p. 5.

218. "The London Stone Masons' Strike," *Industrial Review,* 3 November 1877, pp. 5–6.

219. *Ibid.,* p. 6.

220. "The London Stone Masons' Strike," *Industrial Review,* 9 March 1878, p. 5; PRO Works 12/45/1 ff. 119–20 (8 January 1880), Noel to Treasury lords.

221. "The London Stone Masons," *Industrial Review,* 17 November 1877, p. 3. "The London Builders and the Masons' Strike," *Industrial Review,* 17 November 1877, p. 3.

222. "The London Masons' Strike and Arbitration," *Industrial Review,* 16 February 1878, pp. 4–5.

223. *Ibid.;* "The London Stone Masons," *Industrial Review,* 23 February 1878, p. 6; "The London Stone Masons' Strike," *Industrial Review,* 29 December 1877, p. 5.

224. "The London Masons," *Industrial Review,* 2 March 1878, p. 4.

225. "The London Stone Masons," *Industrial Review,* 9 February 1878, p. 6; "The London Stone Masons' Strike," *Industrial Review,* 9 March 1878, p. 5.

226. "The Masons of London and the Strike," *Industrial Review,* 6 April 1878, p. 4.

227. "The London Stone Masons," *Industrial Review,* 23 March 1878, p. 9.

228. Hilton, *Foes to Tyranny,* p. 164.

229. "The New Law Courts," *Building News,* 16 August 1878, p. 156; "Progress at the New Law Courts," *Builder,* 4 October 1879, p. 1104.

Notes to Chapter 7

1. "Retrospective," *Builder,* 30 December, 1876, p. 1254. A cataloguing of the PRO, undertaken after this chapter was written, has brought to light additional files pertaining to the construction of the law courts.

2. The account of the Doves' work which follows is based largely on "Foundations for the New Law Courts," *Building News,* 25 August 1871, p. 133. See also: "Works in Hand: Foundations for the New Law Courts," *Architect,* 8 April 1871, p. 185.

3. M. H. Port, ed., *The Houses of Parliament,* (New Haven and London: Yale University Press, 1976), p. 197. Also: J.

Mordaunt Crook, "Sir Robert Smirke: A Pioneer of Concrete Construction," *Transactions of the Newcomen Society* 38 (1965–66): 5–22.

4. Port, ed., *The Houses of Parliament,* p. 198.

5. "Foundations for the New Law Courts," p. 133.

6. Reported in "Miscellanea: The Workmen at the Law Courts," *Builder,* 2 March 1872, p. 174; and "Chips," *Building News,* 8 March 1872, p. 206.

7. "Our Office Table: The New Law Courts," *Building News,* 20 February 1874, p. 218.

8. Dates from Augustus W. Tanner,

"Some Recollections of the Late Mr. Street and the Building of the Law Courts," *British Architect*, 1 February 1882, p. 567.

9. "The New Law Courts," *Times*, 25 August 1874, p. 6.

10. This part of the work is best described in "Retrospective," *Builder*, 30 December 1876, p. 1254.

11. This and the subsequent discussion of machinery is based on these sources: "The New Law Courts," *Times*, 25 August 1874, p. 6; "The New Law Courts," *Times*, 1 September 1875, p. 9; "Retrospective," *Builder*, 30 December 1876, pp. 1253–55; "Progress at the New Law Courts," *Builder*, 4 October 1879, p. 1104; and "The New Law Courts," *Building News*, 16 August 1878, p. 156.

12. "The New Law Courts," *Building News*, 16 August 1878, p. 156.

13. "The New Law Courts," *Building News*, 19 May 1876, p. 490.

14. GES's earlier view is reflected in his "On the Probability of Certain Churches in Kent and Surrey Being by the Same Architect, with a Suggestion for a Guild of Architects," *Ecclesiologist* 11 (1850): 31–42. His later, more skeptical attitude toward medieval craftsmanship is seen in *Some Account of Gothic Architecture in Spain*, 2d ed. (London: John Murray, 1869), p. 464; and in his discussion of Christ Church Cathedral, Dublin, quoted in AES, *Memoir*, p. 117.

15. For scaffolding at Parliament see: Port, ed., *The Houses of Parliament*, pp. 208–12.

16. Tanner, "Recollections of the Late Mr. Street," p. 568.

17. "The New Law Courts," *Building News*, 17 January 1879, p. 76.

18. For the numbers of workers see: PRO Works 12/45/2 ff. 16–19 (12 October 1875), GES to Mitford; "The New Law Courts," *Times*, 25 August 1874, p. 6; "The New Law Courts," *Times*, 1 September 1875, p. 9; "The London Stone Masons' Strike," *Industrial Review*, 27 October 1877, p. 4; "The New Law Courts," *Building News*, 16 August 1878, p. 156; "The New Law Courts," *Building News*, 17 January 1879, p. 76; "Progress at the New Law Courts," *Builder*, 4 October 1879, p. 1104.

19. Port, ed., *The Houses of Parliament*, p. 216, table 3.

20. PRO Works 12/45/2 ff. 16–19 (12 October 1875), GES to Mitford.

21. "Miscellanea: Accident at the New Law Courts," *Builder*, 1 May 1875, p. 403; and "The New Law Courts," *Times*, 1 September 1875, p. 9.

22. "Accidents: New Law Courts," *Builder*, 30 September 1876, p. 959.

23. "Miscellanea: Accidents at the New Law Courts," *Builder*, 30 October 1875, p. 983.

24. "Miscellanea: Accident at the New Law Courts," *Builder*, 5 January 1878, p. 25.

25. On Portland stone see: "On the Principal Building Stones Used in the Metropolis: Civil and Mechanical Engineers Society," *Building News*, 11 June 1869, p. 526. This is a report on a talk given by Arthur C. Bain on 2 June 1869. See also Alec Clifton-Taylor, *The Pattern of English Building*, new ed. (London: Faber and Faber, 1972), pp. 68–70. The contract, general conditions, and specifications for the superstructure of the law courts are preserved at the Library of the Property Services Agency, Department of the Environment, Croydon. They provide most of the details that follow.

26. Port, ed., *The Houses of Parliament*, pp. 97–98.

27. GES, "The True Principles of Architecture, and the Possibility of Development," *Ecclesiologist* 13 (1852): 255.

28. "Our Office Table," *Building News*, 24 January 1879, p. 110. The mistake was made in "The New Law Courts," *Building News*, 17 January 1879, p. 76.

29. GES, "True Principles of Architecture," p. 248; and R.A. lecture "Principles of the Art of Architecture," quoted in AES, *Memoir*, p. 342.

30. "Dennett's Fire-proof Constructions," *Building News*, 21 September 1866, p. 626. An example of an advertisement is "The Dennett Arch," *Building News*, 17 January 1868, p. iv.

31. [Patent news], *Building News*, 6 September 1867, p. 623. "Notes on Novelties: Bullivant's Patent Air-proof and Noiseless Sashes and Frames," *Architect*, 3 December 1870, p. 323.

32. Referred to in PRO Works 12/32/1 f. 6 (4 August 1874), Galton to Lennox.

33. PRO Works 12/32/1 ff. 1–4 (3 Au-

gust 1874), GES to Galton. F.5 is a printed plan for the unsuccessful site extension bill of 1868, marked to show the two sites then under consideration. Works 12/32/1 f.7 (19 August 1874), Hunt to Lennox.

34. PRO Works 30/1294 and 30/1295.

35. PRO Works 12/32/1 f.7 (19 August 1874), Lennox memorandum.

36. Reported in PRO Works 12/46/1 ff.8–10 (30 April 1877), W. H. Smith (Treasury secretary) to Noel; and Works 12/34/2 ff.38–39 (31 July 1877), GES to Mitford.

37. PRO Works 12/34/2 ff.38–39 (31 July 1877), GES to Mitford.

38. PRO Works 12/34/2 ff.41–42 (8 August 1877), GES to Mitford. Works 12/34/2 ff.55–56 (19 June 1878), GES to Mitford.

39. PRO Works 12/34/2 ff.41–42 (8 August 1877), GES to Mitford [excerpted in Works 12/32/1 f.8, with approving memo (10 August 1877) by Hunt.] Works 12/32/1 f.13 (19 November 1877), Treasury to Noel.

40. PRO Works 12/43/1 ff.7–8 (10 March 1881), GES to Mitford.

41. "Temple Bar and the New Law Courts," *Builder*, 26 December 1874, p. 1065.

42. "The New Law Courts: Visit of the Architectural Association," *Builder*, 20 May 1876, p. 492.

43. F. H. W. Sheppard, ed., *Survey of London, Volume 38, The Museums Area of South Kensington and Westminster* (London: University of London, 1975), pp. 209–10.

44. Hughenden papers, B/XX/Lx/422a (14 April 1874), Scott to Lennox.

45. PRO Works 12/43/5 ff.11–12 (9 January 1879), GES to Mitford (excerpted in Works 12/42/6 f.1).

46. PRO Works 12/42/6 ff.3–4 (22 February 1879), GES to Mitford.

47. *Ibid.*, (24 February 1879), Mitford and Hunt memos.

48. PRO Works 12/42/6 ff.13–14 (11 December 1879), GES to Mitford. Mitford and Hunt both called it an "enormous improvement" over the February design.

49. PRO Works 30/2032, "New Courts of Justice No. 33. Contract Drawing Detail No. 1. Proposed Altered Position of Gables Carey Street Elevation, Main Building," dated July 1874.

50. PRO Works 30/2062, "New Courts of Justice. Contract Drawing No. 33P. Detail No. 1. Carey Street Elevation. Main Building. Detail of Upper Portion and Gables of Wings," dated April 1877. This shows the triple gable. A pencil sketch suggests that GES later considered a single gable, but a final design of 5 November 1879 preserves the triple feature: Works 30/2077v.

51. Nikolaus Pevsner, *London 1: The Cities of London and Westminster*, 3d ed. rev. (Harmondsworth, England: Penguin Books, 1973), p. 321. In fact, Webb left GES's office in 1858.

52. PRO Works 12/42/5 f.1 (29 March 1876), Earp to GES (copy on GES's stationery).

53. PRO Works 12/42/5 ff.2–3 (31 March 1876), GES to Mitford.

54. *Ibid.* (3 April 1876), Hunt and Lennox memos.

55. PRO Works 12/42/5 f.5 (16 November 1877), GES to Mitford, outlining the program.

56. PRO Works 12/42/5 f.19 (3 July 1880), Tanner to Mitford.

57. Reported in "Our Office Table," *Building News*, 3 September 1880, p. 288; and "Parliamentary Notes: The New Law Courts," *Building News*, 10 September 1880, p. 314.

58. PRO Works 12/42/5 ff.10–11 (4 February 1878), GES to Mitford; and Works 12/42/5 f.18 (3 February 1879), GES to Noel.

59. PRO Works 12/42/5 f.21 (21 July 1881), GES to Mitford.

60. PRO Works 12/45/5 ff.23–24 (4 August 1881), GES to Mitford.

61. PRO Works 12/43/5 f.1 (6 July 1877), Noel to Treasury lords.

62. PRO Works 12/43/5 f.2 (17 July 1877), William Law (Treasury secretary) to Noel.

63. PRO Works 12/43/3 ff.1–2 (27 May 1881), H. Wilson (superintendent of furniture, Office of Works) memo.

64. PRO Works 12/34/2 ff.26–27 (17 July 1878), GES to Noel, referring to the eighteen rooms on the first floor.

65. PRO Works 12/34/2 ff.29–30 (24 July 1878), Tanner to Mitford, enclosing drawings now lost.

66. PRO Works 12/43/5 ff.21–23 (2 April 1880), GES to Noel.

67. PRO Works 12/43/5 ff.25–26 (27 July 1880), GES to Mitford, with Hunt memo (3 August 1880), approving.

68. PRO Works 12/43/2 f.1 (26 August 1880), GES to Mitford.

69. PRO Works 12/43/2 f.12 (23 November 1880), Mitford to GES, reporting invitations to tender; Works 12/43/1 f.19 (14 March 1881), Mitford to GES, reporting invitations to tender.

70. PRO Works 12/43/1 f.16 (5 April 1881), GES to Mitford.

71. PRO Works 12/43/2 f.35 (15 March 1881), H. Cuffe (solicitor of works) memo; Works 12/43/1 f.28 (3 October 1882), J. Mason (chief examiner of works) memo, noting date of western contracts. Lovatt's complaint appears in Works 12/43/2 f.33 (28 February 1881), Holland to Mitford; and Works 12/43/2 f.34 (5 March 1881), Lovatt to Mitford. The delay in signing the eastern contract was due to an error by which the schedule of prices was sent out to be printed instead of being copied by hand. Works 12/43/2 f.33 (1 March 1881), Mitford memo.

72. These drawings are lost. The specifications, which are quoted hereafter, have been preserved. Those for rooms one to four, dated January 1881, are PRO Works 12/43/1 ff.70–86; for rooms five to nine, dated January 1881, are Works 12/43/1 ff.87–100; for rooms ten to fourteen, dated October 1880, are Works 12/43/2 ff.140–59; and for rooms fifteen to eighteen, dated October 1880, are Works 12/43/2 ff.121–39.

73. Reported in PRO Works 12/43/1 f.44 (19 December 1884), AES to Mitford. The date of this fire has not been determined, but it preceded this letter by much more than one year.

74. PRO Works 12/46/1 ff.141–42 (16 August 1881), GES to Mitford. Discussion of present condition with Mr. J. F. Warwick, assistant superintendent and controller of common services.

75. PRO Works 12/43/5 ff.11–12 (9 January 1879), GES to Mitford.

76. PRO Works 12/43/5 f.13 (3 February 1879), Hunt to Mitford; Works 12/43/5 f.14 (10 February 1879), Mitford to GES; Works 12/43/5 f.15 (11 February 1879), GES to Mitford.

77. PRO Works 12/43/4 f.1 (9 December 1879), Henry Leigh Pemberton (solicitor of the supreme court) to Mitford.

78. PRO Works 12/43/4 f.2 (15 December 1879), Noel to Treasury lords; Works 12/43/4 f.3 (29 December 1879), Lingen (Treasury secretary) to Noel; Works 12/43/4 f.4 (30 December 1879), Mitford to GES.

79. PRO Works 12/43/4 f.5 (15 January 1880), GES to Mitford.

80. Jessie was the daughter of William Holland, a partner in the firm until a year before his death in 1879. See: Simon Jervis, "Holland and Sons, and the Furnishing of the Athenaeum," *Furniture History* 6 (1970): 43–61.

81. PRO Works 12/43/4 ff.7–8 (12 February 1880), GES to Mitford, enclosing list of tenders.

82. PRO Works 12/43/4 f.23 (21 February 1880), contract with Collinson and Lock.

83. Juliet Kinchin, "Collinson and Lock," *Connoisseur* 201 (May–August 1979): 47–53. A complete survey of surviving furniture in the building has not been attempted. Conclusions are therefore tentative.

84. PRO Works 12/43/3 ff.1–2 (24 May 1881), GES to Mitford.

85. PRO Works 12/43/3 f.3 (14 June 1881), Mitford to GES.

86. PRO Works 12/43/3 ff.6–7 (16 August 1881), GES to Mitford.

87. Victoria and Albert Museum, Holland Papers, *Sales Journal,* 1880–84.

88. Ironically, this delay was made in part at the urging of GES, in order to have time to test Bulls' work more thoroughly for suspected deficiencies. PRO Works 12/46/1 ff.141–42 (16 August 1881), GES to Mitford, with concurring memos by Hunt and Noel (19 August 1881).

89. The drawings are lost. PRO Works 12/43/4 ff. 10–11 (16 February 1882), AES and Blomfield to Mitford; Works 12/43/3 ff.44–50 (14 February 1882), Gillow and Company tender; Works 12/43/3 ff.51–57 (14 February 1882), Collinson and Lock tender. The tender of Holland and Sons is missing.

90. PRO Works 12/43/3 ff.17–18 (13 July 1882), AES and Blomfield to Mitford, proposing extension of contracts, with approving memo by Shaw-Lefevre (17 July

1882). Works 12/43/3 ff.21–26 (25 July 1882), Gandy furniture schedule.

91. No additional estimate survives, nor do the contracts. The increased furniture order is approved in PRO Works 12/43/3 f.31 (2 August 1882), Callander to Blomfield.

92. Jervis, "Holland and Sons," pp. 43–61. A book on the work of the firm by Edward Joy is anticipated.

93. The apparently incomplete Holland records do not show any major furniture construction for the law courts until the summer of 1883, when they were engaged to furnish the refreshment rooms in the basement. Victoria and Albert Museum, Holland Papers, *Sales Journal*, 1880–84.

94. Background information is provided in Nicholas Goodison and John Hardy, "Gillows at Tatton Park," *Furniture History* 6 (1970): 1–39.

95. Westminster Public Library, Gillow Papers: Estimate Book 28 [120], 12636, 12637, 12638; Estimate Book 29 [121], 12847, 12848, 12849, 12850, 12894; Estimate Book 30 [122], 13051, 13052, 13053, 13054, 13055, 13060, 13073, 13090, 13108, 13109, 13120, 13125, 13131; Estimate Book 46 [138], 536. The photostatic copy of these papers, located at the Victoria and Albert Museum, was consulted.

96. PRO Works 12/42/4 ff.1–3 (8 June 1881), GES to Mitford.

97. PRO Works 12/42/4 f.4 (13 June 1881), Mitford to GES.

98. PRO Works 12/42/4 ff.5–6 (24 August 1881), GES to Mitford; Works 12/42/4 f.7 (31 August 1881), Shaw-Lefevre to Treasury lords; Works 12/42/4 f.8 (12 September 1881), Colin (Treasury secretary) to Shaw-Lefevre.

99. GES, "On Glass Painting," *Ecclesiologist* 13 (1852): 238.

100. Tanner, "Recollections of the Late Mr. Street," p. 569. PRO Works 12/42/4 f.10 (10 December 1881), Tanner to Mitford. Works 12/42/4 f.11 (12 December 1881), Mitford to GES.

101. "Report of the Commissioners Appointed to Advise and Report as to the Buildings Proper to Be Erected and the Plans upon which Such Buildings Shall Be Erected for the New Courts of Justice," *BPP*, volume 20 in 1871, p. 72.

102. GES's plan is PRO Works 12/41/2 ff.5–27.

103. GES's 1877 specifications for this system are PRO Works 12/41/2 f.75.

104. Note on drawing PRO Works 30/1804.

105. The specifications for the adopted design have not been found. They are described by GES in two letters to Mitford: PRO Works 12/41/1 ff.43–44 (8 December 1879); and Works 12/41/1 f.110 (29 January 1881). The fullest description is in "Warming and Ventilation of the New Law-Courts," *Building News*, 17 February 1882, p. 195; slightly modified in "Visit of the Architectural Association to the New Law Courts," *Builder*, 3 April 1886, p. 523.

106. PRO Works 12/42/9 f.7 (27 April 1877), list of tenders.

107. PRO Works 12/42/9 f.22 (28 October 1879), GES to Mitford, with Mitford memo (31 October 1879) and Hunt memo (3 November 1879).

108. PRO Works 12/42/9 f.24 (4 November 1879), Mitford to GES; Works 12/42/9 f.25 (20 November 1879), GES to Mitford; Works 12/42/9 f.26 (25 November 1879), Mitford to GES.

109. PRO Works 12/42/9 f.27 (8 December 1879), GES to Mitford. On the same day, in another letter to Mitford, he called the use of electric light "probable": Works 12/41/1 ff.43–44 (8 December 1879), GES to Mitford.

110. PRO Works 12/42/9 f.28 (3 January 1880), Callander to GES.

111. "Royal Institute of British Architects," *Architect*, 30 April 1881, pp. 308–10. Also reported in "Royal Institute of British Architects: Obituary—Electric Lighting," *Builder*, 30 April 1881, pp. 534–35.

112. PRO Works 12/42/9 ff.29–30 (13 February 1882), AES and Blomfield to Mitford.

113. Crompton's first estimate is PRO Works 12/41/3 ff.1–3 (16 May 1882), Crompton to Shaw-Lefevre. Works 12/41/3 ff.4–11 is subsequent correspondence.

114. PRO Works 12/41/3 ff.12–15 (4 September 1882), Blomfield to Shaw-Lefevre.

115. The Swan lamps at Cragside are shown in Andrew Saint, *Richard Norman Shaw* (New Haven and London: Yale University Press, 1976), plate 98.

116. The search for an alternative power source may be followed in PRO Works 12/41/3 ff.22–35.

117. Completion is reported in PRO Works 12/41/3 f.52 (22 February 1883), H. R. Arthur (for Swan) to Shaw-Lefevre; and Works 12/41/3 f.58 (26 June 1883), J. H. Ivory (for Swan) to Shaw-Lefevre.

118. Complaints: PRO Works 12/41/3 ff.55–56 (30 March 1883), Mitford to Swan; and Works 12/41/3 ff.61–62 (24 August 1883), Potter to Crompton. For the new engines see Works 12/41/4, *passim*.

119. The lighting system as finally constituted is described in "Miscellanea: The Electric Light in the Law Courts," *Builder*, 6 September 1884, p. 342 [reprinted from the *Electrician*]; and "Visit of the Architectural Association to the New Law Courts," *Builder*, 3 April 1886, p. 523.

120. GES, *Remarks and Suggestions on the Scheme for the Completion of St. Paul's Cathedral* (London, 1871).

121. "The Demolition of Temple Bar," *Builder*, 8 August 1874, p. 673.

122. PRO Works 12/38/3 ff.9–14 (3 August 1874), GES to Mitford.

123. PRO Works 12/38/3 f.16 (6 August 1874), GES to Mitford.

124. The Court of Common Council meeting on 17 December 1874 is reported in "Temple Bar and the New Law Courts," *Builder*, 26 December 1874, pp. 1064–65; and "Temple Bar," *Architect*, 19 December 1874, p. 336. The engineer of the commissioners of sewers proposed removal of Temple Bar at their meeting on 16 March 1875. Reported in "Temple Bar," *Architect*, 20 March 1875, p. 179; and "Miscellanea:

Fleet-street and Temple Bar," *Builder*, 27 March 1875, p. 289.

125. "Temple Bar," *Architect*, 30 September 1876, p. 204.

126. First discussed by the City lands committee on 5 March 1877: "Mr. Street, R.A., and the Temple Bar Memorial," *Architect*, 2 October 1880, p. 209.

127. PRO Works 12/38/3 ff.32–33 (26 July 1877), Frederick Brand (City comptroller) to Mitford; Works 12/38/3 f.35 (8 August 1877), GES to Mitford. "Miscellanea: Temple Bar," *Builder*, 24 November 1879, p. 1184.

128. "Miscellanea: Temple Bar," *Builder*, 19 January 1878, p. 73.

129. PRO Works 12/38/2 ff.5–6 (28 April 1880), GES to Mitford.

130. PRO Works 12/38/2, *passim*. GES [letter], "The Common Council and the Temple Bar Memorial," *Times*, 25 September 1880, p. 11, dated 25 September 1880. GES [letter], "Temple-Bar Memorial," *Times*, 29 September 1880, p. 9, dated 28 September 1880. GES [letter], "Temple-Bar Memorial," *Times*, 13 October 1880, p. 11, dated 12 October 1880.

131. "Temple Bar," *Architect*, 14 August 1880, p. 109; and "The Temple Bar Memorial," *Architect*, 13 November 1880, p. 304.

132. "The Design of the Temple Bar Memorial," *Architect*, 20 November 1880, pp. 313–14.

133. "Our Office Table," *Building News*, 1 December 1882, p. 682. The *Times* also criticized the design: [leading article], *Times*, 8 October 1880, p. 7.

Notes to Chapter 8

1. A. W. Blomfield [letter], "Correspondence: The President of the Institute," *Architect*, 23 April 1881, dated 19 April 1881. Also printed in *Building News*, 22 April 1881, p. 467; and *Builder*, 23 April 1881, p. 522.

2. The narrative of GES's last months comes largely from AES, *Memoir*, pp. 270–73.

3. The date of the second stroke comes from "The Late G. E. Street, R.A.," *Builder*, 24 December 1881, p. 777. Arthur

places it a few days earlier, but the *Builder*'s dates seem to be more consistent.

4. "Mr. George Edmund Street, R.A.," *The Guardian* [Westminster], 21 December 1881, p. 1821.

5. The funeral is reported in "Funeral of Mr. G. E. Street, R.A.," *Building News*, 30 December 1881, p. 893; "Funeral of Mr. G. E. Street, R.A.," *Builder*, 31 December 1881, p. 831; and "Notes and Comment," *Architect*, 31 December 1881, p. 427.

6. Simon Jervis, "Holland and Sons,

and the Furnishing of the Athenaeum," *Furniture History* 6 (1970): 45.

7. BL Add. MS. 44786 f.68 (24 April 1879), breakfast list. AES, *Memoir*, pp. 258–59.

8. "The Will of Mr. George Edmund Street, R.A.," *Builder*, 8 April 1882, p. 414. Holland and Sons assessed the furnishings at Cavendish Place and Holmdale at £5447 and £1173, respectively. They also valued the lease at Cavendish Place at £6400 (thirty-four years at £150 p.a.). Victoria and Albert Museum, Holland Papers, Day Book, 1882 (R–Z).

9. PRO Works 12/33/1 ff.206–7 (19 December 1881), AES to Shaw-Lefevre.

10. PRO Works 12/33/1 ff.211–12 (23 December 1881), AES to Mitford. See also AES, *Memoir*, p. 292.

11. The drawings for these are PRO Works 30/2216, 2217[r], 2217[v], 2218, 2219, 2220, 2221, 2222, and 2223. AES also designed some fittings for the appeals court in 1883: Works 30/2213, 2214, and 2215.

12. The drawings for these are PRO Works 30/2225[A–D], 2238, 2239, 2240, 2241, 2242, 2243, and 2244.

13. "Notes," *Builder*, 31 October 1885, p. 595.

14. Cavendish Bentinck in *Hansard*, 3s 279 (21 May 1883): 641.

15. "The Central Hall of the Law Courts," *Punch*, 11 November 1893, p. 217.

16. PRO Works 12/33/2 ff.170–71 (3 August 1884), AES to Mitford.

17. *Ibid.*

18. PRO Works 12/45/3 ff.17–20 (1 March 1883), Hunt to Mitford.

19. PRO Works 12/58/6 ff.2–3 (April 1891). The precise cutoff was 31 March 1885.

20. The opening ceremony was reported best in the illustrated papers. See: "Opening of the Royal Courts of Justice," *Illustrated London News*, 2 December 1882, p. 566; [leading article], *Illustrated London News*, 9 December 1882, p. 586; "The Queen Opening the Royal Courts of Justice," *Illustrated London News*, 9 December 1882, pp. 610–11; "Topics of the Week: Last Monday's Ceremony," *Graphic*, 9 December 1882, p. 627; "Our Illustrations: The Opening of the Royal Courts of Jus-

tice," *Graphic*, 9 December 1882, pp. 627–30; J. D. S., "The Memories of Westminster Hall," *Graphic*, 9 December 1882, p. 635; and supplement to the *Pictorial World*, 9 December 1882, pp. 441–44. See also: "The New Law Courts: The Great Hall," *Builder*, 9 December 1882, p. 746; "Our Lithographic Illustrations: The New Royal Courts of Justice," *Building News*, 8 December 1882, p. 692; and "The Royal Palace of Justice," *Architect*, 9 December 1882, pp. 355–56.

21. The security precautions are recounted in Lord Redesdale (A. B. Mitford), *Memories* (New York: E. P. Dutton and Company, [1915]) 2: 688–90.

22. "Death of the President of the Royal Institute of British Architects," *Builder*, 24 December 1881, pp. 784–85; "Architectural Association: The Late G. E. Street, R.A.," *Builder*, 14 January 1882, pp. 54–55; "Royal Institute of British Architects," *Building News*, 23 December 1881, p. 819; "Architectural Association: The Late Mr. G. E. Street, R.A.," *Building News*, 13 January 1882, pp. 40–41.

23. "The Dean of York on the Late Mr. G. E. Street," *Building News*, 6 January 1882, p. 29; "The Late Mr. Street," *Architect*, 7 January 1882, p. 9.

24. "Canon Barry on the Late Mr. G. E. Street," *Building News*, 6 January 1882, p. 29; "The Late Mr. Street," *Architect*, 7 January 1882, p. 9. Canon Alfred Barry was the brother of E. M. Barry.

25. "Proposed Memorial of the Late Mr. Street," *Builder*, 11 February 1882, p. 176; "Statues, Memorials, &c," *Building News*, 10 February 1882, p. 192; "The Late Mr. G. E. Street," *Architect*, 11 February 1882, pp. 90–91.

26. "The Street Memorial," *Builder*, 8 April 1882, p. 415; "The Memorial to the Late Mr. G. E. Street," *Building News*, 7 April 1882, p. 417; "The Late Mr. G. E. Street, R.A.," *Architect*, 8 April 1882, p. 219; PRO Works 12/34/3 ff.1–3 (19 July 1882), Blomfield to Mitford.

27. A. J. Beresford-Hope [letter], "Correspondence: Memorial to Mr. Street, R.A.," *Building News*, 9 June 1882, p. 711, dated 7 June 1882. PRO Works 12/34/3 ff.5–6 (25 July 1882), Shaw-Lefevre to Treasury lords; Works 12/34/3 f.7 (28 July

1882), Leonard Courtney (Treasury secretary) to Shaw-Lefevre.

28. PRO Works 12/34/3 f.8 (10 December 1884), Blomfield to Mitford.

29. "The Late Mr. Street, R.A.," *Illustrated London News*, 27 March 1886, p. 323; AES, *Memoir*, pp. 294–95.

30. PRO Works 12/42/2 f.12 (10 May 1878), Potter contract.

31. PRO Works 12/42/2 f.17 (24 March 1881), Shaw-Lefevre to Treasury lords; Works 12/42/2 f.18 (31 March 1881), Cavendish (Treasury secretary) to Shaw-Lefevre.

32. PRO Works 12/42/2 f.26 (19 April 1882), Mitford to Christie; Works 12/42/2 f.27 (24 April 1882), E. Dunkin (Christie's assistant) to Mitford; Works 12/42/2 f.33 (1 July 1882), Mitford to Gillett and Bland; Works 12/42/2 ff.36–38 (26 July 1882), Gillett and Bland to Blomfield, enclosing estimate; Works 12/42/2 f.39 (28 July 1882), Blomfield to Mitford; Works 12/42/2 f.40 (9 August 1882), Callander to Gillett and Bland.

33. PRO Works 12/42/2 f.53, designs of old and new dials.

34. In addition to the sources cited above, see: "Miscellanea: A Big Bell for the Royal Courts of Justice," *Builder*, 12 May 1883, p. 657; "The Clock and Bells at the New Law Courts," *Builder*, 22 December 1883, p. 841; and "The Law Courts Clock and Bells," *Illustrated London News*, 29 December 1883, p. 631.

35. PRO Works 12/42/2 f.63 (4 December 1883), Gillett and Bland to Mitford.

36. GES's design, which is lost, was exhibited at the Royal Academy in 1869 (no. 993). See: Basil H. Jackson, ed., *Recollections of Thomas Graham Jackson, 1835–1924* (London, New York, and Toronto: Oxford University Press, 1950), pp. 133–34 and 137.

37. For a general discussion see: AES, *Memoir*, pp. 210–17. GES's report on his own design is reprinted in "Illustrations: Design for Edinburgh Cathedral," *Architect* 11 January 1873, pp. 24–25.

38. Ewan Christian, "The Edinburgh Cathedral Competition: Mr. Christian's Report on the Designs," *Architect*, 22 February 1873, pp. 95–99, dated 30 October 1872.

39. GES is favored generally, although some criticisms are made.

39. GES [letter], "Correspondence: The Edinburgh Cathedral Competition," *Architect*, 4 January 1873, p. 13, dated 30 December 1872.

40. He did, however, submit samples of his previous work to the Truro cathedral building committee in 1878.

41. The vote is reported in "Chips," *Building News*, 9 July 1869, p. 37.

42. "The Royal Academy," *Times*, 9 January 1871, p. 5; "General," *Architect*, 8 July 1871, p. 24.

43. GES, "A Lecture Delivered at the Royal Academy Last Session," *Architect*, 16 December 1871, pp. 299–301; 23 December 1871, pp. 310–12; 30 December 1871, pp. 323–25; and "A Second Lecture Delivered at the Royal Academy Last Session," *Architect*, 17 February 1872, pp. 78–80; 24 February 1872, pp. 88–90; 2 March 1872, pp. 103–4.

44. E. M. Barry, *Lectures on Architecture Delivered at the Royal Academy* (London: John Murray, 1881).

45. "Academy Lectures on Architecture," *Architect*, 4 April 1874, p. 191.

46. AES, *Memoir*, pp. 260, 269. At the same time he was elected treasurer of the Royal Academy, again succeeding Barry. This post was traditionally given to architects.

47. His lectures were printed fully in the *Builder*, *Building News*, and *Architect*, and as an appendix in AES, *Memoir*.

48. AES, *Memoir*, pp. 49–50.

49. AES, *Memoir*, p. 226.

50. For a general account of this controversy, see *ibid.*, pp. 263–66.

51. "Mr. Street and the Institute," *Architect*, 12 April 1879, pp. 213–14.

52. "The Coming Elections at the Institute of Architects," *Architect*, 12 March 1881, pp. 175–76.

53. Published under a cover letter from Edis, dated 6 April 1881: R. W. Edis [letter], "Correspondence: The Presidency of the Institute," *Building News*, 8 April 1881, p. 404; and "Correspondence: The Presidency of the Institute," *Architect*, 9 April 1881, p. 260. Edis's letter alone appears in "The Presidency of the Institute," *Builder*, 9 April 1881, p. 459.

54. William Burges [letter], "Correspondence: The New President of the R.I.B.A.," *Building News,* 1 April 1881, p. 374, dated 29 March 1881. Arthur Blomfield [letter], "Correspondence: Election of President, R.I.B.A.," *Building News,* 22 April 1881, p. 467, dated 19 April 1881. Also printed in "Correspondence: The Presidency of the Institute," *Builder,* 23 April 1881, p. 522.

55. William White [letter], "Correspondence: Election of the President, R.I.B.A.," *Building News,* 22 April 1881, pp. 467–68, dated 20 April 1881; and also printed as "Correspondence: The President of the Institute," *Architect,* 23 April 1881, pp. 295–96.

56. A Former Member of the Council [letter], "The Presidency of the Institute of Architects," *Builder,* 2 April 1881 , p. 420; A One-while Member of the Council [letter], "The Presidency of the Institute," *Builder,* 23 April 1881, p. 522.

57. The *Builder* at first refused to print the "rather violent" letters that it had received. "Miscellanea: The Presidency of the Institute of Architects," *Builder,* 26 March 1881, p. 391.

58. T. R. Smith [letter], "Correspondence: The Presidency of the Institute," *Building News,* 8 April 1881, pp. 403–4; also in "Correspondence: The Presidency of the Institute," *Architect,* 9 April 1881, p. 260; and "The Presidency of the Institute," *Builder,* 9 April 1881, p. 459.

59. T. R. Smith [letter], "Correspondence: The Presidency of the R.I.B.A.," *Building News,* 6 May 1881, pp. 531–32, dated 3 May 1881, enclosing the memo.

60. *Ibid.* Smith reports Jones's offer. The Hayward and Street letters appear in "The Presidential Election," *Architect,* 23 April 1881, p. 294; and "The Presidency of the Institute," *Builder,* 23 April 1881, p. 522. Hayward's letter is dated 14 April 1881; GES's reply is dated 19 April 1881.

61. The election meeting is reported in "The Election of Mr. Street as President of the Institute," *Architect,* 14 May 1881, p.

331; and "Annual General Meeting of the R.I.B.A.," *Building News,* 13 May 1881, p. 561.

62. For a general discussion see: Robert Macleod, *Style and Society: Architectural Ideology in Britain, 1835–1914* (London: R.I.B.A. Publications, 1971), pp. 123ff.

63. GES, "The Opening Address, 1881–1882," *Royal Institute of British Architects Proceedings* 1881–82: 68.

64. "Mr. Street on Bad Building," *Building News,* 11 November 1881, p. 615.

65. H. S. Goodhart-Rendel, "Victorian Public Buildings," in *Victorian Architecture,* ed. Peter Ferriday (London: Jonathan Cape, 1963), p. 99.

66. "The Decline and Fall of British Architecture," *Builder,* 3 March 1877, p. 203. Speech delivered at Whitehaven. He returned to the same theme six years later: *Hansard,* 3s 279 (21 May 1883): 639.

67. "The New Law Courts," *Building News,* 19 May 1876, p. 490. See also: "The New Law Courts," *Building News,* 24 May 1878, p. 519; and "The New Law Courts," *Building News,* 17 January 1879, p. 76.

68. "Architectural Association: The Late Mr. G. E. Street, R.A.," *Building News,* 13 January 1882, pp. 40–41; and "Architectural Association: The Late G. E. Street, R.A.," *Builder,* 14 January 1882, pp. 54–55. The impression of these remarks was modified in J. P. Seddon [letter], "Correspondence: Mr. Street's Churches," *Building News,* 20 January 1882, p. 90, dated 13 January 1882. See Seddon's more sympathetic obituary: "George Edmund Street, R.A.," *Architect,* 24 December 1881, p. 406.

69. P. G. Wodehouse, *Carry On, Jeeves!* (London: Barrie and Jenkins, 1976), pp. 253–54 (first published in 1925).

70. "The Royal Palace of Justice," *Architect,* 9 December 1882, pp. 355–56.

71. "Royal Institute of British Architects," *Building News,* 23 December 1881, p. 819; and "Death of the President of the Royal Institute of British Architects," *Builder,* 24 December 1881, pp. 784–85.

Archival Materials

THE PUBLIC RECORD OFFICE at Kew is the repository of the largest portion of the papers pertaining to the law courts. The Works 12 class of documents contains the correspondence file for the building, the Works 30 class includes more than 1000 relevant drawings, and the Treasury 1 class contains pertinent Treasury correspondence. All of these have satisfactory indices.

The building superstructure specifications and contract are preserved at the library of the Property Services Agency, Department of the Environment, Croydon. The drawings used by the foundation contractor are held by the Drawings Collection of the British Architectural Library (R.I.B.A.), London, where they comprise the U17/2 class. Further important correspondence is to be found among the Gladstone and Layard papers at the British Library, and numerous smaller collections, papers, and drawings are cited in the notes. Street's personal papers were destroyed in the Second World War.

Selected Bibliography

THE FOLLOWING includes only the most important and pertinent recent scholarship, together with selected older works. For further biographical references see chapter 1, n.4. Street's most important writings are cited in chapter 1, nn.7–10.

G. E. Street and His Other Buildings

Clarke, Basil F. L. "Street's Yorkshire Churches and Contemporary Criticism." In *Concerning Architecture: Essays on Architectural Writers and Writing Presented to Nikolaus Pevsner,* edited by John Summerson, pp. 209–25. London: Allen Lane, the Penguin Press, 1968.

Germann, Georg. "George Edmund Street et la Suisse." *Zeitschrift für schweizerische Archäologie und Kunstgeschichte* 29 (1972): 118–30.

Hitchcock, Henry-Russell. "G. E. Street in the 1850's." *Journal of the Society of Architectural Historians* 19 (1960): 145–71.

Humphrey, Stephen. "St. Dionis Backchurch: Victorian Proposals." *London Topographical Record* 24 (1980): 131–45.

Jackson, Neil. "The Un-Englishness of G. E. Street's Church of St. James-the-Less." *Architectural History* 23 (1980): 86–94.

King, Georgina G., ed. *George Edmund Street: Unpublished Notes and Reprinted Papers.* New York: Hispanic Society of America, 1916.

Long, E. T. "Churches of a Victorian Squire." *Country Life,* 29 September 1968, pp. 770–72.

Meeks, Carroll. "Churches by Street on the Via Nazionale and the Via del Babuino." *Art Quarterly* 16 (1953): 215–27.

Millon, Henry A. "G. E. Street and the Church of St. Paul's in Rome." In *In Search of Modern Architecture: A Tribute to Henry-Russell Hitchcock,* edited by Helen Searing, pp. 85–101. New York: Architectural History Foundation; Cambridge, Massachusetts, and London: MIT Press, 1982.

Millon, Judith Rice. *St. Paul's within the Walls, Rome: A Building History and Guide, 1870–1980.* Dublin, New Hampshire: William L. Bauhan, 1982.

Street, Arthur Edmund. *Memoir of George Edmund Street, R.A., 1824–1881.* London: John Murray, 1888. Reprinted. New York: Benjamin Blom, 1972.

Summerson, John. "Two London Churches." In *Victorian Architecture: Four Studies in Evaluation,* pp. 47–76. New York: Columbia University Press, 1970.

The Law Courts

Aslet, Clive. "A Palace for Many Courts: Centenary of the Royal Courts of Justice." *Country Life,* 11 November 1982, pp. 1462–64.

Kinnard, Joseph. "G. E. Street, the Law Courts and the 'Seventies." In *Victorian Architecture,* edited by Peter Ferriday, pp. 221–34. London: Jonathan Cape, 1963.

Port, M. H. "From Carey Street to the Embankment—and back again!" *London Topographical Record* 24 (1980): 167–90.

Port, M. H. "The New Law Courts Competition, 1866–67." *Architectural History* 11 (1968): 75–93.

Summerson, John. "The Law Courts Competition of 1866–67." *R.I.B.A. Journal* 77 (1970): 11–18.

Summerson, John. "A Victorian Competition: the Royal Courts of Justice." In *Victorian Architecture: Four Studies in Evaluation,* pp. 77–117. New York: Columbia University Press, 1970.

Index